VOLUME 1 SOUTH

First published in Great Britain 2008 by Pesda Press
Galeri 22, Doc Victoria,
Caernarfon, Gwynedd
LL55 1SQ
Wales

Copyright © 2008 Gary Latter
ISBN 978-1-906095-06-2

The Author asserts the moral right to be identified as the author of this work.

Maps by Bute Cartographics.
Printed in Poland, produced by Polska Book.

Gary Latter

CONTENTS

📷 *Dave MacLeod on the first ascent of Ring of Steall, Glen Nevis, one of the hardest routes in the book at F8c+. Photo Claire MacLeod.*

"Climb the mountains and get their good tidings. Nature's peace will flow into you as sunshine flows into trees. The winds will blow their own freshness into you, and the storms their energy, while cares will drop off of you like autumn leaves."
– John Muir

SCOTTISH ROCK

The area covered by this book, the Highlands and Islands, lies entirely to the north of the Highland Boundary Fault. With its mountain landscapes, deep glens, lochs, rivers and hundreds of islands, it represents one of the most extensive and least populated semi-natural areas remaining in Western Europe. Scotland can also lay claim to the only true areas of 'wilderness' remaining in Britain, with vast tracts of uninhabited areas in the far North West, and the similarly wild and unspoilt high arctic plateaux of the Cairngorm massif. Often, by choosing your venue carefully, it is possible not just to avoid queues but to have whole mountains to yourself.

Within this incredibly varied setting can be found stunning examples of every sub-sport that rock climbing has evolved. In UK terms, we have the longest mountain routes (such as *The Long Climb* on Ben Nevis); the biggest sea cliffs (St John's Head, Hoy), which also harbour the only multi-day big wall route in the country – the 23 pitch *Longhope Route*; the steepest cliff (Sron Ulladale, Harris). But size isn't everything. In contrast, a myriad of miniature sport routes have appeared in recent years, together with a resurgence of interest in outcrop climbing in general. There has also been the opening up of some wonderfully situated bouldering venues, together with exquisite deep-water soloing on a few esoteric locations.

This book is intended as a celebration of the wealth and variety of great climbing that Scotland has to offer. The selection of routes should have something for everyone, from the athlete to the aesthete. Climbing in Scotland is about more than the rock alone; there is the magnificent and awe-inspiring scenery, the sense of history, the wide open spaces, the clean fresh air and the possibility of solitude.

USING THE GUIDE

All the areas covered are described as approaching from the south, where the majority of visitors originate. Similarly, the routes are also laid out in the order they are encountered from the approach. Each area has an introduction outlining the style of climbing, together with detailed up-to-date information on **Accommodation** and **Amenities** – in short everything the visitor requires to familiarise themselves with an area. Each cliff or crag is described in summary, together with specific **Access, Approach** and **Descent** details clearly laid out. In addition, maps and photo-diagrams illustrate further. Routes are given an overall technical grade alongside the adjectival grade, with the individual pitch grades incorporated within the description. The abbreviations **FA** and **FFA** refer to the first ascent and first free ascent respectively. **PA** refers to the number of points of aid used on the first ascent. There are very few routes containing aid in this book, though in some instances the use of a couple of points of aid may give a more consistent route, and an alternative grade is offered. On a few harder routes, usually unrepeated, rest points were used and this is mentioned in the hope of encouraging subsequent free ascents. **PR** and **PB** refer to peg runner and belay respectively; **F** and **R** to friends and rocks; **BB** and **LO** refer to bolt belays and lower-offs on the sport crags. **TIC** stands for Tourist Information Centre; **ATM** for Automated Teller Machine.

You should have the relevant Ordnance Survey 1:50,000 map and, particularly for the remoter mountain crags, knowledge of how to use a map and compass is assumed. The middle of the Cairngorms or the top of Ben Nevis is not the place to attempt to learn to navigate. The Grid Reference and Altitude refers to the base of the cliff or crag. The approach times quoted are intended as a general guide (racing greyhounds and ramblers/tortoises can make their own adaptations accordingly), along the lines of Naismith's Rule (4.5km per hour and one minute for every 10m of ascent).

I have attempted to consult as many active climbers in Scotland as possible to get a broad range of opinions and a consensus on grades and quality, but the final selection of routes is a personal one. For instance, not all the routes are on immaculate rock, with some of the older routes in the traditional character-building mode. Jim Bell's famous adage, *"Any fool can climb good rock. It takes craft and cunning to get up vegetatious schist or granite."* may be worth bearing in mind.

ACCOMMODATION

Information on a range of budget accommodation is included for each area, from camp sites and youth hostels to private bunkhouses. There are also a number of well-situated mountaineering club huts in all the main mountain areas. These are available for booking by members of the MC of S, the BMC and affiliated clubs. In addition, Tourist Information Centres (**TICs**) are detailed at the start of each main area. These are a good source of information on bed and breakfast, guest house and hotel accommodation. Each area tourist board publishes a **Local Accommodation and Visitor Guide** annually, and these are available free of charge by calling or writing to the respective offices.

EATING OUT

One important point worth bearing in mind, (especially for those used to continental and transatlantic hospitality) is that the majority of Scotland still lurks in the dark ages when it comes to the service industry. Most pubs only serve food over a short period at lunchtime; often 12–2pm, and more importantly, the majority of pubs and hotels stop serving food at 9pm, some at 8pm even! I've had the misfortune to turn up at a restaurant/pub in Skye (in July, the height of the tourist season) to be informed *"We're not serving food: the chef's on his lunch"* – unbelievable. Establishments that are particularly good and worth seeking out are highlighted within the introductory section of each relevant chapter.

ACCESS

The **Land Reform (Scotland) Act 2003** gives statutory access rights to most land and inland water. These rights exist only if exercised responsibly by respecting the privacy, safety and livelihoods of others and by looking after the environment. The Scottish Outdoor Access Code provides detailed guidance on the responsibilities of those exercising access rights and those managing land and water.

- Take responsibility for your own actions and act safely.
- Respect people's privacy.
- Assist land managers to work safely and effectively.
- Care for the environment and take any litter home.
- Keep all dogs under proper control.
- Take extra care if organising an event or running a business.

WILD CAMPING

In the rural areas it is often possible to camp at the side of the road. If in doubt, ask permission locally from farmers and crofters. Remember, lighting fires is illegal (not to mention unnecessary) and remove all litter. It should almost always be possible to camp in the hills, except perhaps in some areas during the stalking season.

CARAVANS

Those wishing to bring caravans please don't – go to the Lakes, the Borders or some other rolling hills well away from the Highlands and Islands. Even better, stay at home and play tiddlywinks or golf, or take up macramé or embroidery or some other suitably sedate pastime. Alternatively, travel under the cover of darkness, preferably at 3am on a Sunday morning.

BIRDS

Some of the sea cliffs are affected by nesting seabirds and should be avoided during the nesting season of April – July inclusive. Almost all birds, their nests and eggs are protected. The proliferation of guano on such cliffs makes it in the climber's interest to choose another venue. In particular, some popular routes, such as the *Old Man of Stoer* and *Hoy*, have the occasional fulmar nest on ledges, and it is definitely in the climber's interest to avoid close encounters, as they have the nasty habit of vomiting semi-digested fish oil onto uninvited visitors. It should still, however, be possible to climb these routes during the nesting season. In the unlikely event of coming across birds of prey (especially peregrine falcons, golden or white tailed sea eagles – all Schedule 1 birds) choose another route or cliff. It is an offence, under the Wildlife and Countryside Act 1981, to disturb any Schedule 1 bird, with fines of up to £5,000 and possible imprisonment. Their continued existence is surely more important than another tick in the guidebook? Information on current restrictions is available from the Mountaineering Council of Scotland (☎ 01738 638227; www.mcofs.org.uk).

SEASONAL RESTRICTIONS

The grouse shooting season is from 12 August (the 'glorious' twelfth) – 10 December and deer from 1 July – 20 October for stags and 21 October – 15 February for hinds. There are few crags or cliffs included where access problems have been encountered in the past. A caring, responsible attitude towards parking, litter, conservation and a polite approach to landowners should ensure that the present situation continues. If any difficulties are encountered, contact the Access and Conservation Officer of the Mountaineering Council for Scotland (☎ 01738 638227; www.mcofs.org.uk). No commercial stalking takes place on National Trust for Scotland properties (such as Glen Coe and Torridon), ensuring access at all times.

DIRECTIONS

All directions (left and right) are given for climbers facing the crag, except in descent. Any ambiguous descriptions also include a compass point, but if you don't know your left from your right, chances are you won't have a clue where the North Pole lies.

CONSERVATION

Try to adopt a minimum impact approach at all times, leaving the place as you would like to find it. Approaches to some of the cliffs can be greatly aided by the use of bicycles. Their use should be restricted to solid paths

such as private and forest roads or rights of way, not soft paths and open hillsides where considerable erosion can occur. Where there is a substantial time-saving advantage, such information is included in the approach information. Where repeated abseils from trees is the norm (such as on Creag Dhubh), slings and karabiners or maillons have been left in place, and their use is encouraged to prevent ringing of the bark, leading to the eventual demise of the trees. Always park with consideration for others, and avoid damage to fences and walls. And of course, as the country code stresses, avoid 'interfering' with animals (Aberdonians and Rick Campbell take note!). Do not leave any litter, including food scraps, finger tape, chalk wrappers and cigarette ends and remove any left by others. Bury or burn toilet paper. Scratching arrows or names at the base of routes can clearly be viewed in a modern light as nothing short of vandalism. Established markings are mentioned to aid identification, and it is hoped no further additions will be thought necessary. Many of the areas covered are within National Scenic Areas (NSA), National Nature Reserves (NNR) and Sites of Special Scientific Interest (SSSI), controlling development and ensuring the retention and preservation of the natural environment.

ETHICS

The vast majority of routes included are in the traditional or adventure mould, where there is little or no protection in situ. The following policy statement on bolts has been drawn up by the Mountaineering Council of Scotland, after consultation with all interested parties.

"The MC of S acknowledge that there is a place for bolts in the future development of Scottish climbing. However, to ensure that the highly regarded ethos of, and future development of, traditional climbing (involving the use of leader-placed and second-removed protection) is not threatened, it is felt that the use of bolts should be limited to the production of sport climbs. There should be no retrospective bolting of established climbs for protection or belays, and there should be no minimalist bolting.

"The production of sport climbs with bolts is acceptable on natural rock only when all the following conditions have been satisfied:

1 *On low-lying cliffs, provided that such development is not against the wishes of the landowner. Bolts are inappropriate on mountain cliffs and sea cliffs.*
2 *On routes where natural protection is absent or is inadequate for the repeated falls that such routes necessitate.*
3 *Where the rock is steep and provides climbs of a high order of difficulty, at the forefront of developments of the day.*
4 *Where there is no historical or anti-bolt ethic.*

"Concerning quarried rock, it is felt that any future develop-ment should only be constrained by points 2 and 4 above. Finally, it is felt that bolts should be located to ensure minimum visual impact and should be placed according to current best practices. It is intended that these principles are not seen as simply restrictive rules, but as a guide to promote the positive development of Scottish climbing, where sport climbing, rather than a substitute for traditional climbing, grows alongside it."

STYLE, PEGS & IN SITU PROTECTION

"Ethics change the experience for others, style only changes your own personal experience."

The use of chalk is no longer a burning issue. Nevertheless, its use should be kept to a minimum, hopefully only on extremes. Chalk has been spotted on descent routes (I kid you not) and on VDiffs, such as *Agag's Groove*, which must be an ultimate low point. Hold improvement is unacceptable on natural rock. If you can't climb a piece of rock with the holds available, leave it unclimbed rather than resort to the hammer and chisel. The use of hammered nuts should be discouraged, as their rapid deterioration soon blocks the placement possibilities for subsequent ascentionists.

Whilst the style a route is climbed in is a personal one, I feel obliged to make a few comments. The use of 'rest points' (i.e. aid) and prior top-roping should be reserved

for routes that are pushing new frontiers. It is true to say that such tactics percolate downwards. Try to give the rock a fighting chance, and approach the route on its own terms, in accordance with local practices. The majority of active pioneers in Scotland have attempted to push standards, and many very audacious leads have been achieved on-sight or ground up.

QUALITY ASSESSMENT

I had originally intended to adopt the Farquhar rating system, with its two extremes of PS and FB, but as hopefully there are no 'pure sh≈@‡' routes herein (unless included for historical interest, or to aid in crag descriptions) and masses of '#µ©k*≈g brilliant' routes, I have decided to opt for the conventional star rating system, with three star routes being of truly outstanding quality. As the climbing in Scotland is clearly superior to anything south of the border, a few exceptional routes have the honour of four stars. These are absolute 'must do's' that would rate amongst the best anywhere on the planet, such is their undeniable brilliance. On a few isolated routes, a wire brush symbol denotes that the route may require prior cleaning in its present state, and the stars assume the route is in a clean state. These are routes which were originally climbed following cleaning on abseil, but at the time of writing have not had much repeat traffic, and may require a quick abseil with a wire brush prior to an ascent.

CLIMATE

"They'll all be doing them when the sun comes out." – Don Whillans.

The Highlands and Islands are dominated by the prevailing southwesterly winds, bringing moist and usually mild air from the Atlantic. In addition, many of the Atlantic depressions pass close to or over Scotland. *"It always rains up there"* is a commonly held myth. It is easy at first sight to confuse a map of annual rainfall with that of a relief map, for the two are closely linked. The wettest belt extends from the Cowal peninsula (south and west of Arrochar) in a broad band as far as the hills just south of Torridon. In the mountains an annual precipitation of between 200–300cm and more is the norm, these dreich figures dropping markedly to 150–200cm on the coastal fringe. Within this broad belt there is much variation. As an example, at Dundonnel at the head of Little Loch Broom the annual rainfall is 180cm; 10km south it is 250cm, and 10km further north in Ullapool the average is 120cm.

The coastal promontories, especially in the north, and the Outer Hebrides receive only 100–150cm. Similarly, low ground around the Cairngorms and the eastern edge of the Central Highlands (such as Craig a Barns and The Pass of Ballater) benefit from the rain shadow effect of the hills further west (70–90cm). The higher ground in the Cairngorms receive around half the precipitation than the hills just in from the main Atlantic seaboard, with an average of 225cm recorded on Cairn Gorm summit. Lying in the centre of the country, their climate is more continental, with warmer summers than on the coasts. Many districts in the north and east have, on average over the four summer months from May–August, a total rainfall of less than 25cm, comparing favourably with the drier parts of England. Throughout the country the driest and sunniest period is from mid-May to the end of June, the next driest from mid-September to mid-October.

In the Outer Hebrides gales are recorded on over 40 days of the year, and in the Northern Isles this figure is even greater, though most of these occur in the winter. Prolonged spells of strong wind are uncommon between May and August. Especially in the Western Isles and along the west coast, May is the sunniest month, closely followed by June. April is sunnier than the popular holiday months of July and August. The temperatures on the west coast and the islands are generally a couple of degrees cooler than inland, with the Northern Isles a couple of degrees cooler again. Finally, in midsummer there is no complete darkness in the north of Scotland, with Shetland receiving about 4 hours more daylight (including twilight) than London.

TIDAL INFORMATION

In general, the tide ebbs and flows twice daily. As a rough guide, the tide takes 6 hours to come in, spends a half an hour 'on the turn', then 6 hours to recede, before repeating the same process. Spring tides occur after a new and full moon, and have the greatest amplitude. Tide tables are published annually for specific areas and are available from yacht chandlers and in many newsagents, or from harbour offices.

WEATHER INFORMATION

Both quality Scottish daily newspapers, **The Herald** and **The Scotsman,** publish detailed forecasts, including synoptic charts, and a hillwalking forecast appears in **The Scotsman** on a Saturday. **Scotland on Sunday** also has a similarly detailed 36-hour forecast and a forecast for the coming week, including specific mountain, coastal and sailing conditions. There are a multitude of recorded weather forecasts, including Weathercall, providing a daily or 5-day outlook. Grampian & East Highlands ☎ 09014 722 074. West Highlands & Islands ☎ 09014 722 075. Caithness, Sutherland, Orkney & Shetland ☎ 09014 722 076. Calls cost 60p per minute. Scottish Television broadcast Scottish Weather forecasts at 1.30pm, 6.28pm and 9.28pm; Radio Scotland (810 AM; 92–95 FM) has detailed outdoor forecasts at 6.28am, 5.58pm and 11.55pm; there is a **Forecast for Outdoor Activities** with detailed conditions for climbers and hillwalkers at 6.58pm on weekday evenings, and at 7.00am and 6.25pm on a Saturday. Many of the better climbing shops in mountain areas display a 72-hour MetFax mountain weather forecast, as do Glenmore Lodge (☎ 01479 861256).

WEE BASTARDS

Little biting creatures, which the vast majority of tourist-orientated brochures and guidebooks fail to mention, can make a massive difference to one's stay in the Highlands and Islands. Of the thirty-four species of biting midge

 For even more information, resources and a bibliography, visit **www.scottishrock.co.uk**

found in Scotland, only four or five species bite humans. By far the worst and most prevalent, accounting for more than 90 percent of all bites to humans is the female of the species *Culicoides impunctatus*, or the Highland Midge. This voracious creature first makes its appearance around the end of May and can persist until the end of September in a mild summer, with early June through to August being the worst periods. They are particularly active on still, cloudy or overcast days, especially twilight (which lasts throughout the night in Scotland in summer). Wind speeds above a slight breeze force them to seek shelter. Mosquitoes and blackfly are less of a problem, though the cleg (or horsefly) feeds mainly during warm bright days. Finally, sheep or deer ticks, small black or brown round-bodied members of the genus *arachnid* rest on vegetation, awaiting a host. The tick sinks its head into the victim's flesh, until it eventually swells up and drops off. Do not pull off, unless with tweezers, as this will leave behind the pincers or mouth-parts. Instead, apply alcohol or insect repellent. There is a multitude of insect repellent commercially available, most containing varying concentrations of diethyl toluamide (DEET). Older natural formulas, such as the very aromatic citronella oil (available from chemists), and those containing lemon eucalyptus oil, seem reasonably effective. The leaves of the bog myrtle, when crushed and rubbed into the skin also seem effective though not very long lasting, necessitating repeated application.

MOUNTAIN RESCUE

In the event of a serious accident requiring medical attention, contact the Emergency Services (999) and ask for Mountain Rescue, Coastguard or Police. Give concise information about the nature of the injuries, and the exact location, including a six-figure grid reference or the name of the route if possible. Try to leave someone with the victim, who should be made as comfortable as possible, if injuries allow. If unconscious, be sure to place in the recovery position, ensuring the airway is clear. In a few instances Mountain Rescue posts (containing a stretcher and basic rescue kit) are located in the hills, and are noted within the introductory text at the start of relevant cliffs.

GRADES

Routes are graded for on-sight ground up ascents, and the climber is assumed to be fully equipped with a wide range of protection devices. On some of the hardest routes skyhooks may be found useful. It goes without saying that people should make their own judgement regarding any in situ equipment encountered including fixed abseil points, all of which will rapidly deteriorate through exposure to the elements. I have tried to be as consistent as possible, though minor regional variations may occur. Any crucial runner information, especially relating to obscure gadgets or hidden or hard-to-place protection has been included where known. Where a route has only received an ascent after extensive top-rope practice this headpointed ascent has been highlighted within the first ascent details where known, in order to record such prior familiarisation.

DISCLAIMER

The author, publisher and distributors of this book do not recognise any liability for injury or damage caused to, or by, climbers, third parties, or property arising from such persons seeking reliance on this guidebook as an assurance for their own safety.

Cliff Ogle & Patricia Littlechild on the spectacular top pitch of Quiver Rib, Terrace Face, Aonach Dubh, Glen Coe – one of the finest Difficult routes in the book.

GEOLOGY

by Dr Darren McAulay & Gary Latter

"For its size Scotland has the most varied geology and natural landscapes of any country on the planet."
- Alan McKirdy and Roger Crofts, *Scotland: The Creation of its Natural Landscape,* Scottish Natural Heritage, 1999

Scotland hosts a wealth of rock types and topography, each of which provides unique characteristics and opportunities to the climber. The intricate geological history has been at the forefront of study; indeed many of the major earth moving mechanisms (e.g. thrust and fault movements) have been understood by analysing relief and rock outcrops throughout Scotland.

Rock climbers cannot escape the fact that geology plays a major role in the formation of their playground and many have more than a passing interest in the subject. An in-depth description of Scottish geology can be found elsewhere, but the following notes give an insight into how rock type influences not only the formation of our vertical arena but affects frictional qualities, hold type/ shape and quality, and the provision of opportunity for the placement of protection.

A BRIEF GEOLOGICAL HISTORY

The age of the Earth is estimated to be in the region of 4,500 million years. Scotland's oldest rock, the Lewisian gneiss, is dated at 2,300 – 2,600 million years, being some of the oldest rocks to outcrop in Europe. The gneiss originally formed part of a huge landmass that included Scandinavia, Greenland and Northeast America. This landmass was uplifted and then eroded to give an undulating landscape that can be seen in the ancient topography of the NW mainland and its namesake of the Isle of Lewis. Around 1,100 million years ago, the gneiss was covered by around 5,000 metres of red sandstone called the Torridonian which was deposited by rivers flowing from the north. Following this and further to the south in more marine waters, sediments were being heated and folded (metamorphism) to produce the Moine schists.

Around 570 million years ago, the sea level rose and a series of sandstones, siltstones and limestones formed on the Torridonian/Lewisian basement – called the Cambrian. The next event, which had major consequences, started around 450 million years ago and involved the collision of two landmasses over 130 million years. The result was the Caledonian mountain belt, believed to be of Himalayan stature, which produced the Dalradian schists, which together with the Moine schists make up most of the Highlands. Aside from the massive folding of the rocks during this time was the series of northeast-southwest trending faults that came into existence. The Highland Boundary Fault, which runs through Arran, Loch Lomond and on to Stonehaven now forms the dividing line between the Scottish Highlands to the north and the Central Lowland Belt to the south. During this period heating allowed molten rock to rise up into the schists, sometimes reaching the surface forming volcanoes (Ben Nevis and Glen Coe) but generally solidifying as granite deeper in the crust (Cairngorms, Starav, Rannoch). At this point Scotland was still connected to a landmass that included North-east America and Scandinavia.

After the Caledonian shake-up a further series of sandstones were produced; the Old Red Sandstones, which are no longer represented in the Highlands but still occur in Orkney and NE Scotland. The period between 360 – 100 million years ago produced various rock types including more sandstones, limestones, coal measures and shales (source of oil and gas) but apart from in the Central Belt these rocks are not widespread and are of little interest to the climber. However, the Great Glen Fault (now filled by Loch Ness) was active at various times in this period causing a lateral tearing of the earth (as the San Andreas Fault does today in California). It has been shown that the area to the north of the Great Glen has moved 100km relative to the south. Major rock forming events were still not finished though, as around 60 million years ago great movement occurred when North America broke away from the European continent. Apart from the obvious geographical (and some say fortunate!) consequence, the earth movements created substantial heating with the result that huge volcanoes were formed along the NW margins of Scotland (a line from Arran to Skye to St Kilda). Subsequent extensive erosion by elements such as changes in climate and periods of glaciation have reduced the mountains and volcanoes to the remnants left today. Fortuitously, these remnants offer a western coastline that is 260 miles from north to south but over 2,000 miles in outline, with 550 Hebridean islands, 40 mainland sea lochs and hundreds of mountains and cliffs to enjoy.

ROCK TYPES

Lewisian Gneiss – Ancient rocks that have undergone such extreme heating and pressure that all trace of original structure has been lost. The Lewisian rocks originally formed part of a great continent that was worn down to a low lying, gentle landscape, subsequently covered (in Scotland) by the Torridonian sandstones. Typically forms rounded and rocky outcrops (due to the lack of jointing) with exceptional friction when weathered, because of the coarse-grained nature and streaked texture that permits the formation of flat, banded holds and rough pockets. It occurs on Lewis and Harris and the Barra Isles, on almost all the worthwhile crags and cliffs in the Gairloch district, including the remote Carn Mor, and in bands in Sutherland, including around Sheigra.

Torridonian Sandstone – Transported by the action of large rivers on the margins of a mountainous continent to the north, the Torridonian deposits generally consist of coarse-grained, red sandstones that contain frequent pebbly bands. The Torridonian exhibits its original bedding, since it has escaped the mountain building forces imposed on many other rock types in Scotland. Good friction and quick drying, the holds often have a rounded feel and friends/cams ensure peace of mind in the sometimes flared cracks and horizontal breaks. The outcrops around Torridon, and almost all the cliffs and crags in Coigach and Assynt, are composed of this rock.

Cambrian Quartzite – Deposited on top of the Torridonian sandstones but with a southeast tilt, this quartzite is the result of heating of quartz-rich sandstones. They are brittle and well jointed which tends towards sharp flat holds. This rock outcrops mainly as resistant summit caps on the hills of Assynt

and Sutherland where frost-shattering forces produce abundant sharp, blocky screes. Further south the extensive Coire Mhic Fhearchair on Beinn Eighe and the Bonaidh Dhonn overlooking Loch Maree are two of the finest examples.

Moinian/Dalradian Schists – These are the predominant rock types of the Highlands, the result of metamorphism (intense folding, alteration by heat and pressure and even melting) caused by the meeting of two crustal plates. They formed a chain of mountains of Himalayan stature as huge folds and thrusts occurred, sometimes causing older rocks to rise up over younger, with the culminating edge being the Moine Thrust which runs from Skye to the north coast near Durness. The metamorphism of original sandstones, mudstones and possibly igneous rocks caused a slaty cleavage to develop which cross cuts the original bedding planes. Hence, the schist crags vary enormously depending on

Stripey Lewisian gneiss.

the local variations in the folding, and can even vary from route to route. At Creag Dhubh, for instance, the majority of the holds are of a horizontal, sometimes sloping nature whereas The Cobbler exhibits a variety of holds from slopers, to jugs and pockets, to quartz knobs. One notable property of the schists is that they offer poor friction when wet or lichenous, particularly the mica-schists in the Southern Highlands. Other locations include Glen Nevis, Craig a Barns, and venues as diverse as Glen Ogle and the alpine Aonach Beag.

Old Red Sandstone – Not a common rock type in terms of climbing (and geographic distribution) in Scotland, with the exception of the Northern Isles and the Old Man of Hoy. It is generally well bedded which results in many horizontal breaks and cracks (often rounded or flared). The friction is good where the rock is clean, the quality is generally impeccable on the dark russet coloured walls and it is at its best on some of the upper sections on Rora Head.

Finger jamming on Cairngorm granite.

Jurassic Sandstone – Although most of the rocks from this period tend to be soft and friable, some climbing can be found. A notable exception is the quartz sandstone of Suidhe Biorach (Skye) which like the Cambrian quartzite has a tendency to produce sharp, flat edges and, where eroded by the sea, has numerous pockets.

Granite – The granites can be found all over the Highlands, formed when large amounts of molten rock rose up through the folds and faults of the Caledonian mountains and solidified. The quality of the granite can depend on the rate at which it cooled. Rapid cooling producing a fine grain such as at Binnein Shuas and Dirc Mhor, whilst slower cooling produces a coarser grain as in the Cairngorms. Typical granite holds consist of cracks and flakes of a rounded nature, which are the product of blocky fractures formed during cooling. In addition ice-scoured slabs can be noted for their absence of holds and scarcity of protection (Etive, Arran and some of the cliffs in the Cairngorms). Gullies, formed by preferential weathering of intrusions and minor faults, tend to be very loose, formed of a fragile substance more closely resembling Weetabix than rock. Many routes follow lines produced by similar intrusions including the quartz vein on *Swastika*, and pegmatite band on *Ardverikie Wall*.

Andesite & Rhyolite – Forming similarly to the granites above, but in areas where the molten rock was able to penetrate the surface, are a range of lavas and granites. Most notably in the Ben Nevis and Glen Coe areas, huge blocks of schists were undermined by molten rock, which caused a subsequent collapse and outpouring of lavas. Although the lavas have long since been eroded away, leaving mostly schist and granite, the collapse (estimated at 1,600m in Glen Coe) resulted in some rocks (mainly rhyolites and andesites) being dropped to a level that was not removed. The rhyolites and andesites are very resistant to erosion compared to the surrounding schists and so make up the higher parts of the mountains. The Ben Nevis complex experienced at least four episodes during the collapse and subsequent granite intrusions and the differential cooling has resulted in a variety of coarseness, the area around the Carn Mor Dearg arête being fine grained as the result of a smaller, later subsidence. The summit block of the Ben consists of a resistant andesite that is the core of the collapse. The main cliffs still rest on schists that are 600m above sea level. Everywhere on the cliffs there is an inward sloping trend that results in good ledges/holds. Both rhyolite and andesite are fine grained, and fracture to give good sharp holds, though some of the best climbing in Glen Coe is on wonderful compact rough bubbly brown-pink rhyolite, at its best when water washed and well weathered. A number of dykes, mainly of porphoritic microdiorite have eroded to give features such as the distinctive *Ossian's Cave* and the descent route down from the Terrace Face, both on Aonach Dubh.

Dolerite & Basalt – Huge basaltic lava fields covered much of the area of what is now the western coast of Scotland. They poured out from huge volcanoes that have long since been reduced to their roots but many layers built up over time. Dolerite is a fine-grained lava and where it was intruded between layers (as a sill) it often cooled in the famed columnar form seen at Fingal's Cave (Staffa) and Kilt Rock (Skye). Basalt is generally unreliable for climbing, but the harder dolerite can form excellent cracks and vertical columns giving sustained jamming, its long parallel cracks being well protected with an ample supply of cams.

Gabbro – This coarse rock is famed for its roughness and great friction. The origin of gabbro is associated with volcanic activity but unlike the dolerite and basalt lavas it solidified deep within the root of such volcanoes. Solidification was slow which accounts for the coarse-ness of gabbro. Subsequent pressuring caused fissures within the volcanic complexes, with the result that much of the original rock was crosscut by smaller basalt intrusions (dykes) that radiate out from the centres; *The Snake* on the Eastern Buttress of Sron na Ciche follows the line of one such prominent dyke. These basalt dykes are fine-grained and less resistant than the gabbros and

although weathering often removes the dykes to form gullies and ledges, caution must be taken when climbing as the rock can be brittle and has poor friction when wet. Gabbro on the other hand retains good friction even in the rain, which is fortunate considering their location on Skye and Ardnamurchan.

In addition to the above, there are lesser outcroppings of other rocks, such as slate, limestone, greywacke and conglomerate throughout the Highlands and Islands, though (with the exception of the conglomerate crags of The Camel and Sarclet) none of the venues are deemed worthy of consideration from a climbing point of view to date. The rapid pace of exploration in recent years, together with the acceptance of the worthiness of rock quality in other parts of the UK, will undoubtedly reveal other venues.

Finally, it should be noted that erosion of the mountains and crags is continually taking place. Notable examples in recent years include two huge rock falls (1995 and 2000) on the right wall of *Parallel B Gully* in Lochnagar, the top corner of *The Giant* on Creag an Dubh-loch, large fresh rock fall scars around the base of *Collie's Route* on Skye's Sron na Ciche, the repositioning of huge chokestones in *The Chasm* on Buachaille Etive Mor, and the collapse of the natural arch that joined the top of the Old Man of Hoy to the mainland cliff as recently as just over one hundred years ago.

Lichen growth considerably changes the appearance of rock. Knoydart.

South Ridge Original, Lower East Face, Rosa Pinnacle,
Cir Mhor. Karen Latter climbing.

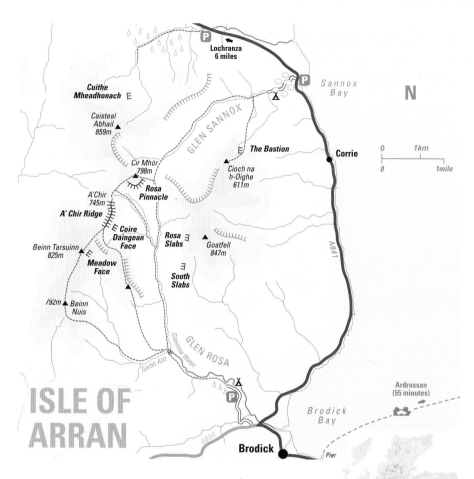

This roughly kidney-shaped island sits in the Firth of Clyde. It is the most southerly (and the most accessible) of the Scottish islands, and a popular tourist destination. It straddles the Highlands and Lowlands, as the Highland Boundary Fault passes through its centre – the 'String Road' (B880) between Brodick and Blackwaterfoot. Arran is often described as 'Scotland in miniature', displaying a wide range of rock types and landforms in such a small (32 x 16km) area. Despite the geological diversity, all the quality climbing is concentrated on the granite cliffs in the mountains to the north-east. A number of outcrops and sea-cliffs have also been climbed on but they do not compare with the bigger cliffs, and a wet day would be better spent exploring the many cafes and pubs. It should be noted that, on occasion, *"The climbing is anything but straightforward yet can be addictive. Arran is all wrong in the same way as a camel is a horse designed by a committee. Whoever thought up this place did so in a distinctly mischievous frame of mind."* – Bill Skidmore, Arran this Summer, 1978 SMCJ

"With the advent of climbing wall training, Arran seems even more baffling and inscrutable"
– Andrew Fraser, 1999

Access: A regular car ferry (Caledonian MacBrayne at the Ferry Terminal, Ardrossan ☎ 01475 674134 www.calmac.com) runs from Ardrossan – Brodick, the main (only) town on the island, taking 55 minutes. There is a regular 7am ferry to the island, making day trips eminently possible (there is also a late ferry back on a Friday). Unless staying for longer than a weekend, taking a car across is expensive (£70+) and other options are worth considering. The two popular camping spots with climbers and hillwalkers, Glen Rosa and Glen Sannox, can be reached by taxi for a few pounds; Sannox also has a regular bus service. There is also a summer crossing from Claonaig (Kintyre) – Lochranza at the north of the island. There is a frequent train service from Glasgow to Ardrossan, reaching Arran just two hours from the city.

Access to all the cliffs on **Beinn Tarsuinn**, **A'Chir**, **Goatfell** and **Cir Mhor**: From the pier at Brodick head north up the main (A841) road for 1.3 miles/2km. Continue straight on along the B880 west for 0.1 mile/0.2km then turn right up a single track road for 0.8 mile/1.3km to limited parking at the end of the tarmac road overlooking the campsite.

A bicycle may be useful, to make the long approach up Glen Rosa more bearable and a much more feasible day trip from the mainland. Mountain bikes can be taken at least as far as the bridge over the Garbh Allt, though the track is pretty rough and hard going. The corner of the Garbh Allt in Glen Rosa takes exactly the same time to reach by taxi or bike.

Amenities: TIC The Pier, Brodick (☎ 01770 302140; www.ayrshire-arran.com). Many cafes and pubs offering lunches, especially around Brodick. Numerous places in Brodick do bike hire, including: Arran Adventure Company, 300m from pier (☎ 01770 302244; www.arranadventure.com) & Brodick Cycles (☎ 01770 302460).

Accommodation: The most popular camping spot for climbers and hillwalkers is the Glen Rosa Farm Site (c. £5 per night for a tent; ☎ 01770 302380) at the end of the single track road at the bottom end of Glen Rosa. No showers. Unfortunately, this usually becomes overrun with drunken weegies* at Bank Holidays. Also beware the midges! Numerous quiet isolated camping spots can be found much further up Glen Rosa, beyond the bridge over the Garbh Allt, the best in the flat ground just beyond where the path splits (due west of the summit of Goatfell, beneath the Rosa Slabs). A fine less-frequented camping spot can also be found near the bottom of Glen Sannox (5 – 10 minutes walk from road), on either side of the track, the best spots in the trees 100m beyond the navigation beacons. **Youth Hostel:** at the north end of the island, at Lochranza (☎ 01770 830631). **Bunkhouses:** Aldersyde Bunkhouse, Lamlash (☎ 01770 600959; www.aldersidebunkhouse.co.uk); Kilmory Lodge Bunkhouse (☎ 01770 870345 or 368; www.kilmoryhall.com). For groups only, there are bunkhouses at Corrie – North High Corrie Croft Bunkhouse (☎ 01770 302203 or 810253; www.arranland.net) and Shore Lodge, at Brodick Castle (☎ 01770 302202; www.nts.org.uk). There are more hotels, guest houses, B&Bs and self-catering establishments than you could shake a stick at. Call **TIC** (above).

*weegies = natives of
Scotland's largest conurbation

For those who go to the hills to get away from people, ignore the 'No Camping' notices (erected by the campsite owner!)

John Dunne on the first ascent of The Great Escape, the Bastion, Cioch na h-Oighe. Photo Dave Simmonite.

ARRAN HISTORY

Early exploration concentrated on the ridges, with the most difficult summit on the island, the superb *A'Chir Ridge* traversed in 1892 by a large party attending an SMC yacht meet at Brodick. Though climbed in January, it was not in winter condition and can be properly regarded as the start of rock climbing on the island. Until the late thirties, Arran earned a somewhat deserved reputation for possessing only loose and vegetated rock. This situation was rectified in 1935 when J. Ramsay and partner

climbed the first route on the best cliff on the island, the *South Ridge* of the Rosa Pinnacle on Cir Mhor. Their ascent included the Layback Crack, later incorporated into the direct version. Three years later, the southern team of Ken Barber and Alfred Pigott climbed the first line on the east face with the hard *Easter Route* which pushed the standard to HVS.

The turning point that altered perceptions with regard to the quality of rock climbing available on the island was the ascent of *South Ridge Direct* in 1941 by Hamish Hamilton and David Paterson. This, together with the addition of a clutch of very good routes during the Second World War, did much to dispel the poor reputation of Arran's rock. Based just across the Clyde at the Admiralty anti-submarine depot at Fairlie was a group of naval personnel comprising Geoffrey Curtis, Gordon Townend and Ken Moneypenny. They made the second ascent of *South Ridge Direct* and went on to add many of the best lower grade routes on a number of cliffs. Amongst these were *Pagoda Ridge* and *Slab and Flake Route* on the Coire Daingean Face, *Caliban's Creep*, *Prospero's Peril*, and *Labyrinth* on Cir Mhor (all 1943). The following year, they added the popular classic *Sou'wester Slabs* to the Rosa Pinnacle, and produced the first worthwhile route on Cioch na h-Oighe with *Midnight Ridge Direct*. They also climbed *Fourth Wall* on the Rosa Pinnacle, returning the following year to add a better finish. Not much of significance was climbed in the following ten years, J.Ashford and D.Burke's ascent of *Sickle* on the Rosa Pinnacle in 1957 being the only route to improve on the standard set by Barber and Pigott's ascent of *Easter Route* almost twenty years previously. On the same face, in 1960, Donny Cameron and Dick Sim climbed *Hammer* on the same day that Davy McKelvie and Bob Richardson put up the adjacent *Anvil*. That same year, Andrew Maxfield climbed the first line on The Bastion of Cioch na h-Oighe with the exhilarating curving fault of *Tidemark*. In 1962 Bob Richardson and Bill Skidmore opened up the Meadow Face of Beinn Tarsuinn with *The Rake*, a hard though messy line, now very much improved with the addition of a clean *Direct Start* from George McEwan and Alastair Walker in 1988. Skidmore and Richardson, with Jim Crawford and John Madden returned to Cir Mhor in 1963 to climb the classic chimneys and cracks of *West Flank Route*.

The mid to late sixties saw the Edinburgh Squirrels (climbing club) active on the island, climbing the first worthwhile routes on the South Slabs of Glen Rosa, with 'Bugs' McKeith and B.Kennelly adding *Blank* and McKeith and Jim Brumfitt *Dogleg*. Further routes succumbed on the Meadow Face, with Mike Galbraith and McKeith

putting up *Brachistochrone* in 1966. Ian Rowe and Ian Dundas climbed the companion line *Bogle* the following year. Around this time, the occasional use of aid was fairly commonplace, either for gardening or to overcome short crux sections on the hardest routes. That same year (1967), Andrew Maxfield and Bob Wilde climbed the fine-looking corner up the left side of The Bastion to give *Klepht*, their ascent involving *"a significant amount of undeclared aid"*. Ian Fulton and J.Shaw added the best line on the Coire Daingean Face with *Mosque*. The following year, Rab Carrington and Fulton climbed the thin slab of *Insertion*. At a very bold and poorly protected E3, this route was for many years the hardest route on the island and is still a pitch that requires a cool head.

Activity continued on the Meadow Face throughout the seventies, with Bill Skidmore and Jim Crawford climbing the striking corner line of *The Blinder* in 1970. In 1975 Ian Duckworth, with John Fraser and W.Smith, climbed the impressively-situated *Brobdingnag*, up the left edge of the main face and freed *Brachistochrone*. The following year, Jim Perrin and partner made free ascents of a number of routes on the cliff including *Bogle*.

Whereas elsewhere in Scotland the main body of Scottish activists were actively freeing existing aid, Arran activists were content to bag first ascents with various quantities of aid. The steep clean walls of The Bastion saw much activity. In 1977 Bill Skidmore and Bob Richardson bagged the fine *Armadillo*, with three points of aid. Over the next few years, Graham Little actively pursued the wealth of plum lines remaining. Despite benefiting from abseil inspections, much aid was used on almost all the new additions. In 1979 Little added *Rhino*, initially soloed using a back-rope with a couple of points of aid, then re-led conventionally a few months later in the company of Skidmore. The route received its free ascent from Pete Whillance and partner in 1983. The big route in 1980 was the controversial *Abraxas*, with three bolt belays and extensive use of aid (twelve points). Little climbed this with his brother Bob, following an earlier attempt with Skidmore who was unhappy with the style and quantity of aid being used. In 1981 Little (and his trademark aid points) cleaned and made a direct ascent of *Klepht* with

Armadillo, the Bastion, Cioch na h-Oighe.
Derek Austin climbing. Photo Andrew Fraser.

four points of aid, soon freed a few months later by Craig Macadam and Andrew Fraser. Both *Klepht* and *Armadillo* subsequently had bolt belays added retrospectively. Little also climbed the fine pillar of *Digitalis* (three points aid and a tension traverse) and with Colin Ritchie climbed one of the best lines on the island with *Skydiver* (four points of aid) up the centre of the Upper East Face of Cir Mhor. The following year Little and Skidmore added *Ulysses* on Cuithe Mheadhonach, which made use of a bolt belay at mid-height. Little provoked further controversy on the same crag two years later when he climbed *Achilles* (E3) with two rivets for aid, which he immediately replaced with a bolt.

In the mid-eighties a number of strong teams made positive inroads into restoring the growing number of 'aid extravaganzas' littering the cliffs to their free state. In 1984 *Skydiver* received a second and free ascent, together with a more logical direct finish from Colin MacLean and Andy Nisbet. The plum line of *Abraxas* received its overdue free ascent the following year from Craig Macadam and Derek Austin, and Macadam with Simon Steer continued the clean up of the untidy aid points littering The Bastion by freeing *Armadillo*. A few days later, Dave Cuthbertson and Kev Howett completed a line up the right side of The Bastion, partially cleaned by Macadam, to give what was then the hardest line on the island with *Token Gesture*, the first E5. The previous week, Macadam with Simon Steer had pioneered the bold *Vanishing Point* up the centre of the great central slab on the Rosa Pinnacle of Cir Mhor. In the space of a few weeks the standard of free climbing in Arran had risen a couple of grades. This development was consolidated the following year. Mark Charlton and Kev Howett produced the boldest slab climbing on the island with *Insertion Direct* straightening out Carrington's bold sixties test-piece.

Activity picked up in the nineties with Howett and Little adding a range of excellent routes of all grades on many of the best cliffs prior to publication of the last guide. During the memorable long hot summer of 1995, on Cuithe Mheadhonach they added the hard *Icarus*. They returned a couple of weeks later, producing their free version of Little's *Achilles* to give what was then the most technical pitch on the island, with a short 6c section to bypass the original aid bolt. On the Meadow Face, Little and Howett added *Blundecral*. A few weeks later, Robin McAllister and Andrew Fraser unwittingly repeated the lower section, adding their *Blunderbuss Finish*, both lines failing to address the main challenge by traversing off onto easier ground. McAllister and Fraser soon returned to add the longest extreme on the island with *Gulliver's Travels*, one of the few routes to break the alliterative trend of route names on the cliff. Robin returned the following year with Dave McGimpsey and, after practising the pitch on a shunt, added the hard and bold *True Finish* to *Blundecral*. Proving that excellent routes of a reasonable standard abound, even on the most popular cliffs, Martin Reynard found *Ariel's Arête* and *Fox Among the Chickens* on the Lower East Face of Cir Mhor, and Little and Howett produced the best route on the South Slabs with *Blankist*. The following year, Howett went on to add the first E6 in the mountains on Arran with *The Brigand* up on The Bastion. Standards took a considerable leap forward in 2001 when Dave MacLeod ascended the obvious central challenge on The Bastion, only to find out soon afterwards that, despite the route requiring further cleaning and the chalk running out, John Dunne had apparently beaten him to it. Despite this controversy, at E8, *The Great Escape* stands as a pointer to the standards achievable by the adoption of headpoint tactics in the mountains. Later that year a clutch of hard additions appeared on the other showpiece cliff on the island, the Rosa Pinnacle of Cir Mhor. Slab maestro Julian Lines on-sight soloed first *West Point* then *Insertion Direct*. He then confirmed what anyone who has climbed with him over the last few years already knows, which is that he is one of the boldest (craziest?) climbers of his generation, when he on-sight soloed a new 100m E5 5c line *Forge* next to *Anvil*. Round the corner Gary Latter added *Incus*, Dan Honeyman headpointed *Hardland*, and MacLeod added a couple of pitches below the impressive (as yet unclimbed!) hanging prow at the top of the East Face – *The Sleeping Crack*.

BEINN TARSUINN
(TRANSVERSE MOUNTAIN)
The next hill north of Beinn Nuis, connected by a grassy ridge.

NR 962 412 **Alt:** 570m
MEADOW FACE 2¼hr

An extensive clean 200m high gradually steepening face, which takes its name from the prominent small area of lush grass below the base. Despite its sunny aspect, many of the routes can take a couple of days to dry after heavy rain, due to a fair bit of vegetation on ledges.

Approach: From the small car park by the Glen Rosa campsite, follow the track up the glen for 2.2km to cross the bridge over the Garbh Allt. Follow the path steeply up the right (north) side of the burn. After 600m, take the right path fork and follow it over the first small hill (Cnoc Breac). From the small col beyond, contour into Coire a' Bhradain and continue NW, roughly following the line of the burn into Ealta Choire.

Descent: Down the right side of the cliff, by a well-worn path which runs underneath Consolation Tor then drop back down into the coire.

1 **The Blinder** ★★   **140m E1 5b**

FA Bill Skidmore & Jim Crawford (2 PA) 21 August 1971;
FFA Jim Perrin & partner August 1976

The striking corner line left of the imposing left edge of the main slabs. The top two pitches call upon old-fashioned chimney techniques and feel as hard as anything on the lower pitches.

1 **35m 5b** Gain the crack from a small ledge and follow it direct until it is possible to traverse left to a belay on a grass ledge.

2 **20m 5a** Regain the main corner and cross a small roof then continue past a grass clump to belay in a small recess.

3 **30m 5a** Climb the groove past a grass section and up to an undercut bulge, which leads to a good stance in a deep chimney.

4 **25m 4c** Climb the chimney via a chokestone to exit onto the floor of great square recess. It is also possible to avoid the main challenge by climbing a line of flakes (poorly protected) on the wall left of the chimney.

5 **30m 4c** Enter a tight slot in the right hand corner and struggle to a boulder bulge, moving onto the left wall above this. Continue left up easy groove to a large flake belay at top.

📷 Alan Ramsay starting up the second pitch of The Blinder.

② Brobdingnag ★★   203m E2 5c

FA Ian Duckworth, J.Fraser & W.Smith (4 PA) April 1975

Follows the great left edge of the cliff. Start on a sloping grass ledge to the right of *The Blinder*.

1 **30m 5b** Traverse right to a small corner. Climb the corner and continue straight up to a large grass ledge.

2 **18m 5b** Climb a grassy groove to an often wet over-hang, turn it on the left and belay below twin cracks.

3 **18m 5a** Climb the cracks to an overhang and step right to a shelf below a shallow chimney. Climb the chimney to a belay below a thin crack in wall.

4 **45m 5b** Climb the crack and swing left to gain a ramp. Move right then left on good holds and follow a corner to belay below a small cave.

5 **12m** Climb up left easily through a remark-able rock arch to belay in a deep hole.

6 **20m 5a** Climb a loose slab to a ledge then directly up a good jamming crack and exit right to a large stance.

7 **15m 5a** Follow the left-hand crack and transfer to the right-hand crack to pull over a jammed block.

8 **45m 4c** Climb a corner and slabs to finish.

③ Blundecral ★★   115m E3 5c

FA Graham Little & Kev Howett 5 August 1995

This varied and interesting route climbs a line on the wall between *Brobdingnag* and *Brachistochrone* taking the obvious break through the band of overhangs at the end of the long roof running left from *Brachistochrone*. Start on a vegetated ledge at a bay to the left of the first chimney of *Brachistochrone* gained by scrambling up the groove to below the chimney then traversing left.

1 **25m 4c** Climb a flake then move right to an obvious groove (which runs parallel to the *Brachistochrone* chimney). Ascend the groove or wall to right then move left to belay at a pointed turf ledge.

2 **25m 5c** Follow the line of a thin diagonal crack up and left to a left-trending ramp which leads to the base of a right-facing corner. Climb this then step left to grasp a huge block/flake. From its top make a difficult step right to gain a rock ramp and belay.

3 **15m 5c** Climb the diagonal undercling to reach

a hidden left-trending groove. Ascend this for 3m then traverse back right across the wall to gain the obvious thin rock ramp. Move right to belay at a small turf ledge. A spectacular pitch.

4 **25m 5c** Climb the fine diagonal rock ramp above to step left onto a continuation ramp. Go up this to a knobbly vein on the wall above. Pull up on to a shelf and move left up this to gain the obvious flake crack, which is climbed to a ledge above. Belay on the right. A bold pitch.

5 **25m 4c** (for the jump!) Walk right along the ledge until a mauvais pas is reached. Jump down on to a grass ledge and grab an enormous flake. Ascend this then blocks to belay on *Brachistochrone* (at the end of the difficult climbing on this route). Scramble up a grassy groove then traverse off right to clear the crag.

③a Blundecral True Finish ★★   30m E5 6a

FA Robin McAllister & Dave McGimpsey (headpointed) 4 August 1996

A significantly harder finish, bold and poorly protected on the crux traverse. From the belay at the top of pitch 4 move left and climb a steep slab on tiny holds to a wide horizontal break. Move left along this break until a step up onto a narrow sloping ramp can be made. Move left again (joining the *Blunderbuss Finish*) to reach and climb a flake crack leading to a narrow chimney. Ascend the chimney taking either fork to reach a wide ledge. Belay well back on a large spike. Either continue up the *Blunderbuss Finish* or traverse right to quit the crag.

③b The Blunderbuss Finish ★★   215m HVS 5a

FA Andrew Fraser & Robin McAllister 31 August 1995

A finely situated left finish, extending the route to the top of the crag and missing out the crux section of the original route.

1-3 **65m** Climb the first three pitches of *Blundecral*.

4 **25m 5a** Climb the diagonal rock ramp, as for *Blundecral*, step left onto a con-tinuation ramp and follow it for 7m to take a spectacularly-situated belay on the ramp.

5 **25m 4b** Continue up the ramp for 3m then move up onto a higher ramp. Follow this leftwards until it leads to a wide grassy fault (*Brobdingnag*). Climb this to a cave belay beneath an arch at 7m.

6 **25m 5a** Quit *Brobdingnag* by jumping onto a grass ledge to the right of the belay. Follow this rightwards and down to its end then take the flake crack leading up to a narrow chimney, taking either fork to gain a wide ledge.

7 **50m 4c** Climb a slab at the extreme left of the upper face to its apex, move right then continue to climb the left-trending flake cracks above.

8 **25m** Pleasant climbing up walls and cracks leads to the top.

4 **Brachistochrone** ★★ **240m E1 5b**

FA Mike Galbraith & Alasdair 'Bugs' McKeith 18 September 1966; FFA Ian Duckworth & party April 1975

"... that thought-provoking slit down the full height of the Meadow Face. To then hear it described as an 'interesting enough struggle' can make a man suspect the approach of old age or a leg-pull." – Bill Skidmore, 1972 SMCJ The left of the two long parallel cracks with 'some remarkable situations' in the lower section. Outstanding climbing if climbed to the terrace and walk-off. Scramble up a groove to the base of the chimney.

1 **45m 4c** Climb the chimney then a flake overhang and the twin cracks above to a belay ledge beneath a huge roof.

2 **15m 5b** Climb twin overhanging cracks through the roof to a block belay in a chimney.

3 **28m 4c** Traverse left up a layback shelf then back right to a ledge. Climb a crack then a further crack past a chokestone to a ledge.

4 **17m 5a** Climb overhanging crack to recess. Swing down left to a steep slab and go up to a grassy ledge and block belay. Walk off here, or:

5–7 **90m** Continue by grassy grooves, slabs, corners and flakes, crossing *Meadow Slabs* to the continuation of the crack in the upper slabs.

8 **45m 4b** Finish up the crack over three overlaps, turning the middle one on the right.

5 **Bogle** ★ **220m E2 5c**

FA Ian Rowe & Ian Dundas 22 July 1967; FFA Jim Perrin & partner August 1976; pitch 5 Varn. George Szuca & Andy Wren 27 May 1991

The right of the two long parallel crack lines splitting the front of the face with a disproportionately hard 6m of ferocious fist jamming on the crux pitch. Scramble up to belay at the base of the crack.

1+2 **60m 4c** Follow the general line of the crack to belay on a slab beneath the large overhang.

3 **15m 5c** Move up onto a pedestal then follow the 'strenuous, slimy' crux crack for 6m then traverse 3m right and up a parallel crack to belay on the ledge above.

4 **25m 5b** Continue up the crack.

5a **15m 4c** Climb the slimy cave by a contorted through route then move left up a slab to belay 6m above.

5b **15m Ungradeable** (XS). If, as reported, the through route is still blocked by turf and rubble, it can be bypassed by an intimidating stomach traverse left along a shallow wet sloping shelf.

6 **30m** Scramble up to the foot of the *Meadow Slabs*.

7 **50m 4b** Follow the continuation of the crack to a large summit block.

8 **25m 4c** Finish up two left cracks.

6 **The Rake Direct** ★ **210m E2 5c**

FA Bill Skidmore & Bob Richardson (2 PA) 18 August 1962; Direct Start: George McEwan & Alastair Walker 21 May 1988

At the bottom right of the main face is a huge slab, bounded on the right with a large groove line. Start at the base of the slab.

1+2 **90m 4b** Climb directly up the centre of the slab to belay on a large grass ledge, beneath a slabby corner containing two small overlaps.

3 **35m 5a** Climb up and left through the overlaps then traverse left to another slabby corner. Climb this then traverse left to belay on top of a huge flake.

4 **15m 5b** Gain and climb the overhanging crack above to belay below a corner.

5 **30m 5c** Go up then round right into a corner, climb this with difficulty (often wet) to gain an obvious

bay on the right. Follow a crack in the slab on the left and rock ledges to belay on a grass ledge.

6 **10m 4b** Climb the corner above to a grass ledge and PB in overhanging cave.

7 **15m** As for pitch 5 of *Bogle*, or from the top of pitch 5, traverse left for 7m, moving up onto a higher ledge to join *Brachistochrone* at the start of pitch 4.

8 **15m** Scramble up to the terrace.

7 Gulliver's Travels ** 300m E2 5c

FA Andrew Fraser & Robin McAllister 20 September 1995

A fine adventure with spectacular positions making up for the relative shortage of new ground. It follows a natural rising traverse, using the leftward trend and ledged nature of the cliff. The longest extreme on the island. Follow the first 5 pitches of *The Rake Direct* to belay in *Bogle*.

6 **30m 5a** Move up to a ledge on the left and follow this left to the crack of *Brachistochrone*. Descend this for 3m past a chokestone then follow a ramp up left past an awkward break to take a spectacularly-situated belay on the ramp 7m beyond the break.

7 **30m 4b** Continue up the ramp for 3m then move up onto a higher ramp. Follow this leftwards until it leads to a wide grassy fault (*Brobdingnag*). Climb this to a cave beneath an arch at 7m then traverse left to a block belay overlooking *The Blinder*.

8 **40m 5c** A sensational and intimidating traverse leads to *The Blinder* (a rope looped over the top of the arch lowers the fall potential). Continue to a chimney which is climbed via a chokestone to exit on to the floor of a great square recess.

9 **30m XS** 4c Finish as for the last pitch of *The Blinder*.

8 The Curver ** 130m E1 5b

FA Rab Carrington & Ian Fulton 14 June 1968

Good delicate slab climbing, though slow to dry. It follows a series of grooves up through the curving overlaps, above and roughly parallel to the original grassy line of *The Rake*. Start near two overlapping slabs, close to the end of pitch 1 of *Meadow Slabs*.

1 **25m** Climb a slab and groove to belay above a damp corner.

2 **25m** Climb the groove on the right for 9m, gain a higher slab on the right then follow the slab corner for 12m. Move out right to reach a small stance and belay.

3 **40m** Move leftwards to gain the base of a narrow slab gangway, and continue to a deep flake crack. Climb this, or the layback shelf on the right to a block belay on a large ledge.

4 **40m** Pull round the edge on the right on quartz holds then follow a line of holds across slabs to finish up a corner.

9 Snakes and Ladders *** 50m E2 5b

FA Colin Moody & Billy Hood 16 May 1998

A slab of perfect rock up right of *The Curver*. Easily seen from the slopes on the right, it contains a vertical heather crack on the right side. The pitch was gained by abseil from chokestones at the top. Traditionalists can alternatively gain the base by two pitches of grassy grooves. Start up a bulge on the left side and follow the crack to a downward-pointing flake. Traverse right for 5m then climb straight up on seams and pocks to the left of the heather crack. A F #2 protects the top section, a R #6 can be threaded just below it.

10 Meadow Slabs * 60m Difficult

FA Geoffrey Curtis, Ken Moneypenny & E.Morrison 20 August 1944

Pleasant climbing up the left edge of the upper slabs. Start at the left end of The Terrace, beneath a chokestoned crack formed by a slab and the wall above. Climb the crack then descend obliquely left on turf ledges towards the base of the blunt skyline ridge. Cross a slab, beyond which will be seen the foot of a 3m chimney which marks the start of the climb proper.

1 **10m** Climb the little chimney which narrows to a crack then gives access to the crest.

2 **20m** Climb a short undercut chimney on the left then easier ground to a belay.

3 **30m** Go slightly right then slant left up a grassy crack to reach a branching chimney. Climb the left wall then above by a slanting crack. Gain a short arête to finish.

GOATFELL
(HILL OF THE WIND)
The highest, most prominent and by far the most popular hill on the island.

SOUTH SLABS (w) 1¾hr

NR 986 409 **Alt:** 420m

A prominent area of clean compact slabs high on the west flank of the hill. The rock is more continuous and cleaner than the main Rosa Slabs, offering far and away the best middle grade friction routes on the island. Generally the rock is climbable anywhere, though protection is often noticeably lacking.

Approach: From the campsite continue up the forestry track and the continuation path to the footbridge over the Garbh Allt after 2km. Cross the bridge and continue up the path close to the west bank of Glenrosa Water for a further 2km then cross the stream and slog steeply up the hillside on the right (300m of ascent) to the base of the slabs.

Descent: By a vague path down the right (south) edge of the slabs.

 Blankist ★★★★   **110m HVS 4c**

FA p1 Dave Bathgate & Jim Renny 21 June 1964;
Graham Little & Kev Howett 20 August 1995

The best route on the slabs taking a direct line up the right on perfect rock. Start 10m right of the left-trending broken fault.

  1 **30m 4c** Climb straight up the holdless slab immediately right of a black streak to reach flakes. Ascend these to belay on a small gravel ledge in a heather groove on the right.

  2 **25m 4b** Move out left and climb slightly leftwards

up a line of perfect pockets moving left to gain
an obvious long thin downward-pointing flake.
Thin moves above this lead to a fine flake belay.
A direct line right of this can also be taken to
belay at a large flake crack further right.

3 45m 4b Climb straight up a bare slab to
move right to gain and follow an obvious rib
(overlooking a long corner to the right) then
up easier-angled slabs to step right to belay at
the base of a short banana-shaped groove. A
memorable pitch – very bold, but steady.

4 10m Scramble up heather to finish.

② Blank ★★★   110m VS 4b
FA Alasdair 'Bugs' McKeith & B.Kennelly 13 September 1963

Great climbing, taking a line near the centre of the slabs.
Start 5m right of the left-trending broken fault.

1 30m 4b Climb the slab boldly, heading for a line
of scoops and flakes then follow these trending
slightly right to belay on a small gravel ledge
in a heather groove (common to *Blankist*).

2 45m 4b Step left, move up then follow a wide
vein running left across the slab until 5m short
of a heather groove. Follow a line of pockets up
a shallow scoop to gain and climb a flake groove.
At its top traverse 3m right, surmount an overlap
then climb straight up on pockets to a ledge.

3 35m 4b Climb directly up the centre of the
big slab. A superb unprotected pitch.

③ Filling in the Blanks ★★★   120m HVS 4c
FA p1 Andy Nisbet April/May 2004;
p2 Gary & Karen Latter 9 July 2005

Superb bold climbing plugging the obvious gap up the
centre of the slabs.

1 50m 4b Climb the first pitch of *Blank* but
instead of moving out right to the belay follow
the lower dyke leftwards then follow a line of
pockets trending leftwards up the slab to belay
at the base of the easy flake groove on *Blank*.

2 60m 4c Climb easily to the break, step up

right onto the slab above and move up
leftwards to boldly climb the slightly
protruding rib above. A superb bold pitch.

3 10m scramble to finish.

④ Dogleg ★★   115m VS 4b
FA Jim Brumfitt & Alasdair 'Bugs' McKeith 21 June 1964

Similarly bold climbing to the neighbouring *Blank*. Start
at the base of the left-trending broken fault.

1 50m 4b Climb the slab to a break in a thin
overlap at 6m, surmount this then up a flake
edge. Trend slightly rightwards up undulating
slabs to gain a short flake groove, up this then
traverse left to a heather groove and up this,
moving up right to belay at base of a groove.

2 50m 4b Climb the easy flake crack in the groove
to an old PR then traverse left until a line of
pockets leads up the fine slab direct into the
curving right-facing corner. Step left and follow
the rib left of the corner, leading
to easier upper slabs.

3 15m Scramble to finish.

⑤ Trundle ★   130m Severe 4a
FA W.Bailey & R.White 1 April 1964

Good climbing up the left side of the slabs. Start 12m left
of the left-trending broken fault.

1 30m 4a Move up into a scoop, step right
then climb up into narrow grooves and
follow these up left to a prominent flake.

2 30m 4a Move up a short way then
traverse right to a thread runner on an
edge. Continue slightly leftwards by a
fading layback crack then over bulges and
slabs to belay on a heather ledge.

3 35m 4a Traverse up rightwards across the fault
to a mossy corner. Climb this then move right
to climb a crack up the slab to a block belay.

4 35m 4a Traverse right along ledges for 5m then
up rightwards past a large knob to finish.

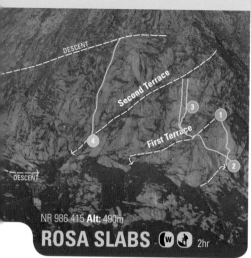

NR 986 415 **Alt:** 490m

ROSA SLABS 🌊 🧗 2hr

The large expanse 500m further north up Glen Rosa from the South Slabs. Two right-slanting rakes, the First and Second Terraces, split the slabs into three sections.

Approach: As for the South Slabs, continuing for a further 0.5km then cross the stream and slog steeply up the heather-clad hillside on the right (midway between the 3rd and 4th burns coming down the hillside) to the base of the slabs.

Descents: Down the left (north) side of the crag, or down either of the Terraces.

① Angel's Pavement ★★   80m HS 4b
FA Neil MacNiven & G.Kilgour 27 July 1960

A very good short route up the lower right side of the slabs. Start by scrambling up rightwards along a grassy rake above the small isolated hanging slab at the bottom right of the cliff.

1 **20m 4a** Climb a prominent vertical crack to break through the overlap by the obvious weakness to a small spike belay on the right.
2 **25m 4b** Follow the obvious line diagonally left then a prominent chain of pitted holds leading up right then climb direct up the slab for 4m to a rounded ledge. Traverse easily left to belay on a small ledge.
3 **35m 4a** Climb direct up the slab, crossing two small overlaps to finish at the upper end of the First Terrace.

② The Perfect Fool ★   170m HVS 4c
FA Andy Nisbet & Alf Robertson 19 April 1981

The best 'non-line' on the slabs, taking the centre of the blankest steepest section. Steady climbing, though protection and belays are scarce. Start about 10m right of *Angel's Pavement*. Climb diagonally left across the clean slab crossing a small overlap until it is possible to go straight up to the terrace at the foot of *Fool's Causeway*. Climb the first 7m of that route then go straight up the slab to an overlap. Surmount the overlap and continue straight up keeping to the rock.

③ Fool's Causeway ★   90m HVS 4c
FA Neil MacNiven & G.Kilgour 27 July 1960

Good climbing up the right side of the middle tier. Start at a thread belay below a smooth water-streaked slab lower down the terrace from the finish of *Angel's Pavement*, gained via either of the two previous routes.

1 **25m 4c** Gain the foot of the slab from the right and follow a very thin grassy crack rightwards to its end then move up to a poor PB in a pocket.
2 **35m 4c** Friction up rightwards to a line of pockets leading to a tiny groove, developing into a layback crack and curving into a small overlap. Continue by an easier groove above then a slab to a ledge.
3 **30m** Finish by easier slabs leading to near the upper end of the Second Terrace.

④ Zigzag Direct ★★   120m Severe 4a
FA Davy McKelvie & Dick Sim June 1958; Direct Start Bill Wallace, Dick Sim & Miss G.Hamilton June 1965

Good sustained climbing on excellent rock in the upper section. Start at a little rib left of the prominent waterslide.

1 **45m 4a** Climb the rib then continue direct to the base of the upper edge.
2+3 **75m 4a** Follow the edge.

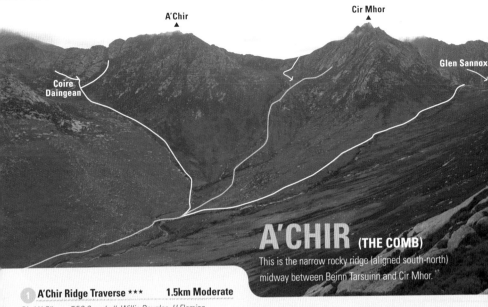

A'CHIR (THE COMB)

This is the narrow rocky ridge (aligned south-north) midway between Beinn Tarsuinn and Cir Mhor.

① A'Chir Ridge Traverse ★★★   1.5km Moderate

FA J.H.Gibson, T.F.S.Campbell, Willie Douglas, H.Fleming R.A.Robertson & Dr Leith 30 January 1892

An excellent ridge traverse with stunning views, usually traversed from south to north, saving the most difficult section to last. The rock is generally superb throughout with much variation possible, with very straightforward paths on the west flank avoiding most of the interesting sections. The best line keeps to the crest of the ridge as much as possible and is obvious and polished at a number of places where the route drops down into a succession of small cols on the ridge. About 300 metres north of the summit lies *'Le Mauvais Pas'*. The northern extremity of

the ridge terminates in a long vertical drop down to a col. About 20m south of this, descend a short wall on the east flank (arrow scratched in rock above) to gain a fine incut dipping ledge (quite exposed) dropping down north towards the col. This peters out near the base, with the final 2 metre section to a good flat landing presenting the only real difficulties on the ridge. Either descend steeply (or jump!) to gain the col. The route continues much more easily to the Cir Mhor col, affording grand views of the Rosa Pinnacle on Cir Mhor. Continuing over Cir Mhor and Goatfell gives a fantastic day's ridge walking.

NR 966 417 **Alt:** 510m   2hr

COIRE DAINGEAN FACE

A series of steep slabby buttresses split by numerous prominent deep gullies. The buttresses are traversed by vegetated ledges resulting in many of the routes being slow to dry after rain.

Approach: From the campsite in Glen Rosa, continue up the forestry track and the continuation path to the footbridge over the Garbh Allt after 2km. Cross the bridge and continue up the path close to the west bank

of Glenrosa Water for a further 3km, where the stream bends round to the left and splits. Stay on the less obvious path, which continues up the left bank for 250m then follow a vague path on the north bank of the stream on the left which leads steeply up into the north-east facing Coire Daingean.

Descent: Down the wide grassy Gully 6, which lies just left of *Slab and Flake Route*, well up and right of the buttress containing *Mosque* & *Pagoda Ridge*.

Gully 6

Boundary Gully

COIRE DAINGEAN FACE

Gully 4

Gully 5

Slab and Flake Route * 125m HS 4b

FA Geoffrey Curtis, H.Dunster & Gordon Townend
19 September 1943

Good initial climbing up the left side of the buttress
between Gully 6 and Gully 7, though grassy higher up.
Start at the bottom left edge of the buttress. The first
two pitches are well worth doing, from where a short
abseil can easily be made from the block into the gully.

1 **30m 4b** Climb the slab edge for 15m
then go diagonally right then back left
again to the edge. Large flake belay.

2 **20m 4a** Climb the flake by either edge (easiest on
the left) then cross a heather terrace to block belay
on the edge. Either abseil off (recommended), or:

3 **15m 4b** Climb a cleft slanting right behind a
further flake containing a chokestone. From the
top left edge of the flake, step across onto the
steep wall opposite (crux) to gain a ledge above.

4 **25m** Follow the rising grass rake on the right to
a rock shelf, and up this leftwards to another
shelf. Move right up a slab to a flake belay.

5 **20m** Climb the corner to a bouldery terrace and
spike (possible belay). Climb the spur behind the
spike and a slab above then go right to a block belay.

6 **15m** Climb the wall and crack which leads to
a grass terrace at the top of the buttress.

Mosque *** 220m VS 4c

FA Ian Fulton & J.Shaw 20 July 1968

An excellent fairly direct and sustained line up the
buttress. Start just left of the slabby toe of the buttress,
where PR and *Mosque* are scratched on rock.

1 **40m 4c** Friction up the widening slab to an
overlap then traverse left to a peculiar 'bulb-shaped
protuberance'. Cross the overlap then move up
to the next overlap. Move down and right to
belay at an old peg just below a small juniper.

2 **30m 4c** Climb the slab above then move right to
a flake on the edge of the next overlap. Surmount
this and continue to yet another overlap. Climb
this and the slab above to a ledge and flake belay.

3 **20m 4b** Climb the bulging wall right of the belay
then a slab and grass to belay beneath an overlap.

4 **20m 4b** Cross the overlap just left of the belay
then climb leftwards to a good small hidden thread
runner. Follow a line of pockets rightwards over
an edge to belay in a small recess on the right.

5 **40m 4b** Climb the recess then move rightwards up

pockets then traverse hard right to a wide grungy
crack in the overlap. Climb this and turf then
boldly up the slab above to belay on the edge.

6+7 70m Finish up the edge overlooking
the gully (as for *Pagoda Ridge*).

⑧ Pagoda Ridge ★★ 225m Severe 4a

FA Geoffrey Curtis & Gordon Townend 25 May 1943

Very good climbing, up the edge overlooking Gully
4. Start just left of the lowest slab, at the toe of the
buttress (PR and arrow scratched on rock).

1 25m Climb a heathery crack which ends in a
sharp flake then traverse left and up to a heather
patch then cross a slab to beneath an overlap.

2 25m 4a Move up onto a sloping shelf (the middle
of three such features). Undercut this diagonally leftwards to the edge and up this to a belay. A fine pitch.

3 20m Follow the edge with one short dog-leg
move right to thread belays at the base of a
pile of blocks beneath a heather ledge.

4 35m 4a Climb a short steep crack above
the heather to a ledge above then up an
easy slab diagonally rightwards to belay
on spikes in a small corner on the right.

5 25m 4a Using the spikes, swing round the arête
on the right and traverse across a slab then step
up and traverse back left to a thread belay on
the edge. Variation: It is also possible to climb
straight up from the spikes and mantelshelf

onto the slab above, eliminating the zig-zag.

6 35m 4a Move up on to the ledge above then
continue quite boldly up the edge in a fine position
to a steep cracked wall. Over this then up broken
ground to a thread belay beneath a huge boulder.

7 40m Continue more easily up
the crest to a block belay.

8 20m Finish over a jumble of boulders.

④ Boundary Ridge ★★ 115m Difficult

*FA Geoffrey Curtis, H.Dunster, Ken Moneypenny & Gordon
Townend 4 July 1943*

Good climbing. Start 15m up from the lowest rocks, at a
notch in the crest of the ridge.

1 20m Climb a slab to a block on the crest then swing
left to a grassy shelf which leads to a block belay.

2 20m Follow the wide crack which leads to a
spike leaning against the wall on the right.

3 20m Climb the wall and crack which
leads to the base of a steep arête.

4 20m Climb the arête to a ledge, traverse
right a few metres then up a steep slab and
broken ground to a platform containing a
jumble of blocks overlooking Boundary Gully.

5 35m Follow the horizontal ledge rightwards past
a pool of water then climb the slab above. Slant
up left to a wall with a Y-shaped crack, and up
this to a rock shelf leading to a final short wall.

📷 *Gary Latter on the first pitch of Slab and Flake Route.
Photo Karen Latter.*

CIR MHOR (THE GREAT COMB) 🏔 🅢 🏔 🚶 2½hr

This distinctive pointed peak dominates the skyline at the head of the long boggy Glen Rosa and is far and away the most spectacular and distinctive of all the Arran hills. A selection of fluted buttresses lie on the south side of the mountain with the superb slabs and steep walls of the Rosa Pinnacle taking pride of place in the centre of the face. Despite the longest approach on the island, it is justifiably the most popular – well worth the effort!

Approaches: (A) Up the forestry track from the campsite and up the path to the footbridge over the Garbh Allt after 2km. Cross the bridge and continue close to the west bank of Glenrosa Water for a further 3km to where the stream bends round to the left and splits. Stay on the less obvious path which continues up the left bank for 350m. The way steepens on the path up the hillside into Fionn Choire. The cliff lies about 300m north-east from the path (half an hour from fork in path).

(B) A slightly shorter approach is possible from Glen Sannox. Park by a telephone box on the east side of the A841 at Sannox Bay. Follow the track west up Glen Sannox past the beacons to cross the stream after a kilometre. Continue up a boggy path close to the right (north) bank of the burn for about 3km to re-cross the burn. A steep path leads up the hillside (200m ascent) to The Saddle. Drop down right slightly then contour round rough ground for almost 1km to the base of the crags.

Descent: Down the right (west) side of Caliban's Buttress. Alternatively, for routes on the right side of the cliffs, descend the broad Sub Rosa Gully between the Rosa Pinnacle and Prospero Buttress, avoiding a short area of slabs low down by either of two forks, easiest by the left (east) fork.

ROSA PINNACLE 🅢 🏔

NR 972 428 **Alt:** 550m

The showpiece cliff on the island, with a range of excellent routes of almost every grade. Many of the routes criss-cross in the middle and upper sections of the cliff, and there is much scope for interchanging pitches.

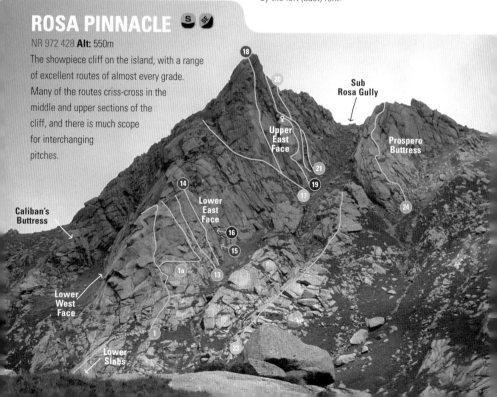

SOUTH FACE, ROSA PINNACLE

1 **South Ridge Direct ★★★★**   **330m VS 5a**

FA J.F. 'Hamish' Hamilton & David Paterson September 1941

A very popular classic, with three harder pitches – the 'S', 'Y' and 'Layback' cracks. The ridge forms a steep nose rising out of a mass of vegetated slabs on the lower face. The first pitch of technical interest is the distinctive S-crack splitting the face of the nose. Start by scrambling up easy grass ledges right of the toe of the buttress.

1 **44m 4a** Follow cracked slabs on the left, leading to ledges on the right. Continue to a right-facing corner. Climb the layback flake on the right then move back left to belay at the top of the corner.

2 **6m** Step left and up easy corner to base of S-crack.

3 **25m 4c** The S-crack leads to a large block belay on a wide shelf. A fine pitch.

4 **10m 5a** The overhanging Y-cracks now loom above. Climb these strenuously (crux) to a belay just above.

5 **45m** Move up to a block-strewn terrace, step round a rib on the left then follow an easy diagonal traverse to belay in the far corner beneath the Layback Crack.

6 **25m 4b** Follow the Layback Crack until a vein runs out right. Follow it across the slab then climb a short easy flake crack to gain a large platform. The corner crack can also be followed in its entirety – *Lovat's Variation*, VS 4b.

7 **25m** Above lies the obvious Three-Tier Chimney on the left side of the crest of the ridge. Follow the chimney to gain the crest of the ridge.

8+9 60m Follow the crest of the ridge in two easy pitches to gain The Terrace beneath the Upper Pinnacle.

10 40m Start in a recess beneath the rightmost of two slabby right-facing corners. Climb either the corner or the slab on the right to gain a fault near the ridge crest. Follow this easily then the blocky chimney above to a long grass ledge.

11 35m Walk along the grass ledge to a little chimney. Climb the slab on its right to the ridge crest. Move round right onto the east face then make an exposed traverse right into an open flake-corner. Climb this to belay in a crevasse.

12 15m Continue easily up the crest to the top of the Upper Pinnacle.

1a **South Ridge Original ★★**   **60m VS 4b**

FA J.Ramsay & party 1935

A worthy alternative, especially if there is a bottleneck of climbers on the S-crack, or to avoid the harder Y-crack.

1 **30m** Traverse right from the foot of the S-crack below the steep wall then climb up into a turfy recess beneath the large undercut corner.

2 **30m 4b** Climb out of the recess into the corner and climb it; then the cracks in the slabby left wall to the block-strewn terrace.

2 **Incus ★★**   **55m E6 6b**

FA Gary Latter 27 August 2001

A series of pitches up the wall left of *South Ridge Direct*, the main centre of interest being the thin flange 15m left of the S-crack. Start on the front face just round right of *Anvil Recess Start* beneath a short groove.

1 **15m 5a** Climb the short undercut groove to layback onto a slab above then more easily up this. Climb easily right across a slab then up past a large flake to belay on a grass clod directly beneath the flange.

1a **30m 5a** A longer better pitch, occasionally climbed as an approach to the S-Crack. Start further right, beneath a left-facing groove. Enter and climb the wide slot in the groove to easier ground then continue by a steep hand crack and cracks just to its left to belay on grass clod above large flake.

2 **10m 6b** Move up the corner and step left across the slab to the flange. Climb this with interest (sustained and well protected) then use a one-finger pocket in the wall above to hand traverse left on a micro-granite vein to superb finishing holds. Belay on the shelf above.

3 **15m 5c** Walk right along the shelf to belay at the base of the curving corner. Climb this, moving up right at its top to a huge thread. Abseil off. Alternatively, climb up leftwards from the top of the corner to gain the block-strewn terrace on *South Ridge Direct*.

LOWER WEST FACE
The superb, generally immaculate slabs extending leftwards up the slope from the toe of the South Face.

3a Anvil Recess Start ★★★   **40m HVS 5a**

FA Bill Skidmore, Jim Crawford & John Madden 16 July 1964

Better than the parent route. Start at a block at the base of a left-slanting corner crack, directly beneath the huge inverted V-shaped recess on the front face of the ridge.

  1 15m 4b Climb the corner crack to a spike belay.

  2 25m 5a Pull round left to gain the slab above, and move up until it is possible to move right to the bottom of a large flake lodged under the right wall of the recess. Climb the flake and step left to the opposite wall then strenuously gain the slab above. Continue more easily by a crack on the right and over a grass tuft then move left to reach the cave belay on *Anvil*.

3 Anvil ★★   **55m HVS 5a**

FA Davy McKelvie & Bob Richardson 6 August 1960

Start at a wide crack a few metres right of *Hammer*.

  1 30m 5a Follow the crack to just left of the corner of a small overlap. Descend 3m then traverse delicately right across the steep slab to gain holds on the slab edge which lead up through the overlap to a sloping platform. Continue up the narrow groove above to belay on a grass ledge.

  2 15m 4b Move up grassy grooves left to belay in a cave.

  3 10m 5a Break out right then follow an easy shelf to gain *South Ridge Direct*.

3b Variation Finish ★★   **25m VS 4c**

FA Bob Richardson & John Madden 1965

From the cave, traverse left and climb a rounded bulging groove to beneath an overhang. Right up a slab then climb a groove and further slabs to finish on *South Ridge Direct*.

4 Insertion ★★   **105m E3 5c**

FA Rab Carrington & Ian Fulton 15 June 1969

A very bold slab climb of its day. Start 1m right of *Anvil*.

  1 45m 5c Climb straight up the steep slab to an overlap, cross this, continue up a further steep slab, trending right to belay a short way beneath the cave on *Anvil*.

  2 30m 4c Traverse up and left beneath the large overhang then ascend the bulging rounded groove (as for *Anvil Variation Finish*) to beneath the overhang. Pull out right onto a slab then move easily left, crossing *South Ridge Direct* to belay below a steep slab.

  3 30m 4c Move up left then traverse horizontally right below an overhanging wall. Continue right round an edge to a crack which leads to the large platform beneath the Three-Tier Chimney on *South Ridge Direct*.

4a Insertion Direct ★★   **105m E5 5c**

FA Mark Charlton & Kev Howett June 1986

A very thin bold first pitch climbing direct up the slab. Start as for *Insertion*.

  1 50m 5c Climb as for the normal route to over the overlap then straight up into a scoop in the centre of the slab. Ascend this then teeter rightwards to take a hanging belay under the big overhang at the base of the *"bulging rounded groove"* of *Anvil Variation Finish*.

  2 30m 5a Gain and climb the groove to below a roof. Move out right up a slab to belay at its top below a bulging wall with a large pocket.

  3 25m 5c Pull past the pocket and smaller ones above. Swing round the edge then climb to reach easier ground on *South Ridge Direct*.

5 Forge ★★   **100m E5 5c**

FA Julian Lines (on-sight solo) 28 July 2001

Bold sustained climbing.

  1 50m 5c Start as for *Anvil*, but where that route goes right continue up the groove and flakes. When it becomes blank, move right onto the slab and up to pockets. Step right and continue up into a scoop with a tiny flake. Exit the scoop on the right and move up to a shallow-angled slab. Just before a bulging section, traverse down and left to reach *Hammer*.

  2 25m 5b Follow a line of pockets up and right until they disappear then go straight up the slab to a horizontal flake-line. Move right to easy ground to belay below the slabby arête on the skyline.

3 25m 5c Using a short crack/pod on the left of the arête, make a thin move to gain the arête. Climb the arête on the right for 3m (easy) then make a hard move left onto a boss/smear and further hard moves up to small holds on the slab. Stretch right to good pockets in the very crest and climb direct to join *South Ridge Direct*.

6 Hammer **   85m VS 4c

FA Donny Cameron & Dick Sim 6 August 1960

Good climbing, starting up the tapering slab just right of *West Flank Route*.

1 25m 4b Climb up onto the slab then move left to a crack and follow this and the small continuation groove to belay midway up the two-tiered chimney on *West Flank Route*.

2 20m 4c Descend a short way then traverse right and follow a good tufty crack to a large belay ledge.

3 40m 4b Follow the crack in the slab to reach a vein of micro-granite near the top. Delicately follow the vein right to a crack which leads to the base of the Layback Crack on *South Ridge Direct*.

6a Pocket Slab Variation **   35m VS 4b

FA Colin Moody & Cynthia Grindley 9 July 2005

Apparently much better than the original. Instead of following the vein rightwards, follow a line of pockets up slightly left then back right. Finish straight up to join *South Ridge Direct*.

7 West Flank Route ****   155m E1 5b

FA Jim Crawford, John Madden, Bob Richardson & Bill Skidmore 3 August 1963

A classic route, taking the line of left-trending open chimneys and cracks. Low in the grade. Start beneath the prominent open chimney in the centre of the main slab.

1 35m 5a Struggle up the two-tiered chimney-like feature, (possible belay at 20m) to a ledge beneath a small overlap in the slab.

2 25m 4b Continue up the long left-slanting diagonal

crack in the slab above to the large overlap. Move right round the corner to belay in a niche.

3 30m 5b Step up and left round an edge into a groove and crack, and follow these to gain a small spike and flake by a rounded layback. Take the right branch of the crack until a move left can be made across the slab. Climb to a horizontal crack then traverse left across the slab (crux) and climb up to a thread belay (on *Sou'wester Slabs*) at the top of a grassy groove.

4 35m 4c Ascend the corner above the belay, and step left to a ledge on the slab edge. Climb the edge to a large overhang, hand traverse 2m left to gain a wall and continue left round a bulge. Climb up easier ground to a belay.

5 30m Climb broken slabs to a short wall then a recess, to finish up a crack leading to The Terrace.

The two prominent chimney systems are *The Sickle* * HVS 4c, 5a, 4c and *The Iron Fist* * E1 4c, 5b respectively.

8 Vanishing Point ***   100m E4 6a

FA Craig Macadam & Simon Steer May 1985

Thin bold slab climbing. Start at the same point as *The Sickle*, at an easy flake system.

1 30m 6a Up the easy flake for 10m then up to flakes in the slab above. Traverse right with difficulty to gain the prominent flake crack. Continue up this with increasing interest, passing two prominent pockets to belay.

2 45m 4c Step right onto the slab and climb direct up this heading leftwards into the lower continuation of the *South Ridge* layback. Up this to belay at the base of the layback pitch.

3 25m 6a Up the corner for 4m then foot traverse left to a shallow groove in the arête. Up this then the thin bold slab above to finish on *Sou'wester Slabs*.

9 Fourth Wall *   125m HS 4b

FA Gordon Townend & Ken Moneypenny 5 August 1945

Good open climbing, with only the last pitch being of any difficulty. Start at the base of a long left-slanting groove, (level with the base of the vertical east wall on Caliban's Buttress).

 1 **50m** Follow the groove then the rib on the left to a block belay just above the level of the right traverse on *Sou'wester Slabs*.
 2 **50m** Continue direct by cracks and grooves to a huge plinth leaning against the face.
 3 **25m 4b** Climb the initial section of the steep narrow chimney to a small ledge then traverse right, descending slightly for 6m until it is possible to climb the delicate and exposed wall. At the top a final awkward step right into an easy groove leads to The Terrace.

10 Sou'wester Slabs ****   100m Very Difficult

FA Geoffrey Curtis, M.Hawkins, H.Hore & Gordon Townend 3 September 1944

The classic lower grade route of the island, consequently very popular.

 1 **48m** Follow *Fourth Wall* to an obvious easy traverse line out right to belay at the base of a shallow left-facing groove.
 2 **45m** Follow the groove to a large flake beneath twin parallel cracks. Continue up the cracks to the right edge of the slab. Step down to the lower slab on the right, and climb diagonally rightwards up a groove to belay at a PR under the great overhang.
 3 **7m** Traverse easily right to join *South Ridge Direct* beneath the Three-Tier Chimney.

Either finish up the last 6 pitches of *South Ridge Direct* (175m), or continue traversing round right onto the east face then up on grassy ledges. Scramble down to the top of the vegetated line of *Old East* (Mod) which leads down diagonally rightwards into Sub Rosa Gully.

11 Arctic Way **   65m HVS 5a

FA Billy Hood & Colin Moody 19 June 1982

Good sustained climbing. Follow the lower section of *Fourth Wall* to belay at the base of the prominent left-facing corner crack, below and right of the huge plinth on *Fourth Wall*.

 1 **40m 5a** Climb the corner then the continuation crack, crossing two bulges to belay below an overlap.
 2 **25m 5a** Move left to a crack through the overlap and go left again to a bulge. Cross the bulge then left up the slab for just over a metre. Traverse right to climb a thin crack then trend left to a block belay at the top.

CALIBAN'S BUTTRESS

NR 972 429 **Alt:** 630m

The buttress immediately left of the Rosa Pinnacle, higher up the slope, level with the base of *Sou'wester Slabs*.

12 Caliban's Creep ***   150m Very Difficult

FA Geoffrey Curtis & Gordon Townend 25 July 1943

Previously a renowned sandbag and *"the hardest Diff in the world"*, it may still prove problematic to those of ample girth. Start on the right of the toe of the buttress, which forms a square-cut overhang.

 1 **25m** Climb diagonally leftwards up slabs to belay amongst a pile of boulders, beneath an overhang.
 2 **25m** Traverse right across the wall on good holds, step down and continue round the edge then up an easy chimney to belay on the right on an area of slabs.
 3 **15m** Continue up the slabby ridge crest to belay beneath the right edge of a short vertical wall.
 4 **20m** *"What have we here? A man or a fish?"* Crawl through the narrow rock tunnel on the right (The Creep) then follow a narrowing ledge round right onto the east face and into a deep chimney on the right. Climb up this to belay on the floor of the great fissure above.
 5+6 **65m** Escape from the fissure then about 60m of *"pleasant, carefree climbing near the right edge finishes the climb"*.

LOWER EAST FACE

The east flank of the South Ridge, between the corner pitch of *South Ridge Original* and *Old East*.

Approach: Up Sub Rosa Gully.

13 The Crack ⋆   45m HVS 5a
FA Ian Cranston, John Earl & Bob Hutchinson 29 May 1973

A fine looking flake crack forms a slim right-facing groove right of the corner pitch of *South Ridge Original*. Start at two parallel cracks in a protruding buttress of crumbly rock in Sub Rosa Gully.

1 **15m 5a** Follow the crumbly parallel cracks then the groove to belay on a grass ledge.

2 **30m 5a** Climb the groove on the left until level with the flake crack. Traverse left to gain the excellent flake crack, which leads to the block-strewn terrace on *South Ridge Direct*.

The following two routes lie right of *The Crack*. From the finish of either, an easy traverse left leads to the belay at the top of the Y-crack on *South Ridge Direct*, where an abseil down *South Ridge Original* is possible.

14 Ariel's Arête ⋆⋆⋆   40m E1 5b
FA Martin Reynard & Dave Musgrove 6 May 1995

A superb pitch following flakes and cracks up the striking edge. Start at a messy bay just right of *The Crack*. Scramble up the bay then move left to a ledge. Climb an awkward little wall then pull into the flake system on the right. Follow this then an amazing thin crack up the edge to gain a rock ledge. Continue up the slab past large pockets to belay at a horizontal fault.

15 Fox Among the Chickens ⋆⋆⋆   40m E2 5c
FA Martin Reynard, Dave Musgrove & Pete Benson 6 May 1995

Right of *Ariel's Arête* is a prominent wall with an obvious pocket high up and three short flake-cracks low down. Start below the centre of the wall. Climb an undercut corner then move left and up to gain the lowest of the cracks; climb these to their top. Make a move right then climb the wall directly, finishing up a short groove.

16 Hardland ⋆⋆⋆   30m E5 6a
FA Dan Honeymann & Tom De Gay (headpointed) 26 August 2001

A stunning route up the pocketed slab. Start just right of *Fox Among the Chickens* and gain the intermittent crack in the slab (good cams in these). From near the top of the second crack, break out left with difficulty to gain the huge pocket. Follow a line of pockets boldly leftwards with a final difficult move to gain the edge of the slab and the top. Either abseil off or continue as for 15.

17 Old East   60m Moderate
FA Gordon Townend & J.Jenkins August 1946

A useful approach or descent, following a vegetated curve cutting up diagonally leftwards below the base of the Upper Pinnacle, linking Sub Rosa Gully with The Terrace.

UPPER EAST FACE

A fine steep buttress rising out of the upper reaches of Sub Rosa Gully.

Approach: Up Sub Rosa Gully, or via a route on either the Lower West or Lower East Faces then descending the diagonal fault of *Old East*.

18 Skydiver Direct ⋆⋆⋆⋆   70m E3 6a
FA Graham Little & Colin Ritchie (4 PA) 1 August 1981; FFA with direct finish Colin MacLean & Andy Nisbet 7 May 1984

Excellent varied climbing with a short well protected crux. In the centre of the cliff is a slim groove splitting the arête. Scramble up (or down) *Old East* to a belay at the base of the arête.

1 **25m 5b** Climb the groove just left of the arête, moving right round the arête at 10m to a small ledge. Continue up the excellent twin cracks in the groove to a small sloping stance beneath the roof.

2 **45m 6a** Undercut round the roof and make contorted moves (crux) to gain the slim groove. Follow the groove and up past a large detached flake to a crack (possible belay – poor). Up the crack to a horizontal break then right to reach a flake. Climb the flake and continue easily on huge holds over the twin roofs above to a recess. Head rightwards up slabs to finish up a short overhanging corner.

19 **The Sleeping Crack ★★★★**   **55m E6 6b**

FA Dave MacLeod & Dan Honeyman 27 August 2001

The attractive intermittent crack in the huge projecting pillar at the right side of the cliff.

1 **15m 6a** Gain the first crack and follow it with increasing difficulty until it is possible to escape left onto the slab. Take a hanging belay on huge thread.

2 **40m 6b** Traverse right and boldly climb a sloping shelf to regain the crack-line. Follow this with hard moves (crux), but excellent protection to an undercut flake. Follow this leftwards then up until beneath the final bulge. Climb rightwards up another flake then make a difficult move up left on finger pockets to gain the finishing slab. Pad easily up this to a flake belay on the terrace (large cams useful).

20 **Labyrinth ★**   **120m Very Difficult**

FA Geoffrey Curtis & Ken Moneypenny 26 September 1943

A popular old-fashioned classic, with all that that implies, based around the central chimney line. Start just below the bottom right corner of the monolithic wall beneath a rock alleyway or vent.

1 **20m** Enter the vent and ascend it, climbing behind a huge jammed block, to exit left. Continue up to gain a grass platform.

2 **10m** Climb the right-slanting groove to belay on a sloping grass ledge.

3 **15m** Traverse left on the horizontal ledge to gain a small undercut corner. Ascend this to belay in the groove above.

4 **30m** Ascend the chimney above, past a grass platform and two sets of chokestones to belay in 'The Eyrie' – the rocky recess beneath the base of the prow.

5 **35m** Traverse rightwards, gaining a little height, to an easy right-slanting grassy rake. Continue along this to belay at a cluster of blocks.

6 **10m** Drop behind the blocks to a recess overlooking Pinnacle Gully then follow the short steep chimney, finishing up a slab.

20a **Labyrinth Direct Finish ★★**   **40m VS 4b**

FA J.Stuart Orr & John MacLaurin May 1951

A much better though noticeably harder finish. From 'The Eyrie', climb easily direct up to the large corner. Climb the corner for 5m then traverse left along two horizontal faults with difficulty to the crest of the final pitch of *South Ridge Direct* and so to the top.

21 **Easter Route ★★**   **95m HVS 4c**

FA Ken Barber & Alfred Pigott Easter 1938

One of the hardest routes from the thirties, following the chimney line just up and right of *Labyrinth*. Start beneath the line of the chimney.

1 **15m** Scramble up to a block below the first chimney.

2 **20m** Follow the chimney to a grass ledge with blocks.

3 **10m** Continue up to a grass patch below a steeper chimney.

4 **12m 4c** Climb the steep chimney until a move right can be made onto a turf-capped ledge.

5 **10m 4c** Two shallow horizontal grooves cross the steep wall above. Using these, go left to the edge of the wall then climb direct to a grass ledge on the left.

6 **8m** Traverse left to the base of the steep curving crack on the right side of The Prow.

7 **20m 5a** Climb the crack with difficulty to a ledge then continue up the final chimney crack.

PINNACLE GULLY AREA

Pinnacle Gully bounds the upper side of the Upper East Face.

22 **The Rosetta Stone ★★**   **12m E1 5a**

FA J.MacLay & William Naismith (top-rope) 1894;
FPA Robin Smith (solo) May 1957

This huge block lies at the top of *Pinnacle Gully*, on the west side of the Pinnacle summit. A fine friction problem, following the left edge of its west side. Descend the same line on all fives!

PROSPERO BUTTRESS

The discontinuous rib bounding the right edge of Sub Rosa Gully, steepening in its upper section.

23 Prospero's Prelude ★　　　　**120m Moderate**

FA Geoffrey Curtis & Ken Moneypenny 26 September 1943

A pleasant useful approach, either to *Prospero's Peril* or the Upper East Face. From near the watercourse in the right (east) branch, gain and follow slabby grooves in the crest.

24 Prospero's Peril ★★　　　　**122m HS 4b**

FA Gordon Townend & Geoffrey Curtis 25 July 1943

Varied and interesting climbing on good rock. Start right of the toe of the upper buttress.

1　**12m 4b** Bear slightly right and gain a slab. Climb the slab until a traverse right can be made into a crack.

2　**20m** Climb a narrow chimney.

3　**30m** Easy climbing, first up chimneys, and then a broad slab to a poor stance on its edge.

4　**15m** Continue up the slab to belay under a small overhang.

5　**15m** Traverse left for 3m. Climb a knee-width groove and then a slab.

6　**30m** Traverse left up a narrowing slab to a foothold on the vertical wall of the gully. The slab above is attained by two delicate and exposed steps to the right. The stance is 15m higher.

CIOCH NA H-OIGHE
(THE MAIDEN'S BREAST)

The distinctive elegant pointed peak of this magnificent mini mountain presents an exquisite panorama from the superbly positioned summit.

Access: From Brodick, follow the A841 north up the east side of the island for 8 miles/13km to park just beyond a telephone box on the east side of the road at Sannox Bay.

Approach: Follow the track west up Glen Sannox past the beacons, to cross a burn after about 10 minutes (0.8km). Head left (south) by a small path following the general line of the Allt a' Chapuill (burn) up the hillside into Coire na Ciche (also known as The Devil's Punchbowl).

1 Midnight Ridge Direct ★　　　　**130m VS 4c**

FA Geoffrey Curtis & Gordon Townend 6 May 1944

Good airy climbing; the only worthwhile climbing on the mountain outwith The Bastion. The route follows the ridge formed by the south-east and east faces (directly below the top of Ledge 1 when viewed from the lip of the corrie). Start just right of a prominent gravelly fan on the right of the corrie lip.

1　**50m** Climb up to the base of the ridge by awkward vegetatious grooves, moving left to gain a thread belay in a little recess 4m right of the arête.

2　**15m 4c** Ascend the short strenuous overhanging scoop to a sloping ledge (crux) then climb a short wall to a grass ledge. Swing steeply left onto the undercut slab above the left end of the ledge and step left to a spike belay on the arête.

3　**25m 4b** Move up and left onto the vertical wall left of the belay and up this on good holds to a small ledge. Continue up a small corner to a grass ledge then over some ledges to climb a short left-facing layback groove leading to a large block belay.

4　**40m** Finish up the much easier pleasant narrow ridge.

Ledge 4

Ledge 3

© Photo Andrew Fraser.

THE BASTION

NS 000 439 **Alt:** 500m

E 🧗 1½hr

An isolated steep clean wall high up in the coire, harbouring a concentration of steep spectacular extremes.

Approach: A series of rightward slanting rakes, numbered 1 – 5 from right to left run across the generally broken and vegetated face. The central rake, Ledge 3 leads with care up to the base of The Bastion.

Descent: The easiest descent is to make two abseils down the line of *Klepht* from the bolt belay at the top. Alternatively, traverse right and carefully descend Ledge 3 back to the base of the cliff.

2 Digitalis ★★ 68m E2 5c

FA Graham Little & Bill Skidmore (3 PA & tension traverse) 4 April 1981; FFA lower pitches Pete Linning & Colin Ritchie 1982; FFA top pitch Gary Latter & Alan Ramsay 25 May 1991

The roofed pillar at the left end of the cliff.

1 **18m 5c** Follow *Klepht* for 12m to a small ledge then traverse left across a slab to a small hold. Continue round the edge to belay in a grassy niche.

2 **15m 5a** Up a corner above a detached pillar to below a roof. Turn the roof on the right and up cracks trending left to a small ledge and belay.

3 **15m 5b** Ascend an awkward corner and then directly up to a small ledge below twin roofs.

4 **20m 5c** Climb the overhang directly above the belay to gain a groove. Move left and up easier rock to a heather ledge and flake runner. Continue

up a slabby groove, trending right to a thread belay on a terrace. Walk off left to gain Ledge 4.

3 Klepht Direct ★★ 55m E2 5c

FA Andrew Maxfield & Bob Wilde (extensive aid) 25 May 1967; Direct Graham Little & Colin Ritchie (4 PA) 16 April 1981; FFA Craig Macadam & Andrew Fraser 10 August 1981

The prominent large open corner at the left end.

1 **27m 5c** Up the corner past a small ledge, move right and climb a corner directly to BB on a grass ledge.

2 **28m 5c** Follow the main crack past a recess until a smaller crack in left wall allows the final corner to be climbed to a grass ledge and good thread belay. Either walk and then scramble off left to gain Ledge 4, or move up right to abseil from the BB on *Armadillo*.

④ The Brigand ★★   60m E5 6b

FA Kev Howett, Graham Little & Lawrence Hughes 1996

The pillar midway between *Klepht* and *Armadillo*, spoilt by a band of disintegrating rock low down on the second pitch. Start a few metres down from *Armadillo* below a prominent left-facing double-roofed groove.

1 **20m 5c** Up the groove to swing out right onto a good flake near the top (good nuts in a small pocket just above). Move left on good holds on the lip to an undercling at the left end of the roof. Continue along the narrow sloping ledge to belay in a crack system.

2 **40m 6b** Climb the crack above the belay to a band of disintegrating rock. Gain a thin hanging flake groove in this band. Struggle up this to reach some pockets and step right back onto real rock again. Climb up to a diagonal flake corner, mantelshelf onto its top then climb pockets in the wall above. Palm left to gain a small flake which leads to a nasty exit onto a sloping ledge on the edge of the pillar. Climb the short open corner above the ledge, pulling out left at the top. A short slab and flake groove lead to a grassy ledge and the BB on *Armadillo*.

Three options exist: Abseil from the BB, finish up the last pitch of *Armadillo*, or drop down left and traverse clear of the face, as for *Klepht*.

⑤ Armadillo ★★   100m E3 6a

FA Bob Richardson & Bill Skidmore 14 July 1977 (3 PA);
FFA Craig Macadam & Simon Steer 29 May 1985

A fine route with a short well protected crux, taking the prominent open groove up and right of *Klepht*. Start below this.

1 **25m 6a** Climb the groove to a roof at about 20m. Make difficult moves round this to a ledge and belay.

2 **35m 5b** Up the groove above then break out right onto some pockets. The easy angled groove leads to a belay.

3 **40m 5b** From the top of the rake climb a series of short overhung corners to a grass ledge. Traverse left, go up then move right into a final easy groove.

⑥ Abraxas ★★★   105m E4 6a

FA Graham & Rob Little (12 PA) 26 May 1980;
FFA Craig Macadam & Derek Austin 1 June 1985

An excellent route in a fine situation. The traverse at the end of the second pitch is often wet. Start directly behind the right end of the prominent arched overhang in the centre of The Bastion.

1 **30m 6a** Traverse leftwards and slightly upwards to the left end of the arch. Move left around the edge to the base of a yellow roof-capped corner. Up this and pull right onto the wall. Move slightly left at a horizontal break then make a difficult move (crux) to gain a hidden finger pocket. Up from this to gain a rightward hand traverse line which leads to a belay just above.

2 **35m 6a** Climb a diagonal finger crack to a narrow sloping shelf. Gain this awkwardly and follow it to reach a vertical water-worn groove. Up this to its top and step left to a sloping ledge. Cross a narrow shelf on the left to gain a niche and BB.

3 **40m 5b** Up a crack on decomposing rock to an undercut flake. Pull left on good holds to reach a crack, up this to a heather ledge. Follow a grassy ramp and continue up further grass to belay well back.

⑦ The Great Escape ★★★   100m E8 6c

FA John Dunne & Andy Jack 21 June 2001

A stunning line breaching the centre of the cliff.

1 **30m 6b** Climb the open groove right of the first pitch of *Abraxas*, crossing a roof to belay on a ledge.

2 **40m 6c** The awesome main pitch. Climb directly up the stunning leftward trending groove to a poor in situ thread runner. Make difficult moves diagonally leftwards to gain the left-hand pincer. Follow this in a spectacular position to belay on the *Tidemark* ledge.

3 **30m 6b** Ascend the obvious scoop past a hard move at about 5m to a spike runner. Continue up the slab above to finish up easier ground.

8 Rhino ★   **80m E2 5b**

FA Graham Little (2 PA, solo using back rope) 3 June 1979; FFA Graham Little & Bill Skidmore 1 July 1979

The prominent pointed flake high on the wall up and right of *Abraxas*. Start at a cairn.

1   **20m 5b** Gain and climb a 3m leftward-facing flake. Mantelshelf and go straight up to a bulge. Pull left to reach a small heather ledge. Climb up to a curious hold (PR above) and step right to a stance on a grass ledge.

2   **20m 5a** Climb straight up on good flakes then by a crack to enter the crux chimney crack (PR above). Climb the chimney and exit left round a chokestone to belay at the top of the flake.

3   **30m 5b** Walk right and climb the corner above a big block. Make a detour on the left wall then continue up the corner to a grass ledge and belays.

4   **10m 4c** Climb the overhanging corner with strenuous finish to a ledge and belay. A short scramble leads to the top end of Ledge 4.

9 Token Gesture ★★   **70m E5 6b**

FA Dave Cuthbertson & Kev Howett 5 June 1985

Climbs the wall right of *Rhino*. Start just right of this.

1   **20m 6b** Make a long reach to gain a hanging flake and climb the shallow scoop directly above then step right to good footholds. Climb a series of flakes diagonally left towards a vegetated flake (good holds). Step back right then up over a bulge and go left on huge hidden pockets, stepping down to a ledge and belay on *Rhino*.

2   **20m 6b** Traverse back out right on the pockets then up to a large jug at the base of the hanging groove. Climb this to its top and step out right and make a difficult move onto the slab.

3   **30m 5c** Climb the wall above via a line of left trending pockets to gain a flake. Go rightwards up an easy ramp and ascend a small groove. Exit left with an awkward move onto a slab which leads right into the final corner of *Rhino*. Finish up this.

10 Tidemark ★★★   **75m HS 4b**

FA Andrew Maxfield & John Peacock 9 June 1960

A fine wildly exposed girdle taking the glaringly obvious (visible from the road!) curving shelf across the top third of the cliff. Start at a rounded flake belay well above the upper end of Ledge 3. This can be gained either by a serious scramble up and left from near the top end of Ledge 3 or by making a 55m abseil from a large flake-boulder at the top of the gully bounding the right end of the face.

1   **30m 4a** Traverse left across two slabs (often wet) to a large split block. Climb over the block then walk across grass to an 'eye-hole' belay, atop the *Rhino* flake.

2   **30m 4a** Follow the magnificent exposed gangway to step left across the slab to a wide crack. Continue more easily up this to belay on a small ledge just left of an overhang. A stunning pitch.

3   **15m 4b** Climb the short flake crack above then traverse left into a heather groove which leads to Ledge 4.

11 Slipway ★   **45m HVS 5a**

FA Bill Skidmore & John Madden (1 PA) 7 June 1975

A good continuation to any of the routes on The Bastion. It lies on the short steep little buttress above Ledge 4, situated almost immediately above the finish of *Tidemark*. Start at a small open corner.

1   **15m 4c** Climb the right wall via a blocky flake and spike then up the left-trending ramp over a block to a small grass ledge on the left.

2   **30m 5a** Gain the ramp above with difficulty. (This point can also be gained by a traverse left from the right end of the ledge, lowering the overall grade to VS). Follow the ramp for about a metre, step down then traverse left to cracks. Go up to a square cut recess and exit left to a large chokestone belay. Scramble to Ledge 5.

CAISTEAL ABHAIL
(CASTLE OF THE FORK/PTARMIGAN STRONGHOLD)

1½hr

NR 970 452 **Alt:** 520m

CUITHE MHEADHONACH
(CENTRAL STRONGHOLD)

A clean 45m high sheet of granite set slightly off the vertical, with a good range of open wall climbs in the higher grades. It is situated on the flank of the ridge projecting north from the summit of the hill, overlooking Coire nan Ceum.

Access: Continue north-west along the A841 beyond Sannox for 1.6 miles/2.5km to park in a car park on the left (south) side of the road, just south of a bridge over the North Sannox Burn.

Approach: Follow a path up the left (south) bank of the North Sannox Burn, through the forest (often boggy). Just beyond the forest, the path passes some waterfalls and a narrow gorge. A short way beyond, cross a smaller tributary stream on the right and head straight up the hillside in the direction of the cliff. 3km/450m ascent.

Descent: Down steep grass at the left side of the crag.

① One Eyed Jacks ★ 45m E3 5c
FA Craig Macadam & Simon Steer May 1984

Serious, with no protection until above the crux. Start 1.5m left of obvious crack near the left end of main face.

  1 20m 5c Climb the wall moving slightly right then back left to gain the obvious flake crack (first runners). Up the flake crack and through the roof to belay as for *Ulysses*.

  2 25m 5b Follow a left trending line to the edge of the crag and up this.

② Ulysses ★ 50m E2 6a
FA Graham Little & Bill Skidmore 9 May 1982

The pale wall dominating the left half of the crag. Scramble along a grass terrace from the left to start 9m right of the vegetated crack.

  1 25m 5c Up a slabby wall trending left until below the right end of a long roof. Move left under the roof to a good thread runner. Surmount the roof direct and climb the wall above until a short left traverse can be made to a small ledge and bolt belay.

2 25m 6a Traverse right to crumbling flakes. Climb these, the crack above and an awkward wall to a small flake. Traverse hard right to shallow corner cracks, up these (PR) and traverse left for 3m under bulging rock. Move over the bulge and up short rock steps to a thread belay at the top.

3 Icarus ✶✶   **55m E5 6b**
FA Kev Howett & Graham Little 22 July 1995

Takes a sustained line on the wall between *Ulysses* and *Achilles* moving left to the belay of the former then tackles the headwall to the left of *Ulysses*. Start as for *Ulysses* 6m right of the vegetated crack.

1 30m 6b Trend right, bypassing the right end of a thin roof, to gain a slight right-facing scoop and small ledge above (*Ulysses* goes up and left from here). Traverse hard right to gain big flat holds. From the top of these traverse slightly left then up via a finger pocket to reach an undercling. Move left to an incipient flake, climb this then make precarious moves over a bulge and up to reach a deep horizontal break. Traverse left strenuously to below twin flakes (F #0). Pull up to stand in the break then teeter left to reach the traverse leading to the bolt belay on *Ulysses*.

2 25m 6b Climb up the flakes and cracks of *Ulysses* to a jug where the route traverses right. Traverse left to a big flake. Pull up then ascend a line of small pockets in the wall above with desperation to a horizontal break. Finish straight up.

4 Achilles ✶✶   **50m E5 6c**
FA Graham Little 29 April 1984 (2 PA);
FFA Kev Howett & Graham Little 6 August 1995

A spectacular and excellent climb taking a fairly central line on the pale wall on the left side of the crag. The description is for the free variation of the route superseding the original line, which controversially employed a bolt for aid. A double small set of Friends is required to adequately protect this pitch. Start about 9m right of *Ulysses* at the highest point of the vegetated terrace. Climb the slabby wall to reach an easy left-facing flake system. From the top of this, a second and fragile flake is gained by difficult moves on the left. A long stretch allows a step up on to the toe of the flake, from where a bombproof R #9 (optional belay) can be placed in a short deep vertical crack. This crack curves left to become a horizontal break. Hand traverse this break until a step up can be made on to a higher break. Move right then make desperate moves to gain a left-facing flake (crux). Pull over this to reach a horizontal break then reach left to gain another flake edge. A horizontal crack, becoming a rail, runs out left. Follow it to reach the obvious crack and flake system which leads strenuously but more easily to the top.

📷 *Gary Latter on Achilles. Photo Karen Latter.*

Punster's Crack, The Cobbler. Britta Dost climbing the second pitch. Photo Dave Cuthbertson, Cubby Images.

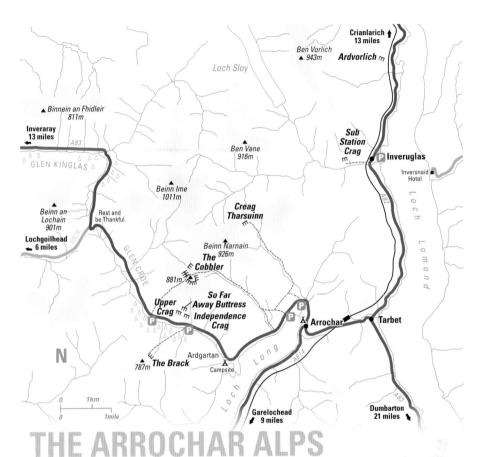

THE ARROCHAR ALPS

The village of Arrochar lies at the head of Loch Long. Five peaks to the north and west are collectively known as 'The Arrochar Alps', but it is the lowest peak, The Cobbler, that dominates, with the highest concentration of quality rock climbing of every grade. Like much of the Southern and Central Highlands, the rock is largely mica schist, folded and contorted, with many quartz intrusions. Many of the neighbouring hills also have good crags and cliffs.

Accommodation: Campsites at Ardgartan (☏ 01301 702293/360; www.forestholidays. co.uk), 2.5 miles/4km west of Arrochar: caravan & campsite in Arrochar at (NN 301 048); Ardlui (☏ 01301 704243; www.totaltravel.co.uk). **Youth Hostels** at Arden, off A82 near Balloch (☏ 0870 004 1136; www.syha.org.uk); Inveraray (☏ 01499 302454; www.syha. org.uk) or Crianlarich (☏ 0870 004 1112; www.syha.org.uk). There are numerous hotels and B&Bs in Arrochar.

Amenities: TICs – opposite Tarbet Hotel (☏ 01301 702260) on A82 on Loch Lomond-side; Ardgartan in Glen Croe (☏ 01301 702432); Inveraray (☏ 01499 302063; visitscottishheartlands.com). Tarbet tearoom 200m along A83 from A82 junction. Small grocers, cafe, restaurants and chip shop all in Arrochar. Bar meals available in hotels.

HISTORY

Not surprisingly, the craggy profile of The Cobbler attracted the attentions of the first climbers in the area, being the most accessible mountains from the Central Belt. The rocks were first explored by the founding members of the Scottish Mountaineering Club, with Willie Naismith and Gilbert Thomson gaining the summit block via *The Arête* in July 1889. A few months later, Thomson returned to pioneer the first ascent of the South Peak by the *South East Ridge*. Five years later, Naismith and Thomson completed *Original Route* up the other side of the same peak. Two years later, in 1896, Naismith and J.S.MacGregor climbed *Right-Angled Gully* over on the North Peak, raising the standard to Very Difficult, particularly for the short steep final wall.

One particular pitch that stands out from this period (in terms of difficulty, not quality, and therefore not described) was the short repulsive slimy crack above the end of the path on *Original Route*. Naismith with James Rennie climbed this in 1898 to give *North-West Crack*, at VS 4c substantially harder than anything else from that era. Another impressive ascent from this period was Harold Raeburn's lead of *The Fold* in 1904, gained by a traverse along Halfway Ledge from Ramshead Gully. Climbed *"in the company of several ladies"*, it later formed the top and crux pitch of *Recess Route*.

The next period of development occurred in the thirties, with the arrival of Jock Nimlin, who dominated new route activity on The Cobbler for over a decade. His first addition was a bold solo ascent of the short *Direct Finish* to *Right-Angled Gully* in June 1930. Amongst the dozen new routes that he put up, are many of the best VDiffs and Severes on the mountain, including the airy *Nimlin's Direct Route* (1933), *North Rib Route* and the popular classic *Recess Route*, which he climbed with John Fox and Bob Ewing in 1935. Prior to the thirties, climbing was very much a sport reserved for the middle and upper classes, with almost all the earlier pioneers staying in hotels or using their own transport on shorter outings. Lack of work during the depression in the thirties forced many working class city dwellers out into the country as a way of filling their time. Nimlin was the founder of the Ptarmigan Club, while his partner on many of the early routes, Andy Sanders, formed the Creagh Dhu Mountaineering Club.

After the Second World War, members of the infamous tough Clydeside club the Creagh Dhu took over as the main activists. Their finest technician, John Cunningham, added his first new route on The Cobbler with *Chimney Arête* in 1947. Teaming up with another talented climber, Bill Smith, the pair went on to add *Deadman's Groove* and *S Crack* on the South Peak. Cunningham also soloed the finely situated *Ardgartan Arête* and climbed the hard lower section of *Direct Direct*. The productive Cunningham-Smith partnership continued with the excellent and varied *Punster's Crack* in 1949. In 1951 Smith and Hamish MacInnes made the first venture onto the South Face of the South Peak with *Gladiator's Groove*, Smith returning the following year to add the bold *Direct Start*, pushing the grade to E1. Also around this period, Cunningham and MacInnes added *Wether Wall*, MacInnes returning the following year with Bill Smith to add the best VS in the area with *Whither Wether*. Smith repeated the route the same month, adding the *Left Hand Finish* which has now become the usual route of ascent. Over on the South Peak, MacInnes climbed *Ithuriel's Wall* with some aid. MacInnes's predilection towards aid climbing earned him the nickname 'MacPiton'. A few years later, in 1955, a large party of Creagh Dhu climbers contributed to the production of *The Nook Direct* with aid used on all three pitches, though the first pitch must have been extreme with only 1 point. The first complete ascent was made by Mick Noon, who was involved

Centre Peak, The Cobbler. Paul McNally climbing.

in all the other pitches. Back on the South Peak, Eric Taylor and A.Crawford added *Dicer's Groove*. The final contribution from this group, bringing this productive period to a fitting close, was Patsy Walsh's ascent of the steep and bold *Club Crack* in July 1957. On an earlier attempt, Walsh took a long fall and was lowered almost unconscious and propped up in a corner while the others went off to pack in more climbing. Walsh returned a few weeks later to complete the climb, followed by about eight other members of the club. The only incursion into the dominance of the Creagh Dhu occurred when a young Robin Smith (then 18 years old) left his mark with the hard *Glueless Groove*.

Nothing of note occurred for a decade. With major big wall routes being established in Yosemite, aid climbing was in vogue. Rusty Baillie and John Amatt spent two days in 1967 aiding a direct line up the wildly exposed pillar beneath the summit of the North Peak, resulting in the spectacular *Baillie's Overhang* (A3), which made use of a number of bolts. Across the way on The Brack, Bill Skidmore, Bob Richardson and Jim Crawford of the Greenock Mountaineering Club similarly spent a couple of days aiding the steep crack-line of *Mammoth*, again A3. The following year, Rab Carrington and Jimmy Gardiner celebrated *McLean's Folly* over on the South Peak, rubbing salt into the wound following an unsuccessful attempt from John McLean. The pace of activity slowed, though Skidmore was actively exploring other cliffs in the area. Throughout the mid-seventies, Skidmore with a variety of partners added a route every summer for four years to the fine neglected Creag Tharsuinn, accounting for all the worthwhile routes on the cliff so far. The results were the fine VSs of *The Tingler* and the superb *Terminal Wall*, followed by *Trilogy*. The final addition *Tremolo* completed the alliterative trend. Throughout the seventies many of the aid points on The Cobbler were tidied up, though actual first free ascents were seldom recorded, as it was just assumed that the routes should be climbed free at the time. In 1978 Dougie Mullin and Alan Pettit freed *Mammoth* on The Brack; at E3 5c, the first route to improve on the standard set by Walsh with *Club Crack* more than twenty years previously.

Standards took a major leap forward in 1979 when Dave Cuthbertson succeeded in climbing the impressive thin hanging crack above up the centre of the scooped wildly overhanging wall above the traverse on *Punster's Crack*. The resultant *Wild Country* heralded the arrival of a new standard, firmly establishing the E5 grade in the Scottish mountains. Significantly, the pre-placed hammered nut used to protect the crux disappeared soon afterwards, and the route has risen a grade to E6 and still awaits an on-sight ascent. Cuthbertson returned the following year, to add a further E5 with the evocatively named *Rest and be Thankful* up the intricate wall left of *Club Crack*.

With an uncanny knack for picking plum lines, the prolific Lakeland activist Pete Whillance, accompanied on this occasion by Pete Botterill, made the first of what turned out to be a series of very productive trips north of the border. The blunt arête dominating The Brack gave him the aptly named *Edge of Extinction*, and again set a new standard at E6. The route received its second ascent from Paul Laughlan in 1987, who abseiled down and placed an additional peg next to a tied off blade. All further ascents have been on-sight. Apparently Murray Hamilton had abseiled down the line prior to Whillance and been dissuaded by the obvious lack of protection.

Just south of the Crinan Canal in Knapdale, Graham Little, with Pete Linning and Colin Ritchie, developed the fine epidiorite crag of Creag nam Fitheach in 1981 and 1982. With almost 20 routes, best of the bunch were *The Prow* and the superb HVS *The Razor's Edge*, with *Crucifixion Crack* the hardest at E2. Though the crag had previously been climbed on in the forties by Alex Small, and in the late seventies by Dave Hayter and friends, they left no record of their ascents.

In the spring of 1985 locals from Arrochar Outdoor Centre Jim Divall & Ray Cluer developed the fine Sub Station

Crag, establishing five extremes, including the best route *Charge of the Light Brigade*, utilising 4 peg runners. Around this time they had also developed a number of roadside crags low down in Glen Croe. In addition to numerous easier routes on the Lower Crag, climbed with students from the Arrochar Outdoor Centre, they added *Crossover* and freed the spectacular twin 2m roofs of *The Hooded Groove* on the imposing Upper Crag. In the middle of February Gary Latter paid a visit. After placing a couple of pegs, he climbed an old top-rope problem to unveil *Pockets of Excellence*. On the Upper Crag, Latter managed to on-sight *Double Clutching*, the name coming from the clods of grass used to pull over the top of the crack. The following year Ronnie Bruce climbed the excellent companion finger crack *Short Sharp Shock*, following a previously aided ascent. The route soon received a flashed second ascent from Murray Hamilton. Over the next few years, Dave Griffiths took over as the main enthusiast, producing a number of gems, including *All Heroes Die Young*, *New Position*, *Aftershock*, *The Sharp Kiss*, and *The Edge of Insanity* with a bolt and peg. These were soon removed by Gary Latter prior to the second ascent. Griffiths later commented that he knew the bolt would be taken out, but was quite happy to receive the publicity. At Creag nam Fitheach, Griffiths got an early start in 1988, climbing *Maneater* in February. He later went on to produce the stunning finger crack *Crystal Vision*, Scotland's answer to Fingerlicker (only better!). The route soon received second and third ascents from Latter and Mark McGowan, McGowan going on to make an audacious solo ascent immediately afterwards. McGowan also stepped in and top-roped then lead the adjacent bold square-cut arête to give the excellently-named *Not Waving, But Drowning*, at E6 6b a significant route strangely overlooked in the historical sections of the last

> Griffiths, belayed by his mother (a non-climber), climbed the best line on The Cobbler's South Peak with Osiris … (which) ranks alongside his Crystal Vision as two of the best single pitches of their grade in the area.

two SMC guides. Griffiths returned to the crag in 1995, producing the fine arête of *The Changeling* after top-rope practise and pre-placing a peg.

Not all the activity was on the outcrops. Griffiths, belayed by his mother (a non-climber), climbed the best line on The Cobbler's South Peak with *Osiris*. The route made use of 3 pegs and an in situ thread, and ranks alongside his *Crystal Vision* as two of the best single pitches of their grade in the area. The previous year, Griffiths had added the short bold arête *Straight Flush* to the small outcrop beneath the North Peak.

The following year on The Cobbler, Mark McGowan and Grant Farquhar added a similar companion pitch to *Rest and be Thankful*, with *Rise to the Occasion* taking the shorter wall to the left. The initial steep crack had been climbed earlier by Griffiths, who lowered from a nut rather than tackle the bold upper wall. The Cobbler still remained the focus of interest throughout the nineties. In 1991 Gary Latter added the bold *Horus* on the South Peak. Two years later, he returned to complete the stunning flying arête of *Wild at Heart*, a route visible in profile from Arrochar. This was the first route to be climbed in redpoint style, with 4 peg runners making it feel almost like a sport route, though with a bold start. The glaringly obvious gaping offwidth slit further right succumbed to the determined duo of Rick Campbell and Paul Thorburn the following year. *Wide Country* completed a fine trilogy of hard contrasting adjacent lines on this scooped wall. A somewhat miffed Mark Garthwaite (who had cleaned the line on abseil some time previously) arrived at the base just as Campbell completed the pitch.

The long hot summer of 1995 saw the rekindling of interest in most of the many remaining lines. Latter and Thorburn filled in the gaps on the fine steep Osiris slab, with two other routes *Ra* and *Geb* in a similar mould. Thorburn plugged an obvious gap nearby with the steep bold *Ethereal*, on which he logged some substantial flight time prior to success. Thorburn also made the second ascents of *Horus* and *Wild at Heart*, and the third ascent of *Wild Country*, without the benefit of the pre-placed nut. Some other obscure wee gems climbed that summer included the jam crack of *A Crack in the Clouds*. The

final route that year was the stunning overhanging prow beneath the summit of the North Peak, which Latter climbed to give *Dalriada*. At E7 this continued the tradition of The Cobbler as a forcing ground for rising standards, first established back in the thirties.

Bringing things up to date, Dave MacLeod added a number of hard routes to Upper Crag in Glen Croe, culminating in the very hard and serious *The Fugue*, a headpointed ascent of a route bolted by Thorburn in the early nineties, before the dinosaurs removed the bolts. Two small but worthy contrasting sport venues have been developed in the last few years. At Ardvorlich Crags, a number of previously climbed lines by various parties including Colin Lambton, Graeme Harrison and John Watson were tidied up and retro-bolted in 2006 by Harrison and Watson to produce a small, worthy and very accessible mid-grade venue.

In contrast, The Anvil, a massive free standing boulder overlooking Loch Goil now hosts some of the best hard sports routes in the area. Dave MacLeod added the first routes late in 2004, including *Hammertime*, returning the following May to add the fine *Anvilfire*. May 2006 saw some great additions, including *Friendly Fire* from Richard McGhee, Dave Redpath's *Spitfire*, reputedly one of the best F8a's in Scotland, and the fine looking *Shadowlands* from Mike Tweedley. True to form, MacLeod went on to add the hardest line on the crag with the testing *Body Blow*, climbing the top half of a project on the very steep North Cave. MacLeod returned in the autumn to complete the hardest sport route in Scotland at the time with his ascent of *Bodyswerve*. This accolade was soon superseded with his ascent of the long and sustained *Metalcore* in May 2007. Malcolm Smith soon got in on the action, making the second ascent of all MacLeod's hardest, in addition to adding a couple of hard crimpy routes of his own with *The Smiddy* and *Black Out*.

BEN VORLICH
(MOUNTAIN OF THE BAYS)

© Alan Leary

NN 306 094 **Alt:** 200m (S) (👤) 20min

SUB STATION CRAG

A fast drying slabby schist crag to the west of Loch Lomond on the southern slopes of Ben Vorlich.

Access: Follow the A82 along the west shore of Loch Lomond 3.5 miles/5.6km north of Tarbet. At Inveruglas park with consideration on the west side of the road by a telephone box 150m north of the approach road, or half a mile/800m further north at the large tourist car park and viewpoint near the power station on the shore of the loch. Travelling from the north the telephone box is 12.9 miles/20.6km south of Crianlarich.

Approach: Follow the tarmac road west up the hillside, taking the right fork just before the sub-station. Cut diagonally leftwards up to the crag.

Descent: Abseil from trees at the top of the crag.

1 The Pylon Effect ★   50m E3 5c
FA Ian Taylor & Colin Moody 3 November 1988

The fine left arête. Start at a short crack left of the great flake. Follow the crack until a leftward traverse leads to a flake on the arête. Climb the arête direct to the top. Belay well back.

2 Charge of the Light Brigade ★★   45m E3 5c
FA Jim Divall & Ray Cluer 1985/6

Good reasonably protected climbing up the left side of the crag. Climb up to the left of the great flake, then the groove to a PR. Head diagonally right, then back left past several PRs to finish direct. Continue more easily above.

3 White Meter ★★   45m E4 6a
FA Colin Moody & Ian Taylor 3 November 1988

Gain the flake and from near its left end move up and step right, then up to a jutting quartz lump. Move up left to a bulge (F #1.5 in horizontal crack), and surmount it using a quartz hold, and up to trees. Quite bold and run-out. Abseil off.

4 Power to the People ★   35m E2 5c
FA Jim Divall & Ray Cluer 1985/6

From the upper right end of the great flake climb direct past a PR to a horizontal break. Cross the small overlap and ascend the groove on the right. Step right to a ledge and continue easily up heather ledges to belay on the right.

5 Current Affair * 　　　　　　35m E2 5b

FA Jim Divall & Ray Cluer 1985/6

Ascends the wall left of the crack-line of 6.

1　**15m 5b** Climb up to gain two thin parallel cracks.
　　Up these, move left to a flake then right to PB.

2　**20m 4c** Move up left past a bulge to a grass ledge,
　　then up heather ledges to belay on the right.

6 Wired for Sound * 　　　　　35m E1 5b

FA Jim Divall & Ray Cluer 1985/6

The crack-line left of a prominent rib at the right end.

1　**20m 5b** Up the crack and wall above
　　to a ledge on the right.

2　**15m 4b** Climb straight up to a grass ledge.

7 Live Coverage * 　　　　　　48m HVS 5b

FA Jim Divall & Ray Cluer 1985/6

The rib at the right end of the crag.

1　**15m 4c** Climb the left side of the rib to
　　a break, then up the slab above.

2　**24m 5a** Up the slab on the right, move left
　　to a small corner and up crack above.

3　**9m 5b** Finish up the overhang above,
　　or walk off right below it.

NN 323 123 **Alt:** 80m **(w) 🧗** 10min

ARDVORLICH CRAGS

A couple of fast drying, sunny, 'sportingly-bolted' adjoining walls on a small knoll on the east side of Ben Vorlich with grand views down Loch Lomond. It should be noted that the routes are not complete clip-ups and the second bolts on some look alarmingly high (possible ground-fall potential) – take care!

© John Watson.

Access: North up the A82, 1.5 miles/2.4 km beyond the viewpoint by the loch side at Inveruglas, turn off west (signposted Ardvorlich House B&B). Park on the left just after the gate, taking care not to block access. **From the north:** the turn-off 2.7 miles/4.3 km south of Ardlui train station (300m south of the traffic lights on the loch side). **Approach:** Head west up the left bank of the stream on the right. Cross the stream and go under the railway at the bridge. Follow a vague path near the right bank, which veers rightwards to the crags. This direct approach has been agreed with the kind permission of the B&B owners (www.ardvorlich-house.co.uk ☎ 01301 704258) – please respect their privacy and adhere to these directions.

1 Magic Carpet Ride * 　　　　　15m F6b

FA John Watson 2002

"You'll need your trad head for this one." The half-bolted, half-pegged route through the steepening overlap near the apex of the slab. Keep your nerve between bolts and pegs – the climbing is never desperate.

2 Snake Eyes * 　　　　　　　15m F6a

FA John Watson 2005

Pull through central roof and move up and left to the meet 3. Step down and traverse left to bigger holds. Follow quartz straight up to a sapling, then easily right to LO.

3 Dilemma ★★   15m F6a+
FA John Watson 2005

Pull on by a quartz crack (crux) and climb up to a thin section moving up and right, finishing direct.

4 Lake Lomond ★★★   12m F6a
FA Graham Harrison, et al. 2004

Climb up behind the saplings to a crux step left onto the wall. Follow the pale wall directly.

5 Drifting from Shore ★   12m F6b/6c
FA Graham Harrison, et al. 2004

The bulge and headwall direct. The crux bulge can be bypassed on the right. Good headwall crimping.

6 The Groove ★   12m F6a
FA John Watson 2002

Good climbing up the juggy central groove and pocketed headwall. Veer left at top to a mantelshelf finish.

7 That Sinking Feeling ★   15m F6a+
FA John Watson 2006

Excellent technical climbing up the left arête. Step right from the arête with crux move to layaways. Up jugs to clip, then more easily on good holds in the groove right of the wee roof.

8 Carnage   5m F6c
FA John Watson 2006

The wee roof is butch. A bolted boulder problem, which can be extended to F7a by bouldering in along the break and boosting for the jug at first bolt, continue on to 7.

Jo George on the fingery Lake Lomond Photo John Watson, Stone Country Press

NN 282 074 **Alt:** 660m. 2½hr

CREAG THARSUINN
(TRANSVERSE CRAG)

This is the hill on the north-east ridge of Beinn Narnain with an isolated buttress of excellent clean schist high in the back of Coire Sugach providing a concentrated selection of good very quick-drying routes. A fine isolated venue, much quieter than the neighbouring Cobbler.

Access: Follow the A83 through Arrochar for 0.6 miles/1km to the large car park (pay & display) by Succoth at the head of Loch Long (NN 294 048).

Approach: Follow a steep path zig-zagging directly up through the trees to begin with for about 1km (330m of ascent), then traverse right along the horizontal path at the top for 600m to an obvious stream. Continue steeply by a small path on the edge of the forest, overlooking the Allt Sugach (stream), then continue in the same direction over rough ground into the coire.

Descent: Either abseil from the bolt belay at the top of the leftmost two routes (leave 2m sling to extend ropes to edge), or down the left side of the cliff.

SUGACH BUTTRESS

The large buttress on the left, split by the left-slanting *MacLay's Gully* – a 'traditional' VDiff. The curving corner formed between 'The Great Slab' and the steep rib left of *MacLay's Gully* is taken by *Slab and Groove* (VDiff.), up which the last two routes start.

 Trilogy ★   **60m HVS 5a**

FA Bill Skidmore & D.Dawson 19 July 1976

Fine climbing, with a sustained first pitch tackling the vertical wall down and right of *Terminal Wall*, just left of the wet fault of *McLaren's Chimney*. Start centrally, beneath the undercut bulge crossing the face.

   1 30m 5a Climb the wall to a bulge. Traverse right

and climb the bulge using high holds to gain a juniper ledge. Climb the crack on the left to enter a groove on the right leading to an overhung recess then move right to a grass ledge.

2 **15m 4b** Return left and climb the vertical wall on good holds to a belay on the right.

3 **15m 4a** Go down and left to finish up a prominent crack.

② Terminal Wall ★★   50m VS 4c

FA Bill Skidmore & J.Johnson 29 June 1975

The fine wall high on the right wall of *MacLay's Gully*. *"The immaculate second pitch … offers bold and exposed climbing; one of the finest pitches at the grade in the Arrochar area. The route is high in the grade."* Belay on the right wall opposite a grassy corner.
Tom Prentice, *Arran, Arrochar and the Southern Highlands*, (Scottish Mountaineering Trust, 1987).

1 **15m 4a** Climb grassy corners to a niche under the large roof. Better belays on left wall.

2 **35m 4c** Continue up the wall to a groove with flakes. Leave this on the left and climb to a crack and groove left of the second overhang. Traverse hard left from the bottom of the crack (crux) to gain the main crack which leads past a sentry box and over small ledges to a ledge. Finish up the crack above. Traversing left lower down raises the grade to HVS.

③ The Tingler ★★   55m VS 4c

FA Bill Skidmore & John Gillespie 23 June 1974

Good climbing up the sharp arête just left of *MacLay's Gully*. Start as for *Slab and Groove*.

1 **5m** – Climb *Slab and Groove* to the base of vertical crack just left of the true edge.

2 **40m 4c** Climb the crack to a flake runner then straight up the steep wall on the left to a thin grass ledge. Move right to an edge leading to another grass ledge.

3 **10m 4c** Climb the wide crack above, swing left round the edge (this point can be gained direct at 5a), then finish direct via a flake with a long reach near the top. Monster bolt belay above.

④ Tremelo ★★   70m E1 5b

FA Bill Skidmore & D.Dawson 19 July 1977

A good route up the steep clean wall high on the left, above The Great Slab. Start as for *Slab and Groove*.

1 **25m** – Climb halfway up *Slab and Groove*.

2 **30m 5b** Traverse right along the large flake, then climb a thin crack up right. Climb a crack over a hard bulge then move up and left to a ledge.

3 **15m 4c** Move right, step off the left end of the flake and finish up the wall just left of *The Tingler*.

📷 *Karen Latter and Gary Benson on the fine main pitch of Terminal Wall.*

THE COBBLER

NN 259 058 **Alt:** 800m 1¼ – 2hr

"That rock had beauty in it. Always before I had thought of rock as a dull mass. But this rock was the living rock, pale grey and clean as the air itself, with streaks of shiny mica and white crystals of quartzite. It was joy to handle such rock and to feel the coarse grain under the fingers."
– W.H.Murray, *Undiscovered Scotland*, 1951

With its distinctive craggy profile, the gnarled contorted mica schist, often studded with quartz, has attracted the attentions of generations of climbers from the Central Belt. Here are to be found as fine a cross section of routes as any mountain. The rock is particularly slippy when wet, (like standing on a wet fish!); though many of the routes dry quickly.

Access: From Glasgow and south: Follow the A82 to Tarbet then turn left and follow the A83 through Arrochar and up Glen Croe to park by the old bridge on the right at (NN 242 061), just beyond the end of the forestry plantations on the east (right) side of the road, 4.7 miles/7.5km

west from the large car park at the head of Loch Long.

From the west: The parking spot is 1.3 miles/2.1km east from the Rest and be Thankful (0.2 miles/0.3km beyond two large lay-bys on the north side of the road).

Approach: (A) Cross the burn by the old bridge and follow a path up the left side to reach a small dam after about 1.5 km. Follow a further path up the ridge (left side of the burn) on the right to reach the col between the North and Centre peaks. 1¼ hours.

(B) The popular alternative approach starts at the large car park (pay & display) by Succoth at the head of Loch Long (NN 294 048), 0.6 mile/1km outside Arrochar. Follow a steep path directly up (through the trees to begin with) for about a kilometre (300m of ascent). The path then contours left round the hillside and follows the right bank of the Allt a' Bhalachain, past the Narnain boulders, before crossing the stream and heading up into the coire. 2 hours.

Accommodation: There are numerous small howffs in the coire, the best being high up, nearest the path (sleeps two). Wild camping anywhere in the hills.

SOUTH PEAK
SOUTH FACE

The steep clean face overlooking Glen Croe.

Descent: From the large grassy terrace at the top of the wall scramble down rightwards and down the well-worn *South East Ridge*. For the single pitch routes on the lower slab, finish up either *Gladiator's* or *Ra*, or abseil from the ledge (sling sometimes in situ).

❶ Ethereal ★★   45m E6 6b

FA Paul Thorburn & Rick Campbell 21 June 1995

Steep bold climbing up the imposing scooped wall in the centre of the face.

  1 **30m 6b** From a flake at the base of the wall, climb up, right then back left to a pocket (F #3). Move up left to shake out (Roller #4 and nuts in slot

down left). Climb with difficulty up wall to gain top of ramp. Follow flakes up then right to belay.

  2 **15m 4a** Direct up occasional rock to top.

❷ Glueless Groove ★★   45m E2 5b

FA Robin Smith June 1957

The shallow steep groove in the centre of the face, best done in one long pitch. Climb the cracked groove (most defined and leftmost) to a large flake and a ledge on the right. Continue quite boldly up the wall immediately above the flake, trending slightly left to some quartz blotches, then up to a ledge. Finish up the groove above.

SOUTH FACE

© Alan Leary

3 Ithuriel's Wall ★★   **45m E2 5b**

FA Hamish MacInnes (some aid) 1952; FFA John Hutchison 1976

The prominent shallow left-facing corner high on the face. Start beneath broken grooves, down and left of the main corner pitch.

1 **10m 4a** Follow the grooves to a large ledge and block belay.

2 **25m 5b** Climb the corner through some bulges to gain the large ledge on 4. Belay in the corner on the right.

3 **10m 5a** Finish up the arête right of the groove.

4 Gladiator's Groove Direct ★★★   **65m E1 5b**

FA Bill Smith & Hamish MacInnes 1951;
Direct Start Bill Smith & Bob Hope June 1952

1 **35m 5b** A bold pitch, following a narrow slanting fault across the top of the slab. Start at a band of quartz at the left end of the slab. Up to a good hold below the quartz then on good holds to the right-slanting gangway. Follow this delicately to a large perched block at its end. Easily to a large ledge and belay.

2 **18m 5a** Move up and left to the base of a large right-facing corner, and up this with hard moves to gain a belay on the ledge on the left.

3 **12m 5a** Crack above to top.

5 Geb ★★   **35m E4 6a**

FA Gary Latter & Paul Thorburn 2 June 1995

A right-slanting diagonal line across the slab. Start up 4 to the quartz band. Traverse this past 2 PRs then up the vague crack-line as for 7 but continue rightwards to finish up the right side of the block.

6 Ra ★★   **65m E4 6a**

FA Gary Latter & Paul Thorburn 1 May 1995

A direct line up the left side of the slab. Quite bold and run out, despite the proliferation of pegs. Start down and right of 4.

1 **35m 6a** Up past PR onto a sloping ledge. Step left and up onto a small ledge above (skyhooks 0.5m above PR & out on right). Climb direct past

3 PRs to the rising traverse shelf on 4. Arrange protection (thin crack out left, or block on right) and climb directly up the wall above on improving holds to belay on a ledge.

2 30m 5c Follow 4, but where that route traverses left onto the ledges climb directly by a vague crack to finish up the last few metres of that route.

 Osiris ★★★   **35m E4 6a**
FA Dave Griffiths 6 April 1988

Immaculate bold slabby climbing. Start at the lowest point of the crag, behind a large fallen boulder. Easily up broken ledges and left to PR below the centre of a roof. Step left and pull through the roof leftwards past a further PR to a thread. Step left and up a thin crack (PR at thread) trending slightly rightwards to finish easily up the left side of a huge perched block.

8 Horus ★★   **40m E6 6b**
FA Gary Latter 20 July 1991

A direct sustained line up the wall right of 7 with only marginal protection. Up to the first PR and cross the roof slightly rightwards with difficulty (tied off PR above – difficult to clip; also Wallnut #1 placement just to its left) to good quartz holds and runner placement (hand-placed PR in a pocket on the left). Move slightly right above a small overlap on small quartz holds past a further hand-placed PR in a pocket, to a good hanging flake and better holds. Directly past a good no-hands rest to gain the base of a diagonal crack and move slightly leftwards (crux) to a prominent side pull (RP #3 in a triangular niche) and up on improving holds, pulling out rightwards to easier ground. Belay on a ledge further back.

SOUTH-EAST FACE
Narrow slabby face overlooking Ardgartan and Loch Long.

1 Ardgartan Arête ★★   **60m VS 4b**
FA John Cunningham (solo) June 1948

1 25m 4b Start 5m right of arête. Up a slab over a bulge (poorly protected) and trend left to grooves in the arête. Up these to a large ledge and belay.

2 10m 4a Climb the wall and cracks to a finely situated ledge just right of the arête.

3 25m 4a Continue either up cracks in the wall above or the wall on the left overlooking the South Face to a large grass terrace. Move out right and scramble to the summit.

2 Ardgartan Wall ★   **60m Very Difficult**
FA Jock Nimlin, Jimmy Wynne, Wattie Neilson & Rab Goldie October 1937

Start about 10m right of the arête, beneath a shallow groove.

1 15m Climb the groove and wall.

2 35m Continue directly up the wall to belay on a grass ledge.

3 10m Traverse left along the ledge and finish up a steep little wall next to an overhang.

3 South East Ridge ★   **100m Moderate**
FA Gilbert Thomson et al. October 1889

Follows a line near the right edge of the face. Also a useful descent. Follow well-worn crampon scratches and eroded paths. Continue to the summit, descend by *Original Route*. Avoid in the wet, as it can be very polished and slippery.

📷 *Paul McNally stepping out on the pleasant, well-protected, S Crack.*

NORTH FACE

 Bow Crack *   **30m HS 4b**

FA Bill Smith, W.Dobbie & Bob Hope June 1952

The crack in the steep wall left of the short prominent gully.

1. **16m 4b** Climb crack over a small bulge to a small
   ledge. Go left for 6m to belay in a small niche.
2. **14m** – Move up and right then
   over ledges to the ridge.

S Crack **   **40m VS 4c**

FA John Cunningham & Bill Smith June 1948

A good sustained pitch up the left-facing cracked groove
in the wall right of the short gully. Follow the hand-sized
crack in the groove, finishing slightly leftwards to a grassy
ledge. Well-protected with large nuts and Fs. Walk off left.

Sesame Groove   30m Very Difficult

FA Jock Nimlin, Miss Jennie Dryden & Bob Peel May 1940

A useful access route to the steep cleaner upper wall.
Start at the foot of grassy traverse and scramble up
grassy corner then groove to overhanging wall. Traverse
right on a small shelf to reach block belay.

Deadman's Groove *   40m VS 4c

FA John Cunningham, Bill Smith & Sam Smith May 1948

The prominent steep groove up the right side of the
overhanging arête. Start at a small ledge just above the
finish of 6. Traverse easily left to a prominent crack and
follow it over two bulges to a small ledge. Enter a groove
on the left and climb it to the ridge. Slow to dry.

McLean's Folly *   42m E1 5b

FA Rab Carrington & Jimmy Gardiner August 1968

The prominent right-trending groove in the face right of 7.
Start just above the finish of 6.

1. **12m 4b** Traverse left onto the open rib
   and follow this for 6m near the edge
   to a niche under an overhang.
2. **30m 5b** Swing right onto the arête and climb
   the steep groove trending right to the top.

Nimlin's Direct Route *   75m Very Difficult

FA Jock Nimlin & Andy Sanders April 1933

The edge formed by the North-East and North-West
faces. Start about 30m up the face, where a ledge runs
out leftwards to the edge. Traverse along the ledge, gain
the edge, and follow this to finish at a conspicuous, semi-
detached block near the summit. Fine open situations.

NORTH-WEST FACE

Original Route *   50m Moderate

FA William Naismith & Gilbert Thomson May 1894

Gain and follow a path along the main grass ledge then
up and right over a short wall in a corner to the top. Very
polished – avoid in wet conditions.

CENTRE PEAK

The Arête **   60m Moderate

FA William Naismith & Gilbert Thomson July 1889

Above the col between the South and Centre peaks is
a 10m hand crack up the centre of a slabby buttress.
Follow this then the natural continuation up the edge to a
perfect finish atop the summit block.

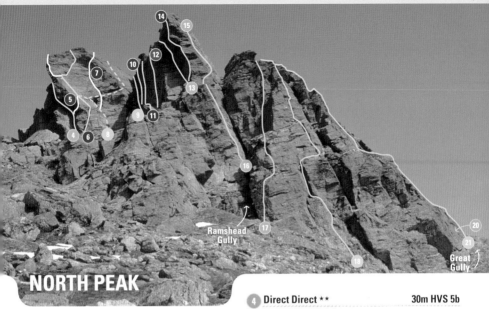

Ramshead Gully

Great Gully

NORTH PEAK

① Chimney Arête ★★   20m VS 4b

FA John Cunningham & Ian Dingwall June 1947

The blunt left arête of the chimney. Serious. The crux is
bypassing the mid-height bulge, round on the left to a jug.
Finish up the slabby right side.

② Right-Angled Chimney ★★   30m Difficult

FA Unknown

The prominent roof-capped chimney. Finish up the slabby
wall on the left. Polished.

③ Cat Crawl ★   35m HS 4b

FA A.Lavery & A.N.Other 1936

Start below prominent fault trending right into larger
groove.

  1 **18m 4b** Direct to the start of the fault and
     traverse it for a few moves then direct up to a
     short left-facing corner. Up this to a good quartz
     spike belay above. (The original route traversed
     the entire fault then up the groove to the spike).

  2 **17m 4b** Bridge up the exposed bulge above for
     a few moves, traverse left on good holds across
     the lip of the overhang then direct to the top.

④ Direct Direct ★★   30m HVS 5b

FA Upper Crack R. Muir & J.Wilson;
Lower Crack John Cunningham 1948

Start in the recess below a hanging left-facing groove.
Climb the bulge (good protection in a crack above) to a
good hold. Up the groove past the spike belay of 3 to finish
directly up a steep crack above, or the wall on the left.

⑤ Wild at Heart ★★★   60m E6 6b

FA Pitch 1 Gary Latter & Brian Beer 3 September 1993;
Pitch 2 Gary Latter & Tom Keenan (redpointed) 27 September 1993

An outrageously exposed top pitch up the edge of all things.
The main pitch attacks the stunning flying arête up the left
edge of the scooped wall above the flake belay of 8.

  1 **25m 5c** Start up 4 to the roof at 12m. Arrange protec-
     tion, step down for 3m then ascend diagonally right-
     wards across the wall to better holds. Up to the roof
     and follow this right to belay on the *Punster's* flake.

  2 **35m 6b** Go up the wall directly above to a crack
     then traverse left to quartz on the edge and up
     to a ledge and two poor PRs. Make committing
     moves leftwards off the ledge with a long reach to
     the first peg runner. Continue with difficult reachy
     moves slightly leftwards past a number of peg
     runners to good finishing holds near the arête.

6 Wild Country ★★★   50m E6 6b

FA Pitch 1 as The Nook Direct Start (1 pt. aid) Bill Smith & Mick Noon 1955; FFA with new top pitch Dave Cuthbertson & Rob Kerr 4–5 July 1979

A seminal route, ahead of its time and a pre-cursor of many hard mountain routes in the eighties. The pre-placed nut used on the first ascent has since disappeared and the route has yet to receive an on-sight ascent. Start in the same recess as for 4.

1 **20m 5c** Climb a widening right-slanting crack past a large flake then easily leftwards up a slab to a block belay, as for *Punster's*.

2 **30m 6b** Up a slab and thin crack then move left to a large flat ledge. Follow a series of overhung ledges rightwards to a good hold at the base of a thin hanging crack. Up the crack (good Wallnut #4 on side), heading for a good small side pull out left (crux) to reach a recess then easily to the top.

7 Wide Country ★★★   40m E5 6b

FA Rick Campbell & Paul Thorburn (both led) July 1994

The evil gaping slit up the right edge of the wildly overhanging face. Follow 8 heading direct for the widening crack. Thrutch up the offwidth crack to gain the niche and exit rightwards. A generous supply of tape, a high pain threshold and a Camalot #4 will all be found to be of use.

8 Punster's Crack ★★★★   50m Severe 4b

FA John Cunningham & Bill Smith August 1949

One of the best routes of its grade in the country with superb positions. Start at a flat rock ledge directly below the prominent deep overhanging crack in the headwall.

1 **20m 4a** Up a short slabby stepped corner then trend left to a large block belay.

2 **15m 4b** Traverse up and right to a prominent wide slot (good large nut runner above for the leader). An awkward step across the slot leads to a shelf. Belay below the cracks at the right end of the ledge.

3 **15m 4a** Move diagonally left and follow cracks up the wonderfully situated steep slab above. Flake belay far back.

9 Right-Angled Gully ★★   35m Very Difficult

FA William Naismith & J.MacGregor 1896

The prominent steep corner-gully at the back of the bay.

1 **17m** Up on polished holds to where it steepens.

2 **12m** Follow the ledge on the right to a thread belay at a large rock just before its highest point.

3 **6m** A final short steep corner on the wall on the left leads to the top.

> **Variation** – *Direct Finish* ★ 10m Severe 4a. *FA Jock Nimlin (solo) 15 June 1930.* Follow the well protected crack up the back of the corner above the belay ledge at the end of the first pitch. Slightly dirty.

10 Rise to the Occasion ★   30m E5 6a

FA Mark McGowan & Grant Farquhar 1989

The short crack and steep wall above. Start beneath the crack, a short way up 9. Climb the thin crack then make difficult moves to become established on the wall above. Continue directly, past a number of horizontal breaks to finish on the large ledge.

11 Rest and be Thankful ★★   45m E5 6a

FA Dave Cuthbertson & Ken Johnstone May 1980

Superb meandering wall climbing, though quite slow to dry. Start at the foot of the right-facing groove in the centre of the wall.

1 **35m 6a** Follow groove to its top (often wet). Traverse left then step down to good holds. Traverse about 3m left then up to a good foothold. Continue up then right to a good horizontal break then up and left to reach a good ledge. Up the wall then easily right to a thread belay.

2 **10m 5a** The wall above at its highest point to the top.

12 Club Crack ★★★   50m E2 5b

FA Patsy Walsh & numerous Creagh Dhu members July 1957

Bold, sustained and strenuous climbing up the steep crack springing out of the cave at the right side of the wall. Start beneath the roof.

1 **40m 5b** Pull direct through the roof above the cave and follow the crack past an ancient and

much fallen-on peg (rounded spike up on right). Continue in the same line, easing towards the top.

2 **10m 4c** Climb the highest point of the wall above the large ledge.

The following three routes start on a sloping grass terrace up and right of *Club Crack*. Thin people can reach the base by squirming through the back of the cave, others by a short rock step on the right.

13 Right-Angled Groove *   48m VS 4c
FA Jock Nimlin (solo) 1934

1 **42m 4c** Follow the slabby open groove, with an excursion on to the left wall high up, to a thread belay on the long grassy ledge near the top. The corner crack can also be climbed throughout at VS 5a.

2 **6m** – Finish up the corner on the left.

14 Dalriada ****   40m E7 6b (F7b)
FA Gary Latter (redpointed) 20 September 1995

Spectacular and very sustained climbing up the wildly undercut prow directly under the summit of the North Peak. Start at the base of the arête at the same point as 13. Up the groove for 3m to a ledge then the flake crack above to 2 PRs. Move right round the arête and up to a superb thread. Straight up the thin finger crack and the arête past a poor PR to a good rest under the roof. Make hard moves left and up to reach the prominent diagonal crack and a line of incut jugs which lead past more PRs to the final capping wall. Continue with interest past two small finger pockets to pull out right to a ledge. Scramble up the ridge to belay just short of the summit.

15 Whither Wether ****   40m VS 4c
FA Hamish MacInnes & Bill Smith August 1952

A wildly exposed pitch, quite run-out in places. Start from a belay just right of the base of 13. Up the centre of the steep wall, trending right. Pull round the edge and up a bold slabby wall to a short vertical crack then follow a leftward trending line to belay just short of the summit cairn.

16 Wether Wall **
FA John Cunningham & Hamish MacInnes September ...

A good pitch, providing a logical start to 15. Start by scrambling up to a grassy ledge about 40m up *Ramshead Gully*, above chockstones and below the deep chimney of the gully. Step left onto the wall and climb direct past a series of small ledges, heading for a small left-pointing flake. Pull over this and up a groove above to a grass ledge at the base of 13.

17 Incubator **   80m 75m HS 4b
FA Above terrace John Cunningham & Ian Dingwall 1948; Below terrace John Cunningham, Bill Smith & Tommy Paul 1940's

A good direct line up the facet overlooking *Ramshead Gully*. Start just right of *Ramshead Gully*, (about 10m up left from the start of 18).

1 **25m 4a** Follow a series of broken walls direct to beneath a steeper wall.

2 **15m 4b** Up the crack in the bulge (above and just right of a small juniper) and the fine corner above to the terrace.

3 **35m 4b** At the back of the terrace is a left-facing corner with twin cracks. Climb the right-hand crack, past a weird phallus at 10m. Move out right past grass ledges to finish by a short crack.

Kevin Howett on the eighties testpiece Rest and be Thankful.

Dave MacLeod on the second ascent of the spectactularly positioned (even if I say so myself!) Dalriada. Photo Dave Cuthbertson, Cubby Images.

18 Recess Route ★★★   90m Very Difficult

FA Jock Nimlin, John Fox & Bob Ewing May 1935
Crux pitch (The Fold) climbed by Harold Raeburn 1904

A popular classic, following the prominent deep
V-chimneys and grooves up the highest section of
the face. Start by a boulder at the left side of a small
amphitheatre just left of the lowest point of the crag.

1 **25m** Follow a left-slanting crack in the slab then
the wide crack in the groove to a belay ledge.

2 **25m** Ascend the chimney past an
overhang. Continue up the deeper chimney
to belay on the Halfway Terrace.

3 **5m** Walk right along the terrace to a belay.

4 **10m** Climb the steep left-slanting groove (The
Fold) on its left wall to belay in a small cave.

5 **25m** Bypass the overhang above on either
side then finish up the chimney.

19 Grey Wall ★   35m VS 4b

FA Willie Rowney & Mick Noon 1952

Exposed slabby climb with a minimum of protection. Start
by scrambling 10m down from the finish of *Ramshead
Gully*. Climb up slightly rightwards for about 10m then
directly up the wall above. A good finish to 17 or 18.

Bounding the right edge of the main face is the
prominent vegetated scree-filled Great Gully, with a
chokestone near its base.

20 Spinal Rib ★★   35m HS 4b

FA Patsy Walsh September 1952

A good exposed pitch up the steep rib on the right wall
of the gully. Scramble up under the chokestone of Great
Gully. Pull up onto the rib and follow it over several
bulges to a good rest beneath the final overhang. Climb
this on the left (technical), or more strenuously on the
right to join 21. Follow this to belay beneath a short wall.
Finish up that route.

21 North Rib Route ★   90m Very Difficult

FA Jock Nimlin & John Fox 1935

Climbs the series of short steep walls on the right
bounding rib of Great Gully. Fine rock and good positions
on the main pitch. Start at a groove at the lowest rocks,
about 6m right of the gully. Start 2m up left from the right
end of the gully wall. Move round right and up a short
crack then pull round onto the right side of the rib and
follow a crack to a large block belay on a ledge.

THE SUGAR WALLS

The short steep walls below the North Peak, about 100
metres below the main face, just above the tourist path.

1 Straight Flush ★★   15m E3 5b

FA Dave Griffiths & Ian Griffiths 26 June 1987

Climb the right side of the arête. Protection is quite
sparse in the upper section.

2 Lumpy Custard ★★   15m E1 5b

FA Gary Latter & Paul McNally 26 April 1995

The centre of the wall, between the arête and the corner.
Start beneath a small flake and follow a direct line to
finish at a small notch in the top of the crag.

CHOKESTONE GULLY

1 A Crack in the Clouds ★★★   20m E3 6a

FA Paul Thorburn & Gary Latter 16 September 1995

100m north of the Sugar Walls is a north-facing gully
wall (Chokestone Gully) containing a perfect hand and
fist crack above a roof low down. Approach from above
by cutting down diagonally left then back right to the
base. Belay to a F #1.5 on the slab behind the route.
Gain a niche left of a crack via a large initial roof on
good holds. Pull into the thin finger crack with difficulty
and follow it on widening jams. Belay on a boulder far
back on the right.

NN 246 034 **Alt:** 620m 🗻 ⛺ 1½hr

THE BRACK

Access: Follow the A83 0.5 mile/0.8km north of Ardgartan to the TIC on the left (west) side of the road. Cross the bridge over Croe Water and park on the right.
Approach: Follow the forestry road west up the Glen for about 1.8km to a stream just beyond the junction with a higher road then cut steeply up the hillside heading slightly rightwards, always keeping to the right side of the stream.
Descent: Down the left (east) side of the crag.

① Edge of Extinction ★★   85m E6 6a

FA Pete Whillance & Pete Botterill 19 May 1980

The big impressive arête in the centre of the main face left of *Mammoth*. The second pitch is serious.

1 **40m 6a** Climb up the overhung recess (as for *Mammoth*) then directly up the crack above to a ledge at 12m. Move up onto the wall just right of the arête (2 PRs) and climb diagonally rightwards to a flake. Up the steep wall above on small holds to a ledge below a prominent hanging corner. Take the corner past a PR at start. Exit left at the top to ledges on the arête. Step down left to peg and nut belays.

2 **45m 6a** Take the right side of the arête for 6m to a small ledge then up a ramp on the left to where it merges onto a steep wall (poor PR and nuts). Climb the wall leftwards to a ledge and continue up until good holds lead back to the arête at 27m. Turn the overlap above on the right, step back left onto the arête and continue easily to the top.

② Mammoth ★★   88m E3 5c

FA Bill Skidmore, Bob Richardson & Jim Crawford (VS & A3) September 1967; FFA Dougie Mullin & Alan Pettit Summer 1978

The prominent hanging crack in the steep left wall of *Great Central Groove*. Start at a cave-like recess down and left of the crack underneath the arête.

1 **18m 5a** Climb up the overhung recess then swing round the right edge to gain a narrow ledge. Continue up the wide crack to belay beneath a prominent overhanging crack.

2 **25m 5c** Climb the wall and crack above the stance which leads to a recess. Continue through the overhang to a ledge (possible belay). Move up right to a grassy ledge then easily to a large ledge and thread belay.

3 **30m 5b** Climb the jam crack which leads to a fine cave belay. Strangely, a bolt appeared here in the early eighties, though adequate natural belays exist.

4 **15m 5a** Continue up the wide crack above the cave to finish up a short corner.

GLEN CROE
(ENCLOSED GLEN/GLEN OF THE SHEEP-PEN)

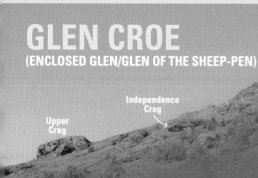

A varied selection of quick drying mica-schist crags on the lower slopes of The Cobbler.

Access: Follow the A83 west beyond Arrochar for 4.8 miles/7.7km to turn right into the old road (signposted 'Honeymoon Bridge car park'; 0.8 miles/1.3km beyond TIC & just east of where the river forms a short narrow gorge on the north side of the road). Park by the picnic tables at the north end.

MIDDLE CRAG

The lowest lying crag of any worth. Unfortunately much frequented by muddy-booted abseilers from the local outdoor centre; consequently suffers from severe erosion and a proliferation of stakes and bolts on top. A number of obvious 15m routes from VS – HVS are worthwhile. The bulging wall in the centre is taken by *Pockets of Excellence* E5 6a. There are also several micro-routes and much **bouldering** just north of here.

UPPER CRAG

The best of the crags so far climbed upon on the lower slopes of the hillside, this severely overhung crag (easily seen in profile from the A83) offers a good selection of fine contrasting pitches.

Approach: Follow the old road north for 100m then a well-trodden path directly up to the base of **Middle Crag**. Skirt round the left edge of this then direct to the crag.

① Outside Edge   10m VS 4c
FA Dave Griffiths & Cameron Bell 12 August 1986

The right edge of the slabby left wall of the crag.

② All Heroes Die Young ★★   15m E3 6a
FA Dave Griffiths 13 September 1986

Follows a line of shallow grooves near the left edge. A thin crack leads to a small ledge, PR then up a shallow bulging runnel passing a further PR and fragile thread to pull blindly onto the rounded slab at the top.

③ The Hooded Groove ★★   20m E2 5c
FA unknown; FFA Jim Divall 1980's

Spectacular climbing up the main open groove which cleaves the main bulk of the crag in two. Direct entry and exit from the relatively straightforward groove is barred by two one-metre roofs. Breach the widest part of the initial roof by a crack. Easily up the groove, finishing by laybacking round the right end of the capping roof.

④ Crossover ★   20m E1 5b
FA Jim Divall 1980s

A leftward trending diagonal line, avoiding the roofs of 3. Start to the right of that route. Climb up and left into the groove, climb it for 8m then move left and finish left around the main overhang.

⑤ The Edge of Insanity ★★   20m E4 5c
FA Dave Griffiths (BR & PR) 13 April 1987;
FA after removal of bolt and peg Gary Latter 7 June 1987

The steep right edge of 3 with some finely situated climbing in its upper reaches. Start beneath a prominent block just right of 3. Climb direct to this then up to a ledge on the left. Move onto a smaller ledge on the right (runners in flake – wobbly!) and stand on this. Make a longish reach straight up for good quartz pockets then swing right onto a giant jug before strolling up the final easy section.

S **10min**

UPPER CRAG NN 257 046 **Alt:** 230m

6 The Fugue ★★★   **20m E9 6c**

FA Dave MacLeod (headpointed) 16 October 2002

Very serious hard climbing taking the steep central wall. Start just left of 7 and climb a short groove to good holds. Place an assortment of dubious gear behind the soft jug on the right. Step left and launch up the overhanging wall with increasing difficulty to a desperate crux move from a small undercut. Move left to a jug in the lip and in a serious position reach rightwards through the bulge to twin finger pockets (wires in left pocket). Climb the steep wall directly above on crimps to a good finishing jug. Very powerful (F8a+) climbing with groundfall potential.

7 Short Sharp Shock ★★   **25m E4 6a**

FA Ronnie Bruce July 1986

In the centre of the crag are twin overhanging finger cracks leading into a niche below a grassy bay. The left crack. Make some awkward moves to become established in the crack, and follow it on good positive finger-locks to a rest just below the top. Pull over on good holds (in situ slings – possible LO) and easily up a slabby crack above.

8 Double Clutching ★   **25m E3 6a**

FA Gary Latter & Colin Gilchrist 5 August 1985

The right crack. Gain the crack with a long reach and climb it to a sharp pull onto a ledge at its top. Easily up a slabby crack to finish.

Down and right of the main crag is a large boulder with a steep front face and a prominent overhung right arête.

9 The Sharp Kiss ★   **15m E3 6a**

FA Dave Griffiths 13 July 1987

Steep technical climbing up the left side of the front face. Start at a large flat boulder on the left. Pull right and go up to a good horizontal break then through the bulge with difficulty (PR) to finish up an easier slab.

10 Tick Tock ★★★   **18m E6 6b**

FA Dave MacLeod (headpointed) July 2002

The stunning bold blunt right arête with a bouldery crux and bold finish. Climb easily from the right to a jug on the right (wire behind) then make a hard move to gain incut pockets on the arête. Make a long reach from here to finish on improving holds.

11 Litterbug ★   **15m E1 5b**

FA Ian Taylor & A.Caren July 1988

Start beneath the blunt rib just left of a large rowan on the far right of the right wall. Ascend the wall, keeping left of the rib to pull onto a slab. Finish up and left and belay well back.

NN 259 046 **Alt:** 230m   10min

NN 259 048 **Alt:** 310m   20min

INDEPENDENCE CRAG

Slightly higher than **Upper Crag**, a little over 100m further right lies a bulging wall containing a prominent deep hanging crack on its right side.

Approach: Traverse right from the base of **Upper Crag**.

A short solo 1 *Imposition* ★ E4 5c tackles the left end of the bulging wall.

2 New Position ★   12m E2 5c

FA Dave Griffiths 14 September 1986

The strenuous though well protected hanging flake crack.

SO FAR AWAY BUTTRESS

The largest crag up and right of **Upper Crag** split by a prominent diagonal break running from right to left with a band of roofs parallel to and above the break.

Approach: Diagonally right up the hillside from **Upper Crag**, a further ten minutes walk.

1 Aftershock ★★   30m E3 5c
FA Dave Griffiths 2 May 1987

Climb the left edge of the buttress to join 2 where it moves into the gully. Pull through the bulge above on side-pulls and continue to the obvious niche in the horizontal break. Traverse right along the break until in the centre of the crag and direct past a poor tied off PR to top.

2 Give us a Break ★   30m E1 5b
FA Gary Latter & Mick Fowler 31 July 1985

The diagonal break. Start below the right end of this. Gain the break and follow it until it is possible to move into the gully. Nut belay above. Scrambling remains.

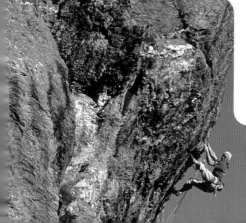

Dave MacLeod on the first ascent of the testing The Fugue. Photo Dave Cuthbertson, Cubby Images.

NN 260 049 **Alt:** 340m 20min

GREAT SLAB

A slabby crag in the recess just up and right of **So Far Away Buttress.**

1 The Incredible Hulk ★★   15m E5 6a

FA Stuart Robinson & Ken Lawson April 1989

Very bold and strenuous. Round the left side of the main slab is an overhanging wall with a thin flared crack starting at one third height. Climb the wall and crack.

2 Lapland ★   20m E1 5a

FA Ian Taylor & B.Williamson 16 August July 1988

Follows a series of overlapping slabs at the left end of the slab. Start on top of a heather-capped block above and left of a rowan. Climb up to the right end of the first overlap, traverse left above the overlap to gain a slab. Cross the next overlap where the slab above forms a bulge to finish up a shallow corner.

3 Fearless ★   25m VS 4c

FA Dave Griffiths (solo) 30 May 1987

Poorly protected climbing up the centre of the main slab. Climb the bulging central rib moving out right to finish.

4 Rock Sculpture ★   25m E3 5c

FA Stuart Robinson & Ken Lawson (2 PRs) April 1989;
FA after removal of pegs Ian Taylor & George Szuca April 1989

Ascends the right side of the main slab. Start up a heathery flake crack to reach the left end of overhangs. Go up on small holds (RP #3 in a thin crack) then trend right to a ledge. Continue directly. PB on slab above.

The Edge of Insanity, Upper Crag. Andy de Klerk climbing.

THE ANVIL

1hr ½hr ¼hr

NS 206 949 **Alt:** 80m

A massive free standing boulder on the east side of Loch Goil opposite and very slightly north of Carrick Castle. The two steep aspects with the routes give very intense climbing on good schist. It requires about 3 days to dry in the winter (apart from the very steep **North Cave** routes, which are almost perma-dry!)

although it seems to stay dry most of the summer. The very sheltered nature enclosed within the forest (extreme midge rating!) precludes activity for most of the summer. Routes here have had few repeats, and grades may change – both F8b+s may be hard for the grade, if not F8c.

Routes are described from right to left.

WEST FACE

The initially 'vertical-looking' face actually overhangs by about 30 degrees.

Access: Turn south from the A83 at the Rest and be Thankful and follow the B828 for 3.3 miles/5km then B839 continuation for 5.8 miles/9.3km to park in large car park on the loch side, opposite the supermarket and post office in Lochgoilhead.

Approach: Follow the road continuation south past the bike hire garage (£10/day, April–Oct; ☎ 01301 703432) then a small steep path on the left (signposted **to forestry track**) after about 1.5km, just before the road starts to descend fairly steeply. Follow this to gain the forestry track and continue along this for about 4km. The crag is just visible 20m uphill from the track, about 200m beyond a long downhill section, beyond the second cattle grid. Alternatively, by waterborne means across the loch from Carrick Castle then jungle bash up the hillside to the forestry track. A small stream runs down the north side of the crag, directly beneath the routes on the **North-West Face** and **North Cave**.

① Way Out West *   **10m F6b**

FA Dave MacLeod November 2004

Follow the right arête to a small ledge then leftwards until possible to make another 'graunchy' rockover onto the final slab.

② Nu Mettle *   **10m F7b**

FA Dave MacLeod November 2004

A devious and technical line up the short shallow groove leading rightwards into 1. Some very sloping holds.

③ Hammertime **   **12m F7b+**

FA Dave MacLeod November 2004

Excellent climbing on rough edges and pockets taking a diagonal line heading rightwards across the front face. Follow 5 to the first bolt then make a difficult step right to a pocket. Continue the diagonal to eventually gain easier climbing and the finishing slab of 1. Made to be climbed!

4 Black Out ★★   15m F8b

FA Malcolm Smith September 2007

Start as for 3 then climb straight up to the top of the obvious flake. Span left to a side pull slot, then climb directly up the right side of the shallow groove on poor crimps.

5 Crossfire ★★   15m F7c+

FA Dave Redpath 21 May 2006

The diagonal cracks splitting the front face. Start up 3 then move left to a series of jugs. Where these end make a hard move into 6 to join it at its first crux. After this keep moving left along a break to gain the LO of 7.

6 Spitfire ★★★★   12m F8a

FA Dave Redpath 21 May 2006

Fantastic sustained climbing *"with nothing much harder than British 6b climbing."* From the large flake move up to a poor rest on sidepulls. The first crux involves gaining the edge, the second a big move off the last pocket.

7 Anvilfire ★★   12m F8a

FA Dave MacLeod May 2005

The left arête. *"Painfully technical."* A technical section up the arête leads to a shake out by the last bolt. Swing left and rock over onto the hanging slab with difficulty to slap for the apex of the arête. A Direct Finish at F7c/+ is possible, crimping with poor feet to a jug.

Dave MacLeod on first ascent of Body Swerve. Photo Dave Brown, Hot Aches Images

NORTH-WEST FACE

The crag now changes aspect with a jumble of huge fallen boulders just to the north.

8 Friendly Fire ★★★   12m F7a

FA Richard McGhee May 2006

Brilliant varied climbing in a magnificent setting. Start at the arête as for 7. Trend leftwards after the first bolt, making bouldery moves to a good jug. Rock onto the slab above to a no hands rest before the final steep section. From the slab, trend rightwards to good spaced jugs in the groove to finish.

9 The Atlantic Strikes Back ★   15m F7c+

FA Dave MacLeod April 2006

Climb the bouldery but fun steepening groove left of 8 to the ledge. Another hard boulder problem leads to the shelf in the middle of the wall above. Follow this rightwards to the LO of 8.

9a Cowal Crusaders   12m F6c

FA Dave MacLeod November 2004

A link up giving pumpy climbing on jugs. Start up the ramp on the left side of the face to gain the ledge. Traverse right across the slab to finish up the steep groove of 8.

10 The Smiddy ★   20m F8b+

FA Malcolm Smith 26 August 2007

Climb 11 for 4 bolts, then break out right up the fingery wall. Short, sweet, and crimpy. Cool moves.

11 Shadowlands ★★★   18m F7c

FA Mike Tweedley 22 May 2006

The impressive cave arête following an obvious crack. Start in the cave. Move steeply up on good holds to a small ledge. Use a large flange to gain positive holds in the crack then follow a powerful sequence to better finishing holds.

NORTH CAVE

Some extremely steep climbing. Climb the in-situ knotted rope to gain a glacis; traverse rightwards then scramble round the edge into the stygian depths of the chasm.

2 Fire Power ★★   10m F8b

FA Dave Redpath 20 May 2007

Climbs the right side of the roof, starting right of the short arête underneath. The meat of the route involves a short crux at the start of the roof (Font 7c+).

13 Blood Fire ★★   10m F8a+

FA Alan Cassidy 8 July 2007

Starting up the corner, a sequence of 4 hard moves (Font 7b+, easier for the tall) leads to a line of better flat holds leading into 13a. Finishing more directly up 14 should make an F9a!

13a Heavy Metal   10m F7b

FA Dave Redpath 2006

Start 13 at mid-height using the adjacent boulder to power out of the cave.

14 Body Blow ★   10m F8b+

FA Dave MacLeod 22 May 2006

Top half of the roof project. Step off the halfway boulder and make very hard (British 7a) moves to gain a good jug. Compose then climb the *"awesome"* headwall with great moves.

14a Metalcore ★★★   20m F8c+

FA Dave MacLeod 2 May 2007

Climb the start of 14, then follow the faint rightward trending crack all the way to the peak of the roof.

15 Body Swerve ★★   20m F8c

FA Dave MacLeod 10 October 2006

"I'm certain it's the hardest sport route in Scotland." – MacLeod 2006. The super steep line through the left end of the cave. Start in the depths of the chasm. Climb up past a large flake to follow very steep ground leading to good finishing holds. Finish up the next route.

16 Amateur Hacker   10m F6c

FA Dave MacLeod 24 September 2006

Climb round the huge boulder and swing onto a shelf which leads to the slanting groove above. Balancy.

Metalcore, Dave MacLeod on first ascent. Photo Claire MacLeod.

NR 782 848 **Alt**: 220m 🏄 🧗 🥾 25 min **(CRAG OF THE RAVEN)**

CREAG NAM FITHEACH

A fine wee crag well away from all the mainstream climbing areas. The rock is an excellent rough epidiorite (chemically similar to gabbro) which dries quickly. There are a number of convenient bolt belays at the top of the crag, placed in the late eighties, apparently by members of staff from Achnamara Outdoor Centre. Although adequate natural belays exist the bolt belays should be left in place.

Access: From the south: turn left off the A816, 2 miles/3km north of Lochgilphead heading west along the B841 on the south bank of the Crinan Canal for 3 miles/4.5km to Bellanoch. From the north: turn right 1 mile/1.6km south of Kilmartin and follow the B8025 south-west across the Moine Mhor for 4.5 miles/7km to Bellanoch. At Bellanoch: head south down the B8025 for just over a mile/1.8 km then take the left fork down the single track C-class road through Achnamara to take a left turn, signposted Kilmichael of Inverlussa. Park on the grass in front of the church. (3.5 miles/5.5km).

Approach: Follow Land Rover track through the yard opposite the church which leads up round past a small hydro building. Continue more steeply up the track through a gate and up through the forest to its end at a small dammed loch. Gain the left end of the crag by boulder hopping.

Descent: Down either end of the crag.

1 Moby Dick ★★   **35m Very Difficult**

FA Alex Small & party 1940s

The pleasant slabby face forming the left side of the obvious arête. Start up the right side of some wedged blocks and climb a fine crack finishing slightly rightwards.

2 Captain Ahab ★   **50m HVS 5a**

FA Dave Hayter & party early 80s

Below the slab is a prominent right-facing corner. Layback this to a ledge near the arête (possible belay). Continue up the obvious line just left of the arête (poorly protected) and finish more easily up the arête.

3 Maneater ★★   **30m E3 5c**

FA Dave Griffiths & Cameron Bell (1 PR) 21 February 1988; PR removed by Gary Latter prior to #2nd ascent 1988

The gaping off-width crack is not quite as ferocious as first appearances might suggest. Climb it mainly using a good finger crack for protection on its right wall. Stroll up the very much easier arête to finish, or lower off from a good spike a short way up this.

4 Temptation *   30m E3 5c
FA Dave Griffiths 20 July 1988

The slim left-facing groove just right of 3. Start behind a rowan. Climb the groove and flake and either finish up an easy arête or move left and lower off a good spike.

5 Crucifixion Crack ***   25m E2 5c
FA Graham Little & Pete Linning 9 October 1982

Excellent well protected climbing. Start immediately right of a rowan tree. Up a ramp to make difficult moves to pull into a triangular niche. Pull over the overlap then hand traverse the diagonal flake-crack leftwards to gain the easy upper arête to finish.

6 Pocket Wall **   20m E1 5b
FA Graham Little & Pete Linning 9 October 1982

The centre of the wall facing 5. Easily up on pockets to a ledge then continue with technical moves to stand on this. Either finish directly or escape out left.

7 The Razor's Edge ***   25m HVS 5a
FA Graham Little 10 July 1981

Superb climbing up the prominent 'Africa-shaped' flake crack on the right flank of the third buttress from the left. Up a rib to a ledge to gain and layback/jam the fine flake crack and a short corner to finish.

8 The Changeling **   30m E5 6a
FA Dave & Ian Griffiths (headpointed) 16 September 1995

The left arête of the pod-shaped groove (*Metamorphosis* E2 5c). Start just to the left of the groove at a wide crack. Up this to stand on top of a block. Now climb direct up the bulging arête (PR) to where the angle eases and swing into a hanging crack on the right. Follow this to where a move left to a ledge can be made. Up a ramp to the top.

9 America **   30m VS 4c
FA Graham Little & Colin Ritchie 6 June 1982

Start in the deep recessed groove 10m right of 8. Climb

to the top of a large flake on the left. Go directly up for 3m, move right into a crack and finish up this.

10 The Trial *   30m E1 5b
FA Graham Little & Colin Ritchie 6 June 1982

Start to the left of an enormous leaning block, which moves; beware! Climb a rib to a small bush. Cross an overhang to gain a roofed niche then direct up the wall above.

11 The Prow *   30m E1 5c
FA Graham Little & Colin Ritchie 5 June 1982

The prominent jutting rib. Using a flake on the left, gain and climb a finger crack parallel to the edge. Up the exposed arête and the short, difficult wall above.

12 Crystal Vision ***   30m E5 6b/5.12a
FA Dave Griffiths 29 July 1988

The Fingerlicker of Scotland – superb sustained finger-jamming with a hard crux – very well protected. Start at the lowest point of the right wall of 11. Climb up and left to good slots then make hard moves rightward to gain the crack. Continue with difficulty to a good resting ledge. Continue up the groove above, exiting out left through a gap to finish up the crux wall of 11.

13 Not Waving, But Drowning **   30m E6 6b
FA Mark McGowan & Stuart Lampard (headpointed) August 1988

The striking square-cut arête. Climb up to below a roof at 6m. Reach round to a horizontal break (protection). Make moves up to a fingertip undercut (Roller #2) then make sequential slaps (crux) to a poor peg runner. Climb an arête, passing a F #2 placement on the left to a good ledge below a bulge (RP #4). An awkward move onto the ledge leads to a precarious move up the wall to a thin horizontal break (RP #2 & #3). Swing round arête to good holds and protection. Follow flake holds to top.

The 10m buttress bounding the far right end of the crag contains a trio of Severes, together with the fine diagonal jam crack of 14 *Chamonix Crack* * VS 4c.

Prince of Thieves, Lower Tier, Erraid. Jules Lines soloing.

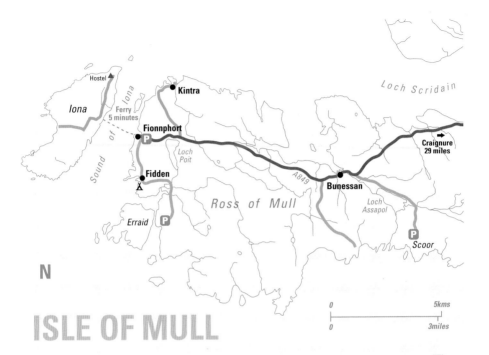

The second largest and one of the most accessible of the Inner Hebrides. Although it is one of the wettest islands of the Hebrides all the climbing described is situated around the west end of the low lying Ross of Mull peninsula, benefiting from a much lower rainfall than the hillier centre of the island.

Access: Caledonian MacBrayne operate vehicle and passenger ferries from Oban – Craignure (45 minutes); Lochaline – Fishnish (15 minutes) and Kilchoan – Tobermory (35 minutes, April – Oct; Sunday June – Aug only). (☎ 01475 650100; www.calmac.co.uk).

Accommodation and Amenities: Bunkhouse & campsite at Shieling Holidays, Craignure (☎ 01680 812496; www.shielingholidays.co.uk). Balmeanach caravan and campsite at Fishnish (☎ 01680 300342; April – Oct) with good friendly café. YH at Tobermory (☎ 01688 302481; tobermory@syha.org.uk); Dervaig Bunkrooms (☎ 01688 400249); innumerable Hotels & B&Bs – TICs at The Pier, Craignure (☎ 01680 812377; info@mull.visitscotland.com) or Main Street, Tobermory (☎ 01688 302182; info@tobermory.visitscotland.com) April – Oct; www.visitscottishheartlands.com.

Wild camping is possible close to all the crags described, though there are few streams for drinking water. There is a small basic campsite (☎ 01681 700427 portaloos and hot showers) at Fidden, 1.3 miles/2km south from Fionnphort, overlooking a fine sandy beach at the north end of Erraid. There are a couple of small supermarkets in Bunessan, pubs in Pennyghael, Bunessan and Fionnphort and a tearoom in Bunessan.

HISTORY

The first recorded routes on the crags described occurred in the early nineties with Colwyn Jones, Steve Kennedy and Dave Ritchie adding a dozen routes to the Lower Tier at Erraid together with a handful of routes on the more extensive Upper Tier. Graeme Little had previously soloed around on these crags, but left the routes unrecorded. Ross of Mull residents Danny Brooks and James Marshall added the first routes on Tolkien Crag on Iona and at Scoor, soon joined by Colin Moody. The trio accounted for over forty additions at Scoor, amongst them *Where Eagles Dare* and *Night Rider* from Brooks and *Kelpie* and *Tystie* from Moody. Moody then developed a range of good crags on Iona, opening up Ireland Wall with *The Good Book*, visiting Johnny Adams soon adding the excellent neighbouring *Heretic*. Moody also initiated development of Raven's Crag. Standards leapt considerably in August 1993 with a productive visit from a motivated Mark Garthwaite. On Raven's Crag he produced *Yabbadabbadoo* and *Mr Muscle*, both E5, soon followed by *The Incredible Dr Sex*. His partner on some of these, Dave Greig, also added some of his own, including *Prodigy*. Garthwaite returned numerous times, notching up a series of further hard additions, *Tweekie Pie* and *See You in Hell Soldier Boy* at Scoor the most impressive, together with a trio of further routes on Raven's Crag, including *Smoking the Toad*. Significantly, the majority of these harder additions were headpointed after prior top-rope practise.

In 1997 Rab Anderson nipped across, adding a couple of hard routes, including the eliminate *Tippidy Doodah* at Scoor. Gary Latter visited, repeating some of the hard routes, as well as adding a few of his own, including *Covenant* and *Skerryvore* on the Upper Tier at Erraid and *God is Dead* to Raven's Crag. Moody, Louise Gordon Canning and Michael Tweedley soon developed the left end of the Upper Tier at Erraid with a range of good easier additions. Rick Waterton also repeated some hard routes on the crags including the second ascent of *See You in Hell Soldier Boy* after a hold fell off, as well as adding *Blood Eagle* to Raven's Crag. Latter returned to Erraid numerous times, adding many further routes

including *Catriona*, and with Jules Lines developed the Paradise Wall as an excellent deep water soloing venue – highlights including *Dreamline* and *Drowning in Adrenaline*. It later transpired that Andy Spink had previously climbed the first route on here with his ascent of *Please Rub Salt into my Wounds!* back in 1996. On a small granite dome overlooking Fionnphort, Tweedley headpointed the short bold slab *Akira*.

Lines returned to Erraid the following year, single-handedly developing many good new crags, on-sight soloing over thirty new routes in a very productive three days in August. Amongst the highlights *The Otter's Breakfast Table* and a further couple of deep water solos on the Otter Walls; the very thin *Jules's Pistachios* to Strawberry Pig Slab and a couple of good lines in Asteroid Chasm. Moody soon added further routes here, later returning in 2005 to establish the fine *Solar Collector*. Lines and Paul Thorburn returned in 2003, developing further crags with Karen's Slab and Red Anvil Chasm, on-sight soloing a couple of routes on the former. In 2006, Moody and Cynthia Grindley added a further fifteen routes to the short though good Mink Walls, *Need an Inch* being the best and hardest of the bunch.

📷 *Caroline, Mink Walls, Erraid. Colin Moody on first ascent. Photo Cynthia Grindley.*

SCOOR

NM 410 188 E) (W ⚓ 20min

A fine assortment of schist crags on the south coast of the Ross of Mull. The area has a pleasant holiday atmosphere with a fine sandy beach in an idyllic setting. A herd of wild goats is in residence and there are often Golden Eagles around.

Access: Follow the A849 west across the island to Bunessan. Turn left (south) 200m beyond the school and follow the minor C-class road which becomes a rough though driveable track east past Loch Assapol, curving round right (south) to park overlooking ruined chapel (2.4 miles/3.8km from Bunessan).

Approach: Follow the track which heads out south-west (not the continuing road to Scoor House). At the third gate the beach is straight ahead. All are within 5 minutes from the beach. Garbh Eilean is the rough rocky 'island' straight ahead, while **Dune Wall**, **Beach Wall** and **The Slab** are all to the left (east), the latter hidden from view.

Tystie, The Slab. Gary Latter climbing. Photo Karen Martin.

GARBH EILEAN
(ROUGH ISLAND)

The 'island' on the left side of the beach. It becomes tidal only on spring tides or following a big storm when the sand is washed away.

HORSE WALL E)

A clean gently overhanging wall on the tiny tidal island opposite **Beach Wall**.

1 LaURACHEVAL ★★   13m E3 5c
FA Mark Garthwaite & George Szuca 5 September 1993
The left-slanting crack on the right side of the wall starting at the right edge of the dark stained wall.

2 See You in Hell Soldier Boy ★★★   14m E6/7 6b
FA Mark Garthwaite (headpointed) 15 October 1994
Start at good holds 1m left of the black-stained wall. Move up to a short sharp flake and move left to a very sharp finger jug, shake out and gear. Make very thin technical moves up the wall above to reach the diagonal crack. Pull out right to a finger hold, stand in the crack and reach over the top to finish. RPs and HBs #2 - #5 essential.

3 Eat My Shorts ★★   13m E5 6a
FA Mark Garthwaite & Colin Moody 25 September 1994
The layback crack at the left side of the wall. Flared and quite difficult to protect.

4 Wild Swans ★   11m E1 5b
FA Colin Moody & Mark Garthwaite 15 October 1994
The crack up on the left.

5 Photo Finish ★   8m E3 5c
FA Colin Moody & Louise Gordon Canning 28 June 1997
A bold start above a poor landing. Left of 4 is a small slanting overlap. Climb up right to the right end of the overlap, step left and climb the crack.

DUNE WALL (w)

The first small wall left (east) from the approach. From a distance a coating of black lichen gives an impression of wetness but the wall dries quickly. If natural belays are found lacking there is a stake well up from *Wallcreeper*.

From the left are 1 *The Arête* HVS 5a; 2 *Flick-flake* HVS 5a – the groove and sharp layback crack immediately right & the thin crack of 3 *Tippidy Doodah* ∗ E4/5 6b. The shallow corner is 4 *Red Shafted Flicker* E1 5b.

5 Wallcreeper ∗   10m E2 6a
FA Colin Lambton, Colin Moody & Mike Rosser 1994

Climb the scoops in the centre of the wall. A steep start gains a left-sloping ramp. Mantel out right then make a thin move (crux) to good holds below the top.

6 The Crystal Ship ∗   10m E4 6a
FA Tom Charles-Edwards 1996

The blind groove just right of 5.

7 Troglodyte ∗∗   10m HVS 5a
FA Colin Moody & Allan Petrie 27 September 1993

Climb the crack to the overhang, step left and layback to the top.

The crack to the right is 8 *Thorns* HVS 5a.

9 Dune Chough ∗   10m VS 4c
FA Colin Moody & Allan Petrie 27 September 1993

The cracks on the right side of the wall. Climb up to a small overlap, step right and follow the flakes.

Tweekie Pie, Beach Wall. Gary Latter climbing. Photo Karen Martin.

BEACH WALL AREA (w)

The short wall and the rocks beside it overlooking the boulders at the east (left) end of the beach. There is a large patch of ivy at the left end.

1 Better Than a Poke in the Eye *   8m E4 6a

FA Mark Garthwaite 29 August 1993

The right-slanting crack at the left side of the crag just right of the ivy.

The crack and wide corner crack is 2 *Fungy* VS 4c.

3 The Reality Dysfunction **   15m E6 6a

FA Niall McNair May 2004

The prominent square-cut arête - low in grade but serious. Start on the arête and the 'drainpipe' feature before moving onto the arête proper at half height. Crux right at top.

4 Waves and White Water **   15m HVS 5a

FA Danny Brooks & James Marshall October 1991

The prominent square-cut corner, often with a wet spring at the base.

5 Tweekie Pie **   15m E5 6c

FA Mark Garthwaite 5 September 1993

The thin cracks up the right wall of the big corner of 4. A very thin and technical crux is at the top, protected by RPs. Climb the thin crack to good edges in the horizontal break at two thirds height (small rocks). Move right then back leftwards up the shallow diagonal crack to a desperate thin section to better holds, finishing on a superb flake over the top. Belay stake in the bracken.

6 Sylvester *   15m E2 5c

FA Mark Garthwaite & Colin Moody 29 August 1993

The w-i-d-e crack right of 5. Take some large cams!

7 Runout *   15m VS 4b

FA James Marshall & Danny Brooks March 1992

Left of 9 is a recessed area, left again is another ridge. Climb this ridge to a bulge then the left-slanting crack on the left. Strenuous.

8 Bluebell Blues *   15m E1 5b

FA Danny Brooks February 1993

The left wall of 9. Gain the base of the left-slanting ramp, up this and the corner and step right to finish.

9 Kilvickeon **   20m E2 5b

FA Danny Brooks March 1992

There is a boulder field west of The Slab and west again is a ridge. Start left of the base of the ridge. Climb a difficult overhanging layback then move right to gain a foot ledge. Move back left onto the arête and straight up to finish.

10 Mink *   15m VS 4b

FA Danny Brooks 1992

The ridge high in the boulder field left of The Slab. Start up the right edge and finish up the left edge then traverse the neck to gain the boulder field. Although the crux is low down this is a bold route to lead and second – probably best soloed.

THE SLAB

Situated behind **Beach Wall** out of sight on the
approach. The starts of the first three routes are affected
by high tides. Protection is often behind flakes which
might not take a big fall; therefore the adjectival grade is
often higher than expected. Routes from right to left.

1 Head Butts *   15m E2 5b

FA Danny Brooks & Colin Moody 18 October 1992

There is a small overhung niche at the right end of the
crag. Gain this, climb the overhang to the ledge then
continue up the crack in the shallow corner.

2 Tystie **   15m E3 6a

FA Colin Moody & Neil Horn 14 June 1993

The thin twin cracks just left of 1 with the crux near the
top. Protection is *"a bit funky"*.

3 Bonxie *   15m E3 6a

FA Gary Latter & Louise Gordon-Canning 7 August 1997

The prominent thin twin cracks in the wall left of 2. Make
a hard bouldery start past a good friend slot at the start
to better holds, finishing directly by good flakes in the
upper wall.

4 Sawfish Crack *   15m E1 5b

*FA Colin Moody, James Marshall & Danny Brooks
28 September 1991*

Start 6m left of the niche of 1 directly below a short
left-facing corner. Climb to a triangular overhang, step
right and follow the sharp crack leading to the finishing
corner.

5 Pocket Razor *   15m Severe 4a

FA Danny Brooks & James Marshall August 1991

Further left is a shallow corner crack. Start up this then
move up rightwards on sharp flakes to finish up the final
corner of 4.

6 Chough-less **   15m VS 4c

*FA Colin Moody, Danny Brooks & James Marshall
28 September 1991*

The shallow corner crack.

7 Splitting Hares *   18m E3 6a

FA Michael Tweedley & Cynthia Grindley 2 June 2002

The thin crack right of 8. Wimp onto that route
near the top.

8 Everything Flying By ★★   20m E1 5b
FA Colin Moody & Danny Brooks 19 August 1992

Left of the upper half of 6 are three thin vertical cracks. Move up left to gain and climb the left crack.

9 Seal Show ★★   20m HVS 5a
FA Colin Moody & Danny Brooks 20 October 1991

In the centre of the slab are two prominent faults starting as shallow chimneys. Follow the right fault, stepping right at the top. High in the grade.

11 Turnstone ★   25m E2 5b
FA Colin Moody & Mark Shaw 12 July 1994

Left of the left fault (10 *Greased Lightning* E1 5a) is a thin crack and left of this an easier crack, which is gained from the top of the highest boulder. Climb up passing a block at 7m then climb up to and over the bulge at two small overlaps to reach a flake. Follow the flake right to

a rock-scarred recess in the fault and finish directly to belay well back.

12 Where Eagles Dare ★★★   25m E1 5a
FA Danny Brooks & Sean Morris October 1992

A fine intimidating wander. Start 7m left of the left fault just left of 10 and left of where the cliff base steepens. Climb a crack for 4m then move left 1m and follow another crack to the small overhangs. Step left and climb the open chimney for 2m. Hand traverse left across the wall to a sapling then direct to the top.

13 Hit and Run ★★   25m E2 5b
FA Colin Moody & Andrew Pedley 22 August 1993

A good route crossing 12. A bold start but low in the grade. Start 3m left of 12. Climb the crack direct to below the right side of the crescent-shaped overhang. Step right to join 12 up the open chimney and continue up and right to finish.

📷 *Didn't think I was that strong! Bouldering on Fionnphort beach, Ross of Mull. Photo Karen Martin.*

Slab & Crack

NM 304 237 **Alt:** 50m 10min

FIONNPHORT
SLAB AND CRACK

A fine wee dome of perfect rough granite.

Access: Park at the east end of the car park by the ferry terminal at Fionnphort.

Approach: Follow the road down past the graveyard then cut right behind the rightmost house to pick up a well-worn path cutting up just west of the wall.

1 Akira ★★★   **9m E6 6b**

FA Michael Tweedley (headpointed) August 2001

The crack terminating just beyond mid-height. Easily up crack then move left to an *"obvious wee grey blobby hold"*. Follow a sequence of tiny holds right to above the crack then make a lurch for the final holds (6a).

Bouldering: There is a wealth of good bouldering at a variety of excellent venues. The gabbro at the fine sandy beach at Laggan Sands on Loch Buie is a fine venue. There is also some good bouldering on fine granite bluffs scattered across the hillside of Catchean overlooking Fionnphort and at Kintra about 20 minutes east round the coast from the cottages.

📷 *Bouldering on perfect granite – hillside north of Fionnphort.*

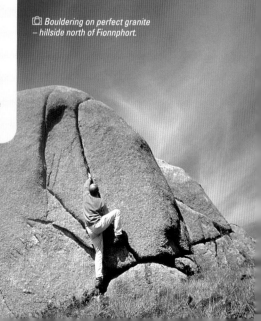

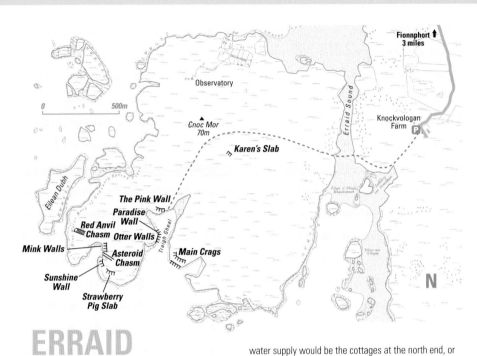

ERRAID

Erraid is a small tidal island situated just off the west-most point of the long peninsula of the Ross of Mull. It is accessible by foot across the sands most of the time, though the shifting level of the sand or spring tides may necessitate wading for approximately 2 hours either side of high water. The climbing is on a range of short but superb granite crags located close to the popular yacht anchorage Traigh Gheal (white sands) at the south-west corner of the island. The island featured in Robert Louis Stevenson's classic Scottish novel *Kidnapped*. Stevenson stayed for a short time at the north end of the island. The earlier uncredited routes were all climbed by combinations of Colwyn Jones, Steve Kennedy and Dave Ritchie in July 1990 and April 1991

Accommodation and Amenities: The area around Traigh Gheal is a perfect haven, with beautiful white beaches and some fine wild camping. A small stream runs into Traigh Gheal, though during prolonged dry spells this dries out. Alternatively, the nearest fresh water supply would be the cottages at the north end, or the farm at Knockvologan. With lots of thick bracken, midges and ticks can be a problem.

Access: Follow the A849 west across the island to its end at Fionnphort. Turn left (signposted Columba Centre & Fidden) at the car park and follow the narrow C-class road southwards for 3 miles/4.8km to park on the left, at Knockvologan Farm.

Approach: Follow the farm track south, bending round west down to the sands. Walk or wade across Erraid Sound and head west for 700m then south-west to arrive at the wonderful Traigh Gheal (35 min). For the **Main Crags**, scramble round the shore on the left to pick up a path cutting up then contouring right to arrive at the left end of the **Upper Tier** (10 min). The **Pink Wall** lies just a few minutes west of the beach, overlooking the small west-most beach. The **Paradise** and **Otter Walls** are about 5 minutes south from here. **Strawberry Pig Cliff** and **Sunshine Wall** lie about 5 minutes from here due south-west. **Asteroid Chasm** and **Mink Wall** are 10 minutes due west of the **Paradise Wall** on the west coast and **Red Anvil Crag** less than 10 minutes from here to the north-west.

MAIN CRAGS

LOWER TIER NM 295 191 45min

A small enclosed bowl at sea level. Only a couple of the routes on the right side of the crag are tidal, though the crag could be affected by rough seas.

Descent: Scramble down the left (east) side of the slabby middle tier then negotiate a unique little narrow rock archway (fixed rope in situ) to gain the centre of the crag. There is also an easy (Mod) descent down the V-gully at the west end of the crag, behind the Sentinel. Routes on the right side of the crag can also be gained by an easy scramble in from the east at low tide.

The cracks in the gully wall at the back of the Sentinel are from the left: VDiff, VS 4c and VS 4c.

1 Fools Gold   8m E2 6a

FA Julian Lines & Paul Thorburn June 2004

Start below flying fin left of two main arêtes. Boulder up seam onto ledge on right. Finish up easy corner.

2 Sentinel **   12m HVS 5a

The most prominent crack splitting the sea-ward face. Climb the cracks to a wide ledge before stepping back left to the main crack.

2a Sentinel Direct *   4m E1 5b

Climb the steep cracks just left of the start of the ordinary route which is joined just above the ledge.

3 Daylight Robbery ★★   10m VS 4b

The next crack right of 2, with a bouldery start.

4 Mullman ★   8m HVS 5a

The next crack to the right, starting up a short slab.

5 Erraid Shelter ★★   8m E2 5b

FA Julian Lines & Gary Latter (on-sight) 16 July 2001

The short arête above the upper ledge, left of the arch.

6 Weeping Corner ★   7m HVS 5a

The obvious black corner just right of the archway.

7 Davie ★★   8m E3 6b

FA Julian Lines & Gary Latter (on-sight) 18 July 2001

Surprisingly independent climbing up the right arête of 6. Place a low runner in the groove and move right to good jug on the arête (sling). Attain a standing position on this then continue up the arête and crack pleasantly.

> The shallow groove/arête on the right side starting up 8 was also climbed at E2 5c.

8 Flood Warning ★★   9m E2 5c

FA Colin Moody & Billy Gordon Canning 29 June 1997

Start a few metres right of 6. Climb an awkward bulge then the twin cracks.

9 Tarzan★   10m HVS 5a

Climbs the wall and crack starting at the right end of the undercut section a metre right of 6.

10 Jane   10m VS 5a

A difficult well protected start to gain the left side of the large incut ledge, finishing more easily up the deep corner.

11 The Hole ★★   8m HVS 5a

The crack on the left wall of 12.

12 Jungle Book ★   8m VS 4b

The obvious corner a metre right of 10.

13 Spiral Arête ★   10m HVS 5a

Start up a short corner and slab to the right of the arête. Spiral back up left and finish up a short corner.

14 Prince of Thieves ★   10m E1 5b

Sustained climbing up the striking crack on the wall just right of 13.

15 Moody's Blues ★   10m E2 5b

The next crack to the right. Gain a small incut ledge from the right. Climb a thin crack to a ledge, reach right and follow the deep crack.

> The two short cracks round to the right are Moderate and Difficult respectively.

MIDDLE TIER

This gives some fine easy-angled 18m routes on immaculate rock, generally climbing anywhere at Moderate – Difficult.

Davie, Jules Lines on first ascent.

UPPER TIER

NM 295 191 **Alt:** 30m  45min

Much steeper than the lower tier, with many short brutal pitches, often with hard bouldery starts above perfect flat grassy landings.

Descent: Down either side of the crag, the east descent by the easy rock ramp right of the highest section.

The first three routes are on the large block up and left of the main crag.

LEFT SIDE

Left-Hand Route   **9m Severe 4a**

FA Colin Moody 10 August 1997

Climb corner/chimney on left side of boulder then continue up the crack above.

The Goupher Hole ★★   **11m VS 4c**

FA Colin Moody & Derek Stuart 11 August 1997

Gain the shelf right of 1, step up then follow break right to finish up the scoop.

One Dead Puffin ★   **9m HVS 5a**

FA Michael Tweedley 11 August 1997

Climb the corner on the right to the break, move left and finish up the arête.

The short right-facing corner crack beneath the boulder is Severe 4a.

Ledge Route ★   **12m VS 4b**

FA Colin Moody 10 August 1997

Climb a jam crack then go directly up the slab above (bold), which faces the boulder.

Smelly Mussels ★   **9m HVS 5a**

FA Michael Tweedley & Louise Gordon Canning August 1997

Climb the left side of the block left of 6. Traverse into the centre of the block and finish up the crack with an awkward finish.

The arête on the left is 5a VS 4c; the short chimney further left Severe 4a.

The Dead Pool   **9m Severe 4a**

FA Colin Moody 10 August 1997

Right again are two huge blocks. Climb the V-notch between them and finish up the ramp on the right.

Bacteria Soup ★   **12m Severe 4a**

FA Colin Moody 10 August 1997

Right of 6 is a heather ramp with a short face on the right. Climb the flakes and jam crack in the centre of the short face. Step right and finish up the corner.

Blood Orange ★   **12m Severe 4a**

FA Derek Stuart, Colin Moody & Michael Tweedley 11 Aug 1997

The corner on the right to the shelf then move right and finish up a further corner.

9 Tyke's Lead ★   **11m Very Difficult**

FA Louise Gordon Canning, Karen Martin & Colin Moody 10 August 1997

The chimney near the left side of the highest section of the crag. Above the chimney, step out left past a small spike then finish right, or up the arête at Severe 4a.

10 Misunderstanding ★   **11m VS 4c**

FA Louise Gordon Canning & Michael Tweedley August 1997

Start right of the chimney. Move up then left towards the chimney then finish up the steep ramp out right.

11 Pharos ★   **8m E2 5c**

FA Gary Latter (on-sight) 26 August 2000

The widening crack just right of 10.

12 The Round House ★   **10m E1 5c**

FA Julian Lines (on-sight solo) 22 August 2002

Step off the right end of the boulder and make an awkward move to gain a grey foothold. Layback the flake to gain a grey jug and finish on jugs.

13 Covenant ★★★   **12m E4 6a**

FA Gary Latter & Colin Moody 10 August 1997

The prominent steep crack up the highest section of the crag. Sustained and well protected.

14 Nite Lites ★★   **10m E1 5b**

FA Colin Moody, Cynthia Grindley & Stephen Porteus 29 July 2000

The crack just right of 13, easing after a bouldery start.

RIGHT SIDE

15 **Access Route** *   **12m Difficult**

Climb by either of the two wide cracks up the slabby section in the centre of the crag, where it changes direction.

16 **Chickenhead** *   **10m E2 6a**

FA Gary Latter (on-sight) 16 July 2001

The groove and short steep crack right of the slab where the crag changes direction.

17 **I Hear of the Red Fox** *   **10m E1 5b/6b**

FA Julian Lines (on-sight solo) 22 August 2002

Start just left of 18. Reach, jump, scratch! for a jug, go up to undercuts and stretch right into 18 for a move to gain a jug then go diagonally left to finish through a small crack in thc headwall.

18 **Walls without Balls** *   **12m E1 5b**

FA Dave Ritchie early 90s

The obvious deep crack in the wall just left of the ledge at ⅔ height. Awkward bouldery start.

19 **Skerryvore** **   **12m E3 6b**

FA Gary Latter (on-sight) 10 August 1997

The steep crack leading to the left side of the ledge at ⅔ height. A difficult bouldery start leads to better holds in the niche at half height. Continue with interest to gain the ledge. Finish easily above.

20 **Stealth** *   **10m HVS 5b**

FA Steve Kennedy early 90s

Climbs the right crack to gain the upper ledge. Hard bouldery start.

21 **RLS** **   **10m E2 5b**

FA Gary Latter (on-sight) 10 June 2001

The rightmost of two crack systems just right of 20, starting up short easy right-facing groove.

22 **A Helping Hand** **   **10m E2 5b**

FA Gary Latter, Louise Gordon Canning & Colin Moody 10 August 1997

The deep wide central crack. Large cams useful.

23 **Catriona** *   **10m E4 6b**

FA Gary Latter 26 August 2000

The fading cracks in the wall just right of 22. Climb up to ledge from right then cracks to horizontal break and good Fs. Continue straight up past flange to a rounded finish.

24 **Oliver** *   **13m VS 4c**

FA Steve Kennedy early 90s

Start just left of the base of the descent ramp. Follow a steep flake up leftwards then direct by wide cracks.

25 **Fagan** *   **10m HVS 5a**

FA Dave Ritchie early 90s

The wall and short crack above the base of the easy descent ramp.

Stonecrop Groove ★★   **6m E3 6a**

FA Julian Lines (on-sight solo) 16 July 2001

Left-facing groove up the left side of the short wall beneath the descent ramp.

 Minor ★   **9m HVS 5a**

FA Colin Moody & A.N.Other 1990's

Left-facing flake, finishing up jam crack.

28 **The Vagabond** ★   **10m HVS 5a**

FA Gary Latter (on-sight solo) 17 July 2001

Right-facing groove, stepping up left onto ledge to finish up jam crack.

29 **The Merry Men** ★   **8m HVS 5a**

FA Gary Latter (on-sight solo) 26 August 2000

Towards the right end of the crag is a prominent roofed recess. Climb the crack up the right wall.

30 **The Dynamiter** ★   **12m HVS 5a**

FA Gary Latter (on-sight solo) 17 July 2001

There is a short blunt arête at the far right end of the crag. Climb the cracks immediately to its right, scrambling to finish.

31 **Right Slab** ★   **35m Difficult/Very Difficult**

FA Colin Moody (on-sight solo) late 90s

At the far right end of the crag is a narrow easy-angled slab. Climb it, stepping out left to avoid a thin section, or climb it direct.

KAREN'S SLAB   NM 297 197 30min

Isolated clean slab 300m NE of the beach.

1 **Sophie** ★   **12m E2 5b**

FA Julian Lines & Paul Thorburn (on-sight solo) June 2004

The slab. Start up crack, step right and up to another crack.

2 **Holly**   **12m E3 6a**

FA Julian Lines & Paul Thorburn (on-sight solo) June 2004

Thin slab on left with hard start.

Walls without Balls, Upper Tier.
Jules Lines climbing.

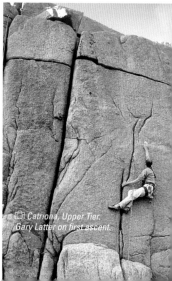

Catriona, Upper Tier.
Gary Latter on first ascent.

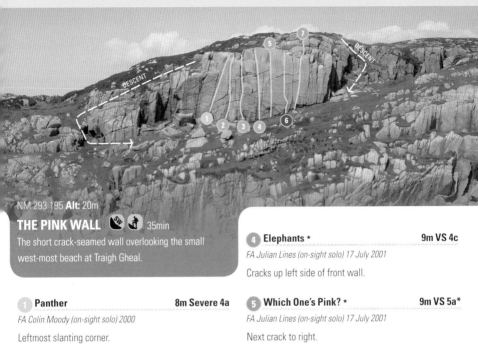

NM 293 195 **Alt:** 20m

THE PINK WALL 🖐 🧗 35min

The short crack-seamed wall overlooking the small west-most beach at Traigh Gheal.

① Panther   8m Severe 4a

FA Colin Moody (on-sight solo) 2000

Leftmost slanting corner.

② Pink One *   9m HVS 5a

FA Julian Lines (on-sight solo) 17 July 2001

Twin cracks left of corner.

③ Floyd *   9m HS 4b

FA Gary Latter (on-sight solo) 26 August 2000

Corner.

④ Elephants *   9m VS 4c

FA Julian Lines (on-sight solo) 17 July 2001

Cracks up left side of front wall.

⑤ Which One's Pink? *   9m VS 5a*

FA Julian Lines (on-sight solo) 17 July 2001

Next crack to right.

⑥ Pinky *   10m E1 5b

FA Gary Latter (on-sight solo) 17 July 2001

Central crack.

⑦ Perky *   10m VS 4c

FA Gary Latter (on-sight solo) 17 July 2001

Crack up right side of wall.

📷 Pinky. Gary Latter on first ascent.
Photo Jules Lines.

NM 293 193

PARADISE WALL 40min

A fantastic deep-water soloing venue, on the west side of the bay, about 100m south of the small westerly beach.

Approaches: Routes 1 and 2 are approachable at all states of the tide, 3 at mid-low tide and the start of 4 is only reachable at low tide. For routes 1–3 descend a short chimney (Severe) on the east face, about 6m south of the wall then left along ledge to gain a flake line which allows a fine descending traverse down rightwards (5b) to the base of the routes. Route 4 is gained by scrambling down the easy ridge just north of the chasm forming the wall.

DESCENT

1 The Brine Shrine ★★★ 12m XS 5c S0

FA Julian Lines (on-sight solo) 16 July 2001

The offset slanting off-width at the left side. A jammed chokestone low down is helpful, as are holds on the walls on either side. From a rest in the wide horizontal near the top, finish either directly up the wall, or hand traverse out left. High in the grade.

2 Please Rub Salt into my Wounds! ★★
10m XS 5c S0

FA Andy Spink (on-sight solo) 1996

The flaky central crack, with the crux passing a small spike low down. Finish on a good jug and excellent jams. Low in the grade.

3 Dreamline ★★★ 12m XS 6b S1

FA Gary Latter (on-sight solo) 17 July 2001

The stunning hanging finger-crack (crux), widening to hands in its upper reaches. Finish by stepping into a recess out right.

4 Drowning in Adrenaline ★★★ 15m XS 6a S1/2

FA Julian Lines (on-sight solo) 18 July 2001

A fantastic rising traverse line. Start by bridging across the chasm (short people need not apply!) to left-facing flake a few metres right of the large schist intrusion Move up left into the intrusion then gain the good flake out left and follow it into 3. Move up this to follow the next break out left to a reasonable rest in the next crack. Continue out left on the lower (cleaner) of two breaks, hand traversing the final wide slot of 1 to finish. Diving/jumping from the finishing ledge is obligatory.

Dreamline. Gary Latter on first ascent
Photo Jules Lines.

THE OTTER WALLS 🄴 🏊 🚶 40min

Adjoining The Paradise Wall on the seaward side.
Routes from right to left.
Descent: Climb or abseil down *The Longest Yet*.
NM 293 193

⑤ Amphibian ★★   14m VS 5a

FA Julian Lines (on-sight solo) 20 August 2002

Climb the obvious square-cut groove. Low tide needed.

① Gourmet Crab Crack ★   12m HS 4b

FA Julian Lines (on-sight solo) 20 August 2002

Cracks to the right of 2.

Note: The line to the left of 5 has not been climbed. The first half is E1 5b and very good but the second half needs a brush.

About 30m left (south) of 5 are some slabby rock shelves about 8m above the sea. This is where the next two routes start.

② The Longest Yet ★   18m Severe 4a

FA Gary Latter (on-sight solo) 18 July 2001

The prominent open chimney.

③ The Otter's Breakfast Table ★★★   15m E3 5c

FA Julian Lines (on-sight solo) 21 August 2002

Beautiful climbing on beautiful rock. Start 5m left of 2 on a large barnacle-encrusted boulder (the breakfast table). Climb a slanting groove/crack up the centre of the concave wall. Where it steepens, move rightwards on flakes to reach a large flake on the right edge. Continue up this to a jug and finish at twin cracks and a chockstone hold.

⑥ Tarka ★   15m XS 6a S0

FA Julian Lines (on-sight solo) 21 August 2002

Start at the inland end of slabby shelves and climb down on to a flaky/juggy wall. Move right for 4m to a large granite chockstone. Squirm out above into a roof, slap for a grey nubbin and climb a flake on the right to a big jug. Ramble up a slab to finish.

④ Black Eye Rib ★   12m E1 5c

FA Julian Lines (on-sight solo) 20 August 2002

Start on the right side of an obvious rib, low tide necessary. Make crux moves on undercuts and barnacle-encrusted footholds to reach better holds (or start from further right, as per 3 and traverse at 5b). Climb the arête on the right then swing left around the arête to a spike and continue on its left.

⑦ Ring of Bright Water ★★   XS 5b/c S0

FA Julian Lines (on-sight solo) 21 August 2002

From the seaward end of the shelves, go down easy slabs with grey nubbins and traverse along just above the water line (best done at high tide) – technical in places. Cross the flaky/juggy wall to the chockstone and then rightwards across a square-cut bay, along jugs to where the rock changes direction 90 degrees and becomes very steep (6a above boulders, so no longer DWS). Here, rock up onto a slab for a rest and then reverse. If done like this then there is good water underneath all the way.

NM 290 192 **Alt:** 20m (w) 45min

STRAWBERRY PIG SLAB

A pleasant 8m slab on the peninsula to the west, with some obvious red intrusions, one of which looks like a pig.

All routes Julian Lines (on-sight solo) 19 August 2002, except Jules' Pistachios 21 August 2002.

 Jo's Plums ★   **8m VS 4c**

An obvious straight crack at the left end.

2 Dari's Bananas ★   **8m HVS 5a**

Broken cracks.

3 Strawberry Pig ★   **8m E2 5b**

Start at a short crack and make a hard move right to gain the pig then direct up the slab.

4 Jules' Pistachios   **8m E5 6b/c**

Start directly below the pig and climb up to a red blotch to the right of the pig. Scratch desperately to the top.

5 Raspberry Lips ★   **10m E3 6a**

Make hard moves to gain an undercut in an overlap. Go right and finish as for 6.

6 Ripe Mangoes ★   **8m E1 5b/c**

Go up past a red blotch and continue direct.

7 Rotten Pineapple   **8m VS 4c**

An obvious dog-leg at the right end.

Asteroid Chasm

Strawberry Pig Slab

Mink Walls

Sunshine Wall

NM 290 192 **Alt:** 10m

45min

SUNSHINE WALL

About 50m down and left (facing in) from **Strawberry Pig Slab**. A small crevasse forms the right side of the crag.

All routes by Julian Lines (on-sight solo) 21 August 2002.

1 Melanoma   **10m Severe 4a**

The initial corner.

2 Hydrogen   **10m E2 5b**

Climb the arête initially on the left via a flake then on the right.

3 Daniel's Dihedral ★   **10m VS 4c**

The off-width corner.

4 Vermelho Quente ★   **10m E1 5b**

The obvious arête where the crag changes direction, using the crack on its right side.

5 Spidery Cracks ★   **10m VS 4c**

The spidery cracks!

6 Black Square ★   **10m HVS 5a**

The crack with the black square.

7 Sun Spots ★   **10m HVS 5a**

A crack with a hanging corner and red blotch.

8 Grey Matter ★   **10m E1 5b**

A crack and roof with an aerated flake.

9 Where's Your Tan, Karen? ★   **10m E1 5b**

Go up to a short corner in an overlap. Pull through and up a hand crack.

10 Topping up your Tan ★   **5/10m E1 5b**

Either start from low down by a tongue of flake, or bridge across the void to gain grey footholds. Make delicate face moves using a small ear-type flake.

11 Anticyclone ★★   **10m E1 5b**

Great climbing into the A-shaped roof and wall above.

12 Rays   **8m VS 5a**

A hand crack through a bulge.

13 Is this Scotland?? ★   **8m E2 5c**

The centre of the roof via a big hold then veer left along a diagonal.

14 Ellipse   **10m HVS 5b**

Start right of an arching flake. Move left to a bulge and climb twin cracks to the top past a red knob.

ASTEROID CHASM

NM 289 193 🪨🪨🪨🪨🪨 45min

A stunning piece of rock architecture approx. 4m wide, caused by the erosion of a basalt dyke. The SW facing wall is just off vertical; the NE facing wall just overhanging. Also a huge block (the asteroid) wedged in the top. **Nesting restrictions:** Shags nest here and the crag should be avoided May – July.

Approach: About 45 min from the car park – see map.

SOUTH WEST FACING WALL

1 Black Hole ★★   26m E1 5c

FA Colin Moody & Cynthia Grindley 21 September 2002

Towards the right end of the wall is a right slanting ramp. Make thin moves to gain the ramp, follow it to the ledge then climb the steep corner crack. The start is slow to dry and was a bit damp.

2 Space Traveller ★★   28m E1 5b

FA Julian Lines (on-sight solo) 20 August 2002

The central curving twin cracked corner.

3 Solar Collector ★★★   20m E2 5b

FA Colin Moody & Cynthia Grindley 7 August 2005

Twin cracks up the corner across from 5. There is a large boulder at the start.

NORTH EAST FACING WALL

4 Milky Way ★   22m HVS 5a

FA Colin Moody & Cynthia Grindley 14 September 2002

The west facing crack on the prow inland from the branch in the chasm. Perhaps only VS?

5 Asteroid Groove ★★   22m HVS 5a

FA Julian Lines (on-sight solo) 19 August 2002

The tapering hanging groove. Move left into the groove and climb to its top and a ledge (nest in summer). Move left and continue up the obvious line to finish by the asteroid block.

6 Mars Watchers   22m VS 4b

FA Colin Moody (solo) 27 August 2003

Gain the shallow chimney right of 5. Follow the ramp up left, go over a bulge and finish up the wide corner crack. The easy start was not climbed, but had been climbed before with a low tide.

Further right are some amazing-looking crack lines.

(7) Infinitesimal   8m VS 4c
FA Julian Lines (on-sight solo) 20 August 2002

Tapering crack in a square-cut corner near the seaward end.

NM 289 194 **Alt:** 10m  45min

MINK WALLS

About 50m north from **Asteroid Chasm** lies a red slab with an arching overlap at the right end, with walls extending leftwards for 50m.

(1) Pond Filler *   13m VS 4c
FA Colin Moody & Cynthia Grindley 3 June 2006

Obvious crack at left end, where wall increases in height. Start at left side of pool and either climb direct or from the left. Final moves avoidable by a ledge.

(2) Pond Life   8m E1 5a
FA Colin Moody & Cynthia Grindley 23 July 2006

Off width crack in left-facing corner at right side of pool.

(3) Abby *   8m VS 5a
FA Julian Lines (on-sight solo) 19 August 2002

Shallow corner just right of 2.

(4) Emma *   8m E1 5a
FA Julian Lines (on-sight solo) 19 August 2002

Just to the right are some flakes. Climb these and a shallow unprotected groove.

(5) Orbit *   7m E2 5c
FA Colin Moody & Cynthia Grindley 23 July 2006

Right of 4 is a thin crack with a wider section 2m from the top.

(6) Toad Hole   7m Severe 4a
FA Colin Moody & Cynthia Grindley 3 June 2006

Right of 5 is a black left-slanting seam. Climb a short right-facing corner to gain a ledge at the black seam then crack above slightly leftwards.

(7) Toad Crack *   7m HVS 5a
FA Colin Moody & Cynthia Grindley 3 June 2006

The fine crack just right.

(8) Just Spitting *   7m HVS 4c
FA Colin Moody & Cynthia Grindley 1 July 2006

Gain a flake left of 9 and continue up it. Protection can be placed before the top.

(9) Jammer   7m HVS 5a
FA Colin Moody & Cynthia Grindley 3 June 2006

The corner crack.

10 Caroline ★   8m VS 4c

FA Colin Moody & Cynthia Grindley 3 June 2006

Start just right of 9. Climb up to an undercut flake and
then the flake.

11 Interrupted by Canoes ★   8m E1 5b

FA Colin Moody & Cynthia Grindley 3 June 2006

Good climbing up the cracks and flakes to the right.

12 Wrecked   8m HVS 5a

FA Colin Moody & Cynthia Grindley 25 June 2006

The next line to the right, finishing up a right-facing flake.

13 Neanderthal ★   8m E1 5b

FA Colin Moody & Cynthia Grindley 1 July 2006

Climb a jam crack and continue up a thinner crack.

14 Need an Inch ★★   8m E2/3 5c

FA Colin Moody & Cynthia Grindley 1 July 2006

The hairline crack.

15 Red ★   8m VS 4c

FA Colin Moody & Cynthia Grindley 25 June 2006

The cracks at the right end of the short wall.

16 Access Route   8m Very Difficult

FA Colin Moody & Cynthia Grindley 3 June 2006

The vegetated corner is useful.

17 The Mink ★★   15m E2 5b

FA Julian Lines (on-sight solo) 3 June 2002

A fine route. Climb the right side of the slab, just right
of a hairline crack, to gain the start of the overlap/arch
on the right. Follow the overlap leftwards to finish up a
corner-groove.

18 Helga   15m VS 4c

FA Colin Moody & Cynthia Grindley 13 August 2006

The left-facing corner crack and the continuation crack
just right of 17.

Stealth, Upper Tier. Jules Lines climbing.

RED ANVIL CHASM

NM 287 195 🦅 🖐 🏔 🏃 45min

The same dyke as **Asteroid Chasm** but a further 400m NW. Probably climbable at high tide. There is also a superb west-facing bouldering wall just round the corner, above a platform.

NE FACING WALL

1 **Red Anvil** ★   **15m E3 5c**

FA Julian Lines (on-sight) & Paul Thorburn (both led) June 2004

Climb cracks to the anvil then take the easiest line out right.

SW FACING WALL

10m high wall 40m long wall sporting many steep pumpy crack lines (6 unclimbed!). The obvious groove in the centre has a loose block at the top and is also unclimbed.

2 **Stork's Crack** ★   **8m E3/4 6a**

FA Paul Thorburn & Jules Lines (on-sight) June 2004

Thin crack starting off block 4m left of the groove. Awkward to protect.

3 **Paz irmao** ★   **10m E1 5b**

FA Julian Lines & Paul Thorburn (on-sight) June 2004

Crack 2m right of the groove.

4 **Stork's Easy Crack** ★   **10m HVS 5a**

FA Paul Thorburn & Julian Lines (on-sight) June 2004

Next crack 2m right of 3.

📷 *Bouldering Wall, north west of Red Anvil Chasm*

IONA

"We are now treading that
illustrious Island, which
was once the luminary of
the Caledonian regions,
whence savage clans and
roving barbarians derived the
benefits of knowledge and
the blessing of religion"
– Dr Johnson

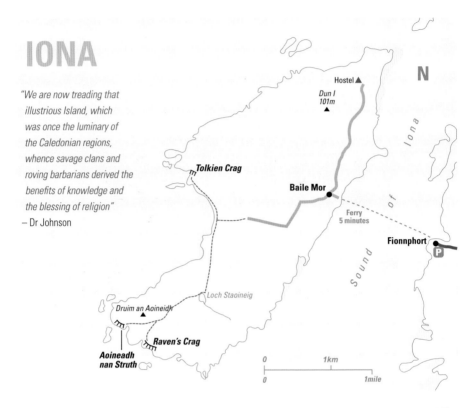

An incredibly popular (over 200,000 visitors a year) little island off the west coast of the Ross of Mull for those of a religious bent since an Irish murderer fled there in exile back in the 6th century. It is also the burial ground of 48 Scottish kings and the remains of an Iron Age fort are still evident. It is worth mentioning that the majority of visitors rarely stray from the paths and despite the commotion it is still possible to find solitude. The island has only been regarded as a climbing venue since the 90s.

Access: A regular passenger ferry (a 5 minute crossing) from Fionnphort at the west end of the A849 on the Ross of Mull to the jetty at St Ronan's Bay in the centre of the east side of the island. In summer (end March – early October) the first ferry crossing is at 08.45 with the last return 18.30 (10.00 and 17.15 on Sundays).

Amenities: From the jetty, turn right for spiritual replenishment. Turn left for Martyr's Bay Restaurant for tea, coffee and meals and the only pint on the island. The general store by the pier also does bike hire (£5 per day) which may make a day trip a more reasonable option.

Accommodation: There are no official campsites but the heathery knolls at Loch Staoineig are good for wild camping. There are also many isolated beaches around the south west coast (carry drinking water with you). Officially, free camping is only permitted at the north end of the island – ask permission at the croft or call Mrs McFadyen on ☎ 01681 700341. Iona Hostel at north end of island, 1.3 miles/2km north of pier www.ionahostel.co.uk; info@ionahostel.co.uk; ☎ 01681 700781; £17.50/night). Numerous B&B establishments and a couple of hotels.

Note: Mountain bikes would make a day trip much more productive/ feasible and could be taken within few hundred metres of Tolkien Crag and about 30 minutes from all the southern crags.

PORT BHAN – TOLKIEN CRAG

NM 264 244 30min

A short non-tidal crag at the back of the beach of particular interest to wee hairy-toed climbers. The crag is nothing special but in an idyllic setting right off the beach.

Approach: As for the other crags as far as the golf course then follow the track westwards towards the shore. Turn right and follow the fence north-west, go over a style and cross a field to a second sandy beach and the crag.

Descent: Down either end or scramble down the open gully between *Hairy Toes* and *The Shire*.

---

1 Hairy Toes ★   **25m Severe 4a**

FA Colin Moody (on-sight solo) 1990s

Climb up over a block then the centre of the red slab above.

---

2 The Shire ★   **15m Very Difficult**

FA Danny Brooks, John Ferrie & Ian Taylor 15 February 1993

The easy angled blunt arête at the right side.

---

3 Cracks of Mordor ★   **15m VS 4c**

FA Danny Brooks, John Ferrie & Ian Taylor 15 February 1993

Start left of *The Shire*. Climb straight up to twin cracks then climb them.

The wall just left is also VS, the grey corner to the right 4 *Gollum* HVS 4c

---

5 Smaug ★★   **25m HVS 5a**

FA Danny Brooks 15 February 1993

Start just left of 4. Climb the wall to a small overhang then move right onto the arête. Climb up and left above the overhang to a small ledge, continuing to a larger ledge above. Move up right to a horizontal break and a large ledge then over a bulge to finish. The overhang can also be breached direct by a long reach.

---

6 My Precioussss ★   **25m HVS 5a**

FA James Marshall, Gail Hutter & Danny Brooks October 1991

Climb a break up and right to a small roof then move round the side of this and finish up the groove.

---

7 Bilbo and Friends ★   **25m Severe 4a**

FA Danny Brooks, Gail Hutter & James Marshall October 1991

Follow the ramp-line before the overhanging wall up right to a ledge. Move left and finish up the groove.

---

8 Yan's Route ★   **25m HVS 5a**

FA Ian Taylor, John Ferrie & Danny Brooks 15 February 1993

Start up 7. At 4m go left across the steep wall to a jug and sloping crack. Finish directly.

9 *Snip Snap* E4 6a ascends the short overhanging wall at the left side of the crag.

RAVEN'S CRAG LAYOUT

APPROACH

Menhir

Main Wall

Main Wall Continuation

The Pulpit

The Altar

The Menhir

NM 255 220 **Alt:** 50m 1hr

MAOL NA CICHE
RAVEN'S CRAG

A long wall of generally gently overhanging gneiss on the coast at the south-west end of the island. The crag is set back about 50-100m from the sea. A few of the routes climb veins of darker (and softer) amphibolite.

Approach: Turn left at the ferry slip on the road heading south for 0.7km before turning right and following the road that runs west towards the golf course. At the road end follow the fence south (left) which meets a rough road heading up the hill to Loch Staoineig. Continue south over the track for a few hundred metres. The hill Druim an Aoneidh soon comes into view to the right. Head for the summit cairn then bear left (due south) to descend a shallow open U-shaped gully leading down to the left (north) end of the crag (overlooking the stony beach of Port nan Struth).

Nesting restrictions: A pair of ravens occasionally nests at the right end of the crag (route 21). If present (not there 2005) avoid the cliff from March-June.

Layout: The wall runs in a straight line with three rocks standing proud of the main face; The Menhir stands guard over the left end; roughly in the centre is The Pulpit, with the gap behind filled with large boulders. Right of The Pulpit is the impressive overhanging prow of The Altar. At the right end of the cliff the rock turns to face east and diminishes in height.

THE MENHIR

(1) Welly Route　　　　　　　**10m Difficult**

FRA Colin Moody (in his wellies!) 12 December 1992

The easiest way up the block. Either descend by the same line or attach a rope to the thread at the base and abseil down the west side.

MAIN WALL

The right-facing corner and short wall right of The Menhir is 2 *Eric the Red* ★E2 5b.

(3) Rod, Todd, This is God ★★　　　　**20m E4 6a**

FA Mark Garthwaite & Colin Lambton 24 September 1994

The thin crack in the red wall just right of the corner of 2, protected by RPs. Finish by a corner crack.

The Altar

4 Allah Be Praised *   **25m E3 5c**

FA Colin Moody, Michael Tweedley & Louise Gordon Canning 24 August 1997

Climbs the recess left of 5. Follow the left-slanting crack which gets better with height, step right when it ends. Go over a bulge then finish up the easy groove.

5 Yabbadabbadoo **   **20m E5 6a**

FA Mark Garthwaite & Dave Greig 28 August 1993

The left crack in the dark band of rock. A bold start leads to a small sloping ledge and gear. Move up right to the pocket on 6 (F #2.5). Move back left and climb the crack through roofs.

6 Mr Muscle **   **20m E5 6b**

FA Mark Garthwaite & Davie Greig 30 August 1993

The right crack in the dark rock band. Climb straight up to a pocket (F #2.5). Difficult moves lead to the roof (small friend in undercut slot). Move right to a jug on the lip and finish directly up the wall.

7 God is Dead **   **20m E4 6a**

FA Gary Latter & Colin Moody 8 August 1997

The crack up the black seam in the arête. Start on the arête. Up to the groove and up this steeply to good holds at its top. Continue more easily up the arête, moving left to finish past a hollow-sounding flake.

8 Jehad *   **20m E2 5b**

FA Colin Moody & Stella Adams 19 June 1993

A fine line, though spoilt by some dubious black rock. The central corner system, trending slightly right. A nest was built by a big black bird on the route in 1994 but the grade remains the same.

9 Crusade * 30m E2 5b

FA Colin Moody & Allan Petrie 26 September 1993

Right of the central corner of 8 is a small pinnacle half way up the cliff. This route climbs the crack on the left side of the pinnacle. Start below the crack. Climb a green slab that stands proud of the cliff base then continue up the crack, stepping left at the top of the pinnacle.

10 Solar Temple * 25m E2 5b

FA Gary Latter & Colin Moody 8 August 1997

The shallow right-facing groove at the right side of the pinnacle. Climb a lichenous slab then over a bulge and up a groove to the pinnacle. Step right and up the wall on good incut holds.

11 Waco * 20m E2 5b

FA Dave Greig, Colin Moody & Mark Garthwaite 28 August 1993

Start just left of the shallow cave. Climb the short right-facing corner and continue directly above.

12 Cul Dreimne * 20m E2 5b

FA Dave Greig, Colin Moody & Mark Garthwaite 28 August 1993

Pleasant climbing but slow to dry. Start to the right of the shallow cave. Step left off the boulder and climb steeply to easier ground. Continue to a steepening then climb the slanting crack on the left to finish up the short wall.

THE PULPIT (W)

Many of the routes tend to be a bit unbalanced with steep starts and easier finishes.

13 Passage ** 20m VS 4b

FA Colin Moody & Neil Horn 12 June 1993

Pleasant climbing up the prominent right-slanting ramp. Climb the crack and follow the ramp right until it runs out at a further crack which leads to the top.

14 Parable * 20m E1 5b

FA Colin Moody & Neil Horn 12 June 1993

A good route cutting through the ramp. Start 1m left of the left-slanting crack. Step up and right and follow the

crack to the ramp. Continue in the same line over the bulge at a notch and direct to finish.

15 Fire and Brimstone * 18m E3 5c

FA Colin Moody & Mark Shaw 20 August 1994

The red wall. A fine start but the upper half is a bit disappointing. Right of the crack of 14 is a short black crack at head height. Climb past the crack to reach the small ramp and follow this to its end. Pull out left and carry on up, trying to avoid 16.

16 Scripture * 18m E1 5b

FA Colin Moody & Stella Adams 19 June 1993

Start up a bulging crack and follow it to the arête to a finish shared with 13.

17 Apocrypha * 18m E1 5b

FA Colin Moody & Neil Horn 12 June 1993

Just right of the previous route are two seams of dark rock. Follow the right seam then the corner above on large flakes.

THE ALTAR 🌤️

18 The Incredible Dr Sex *** 12m E6 6b

FA Mark Garthwaite 4 September 1993

The stunning arête of the pinnacle. Start 1m left of the arête. Move up right to a jug on the arête and gear. Move up and slightly right to small flat holds then make some hard moves to gain and use an undercut on the right. Gain the next break and gear. More hard climbing leads direct to the top.

19 Blood Eagle ** 12m E5 6a

FA Rick Waterton September 1997

Start just left of 20. Climb up leftwards past a R #1 placement on the right, finishing at an obvious slot.

20 Smoke Yourself Thin * 11m E4 6a

FA Mark Garthwaite & Colin Moody 24 September 1994

Start near the right side of the pinnacle. Move up to then climb the left-leaning shallow groove. Continue up, stepping right at the top.

MAIN WALL (CONTINUATION)

21 The Bantry Boat ★   **20m E3 5c**

FA Colin Moody & Tom Charles-Edwards 22 July 1995

Below the nest are two corners. Climb the shallow left
corner and move right, brushing past the nest. A steep
wall then easier climbing leads to the top.

22 Smoking the Toad ★★★   **20m E5 6b**

FA Mark Garthwaite & Colin Lambton 24 September 1994

Start on the shelf at the prominent crack in the centre
of the red wall, right of the nest. Make a series of long
reaches on good holds to a PR. Hard moves above lead
to a good shake-out and gear under the roof. Pull through
the roof and finish direct. (The peg was placed in 1993
and should probably be replaced with a stainless one –
maybe E6 in current state?).

23 Prodigy ★★★   **25m E4 6a**

FA Dave Greig & Mark Garthwaite 30 August 1993

Climbs the right side of the red wall. Climb the grey crack,
step left and climb a ramp to a small overhang. Move
up right to main overhang and traverse left under the
overhang to its lip, then up and over.

EAST FACE

24 Mental Torment ★★   **20m E1 5b**

*FA Colin Moody, James Marshall, Danny Brooks
& Andrew Pedley 21 August 1993*

The stepped corner at the left side of the face. Worthwhile.

*God is Dead.
Gary Latter on first ascent.
Photo Karen Martin.*

AOINEADH NAN STRUTH

This is the most south-westerly point on the island. There are three crags, described from south to north all within a short 200m stretch of the coast.

Appr: As for **Raven's Crag** to the summit cairn of Druim an Aoineidh then head due west, dropping down a short easy gully and across flat ground above the stony beach.

NM 253 223 🇸 🇸 🚣 👣 1¼hr
IRELAND WALL

The highest and most impressive of the crags on the headland directly opposite the north end of the long rocky island just offshore. Only the last two routes are tidal, though some of the others may be affected by rough seas.

Descent: Walk down an easy shelf descending northwards underneath the west face of the crag.

> 1 *The Shelf* is Difficult; leftward line, crack to finish up an easy corner is 2 *Sash Verte* VS 4c; 3 *Vatican City* Severe 4a follows crack then flake on right to corner crack.

4 Chinatown * 25m E3 5b
FA Steve Scott & John Adams 19 June 1993

Follow the crack up the black seam 10m right of the corner. Some loose rock.

5 The Good Book ** 30m E1 5b
FA Colin Moody & Billy Hood 2 May 1993

The fine looking wide corner crack.

6 Heretic *** 30m E3 5c
FA John Adams & Steve Scott 20 June 1993

Excellent climbing on immaculate sea-washed rock, tackling the prominent crack up the centre of the south-facing wall at the base of the shelf. Follow an easy flake line leading rightwards to the crack. Cross the roof on good holds and move steadily up the wall above, finishing more easily up the upper crack. Belay well back.

NM 253 224
GULLY WALL 🇸 🇼 👣 1¼hr

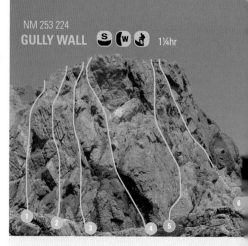

At its south end a deep narrow chasm cuts back into the hillside, containing a huge chokestone near its top.

Approach: From near the base of the shelf at **Labrador Wall** traverse south with some easy scrambling to gain a wide ledge running along the base of the crag.

1 The Black Streak * 12m Very Difficult
FA unknown early 90's

The obvious line at the left side of the crag.

2 A Vicious Streak * 15m Severe 4a
FA unknown early 90's

Follow the crack a few metres left of 3 then right to finish up a shallow corner.

3 The Quartz Crack * 15m Severe 4a
FA unknown early 90's

Look for a prominent shallow quartz groove. Climb this and direct up the wall above.

4 Drunken Biker's Route * 15m Very Difficult
FA Colin Moody, Billy Hood & John Ferrie 1993

Start 2m left of the arête, where the crag changes direction. Follow a shallow left-slanting groove to underneath the overhanging headwall. Step out left past a spike and finish easily.

5 The Man of Riou ★ 15m VS 4c

FA Colin Moody & Billy Hood 1 May 1993

Start a short way right of the arête. Move up then step left onto a steep ramp then continue directly above.

6 L'Homme d'Iona ★ 20m HVS 5a

FA Colin Moody & Billy Hood 1 May 1993

Climb up to the shallow overhang corner, up this swinging out left and finishing direct.

7 Il Uomo Di Roma ★ 20m E2 5b

FA Colin Moody & Louise Gordon-Canning 12 July 1997

Start round right of 6. Climb an easy left-slanting ramp to a ledge and huge flake. Climb up right through an overhang right of the flake to a jug. Pull left into a crack then climb straight up to finish over a bulge.

8 Pontificating ★ 20m E3 5c

FA Colin Moody & Louise Gordon-Canning 20 September 1997

Climb the easy left slanting ramp, as for 7. Step right above an overhang and traverse right below the overlap to follow the fault line to the top.

9 Pope on a Rope ★★ 20m E2 5b

FA Colin Moody & Louise Gordon-Canning 12 July 1997

Start up another easy left-slanting ramp. Move right to gain and follow the line of corners.

10 Up Popes Another ★★ 20m E1 5b

FA Danny Brooks, Colin Moody & Louise Gordon-Canning 22 September 1996

Scramble into the gully until under the huge chokestone. Follow the crack which slants out left below it.

11 Blood Donor ★ 20m VS 4b

FA Colin Moody, Louise Gordon-Canning & Danny Brooks 22 September 1996

Start at a puddle in the gully gained by scrambling into the labyrinthine depths beyond 10. Follow a direct line.

12 Haemoglobin ★ 25m VS 4c

FA Danny Brooks, Colin Moody & Louise Gordon-Canning 22 September 1996

Start at the puddle. Move farther into the gully, easily past the chokestone then direct up the wall.

Passage, Raven's Crag. Colin Moody climbing. Photo Cynthia Grindley.

NM 253 223 1¼hr

LABRADOR WALL

Approach: Down an easy-angled wide ramp running under the base of the crag.

Descent: Down an easy gully down the right side of the **Orange Wall** or down the right side of the crag. The last four routes are on the small **Orange Wall** at the base of the shelf.

① Force 5 *   10m E1 5a
FA Barney Vaucher & Colin Moody 1993

Start in the centre of the scooped wall up right of 2. Climb the depression to a bulge, finishing up the steep flake out left.

The right facing corner crack is 2 *Quack* HVS 5a.

③ Infidels *   12m E4 6a
FA Gary Latter 9 August 1997

Well protected climbing up the left side of the orange arête left of the square cut corner of 2. Climb the front face onto a ledge then a line just left of the arête to a good diagonal crack. Step right onto the arête, finishing on a good jug.

The recessed wall is 4 *Another Day* HVS 4c

⑤ Checking Out *   12m VS 4b
FA Colin Moody (solo) May 1993

Start just right of the arête. Climb steeply up then step left and climb the rib.

⑥ Looking Around *   12m Severe 4a
FA Colin Moody (solo) May 1993

Start just right of the descent gully, right of an arête. Pull onto a shelf right of the corner then up and left to finish up the corner.

ORANGE WALL

⑦ Fault Thing *   8m Severe 4a
FA Colin Moody (solo) early 1993

The left-slanting fault bounding the right edge of the wall just left of the easy descent gully.

⑧ Crack Thing *   10m E1 5b
FA Colin Moody, Billy Hood & John Ferrie 1993

The short crack on the right side of the wall, moving into 7 near the top.

Crack Thing. Gary Latter climbing
Photo Karen Martin.

9 **Magnetic Wall** ★   12m E1 5b

FA Colin Moody & Billy Hood May 1993

Start in the centre of the wall. Climb over a bulge on
improving holds, heading leftwards to finish up the
prominent flake crack.

10 *Chargold* VS 4c tackles the innocuous looking crack.

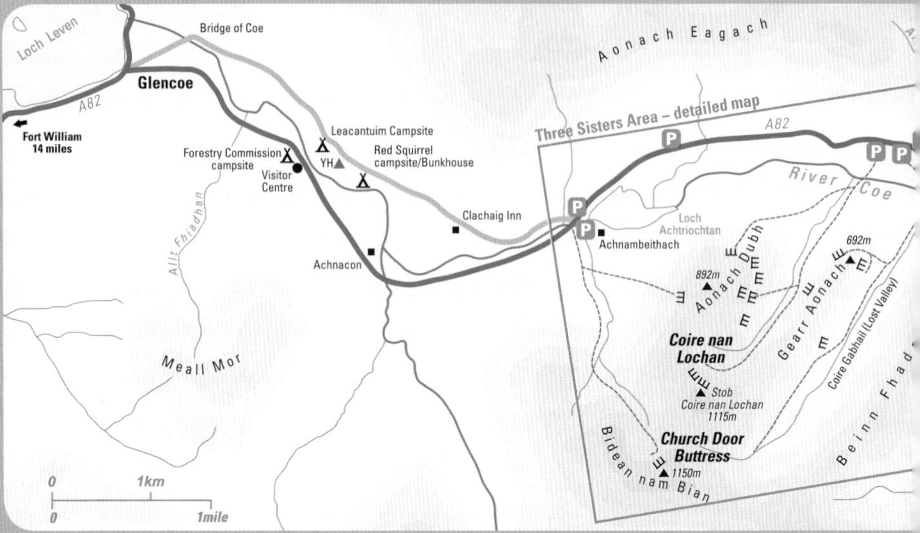

Loch Leven

Bridge of Coe

Glencoe

A82

Fort William
14 miles

Forestry Commission
campsite

Visitor
Centre

Leacantuim Campsite

YH

Red Squirrel
campsite/Bunkhouse

Clachaig Inn

Achnacon

Allt Fhiadhan

Meall Mor

Aonach Eagach

Three Sisters Area – detailed map

A82

River Coe

Loch
Achtriochtan

Achnambeithach

Aonach Dubh

892m

Coire nan
Lochan

Stob
Coire nan Lochan
1115m

Church Door
Buttress

1150m

Bidean nam Bian

Gearr Aonach

692m

Coire Gabhail (Lost Valley)

Beinn Fhada

0   1km

0   1mile

Buachaille Etive Mor.

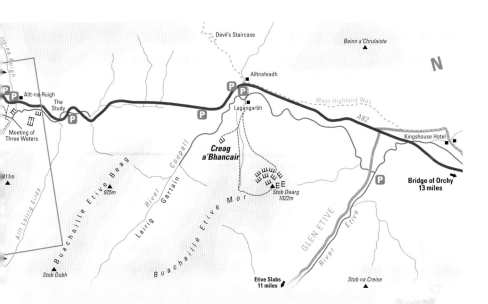

GLEN COE & GLEN ETIVE

COE & ETIVE

Glen Coe is probably the most famous of all highland glens, and certainly the most notorious, due to the tourist industry built around the infamous massacre back in 1692. Here are to be found some of the most accessible mountain routes around, rather like an altogether grander version of the Llanberis Pass. There are a superb range of climbs, from short roadside crags through to some of the most alpine routes in the country and everything in between, including the only mountain sport climbs in the UK. All the worthwhile rock climbing lies on the south side of glen.

The Glen runs west from the headwaters of the River Coe at the tiny Lochan na Fola, underneath Buachaille Etive Beag for 6 miles/10km to open out at the long sea loch of Loch Leven. The name (from Gleann Comhann) means narrow glen, popularly though wrongly supposed to mean the glen of weeping, due to the massacre. Although the distinctive conical Buachaille Etive Mor technically lies at the head of Glen Etive, by long custom Glen Coe stretches four miles further east to the head of Glen Etive. Glen Etive (Horrid Stormy Glen) is a fine picturesque glen with a more open pastoral nature than neighbouring Glen Coe. The River Etive has some splendid pools and a number of fine (though increasingly popular) roadside camping spots, while the backdrop of shapely mountains, from Buachaille Etive Mor and Beag at the head of the glen, Ben Starav across the loch and the distant Ben Cruachan afford a serene ambience lacking on most of the Glen Coe cliffs.

"Glencoe itself is perfectly terrible. The pass is an awful place. It is shut in on each side by enormous rocks from which great torrents come rushing down. In amongst these rocks on one side of the pass … there are scores of glens, high up, which form such haunts as you might imagine yourself wandering in the very height and madness of a fever …"
– Charles Dickens, 1841

Accommodation: Wild camping is still tolerated north of the river at the rear of the Kings House Hotel (though rather ungraciously, they actively discourage the use of the toilet facilities within) and between the road and the river in the upper reaches of Glen Etive, though is generally discouraged elsewhere in Glen Coe. About a third of the way down the back road from Clachaig Inn – Glencoe village lie the **Youth Hostel** (☎ 01855 811219) and Leacantuim Farm Bunkhouse and Red Squirrel campsite (☎ 01855 811256; www.redsquirrelcampsite.com). The National Trust campsite (☎ 01855 811397) is located in the forest on the west side of the A82, 1.1miles/1.8km SE of Glencoe village. There are also caravan and campsites nearby at Invercoe (☎ 01855 811210; www.invercoe.co.uk), 0.3 miles/0.5km from Glencoe village; at Caolasnacon (☎ 01855 831279; www.scottishcampingguide.com), 3.5 miles/5km down the B863 road to Kinlochleven; All Seasons Cabins & Campsite, Kinlochleven (☎ 01855 831539; www.macdonaldhotel.co.uk); Corran Caravans, Onich (☎ 01855 821208). Also By the Way Hostel & Campsite, Tyndrum (☎ 01838 400333; www.tyndrumbytheway.com)

Bunkhouses: Blackwater Hostel and Campsite (☎ 01855 831253; www.blackwater-hostel.co.uk) and West Highland Lodge (☎ 01855 831471), both Kinlochleven; Inchree, Onich (☎ 01855 821287; www.inchreecentre.co.uk); Corran Bunkhouse, by Corran ferry (☎ 01855 821235; www.corranbunkhouse.co.uk). Also Strathfillan Wigwams, Tyndrum (☎ 01838 400251; www.sac.ac.uk/wigwams); West Highland Way Sleeper, Bridge of Orchy Station (☎ 01838 400548; www.westhighlandwaysleeper.co.uk).

Mountaineering Club huts at Lagangarbh (SMC; NN 222 560); Blackrock Cottage, White Corries (Ladies Scottish CC; NN 267 531); Inbhir-fhaolain, Glen Etive (Grampian Club; NN 158 507); Smiddy, Glen Etive (Forventure; NN 116 457); Waters Cottage, Kinlochleven (FRCC; NN 183 617); Alex Macintyre Hut, Onich (MCofS/BMC; NN 046 612): Manse Barn, Onich (Lomond MC: NN 033 613).

Amenities: The Clachaig Inn (☎ 01855 811679 or 811252; www.clachaig.com) and the Kings House Hotel (☎ 01855 811259; www.kingy.com), located at either end of the Glen, are the two most popular places for an après climb pint for most climbers. Both also offer bar meals though the Kings House stop serving at 8.30pm! All the other hotels en route to Fort William also serve bar meals. For provisions, there is a late opening Spar supermarket in Ballachulish village, 1 mile/1.6km west of Glencoe village. There are also a couple of small grocery shops and a post office in Glencoe village together with a couple of cafés – try Crafts & Things at Tighphuirst. Petrol Station in Glencoe village. **Outdoor shops:** 3G Mountain Sports (☎ 01855 811402; www.icefactor.co.uk) is conveniently situated at Tighphuirst, on the south side of the A82 just west of Glencoe village. For the occasional wet weather retreat (not that it rains much in Glen Coe!), the **Ice Factor** is an indoor climbing complex – Leven Road, Kinlochleven (☎ 01855 831100; www.icefactor.co.uk) containing leading and bouldering walls, ice wall, café and gym. There is also a brewery next door!

ETIVE SLABS HISTORY

The slabs were first climbed on in 1954 by a Cambridge University team comprising Eric Langmuir, Mike O'Hara and J. Mallinson. Their ascent of *Spartan Slab* opened the way to a whole new realm of routes on the exposed granite sweep. It was three years before any more routes appeared, when Creagh Dhu members John Cunningham, Mick Noon and Bill Smith unleashed *Agony* – the first use of aid climbing on a large scale in Scotland. Cunningham and Noon returned the following day to climb the larger corner system just to the left to give the classic *Hammer*. Later that summer Noon returned with Eric Taylor to force the first route to breach the centre of the slabs with the bold *Swastika*. Almost all the additions originally employed the odd aid point or tension traverse, all of which have been whittled away over the years, often helped by the widening of cracks due to repeated pegging.

The impressive pairing of Cunningham and Robin Smith teamed up in 1959 for *The Long Wait*, a line previously attempted by Cunningham and Noon and also by Don Whillans. The following year Jimmy Marshall and his fine eye for a line produced *The Pause*, finding a way up the centre of the slabs at a surprisingly reasonable grade along with *Jaywalk*. In the sixties John McLean and Bill Smith produced the excellent *The Long Reach* and Dougal Haston the hard and serious *The Big Ride*. Later,

John Jackson and Rab Carrington climbed *The Pinch* to produce the hardest route on the slabs. The crux pitch was the scene of some epic falls into the *Agony* corner prior to a successful repeat. A few years later Carrington and McLean slotted in *Tous les Doux*. John Newsome and party climbed one of the boldest pitches on the slabs yet with *The Band of Hope*. Aberdonians Dougie Dinwoodie and Greg Strange added *Groundhog*. Ian Nicolson repeated many of the routes around this time in addition to making audacious solo ascents of *The Pause* and *The Long Reach* in a day.

By the late seventies the emphasis was on aid eliminations. Willie Todd and Murray Hamilton freed the top pitch of *Swastika*, Hamilton freed *Groundhog*, and Brian Duff and Todd dispensed with the last aid on the slabs with their free ascent of *Agony*. Two weeks later Hamilton, Brian Duff and Derek Jamieson added *Pinch Direct*. Throughout the eighties Rab Anderson filled a number of gaps including the excellent *Direct Finish* to *The Pinch*, later adding a trilogy of good shorter routes on the right flank in 1991. More recently, in 1998 Dave Cuthbertson added the hardest route with *Angel*, the two hardest pitches crossing the overlap and the final steep headwall. In contrast to the thorough inspection, Julian Lines pushed the limits of thin friction climbing on the slabs in 2000 with the very bold *Gecko*, impressively climbed on-sight.

📷 *The Pause, Etive Slabs. Rob Kerr climbing.*

GLEN COE HISTORY

The first recorded 'climb' was the ascent of *Ossian's Ladder* in 1868 by local shepherd Neil Marquiss. Following an early repeat in the 1890s William Brown commented: *"Hands, knees, toes and eyelids had to be awkwardly spread over a mixture of mud and vegetable, which affords a support as treacherous as it is dirty, and which no respectable mountaineer, having respect for his Norfolk, will care to depend on."* Today the route is no better, with little to recommend it. The first true mountaineer to visit Glen Coe was Norman Collie in the 1890s, scrambling up the tottering scree-filled depths of Great Gully on the Buachaille and later in early April 1894 climbed an unknown *"rather difficult climb up the face of Aonach Dubh just to the left of Ossian's Cave."* Collie, accompanied by Joseph Collier and Godfrey Solly also recorded a number of other easy routes that same year. The first route of any merit was pioneered in July 1895 when William Tough, Rose Brown and William Brown climbed North Buttress on Buachaille Etive Mor. Climbed in torrential rain, the route can justly be regarded as the first proper rock climbing on continuous clean rock of any length in Glen Coe. The following year William Naismith and William Douglas made the first

January Jigsaw, Rannoch Wall, Buachaille Etive Mor. Giles Ruck climbing.

ascent of Crowberry Ridge, by what has since come to be known as Naismith's Route. The ever popular *Curved Ridge* was climbed solo by G Bennett Gibbs the following year, finding the climb *"not difficult"*. How right he was, as the route is rated Moderate. Harold Raeburn, John Bell and Graham Napier opened up Church Door Buttress on Bidean Nam Bian with their ascent of *Flake Route* in 1898. A strong southern team comprising Lakeland cragsmen George and Ashley Abraham along with Jim Puttrell and Ernest Baker made the audacious ascent of *Crowberry Ridge Direct* in May 1900. Graded at Severe this was a significant step forward in standards. Raeburn with Mr and Mrs Inglis Clark made the second ascent three years later. That same year WC Newbigging and party ascended *D Gully Buttress*.

With the interruption of the Great War it was 1920 before the next routes were recorded. In April that year R.F. Stobart and Mr and Mrs Noel Odell made the first ascent of *The Chasm*, at VS 4c another significant breakthrough of a compelling line that had defeated previous attempts by many of the leading climbers around the turn of the century, including Bell, Raeburn and William Ling. The *Direct Finish* was forced in 1931 by Iain Jack and Gordon Robinson. In the autumn of 1920 another strong southern team comprising Morley Wood, John Wilding and Fred Piggott entered into the very bowels of Bidean's Church Door Buttress, producing the classic and unique *Crypt Route*. The next route of any worth was *North Face Route* on the Buachaille from Jim Bell and Sandy Harrison in 1929. Climbing either together or with other partners, most notably Colin Allan, this pair accounted for more than twenty first ascents throughout the early thirties. One of the best of these was *Pinnacle Face* on Aonach Dubh's West Face from Bell and Allan. One development that was to dramatically alter the pace of development was the opening of the new road in 1931. Prior to this it was easier to reach Ben Nevis (by rail). The first route on the impressive pink sweep of Rannoch Wall fell to George Williams, G.F. Todd, Graham MacPhee and Iain Jack in 1934. *Route 1* (originally called simply Rannoch Wall) had actually been climbed the previous year but left unrecorded as Williams had required a top rope to safeguard the final difficult exit. Two years later Hamish Hamilton, Alex Anderson and Alex Small beat Bill MacKenzie's rival party by a few minutes to the base of *Agag's Groove*, thus adding what today is possibly one of the most trodden routes in the country. MacKenzie, Bill Murray and party made the second ascent immediately afterwards. Standards continued to be pushed forward with the ascent of what remains one of the hardest gully climbs in the country with Jock Nimlin and party's ascent of the impressive cleft of *Raven's Gully*. The following year (1938) a strong team comprising Bill Murray, Archie MacAlpine, Kenneth Dunn and W.G. Marskell took advantage of a dry spell to snatch *Clachaig Gully*. This was another glaringly obvious gully that had attracted (and repelled) the attentions of such luminaries as George Abraham and Norman Collie around the turn of the century.

By the end of the decade Rannoch Wall became the focus of attention. Iain Ogilvy and Miss Esme Speakman produced two bold ventures for the day when they pioneered the classic *Red Slab* and *Satan's Slit*, climbed on the same day in 1939. The same pair returned a few months later in January 1940 to complete *January Jigsaw,* taking a direct line cutting through the groove of *Agag's Grove*. The Second World War slowed things down considerably, though less so than the First, as climbing still occurred. During the war R.G. Donaldson and G.R.B. McCarter added *Bottleneck Chimney* and its logical continuation *Hangman's Crack* to the East Face of North Buttress.

The years following the war saw the emergence of one of the most forceful groups of Scottish climbers, the Creagh Dhu Mountaineering Club. Operating out of their hut Jacksonville at the base of the Buachaille they dominated activity on that mountain for over a decade. First on the scene were John Cunningham and Pat McGonigle with *Crow's Nest Crack*. McGonigle also added *Shattered*

Crack, both on the East Face of North Buttress. A few months later Cunningham and Bill Smith hinted at things to come on the Rannoch Wall with *Autumn Slab*, which later became the first pitch of *Whortleberry Wall*. At HVS this was the first route to match the standard of *Raven's Gully* almost ten years previously. Round the corner, Kenny Copland and Bill Smith led *Fracture Route* after another party had top roped the line.

In May 1947 Bill Murray and Donald McIntyre developed the previously overlooked East Face of Aonach Dubh, adding four new routes on the same day including such classics as the *Bow-string*, *Archer Ridge* and *Quiver Rib*. The following month John Cunningham made his historic ascent of *Gallows Route*, at E2 5c the first extreme in the mountains in Scotland, fully matching the top standards down south. The following year Cunningham, Bill Smith and Tommy Paul repeated *Raven's Gully*, adding the fierce and seldom climbed *Direct Finish* at E1 5a. The following month Cunningham and Smith shifted their attention to the fierce looking wall

> The following month (June 1947) John Cunningham made his historic ascent of Gallows Route, at E2 5c the first extreme in the mountains in Scotland, fully matching the top standards down south.

further left. Their *Guerdon Grooves* at HVS 4c marked an important psychological breakthrough and led the way for a clutch of high standard routes that would later fill all the available lines on this steep intimidating cliff.

In 1951 Hamish MacInnes pegged his way up the aptly named *Engineer's Crack* on the North-East Face of Crowberry Ridge, the first instance of such mechanical practises in the glen. Other harder routes appeared on the Rannoch Wall the following year with *Peasant's Passage* (Bill Rowney and MacInnes) and *Wappenshaw Wall* (Bill Smith and MacInnes). Later that year Pat Walsh with MacInnes and Tommy Lawrie produced the first route to venture onto the left side of Slime Wall with *Bludger's Route*. In early May 1954 J.M. Brockway, Stewart Orr and the Stewart family opened up the fine secluded Mome Rath Face above the Lost Valley with

The Wabe, *Mome Rath* and *Outgrabe Route* on successive days. Around this time, in 1956 Walsh renewed his association with Slime Wall, climbing five new routes in the space of two months, including *Revelation* and *Bloody Crack*, which he thought as hard as any in the Coe. A recent ascent suggests E2 5b/c. Later that year, Cunningham and Smith produced *Whortleberry Wall* up the centre of the Rannoch Wall. Other Edinburgh based climbers were starting to feature around this time with Jimmy and Ronnie Marshall, George Ritchie and Archie Hendry the most prolific. In 1957 Jimmy Marshall added the very fine crack of *Spider* to the East Face of Aonach Dubh. On Slime Wall Marshall also contributed the link pitch, combining the lower section of *Bludger's Route* with the upper flake of *Revelation* to give an excellent outing. One other noteworthy addition was *Pegleg* on the Buachaille, again from Marshall.

1958 saw some of the best routes of their standard appear. On the West Face of Aonach Dubh Marshall succeeded in finding a way up the centre of the towering E Buttress. Starting up the great central corner *Trapeze*, named after some of the rope antics involved, had already repelled a young Robin Smith. Not to be outdone, Smith, then nineteen years old, produced what many regard as one of his most inspired pieces of climbing. Breaching the centre of Slime Wall, the bold and intimidating *Shibboleth* fully matched if not exceeded the contemporary standards south of the border. The following month Cunningham and Noon got their teeth into *Carnivore* on Creag a' Bhancair after Don Whillans (with Cunningham) had cracked the serious crux entry pitch. Whillans later returned in 1962 to add what has now become the standard way, nicknamed *Villains Finish*. Cunningham also added a fierce route adjacent to his ground-breaking *Gallows Route* though unlike its predecessor *Bluebell Grooves* used a considerable amount of aid.

... in 1956 Walsh renewed his association with Slime Wall, climbing five new routes in the space of two months, including Revelation and Bloody Crack, which he thought as hard as any in the Coe.

The following year also saw a number of significant ascents. Smith climbed the great central corner-line on Aonach Dubh's North Face to give the classic *Yo-Yo*. With John McLean he returned to add the bold and sustained *True Finish* to *Shibboleth*, completing one of the truly great rock routes. Later that year Marshall and McLean added the excellent neighbouring *Apparition*. Other new names started to appear on the scene including 'the Currie lads' Dougal Haston and James 'big Elly' Moriarty. Amongst numerous additions the pair contributed the steep *Hee-Haw* on E Buttress. Haston and Marshall also added another hard line to Slime Wall with *Lecher's Route*. On Gearr Aonach Smith succeeded where Marshall had failed, producing the pointedly named *Marshall's Wall*. The following year Smith and Jimmy Gardner completed the classic E Buttress trilogy with the exhilerating *The Big Top* tackling the wildly exposed left edge of the *Trapeze* corner. Creagh Dhu climbers Davie Todd and Willie Gordon produced *Superstition* on Slime Wall the following year. Yet again Marshall showed his superb eye for a line with the discovery of the finest line up in Coire nan Lochan with the superb corner of *Unicorn*, climbed in 1967. Aid climbing was in vogue and Dave Bathgate and Arthur Ewing climbed *Flip-out* up the left wall of Ossian's Cave. A fortnight later Bathgate and Bugs McKeith went on to peg their way up the central line on the Lower North East Nose to give *Freak-out*, in addition to climbing on aid the line now taken by *The Clearances*. Wull Thomson and John Hardie made the long trek up to Bidean's Church Door Buttress several times, before finding conditions dry enough for an ascent of *Kingpin*. Kenny Spence and John Porteous repeated many of the hard routes as well as adding a number of their own including a hard *Direct Start* to *Lecher's Route*. Spence also climbed the line later recorded as *Massacre* on Aonach Dubh's North Face, but left it unrecorded as he used two points of aid on what he considered to be a free route. On Slime Wall Ian Nicolson and Con Higgins added the hardest route yet with the bold and intricate *Apocalypse* up the groove system right of *Shibboleth*. The same pair also added one of the best HVS routes on the Buachaille with their *Line Up* up the centre of the Rannoch Wall.

The early seventies was a quiet period of consolidation in Scottish climbing, much of the activity centring upon repeats with little in the way of important new additions. The exceptionally dry summer of '76 saw the first significant new routes for a number of years. Nick Colton and Willie Todd solved a long-standing problem on Creag a' Bhancair, first attempted many years before by the Creagh Dhu. The result was the serious *Le Monde*, at E4 5c an impressive on-sight achievement and one of the first E4s in the country. Up on Aonach Dubh's North Face Ed Grindley climbed the impressive steep hanging crack-line in the wall left of *Yo-Yo* to give *The Clearances*. Climbed over two days from the ground up, the top pitch used a 'gardening peg' (aid) undeclared at the time. This was soon freed on the second ascent by Murray Hamilton and Derek Jamieson the following year. 1977 saw the arrival of a new generation of climbers comprising Dave Cuthbertson, Murray Hamilton, Derek Jamieson and Rab Anderson from Edinburgh and Willie Todd, Ken Johnstone, Dougie Mullin and Kenny McLuskey from Glasgow, all intent on relieving the existing routes of their sometimes overblown reputations and their overuse of aid. Cuthbertson substantially freed *Freak-out*,

with the exception of one lonely peg for aid. Soon the adjacent *Crocodile* was produced, Cuthbertson and Hamilton returning to complete the route the day after Todd and Anderson had climbed the first two pitches. Up on Aonach Dubh's North Face Ken Johnstone added *Eldorado* with some aid. Round on the less foreboding East Face a large number of good short routes were added including *Lady Jane*, *Solitude* and *The Fly*, all from Cuthbertson, who with Todd also climbed the serious *Bannockburn* on E Buttress. The following year Johnstone produced the steep *Spacewalk* with a sling for aid. Up on Slime Wall Hamilton added the hard *Grogblossom*. The following year Dougie Mullin made a fine free ascent of *Freak-out*.

A new guidebook appeared in 1980, the first in a new series of selective Rock and Ice guides, complete with action photos, though strangely with E grades and no technical grades. Summing up in the historical, the author managed to display a serious case of foot in mouth disease with the statement, *"What is fairly certain is that most of the major lines have now been climbed. Future pioneers will have to be content with climbing the very hard spaces in between"* – Ken Crocket, *Glen Coe and Glen Etive* (Scottish Mountaineering Trust, 1980). On the contrary, clearly there were many fine unclimbed lines around. That same summer Hamilton freed *Eldorado* and *Spacewalk*.

The real breakthrough was Pete Whillance's ascent of the obvious modern counter-diagonal line to *Carnivore* on Creag a' Bhancair giving *The Risk Business*, the first E5

Satan's Slit, Rannoch Wall, Buachaille Etive Mor. Kim Hawker & Jo George climbing. Photo Dave Cuthbertson, Cubby Images.

in the Glen. Pre-cleaned on abseil, the route waited four years before it saw any repeat ascents.

Cuthbertson adopted similar abseil inspections prior to ascents of two bold contrasting E6s on Aonach Dubh with *Revengeance* and *Prophet of Purism*. Throughout the eighties other glaringly obvious lines fell, with Whillance snatching another plum with the excellent *The Lost Ark* up on Church Door Buttress. This route was soon given a superb companion with *Temple of Doom* from Hamilton, Rab Anderson and Graeme Livingston. Mick Fowler returned to E Buttress to add the hard *Hamburg*. On Creag a' Bhancair Cuthbertson produced two very bold hard additions with *Gone with the Wind* and *Romantic Reality*, raising the standard with the latter route to E7. Cuthbertson and Livingston controversially bolted (albeit sparsely) two lines on Creag a' Bhancair's Tunnel Wall in 1986. Both *Uncertain Emotions* and *Fated Path* originally employed three bolts apiece, creating bold fingery routes with long run-outs, at E6 and E7 respectively. Livingston returned the following year to add another hard bolted route with *Admission* along with a couple of good traditional lines on the crag including *Twilight Zone*. Cuthbertson also completed another sport line on the wall with *The Railway Children*. Mark McGowan and Paul Laughlan repeated many of the hardest routes on Creag a' Bhancair, McGowan adding his own *Creag Dhont Woll*. Laughlan returned in 1990 to complete the hardest line on the Tunnel Wall at the time with *The Tribeswoman*.

In the late eighties Kev Howett and Mark Charlton added four good extremes on The Bendy, including the very fine under-rated *In Seine* (from Charlton) and the best route *The Roaring Silence* from Howett. Gary Latter added the hardest with *Quietly Burning* in addition to a couple of good pitches in the nearby Allt Doire Beith with *The Sweltering* and *Smouldering*.

On Gearr Aonach Andy Nelson added *Eyes of Mica* cutting through *Marshall's Wall*.

In 1991 on Creag a' Bhancair Grant Farquhar led the serious *Up With the Sun* after top-roping, proving that the Tunnel Wall could be climbed without bolts. In stark contrast, the top pitch was climbed entirely on-sight.

During the long hot summer of 1995 two new crags on the West Face of Gearr Aonach were developed, with Paul Thorburn and Gary Latter getting there first, adding *A Sweet Disregard for the Truth*. Soon Cuthbertson and Anderson arrived, dubbing the crag The Yosemite Walls and adding a handful of routes including *Rock Lord* and *Magnitude* from Cuthbertson and *Boiling Point* from Anderson. Thorburn later returned, unwittingly making the first ascent of *The Mystery Trend* in the belief that he was repeating one of the other pair's routes. He also returned to make a bold on-sight ascent of *Glorious Youth*, coping with poor rock and doubtful protection. Other excellent finds that summer included Martin Crocker's ascent of *The Dispossessed* up the crack-line right of *Eldorado* on the North Face of Aonach Dubh. On the incomparable Slime Wall, Cuthbertson squeezed in the superb *The New Testament*. High up on Church Door Buttress, Latter and Thorburn added *Lost Arrow* and *The Holy Grail* and traversed the Tunnel Wall to give *Tunnel Vision*. Thorburn and Cuthbertson both led the hardest traditional route on the cliff, their ascent of *Symbiosis* producing Scotland's first E8.

That summer both Anderson and Cuthbertson retro-bolted both of Cuthbertson's lines *Uncertain Emotions* and *The Railway Children* on the Tunnel Wall, creating safe Euro-style sport climbs in addition to placing lower off bolts lower down. Later, in 1998 the same pair retro-bolted Livingston's routes *Admission* and *Fated Path*, with the remaining line *The Tribeswoman* receiving the same treatment in 2001. These actions occurred despite the fact that all the routes had been climbed on-sight by several bold climbers, notably Dougie Hall in 1989 and more recently Ian Vickers who ticked the wall in an afternoon in 1997. Not all additions were in the upper grades, with Latter adding a number of good lower grade routes on a range of venues including some excellent V.Diffs up on the Mome Rath Face with *Brillig* and *Toves*. The superb Church Door Buttress yielded another excellent route in 2002 – Latter and Pete Craig exploring *Fundamentalists*. Finally, in 2004 Dave MacLeod completed a couple of obvious gaps up the left side of the Tunnel Wall with *The Third Eye* and *Axiom*.

📷 Agony, Etive Slabs. Gareth Parry climbing the first pitch. Photo Dave Simmonite.

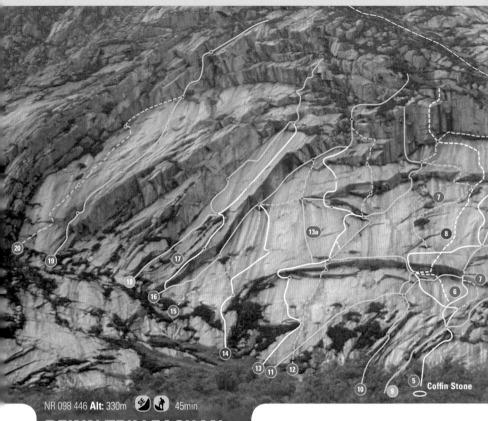

NR 098 446 **Alt:** 330m 45min

BEINN TRILLEACHAN
(HILL OF THE OYSTERCATCHER)
ETIVE SLABS

These granite slabs, unique to Scotland, lie on the slopes of Beinn Trilleachan above the head of Loch Etive. Exposed on the bedding plane at an angle of around 40°, they are generally smoother and with fewer cracks than granite which has cooled quicker nearer the surface. Several planes are separated by overlaps and walls, providing strenuous interludes to the more usual delicate 'padding'. Faith and friction are probably the two best attributes to endow a climber here, not to mention a cool head. With the exception of the corner lines on the left and *Spartan Slab* all the routes involve often quite long run-out sections of padding on bold open slabs, often including smooth holdless sections climbed on friction alone. It is recommended that new visitors choose a route lower than their usual leading standard as many find the climbing particularly bold on first acquaintance.

Access: Turn off south from the A82 about a mile/1.6km west of the Kings House Hotel down the single track road which runs down the entire length of Glen Etive. This culminates at an old dilapidated pier at the head of the long sea inlet of Loch Etive (13 miles/21km). Park here.

Approach: From the parking spot adjacent to the pier go behind an old building and gain a path (very boggy at first) which heads diagonally across the hillside in the direction of the slabs, crossing a stream and negotiating a short rock step just beyond. A large flat boulder, the 'Coffin Stone' lies at the base at the right end of the main slabs, providing a convenient gearing up spot.

Descent: Carefully traverse right along a narrow path

across the top of the slabs and scramble with care down the prominent worn path bounding the right (north-east) edge of the slabs. Great care should be taken not to dislodge rocks onto parties on the slabs below.

The following three routes climb the shorter, less steep slabs on the right. Descend by traversing right on heather to gain the lower section of the path.

❶ Vein Rouge ★★   95m HVS 5a
FA Rab & Chris Anderson 1 June 1991

Start left of three short cracks at the base of the brownish leftmost slabby tongue.

1 **35m 4c** Make a few moves up to gain first one pocket then another. Continue over some small steps then move up right into an obvious scooped depression in the wall, which leads to a grassy handrail.

2 **30m 5a** Ascend the crack above and continue to small ledges. A quartz band runs up the slab above. Move across and up right to belay at a crack.

3 **30m 5a** Move back down left to the start of the quartz band and follow this to the top then scramble to a belay in the corner.

❷ Raspberry Ripple ★★   90m E1 5a
FA Rab & Chris Anderson 1 June 1991

A very good second pitch climbing the rippled slab up the left side.

1 **40m 5a** Climb *Vein Rouge* to where it goes right into the scooped depression. Continue above, passing right of a heather ledge. Go up slightly left and continue to a small ledge at the base of the crack.

2 **50m 5a** The slab above is seamed with ripples. Follow the crack-line which leads

to the rightmost ripple and climb this to a pocket midway up it (F #1.5). Continue up the ripple to holds and easier ground leading to a belay in the corner on rope stretch.

③ Seams Blanc ★★ 95m E2 5b

FA Rab & Chris Anderson 1 June 1991

An excellent second pitch. Start at the base of the lower rightmost narrow tongue of rock.

1 **30m 5a** Climb the tongue, heading for a prominent short corner in the wall. Climb this then move out left to a small ledge.

2 **35m 5b** Follow the seam directly above then the superb pegmatite vein directly above to share a belay with *Vein Rouge*. Steady but unprotected.

3 **30m 4c** Continue straight up the slab above then by grass steps to belay in a short corner.

④ Ba's ★★ 235m E1 5a

FA John McLean & Bill Smith August 1962

Good sparsely protected climbing. Start at the same slabby tongue as *Vein Rouge*.

1 **35m 4c** Climb diagonally right to a small groove then direct to belay on a sloping ledge under a wall.

2 **40m 4c** Climb the wall on the right then start up a thin crack in the slab above, continuing left on a red band to ledges and a poor flake.

3 **20m 5a** Traverse left along the ledges for 6m then up left to belay on a ledge in a grassy corner.

4 **20m 5a** Climb the corner at the left end of the ledge then another steeper corner to belay in the groove above.

5 **15m 5a** Climb the wall above and descend to belay on *Spartan Slab*.

6 **45m 5a** Go left across the slab to a rightwards sloping groove (not the first groove) which is followed until a traverse left can be made to belay on *The Pause*.

7 **45m 5a** Trend up leftwards to a fault which leads horizontally left to a sentry box. Climb up a crack to some trees.

8 **15m 5a** Finish up the corner on the left, as for *The Pause*.

⑤ The Long Reach ★★★★ 220m E1 5b

FA John McLean & Bill Smith (1 PA) June 1963

An excellent direct line up the centre of the slabs. Start behind the Coffin Stone.

1 **35m 5b** Climb the centre of the slab to an overlap which is crossed to belay on the left as for *Spartan Slab*.

2 **40m 5b** Climb the twin grooves above onto a slab then step left along a small snaking dyke. Step boldly up left then trend diagonally up left across the slab crossing a small groove to belay by a small tree beneath the moustache.

3 **25m 5a** Cross the overlap above and left (as for *Swastika*) on good holds then traverse the lip rightwards to ledges beneath a thin grassy break. Continue up and right for 5m to belay in small left-facing corner on *The Pause*.

4 **30m 5b** Traverse left for 3m. then straight up past a quartz pocket to a small corner formed by a shallow right-facing groove and its continuation overlap. Make a *"long reach"* out left, then climb direct to belay on grass ledge near the left side of a small overlap.

5 **40m 5b** Cross the overlap and a bulge in the slab above, then direct to beneath the main overlap. Traverse right to belay beneath an overhung groove in the overlap.

6 **35m 5b** Move up left to below the groove. Gain the groove using a jug on the left wall (bold) and climb it to a ledge. Traverse left to gain a 'sentry box' and thin cracks leading to the tree-lined ledges.

7 **15m 5a** Finish up the final corner of *The Pause*.

⑥ The Band of Hope ★★ 215m E3 5c

FA John Newsome, Colin Stead, Ian Anderson & Ken Crocket 14 August 1971

A direct line between *The Pause* and *The Long Reach*.

1 **35m 5b** As for *The Long Reach*.

2 **40m 5c** Step left onto a spike and climb to the left end of the small snaking dyke on *The Long Reach*. Go up right for 6m to a hold (not visible from below) and continue up the slab slightly right then leftwards to

reach the left end of the Crevasse. A serious pitch.

3 15m 5a Gain the slab directly above then
move into the groove on the left and
climb this over a bulge to a ledge.

4 40m 5a Continue straight up by
bulges and small overlaps to belay in a
black corner below a larger overlap.

5 35m 5a Climb straight up and belay below the
short overhanging corner of *The Long Reach*.

6+7 50m 5b, 5a Finish as for *The Long Reach*.

❼ The Long Wait ★★   255m E2 5b
FA John Cunningham & Robin Smith September 1959

A long sustained route. Start behind the Coffin Stone.

1 35m 5b As for *The Long Reach*.

2 40m 5a Ascend twin grooves above to the large
pocket on *The Long Reach*. Continue slightly right
up a line of weakness in the slab to the overlap,
traverse left and pull up into the Crevasse.

3 15m 5a Gain the slab directly above then
move into the groove on the left and
climb this over a bulge to a ledge.

4 25m 5b Descend diagonally left to an old PR
just above the overlap then back up left to
the right end of a grass ledge in a corner.

5 25m 5b Go up the corner to a P scar at 6m then
break out left and move up left to follow the
slab left of a grass column. Step right to belay.

6 30m 5a Follow the flange up right, continuing
to belay at the top of another grass column.

7 35m 5b Move left to a diamond-shaped
break in the overlap and cross this rightwards.
Continue by a shallow groove and flange left
until a traverse left can be made to belay at the
right end of a grass ledge as for *Swastika*.

8 35m 5b Climb the slab to a small niche, move up
left and ascend a corner to gain a tree-lined ledge.
Traverse right to the base of *The Pause* corner.

9 15m 5a Finish up the vertical
corner as for *The Pause*.

❽ Angel ★★★   215m E7 6c
FA Dave Cuthbertson & Joanna George 3 July 1998

A superb route with difficulties found on steeper rock
than you might think! Take a good selection of very small
to medium cams. Start at the foot of *The Long Reach* slab.

1 30m 5c Climb up and right via a pocket to the
right side of a thin overlap at 6m. Gain and
follow a quartz vein above eventually gaining
The Long Reach. Belay as for *Spartan Slab*.

2 40m 5c As for *Band of Hope Direct*: Follow *The
Long Reach* as far as the left end of the horizontal
quartz band. Now move up and right to climb an
intermittent groove/flange to join the crux traverse
of *The Pause* beneath the big overlap. Traverse
left to belay at the small tree on *Swastika*.

3 15m 6c Traverse right for 5m until beneath a
vague crack cum groove close to the widest part
of the overlap. Make a difficult move to gain the
obvious small ledge on the lip (shallow placement
for a Metolious cam #00 or smallest Alien at the
back of the ledge). Mantelshelf onto the ledge
and, if successful, continue for 5m to scoop ledges.
Above and to the left, a thin grassy break provides
excellent belays using small nuts and cams.

4 55m 5c The rippled slab between *The Long Reach*
and *The Long Wait*. Climb up and slightly right
to a pocket. Trend right again to a small pocket
(Roller #3) then back left to another pocket (Roller
#5) and continue to a scoopy ledge tapering up to
the right, above which another pocket provides
an assemblage of cam protection. Go up and left
to an overlap and via a vague ripple, pad up and
slightly right to a pocket (Quadcam #4 or similar).
Continue up the ripples to a right-facing flake and
so to the left end of *The Long Reach* intermediate
overlap. Take the slab directly above and go
over a small bulge on good but slightly mossy
rock to a belay at the top of a grass column (3m
beneath the second big overlap and 8m right of
the diamond-shaped overlap of *The Long Wait*.

5 50m 5c Trend up and right to a pocket in the slab
beneath a short undercut wall in the main overlap.

Pull directly onto this using an obvious small flange and gain the easy-angled slab above. Climb a left-facing flake and near its top step right past a pocket to reach a left-trending band of quartz leading to the tree-lined ledge beneath the final wall. After the flake this section is more or less unprotected. Either belay at the left end of the tree-lined ledge at the foot of a vegetated corner (later descend 5m for a belay for the last pitch) or traverse horizontally left before reaching the ledge and belay in the corner beneath the undercut left arête of the terminal wall.

6 **20m 6b** To the right of the undercut arête is a dark streak in the side wall above an overlap. Pull into the short crack above the overlap and awkwardly attain a standing position (F #0 or similar cam backed up with a nut). Above this is a placement for an RP #1 and above that, an HB offset #1 on its side was used). Step up and make a long reach left for a thin break issuing from a stepped ramp (F #0 or #0.5 useful). Follow this break down towards the left arête and make thin moves up to gain the next break. There is a reasonable hold towards the left side of the shoulder from which a position can be attained to place a small Alien or Metolious cam #0. This placement is crucial as the crux is above. Gain the next break (nut and F #0) and continue up the arête to an exciting finish. For the belay a F #0 located 3m to the left and a F #0.5 or #1 in crack 3-4m above.

9 **Spartan Slab ★★★**   **210m VS 4c**
FA Eric Langmuir, Mike O'Hara & J.Mallinson (3 PA) 14 June 1954

The easiest worthwhile route on the slabs and consequently very popular. It follows an increasingly exposed rightward trending diagonal line close to the right edge of the main slabs. Start about 5m left of the Coffin Stone, at the most defined groove.

1 **40m 4a** Climb the groove to its end then move rightwards across the slab to a ledge.
2 **25m 4b** Climb the slab and undercut flake heading up rightwards to a good ledge beneath the right end of the overlap.
3 **35m 4c** Move left and up to a recess beneath the

roof. Make an au cheval move to get established over the lip. Continue up the gaping crack to a good horizontal crack. Traverse this right and continue round the rib to a belay near the edge of the slab.

4 **35m 4c** Climb the cracked groove above for 7m, step left into another crack and up to the overlap. Step down right with difficulty to gain a good flange. Cross the overlap and continue up good cracks to a belay.
5 **50m 4c** Continue with interest up the shallow right-facing, right-trending groove (sustained) which leads to an easier crack near the top. Belay at a rowan tree in a bay.
6 **25m** Climb cracked blocks directly above the tree to gain a ledge with some trees. Finish up the easy chimney fault on the left.

10 **The Pause ★★★**   **210m E1 5b**
FA Jimmy & Ronnie Marshall, George Ritchie & Graham Tiso (4PA /1 tension) July 1960

Start at next groove to the left of *Spartan Slab*, 10m left of the Coffin Stone.

1 **25m 5a** Climb the groove, moving left high up to climb another groove to a large spike-hold. Swing out left and belay next to a tree.
2 **20m 4c** Step right and ascend the layback crack on the lip of the groove then more easily to belay next to a small tree.
3 **40m 5b** Move up to the small block overlap, traversing around its right side to beneath the main overlap. Continue traversing delicately right (often wet) into the Crevasse.
4 **40m 5a** Gain the slab directly above then move into the groove on the left and climb this over a bulge to a ledge at 15m. Traverse right for 3m and climb a faint line of cracks to a small overlap. Move right to belay.
5 **40m 4c** Continue up right to the right end of the higher overlap then climb a thin crack to an easy groove leading to a grass ledge beside an overlap.
6 **30m 4c** Climb the overlaps on the left to the base of the final slab then traverse left

to an undercut edge near the right side of the slab (5m right of *The Long Reach* sentry box). Go up the edge to gain grass ledge.

7 **15m 5a** Finish up the steep vertical corner on the left.

11 Swastika ★★★   200m E2 6a

FA Mick Noon & Eric Taylor (some aid) 25 June 1957;
FFA Willie Todd & Murray Hamilton 17 June 1977

Excellent climbing, though the top pitch is much harder and a bit out of character with the rest of the route. Start below the rightmost of twin parallel cracks in a clean slab 40m left of the Coffin Stone.

1 **35m 5a** Take the right-slanting crack to a heather ledge.

2 **25m 4b** Move right across the ledge to a slab beneath a small block overlap.

3 **10m 4c** Climb the slab crossing a small overlap to belay beneath the main overlap.

4 **25m 5a** Step up right and attain a standing position on the lip with interest. Traverse left along 'the moustache' to a grass ledge.

5 **35m 4c** Climb the quartz band above to a tree belay.

6 **30m 5a** Move up right to a ledge then climb the second quartz band above.

7 **20m 5c** Traverse left beneath the upper overlap for 2m then a short corner and groove, moving up left to a tree belay beneath the final corner.

8 **20m 6a** Climb the steep awkward crack (very well protected) just left of the main crack, moving up and right to climb a corner to a ledge, finishing with a layback. Alternatively, the top pitch of *The Pause* provides a more reasonable finish.

12 Tous les Deux ★★   195m E2 5c

FA Rab Carrington & John McLean (1 PA & combined tactics) May 1970; p 2 Brian Robertson, Dick Holt, Fred Harper & Bugs McKeith 11 October 1964

A direct line left of *Swastika*, crossing numerous overlaps with interest. Start at tree right of *Swastika*.

1 **30m 5a** Climb a slab and corner to a grass ledge.

2 **35m 5a** Move up right to ascend a line of weakness up the slab, crossing a small overlap to the main

overlap which is followed rightwards to a belay.

3 **10m 5b** Surmount the overlap and up to the ledge on *Swastika*.

4 **35m 5a** Climb a quartz band for 5m then the slab and slim corner on the left to a ledge and small tree on *Swastika*.

5 **10m 5a** Climb a slab to beneath the overlap.

6 **30m 5b** Climb the large overlap above. This is accomplished by entering from the left and leaving by a dubious flake. Move up to belay below the next overlap.

7 **25m 5c** Climb the steep corner (crux) onto a slab then go up this to a wall and traverse left to the tree belay on *Agony*.

8 **20m 4c** Climb the wall behind to easy ground leading diagonally right.

13 The Valkyrie ★★   205m E2 5b

FA Brian Robertson & Fred Harper (1 PA) October 1965

A fine direct line left of *Swastika*. Start left of *Swastika* beneath the left-most of two long parallel cracks.

1 **25m 4c** Climb crack to belay on a heather ledge.

2 **30m 5a** Move up and left to a small ledge then straight up the slab to a 'cave' below the overlap.

3 **15m 5b** Traverse left for 3m, cross the overlap then follow the lip back right to the belay on *Swastika* at the foot of the quartz band.

4 **30m 5b** From the centre of the ledge move up slightly leftwards to a small quartz pocket then follow a ripple diagonally up right (5m left of the quartz band) to gain a slender corner (long run-out). Climb this leading to the ledge and tree on *Swastika*.

5 **10m 4b** Move up left to a flake belay beneath an overlap.

6 **20m 5b** Cross the overlap and continue slightly rightwards up a slab to belay at a horizontal crack.

7 **30m 5b** Continue up the slab and cross the next overlap. Step right then up a sloping corner and pull up left to join *Agony*.

8+9 **45m 5a, 4c.** As for *Agony*.

13a The Pea Brained Variation ★★   50m E3 5c

FA Andy Nisbet & A.Clifford May 1984

A bold and sustained direct variation on pitch 4 with some excellent blank padding. From the left end of the ledge go up slightly left then right then back left to an obvious red pocket with an ancient chipped spike (poor runner). Go straight up for 5m to a small ledge and protection on the right then head up the blank slab diagonally to gain the left end of the overlap. Traverse right 10m to regain the normal route.

14 Gecko ★★   175m E6 6a

FA Julian Lines & Brian Davison (on-sight) 13 August 2000.

The blank slab to the right of *The Big Ride* provides the meat of this route. 15m left of the start of *Swastika* is a heather bay bounded on its left by a tongue of slab which nearly reaches the approach path. Start up the right rib of this tongue next to the heather bay.

1 **25m 5a** Climb the right rib of the tongue of slab then cracks in the slab to heather and a sapling belay.

2 **35m 5c** Move up left onto slabs and follow holds up and slightly left into the base of the left-facing groove. Step right and follow quartz veins leading diagonally right to level with the *Frustration* ledge. Belay 5m to the left of this by a clump of heather.

3 **30m 6a** Climb quartz veins above to an unhelpful pocket at about 8m. Committing and sustained moves lead to a flake/ledge. A short slab above leads to a traverse to the *Agony* belay.

4 **40m 5c** As for *The Big Ride*.

5 **45m 5a** Follow *Agony* pitches 4 and 5.

15 The Big Ride ★★   145m E3 5c

FA Dougal Haston & Robin Campbell (2 PA & 2 tensions) August 1964; FFA Rab Carrington & Ian Nicolson 1970s

A direct line up the steep slabs right of *Agony*. Start below a crack in the slab just right of *Agony*.

1 **30m 5b** Climb the crack for 18m to a PR then traverse right into a grassy groove and climb it to a ledge.

2 **30m 5c** A bold pitch. Ascend the thin cracked fault above to a grass ledge in the corner.

3 **40m 5c** Traverse right 5m then climb up to a crack. Use a small pocket on the right to gain a weakness and follow this boldly to a ledge with old PRs. Continue to the next overlap and belay in the corner.

4+5 **45m** As for *Agony*.

16 Agony ★★★   150m E2 5c

FA John Cunningham, Mick Noon & Bill Smith 6 April 1957; FFA Brian Duff & Willie Todd 4 June 1978

Excellent climbing up the great sweeping corner. Slow to dry, the route is in the sun until shortly after midday, after which it weeps when the corner comes into the shade.

1 **35m 5c** Up the corner to an old PR at 12m (just above good holds on the left wall). Move right across the slab heading for a small recess and protection in a flake just right again. Step back left and up the slab to a shallow left-facing flake and more easily up this to an overlap. Pull through this to belay.

2 **35m 5c** The sustained corner above to belay on a damp heather ledge at the base of the next corner.

3 **35m 5c** Often wet in the lower section, though still climbable in such conditions. The corner to the roof then round right to belay at an old ring peg 5m up and right of the top of the corner.

4 **25m 5a** Up the corner, traverse right and up the short corner and overlap to the capping wall. Traverse left to belay at a tree.

5 **20m 4c** Climb the wall behind the belay to easy ground leading diagonally right.

17 The Pinch Superdirect ★★★★   215m E3 5c

FA John Jackson & Rab Carrington 18 April 1968; Direct Start: Murray Hamilton, Brian Duff & Derek Jamieson 18 June 1978; Direct Finish Rab Anderson & Kenny Spence 31 March 1984

A superb combination taking the inset corner and slab overlooking *Agony*. Start as for *Agony*.

1 **37m 5c** Climb the first 3m of the *Agony* corner then move up onto the inset wall above. Continue up the corner past a narrow section to a PB.

2 **23m 5c** Continue up the corner to belay on a ledge. Running the first two pitches together on a 60m rope gives a stunning pitch.

3 **20m 5c** Move up right to a thin crack then climb up right past 'the pinch' to an obvious quartz pocket. Step right almost to the edge and climb a crack to belay just beneath a small overlap.

4 **40m 5b** Climb the crack direct, crossing a small overlap to a finger-slot 4m below another overlap. Either move right then up and left above the overlap or go up then left beneath the overlap. Both ways lead to a belay on *Hammer*.

5 **40m 5a** Climb up the slab above then corners onto the upper slab, traversing left below the final wall to a belay.

6 **25m 5c** Climb the steep chimney, move up to a ledge then up walls and across to a recess and tree.

7 **30m 5a** Climb the crack to the right of twin cracks to finish up slabs.

18 Hammer ★★★   150m HVS 5a
FA Mick Noon & John Cunningham (1 tension) 7 April 1957

Excellent climbing up the big corner bounding the left side of the slabs. Scramble up to the base of the corner.

1 **15m 4a** Climb the corner to a tree belay.

2 **35m 4b** Ascend the cracked slab just right of the corner to belay near the top of a heather cone.

3 **25m 5a** Follow a shallow scoop leading obliquely up left (crux) into the main corner, which leads pleasantly to a good ledge and tree belay.

4 **40m 5a** Continue up the corner for 20m, traverse delicately right for 3m then follow cracks to a large overlap. Move right into a recess and pull over into the base of a corner.

5 **35m 4b** Move up the corner then undercut the overlap and climb diagonally up right to gain the top.

19 Jaywalk ★★★   210m E2 5c
FA Jimmy Marshall, James Moriarty & Jimmy Stenhouse (4 PA) September 1960; FFA unknown

A very fine route, much less popular than the routes further right and not visible from the Coffin Stone. The crux sections gaining and leaving the upper slab are steep and well protected. Continue along the path beyond *Hammer*, up and along a ledge then by steep grass tufts to beneath the right edge of the slab 15m right of the vegetated left-bounding corner of *Sickle*.

1 **30m 5b** Ascend the two-tiered groove and its right-trending continuation to gain the upper slab. Step left then up to a belay.

2 **45m 5a** Move right and follow a series of grooves, then the left rib to a belay.

3 **45m 5a** Ascend the groove to a grass patch, move left a metre and continue by smooth slabs and a shallow scoop leading to large grass ledge.

4 **10m 4b** Continue to a grass ledge and prominent small tree.

5 **35m 5c** From the thin grass ledge above surmount a short wall past a spike then climb the crack and groove above, moving right and laybacking into a grassy corner leading to a belay.

6 **45m 4c** Continue up the grassy corner past a short slabby section then up heather to a right traverse leading to the descent path.

20 Groundhog ★★   195m E3 5c
FA Dougie Dinwoodie & Greg Strange (2 PA & 2 tensions) 23 September 1972; FFA Murray Hamilton & Pete Greenwell 3 June 1978

Another very good route ascending the slabs between *Jaywalk* and *Sickle*. Start at the base of the vegetated *Sickle* corner.

1 **35m 5c** Move up right and climb up cracks past a flake, moving up right to an obvious break in a big overlap. Gain the upper slab using the crack on the right and move up then left to big holds. Move up to a ledge and climb the obvious crack to the belay ledge.

2 **45m 5a** Continue up a crack-line and grooves in bulging slabs (never far right of grass patches) to finish by a short left traverse to belay next to a loose flake in the corner.

3 **45m 5a** Climb the corner and go up right to a small circular depression on *Jaywalk*. Go straight up then left to belay in a flanking corner.

4+5 70m 5b,– Climb up to the big grass ledge of *Jaywalk* and finish as for that route.

Crowberry Ridge
Raven's Gully
East Face North Buttress
Great Gully
Lagangarbh Buttress
Great Gully Upper Buttress
Rannoch Wall
Slime Wall
D Gully Buttress
Curved Ridge
Crowberry Basin
Great Gully Buttress
Central Buttress
Waterslide
APPROACH
APPROACH

(BIG HERDSMAN OF ETIVE)
BUACHAILLE ETIVE MOR

'The Buachaille', as it is affectionately known by generations of climbers, holds a special place in the history of Scottish climbing. It's distinctive conical shape, most striking when approaching over Rannoch Moor from the east, makes it easily the most iconic of all Scottish mountains. The mountain is actually a 7km long ridge with four tops, all the climbing concentrated on its most northerly top, **Stob Dearg** (red peak) the highest and most impressive.

Access: Park on the south side of the A82 at Altnafeadh (just west of a small stone barn), 1.8 miles/2.9 km west of the Glen Etive turn-off. Parking is also available in a long lay-by on the north side of the road 100m further west or down the rough track (4WD territory) nearer the river.

STOB DEARG NORTH-EAST FACE

Approach: Follow the path crossing the River Coupall by a footbridge then beside Lagangarbh Cottage. Follow the path cutting left after 200m, which ascends diagonally left across the hillside to the Waterslide.

Descent: Both *Curved Ridge* and *North Buttress* provide convenient scrambling descents. The lower section of *Curved Ridge* can be avoided (i.e. easier and much quicker) by going down **Easy Gully**, with a short step into the lower reaches of **Crowberry Gully**, picking up the approach path lower down just after crossing the stream. From the summit: follow the path south-west then west to flat bealach at the top of Coire na Tulaich. This is steep but straightforward – head diagonally left down a vague path then convenient scree slopes to gain the path above the west side of the burn. In the spring the large snow slope can be avoided either by descending the bergschrund on the east side or continuing north-west and down the ridge of Stob Coire na Tuileachan, skirting underneath the base of the west face of Creag na Tulaich.

NN 223 548 **Alt:** 630m  1¼hr

NN 224 545 **Alt:** 750m

LAGANGARBH BUTTRESS

The most westerly buttress on the north face with the top of the distinctive gaping slit of Lagangarbh Chimney visible from the car park. It has three faces bounded on either side by grassy gullies, its more broken west face overlooking Coire na Tulaich.

Approach: Leave the approach path at the first scree slope after 20 minutes and scramble up the rough slabby rocks to gain a right-slanting gully that runs up beneath the buttress. In the wet follow the heathery slopes left of the approach rocks.

Descent: Down the grassy gully on the right side.

① Lagangarbh Chimney ★★   60m Very Difficult
FA P.Barclay & A.Ramsay September 1930

Excellent entertaining climbing up the huge gaping slit cleaving the centre of the face. Start by scrambling up from the gully to the base of the chimney.

  1 35m Climb the chimney over three strenuous chokestones to belay on the left beneath the final chimney.

  2 25m Continue up the final more open chimney.

GREAT GULLY BUTTRESS

A good compact buttress overlooking the upper reaches of Great Gully.

Approach: Follow the path from Alltnafeadh, which crosses the great gash of Great Gully after about 30 minutes. The buttress on the right side gives a fine scrambling approach on immaculate rough water-worn rock. Routes from right to left.

Descent: Scramble down to the right.

① Sundown Slab ★★   50m Severe 4a
FA Ian Clough & party 23 August 1967

Start at the leftmost of two grooves below and left of a prominent jutting flake. Climb the groove then go left by delicate slabs and open grooves to the top.

② Ledgeway ★★   55m HS 4a
FA Bill Smith & Bob Hope 7 September 1952

Poorly protected. There is a 10m rib about 10m left of the right end of the face. Start at a groove immediately right of the rib.

  1 10m 4a Climb the groove to a grass ledge.

2 20m 4a Traverse right and up from the left end
of the ledge to a shallow white-scarred fault.
Follow this to pass a bulge on the left then climb
up leftwards to the belay on *Direct Route*.

3 25m 4a Climb the flake then the crack
to finish up the open groove above.

2a **Direct Start** *   40m VS 4c

FA Jimmy Marshall 17 June 1956

Start just down and right of the normal start. Follow a
fault to join the normal route at the shallow white-
scarred fault.

3 **Direct Route** **   55m VS 4b

FA Sam Smith & Ian Dingwall October 1946

Similarly bold climbing to the adjacent *Ledgeway*.

1 10m 4a As for *Ledgeway*.

2 20m 4b From the left end of the ledge move
up and slightly left for about 5m then head for
a right-sloping shelf. Step up onto the shelf
and continue up the fractured fault above to
belay at a large pointed flake on grass ledge.

3 25m 4a Climb short steep wall left of the flake
then finish up the slightly left-trending weakness.

4 **June Crack** **   60m VS 5a

FA Bill Smith & John Cunningham 12 June 1948

The prominent rightmost of triple cracks.

1 10m As for *Ledgeway/Direct Route*.

2 20m 4c From the left end of the ledge climb
up and slightly left for 5m to gain and follow
the prominent crack with an excursion onto
the left wall to belay on a small shelf.

3 30m 5a Enter and climb the crack above
either direct (hard but well protected) or
by a short deviation on the right. Continue
up the crack, finishing more easily.

5 *Playmate of the Month* E3 6a takes the prominent
thin crack between 4 & 6.

6 **July Crack** **   50m HVS 5a

FA Robin Smith & Andrew Fraser June 1958

Fine sustained climbing up the thin central crack.

1 12m 4a Climb straight up to belay
on a ledge below the crack.

2 38m 5a The crack.

7 **August Crack** *   50m VS 4b

FA Bill Smith & John Cunningham 3 August 1955

The leftmost of parallel triple cracks.

1 12m 4a As for *July Crack*.

2 38m 4b Make a slightly descending traverse left for
5m to a thin crack. Follow this and the steep fault
above to finish. This pitch can also be gained direct.

GREAT GULLY UPPER BUTTRESS

Approach: Either by a route on Great Gully Buttress
or by scrambling up the right side of that buttress.
Descent: Down the left side of the buttress.

1 **Happy Valley** *   30m E1 5b

FA Ian Nicolson summer 1969

The steep wide crack 10m left of the central chimney-crack.

2 **Yam** *   40m E1 5b

FA Alec Fulton & John Cullen summer 1963

The chimney-crack cleaving the centre of the face with
the crux crossing the roof at one third height.

3 **Yamay** **   40m E2 5b

FA Ian Nicolson & Kenny Spence 1 September 1968

The prominent crack and corner between 2 & 4. Climb to
a small roof, traverse the wall on the right and climb the
corner above. The 3a Direct Start is E2 5c.

4 **May Crack** ****   35m VS 5a

FA Bob Hope & Bill Smith 6 May 1952

Superb rock and protection make this one of the best
single pitches around. Start at a detached block right of 3.
Follow the thin crack which becomes wider and more
distinct in its upper half.

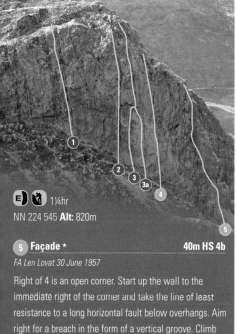

E 🕐 1¼hr
NN 224 545 **Alt:** 820m

5 Façade ★   **40m HS 4b**

FA Len Lovat 30 June 1957

Right of 4 is an open corner. Start up the wall to the immediate right of the corner and take the line of least resistance to a long horizontal fault below overhangs. Aim right for a breach in the form of a vertical groove. Climb the groove and trend left on the steep wall above to finish.

SLIME WALL   🧗 🕐 1hr
WEST FACE OF NORTH BUTTRESS
NN 223 545 **Alt:** 750m

Approach: To the base of Great Gully Buttress then contour left, crossing the gully to reach the base.

Descent: From the top of the cliff scramble up and rightwards and traverse above the top of *Raven's Gully* to follow a diagonal shelf leading down into the tottering confines of **Great Gully**. Either tread warily down this (much loose scree) or more pleasantly, go down the crest of **Great Gully Buttress** heading back right into the gully near the base.

1 Bludger's Revelation ★★★   **157m HVS 5a**

FA Bludger's Pat Walsh, Hamish MacInnes & Tommy Lawrie 21 September 1952; Revelation Pat Walsh & Charlie Vigano June 1956; Link Pitch Jimmy Marshall, J.Griffin, G.Adams & Ronnie Marshall July 1957

"I thought it was one of the most wonderful climbs on the hill, climbing up these long and beautiful silver-grey

A superb and atmospheric sheet of excellent rough compact bubbly rhyolite, which overlooks the tottering scree-filled depths of **Great Gully**. Despite modern protection and sticky boots many of the routes still have fearsome reputations; protection is not always abundant, the holds are sloping and exhilarating exposure makes the Slime Wall a memorable climb. It requires several days of dry weather to come into condition and a few of the routes almost always contain short seepage sections.

grooves leading up to the flake of Revelation." – Jimmy Marshall, *The Edge* 1994

Fantastic climbing threading a line up the left side of the face. Start beneath the left of two parallel grooves, 10m down from the base of *Raven's Gully*, where the face turns to face towards the road.

1 18m Climb up to belay at the base of the groove.

2 24m 5a Climb a detached flake to the right of the groove then step left into the groove and follow it on good holds to a ledge.

3 30m 4c The link pitch. Move left to the edge, climb up for 2m then traverse left into a vertical crack and follow this to a ledge and corner. Move round the edge onto the wall and climb excellent slabby rock to move left to belay.

4 35m 4c Step back right into the groove and up this rightwards following a line of good flat holds leading to the prominent wide flake crack. Follow this, turning the overhang on the left to belay at the right end of a narrow ledge where the flake starts to cut back right.

5 50m 4a Move right along the crest of the flake for 5m then directly to easier ground. Scramble off leftwards.

❷ Lecher's Superstition ★★★ 120m E2 5c

FA Dougal Haston & Jimmy Marshall (2 PA) June 1959;
Superstition Davy Todd & Willie Gordon 1962; Lecher's Direct
Kenny Spence & John Porteous August 1968

Another fine combination.

1 18m As for *Bludger's Revelation*.

2 27m 5c Climb detached flake behind to reach the foot of the groove. From top of flake step left onto steep wall and pull up onto the arête (crux). Return right to the groove and climb it for 15m then move left 3m to belay just above the crux pitch of *Bludger's*. Slow to dry.

3 35m 5b Step right and ascend the prominent crack to belay at the top of the main pitch of *Doom Arête*.

4 15m 5b Climb the groove above for 10m then move up and right to an awkward belay in a corner (3m left of *Revelation* flake).

5 25m 4c Move up and left to finish up a prominent crack leading to easier ground.

❸ Grogblossom ★ 110m E4 6a

FA Murray Hamilton & Derek Jamieson 17 June 1978

Climbs the steep wall left of *Shibboleth* groove.

1 30m 4b As for *Shibboleth* pitch 1.

2 40m 6a Trend left across the wall to an old PR, climb the roof to easier ground (*Shibboleth* is immediately right). Continue up the wall for 12m to a good ledge and poor PR. Step right and climb the right arête of the groove to a poor resting place. Continue to an undercling, step left and make a move up the wall to belay on *Revelation*.

3 40m 4b Trend left 3m to a black groove, climb this for 15m then move right to join the *Revelation* flake. Follow this to top.

❹ Shibboleth & True Finish ★★★★ 165m E2 5c

FA Robin Smith & Andrew Fraser 14 June 1958;
True Finish Robin Smith & John McLean June 1959

The finest route of its grade and length on the planet! Smith's finest achievement and one of the hardest leads of its day. Start 10m left of the base of *Raven's Gully*.

1 25m 4b Trend rightwards up grooves and a slabby ramp to twin blocks on a large ledge.

2 20m 5c Climb the crack for 5m then move left for 3m and move up and right into a left-facing groove (often wet) past an old PR (crux). Follow this to belay on a small ledge.

3 20m 5a The groove above then trend boldly leftwards across the wall to belay.

4 25m 5b Climb a delicate wall on the right (old PR and thread in a shallow groove on the left), heading for a small isolated overhang. Up the short corner directly above and continue to belay at old Ps below an overhanging wall.

5 40m 5b The shallow groove directly above then right along a ramp (the Original Finish, 35m 4b continues up the wall then right up grooves, finishing by a short overhanging corner). Traverse right to a good spike, move up and traverse right to a hanging groove. Easier up this to belay on a ledge.

6 35m 5c Traverse right above the void on good flat holds to the recess at the base of the crack springing from the roof of the Great Cave. Up the crack and continue more easily up the V-groove to finish.

5 The New Testament ★★★★   133m E4 6a

FA Dave Cuthbertson & Joanna George 6 August 1995

A superb route *"one of the best in Glen Coe"*, taking a direct line up the centre of the cliff.

1 25m 4b As for *Shibboleth*.

2 27m 6a Climb corner above for 6m then follow a little stepped overlap going left to enter an obvious groove. (The slim hanging groove immediately right of the *Shibboleth* groove). Negotiate the 'slime factory' and enter the groove. At its top move right into a wet corner. Climb the corner and its right edge (there is another slim corner to the right which you enter towards its top). Climb the mossy thin cracks to belay on the left.

3 27m 5c Climb up and left from the two fingers of rock (forming the V) and climb a slim groove to a 3m tapering crack/groove. Trend left and follow a shallow groove/rib which becomes parallel and close to *Shibboleth's* 4th pitch. This leads to the right side of *Shibboleth's* isolated overhang. From a jug rail climb the wall above and enter a small left facing corner to reach a ledge and belay on *Apparition*.

4 27m 5c Step right and climb two tapering cracks to a ledge. Go up and right to a sloping shelf leading to the right edge of this steep section of cliff. Climb up and left to a square-cut hold then continue to a good side-pull beneath the bulge. Move left and join *Shibboleth True Finish* at the traverse into the hanging groove. Belay on a ledge above.

5 27m 5c From approximately half-way along the belay ledge climb a brown streak to gain the obvious stepped right-trending crack. Climb this in a fine position to easier ground.

6 Apparition ★★★   145m E1 5b

FA Jimmy Marshall & John McLean September 1959

Another superb climb often overlooked in favour of the more celebrated *Shibboleth*.

1 30m 4c As for *Guerdon Grooves*.

2 45m 5b Climb the prominent groove, stepping left into a parallel corner which leads to a square-cut roof. Pull over and climb a steep groove to a ledge then ascend the slab on the right to belay in a recess beneath a grass ledge.

4 35m 5a Climb up to then follow the diagonal crack in the steep wall leading to a slim ledge. Traverse left along this to join the slim groove and ramp of *Shibboleth* (pitch 5).

5 35m 4b The original *Shibboleth* finish. Continue up the wall trending right up grooves leading to a platform, finishing up a short overhanging corner.

7 Raven's Gully ★★   135m HVS 5a

FA Jock Nimlin, Barclay Braithwaite, Norman Millar, John McFarlane & Garry McArtney 13 June 1937

One of the hardest gullies in the country, setting a new standard in its day.

1-3 Three short pitches lead to a belay in a cave beneath a huge chokestone blocking the gully.

4 5a Climb the left wall until possible to pull over using a high hand hold above the slot. Belay well up the scree slope above.

5 4c Continue up narrow chimney past a jammed block then a deceptive groove.

6 18m 4c 'The Bicycle Pitch.' Ascend the left wall on small holds for the first 9m. Above pitch 8, traverse left round the rib into grooves parallel to the gully and climb 45m of easier ground to a grass platform above the caves of the *Direct Finish*. Finish either by a narrow 3m chimney, or traverse left across slabs and ascend 12m chimney and fold.

7a Direct Finish ★★★   50m E1 5a

FA John Cunningham, Bill Smith & Tommy Paul 30 May 1948

At the top of Pitch 8 continue directly up the gully to chokestones and caves, climbing the first on the right then traversing onto the left wall to gain a dark cave. Strenuous bridging leads to rock shelves leading out left beneath huge chokestones to a grass ledge leading to the penultimate pitch of the ordinary route.

CUNEIFORM BUTTRESS 1hr

NN 223 545 **Alt:** 800m

The shorter upper continuation of the face, separated from Slime Wall by *Raven's Gully*, taking its name from the curious wedge-shaped markings evident at its base.

8 Raven's Edge **   170m VS 4c

FA Dave Bathgate & Jim Brumfitt May 1964

A magnificent route without being too taxing, the highlight being the exposed final pitch.

1+2 60m Climb the left edge of Cuneiform Buttress to a point 12m above the fourth pitch of *Raven's Gully* at a large block belay below a vertical wall.

3 25m 4c Climb the wall then traverse left to the foot of a prominent corner. Climb the corner to a ledge and belay.

4 25m 4c Continue up the corner to belay on a platform.

5 30m Climb easily to a thread belay below the big roof on the extreme left edge of the buttress.

6 30m 4b Traverse left under the roof to emerge on the exposed right wall of *Raven's Gully* and finish up the deep crack which splits the wall.

8a Direct Finish *   30m HVS 5a

FA John Porteous & M.MacDonald June 1970

From the thread belay at the top of pitch 4 climb the steep wall on the right. Finish up the chimney and twin cracks above.

NORTH BUTTRESS

1 North Buttress *   200m Moderate

FA William Brown, William Rose & William Tough July 1895

The broad easy-angled buttress lying immediately left of *Great Gully*, which is the second large scree funnel (stream) encountered on the approach path about 30 minutes from the car park. The base is distinguished by two prominent boulders low down. From the approach path scramble up heather and occasional rocky steps to the base of the buttress proper. Traverse left along a path immediately under the base (not obvious from below) to gain an open chimney in the centre of the buttress. Climb this for 20m then move diagonally right round the corner following the obvious (well-scratched) line to return back left. The route is well marked above, gradually easing leading directly to easy ground not far short of the summit cairn.

Cliff layout viewed from approach path at the Waterslide.

Rannoch Wall

East Face North Buttress

Curved Ridge

D Gully Buttress

Central Buttress

1hr

EAST FACE OF NORTH BUTTRESS

NG 226 546 **Alt:** 700m

Green Gully

The left side of the sprawling **North Buttress**
is more open and has a sunnier aspect than the dark
and often gloomy west side (**Slime Wall**). Quick drying
with a good spread of grades and much quieter than the
adjacent Rannoch Wall.

Approach: Scramble up as for **North Buttress** and
traverse up leftwards or continue along the path up past
the **Waterslide** into Crowberry Basin then follow a path
out rightwards and up to the base.

Descent: Traverse right and scramble down **North
Buttress** or abseil from the top of the lower tier,
retrieving the anchors on completion of a second route.

1 Brevity Crack *   50m HVS 5a

FA Pat Walsh & Charlie Vigano summer 1954

A hanging crack starts about 5m up near the left end of
the wall. Climb easily up to it then ascend the crack with
more interest, easing higher up.

2 Shackle Route **   75m Severe 4a

FA S.Cross & Miss A.Nelson June 1936

The wide crack splitting the left side of the face.

1 **45m 4a** Ascend the crack past a 'sentry box' (possible
   belay) on the left at 20m to easier ground near the top.

2 **30m 4a** A slender pinnacle/flake with a jammed
   block to its left lies directly above. Climb either
   the black groove right of the pinnacle or over the
   jammed block to gain a left-slanting groove. Finish
   over a steep wall leading to easier ground.

3 Shattered Crack *   45m VS 4c

FA John Cunningham & Pete McGonigle 23 June 1946

The long thin crack 3m right of *Shackle Route*. Ascend
the wall on good holds past a large loose block heading
towards the block overhang. Climb through this by a
crack, finishing more easily.

4 Crow's Nest Crack **   85m VS 4c

FA John Cunningham & Pete McGonigle 24 June 1946

Good sustained climbing taking the crack above an
overhung grassy recess. Start on a small flat ledge 2m
left of the recess.

1 **45m 4c** Move up for 3m then trend slightly right for
   7m to an awkward move at a corner. Traverse right
   into narrow crack and climb this, then make a long
   step left beneath a small roof onto a slab. Climb this
   to regain the crack where it is split by an overhung
   nose, following the leftmost crack to the terrace.

2 **40m 4a** Move up rightwards from the black groove
   of *Shackle Route* to follow a prominent crack.

5 Mainbrace Crack **   50m HVS 5a

FA Pat Walsh & Bill Smith August 1955

Another fine route. Start at a groove 4m right of 4.

1 **25m 5a** Climb to small overhang at 3m and
   continue up a crack to below another overhang.
   Traverse left 4m and up a fault to where

a step left can be made to a belay.

2 25m 5a Continue up a wide crack for 5m and traverse right to a small ledge below an arête, which is climbed spectacularly to finish.

6 White Wall Crack ★★   50m E1 5b
FA Bill Smith & G.McIntosh (2 PA) August 1955;
FFA Brian Robertson 1963

Round the edge is a noticeably white wall bounding the left side of *Bottleneck Chimney*.

1 35m 5b Climb the thin corner crack to pull onto a sloping ledge at 15m. Make a long step onto the rib on the right and climb to a ledge. Traverse left round a corner for 6m then climb up the open groove of *Mainbrace Crack* then traverse left to belay.

2 15m 4c Follow the wide crack of *Mainbrace Crack* and so to a small ledge on the arête. Leave this by an awkward step down, continue right for 5m to finish up a shallow rib.

7 Bottleneck Chimney ★★   40m HS 4b
FA R.Donaldson & G.McCarter summer 1941

Good well protected climbing up the obvious dark slot visible from the road. Climb the chimney, negotiating the bottleneck strenuously by good holds up on the right. Finish more easily.

8 Bluebell Grooves ★   40m E3 6a
FA John Cunningham & Frith Finlayson (5 PA) August 1958;
FFA Willie Todd & Dave Cuthbertson 3 June 1978

Worth doing as the quality of the rock improves notice-ably on the upper section. Start immediately right of 7.

1 20m 5c Climb the sustained undercut groove on dubious rock to belay on a small grass ledge.

2 20m 6a Traverse right a few metres then ascend the overhung groove using holds on its left wall. Continue steeply to finish.

9 Gallows Route ★★   25m E2 5c
FA John Cunningham & Ian Dingwall June 1947

A serious and historic piece of climbing, the first extreme climbed in the Scottish mountains. A broad nose projects

from the right end of the terrace split by a shallow chimney. Start by scrambling up to belay at the top of the chimney. Descend 3m and traverse left 3m to gain a steep scoop. Climb this, crossing an overhang on the left then a second scoop, turning an overhang on the right. Continue by a third scoop then traverse left to better holds and a belay. Scramble to finish.

10 Creag Dhon't Woll ★★   20m E5 6b
FA Mark McGowan & Cameron Bell September 1987

Bold climbing up the centre of the short compact wall right of 9. Climb up easily to belay as for 9. Ascend the white groove above to a good rest below a thin crack. Arrange protection in a hidden undercut on the right (F #1) then make awkward moves up the wall to a good slot and protection. Further hard moves up the crack lead to an easier finish.

UPPER TIER

Separated from the main lower tier by a long grassy upward curving terrace known as **Green Gully**. Approach via a route on the lower tier.

11 Hangman's Crack ★★   30m MVS 4b
FA R.Donaldson & G.McCarter summer 1941

The prominent corner cleaving the centre of the crag. Scramble up to belay at the base. Move up and slightly right, make an awkward mantelshelf (crux) and move left into the corner which is followed throughout.

12 Garrotte ★★   30m VS 5a
FA John Cunningham & Mick Noon 4 August 1955

The prominent thin crack 3m right of 11. Climb the crack past a nook at 12m. Continue up past a grass ledge to finish on easy ledges.

13 Gibbet ★★   30m HVS 5a
FA Eric Taylor & Bill Smith 9 September 1956

Climb 12 to the first bulge then make a delicate traverse right into a clean-cut groove. Climb the groove.

The hanging groove just right is 14 *Gibberish* E2 5c.

D GULLY BUTTRESS 1hr

1 D Gully Buttress ★   **150m Difficult**

FA W.Newbigging & party 13 October 1903

On approach up the scree just beyond the **Waterslide**, the obvious slit of D Gully lies almost directly above. This route follows the buttress to the left of the gully. Start at the base of the gully and follow easy rocks leftwards. At about half-height a steep 10m wall is encountered. This is Hell's Wall, a poorly protected Severe 4a on sloping holds. Outflank this on the left and regain the buttress. Continue to the top and traverse right to gain the upper section of *Curved Ridge*.

NG 227 544 **Alt:** 530m   1hr

CENTRAL BUTTRESS – NORTH FACE

Lies obliquely up left from the **Waterslide**, well seen in profile. Though very good in their own right the routes also provide logical approaches to the Rannoch Wall. A grassy gully leads up left to form Heather Ledge at just over ⅓ height.

Descent: Traverse easily right above the top of D-Gully to gain *Curved Ridge*.

1 North Face Route ★★   **240m Severe 4a**

FA Jim Bell & Alexander Harrison summer 1929

A good long route and a fine approach to the Rannoch Wall. Start by scrambling up easy slabs to a recess beneath a bollard at 3m at the lower north-east edge of the buttress.

1 **30m** Follow a series of shallow grooves to a ledge.

2 **25m** Move up leftwards and follow the wide left-most crack on huge holds to belay at its top.

3 **40m** Scramble easily up to belay at the top right end of Heather Ledge.

4 **25m** Move up a short way then traverse right round the edge on good holds and up a shallow cracked groove to underneath the overhung recess. Traverse right and drop down to belay on ledge beneath a steep wall.

5 **25m 4a** Climb the wall (crux – quite well protected) to gain a right-slanting shelf at 3m.

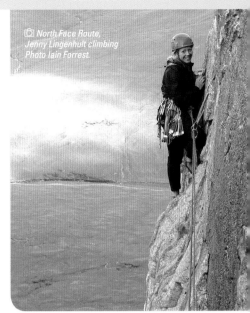

North Face Route, Jenny Lingenhult climbing
Photo Iain Forrest

Go easily along this then up rightwards to belay at the base of a deep overhung chimney slot.

6 **25m** Go up the chimney, stepping left and up the wall at 10m then step back right into the chimney above the overhang. Continue more easily to belay on the right.

7 **40m 4a** Move left down the rock-strewn ledge to near its end then make difficult moves up to climb a crack near the edge then the edge above.

8 **30m** Continue up the edge above on immaculate rock. Scramble up easily then traverse rightwards above the top of D-Gully to gain *Curved Ridge*.

UPPER TIER

2 Hiccup ★★★   **75m VS 4c**

FA Brian Robertson & Jimmy Houston 24 September 1962

Climbs the steep wall just left of the edge. Start below a prominent crack on Heather Ledge 3m left of the large belay at the start of the traverse on the *North Face Route*.

1 **35m 4c** Climb direct up the crack then the left-most of twin cracks to PB on small ledge.

2 **40m 4c** Move up right and finish up the arête.

NG 227 543 **Alt:** 500m 🏔️ 🚶 1hr

CENTRAL BUTTRESS – SOUTH FACE

An excellent quick drying buttress with the obvious exception of Waterslide Gully.

Approach: Scramble round left from the base of the North Face.

Descent: Easiest by two abseils, first from a large block at the top of *Pontoon* then from the flake on *Pegleg* (slings usually in situ). Alternatively traverse right to gain *Curved Ridge*.

1 Plumbline ★★ **75m VS 4b**

FA Jimmy Stenhouse & Jimmy Marshall June 1962

Good sparsely protected climbing up the rib just left of a shallow grassy depression defining the right edge of the face.

1 35m 4a Ascend a small corner continuing directly to a spike belay.

2 15m 4b Move right and follow a steep crack to belay close to the 'neck' of Waterslide Gully, the line of the watercourse.

3 25m Finish up cracks and the slab above.

2 Waterslide Corner ★★ **70m E1 5b**

FA Dave Jenkins & Ian Fulton August 1970

Start beneath the watercourse.

1 20m 4a Climb by steep red slabs up to the prominent shallow groove.

2 30m 5b Climb straight up the steepening groove. Step right, climb a smaller corner on the right for 3m then step right onto a steep wall. Climb this delicately to finish with a tricky move onto a sloping ledge.

3 20m Finish more easily up a groove above.

3 Pegleg ★★ **90m HVS 5a**

FA Jimmy Marshall & George Ritchie September 1957

Good sparsely protected climbing up the centre of the wall. So named as there may be much standing around on one 'shaky' leg at the crux! Start 7m left of *Waterslide Corner* at a reddish, clean-cut left-slanting rake.

1 20m 4a Climb the left-trending weakness to belay on the second large ledge.

2 35m 5a Go up slightly right on steep, water-worn rock then traverse hard left (crux) above the belay to gain a ledge. Ascend the steep groove above then traverse right to a crack. Climb it to reach the top of a large flake (slings in situ).

3 35m 4a Continue more easily to finish up a steep crack.

4 Pontoon ★★★ **80m E1 5b**

FA Jimmy & Ronnie Marshall & James 'Big Elly' Moriarty April 1959

Another excellent route with two contrasting pitches. Bold and fingery on the first; strenuous and well protected on the second. Start about 12m up left from the base of *Pegleg*.

1 40m 5a Ascend the grey wall on the left side of the grey rib. Move up left to reach a thin crack and climb this to step left to below the main crack.

2 40m 5b Avoid the initial grassy section by a deviation on the left then climb the steep crack for 25m. Continue up a thin crack in the smooth slab (crux) leading to easier ground and the terrace.

5 Gravity and Grace ★★★ **55m E2 5c**

FA Willie Todd & Ian Rae June 1986

Another bold pitch giving good climbing on rough rock up the wall left of *Pontoon*. From the foot of the easy gully just left of *Pontoon* scramble up to a belay on a heather ledge at the foot of a shallow, left-facing corner. Climb the corner and crack above. Move left below a smooth wall and cross this back right, passing a tiny spike to the foot of a steep crack. Climb the crack to gain a left-slanting ramp/groove. Follow this to a break below the final overhang. Cross the overhang and belay in a small corner on the left.

 Curved Ridge. Climbers Malcolm & Karren Smith.

CLIMBS ABOVE 🧗 1¼hr
CROWBERRY BASIN

The large basin below the base of Crowberry Ridge where **Easy Gully** and **Crowberry Gully** diverge.
Approach: Just beyond the **Waterslide** the path zig-zags up the scree before leading out right to the **Crowberry Basin**. From the **Waterslide** climb steeply up on a variety of well worn paths over scree, veering slightly right but keeping to the left side of the stream that runs down over the **Waterslide**. Follow the path to cross the watercourse by a line of good holds rightwards up a slab above an exposed drop into the gully. Further scrambling over one short rock step soon leads to the base of *Curved Ridge*.

CURVED RIDGE

① Curved Ridge ★★★   240m Moderate
FA G.Bennett Gibbs July 1896

A great way up the mountain with grand views of the Rannoch Wall. The base of the ridge proper starts at about 680m. *Curved Ridge* lies almost directly above the Crowberry Basin, separated from the large dome-shaped Rannoch Wall by the mainly scree-filled *Easy Gully* just to its right. The line up the ridge is open to much variation but the best line sticks fairly close to the crest, keeping

out of the side wall of the gully which is a bit loose. If in doubt look for the crampon scratches! About two thirds of the way up the ridge levels out, affording excellent views of the Rannoch Wall and a popular luncheon spot. Above, trend slightly left, a short slabby left-facing corner close to the top marking the last of the difficulties. A large cairn marks the top of the ridge from where loose scree leads up then rightwards into Crowberry Gap, behind the tower. The summit lies less than 10 minutes from here.

CROWBERRY RIDGE

This lies between **Easy Gully** on the left and the deep recesses of **Crowberry Gully** on the right. I reckon it should actually be called Blaeberry Ridge – *"The writer's chief difficulty so far (in reaching the foot of the ridge, has been to get his companion past the clumps of ripe crowberries growing everywhere, and this circumstance has suggested a name for the climb."* – The botanically challenged William Naismith, who made the first ascent of *Naismith's Route* with William Douglas in 1896. Anyone who has tasted crowberries *(Empetrum nigrum)* will concur that he's actually describing blaeberries *(Vaccinium myrtillus)*, also known as whortleberry or bilberry in Scotland, an altogether more enticing approach appetiser.

NG 226 544 **Alt:** 760m   1¼hr

SOUTH EAST FACE – RANNOCH WALL

8

7

6

5

4

3

2

1

9

10

11

12

13

14

Curved Ridge

Abraham's
Ledge

First
Platform

Easy
Gully

The distinctive mass of the Rannoch Wall sweeps round from the broad broken **Crowberry Ridge**, overlooking the upper reaches of **Easy Gully** and *Curved Ridge*. Quick drying and with many superb exposed routes it is perhaps justifiably the most popular cliff in the glen. Apart from the two easiest classics, *Agag's Groove* and *January Jigsaw*, the majority of the routes are fairly bold. Catches the sun until mid afternoon.

Approach: Via scrambling up the lower section of *Curved Ridge* then dropping down into **Easy Gully** to gain the base. The upper section of *Curved Ridge* can also be accessed via a route on **Central Buttress** or **D Gully Buttress**.

Descent: Traverse easy slabs left then continue diagonally leftwards to gain an exposed path traversing left immediately above the top of the cliff with a couple of short steep steps (Moderate) to gain the top of *Curved Ridge* (cairn). Descend this back to the base. Faster alternatives include abseiling down from a nut belay near the top of *Satan's Slit* to the large block belay on *Agag's Groove* (2x 35m), retrieving the gear on a subsequent ascent; or by scrambling right and down *Crowberry Ridge*.

1 Grooved Arête ★★★   80m VS 4b
FA John Cunningham & Bill Smith October 1946

Superb poorly protected climbing up the right edge of the wall. Start at a square-cut groove on the right side of the arête just left of the prominent polished 6m chimney leading up to the First Platform on the North-East Face.

1   **45m 4b** Climb the groove direct on small holds, stepping left and up the arête overlooking *Agag's Groove* at about 20m (possible belay on *Agag's* on left). Traverse back right into the groove (above a more difficult bulging section) and follow this with better protection, trending left to belay beneath a groove.

2   **35m 4b** Climb the exposed groove, soon leading to easier steps slightly rightwards up the broad ridge on immaculate rock.

2 Agag's Groove ★★★★   105m Very Difficult
FA Hamish Hamilton, Alex Anderson & Alex Small August 1936

A well-trodden classic giving spectacular exposed climbing on good holds. It follows the left-curving groove starting from the right edge of the wall, clearly visible from the road. Start at a large rectangular detached block at the extreme right edge of the face.

1   **30m** Climb the crack above the block leading into the groove. Follow this to a huge block belay at the base of a wide crack in the groove.

2   **25m** Continue up the easy ramp above to a large block belay or N & PB on a ledge just above.

3   **30m** Continue in the same line to a sloping shelf leading out left onto the exposed nose. Continue steeply up the cracked groove above on superb incut holds. Move left to a block belay. A stunning pitch.

4   **20m** Move left along the ledge and follow fine cracks on good holds to an abrupt finish.

3 January Jigsaw ★★★   75m Severe 4a
FA Iain Ogilvy & Miss Esme Speakman 10 January 1940

Excellent sustained climbing following a line cutting through *Agag's Groove*. Start from the pinnacle on the ledge midway between *Agag's Groove* and a large semi-detached flake in **Easy Gully**.

1   **20m 4a** Climb a short right-facing square-cut groove then move up and left on large steps to a large flake. Traverse hard right along a ledge to a flake belay directly above the start.

2   **20m** Move right and follow a flake and wall leading to the block belay on *Agag's Groove*.

3   **15m 4a** Step off the top of the block and traverse right (not easy to protect) round the corner into a slanting groove. Follow this into a triangular niche (The Haven) then traverse left and move up to belay next to a metal spike below the overhanging crack of *Satan's Slit*.

4   **20m 4a** Traverse up and right round an edge into a groove. Climb it for a couple of metres then move left and up a steep wall. Either finish direct or by an easier groove on the right.

④ Satan's Slit ★★   **85m VS 4c**

FA Iain Ogilvy & Miss Esme Speakman 5 September 1939

A good counter-diagonal line to *Agag's Groove* crossing
that route at mid-height. Start at the base of the easy
chimney up the left side of the large semi-detached flake
at the base of the wall.

1   **30m 4a** Follow the chimney and steep easy
    ground to some prominent flakes. Traverse
    left 6m then move back rightwards to
    belay immediately above the start.
2   **18m 4b** Climb on small holds for 6m, moving
    slightly left then traverse delicately right
    (quite bold) to belay in *Agag's Groove*.
3   **15m 4a** Follow *Agag's Groove* for 5m then break
    right up a shallow scoop and climb direct to a
    small stance beneath an overhanging crack.
4   **18m 4c** Follow the crack, soon easing after the
    initial 4m, continuing more easily to finish.

⑤ Line Up ★★★   **75m HVS 5a**

FA Con Higgins & Ian Nicolson 1 June 1969

Excellent climbing aiming for the prominent slim corner
high on the face. Start below a prominent narrow overlap
in the centre of the reddish slab.

1   **25m 4c** Climb up to the overlap then straight
    up to the left side of a small hanging slab
    belay. Move up and right to belay ledge.
2   **25m 4c** Climb corner above for 5m, step left and
    continue to belay at the base of the upper corner.
3   **25m 5a** Climb corner and roof direct.

⑥ Whortleberry Wall ★★   **105m HVS 4c**

*FA Pitch 1 John Cunningham & Bill Smith October 1946; John
Cunningham & Bill Smith 16 September 1956*

A bold meandering route. Start at the left side of the slab
a few metres left of *Line Up*.

1   **30m 4c** Move up then trend right, heading for the
    left side of the small hanging slab (common to
    Line Up). Move up and right to belay on ledge.
2   **20m 4c** Traverse horizontally left for 5m
    then gradually upwards to a shallow groove
    which leads to a small juniper ledge.

3   **25m 4c** Traverse horizontally right for a metre
    then make an upward traverse to the groove
    of *Line Up*. Step right round the edge and cross
    the face rightwards to a belay on small ledge.
4   **30m 4b** Climb the crack directly
    above, finishing up easier ground.

⑦ Peasant's Passage ★★   **68m HVS 4c**

FA Willie Rowney & Hamish MacInnes July 1952

Bold climbing up the shallow corner near the left side of
the wall, just before the final pitch of **Easy Gully**.

1   **15m 4c** Ascend the corner for 5m then move
    right onto the rib. Traverse right across
    slabs then along narrow ledge to PB.
2   **18m 4c** Go up round the edge to a steep wall with
    a shallow crack. Climb to the left for a metre then
    follow easier broken rocks to the right to a belay.
3   **35m 4b** Ascend the steep corner on the
    right to a white spike, move onto the rib
    on the right and continue directly.

⑧ Wappenshaw Wall ★★   **70m VS 4b**

*FA Bill Smith & Hamish MacInnes July 1952;
Var. to p 1 Bill Smith & G.McIntosh 5 June 1955*

Good atmospheric climbing. Start up left of *Peasant's
Passage* above the rock pitch in **Easy Gully**, gained from
Curved Ridge.

1   **25m 4b** Climb the right-trending corner until it
    is possible to move down and follow an obvious
    traverse line leading to a block belay.
2   **35m 4b** Move right under a large overhang to a
    rib, go straight up under a small overhang then left
    past a detached block. Follow the steep grooves
    above moving left onto a shelf. Where it broadens
    follow the prominent fault to right to a belay.
3   **10m 4a** Move back left and finish up a short wall.

Curved Ridge

Upper Ledge

Abraham's Ledge

APPROACH

Easy Gully

CROWBERRY RIDGE, NORTH-EAST FACE

All the routes start from the First Platform, a terrace reached by a short polished chimney (Difficult) leading from **Easy Gully** to its left end.

Descent: For the first 5 routes, descend as for the **Rannoch Wall**. Alternatively abseil back down the wall (25m from in situ sling & maillon on spike at top of second pitch of *Fracture Route*).

9 Symposium ★★ 70m E2 5c

FA Andy Tibbs, Dave Hainsworth & Alan Winton 4 May 1985

A good sustained pitch up the thin cracks just left of the more prominent *Engineer's Crack*.

1 **30m 5c** Climb cracks directly, moving left at the top just above a small overlap. Continue up easier ground to belay on the right.

2 **40m** Finish up *Fracture Route*.

10 Engineer's Crack ★★ 65m E1 5b

FA Hamish MacInnes, Charlie Vigano & Bob Hope September 1951; FFA Kenny Spence 1960s

The fine crack 5m left of *Fracture Route* gives a good sustained pitch.

1 **25m 5b** Climb the crack to a small ledge, continuing up the thin crack above to traverse right to the belay at the top of the main pitch on *Fracture Route*.

2 **40m** Finish as for *Fracture Route*.

11 Fracture Route ★★ 65m VS 4c

FA Kenny Copland & Bill Smith October 1946

Start at a pillar lying against the wall.

1 **15m** Easily up the pillar to a belay.

2 **10m 4c** Go up the left-most V-crack then with more difficultly past two mantelshelf moves to a belay.

3 **40m** Traverse left round the edge and follow a crack left of the nose.

12 Dingle ★★ 35m HVS 5a

FA Dougal Haston & James Stenhouse September 1958

Sustained well protected climbing up the prominent corner.

1 **10m** Follow a narrow wall to belay beneath the corner.

2 **25m 5a** The corner, finishing by easier slabs on the ridge.

13 The Orphan *   35m VS 4c

FA Colin Read, Colwyn Jones & Geoff Swainbank 3 Sept 2000

The prominent left-facing corner right of *Dingle*. Climb the corner crack until it abuts a small overhang, pull out left and go up until a step right to a ledge. Climb crack pulling out right to avoid a loose block then directly up a short wall. Either finish up *Direct Route* or abseil off.

14 Direct Route **   237m Severe 4a

FA George & Ashley Abraham, Jim Puttrell and Ernest Baker May 1900

"Forty feet of boulder climbing – not justifiable by the ordinary run of climbers" – SMC members after a failed attempt in 1905. *"George Abraham led up in brilliant style. Anxiously we watched him quit the platform, stepping out upon a tiny ledge with his left toe, and, moving cautiously leftward and gradually up, disappear from our sight. The rope went out by inches, and we waited in dead silence for a shout to say that the distant platform was won. The shout was a long time coming"* – Ernest Baker, *The Highlands with Rope and Rucksack*, 1923
A remarkable lead at the time. The crucial second pitch is much harder – out of character with the rest of the climb. Start about 10m from the right end of the First Platform.

1   **20m** Up left-facing grooves and a crack in the wall above which leads to Abraham's Ledge.

2a   **12m 4a** The crux. Move left round the rib and up past two polished foot-holds to enter a smooth scoop. Move up this slightly rightwards to better holds and continue to belay on the Upper Ledge.

2b   **30m** There are numerous variations out right avoiding the main challenge: **Greig's Ledge**, Difficult, climbs up from the right end of Abraham's Ledge for a short way to traverse right into an open corner. Make an awkward move traversing right round the right edge to gain the ledge. Make a rising traverse left from the far end of the ledge to gain the Upper Ledge.

3   **30m** From left side of ledge climb steeply to belay on a shelf where the angle eases.

4   **25m** Move left to the crest and up to a belay at the top of the right side of the Rannoch Wall.

Continue much more easily up broken ground then by a narrow ridge to the base of Crowberry Tower (110m). Climb this easily by an obvious line on its north side (40m). The easiest descent is by a spiralling line down ledges on its west flank leading into Tower Gap. The summit lies less than 10 minutes up the slope from here.

SOUTH-EAST FACE OF STOB DEARG   ⚓   20min

Much quieter (and sunnier) than the more frequented cliffs on the north-east side of the mountain.
Access: Drive down the single track road down Glen Etive and park on the left after 0.9 miles/1.5km, or at a long lay-by on the left (south-east) side of the road, 0.5 miles/0.8km further on, directly beneath *The Chasm*.

Approach: Direct up the hillside from the road to the lower reaches of *The Chasm*.
Descent: From the top of *The Chasm* traverse left and descend slopes south-east into Glen Etive, easiest further left. For other routes either go over the summit and down the path via Coire na Tulaich or traverse right and descend *Curved Ridge* and the lower reaches of **Easy Gully**, heading south from just above the Waterslide across the moor back to Glen Etive.

1 The Chasm ****   450m VS 4c

FA R.Stobart, Noel & Mrs Odell 13 April 1920 (partial winter ascent); Direct Finish Ian Jack & JG Robinson 30 August 1931

"A grand day of strenuous rock work in magnificent surroundings." – Jim Bell

The prominent stepped gully cleaving the south-east face of Stob Dearg some 1.5km down Glen Etive beyond Coupall Bridge. Flanked by shorter, easier and less distinct gullies on either side it is one of the longest and best gullies (and routes!) in the country, mainly on good clean rock. It retains its hardest pitches to the end; the exit out of the Devil's Cauldron. The first climbing starts about 20 minutes above the road at NG 227 536, about 370m. The route follows in general the line of the watercourse with obvious route finding for most of the way. A selection of the most interesting pitches includes:

5 **25m** The Red Slab. Start up a shallow scoop on the left wall close to the watercourse. Climb the slab (loose and poorly protected) trending out right at the top. Belay further back.

6 A huge chokestone (dislodged in July 1976!) blocks the way. Bypass this by the corner on the right wall.

8 **30m** The 100 foot pitch. A huge dyke now crosses the gully. Climb the steep clean wall 6m right of the main watercourse on good holds and immaculate rock. An excellent pitch.

9 **15m 4a** The Piano Pitch. Step down and cross the watercourse to the left wall. Move up for few metres then make a right traverse *"above a small but beckoning pool"*, ending by a difficult move onto a sloping chokestone.

10 **25m 4c** The Converging Walls. The gully now narrows to less than 2m. Scramble up easy steps right of the watercourse to a large ledge beneath the clean smooth walls. Follow a line of holds up and left on the left wall to stand on top of large chokestone then bridge both walls towards the back of the gully. Large boulder belay further back. An exhilarating pitch.

11 **20m** Above, another huge chokestone bars the way. Bypass this on the right by a line of good holds starting close to the back.

12-14 A number of short easier pitches lead obviously to the main fare:

15 **18m** The Devil's Cauldron. Climb directly up the watercourse to belay in a cave.

16 **22m 4c** Chimney well out from the cave heading for a prominent foothold on the right wall. Gain and pass two small chokestones about 3m apart where back and foot work or straddling leads to a gradual easing in the difficulties. Approximately 300m of scrambling leads to the summit ridge and a short stroll to the summit itself.

1a The South Wall of the Chasm ★★   30m VS 4b
FA Jim Bell, Colin Allan & Miss Violet Roy June 1934

The easiest (i.e. driest!) finish out of The Devil's Cauldron. The technical grade is Severe 4a but the finish is normally damp and graded accordingly. Start on the left wall at a chimney. Climb this to a runner at 6m then make very awkward moves to gain a ledge on the right wall. Traverse right round the edge onto a broad ledge then follow the easiest line to finish.

2 The Chasm to Crowberry Traverse ★
1000m Moderate
FA George Tertius Glover & Collinson 10 April 1898

A natural slanting line sweeping across the South-East Face. The line starts beneath the first steep wall on the north (right) side of *The Chasm* where a well marked path shows the way. This leads past scree slopes to pass underneath an impressive undercut wall on the left about halfway along. Move out right round the corner at a steepening and cross the top of the left fork of Lady's Gully, coming up from the right. Continue up smooth, often wet rock then go up a rounded broken rib to the right of a wet groove. Continue slightly right up a shallow recess then up scree slopes fairly directly to gain the large cairn at the top of *Curved Ridge*.

NN 217 553 **Alt:** 430m

CREAG A' BHANCAIR

30min

" ... VERTICAL AND BULGING IN GREAT PORPHORYTIC WALLS OF APPARENT IMPREGNABILITY. "
– Jimmy Marshall, *Hard Rock*, 1974

DESCENT

DESCE

Tunnel Wall

An extensive low lying cliff with a collection of extremes. It is the most accessible mountain cliff in Scotland (aside from the practically roadside crags above the Bealach na Ba in Applecross). All the worthwhile routes are in the extremes – the cliff contains the highest concentration of hard climbing in the glen. The Tunnel Wall usually stays dry most of the summer, though the upper section of the main cliff can weep for a few days after prolonged rain.

Approach: Follow the path from Alltnafeadh crossing the River Coupall by a footbridge then by the side of Lagangarbh Cottage and up into Coire na Tulaich. After about 1km break off right from the path (by some large boulders) and cut across the wide rocky (usually dry) stream bed to pick up a path which cuts underneath the base of a number of small outcrops. Continue up this to arrive at the right end of The Tunnel Wall.

Descent: From the top of the cliff traverse right (south-west) on rough slabs then continue to gain some shallow vague gullies. Descend these and traverse back east to the base of the cliff.

Routes are described as approached, first from *The Risk Business* going right then left from that route.

❶ The Risk Business ★★★   100m E5 6a

FA Pitches 1 & 2 Pete Whillance & Ray Parker 28 & 29 May 1980; Pitches 3 & 4 Pete Whillance & Pete Botterill 24 August 1980

A grand route with three varied pitches starting up the prominent leftward-slanting fault bounding the right margin of The Tunnel Wall. Start at a large rowan tree beneath the line.

1 **25m 6a** Move up left to a small ledge and poor protruding PR. Move up to a good F #2 placement under the overlap. From the PR traverse left 3m then make difficult moves up and left to reach better holds. Continue up on widely spaced holds until a short traverse left leads to a ledge and PB at the base of a prominent groove.

2 **15m 5c** Climb the groove boldly to grass ledges then easily up right to the PB below *Carnivore Direct.*

3 **30m 6a** Walk 6m left along the ledge and up a short wall to a ledge below a small overhang. Take

THE TUNNEL WALL

In the centre of the crag is an extensive dome-shaped overhanging pink wall so called due to its supposed resemblance to the side walls of a railway tunnel. Here are to be found the only bolted sport routes on any mountain cliff in the UK. The sport routes are all long sustained tests of stamina; all except the routes at either end require a 60m rope and around a dozen quickdraws.

❸ Up With the Sun ★★★   100m E7 6b

FA Grant Farquhar & Gary Latter 29 July 1991

A direct uncompromising line filling the obvious gap cutting through *The Risk Business*. Start 6m down left from the tree at a prominent triangular foot hold.

1 **50m 6b** Go leftwards and up on cleaned edges to a thin crack. Make difficult moves through bulge right-wards to better holds and up rightwards to the PR on *TRB*. Along this to just before the belay and up a shallow groove in the arête past overlaps to pull

the overhang on its left and climb a short groove to where it ends at another small overhang. Pull over this and up to a ledge. Climb the shallow groove-line above to a grass ledge and belay.

4 **30m 4b** Continue up in the same line to the top.

❷ Walk With Destiny ★★   100m E2 5b

FA Dave Cuthbertson & Dougie Mullin 28 May 1978

Good sustained climbing up the central crack and wall above. Start at the base of a slim groove.

1 **40m 5b** Follow the groove until it is possible to gain a crack system by a left traverse. Follow this with a slight deviation on the left and continue to a ledge and belay. Walk left a little to the right end of the *Carnivore* traverse.

2 **18m 5b** Climb the wall and bulge to a horizontal break. Cross the bulge above and continue to a ledge and belay.

3 **42m 5a** Climb the shallow groove above then continue up the wall above to a ledge and belay. Easily to the top.

onto the capping wall with difficulty. Continue directly to join the belay below *Carnivore Direct Finish*. Note: the lower section of this pitch was climbed after top-rope practise then led using three ropes.

2 **20m 6b** Move out leftwards above the belay to a prominent undercling and climb directly through this with difficulty to gain a mysterious old in situ thread. Step left and directly to a roof and protection. Traverse diagonally leftwards to share the belay at the top of the third pitch of *TRB*.

3 **30m 4b** Easily to the top.

❹ Symbiosis ★★★   35m E8 6b

FA Paul Thorburn & Dave Cuthbertson (both led) 11 September 1995

The shallow groove system right of 5. Very serious in its lower half, sustained with difficult but sound protection above – a comprehensive selection of micro wires is required. Start below an undercut left-trending flake-line above a rocky ramp. Follow the undercuts then move up past a poor skyhook. Move up left then back right to gain better protection in a flake. Traverse left to near 5 then follow the faint crack-line to the bulge guarding entrance to the scoop. Gain this then exit right and move up to follow 1 to the stance.

5 Uncertain Emotions ★★★   25m F7b
FA Dave Cuthbertson June 1986; retro-bolted 1995

Follows a line of scoops bounding the right edge of wall. Start at a small flat boulder at the far right end of the wall just before the cliff starts to slope up to the right. Pull over the initial block overhang and climb steadily up the shallow groove to an overlap. Move slightly right to gain a small but positive hold. Continue up and rightwards on improving holds to a second overlap. Pull over this using a good ramp hold and continue to a good shake-out beneath the top bulge. Climb up and rightwards into the middle of the wall above the bulge to finish abruptly at a LO.

6 The Railway Children ★★★   27m F7c
FA Dave Cuthbertson 3 July 1987; retro-bolted 1995

Excellent climbing up the right edge of the upper wall with a short technical section. Gain the shake-out in the top recess on 5 just before that route breaks out right. Hand traverse left on a slightly descending break then climb the hard wall on side-pulls and pinches to gain better holds. Easier climbing soon leads to a LO.

7 The Tribeswoman ★★★   30m F7c+
FA Paul Laughlan summer 1990; retro-bolted 2001

Essentially a long direct start to 6, making it independent of 5. Start beneath the prominent right-trending hand-rail. Climb up on undercuts to the left end of the hand-rail and follow a direct line to finish up the crux wall of 6.

8 Fated Path ★★★★   30m F7c+
FA Graeme Livingston July 1986 ; retro-bolted 1998

An outstanding pitch direct up the centre of the wall. Start in the middle of the wall at the left side of a block in the initial roof. Move left from the block and then

directly up until it is possible to swing right into a shallow groove. Traverse rightwards to a small overlap with good holds above. Climb the wall above past three obvious horizontal breaks which cross the wall at about 7m intervals with hard moves past the third break. Continue more easily up the final less overhanging headwall to a LO.

9 Admission ★★★   30m F7c+
FA Graeme Livingston 20 June 1987; retro-bolted 1998

A parallel line just left of 8 giving more powerful climbing. Start under a small bulge about 6m left of 8. Climb up to a small ledge then rightwards through the bulge to gain a stopping place. Climb the wall above to reach the left end of a small overhang. Move rightwards underneath it and surmount it on large undercuts. Attain a standing position on a small ledge then using a prominent undercut move rightwards then back left to a LO.

10 Axiom ★★★   30m F8a
FA Dave MacLeod (redpointed) May 2004

A brilliant parallel line left of 9. Start up 11 to the second bolt then break off rightward with increasing difficulty to a hard section on sidepulls to gain good edges in a vague niche (technical crux). More sustained climbing leads through the bulge to a decent rest. Move up then rightward to another difficult section, finishing slightly easier.

11 The Third Eye ★★★   25m F7c
FA Dave MacLeod (redpointed) May 2004

Superb technical climbing up the pale wall and bulge up the left side. Start just right of a small cave. Difficult climbing leads to a boss and rest. A thin sustained section up the pale wall gains a line of good holds below the bulge, which is crossed on good holds to a good rest. The final black wall is breached using small crimps leading to a LO at the big horizontal.

12 Tunnel Vision ★★★   30m E4 6a
FA Gary Latter & Paul Thorburn 4 September 1995

Traverse the prominent break from the belays of 16 to 1. Fine positions and very well-protected.

Fated Path, Graeme Livingston on an early repeat of his own route.

13 Romantic Reality ★★★   **100m E7 6b**

FA Pitch 1 Pete Whillance & Derek Jamieson 31 July 1980;
Pitches 2 & 3 Dave Cuthbertson & Kev Howett May 1984

A stunning route, the main pitch breaching the pale wall
dominating the upper left side of the cliff. Start 15m right
of *Le Monde* and just left of The Tunnel Wall.

  1 25m 6a Up a short steep wall to a ledge at 5m.
      Continue up to a little block and move left to a
      ramp then up an overhang barrier, pulling over into
      a prominent rightwards-slanting crack. Follow the
      crack and where it ends climb steeply over a bulge
      and up to the grass ledge and PB on *Carnivore*.

  2 25m 6b Up a short wall to a slab beneath the
      overhang. Pull over this on sloping holds to a
      short diagonal crack and protection. Move left
      and up a groove to an overlap. Pull out right and
      ascend blindly to a 'thank God' hold. Up over a
      bulge to belay at the left end of a cleaned ledge.

  3 50m 5b From the right end of the ledge
      pull rightwards onto the wall and
      ascend this to easier ground. Finish up a
      right trending ledge and mossy rock.

14 Le Monde ★   **50m E4 5c**

FA Nick Colton & Willie Todd (on-sight) 4 June 1976

Of historical interest. A very bold on-sight effort. Start
20m right of 16 at a groove beside a small pedestal.

  1 25m 5c Climb groove until it fades, traverse right
      to shallow scoop, climb the scoop and bulge,
      step left then go straight up to the PBs on **16**.

  2 25m 5a Follow the leftward-slanting ramp/
      fault to a PB below roof. Abseil descent.

15 Twilight Zone ★★   **40m E5 6a**

FA Graeme Livingston & Alastair Ross 20 June 1987

A bold single pitch climbing a weakness in the wall left
of 14 to finish up an obvious cleaned white streak. Start
beneath a small bulge below a gap in the overhang.
Climb the groove boldly to a serious section through the
bulge (R #2) then join 16. Climb the steep wall above to
gain the top of the *Le Monde* ramp. Climb directly up from
here until it is possible to hand traverse right on spikes
to the bottom of the white streak. Ascend the wall above
directly with some technical moves at the top then climb
the slab above to an in situ PB. Abseil descent.

16 **Carnivore** ★★★   **170m E2 5c**

FA John Cunningham & Mick Noon (some aid) 9 August 1958;
Direct (Villains) Finish Don Whillans & Derek Walker 13 June 1962

The first route to breach the main wall, and then only after several attempts by many of the leading climbers of the day. It follows a rising rightward traverse line amidst impressive surroundings. Start about 10m down right from the left end of the cliff, at a bulge beneath a right-trending weakness.

1 **40m 5b** Pull over the bulge and move up rightwards on good holds to a well-hidden thread runner. Continue up by a vague groove to a small ledge and PR at the start of the traverse. Climb down rightwards to gain a line of better holds and follow the fault more easily rightwards to a shelf which leads to a point beneath a long ledge. Climb up steeply onto the ledge then walk right to a PB at the end of the ledge. It is wise to protect the second by back-roping from the PR at the start of the traverse (karabiner often in situ).

2 **20m 4b** Climb the slabby green scoop on the right to a ledge.

3 **20m 5a** Climb over ledges and an obvious line of weakness to a right slanting crack. Climb this to belay on small shelf beneath overhanging black recess.

4 **40m 5c** Climb up into the recess, up this and the layback crack above which leads to the base of a slim groove. Stand in this with difficulty then continue easily to a ledge.

5 **50m** Continue easily past some ledges to the top.

16a **Original Finish** ★★   **110m E3 6a**

FA John Cunningham & Mick Noon (some aid) 9 August 1958;
FFA S.Wilson & T.Marr Easter 1969

4 **20m 6a** Traverse right across the slab, take a horizontal crack beneath overhangs and at 6m climb the overhang. Continue right with difficulty to gain a sloping ledge. Follow this to a small cave and PB.

5 **15m 5c** Continue traversing right on often wet underclings to a large grass ledge and belay.

6 **25m 4c** Traverse left and up for 9m, move left under a bulge and across to a grass ledge then up the wall to a small ledge and belay.

7 **35m** Climb straight up to a large grass ledge.

8 **15m** Climb the wall above to belay beneath a large boulder.

Nearing the end of the difficulties on the first pitch of Carnivore. Photo Dave Simmonite.

📷 *Snickers Boy, North-West Face, Gearr Aonach with Aonach Eagach in the background. Karen Latter climbing.*

THE THREE SISTERS AREA

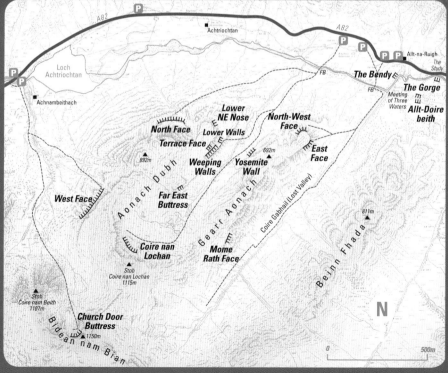

ROADSIDE CRAGS

NN 182 563 **Alt:** 250m
2min

GLEN COE GORGE

About 100m downstream from the waterfall that flows from the Allt Lairig Eilde into the River Coe near the top of the glen. The climbing is on the steep crag facing the road, due south of The Study.

Access: Park at a small parking bay just south of The Study on the north side of the road, or in the lay-by on the south side overlooking the waterfall 100m further east.

Approach: Scramble down easy rocks and jump across the river about 50m downstream from the prominent crack of *Chariots of Fire*.

Descent: Abseil from trees at the top of the crag.

1 Chariots of Fire ★   **40m E1 5a**

FA Martin Lawrence & Rab Anderson 26 June 1981

The widening crack. Near the top climb the wall on the left. Tree belay far back.

2 Delusions of Grandeur ★   **35m E2 5c**

FA Andy Tibbs & G.Jones 8 May 1988

Left of 1 is a thinner steeper crack. Follow this to exit right to a wide ledge at 20m (possible belay). Finish up the corner crack and easier ground above.

THE BENDY

The steep wall overlooking the pool where the River Coe bends shortly before The Meeting of Three Waters. It is very sheltered, fast drying, and must be one of the most accessible crags in the Highlands. After prolonged wet spells the bottom of the routes are often saturated with spray from the waterfall but the routes remain climbable. On first appearances the crag is smooth and holdless, split into two adjoining walls by a vegetated groove. The right wall is just off vertical whilst the left gently overhangs.

Access: There is limited parking for a couple of cars on the north side of the A82 at Allt-na-ruigh (NN 175 566), the white cottage on the north side of the A82 opposite Beinn Fhada – the eastmost of the Three Sisters.

Approach: Descend the left (east) bank of the Allt-na-

NN 175 565 **Alt:** 160m
5min

ruigh to scramble down to the base of the cliff.

Descent: Abseil from trees at the top or walk left (south) about 50m and scramble down and back up the riverbank.

> The obvious cleaned line up the left side of the crag is *Jim'll Fix It* ★ E2 5b.

1 The Roaring Silence ★★   **20m E4 6a**

FA Kevin Howett & Mark Charlton 7 April 1987

The best pitch on the crag giving reasonably well protected climbing up a series of thin incipient cracks running up the left edge of the crag. Start below the left end of a long low ledge system at 6m. Up past a good side-pull on the left to gain holds at the left end of the ledge. Step right and direct up a wall past a bulge to eventually

ALLT DOIRE-BHEITH 🅂 🔷 🔷   10min
(STREAM OF THE BIRCH GROVE)

NN 179 562 **Alt:** 250m

The hidden gorge on the lower slopes of Beinn Fhada above The Meeting of Three Waters. The main crag is a long slightly slabby wall facing away from the road. With the exception of *Squirrel's Crack*, an extra rope is required for a satisfactory belay to the boulders 50m further back.

Access: Park where the old road leaves The Study at NN 179 565 or further east as for Glen Coe Gorge.

Approach: Drop down the hillside to cross the River Coe then head due south for 300m to the top of the crag.

Descent: Down either side of the crag.

1 Sweltering ★   **20m E3 5c**

FA Gary Latter & Paul Farrell 19 July 1987

A direct line through the roof at its widest point left of the central crack. Climb an easy stepped corner and up to the roof. Undercut this leftwards to good holds. Step right round the bulge and make a long reach to the next break. Climb directly to the top.

2 Squirrel's Crack ★   **20m HVS 5a**

FA probably The Squirrels 1960s

The central crack. Belay close to the edge at the top.

reach good F #0.5 or #1 placement in a diagonal crack on the left. Pull over a second bulge rightwards to a good stopping place and finish up a short technical wall.

2 In Seine ★★   **25m E3 5c**

FA Mark Charlton & Kev Howett 8 April 1987

Climbs an obvious natural line up the right side of the left wall. Strenuous and well protected on good holds. Start at the base of the central vegetated ramp. Up this for a few feet then break out left and up a thin crack-line to gain the right side of the long ledge system. Step right and up the wall on good holds to reach a triangular niche. Move diagonally right to the wall to good holds beneath an arching overlap. Pull over this slightly leftwards to finish past a good spike just below the top.

3 The Smouldering ★   **25m E4 6a**

FA Gary Latter 16 June 1987

Start to the right of the central crack just left of a steep smooth slab. Up to good footholds and undercuts, pull right onto a slab with difficulty and continue boldly to twin breaks. Step right at the break and up to a diagonal line of holds and a good nut crack. Pull out slightly right and up to finish.

4 Neeh ★   **20m E1 5a**

FA Gary Latter, Paul Thorburn & Paul McNally 9 June 1995

At the right end of the crag are a cleaned slab and a very shallow left-facing groove. Up the slab or the easier groove then the wall direct to a good break. Direct above past another break to finish easily.

> A small leaning wall low down on the south side of the gorge catches the evening sun and contains four micro-routes from E1 – 2. *Sin Nombre* ★ E1 5b takes the well protected groove and thin crack on the right.

5 Inertia ★   **10m HVS 5a**

FA Davy Gunn & Mark Tennant May 1997

Further up the gorge is a steep wall high up in the trees with a deep crack hidden by a birch tree. Well protected climbing up the crack leads to a birch tree and the top.

GEARR AONACH

The Bidean nam Bian massif throws out three long blunt ridges to the north, popularly dubbed 'the three sisters of Glen Coe'. Beinn Fhada, Gearr Aonach and Aonach Dubh, become progressively steeper, rockier and more impressive from east to west.

The varied cliffs of both Gearr Aonach and Aonach Dubh contain the most accessible easy to mid grade mountain routes in Scotland (excepting the handful of routes on the practically roadside crags above the Bealach na Ba in Applecross).

Access: Park at the upper (eastmost) of the two main car parks on the south side of the road.

NN 166 561 **Alt:** 460m

50min

NORTH FACE

An atmospheric cliff with fine exposed situations.

Approach: Cross the River Coe by the eastmost of the two bridges and follow a well worn path towards The Lost Valley. Break off up right on a more broken path about 100 metres beyond a stile just before the path starts to level out. Follow this, breaking off right again about 100 metres before a large 5m high boulder. A vague path leads up slightly leftwards to the base of the zigzags then bears right along a wide grassy shelf until the face comes into view. Head more steeply directly up to the base.

Descent: Down the zig-zags, an obvious scree-filled path running beneath steep cliffs on the north-east nose of the hill with a couple of easy rocky steps about halfway down.

① Preamble ★★   170m Severe 4a

FA Jimmy Marshall, Len Lovat & George Ritchie May 1957

Good climbing up the left side of the face with an excellent main pitch making up for a scruffy approach. Start below a grey tongue of rock 12m left of a pointed boulder.

1 **30m** Climb rock then vegetation to belay in a grass niche below a short V-chimney.

2 **40m 4a** Climb the awkward chimney then trend right and follow cleaner rock to the ledge beneath the rhyolite band.

3 **30m 4a** Follow the superb black stained groove to a belay.

4 **30m 4a** Continue up the groove to a slabby ledge. Move left along this into a chimney and follow this to a large ledge on the right.

5 **40m** Walk right and follow a line up the wall 10m right of the chimney to finish.

NORTH-WEST FACE

The following routes all start from the girdling ledge delineating the transition from the lower augite-andesite to the wonderful pink rhyolite.

Approach: Scramble up to a small isolated rowan on the left. Traverse grass and rock rightwards to a tree belay on the far right (50m). Make a short steep step up then trend diagonally left to gain the right end of the ledge system (40m). On first acquaintance it may be prudent to rope up for the approach – about Very Difficult, but quite vegetatious and often wet.

② Snickers Boy ★★   80m VS 4c

FA Roger Palin, Scott Muir, Gary Latter & Darren McAuley 18 June 2000

A good direct line up the clean right side of the face, drying much faster than *Marathon Man*. Start beneath a shallow left-facing groove 6m left of the right end of the ledge.

1 40m 4b Climb a direct line following the general line of the groove, moving slightly right for protection before returning left to climb direct to belay on a large grass ledge. An excellent pitch.

2 40m 4c Climb direct above the belay to gain the right end of a left-slanting ramp and follow this with a tricky move moving up onto the rib at its end. Continue up, escaping right into the VDiff. grooves of *Meander* and finish up this.

③ Marathon Man ★★   95m HS 4b

FA Aysel & Ken Crocket May 1978

Start at the right end of a low belt of overhangs, at the base of the black streaked wall. Thread and nut belay in right side of the rounded bowl on *The Walk*.

1 45m 4b Climb straight up by grooves and cavities to a ledge. A fantastic pitch, though slow to dry.

2 38m 4a About 10m above is an open left-trending gully with a rib of steep, clean rock on its left. Climb up to the rib, step onto it from the left and follow it directly on perfect rock to a ledge and flake belay.

3 12m – Step left and climb the awkward wall above to easier ground. Scramble to finish.

④ The Walk ★★★   85m Very Difficult

FA Jimmy & Ronnie Marshall May 1957

Start at the same point as *Marathon Man*.

1 45m Climb diagonally leftwards on the lip of the overhangs into a rounded bowl. Continue diagonally leftwards following an obvious line of holds then trend slightly rightwards to belay on large grass ledge. An immaculate pitch.

2 40m Move out left and follow a left-trending line to finish up broken ground.

⑤ The Prowl ★★   75m Severe 4a

FA Dougal Haston & Jimmy Marshall March 1959

Make an exposed scramble left along the narrow grass ledge from the base of the above routes past a bulge in the overhangs (crawl) to a prominent recess 9m beyond a large rowan.

1 30m 4a Climb the short steep open chimney to a small bay. Leave the bay by a crack on the left and follow this to belay on a grass ledge on the right. A direct line directly above the start can be followed at the same grade on good clean rock.

2 45m 4a Continue directly up the wall above on good holds just right of a vegetated crack, finishing just left of another short crack further right.

⑥ The Cheek ★★   95m Severe 4a

FA Hamish & Mrs M MacInnes Summer 1968

1 30m 4a Climb *The Prowl* to the small bay. Move left round the steep corner then go diagonally left to a small ledge on the edge of the wall. Traverse round left horizontally then down to a groove. Climb this to a block.

2 20m 4a Climb the chimney above directly to a ledge.

3 45m – Finish more easily up a wall of fine rock on the left.

NN 167 559 **Alt:** 440m

EAST FACE 40min

A varied cliff extending left from the Zig-Zags to just before a large stone shoot which descends into the large boulder field just before the head of The Lost Valley.

Approach: As for the North Face to pick up the path leading up to the base of the Zig-Zags then contour left to gain the right end of the cliff.

Descent: Either abseil from trees or walk off right and down the Zig-Zags, the prominent well-worn path containing a few easy scrambling sections about halfway down.

1 Hairy Kipper ** 58m Very Difficult

FA Alistair 'Bugs' McKeith April 1966

Good well protected climbing with fine positions. Start a few metres along the first zig just left of a roof. Scramble up a shelf leading left to a crack on the right wall at 6m.

1 35m Climb the crack, traverse right and slightly up for 10m on good ledges. Move back leftwards up cracks to a ledge below a block recess.

2 23m Move up rightwards then climb the open fault to belay at a rowan in a small recess.

2 Harebell Wall * 45m Severe 4a

FA Gary Latter & Margaret King 28 August 1999

Another fine well protected pitch. Start up the short vertical crack 6m left of *Hairy Kipper*. Climb the crack then move leftwards and up on good holds, veering slightly right to prominent crack in headwall. Climb this which leads into a short left-facing groove. Exit either directly or steeply rightwards then direct to belay on birch tree.

3 High Flying * 75m Very Difficult

FA Alistair 'Bugs' McKeith 30 April 1966

Start at the lowest buttress a few metres left of the start of the Zig-Zags, separated from the main face by a wide shelf.

1 30m Climb the small buttress, walk back to belay in a short corner. Alternatively scramble up the shelf as for *Hairy Kipper*.

2 45m Climb a cracked wall to a ledge beneath a prominent cube of rock (possible belay). Continue up the steep wall just right of the cube on good holds to a tree belay on the terrace.

4 Eyes of Mica ★★   30m E4 6a

FA Andy Nelson & Kev Howett 17 June 1988

Start up the wall just right of the diagonal fault of *Marshall's Wall* about 50m up left from the start of the Zig-Zags. Climb the wall to a horizontal crack. Pull over a bulge and then go left into the pink scoop of *Marshall's Wall* (PR). Climb the thin crack and wall above to the right end of the final steep wall with a long reach to better holds. Abseil descent from in situ ring peg.

5 Marshall's Wall ★   80m E2 5b

FA Robin Smith & George Ritchie May 1960

A good though wandering route following a natural weakness up the crag. Start just right of an overhung recess.

1 **20m 5b** Gain and follow thin cracks leading up left to steeper rock. Move out right above the bulge. Step down to a cramped P & NB in a small recess.

2 **20m 5b** Traverse right 3m then up onto a ledge. Traverse right (quite bold) for 3m to a small ledge. Move up then back left to P & NB on grass ledge.

3 **40m 4c** Move left and climb to ledges, finishing by a short steep corner.

6 Via Dolorosa ★★   100m HVS 5a

FA Brian Robertson & Bugs McKeith 23 May 1964

Start at the base of the wide crack, which lies just left of a yellowish recess.

1 **50m 5a** Ascend the crack to overhangs (possible belay) then traverse left 6m. Continue directly for about 15m then move back right to belay.

2 **10m 5a** Move right to a belay.

3 **40m 4b** Ascend the wall above, finish up a short crack.

7 The Mappie ★★   85m VS 4c

FA James Moriarty & Jimmy Marshall April 1959

Start beneath a clean thin crack 5m left of a wide crack.

1 **45m 4c** Climb up to just beneath the left end of the roof then traverse diagonally left for 12m to a small ledge. Go directly up thin cracks then back rightwards to a stance and spike belay above the start. It is more difficult to leave the traverse line sooner.

2 **40m** Continue more easily directly up the wall. Belay far back.

8 Herbal Mixture ★   70m HS 4b

FA Jimmy & Ronnie Marshall & George Ritchie September 1957

Good climbing despite the name. Start beneath the left end of the overhangs about 10m left of a wide diagonal crack.

1 **30m 4b** Climb heather grooves up and left to a ledge at 15m. Continue up and left to a good ledge in a corner.

2 **40m 4b** Move up slightly right to a ledge at 12m then up and left across the final steep wall (poorly protected) finishing on easier ground.

High Flying. Catherine Sibley climbing.

> *"Twas brillig, and the slithy toves*
> *Did gyre and gimble in the wabe:*
> *All mimsy were the borogroves,*
> *And the mome raths outgrabe.*
> *"Beware the Jabberwock, my son! ... "*
> from *Jabberwocky* – Lewis Carroll

NG 162 554 **Alt:** 550m

1¼hr

MOME RATH FACE

A large impressive face in a delightful situation overlooking the upper reaches of Coire Gabhail (Corrie of the Booty, but more commonly known as The Lost Valley). The face takes a lot of drainage but is well worth a visit after a period of dry weather. The face can also be used to provide a useful approach to the routes on Stob Coire nan Lochan (35 minutes) or Far Eastern Buttress on Aonach Dubh (about 20 minutes).

Approach: Cross the River Coe by the eastmost of the two bridges and follow a well worn (very popular with the touroids) path up into Coire Gabhail. Head across the flat grass and screes to pick up the path again and follow this for 100m then head diagonally left up the hillside then by easy scrambling up the lower reaches of the left-slanting Lost Leeper Gully to gain the left end of the lower cliff. The main face can be gained by continuing scrambling up the gully at about Moderate.

Descent: Scramble back from the cliff to reach easy ground then walk a long way left to reach easy angled slopes beyond a large open gully. Descend to join the well-worn path close to the west bank of the Allt Coire Gabhail.

LOWER CRAG

Right of the open Lost Leeper Gully. From the top of the routes scramble up the right-slanting fault for 70m to the grassy terrace at the base of the main face. All the routes lead to a belay on a small rowan towards the left end of the grass ledge at the top.

1 Slimcrack * 45m Severe 4b
FA Ian Clough & C.Slesser 17 October 1965

The prominent diagonal crack near the centre of the wall. Follow the crack with difficult moves on the right wall at mid-height (overhead protection at this point) leading to tree belay on the left

2 The Burning * 50m E1 5a
FA Andy Tibbs & S.Cameron 12 May 1990

Start midway between 1 and the left edge of the large brown streak. Climb the wall directly (possible belay at 25m), continuing more easily up the upper wall.

3 Batura Wall * 50m HVS 5a
FA Andy Tibbs & H.Shannon 2 July 1989

Start immediately left of the large brown streak. Climb up then left along an obvious break to a small ledge beneath a bulge. Traverse left above the bulge then up a crack then the easier wall trending left to finish.

4 Flake Groove * 65m Very Difficult
FA Ian Clough, G.Brown, J.Donnison & R.Logan 12 June 1967

The wide right-slanting fault towards the right end of the face is slow to dry.

1 **25m** Climb the groove, passing a large flake at 20m with care to belay on ledge a short distance above.

2 **10m** Make an airy traverse left then move up to a small thread belay.

3 **30m** Continue leftwards up walls and slabs.

MAIN FACE

5 Rainmaker *** 70m VS 4b
FA Ronnie Marshall & James 'Big Elly' Moriarty 13 Sept 1958

A frabjous route on perfect rock up the large left-facing recessed corner at the left end of the cliff – one of the best routes of its grade in the Coe.

1 **20m 4b** Climb the corner (bold at first) to better holds and protection, to belay on a large ledge.

2 **15m 4b** Continue up a short wide crack to pull out of a recess on huge holds.

3 **35m 4b** Continue up to beneath a formidable-looking bulge. Layback round this in a fine position then more easily above to belay on grass ledge at top. Scramble right and up to finish.

6 Slithy ** 120m Severe 4a
FA Ian Clough, P.Macleod & R.Morgan 18 August 1967

Good climbing up the left side of the wall. Start at the left end of the alp beneath a rib with grooves on either side.

1 **20m** Move up left and follow the groove round left of the rib awkwardly to a ledge.

2 **25m** Continue up the cracks above.

3 **30m** Continue up the fault to a bulge then move left to a prominent chimney.

4 **45m** Ascend the chimney, exiting left to a grassy bay. Finish up a big flake leading to easier ground.

7 Toves ** 110m Very Difficult
FA Gary & Karen Latter & Colin Whiston 3 September 2000

Good climbing with a superb final pitch. Start beneath the next groove right of *Slithy*.

1 **20m** Ascend the groove passing a steep bulge on the left, continuing more easily to a good ledge and block belay.

2 **40m** Continue directly up the cracks above to belay on a ledge.

3 **50m** Continue up the fault on excellent holds and protection to level with a rowan in a bay out left. Step up right into the fine hanging groove and finish up this, passing some blocks near the top. Scramble to finish.

8 Brillig ★★ 110m Very Difficult

FA Dr Patricia Littlechild, Cliff Ogle & Gary Latter 21 July 2000

A good direct line cutting through the easy shelf of
Mome Rath Route finishing up that route's final pitch.
Start beneath an open groove 3m left of *Outgrabe Route*.

1 **40m** Move up into the V-groove and climb
   steps in the slabby left wall then direct by the
   crack-line to block belay on the wide shelf.
2 **30m** Move out right and follow fine slim vertical
   groove to a good ledge on the right at the top.
3 **40m** Traverse leftwards and finish
   up *Mome Rath Route*.

8a *Direct Finish* ★VS 4b climbs out left round the first
roof, traversing back right to climb slightly rightwards
through the upper bulge leading to easy ground.

© *Cliff Ogle and Patricia Littlechild on
the first ascent of pitch 2 of Brillig.*

9 Outgrabe Route ★ 115m Very Difficult

*FA Ian Clough & party 6 June 1966; pitch 3 J.Brockway & Stewart
Orr 17 May 1954*

Start beneath two prominent crack-lines 10m down and
left of *Mome Rath Route*.

1 **35m** Climb to a recess then move left up
   a short slab corner to the leftmost crack,
   which leads to a large block belay.
2 **30m** Continue directly to the large
   grass ledge of *Mome Rath Route*.
3 **50m** Follow a direct line just left of the chimney.

10 Mome Rath Route ★★ 120m Very Difficult

FA J, Mrs M & Miss C Stewart 16 May 1954

Start at the base of an easy angled grey shelf slanting left.
Climb easily up the shelf to belay on a good grass ledge
at the base of an open chimney. Continue directly, pulling
steeply out rightwards at the top. Scramble to finish.

11 Jabberwock ★★ 100m VS 4c

FA Ian Clough & C.Kynaston August 1966

Start beneath the vertical crack up the wall just right of
Mome Rath Route.

1 **50m 4c** A fantastic pitch on wonderful
   rough pocketed rock. Climb the crack to
   belay on large overhung ledge on the left
   (past possible belay on ledge at 30m).
2 **20m** Climb easily up rightwards across slabs
   and up an easy-angled left-facing groove
   to belay at the base of a steep crack.
3 **30m 4c** Climb the steep crack directly above
   on good holds until it is possible to swing
   onto large holds on the left edge. Continue
   more easily up the wall to the top.

The obvious direct continuation of the crack is 11a
Borogroves ★HVS 5a.

12 The Wabe ★★★ 95m Very Difficult

FA J.Brockway, Stewart Orr & D.Parlane 15 May 1954

Excellent and sustained climbing on very good rock.
Start beneath the wide flake crack 8m right of the grey

shelf of *Mome Rath Route*.

1 50m Climb the flake and continue trending up left then fairly directly, crossing an overhang on the right on good holds. Trend left to spike belay beneath an easy left-facing slabby corner. Other belays possible.

2 45m Climb the slab and corner (as for *Jabberwock*) then traverse easily right along ledge to the right side of a large open recess. Climb up then move diagonally left along a prominent hanging slab above the roofs. Continue direct to belay in a recess. Scramble to finish.

13 Whimsy ★★   95m Severe 4a
FA Ian & Niki Clough 28 August 1966

Very good climbing up the shallow left-facing groove near the right side of the face. Approach the base of the route by scrambling along a grass terrace from the right.

1 45m 4a Climb the groovc and con
tinue up the easier upper groove to belay beneath prominent twin cracks.

2 50m 4a Climb the right crack for 6m then traverse

left steeply on good holds and up the left-hand crack which soon eases. Continue in the same line to belay up on the left. Scrambling remains.

14 Gyre ★★   125m HVS 5a
FA Gary Latter, Tom Cameron & Scott McQueen 26 July 2000

A good direct line up the cracks just right of *Whimsy*. Start 3m right of *Whimsy* beneath a hanging groove.

1 50m 5a Climb the crack which leads to the right side of a bulge. Step left and cross the bulge on good holds past two grass clumps then continue up the easy groove. Climb the fine rib on the right edge to belay beneath the right-most crack as for *Whimsy*.

2 25m 5a Traverse rightwards to a hidden hanging groove. Move up this for a couple of metres then traverse back left to cracks and climb direct on excellent pockets leading to a belay beneath a large flake on the right.

3 50m – Continue direct on easy excellent rock passing triple blocks to belay at the very top of the cliff.

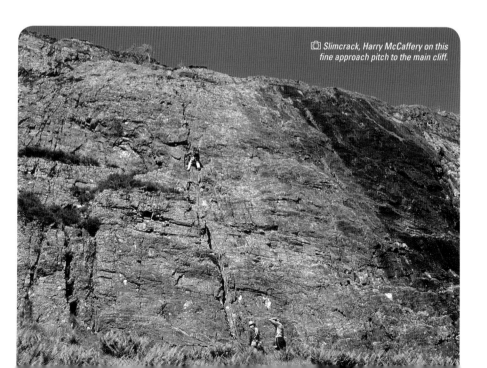

📷 *Slimcrack, Harry McCaffery on this fine approach pitch to the main cliff.*

YOSEMITE WALLS

NN 161 558 **Alt:** 430m (W) 35min

The prominent overlapping wall directly opposite the Lower Walls on Aonach Dubh.

Approach: From the lower of the two main car parks on the south side of the road (NN 168 569) follow the path down the hill to cross the River Coe by the lower bridge. Continue up the path then steeply directly up the hillside to the base of the cliff.

Descents: Traverse right crossing the gully bounding the right edge of the crag to some large boulders then contour back to the foot of the crag. Alternatively abseil from one of the trees overhanging the top of the square-cut recess in the centre of the crag.

① Rock Lord ★★★   30m E7 6b

FA Dave Cuthbertson & Rab Anderson 26 June 1995

In the centre of the overlapping wall an obvious right-facing corner provides the first weakness through the lower steeply overhanging barrier. Start about 4m to the left of the corner at an undercut cave. Difficult initial moves lead to a PR (pre-clipped on FA). Better holds lead up and rightwards to a break level with the top of the aforementioned corner. Move left and up to good holds at a break protected by an assortment of cams and small wires. Continue up the overhanging wall on undercuts to the final bulge. Pull over this (crux) and trend slightly left to a break. Now move up and right on mossy rock to a hollow flake. Step left and up to tree.

② A Sweet Disregard for the Truth ★★★   35m E6 6b

FA Paul Thorburn & Gary Latter (both redpointed) 13 June 1995

Follows a direct line through a series of roofs in the centre. Start beneath a short right-facing groove at the left end of the long roof. Up an easy slab and groove to a break. Step left and pull up leftwards to a good slot

(R #9). Pull right and up to a good hold then direct to good undercuts under the first roof. Undercut rightwards then up to good jams. Step left to good holds at a large perched block then either direct or leftwards to a good small ledge then on good incut holds to an incut ledge. Step right and more easily up the right side of a crack to a nut and tree belay on a cleaned ledge.

3 Boiling Point ★★   30m E4 6a
FA Rab & Chris Anderson & Dave Cuthbertson 25 June 1995

The slim groove in the wall which runs into a crack-line just left of the arête. Direct entry to the groove is possible but prevented by very wet slabs beneath the bulge. Climb up to the right side of the arête, swing around left and traverse to the base of the groove. Climb the groove and the ensuing crack to reach the top of the crag.

4 The Mystery Trend ★   25m E4 6a
FA Paul Thorburn & Gary Latter 9 August 1995

The right arête. Scramble up easy slab to belay

underneath the arête. Move up a groove to gain and follow a left-slanting crack through a low blocky overhang. A thin crack leads to the right side of the mid-height roof. Traverse left under this and make difficult moves round the arête. Continue up then right to easy ground.

5 Magnitude ★★   30m E5 6a
FA Dave Cuthbertson, Chris & Rab Anderson 25 June 1995

A steep sustained pitch up the wall right of the arête. Just right of the start of 4 is a second shorter shallow left-facing groove. Climb this (spike runner on the left wall) which is only adequately protected, to a rest beneath the right side of the overlap. Pull leftwards round this to a more comfortable position and good protection. Follow the thin crack above with increasing difficulty, culminating in a bold move out left beneath the large capping roof. Finish more easily up a groove.

The steep cracked arête right of the central alcove is
6 *Three Tarp Shugs* ★ E2 5b.

📷 *Rick Campbell crucifying himself on The Mystery Trend.*

AONACH DUBH

Stob Coire
nan Lochan

DESCENT

Far Eastern
Buttress

Terrace
Face

Lower
NE Nose

Weeping
Walls

Lower
Walls

APPROACH

APPROACH

THE LOWER WALLS

A long low line of walls (often water-streaked) below the Weeping Walls and the Lower North-East Nose.

Approach: From the lower of the two main car parks on the south side of the road (NN 168 569) follow the path downhill to cross the River Coe by the lower bridge. Continue up the path, leaving the main path 100m beyond where it crosses an open scree gully and a small stream just before a steep section. Follow the less obvious old path to a large boulder just above the prominent waterfall. Cross the stream and continue up a vague path steeply leftward.

Descent: Down either end of the crag or by abseil.

 Thing of Beauty ★★   **40m E3 5c**

FA Gary Latter & Dave Greig 17 August 1993

A direct line up the left edge of the face just right of the wet crack. Start up 2 and climb direct up the diagonal crack past a series of horizontal breaks to a bold run-out section. From the ledge step left and up a blocky dyke to belay in short twin corners.

2 Lady Jane ★★★   **25m E2 5b**

FA Dave Cuthbertson & Derek Jamieson July 1977

Bold steady climbing on immaculate rock. Start 5m right of the wide wet crack. Climb direct by a faint depression to a prominent diagonal crack. Follow this rightwards to a wide horizontal break then direct (left of a wet streak) to small tree. Abseil descent (sling in situ).

3 Charlotte Anne ★★   **25m E4 6a**

FA lower half – (as Mr Bates) Rab Anderson 12 June 1988;
Direct Finish Paul Thorburn & Gary Latter 12 June 1995

A good direct line cutting through 2. Start just right of that route at a short leftward sloping ramp. Move up and make difficult moves over the bulge then direct up the wall heading for a shallow pale groove (3m left of a tree). Gain the groove with a hard move then boldly on improving holds to finish.

4 Sir Chancealot ★★   25m E1 5b

FA Brian Duff & Kenny McLuskey 27 May 1978

A good pitch up the centre of the wall right of 2 heading for a tiny tree on the ledge. Start 10m right of 2. Climb direct to a short right-trending ramp then the wall above, trending slightly right near the top to a thread belay in the cave 2m left of the tiny tree. The top pitch (through the roof above the belay – E2 5c) is probably not worth doing. Descend by abseil.

5 Name Unknown ★★   30m VS 4c

FA the ancients, sometime in the dark ages

The most prominent feature of the wall is a stepped left-trending groove. Climb this. The continuation above is often wet. Climb the rib either side to a thread belay right of a tiny sapling. Abseil descent (sling in situ).

6 Double Exposure ★   70m VS 4b

FA Ken Crocket & Chris Gilmore May 1978

Some 6m right of the lowest rocks is a corner with small, multi-coloured slabs. Start below the corner.

1   **25m** Climb the corner for 15m, break out right and go up to belay under a roof.

2   **45m 4b** Move up and left for a few metres, step onto a steep wall, move right up to a block then follow a groove on the left. Easier rocks lead to the top.

7 Lament ★★   55m Severe 4a

FA John Cullen & Charlie Vigano April 1951

Start 20m up right from the lowest rocks beneath a left-slanting corner with a tiny rowan at the base.

1   **35m 4a** Climb the corner to pull out right at the top. Follow a direct line for 20m, move right and up a shallow groove leading to a belay in a recess.

2   **20m** Climb more easily directly to finish.

8 The Challenge ★★   20m E3 6a

FA Dave Cuthbertson, Rab Anderson & Dougie Mullin 27 May 1978

50m right of the wall containing *Lament* is a short undercut buttress just right of a scrappy chimney capped by a large roof. Start 2m right of the chimney. A fierce bouldery start leads past a good nut slot to good holds at 5m. Step left and continue directly up a faint crack-line to a large ledge level with the rowan on the left. Move out rightwards to belay on a lcdgc above. Scramble off right along a grassy ledge to abseil from a small rowan.

9 Sticky Fingers ★   20m E2 5c

FA Ken Johnstone & Pete Greenwell 27 May 1978

3m right of 8 is an overhanging blocky fault. Climb the fault to a break through the bulge to a ledge on the right. Climb the wall above to belay on a ledge at the top. Scramble off right to abseil from a small rowan.

NN 159 560 **Alt:** 430m   40min

LOWER NORTH-EAST NOSE

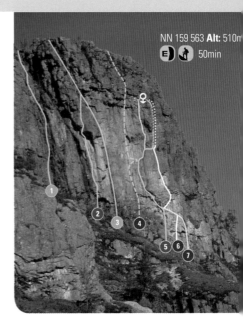

NN 159 563 **Alt:** 510m

E | 50min

A good gently overhanging cliff with a varied collection of steep extremes, many staying dry during the rain.

Approach: As for The Lower Walls approach to cross the stream above the waterfall, drop down again and cross the top of a further wooded stream to gain and cross a grass rake.

Descent: Either make a 50m abseil from a small tree at the top of *Spacewalk* or down broken ground at the left side of the cliff.

1 Turnspit * 60m VS 4c

FA Dougal Haston & Robin Smith October 1961

Climbs a line close to the right edge of the slender buttress at the left extremity of the cliff. Start a few metres up from the right edge in the grassy gully.

1 30m 4b Climb the steep wall then move right and up the groove in the edge which leads to a poor belay.

2 30m 4c Continue up the groove then out onto the left wall. Climb past a creaking flake and finish up the wall above.

2 Stormtrooper * 60m E3 6a

FA Kenny McCluskey & Colin McLean 11 June 1978

The steep wall and overhangs at the left side of the face between *Boomerang* and *Little Boomerang*. Start below the right crack.

1 40m 6a Climb the crack to the first overlap and go left a metre into a broken crack. Climb this trending rightwards into the centre of the wall. Continue up to a small ledge under the roof. Climb up the left side of the roof to good holds then traverse rightwards through overhangs on a horizontal crack and up to the belay ledge on *Boomerang*.

2 20m 4a Finish up *Boomerang*.

3 Boomerang * 90m HVS 5b

FA John Cunningham & Mick Noon 2 August 1955

A good main pitch following the left curving corner at the left side of the main face.

1 30m 5b Climb the wall and crack to a ledge and over a steep section above (crux). At the top make a long step left to a large ledge.

2 30m 4b Continue up the crack to reach a small cave and chokestone belay.

3 30m Finish up the grassy crack.

4 Freak-Out *** 65m E4 6a

FA Dave Bathgate & Bugs McKeith (A3) 1 July 1967;
Aid reduced to 1 PA by Dave Cuthbertson April 1977;
FFA Dougie Mullin & Jim Melrose May 1979

The crag classic, taking the central vertical crack leading to the prominent A-shaped roof at half height. Start by scrambling up to a ledge and tree at the base of the crack.

1 20m 5c Climb the wall to gain the crack, which leads to a short traverse and a small ledge and belay on the right.

2 30m 6a Regain the crack and follow it to a rest of sorts in the niche. Pull over the roof on good holds then continue up the crack to an inverted flake poised beneath the final roof. Pull out on undercut jams leading rightwards through the roof to easy ground.

3 15m Finish easily up the unpleasant wall above.

5 **Crocodile** ★★★   **50m E3 6a**

FA Pitches 1 & 2 Willie Todd & Rab Anderson 4 June 1977;
Pitch 3 Dave Cuthbertson & Murray Hamilton 5 June 1977

Start at a left-curving line of overhangs 5m right of
Freak-Out.

1 **20m 5c** Climb steeply to the overhangs then pull out
right to gain a small ledge. Continue up the shallow
groove above to P and nut belay on small ledge.

2 **10m 5b** Follow the groove on the right for
6m then traverse right round the edge of the
wall to a ledge below a prominent groove.

3 **20m 6a** Climb the groove with difficulty to a
ledge at the top. Hand traverse this easily left
then scramble up leftwards to the tree belay
on *Spacewalk*. Abseil descent.

6 **Revengeance** ★★   **55m E6 6b**

FA Pitch 1 Dave Cuthbertson, Rab Anderson & Martin Lawrence
26 June 1981; Pitch 2 Dave Cuthbertson 27 June 1981

A slightly hybrid direct line up the wall right of *Crocodile*,
starting as for that route. A bold main pitch.

1 **25m 6b** Climb the crack in the bulge rightwards
to join *Spacewalk* and up this to its junction

with *Crocodile*. Step right and climb the wall to
a tiny overlap (least prominent of several – good
stopper #2 at right end in thin diagonal & RP #4
in slot to right). Step right again and continue
with difficulty up the wall, easing with height, to
belay at the end of *Crocodile's* second pitch.

2 **30m 5c** From the top of cracked blocks climb
the wall and very shallow groove parallel and
right of *Crocodile* then overhang direct to top.

7 **Spacewalk** ★★★   **45m E5 6b**

FA Ken Johnstone & Pete Ogden (1 PA) 17 April 1978;
FFA Murray Hamilton & Dave Cuthbertson May 1980

A good steep line up the wall right of *Freak-Out* with a
short well protected crux section. Start directly beneath
steep crack in steep wall about 6m below and to the right
of the start of *Crocodile*.

1 **25m 5c** Up the crack then up and
slightly right to roofs. Pull through the
roofs on the left to join *Crocodile* at old PR.
Continue to belay common to *Freak-Out*.

2 **20m 6b** Up a groove on the right past an old PR
to underneath a roof. Step left, up a short groove
and continue up then right to a tree belay.

📷 *Mark Glaister on the first pitch of Crocodile.*
Photo Dave Cuthbertson, Cubby Images.

Far Eastern
Buttress

Barn
Wall

Terrace
Face

DESCENT

DESCENT

DESCENT

Weeping
Walls

AONACH DUBH EAST FACE

WEEPING WALLS

A fairly extensive off-vertical wall with distinctive drainage weeps down its left side. Away from the weeps some of the routes dry reasonably quickly. There is a large flat-topped boulder at the base of the centre of the cliff. Routes from right to left.

Approach: As for The Lower Walls then continue by a well-worn path that leads diagonally up left underneath the cliff.

Descent: Follow a vague path then descending shelves down rightwards (facing out). Go up slightly across a slab just beyond *The Lower Bow* then down a final short step (see diagram). For routes from *Quietude* leftwards scramble left along grass ledge and drop down to a lower ledge. Either abseil (25m) from tree or scramble down from far end of ledge.

 **Drainpipe Corner ★★** **50m Severe 4a**

FA Bill Smith & Charlie Vigano summer 1951

A good sustained route up the right-bounding corner, though often a watercourse.

1 **23m 4a** Climb the corner, steeply at first to belay at a good ledge where the angle eases.

2 **27m 4a** Continue up the corner to belay on a birch at the top. Descend by abseil or scramble.

2 Eve's Arête ★ **65m Very Difficult**

FA J.Buchanan, J.Forbes, F.Jack, G.Skelton 14 September 1969

The highlight is a fine exposed rising traverse. Start at a short stepped groove just left of the right edge of the wall and just right of where the path gains the base of the crag.

1 **20m** Climb slightly leftwards then trend back right to nut and thread belay just right of the right end of a long narrow grass ledge.

2 **15m** Move up a few metres then follow obvious traverse line on large holds rightwards.

3 **30m** Continue more easily by cracks and grooves up the slabby left side of the arête to tree belay on large heather ledge at top. Either abseil off (50m) or scramble up the blunt edge and easy slabs leftwards above the large rowan at the left end of the ledge.

3 Curving Crack ★★ **85m Severe 4a**

FA Len Lovat 5 October 1952

Start 5m right of the large block in the centre of the face.

1 **20m** Climb up directly to belay at a small rowan at the base of the crack.

2 **30m 4a** Climb the crack and the wall above to belay on a long ledge.

3 **35m** Continue more easily up broken rocks above.

WEEPING WALLS

NN 158 558 **Alt:** 480m

45min

4 *The Straight Climb* ★ VS 4b takes a direct line between the two cracks.

5 The Long Crack ★★   90m Severe 4a

FA Len Lovat & J.Johnstone 6 June 1953

Follows a diagonal crack leading to the rowan in the centre of the top of the main section of the wall. Start just behind the right side of the large block boulder at the base.

  1 22m 4a Climb fairly directly to belay down left of the start of the crack.

  2 28m 4a Move out right and follow the crack mainly on its right side then direct to the rowan.

  3 40m Continue trending leftwards to belay far back.

6 Weeping Wall Route ★★   90m Severe 4a

FA Douglas Scott & J.Henderson August 1947

Excellent sparsely protected climbing, though slow to dry, following a slightly left-trending fault up the right edge of the weeps. Start just left of the block boulder.

  1 15m – Climb direct to belay in a recess beneath the fault.

2+3 75m 4a Follow the fault which leads slightly left to a small block above a bulge. Pull over the block and follow parallel grooves then more easily directly to the Terrace. Finish more easily up the slabby wall above.

The following 7 routes all end at a long narrow grassy terrace. Either finish more easily by about 25–30m of easy angled rock or traverse left to abseil (25m) from a tree at the far left end of the terrace.

7 Quietude ★   50m HVS 5a

FA Dave Cuthbertson & Willie Todd 9 July 1977

Start beneath a prominent black overhang, 15m right of the prominent cracks of *Spider*.

  1 12m Climb the wall to a ledge below the overhang.

  2 38m 5a Cross the overhang by a left-slanting crack to a ledge. Continue leftwards up the wall to a shallow groove and up this to the terrace.

8 Short But Sweet ★★   50m E2 5c

FA Dave Cuthbertson & Roy Williamson Summer 1981

Bold climbing taking a line midway between 7 & 9. Go up the lower wall to the right end of the grass ledge then continue up the wall, starting past two prominent finger pockets, moving up and right to a slight overlap. Step left and climb the steepening wall with final tricky moves about 2m left of the final corner on *Quietude*.

9 Solitude ★★★   48m E3 5b

FA Dave Cuthbertson, Rab Anderson & Willie Todd 3 June 1977

Fine bold wall climbing on immaculate rock.
Low in the grade.

1 **8m** Climb steep wall to the ledge below the crack-line of *Spider Right-Hand*.

2 **40m 5b** From the right end of the ledge climb straight up to a prominent block at 6m then directly up the wall above to the terrace.

10a Spider Right-Hand ★★★   43m VS 4c

Excellent reasonably-protected climbing tackling the rightmost of the twin cracks bounding the left margin of the prominent dark seepage stain. Slow to dry.

1 **8m** Scramble up past a heathery ledge at 6m to the base of the crack.

2 **35m 4c** Climb the crack leading into a shallow groove in its upper reaches and follow this to belay on terrace.

10 Spider ★★★   43m HVS 5a

FA Jimmy Marshall, Ronnie Marshall & Archie Hendry April 1957

Excellent sustained sparsely protected climbing.

1 **8m** Scramble up past a heathery ledge at 6m to belay below the leftmost of the twin cracks.

2 **35m 5a** Move up and climb a shallow right-facing groove to its top then move up right to good holds and protection. Move up to a small foot-ledge then a vague hidden crack to finish directly.

11 The Fly ★   42m E3 5c

FA Dave Cuthbertson & Willie Todd 9 July 1977

A serious pitch up the wall left of *Spider*. Start at a prominent crack 10m left of *Spider*.

1 **12m 4c** Climb the crack to a ledge on the right.

2 **30m 5c** Climb directly up the wall above then move up and left into a scoop. Move slightly left then up the wall above to belay on the terrace.

12 Bivvy Wall ★★   42m E3 5b

FA Dave Cuthbertson & Paul Moores August 1994

More attractive than *The Fly* but equally serious. Start just right of an obvious crack. Climb the wall (without using the crack). Now make an awkward move up the arête then trend slightly right to a scoop (poor wires and spike). Climb the wall above to gain a line of holds trending slightly right. Easier climbing leads to the terrace.

📷 *Drainpipe Corner, Weeping Walls, Chris Dunn climbing.*

NN 157 557 **Alt:** 520m

BARN WALL 🏔️ 🥾 50min

The extensive easier angled continuous mass of rock bordering the left margin of the Weeping Walls.

① Lower Bow *   65m Moderate

FA Donald McIntyre & Bill Murray (both solo) May 1947

This forms a prominent easy-angled open chimney fault higher up. It starts as a shallow right-slanting groove, 2m right of a small rowan and at the base of a slanting shelf.

1 25m Climb the groove which soon leads to an easy-angled slab.

2 40m Continue more easily up the open fault.

NN 157 558 **Alt:** 600m

TERRACE FACE 1hr

This lies above The Terrace with the fine barrel-shaped buttress at the left side harbouring some ultra-classic easier routes.

Approach: Either by a route on the **Weeping Walls** or the right side of the **Barn Wall** or by scrambling easily up the descent route, which starts as for *The Bowstring*.

Descent: Gain a small worn path heading right (north) then scramble down a narrow gully formed by an eroded basalt dyke (often wet). At the base of this a narrow scree cone leads back down to The Haven. Alternatively, make a 45m abseil from in situ sling on block just below the top of *Arrow Wall*, which can be gained by a traverse from the top of the adjacent routes.

① Quiver Rib ★★★★   55m Difficult

FA Donald McIntyre & Bill Murray May 1947

Superb steep well-protected climbing with improbable situations for the grade. Start at the left side of the buttress just right of a wide chimney.

1 25m Climb the rib then move up right to belay beneath a steep wall.

② The Bowstring *   115m Difficult

FA Donald McIntyre & Bill Murray May 1947

Steady climbing on good clean rock. Start at the same point as the descent route, 20m left of the *Lower Bow* on a shelf with small rowans at its right end.

1 20m Climb straight up then slightly right up a glacis to belay in a short left-facing corner.

2 45m Climb the corner and a short steep crack then more easily, veering left into an open chimney for a few moves before returning to climb the right side to belay on a large ledge. Either walk right to the base of The Terrace Face or:

3 50m Continue up the left side of the chimney.

③ Barn Wall Route *   110m Moderate

FA Donald McIntyre, Trevor Ransley & Bill Murray May 1947

Follow the 'line of least resistance', starting from the highest section of the base of the wall.

2 30m Continue in a fine position up the left-trending shallow groove above the belay.

② Arrow Wall ★★★   60m Very Difficult

FA Len Lovat & J.Johnstone 7 June 1953

Another excellent route through some unlikely territory for the grade. Start midway between *Quiver Rib* and *Archer Ridge*.

1 30m Follow the shallow groove avoiding an overlap at 12m on the right. Continue in the same slightly wandering line to belay on the ledge as for *Quiver Rib*.

2 30m Climb the steep black groove directly above the belay on good holds and continue in the same line to the top.

③ Wounded Knee ★★   60m Severe 4a

FA Ken Crocket & Brian Dullea 14 April 1991

Good though fairly sparsely protected climbing up the wall to the left of *Archer Ridge*. Start midway between *Arrow Wall* and the arête.

1 25m 4a Climb a steepening groove to belay on a ledge on the left.

2 35m 4a Step left onto a steep wall, climb up and left for a few moves then traverse across the bulging wall rightwards to the edge. Continue on good holds to the top.

4 Archer Ridge ★★★   60m Very Difficult

FA Bill Murray & Donald McIntyre May 1947;
Direct Len Lovat, Ian McNicol & A.Way May 1954

The blunt right-bounding rib completes the trilogy of classics. Start at the left side of the rounded ridge.

1 35m Follow the crest (possible belay on the right at 25m) then out slightly rightwards beneath a steeper wall. Continue back up and left onto the crest which leads to a belay in a short corner recess.

2 25m Move out right a short way then follow a crack and the short final steep wall which leads to a belay a short way back. The *Direct* (Severe 4a) follows the crest to the left, moving steeply up slightly left from the belay. With careful rope management, possible in one superb 50m pitch, moving up left to gain the block belay just below the top of *Arrow Wall*.

High up in the centre of the face is a distinctive recessed crag above a large heather and rowan tree infested bay known as the Basin. Gain the base by easy scrambling from the left.

5 De Vreemde Stap ★★   40m HVS 5b

FA Martin Hind (Harpic) & H. Van Ryswick July 1978

A useful direct entry to the Basin. Start about 10m right of a chimney high up on the left side. Climb a shallow groove until a wide step right and up to gain the continuation groove. Climb this then by a left-trending crack leading into The Basin.

The following two routes are situated above the Basin. High up is an area of distinctive curving grooves. This route takes a line left of the distinctive pink slab.

6 Hesitation ★★   60m HVS 5a

FA John Cunningham (1PA) 3 July 1966;
FFA Ken Crocket & Ian Fulton summer 1972

Good climbing with a steep finale. Start above and left of the trees beneath an obvious shallow groove left of a slabby scoop.

1 45m 4c Climb the groove then head up and right to a ledge at 35m. Climb diagonally right to a small stance in the large groove capped by a huge roof.

2 15m 5a Climb up to the roof, traverse left 5m then follow an overhanging groove out right (crux) to finish on a large ledge.

7 Terrace Arête ★   35m VS 4b

FA Patsy Walsh & John Cullen May 1954

Bold climbing taking the stepped arête delineating the right edge of the crag. Climb the lower arête on good holds to a large ledge. Step out left with some tricky moves to become established on the arête proper and continue on improving holds to protection. Continue more easily up a shallow groove in the arête.

[Ⓒ] *Archer Ridge. Graham Bremner climbing*

NN 154 555 **Alt:** 740m 1hr

FAR EASTERN BUTTRESS

An excellent crag of rough rock, possibly some of the best in the glen. Well worth the extra walk to escape the crowds.

Approach: Continue up the path on the left side of the stream, crossing the stream where it starts to level out above the waterfalls then head directly up to the base of the crag. 1 hour. Alternatively, from the other cliffs lower down on the East Face continue up the hillside underneath the cliffs for a further 15 minutes beyond Barn Wall.

Descent: The easiest descent is by moving up and left and down the large wide grassy gangway sloping down underneath the small crags bounding the left side of the crag. Alternatively, from the top of the narrow gully bounding the right side of the crag containing a chokestone, traverse a small rock shelf round the corner and down easy slabs then skirt round to the base of the crag.

① Farewell Arête ★　　　　　**70m Very Difficult**

FA Ken Crocket & Alistair Walker 19 May 1990

At the right edge of the buttress is a deep gully. This route follows the arête forming the right wall. Climb the arête with a step left at 6m then continue to a ledge and belay. Continue more easily in a further two pitches (or one long pitch) in the same line.

The following two routes start by scrambling up 15m to a belay at the base of the wall.

② Shibumi ★★　　　　　　　　**45m VS 4b**

FA Ken Crocket & G.Jefferies 12 May 1990

A good pitch on excellent rock up the rightmost of two parallel right-slanting cracks. Move right to good foot-holds before the corner then follow the crack leading to easier ground at the top of the corner. Finish up the edge.

③ Satori ★★　　　　　　　　　**45m VS 4b**

FA Ken Crocket & G.Jefferies 12 May 1990

The left crack. Start beneath the left arête of the wall. Climb up then move right into the crack and follow this and the direct continuation to belay far back.

④ Yen ★　　　　　　　　　**75m Very Difficult**

FA C.Kynaston & J.Garster 29 August 1966

Start 8m right of *Nirvana Wall* near the right edge of the slab.

1　**25m** Climb steep slabs to beneath a steep cracked wall.

2　**50m** Move right and climb the crack with difficulty to a grassy ledge. Finish up the groove.

5 **Nirvana Wall** **   **60m Severe 4a**

FA Ian Clough, C.Kynaston & J.Garster 26 August 1966

The highlight is a well positioned thin crack and groove up the highest, central section of the crag. Start by some wonderful quartz streaks towards the left end of an immaculate smooth slab.

    1 **35m 4a** Climb the thin crack then continue up easier ground to belay beneath the steep upper crack.

    2 **25m 4a** The thin crack, finishing up the right-facing roof skirting the right end of the roof. An excellent well protected pitch. Thread belay 15m further back.

6 **Eastern Promise** **   **65m E1 5b**

FA Rab & Chris Anderson 6 July 1991

A good little route following the arête and thin crack-line left of *Nirvana Wall*. Start beneath a grassy groove.

    1 **40m 5a** Go up the groove a short way then into a thin crack-line on its right wall. Climb this and the arête to a block belay beneath the upper wall.

    2 **25m 5b** Step down right then follow the thin crack up the centre of the wall past the right side of the wall to the roof. Pull rightwards through this then move back left above it and up to the top.

7 **Rough Slab** **   **50m Severe 4a**

FA Bob Richardson, Peter MacKenzie & Bill Skidmore 2 September 1962

A fine aptly named route up the left side of the face. Start beneath a groove in the clean wall overlooking the broken gully on the left. Follow the groove past a large block to a good ledge beneath small overlaps. Traverse slightly right and climb a groove through the overlaps. Move round left above to finish up a fine steep clean slab.

Nirvana Wall, Karen Martin climbing.

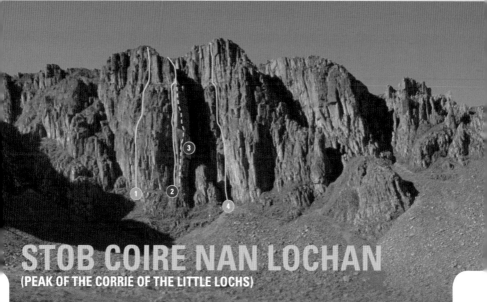

STOB COIRE NAN LOCHAN
(PEAK OF THE CORRIE OF THE LITTLE LOCHS)

This north-east facing corrie formed by the long ridges of Aonach Dubh and Gearr Aonach harbours some of the finest situated routes in the glen. Care should be taken with perched blocks, particularly near the top.

Approach: From the lower of the two main car parks on the south side of the road (NN 168 569) follow the path down the hill to cross the River Coe by the lower bridge. Continue steeply up the path on the left (east) side of the stream up into the corrie.

Descent: Traverse right and down the well worn path and easy-angled ground beyond the right (north) end of the cliffs.

SOUTH BUTTRESS NN 147 551 **Alt:** 900m 1½hr

The leftmost clean buttress.

1 Tilt ★★   135m VS 4c

FA Ian Clough & John Hardie (1 PA) 28 May 1966;
Variation Start Ian & Niki Clough 25 June 1967

Start near the centre of the buttress, beneath a deep-cut chimney which starts at 20m.

- **1** **40m 4b** Climb a line of cracks to the chimney then the chimney to the base of the groove.
- **2** **20m 4c** Climb the groove until above an overhang. Move right and up wall to a huge flake.
- **3** **20m 4c** Follow grooves which lead to a terrace.
- **4** **25m 4c** Traverse left along the terrace then up a wall to awkwardly enter a V-groove chimney. Follow this.
- **5** **30m** Continue easily to finish.

2 Unicorn ★★★   120m E1 5b

FA Jimmy Marshall & Robin Campbell 18 June 1967

The classic line of the corrie taking the eye-catching left-facing corner. Start by scrambling up leftwards to the base of the corner.

- **1** **50m 5b** Climb the corner for 8m then move right and up the right rib for about 10m to step back left into the corner. Follow this to belay next to a PR at a small foot ledge.
- **2** **40m 5a** Continue up the wide crack in the corner. At the top carefully negotiate some tottering blocks to belay in a chimney formed by two large (solid) blocks.

3 30m 5a Move round right and up a short steep chimney to a large flake. Move out right and up good flake cracks which lead abruptly to easy ground. Belay further back. Scramble up the easy ridge above to finish.

> From the base of the final pitch, an abseil descent is possible (slings usually in situ) then climbing *Scansor* (climbing the final chimney common to both only once).

③ Scansor **   120m E2 5b
FA Paul Braithwaite & Geoff Cohen 2 September 1972

A well situated route up the pillar right of *Unicorn*, though the quality of the rock does not come up to the standard of its superior neighbour. Care should be taken with loose flakes. Start at the same point as *Unicorn*.

1 45m 5b Follow the obvious groove right of *Unicorn* to a small ledge on the arête. Move up left and climb the steep crack to level with a small roof on the left. Traverse right and continue by a steep arête to belay at a block.

2 25m 5b Make an awkward move to an upper ledge on left. Go up the wall then traverse right to a small foot-hold in the centre of a pillar. Now make several strenuous moves up and right to a ledge and belay.

3 20m 4c Follow the groove on the right to ledges then up and left across a minefield of loose blocks to belay in a chimney formed by two large (solid) blocks.

4 30m 5a Finish up the top pitch of *Unicorn*.

CENTRAL BUTTRESS   1½hr
NN 146 551 **Alt:** 900m

④ Central Grooves **   115m VS 4c
FA Ken Bryan & R.Robb (1 PA) 3 July 1960

A popular route up the prominent groove-line cleaving the centre of the buttress. Start at the base of the groove.

1 25m 4c Climb the groove to belay on small ledges.

2 20m 4c Continue up the grooves to belay at the top of a pedestal on the left.

3 50m 4c Continue in the same line to a block belay on a broad terrace.

4 20m Finish easily up the crest.

📷 *Looking north over Aonach Eagach from Stob Coire nan Lochan. Tom Cameron quenching his thirst.*

NORTH FACE OF AONACH DUBH

The great gaping slit of Ossian's Cave dominates this broody atmospheric face. The base of the cliff rises immediately above Sloping Shelf, a diagonal fault that runs up right directly beneath the base of the cliff. This forms the boundary between the scrappy lower andesite band and altogether more appealing rhyolite layer above.

Approach: From the lower of the two main car parks on the south side of the road (NN 168 569) follow the path down the hill to cross the River Coe by the lower bridge. Cross the burn and head diagonally right up the hill side,

skirting round either side of a couple of small crags low down. A ledge system leads up right to the base of the Sloping Shelf, which in turn is followed by crossing a deep stream-filled gully (path high up). Just beyond this a short awkward greasy slab regains the path leading up under the cliff. There is a stream running down the shelf directly underneath the base of the crag.

Descent: Routes end on Pleasant Terrace (a bit of a misnomer). Follow this carefully (much loose rock) to make a 35m abseil from an in situ PB near its right end.

NN 155 564 **Alt:** 600m N 1½hr

Pleasant Terrace

Sloping Shelf

① Ossian's Ladder   **45m Hard Very Vegetated**

FA Neil Marquiss 1868

The first recorded 'climb' in the glen – of historical interest only. Recommended if you're insane or into botany in a big way. The route consists mainly of copious

quantities of lush vegetation. The cave itself has been formed by a huge block falling out of a dyke, leaving behind a broken 45 degree sloping base.

❷ Eldorado ★★★   125m E5 6b

FA Ken Johnstone & Mark Worsley (3 PA) 22 June 1977;
FFA Dougie Mullin & Murray Hamilton 17 May 1980;
FA Top Pitch Dave Cuthbertson & Ken Johnstone 18 May 1980

Excellent sustained climbing up a series of cracks
through the bulges in the wall left of *The Clearances*.
Start just right of obvious crack.

  1 18m 5c Move up and left into the crack
       and climb this to belay on the left.

  2 40m 6b Follow the groove to an overhang, step
       right to climb a very short corner. Step left above
       a roof onto a steep wall and a good resting spot.
       Follow the overhanging crack over a second smaller
       overhang with difficulty then go up and left to a
       large ledge. Continue up beside a crack to a terrace.

  3 40m 5c Follow the groove just right of the arête (the
       second most obvious groove left of 4) boldly until it
       is possible to traverse right to the poor belay on 4.

  4 25m 5a Continue up the rib to Pleasant Terrace.

❸ Repossessed ★★★   40m E5 6a

FA Martin Crocker 30 June 1995

A sustained and superb pitch following a direct line
above the roof where *Eldorado* steps left. Follow the
main pitch of *Eldorado* for 10m to the roof. Step right to
an undercut and up a wide crack to better holds. Continue
more easily to the overhanging wall above and up this
to awkward sloping jugs (crux). A long reach gains better
holds and easier ground leading to the long shelf. Belay.

*Eldorado, Tim Rankin &
Guy Robertson climbing.
Photo Dave Cuthbertson,
Cubby Images.*

❹ The Clearances ★★★   105m E3 6a

FA Ed Grindley, Cynthia Grindley & John Main August 1976
(climbed over 2 days & some aid used);
FFA Murray Hamilton & Willie Todd 1977

The hanging crack-line in the wall left of *Yo-Yo*. A
sustained classic with a bold lower section.
Start 6m left of *Yo-Yo*.

  1 45m 5c Gain the left-slanting shelf and follow
       this, then move diagonally left on the slab above.
       Move up right to a small ledge (PR) then boldly
       up the wall past a poor PR to step right into the
       crack and follow it more easily to a shelf.

  2 40m 6a Move up the shelf and follow the
       shallow left-facing groove 5m left of the
       corner to an old nut under the roof. Step right
       under the roof (crux), pull over on good holds
       and continue to a poor belay on small ledge.

  3 20m 5a Continue more easily to the top.

❺ Yo-Yo ★★★★   90m E1 5b

FA Robin Smith & David Hughes May 1959

The great corner of the crag. The bottom 15m often seeps.
On the first ascent Smith spent 4 hours drying the rock
with a towel (hence the name). Start directly beneath
the corner.

  1 35m 5b Move left round an overhang and up
       the left-facing groove. Pull right 6m above
       the ground to climb black seepage streaks
       leading slightly rightwards to the corner
       proper. Up this to belay on a large shelf.

  2 25m 5b Continue up the corner/chimney
       to belay above the main overhang.

  3 30m 5b Continue in the same line with a
       short excursion to the left near the top.

❺ₐ Yo-Yo Continuation ★   60m VS 4c

FA Robin Smith & James Moriarty May 1960

  4+5 60m Continue the line above Pleasant Terrace
       by following the grooved arête and a short
       overhanging corner to the top of the face.

Repossessed, Paul Thorburn on second ascent.

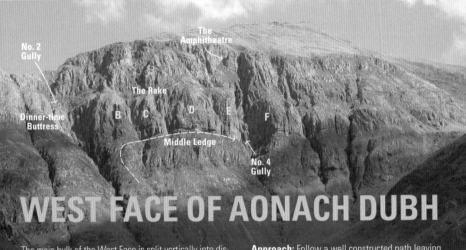

WEST FACE OF AONACH DUBH

The main bulk of the West Face is split vertically into distinct buttresses by six prominent vertical gullies. There are also two horizontal terraces across the face, effectively dividing the buttresses into three tiers. The lower narrow ledge is called Middle Ledge and lies at the base of all the routes. Above is a broader sloping terrace known as The Rake. The lower tier is composed of loose vegetated andesite of no interest to the rock climber. In contrast the steeper middle tier of rough pink rhyolite contains the bulk of the climbing. The one other area of interest is the miniature corrie-like feature of The Amphitheatre, situated between the upper tiers of E and F Buttresses.

Approach: Follow a well constructed path leaving the A82 at the west side (right) of the bridge over the outflow of Loch Achtriochtan directly opposite the Clachaig turn-off. This leads steeply up the hillside, higher up keeping close to the right (west) bank of the Allt Coire nam Beithach.

Cross this stream below the lowest waterfall and head steeply up to the base of **Dinner-time Buttress**, then cross **No. 2 Gully** on the right, low down and climb its right flank (below **B Buttress**) to gain the left end of **Middle Ledge**. Follow this right to the buttress of your choice.

B BUTTRESS   1¼hr
NN 144 555 **Alt:** 600m

The furthest left rock buttress above the left end of Middle Ledge immediately above the approach path up the lower buttress.

Descent: To return to the base of the cliff traverse right (south) along The Rake and down No.4 Gully (see Descent details for E Buttress) then traverse back north along Middle Ledge. The fastest route back to the road is by the easy upper section of No.2 Gully to below Middle Ledge to where it steepens then traverse out right (north) and down Dinner-time Buttress.

1 Bumblebee ★★   **115m Very Difficult**
FA Paul Brian & Robin Campbell July 1972

Good climbing on excellent rock. About 30m above the lowest rocks on the right flank of the central rib is a system of grooves leading to a final crack. Start right of the deep crack in the rib and climb direct up to gain the grooves. Follow the grooves to finish up the final crack.

Direct Route ★★   120m Severe 4a

FA A.Parker & Hamish Nicol June 1948

Climbs the face left of the pinnacles, cutting through a prominent area of red rock just above mid-height. Start 10m left of a long vegetatious groove, at a vertical rib.

1 **20m 4a** Climb the corner left of the rib then continue on slabs to beneath a wall.

2 **40m 4a** Move right then up the steep wall and the easiest line to the top of a grass rake.

3 **40m** Climb direct over the centre of a bulge then by slabby rock.

4 **20m** Continue in the same line to finish.

The Pinnacle Face ★★   90m Very Difficult

FA Jim Bell & Colin Allan May 1932

The right side of the buttress is crested by triple pinnacles. Start beneath a left-slanting chimney 12 metres left of the right end of the face.

1 **30m** Climb the chimney to a ledge and spike belays on the right.

2 **30m** Step right and continue up the grassy slabs and corner left of the shattered arête to a ledge beneath a chimney. Climb the chimney past a recessed cave to belay in a corner on the right.

3 **30m** Climb the corner then the crack up the right side of the pinnacle then more easily to its top. Scramble into the gap for the customary photo on the renowned Pinnacle Flake. Exposed moderate scrambling to the right leads to the main face.

E BUTTRESS

NN 144 555 **Alt:** 600m   1½hr

This is the impressive steep buttress left of No. 4 Gully with its finest feature, the south-west face overlooking the gully.

Descent: Traverse right and descend a sloping shelf into **No. 4 Gully**, then scramble down this with care.

Original Route ★   70m Severe 4a

FA Jimmy Marshall & George Ritchie September 1958

On the approach along Middle Ledge the wet and slimy Amphitheatre Scoop will be seen dividing D and E Buttresses. Continue round an edge on Middle Ledge until a point where a shallow scoop comes into view to the left of the buttress crest.

1 **10m 4a** Go up to an overhang and belay.

2 **20m 4a** Traverse left and up a steep wall to a slab then the slab to a grassy scoop.

3 **40m** Traverse right to the crest and scramble up excellent rock to finish.

Consolation ★   80m VS 4c

FA Ian Clough & G.Grandison 23 April 1962

Start right of the crest at a large spike at the base of a heathery groove.

1 **20m 4c** Follow the groove to below twin cracks.

2 **18m 4b** Gain the right-hand crack and ascend it to a recess below an overhang. Move left round a rib to belay at the base of a small chimney. Either descend by abseil (saves the long descent!) or:

3 **12m** Move up then left to a good belay.

4 **30m** Climb pleasant slabs to finish by easy scrambling.

The Big Top ★★★   160m E1 5b

FA Robin Smith & Jimmy Gardner August 1961

A classic. The highlight is a spectacular wildly exposed pitch up the left arête of the huge leaning left wall of the *Trapeze* corner. Start at a block belay below the arête.

1 **35m 4c** Go up left for 15m, climb a slabby corner and then up and right to a belay on top of a large flake.

2 **35m 5a** Climb the arête to the left and a bulge above. Continue by a crack on the edge of the arête to an easing of the angle. Belay at the base of a large flake.

3 **45m 5a** Move right into a diagonal line of slabby grooves and climb these until it is possible to move left into a 3m crack. Climb the crack to a large ledge and belay.

4 **45m 5a** Now climb a huge flake on the right to reach a wall. Move left up the wall and then right and traverse right across a groove to a slab. Climb the slab and a wall and finish up a broken groove to the top.

Salome ∗   **30m E5 6a**

FA Kev Howett & Gary Latter August 1987

A useful alternative first pitch to *Prophet of Purism*, following a more direct line up the left side of the awesomely steep wall close to the left arête. Start on the large platform just above the rowan tree below the wall where a large flake sits at the base of the route. Step off the flake and follow two thin parallel cracks running vertically up the wall until forced to make a thin move out left to an obvious diagonal hand-rail. Follow this left (F #2 placement halfway along) and make some committing moves to gain large flakes where the hand-rail fades. Gain the recess up on the right and exit directly upwards on poor rock and poor protection until an impasse is reached. Move diagonally left to belay at the base of the large flake on *The Big Top*.

7 Prophet of Purism ∗   **125m E6 6a**

FA Dave Cuthbertson & Roy Williamson summer 1981

The main pitch climbs a wandering line up the big leaning wall left of *Trapeze*, the steepest continuous wall in the glen. Start about 6m down and left from the *Trapeze* corner.

1 **30m 6a** Traverse up and left to a groove, up this and left across a wall to a small groove. Step down to good holds and continue traversing left for about 6m to a recess. Up an overhanging wall to an in situ nut. Continue up and left to join *The Big Top* at the flake crack.

2 **35m 5c** Up the flake crack then traverse right to gain a thin diagonal crack. Follow this for a short way then move up to a big block not far under the belay ledge on *The Big Top*. Move right and follow a line of holds to a flake, move left and up a groove then left from this and up to a ledge.

3 **30m 5a** Up twin grooves above, step left and up to belay at the foot of the huge flake on *The Big Top*.

4 **30m 5b** Up a corner above to PR on *The Big Top*. Finish direct up the undercut flake and groove above.

8 Trapeze ∗∗   **130m E1 5b**

FA Jimmy Marshall & Derek Leaver summer 1958

Start down and right of the large corner near the left edge of some vegetated rakes.

1 **15m** Scramble up the rakes to the base of the corner.

2 **20m 5b** Climb the strenuous corner to beneath an overhang.

3 **40m 4c** Turn the overhang on the left and follow the now easy corner to slabs, continuing to a mossy bay.

4 **5m** Traverse right to a well defined platform.

5 **40m 5a** Quit the platform on the left and climb a steep wall to a ledge and corner above. Turn the corner on the right and make an ascending right traverse to a groove and crack. Climb these to a slab below an overhang and traverse right to a rock bay and belay.

6 **10m** Now follow a groove rightwards and finish by a short crack.

9 Hee-Haw ∗   **135m E1 5b**

FA Dougal Haston & James Moriarty 21 June 1959

This routes completes the original E-Buttress trilogy, though there is some loose rock around. It climbs the steep wall above and right of *Trapeze*. Start by scrambling 50m up No. 4 Gully beneath the rightmost of two impressive hanging cracks in the south wall of the buttress.

1 **25m 5b** Climb a steep groove on the crest of a small buttress, to a grass ledge.

2 **25m 4b** Climb a crack in a corner then up a loose steep wall to belay beside a detached block below a prominent crack.

3 **25m 4c** Climb the prominent crack, which overhangs to a point below a large overhang. Go up rightwards by a steep wall to a ledge and belay.

4 **40m 4c** Traverse left into a steep groove, which is followed to its conclusion. Go left about 25m to reach a small stance on a slab.

5 **20m** Climb the slab and finish by an overhanging crack near the top of the buttress.

10 Hamburg ★★   **100m E4 6a**
FA Pitches 1 & 2 Mick Fowler, B.Craig & L.Smyth 25 August 1984;
FA Upper pitches Mick Fowler & B.Craig 27 August 1984

The prominent crack below the *Direct Finish* to *Hee Haw*, gained via the wall below. Start 6m left of the small buttress projecting from the base of *Hee Haw*.

1. **19m** Climb diagonally up left to belay on grass ledge 6m below and left of the *Hee Haw* stance.
2. **28m 5b** Surmount the short steep wall and ascend the easy right-slanting flake to its top. Step left and up to loose blocks (PR). A difficult pull straight up on dubious holds leads to better holds and a belay ledge below the crack.
3. **25m 6a** Gain a narrow ledge below the crack and climb it to a junction with *Hee Haw* at the groove of the direct finish. An excellent and strenuous pitch, though usually wet
4. **28m 5a** Finish up the steep groove above (the *Direct Finish* to *Hee Haw*).

THE AMPHITHEATRE   1½hr
NN 144 554 **Alt:** 750m

A miniature hanging corrie-like formation with excellent rock scenery situated above The Rake midway between the upper tiers of E and F Buttresses.

Approach: From E Buttress scramble up No. 4 Gully then diagonally left up easy-angled slabs to gain The Rake. Traverse left along this.

11 North Ridge ★   **60m Moderate**

This impressive narrow ridge of excellent rough grey rock forms the left edge of the amphitheatre.

12 North Ridge, South Wall ★★   **60m Severe 4a**
FA Dougal Haston, Jimmy Marshall & James Moriarty May 1959

Climb a series of short steep cracks on the right flank, about 6m from the crest. The route is rather artificial but offers good sport on excellent rock.

Trapeze, Dave Griffiths on the main (crux) corner pitch.

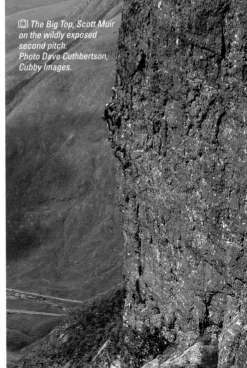

The Big Top, Scott Muir on the wildly exposed second pitch.
Photo Dave Cuthbertson, Cubby Images.

BIDEAN NAM BIAN
(PEAK OF THE MOUNTAINS)

The highest mountain in Argyll at 1150m, the massif projects the long ridges of Beinn Fhada, Gearr Aonach and Aonach Dubh to the north. These ridges mostly obscure views of the summit from the road except from Loch Achtriochtan where the twin buttresses of Diamond and Church Door are visible beneath the summit screes. The former is broken and vegetated, unlike its superlative neighbour.

NN 143 544 **Alt:** 950m   2hr

CHURCH DOOR BUTTRESS

"This is just wonderful, totally brilliant – there's even some sheep" – Paul Thorburn, below base of cliff, 1995

One of the finest cliffs in Glen Coe, it also happens to be the furthest from the road. With the base of the routes lying at an altitude of 950m/3200 feet, the summit lies just a few minutes away from the top of the cliff. The routes are relatively slow to dry and it is unlikely those on the West Face will dry out before June due to the large quantity of vegetation on the slopes above.

Access: Park on the south side of the A82 next to the outflow of Loch Achtriochtan opposite the Clachaig turn-off.

Approach: Follow a well constructed path leaving the A82 at the west (right) side of the bridge over the outflow of Loch Achtriochtan directly opposite the Clachaig turn-off. This leads steeply up into the coire beneath the crags of Stob Coire nam Beith (1 hour +) and continues up to the flat coire floor beneath the broken Diamond Buttress. From here scramble up screes to the base of the cliff.

Descent: From the top of the routes go to the summit then down to the col on the right. Descend steeply down the scree slope running back underneath the base of the cliff. This slope holds much snow well into June and in such conditions the buttress crest further left (facing out) should be followed. In favourable conditions a shorter descent can be made by traversing right (west) across the screes about 50m short of the summit, heading for just above a large pink boulder then diagonally left to gain the scree slope at the base of the cliff. Alternatively, a 50m abseil from a flake at the top of *Temple of Doom* gains the base on rope stretch.

EAST FACE

Go up the scree-filled gully between **Diamond** and **Church Door Buttresses** to a prominent chimney opposite the neck of Collie's Pinnacle on the left.

1 Flake Route ★★   **130m Very Difficult**
FA Harold Raeburn, John Bell & Graham Napier July 1898

"I went forward to the end of the ledge to try and field him should a slip occur, while Napier jammed himself in a hole in the ledge, worked Raeburn's rope over the small hitch and anchored me. This time Raeburn was successful, and wild cheers broke out ... " – Bell.
The original route up the buttress. A huge flake is separated from the buttress by a crack. Ascend the crack to the crest of the buttress. Make an awkward step up and right then direct until a traverse left leads to an arch formed by two enormous boulders. Cross the arch and ascend the shallow chimney (crux). Finish steeply to easy ground.

2 Crypt Route ★★★   **135m Very Difficult**
FA R.Morley, M.Wood, John Wilding, & Fred Piggott 15 September 1920; Gallery Variation: Ian Norris, P.Barker & A.N. Other 15 July 1952

A unique subterranean excursion into the very bowels of the cliff, of interest to speleologists, troglodytes and other such perverts. The only route in the country where a torch is de rigueur. Ascend the chimney for 20m to a corridor cleaving into the cliff. Go to the rear of the corridor where there is a choice of routes, though the honeycomb of subterranean passages are all rather similar!
The Tunnel Route: through a narrow passage in the left wall to a chamber then another tunnel to a further chamber from which a long narrow tunnel leads upwards to a 0.5m diameter hole in the cliff face 6m beneath the right end of the arch. Ascend easy slabs for 6m to another hole in the lower right end of the arch.
The Through Route: through the cave-like end of the corridor to a smaller cave, exiting this with interest using the top of the chokestone. Continue past a grass ledge, a jumble of boulders and a cracked block to the arch.
The Gallery Variation: From the second cave of *The Through Route* enter another chimney in the fault to gain a smaller third cave. Enter the 'gallery' (2m x 1.3m x 6m) above, descend 1.3m from the 'gallery' floor, and facing out, traverse rightwards 15m to climb up to the arch. All three variations finish by *Flake Route*.

Top tips: (1) take long stick and big hook to recover head torches and assorted gear from deep pit **(2)** light breakfast and no lunch recommended **(3)** head torches no use – better off with mouth-held hand torch **(4)** leave rucksacks at base!

WEST FACE

3 Fundamentalists ★★★   **100m E4 6a**
FA Gary Latter & Pete Craig 15 September 2002

The crack-line at the left side of the face just left of *Lost Arrow*. Start at the block belay as for that route.

1 25m 5b Move up leftwards onto a ledge then up left over blocks. Step right and climb a wall above the block to belay on the right as for *Lost Arrow*.

2 25m 6a Climb the slab on the left into the base of the grey corner. Step right into the crack with difficulty and follow it past an old PR to belay in a small recess just right of the prominent square-cut roof.

3 20m 6a Undercut left and pull spectacularly round the roof. Climb the crack above to a good no hands rest on top of the huge block forming the roof. Continue steeply on good holds to belay on a ledge. A superb pitch on impeccable rock.

4 30m 5c Move diagonally up left and climb a short arête on its front face. Continue trending leftwards to a deep corner crack. Step left and climb a short finger crack with difficulty to belay on a ledge above. Scrambling remains.

④ Lost Arrow ★★★   100m E3 6a
FA Gary Latter & Paul Thorburn 10 August 1995

The crack and corner system up the left side of the clean face left of *Kingpin*. Start at a block belay at left end of grassy ledge.

1 25m 4c Up a groove and wide crack to belay on a slab below a small roof.

2 35m 6a Pull through a crack in the lower roof to a slabby ledge beneath a crack in the right side of the roof. Pull through this and up a crack (crux) past an old PR on the left. Continue up the crack to a long sloping ledge on the right wall where the crack narrows and bends. Pull out right to the edge of groove and up midway between both to the easier groove. Thread and nut belay beneath main corner. A superb well-protected pitch on immaculate and very rough rock.

3 40m 5c Climb the rib 3m right of the corner (good nut high in the corner) and move back into the corner. Easily up this and traverse right under the first roof and up a flake to the large capping roof. Undercut this right with a hard move pulling round the right edge of the flake to belay. Scramble up then left to summit screes.

⑤ Kingpin ★★★   105m E3 6a
FA Wall Thomson & John Hardie (some aid) 17 August 1968;
FFA Pitch 1 Murray Hamilton & Dave Cuthbertson 1977;
FFA Complete Dave Cuthbertson & Dougie Mullin 1978;
Direct Finish Murray Hamilton & Rab Anderson summer 1982

A brilliant sustained route, following a direct line up the left side of the prominent pillar up the highest central section of the face. Start just right of a block belay directly beneath a prominent large arrowhead-shaped recess. Pitches 1 and 2 may be better run together.

1 20m 6a Climb crack to a slab then left and up to a steep shallow groove and up this with difficulty to swing right to a poor belay at a groove junction.

2 20m 5c Move up right and follow a black groove (often wet) to an awkward mantelshelf onto a small ledge beneath the short hanging chimney. Up this and step left at its top to belay on a ledge.

3 30m 5b Move back right and up the fine sloping ramp to a small hooded recess. Exit slightly left then up to a ledge. Continue to belay at the foot of the prominent corner.

4 35m 5c Follow the corner to the roof, step left and up the continuation corner above. Swing right at its top to finish up a prominent short flared chimney.

⑥ The Lost Ark ★★★   90m E4 6a
FA Pete Whillance & Ray Parker 27 July 1983

Excellent sustained climbing. Just right of the pillar of *Kingpin* is a large open white-speckled groove.

1 45m 6a Up the left side of the groove then the wall to the roof on the arête. Step left and climb boldly up the left side of arête on rounded side pulls for 5m (crux) to better holds. Move up right and traverse right across the top of the groove in a sensational position to an old PR. Move straight up to good ledge and belay at base of corner.

2 45m 5b Climb the corner above to a good ledge then past a large keyed in block. Avoid the dirty section by moving out onto the right wall then back into the corner. Continue more easily leftwards to finish up the final chimney of *Kingpin*.

⑦ The Holy Grail ★★   35m E5 6b
FA Paul Thorburn & Gary Latter 8 August 1995

A fine sustained pitch with good protection between *The Lost Ark* and *Temple of Doom*. Climb the prominent easy lower V-groove and the shallow white groove above to a roof. Pull out left to a good rest then make hard moves up rightwards into the stepped upper groove and up this to pull to belay as for *Temple of Doom*.

8 Temple of Doom ★★★★   75m E3 6a

*FA Murray Hamilton, Rab Anderson & Graeme Livingston
21 July 1984*

The prominent V-groove and hanging stepped corner
gives superb, well-protected climbing.

1 **30m 6a** Climb the easy lower groove to a
large flake. Up the smooth groove above past
bombproof runner placements and swing left
at the top to a large hanging flake. Pull over
this and belay beneath deep V-groove.

2 **45m 5c** Move right and easily up crack for 6m then
step back left. Pull over the roof above and continue
in a superb position up the hanging stepped corner
system. At the top of this follow the continuation
crack for a short way until it is possible to step right
into the corner on the right. Up this to the top. A brilliant pitch – the situations are strictly space-walking.

9 The Last Crusade ★★   50m E3 5c

FA Rab Anderson & Johnny May 30 May 1992

The prominent V-groove (another one!) and wall right
of *Temple of Doom*. Start just below a huge block at
the base of the crag beneath a wide crack in a shallow
corner.

1 **10m 5a** Climb the corner crack, pull out left to ledges and move up left to the foot of an open corner.

2 **20m 5c** Move right then up to the foot of the
V-groove. Climb the groove to its top, swing
out left then move across to climb steeply up
the left side of a small roof (F #4 useful, though
not essential) and pull onto a small ledge.

3 **20m 5c** Climb the cracks in the wall above.

*Temple of Doom. Gary Latter climbing
first pitch. Photo Paul Thorburn.*

STAC AN EICH (STAC OF THE HORSE) NN 031 593 **Alt:** 100m 5min

A steep little granite crag in the woods of Leitir Mhor (Lettermore) overlooking Loch Linnhe. Many of the routes stay dry all summer, though it is very sheltered and midges can be a problem late in the season.

Access: From the roundabout south of the Ballachulish bridge, head west down the A832 Oban road for about 1.3 miles/ 2km. Turn off left about a kilometre beyond (south) of the old ruined Ballachulish pier up a forestry track (signposted 'The Monument') just before a telephone box. Drive through a gate and up the forestry track for a couple of hundred metres to park at the bend.

Approach: Continue up the track then steeply directly up the slope at the next bend.

Descent: By abseil from trees or fight through the undergrowth and down the steep vegetated descent gully at the right end of the crag.

The crag is dominated by an imposing wall in the centre, split by three short groove lines. Right of this is the central corner line of *Marathon* then a further overhanging wall split by a couple of cracks bounded on the right by an easier angled area of rock.

---

1 Let Sleeping Dogs Lie ★★ 21m E4 6b

FA Murray Hamilton & Rab Anderson 19 May 1985

The deceptive central groove with a perplexing crux. Climb the groove to a good flat hold, make a long reach for a side pull on the right then regain the groove (crux) which leads to easier ground. Move up onto the slab and belay.

2 Seal of Approval ★★ 24m E4 6a

FA Gary Latter & Ian Campbell 6 July 1985

A spectacular line across the centre of the crag. Start beneath twin cracks in the centre of the overhanging wall just right of the previous route. Up twin cracks to gain a scoop. Up this and a flaky groove to good incut holds (nut placement in undercut). Swing right from here into a shallow groove system. Pull leftwards from the top of this to a tree belay. Either scramble up broken ground or abseil off.

 Bill's Digger ★★★   **25m E5 6b**

FA Dave Cuthbertson June 1984

Excellent well protected climbing with a very reachy, contorted crux. It takes the shallow, stepped groove in the arête delineating the centre of the crag. Pull over the initial bulge leftwards on improving holds and move up to a thread runner in a recess. Continue up the steepening groove with a powerful reachy move to gain good holds in a horizontal break. Step right and continue up an easier crack.

4 Marathon ★★   **30m E1 5b**

FA Ed Grindley, Mike Hall & Fiona Gunn 14 November 1981

The central corner line. Well protected, with some weird moves. At the top traverse left onto the slab to belay on the rib. Either scramble rightwards to finish or abseil off.

5 Gunslinger ★★   **25m E3 5c**

FA Ed Grindley & Davy Gunn 22 October 1981

Well protected, strenuous climbing on big holds up the deceptively steep cracks in the highest part of the wall right of 4. Start at an undercut flake. Up this and the crack above, passing a small resting ledge at mid height to finish on good blocks. Tree belay further back.

6 The Monument ★   **10m E3 5c**

FA Ed Grindley 26 March 1982

The crack and capping roof at the right end of the frontal face. Enter the ramp and up a crack to pull over the roof on good holds. Trend easily rightwards to a belay.

The crag continues round right to form a shorter, easier angled west-facing wall.

7 Appin Groove ★★   **9m HS 4b**

FA Ed Grindley 1981

The left-facing layback groove at the highest point of the wall.

Let Sleeping Dog's Lie. Rick Campbell climbing.

Excalibur, Garbh Bheinn.
Dave Cuthbertson climbing the second pitch.
Photo Jo George, Cubby Images.

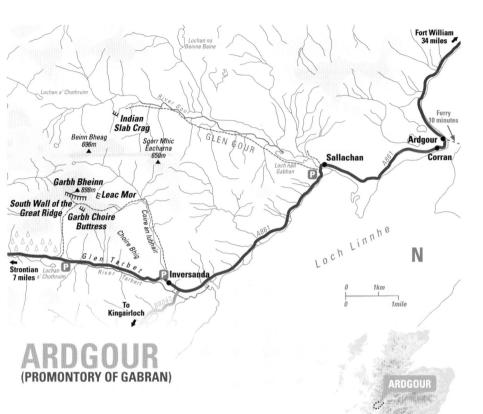

ARDGOUR
(PROMONTORY OF GABRAN)

This is the mountainous district west of Loch Linnhe. Travelling from the south the skyline west of the Ballachulish bridge is dominated by the prominent notched outline of Garbh Bheinn. Being further west and lower lying the district often benefits from fine clear weather when Glen Coe is enshrouded in cloud. It is also considerably quieter.

Accommodation: Wild camping anywhere in the hills, though permission from the estate may have to be sought during the stalking season – enquire at Inversanda House. A better option (sea breeze to dissuade midges) may be to camp on one of the many beaches (plenty of driftwood) thus avoiding the attentions of the landowners.

Caravan & campsites: Glenview Caravan & Camp Park, Strontian (☎ 01967 402123); Resipole Farm Caravan & Camp Park, Resipole (☎ 01967 431235; www.resipole.co.uk). Corran Hotel by the ferry is nearest pub. **Bunkhouses:** Ariundle Centre, Strontian (☎ 01967 402279; www.ariundlecentre.co.uk); Lochaline Dive Centre (☎ 01967 421627; www.lochalinedivecentre.co.uk). Numerous B&Bs locally – **TIC** at Strontian (Easter – Oct; ☎ 01967 402131). Chalets and self-catering accommodation further west in Strontian and Salen. **Amenities:** Spar supermarket and petrol station at Clovullin just off the A861, 1 mile/1.6 km west of the Corran ferry.

"On the one hand ranged a vast array of the mainland mountains … on the other the Atlantic Ocean and the small isles of the west. This truly is the combination to which the Scottish hills owe all worthiness – rock, water, and the subtle colours of the seaward atmosphere."

– W H Murray, Undiscovered Scotland. (J M Dent & Sons,1951)

ARDGOUR HISTORY

The first route here was the classic *The Great Ridge* climbed by John Bell and Willie Brown back in 1897. Ken Barber and J Lomas climbed the long *Route II* up all four tiers of Leac Beag in 1939, improving on the earlier wandering *Route 1*. In 1952 Dan Stewart and Donald Mill had a productive weekend, adding a number of routes including *The Great Ridge Direct Start* and the fine *Scimitar*. A few years later, Jimmy Marshall and Len Lovat added further good lines with *Sgian Dubh* and *Razor Slash*, Marshall returning with others to snatch the superb *Butterknife*. Other harder routes were added throughout the sixties, including further additions from Marshall (*The Clasp*) and Robin Smith (*The Peeler*), but some of the best finds were in the seventies. Ken Crocket and Colin Stead added the improbable *Excalibur*. Les and P Brown and Ian Davidson opened up the fine

Indian Slab Crag in Glen Gour with a number of good routes, including *Indian Slab* and *Outrider*. Later, in 2000, Colin Moody and Cynthia Grindley added *Time Traveller* and the superb *Mullennium*. Dougie Dinwoodie raised standards with his ascent of *The Pincer* in 1978, but it was Murray Hamilton who took things further with a series of contrasting adjacent routes, first with *Chela*, then *Tru-Cut*. Pete Whillance added the bold *White Hope* in 1984, and a couple of years later Hamilton succeeded on one of the most impressive pitches in the mountains with the technical and very sustained *Kelpie*. His second on this occasion, Rab Anderson returned in the nineties to climb two of the three remaining cracks on this steep wall with *Cutlass* and *Sabre*, and later contributed *The Contender*. The final central crack gave Paul Thorburn *The Epeeist* in 1996.

Paul Thorburn on-sight on the first ascent of Leviathan

NM 916 645 **Alt:** 550m

GLEN GOUR
INDIAN SLAB CRAG

Glen Gour is the large flat-bottomed glen running west from Sallachan, north of Garbh Bheinn and just south of the Corran ferry. Despite being north-facing, this fine gneiss crag dries remarkably quickly and receives a fair bit of sun due to its open aspect and low angle. The routes give excellent climbing with fairly spaced protection, generally on superb rock.

Access: From the Corran Ferry, follow the A861 road west for 2.4 miles/3.8km to a small loop road running close to the north bank of the river flowing into Camas Shallachain. Park on the south side of the bridge.

Approach: Follow the track west close to the south side of the river and Loch nan Gabhar then along the south side of the glen until it peters out after about 5.5km. Head diagonally left up the hillside to the base of the cliff. Although rough going at first, **mountain bikes** can be taken 3.5km along the glen as far as the sheepfold (free on the ferry).

Descent: From the large heather terrace at the top, traverse left and across the stream bed then down the slope just to its right (east), re-crossing the stream lower down and slanting down left to regain the base.

① Outrider ★★   **80m VS 4b,4b,4b**
FA Les & P Brown Easter 1972

The prominent left-facing corner at the left side. Walk up left to a path crossing the crag. Ascend the initial slab then move right above the tree to gain the initially grassy corner. Continue up the slab left of the corner. Best climbed in three pitches (no obvious belay at mid-height).

② Ambush ★★   **40m VS 4c**
FA Mike Pescod, Rose McKie & Donald King 15 May 2003

The left edge of the hanging slab above *Outrider*. Climb *Outrider* to above the tree and step right to belay in the higher corner.

③ Time Lord ★★   **205m VS 4c**
FA Colin Moody & Cynthia Grindley 1 July 2000

Slightly better protected than *Indian Slab*. Start right of a vertical grassy crack up and left of *Indian Slab*.

  1 50m 4c Climb up using a flake then direct to belay beneath the path. Walk left to belay at the base of the rib.

  2 40m 4a Climb the rib and continue to belay beneath a black bulge.

  3 50m 4b Move left round the bulge to follow the left edge of the obvious slab.

  4 50m 4a Straight up.

  5 15m 4a Finish up left on ripples.

4 **Indian Slab ★★**   **190m VS 4b**

FA Ian Davidson & Les Brown Easter 1972

Good climbing, particularly on the first and third pitches.
Start at the base of the black-streaked slabs, down and
left of a steep section.

1 **50m 4b** Follow the slab to a grass
   ledge beneath a steepening.

2 **50m** Continue up to cross the path then
   follow ribs and heather leading up left
   to beneath the prominent slab.

3 **50m 4b** A superb sustained pitch. Climb
   the slab crossing the overlap at 30m.

4 **40m 4a** Trend up right to finish.

5 **Mullennium Direct ★★★**   **200m Severe 4a**

FA Colin Moody & Cynthia Grindley 1 July 2000;
pitch 1 Gary Latter & Jeremy Birkbeck 16 August 2002

Four excellent full length pitches towards the right side
of the slab. Start at the very toe of the crag, down right
of the shelf at the base of Indian Slab.

1 **50m 4a** Move up right over initially broken
   ground to gain the superb smooth slab and follow
   this, taking the cleanest line trending slightly
   right to gain the base of the original route.

2 **50m 4a** Ascend the pale slab to belay a few
   metres left of a group of small rowans.

3 **50m 4a** Traverse left to the edge and
   ascend the slab overlooking Indian Slab.

4 **50m 4a** Continue directly to finish.

PALE FACE

Obliquely up and left of the main crag, on the opposite
side of the open gully is an obvious pale slab.
Descent: Down the right side of the crag.

6 **Paleface ★★**   **30m VS 4c**

FA Gary Latter (on-sight solo) 16 August 2002

The prominent thin crack. Climb the crack, finishing by an
easier ridge at the top.

7 **Sun Dance ★**   **30m E2 5a**

FA Donald King, Rose McKie & Mike Pescod 15 May 2003

The front face of the slab.

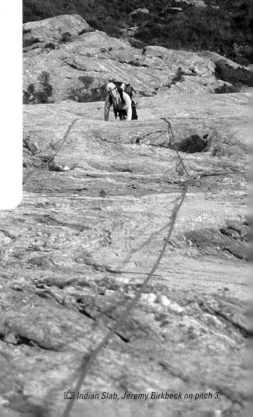

📷 Indian Slab, Jeremy Birkbeck on pitch 3.

GARBH BHEINN
(ROUGH HILL)

The most southerly significant outcropping of gneiss in the country, Garbh Bheinn is an excellent mountain with as varied a range of routes as anywhere, from one of the best ridges on the mainland to a clutch of excellent extremes, and everything in between. The fact that the summit lies just below the three thousand foot mark makes it all the better for that, being devoid of all those boring Munro-baggers. The panorama from the summit is stunning – choose a fine clear day and savour.

Access: Take the ferry over Loch Linnhe at the Corran narrows to Ardgour (7.00-21.00 in summer; 10 minutes crossing time) and follow the A861 south-west (left) for 7 miles/11 km, turning off right 0.3miles/0.5km beyond the Kingairloch turn off, onto the old road which loops round. Park just before the old bridge.

Approach: (A) Follow a stalkers path on the right side of the stream (Abhainn Coire an lubhair) up the very boggy strath of Coire an lubhair (Corrie of the Yew Tree) to cross the stream after about 4.5km (1 hour). Continue steeply south-west up the right side of the burn emanating from

the Garbh Choire Mor to reach the base of the cliffs.
(B) For routes on the **South Wall of the Great Ridge**, a faster, drier and steeper approach up the coire at the back can be made. Drive a further 2 miles/3km west along Glen Tarbert to park on the old road on the left overlooking a tiny lochan (100m before the road crosses the Allt a' Chothruim). Follow a vague path steeply up the right (east) bank of the burn flowing down Coire a' Chothruim (Corrie of the Balance, unnamed on 1:50,000 map, but immediately south of the summit) then slog up hillside rightwards (north-east) to the bealach between Sron a' Gharbh Choire Bhig and Garbh Bheinn. From the bealach continue left up the ridge by a path then cut across easy-angled slabs to gain the upper left end of the **South Wall of the Great Ridge.** 1.25 hours.
(C) An alternative approach to the bealach, much drier underfoot than the first described and not as tortuous as the second, is to cut up left from the old bridge and follow the ridge which eventually drops down into the bealach 1.75 hours.

Descent: Head left (west) along a well worn path along the summit ridge and down to the left end of the cliffs, or continue further to a path into the coire from the bealach.

LEAC MOR (GREAT SLAB) 1¾hr

NM 909 627 **Alt:** 550m

This large secluded cliff lies on the east flank of the mountain, out of sight from the coire. It is divided into four tiers by three terraces, the third tier the Leac Mor.

Approach: Either contour right from low in Garbh Choire Mor, or continue west up the glen by a good path on the north side of the stream then cutting across directly up to the base.

Descent: Either continue up to the summit and down the path to the bealach or from the top of the cliff descend north-west down the ridge to a small col then follow a vague path down a steep grassy slope to arrive just east of small lochan. Head back down the glen by a good path on the north bank of the burn.

---

1 **Route II** ★★   **365m Very Difficult**

FA Ken Barber & J.Lomas July 1939

A long sustained route up the full length of the cliff. Start beneath the left edge of the first tier (the first 100m is avoidable by walking round the left side).

1 **40m** Climb the left edge of slabs to a ledge on the left.

2 **50m** Step back right and up an easy grassy groove.

3 **10m** Easy slabs. Walk over to base of the next tier.

4 **35m** Start just left of the left edge of a smooth pale wall. Up a slab to a vertical crack; up this and a groove to belay beneath a short vertical wall.

5 **40m** Traverse diagonally right to the end of a steep wall then go up to the base of a long narrow grassy chimney on the next tier.

6 **40m** Climb a narrow grassy vertical fault to belay in a grassy alcove 5m above a large block.

7 **45m** Traverse right then up right-wards by cracks/grooves.

8 **35m** Continue straight up.

9-10 **80m** Either finish by any line on the final tier (Difficult) or scramble up left for 150-200m, skirting beneath the final tier.

📷 *The Peeler, Scott Muir starting up the second pitch. Photo Dave Cuthbertson, Cubby Images.*

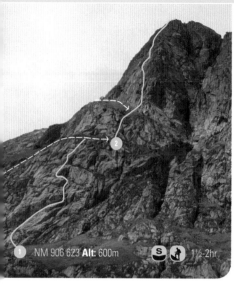

NM 906 623 **Alt:** 600m 1½-2hr

📷 *The Great Ridge. Rob Kerr climbing.*

LOWER CLIFF

The cliff left of the obvious *Great Gully*.

The Great Ridge Direct Start ★★
165m Severe 4a

FA Dan Stewart & Donald Mill 12 April 1952

A good sustained approach to the upper ridge. Start down and right of the prominent right-slanting ramp on the right side of the crag.

1 20m Up the shallow steep ramp, starting on huge pockets then slightly left to belay at base of huge right-sloping ramp.

2 50m 4a Up the ramp (belay possible at 25m, at block just right of old PR) and continue in the same line to move up a steep flake then a short slab to belay on a long grassy ledge.

3 20m Move left round the edge and up easy slabs to belay on grassy ledge below a prominent flake chimney.

4 30m 4a The awkward chimney then leftwards over jumbled blocks then up a slab by a wide crack. Flake belay on the left at the back of a grass slope above.

5 45m Scramble up right then follow a rib, traversing right then up grass to a block belay up to the left of the base of *The Great Ridge*.

The Great Ridge ★★★   250m Difficult

FA John Bell & Willie Brown April 1897

A fine long mountaineering expedition, especially when combined with the *Direct Start*, with a stunning somewhat abrupt finish right on the summit of the hill. The ridge projects south-east from the summit, with the distinctive *Great Gully* cutting deeply into the face just to its right. The climbing becomes very much easier just below half-height. Continue up left from the base of the *Direct Start* to just before the base of a steep 50m cliff just beneath the bealach. Ascend a short step then traverse diagonally right along a grassy rake which leads almost into *Great Gully*. Climb the right edge of a slabby buttress overlooking a shallow open gully then walk up right to a block belay just up left from the base of the ridge proper (45m). Climb over sharp flakes left of the edge and move right to the crest. Continue up this to belay at the base of a short steep V-groove (35m). Climb the groove on good holds then a short ramp on the left (15m). Continue easily up grass to beneath a steep wall. Traverse left along the ledge then climb diagonally right to regain the crest of ridge. Continue up this to belay on the ledge above (40m). Continue up the crest, outflanking a steeper section on the left to a large grassy ledge. Climb a short right slanting grassy gully on the left, with a short rock step at its top then more easily up the obvious line to easier rocks leading to the summit cairn.

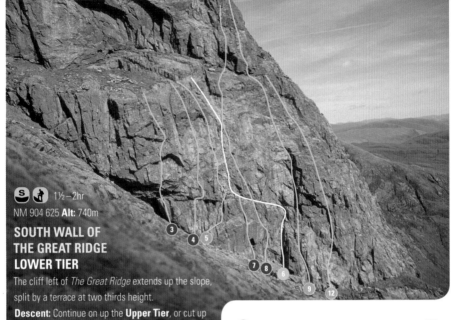

S **(🧗)** 1½–2hr

NM 904 625 **Alt:** 740m

SOUTH WALL OF THE GREAT RIDGE LOWER TIER

The cliff left of *The Great Ridge* extends up the slope, split by a terrace at two thirds height.

Descent: Continue on up the **Upper Tier**, or cut up the easy-angled slabs leftwards beneath the base of the **Upper Tier** then down the path to the bealach.

③ Brack *   40m E3 5c
FA Murray Hamilton & Rab Anderson 21 June 1986

A good steep airy pitch up the left side of the crag. Start at a short prominent arête. Climb the arête to the break, pull left over the roof (crux) and cross the next bulge to the wall above. Move right and pull over the third roof at a break then continue passing left through two bulges to finish on the terrace.

④ The Gay Blade **   40m E3 6a
FA Gary Latter & Paul Thorburn 24 June 1996

The prominent thin crack-line up the wall left of *Scimitar*. Start 3m left of the broken rising ledge system of *Scimitar*. Climb the initial cracked wall with difficulty (crux) to move right at the prominent horizontal break to easier ground. Continue up the crack, moving right on side-pulls into the steep finger crack which soon relents. Continue more easily in the same line, past a short steep wall near the top.

⑤ Scimitar **   105m VS 4c
FA Dan Stewart & Donald Mill 13 April 1952

From the base of the broken rising ledge system, about 30m up left from the huge boulder at the base of *Butterknife*.

1 **30m 4c** Follow the ledge up right until it becomes horizontal. Go up a steep crack above the left end to an overhang, move right spectacularly to good holds on an edge. Move up and left to a ledge and belay at the base of a corner.

2 **25m 4a** Continue directly up slab and open chimney leading to the terrace.

3 **50m 4b** Climb a smooth vertical groove then move right to a flake. Continue either up the left-facing corner or the slabs on its left leading to easier angled slabs to finish on the crest of the ridge.

⑥ Razor Slash *   75m Severe 4a
FA Jimmy Marshall, Len Lovat & Archie Hendry 1 April 1956

Start at the huge boulder set against the face about 30m down from *Scimitar*.

1 **25m 4a** Climb the boulder and step into a dièdre which is climbed to a platform.

2 **20m 4a** Traverse horizontally left along the ledge

for 8m to the base of an obvious layback slab edge. Climb this ledge, occasionally laybacking, and at the top move out delicately over a nose (crux) then right and back left to belay.

3 **30m 4a** Follow the left diagonal fracture cutting across the prominent chimney of *Scimitar* to finish on the terrace.

7 Leviathan *   20m E3 6a
FA Paul Thorburn, Neil Craig, Rick Campbell & Gary Latter 28 June 1997

The wide overhanging crack left of *The Golden Lance*, so named because it is *"nasty, brutish and short."* Gain the crack and follow it forcefully to end on a broken ledge. Scramble off left and down easy ground.

8 The Golden Lance *   98m E2 5c
FA Rab Anderson & Alan Russell 30 June 1984

The prominent thin crack-line left of *Butterknife*. Start on top of the large boulder.

1 **18m 5c** Climb the thin crack then up left and back right to belay on the traverse ledge of *Razor Slash*.

2 **40m 5c** Step right and climb the thin crack-line then over a short leaning wall. Continue in the same line to the terrace.

3 **40m 5b** Above is a short corner terminating at a small roof. Climb the corner and pull over rightwards to reach easier ground. Move up and leftwards into the centre of the wall then climb up to a short leaning wall. Pull over this and finish up easier ground.

9 Butterknife ****   105m HS 4b
FA Jimmy Marshall, Archie Hendry, George Ritchie & Ian Haig 15 September 1956

Stunning climbing, with a particularly fine second pitch. Start directly beneath the main corner, 10m right of the large slanting boulder leaning against the base of the crag.

1 **25m 4a** Up the groove which slants left to belay on a block-strewn ledge below the corner crack.

2 **25m 4b** Up the superb corner on excellent holds to belay at its top. Well protected – large hexes/Fs useful.

3 **25m 4a** Easily up the slab above to belay below a roof at the right end of the terrace.

4 **35m 4b** Cross a small roof low down and follow a direct line to the top.

4a **VS 4c** *Direct Finish* – A fine 45m pitch takes the prominent thin vertical crack midway between the short left-facing corner of *The Golden Lance* and the original finish. Cross the initial overhang on good holds and follow the crack over a steepening to a short diagonal left-slanting crack. Up this and trend slightly rightwards on easier ground to join the crest of *The Great Ridge*. Well protected.

10 Bodkin *   75m E1 5a
FA Ken Crocket & Stuart Smith 10 June 1979

The right arête of *Butterknife*. Start 3m right of that route.

1 **25m 5a** Climb to a steepening at 15m, step left (crux) and continue up and left to belay on the edge below some bulges.

2 **25m 5a** Move right then up to an overhang. Move left to the edge and continue more easily up this.

3 **25m 4a** As for *Butterknife* to the terrace.

11 Poniard **   60m HVS 5a
FA Gary Latter & Dave Greig 28 June 1997

Surprisingly reasonable climbing up the wall between *Butterknife* and *Mournblade*. Start 10m right of *Butterknife*, beneath a prominent shallow pale groove. Climb the groove then move rightward and climb to an undercut flange beneath a small overlap. Cross this and the main overhang above on good holds. Move up a short way to another overlap, step left and finish up the groove, easing towards the top.

12 Mournblade **   65m VS 4b
FA Ken Crocket, Colin Grant & J.Hutchinson 31 July 1976

The corner parallel to and 12m right of *Butterknife*. Start at a rough flake 6m right of *Butterknife*.

1 **30m 4b** Climb up then right to the base of the corner. Follow the corner, step right into a groove and climb it to a good stance at a pinnacle.

2 **35m** – Climb the bulge directly above on good holds and continue more easily up the wall on the left.

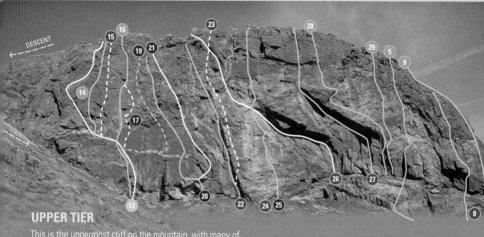

UPPER TIER

This is the uppermost cliff on the mountain, with many of the routes ending just a few metres short of the summit.

Approaches: Head steeply up the back of the coire to the bealach then by a path towards the summit, cutting down easy-angled slabs along the base of the crag. Alternatively the right end of the grass terrace at the base can be gained by following *The Great Ridge Direct Start*. Another possibility is by scrambling up a rocky step at the base of Bealach Gully Buttress (at the foot of the prominent deep gully) then cutting rightwards and up by grass and wood rush. Avoid in wet conditions.

Descent: Follow the well worn path left down the summit ridge to the bealach.

13 Sgian Dubh ★★　　　　　　　**42m Very Difficult**

FA Jimmy Marshall & Len Lovat 1 April 1956

Fine steep climbing up the left side of the wall. Start beneath the prominent deep chimney, just left of the very impressive smooth overhanging wall.

1 **12m** Climb the open chimney, making use of a fine hand crack in the back, to a ledge. Walk along the ledge to belay in its centre.

2 **30m** Climb diagonally leftwards following a line of flake cracks to beneath a bulge. Step left and pull up on good holds to gain the base of an easy-angled right-slanting ramp. Go up this then steeply on good flakes to a thread and nut belay on the ledge above. Scramble up to finish.

14 Sala ★　　　　　　　　　　**30m HVS 5a**

FA Alan Taylor & Rab Anderson 20 June 1982

Climb a flange/crack just left of *Menghini* to where a diagonal crack comes in from the right and continue up to a ledge. Move right and finish up the wall above.

15 Menghini ★★　　　　　　　　**30m E1 5a**

FA Alan Taylor & Rab Anderson 20 June 1982

The prominent crack just left of *The Peeler*.

16 The Peeler ★　　　　　　　　**47m HVS 5b**

FA Robin Smith & James Moriarty June 1961

The hard climbing is well protected and concentrated in the first 9m. Start on the outer edge of the *Sgian Dubh* flake.

1 **12m 4b** Climb the crest of the flake to belay on the platform.

2 **35m 5b** Climb the groove on the right to pull up and leftwards round a roof. Continue up a short steep crack which soon falls back into a groove leading to the top.

17 Cutlass ★　　　　　　　　　　**60m E4 6b**

FA Rab Anderson 6 June 1992

The leftmost crack-line on the leaning wall, immediately right of *The Peeler*. Good climbing, though a bit close to *The Peeler* at times.

1 40m 6b Climb the awkward short groove in the arête just left of *Sgian Dubh* to gain ledges. Climb to beneath the roof, pull round left then move up and right to follow the prominent left-slanting crack to a junction with *The Peeler*. Either belay here or move up and right to a grass ledge.

2 20m Easy ground to top.

18 Sabre ★★   60m E5 6b
FA Rab & Chris Anderson 6 June 1992

Excellent climbing up the thin crack near the left side of the leaning wall.

1 40m 6b Climb the initial corner of *Sgian Dubh* to the ledge. Place the high runners on *Cutlass* and extend them then hand traverse out right for 3m to attain a standing position below the crack. Climb the crack to beneath a small roof, step up left and pull up to easier ground. Move up and climb the cracks in the wall to the right of *Cutlass* to reach a grass ledge.

2 20m Easy ground to top.

19 The Epeeist ★★★   50m E5 6b
FA Paul Thorburn & Gary Latter 23 June 1996

Excellent varied climbing up the central blocky crack in the leaning wall, directly above the very prominent black seep. From the top of the initial chimney of *Sgian Dubh*, first hand then foot traverse the shelf out right with increasing difficulty to the base of the crack. Pull the ropes and move the belayer to below (or drop a 3rd rope). Up the crack with a hard move low down to follow excellent holds which lead out left near the top. Finish up the easier wall above on excellent rock to spike belay. Scramble off.

20 Kelpie ★★★★   45m E6 6b
FA Murray Hamilton & Rab Anderson 21 June 1986

A stunning line, giving one of the best routes of the grade anywhere. Start 5m right of the hanging flake, at the right side of the leaning wall.

1 25m 6b Pull over the roof and up to good nuts in the crack. Traverse left into the steep hanging flake and up this with hard moves up slightly rightwards to good holds at the base of the crack. Powerful sustained climbing up the crack leads to a belay at the top of the leaning wall.

2 20m 5b Continue up the crack leftwards until a groove can be followed to easier ground leading to the top.

Menghini, Jules Lines climbing.

📷 *Jo George on the second pitch of Sgian Dubh. Photo Paul Thorburn.*

 21 Tru-Cut ★   **50m E4 5c**

FA Murray Hamilton & Rab Anderson 13 June 1982

Start as for *Kelpie*. Gain the groove above the initial overlap from the left. Follow this to pull out left and continue up to a move right to reach a ramp/groove. Follow this over the initial bulge to reach a belay, or continue to the top.

22 Chela ★   **45m E3 6a**

FA Murray Hamilton & Al Murray May 1981

The prominent smooth left-facing groove. Bold & sustained.
- **1 25m 6a** Climb the groove to a nut belay.
- **2 20m 5b** Continue more easily directly above.

23 The Pincer ★★★   **50m E2 5b**

FA Dougie Dinwoodie & Bob Smith August 1978

Fine open climbing up the right side of the right arête of the *Chela* groove. Follow the arête, passing the left side of a bulge to reach a small overhang. Turn this on the left to enter a steep corner, and follow this and its left arête to finish.

24 The Contender ★★★   **50m E3 5c**

FA Rab & Chris Anderson 11 August 1994

Brilliant sustained climbing following the thin hanging crack up the left side of the white wall. Many small wires (R #1 – 5) required. Start in the centre of the wall, behind a prominent projecting block embedded in the ground. Climb directly to the right end of a short left-slanting crack at 6m and follow this to gain a jug up on the left. Move up to a large rounded pocket, step left and follow a thin crack over bulges into a groove. Cross a bulge at the top of the groove and follow a ramp a short way then swing out right and up a short crack to ledges. Ascend a niche then a rib on the left finishing up a slab to a thin grass ledge just below the top.

25 White Hope ★★★   **50m E5 6a**

FA Pete Whillance, Murray Hamilton & Rab Anderson 5 May 1984

Excellent sustained climbing, following a direct line up the centre of the clean white wall. Start immediately behind a large embedded flake, below a thin vertical quartz seam in the centre of the wall. Climb this to a right-slanting flake at 12m. Make hard moves directly up from its right end to gain jugs beneath a small isolated roof. Pull over its right side and climb direct, moving slightly left then back right to below the final leaning wall. Move up leftwards to a short crack and pull over to a belay. Scramble to the top.

26 The Clasp ★★   60m E1 5a

FA Jimmy Marshall April 1960

A left-trending line below the leftmost end of the lower of the two large roofs. Start beneath the right end of the roof.

1 **12m 4b** Climb the steep wall and trend left to a belay.
2 **48m 5a** Continue up under the roof, traverse left to a shallow groove then up to a chimney trending left to the top.

27 The Foil ★   80m E2 5c

FA Paul Moores & Mick Tighe (1 PA) 29 May 1978

Sparsely protected climbing across the steep wall sandwiched between the two roofs. Start at a short wall beneath the right end of the upper roof.

1 **40m 5c** Move up to the roof, move left directly below it and follow it left with difficulty to where it fades. Exit left onto steep slabs.
2 **40m** Finish up the cracks in the slab.

28 Excalibur ★★   80m HVS 5a

FA Ken Crocket & Colin Stead 10 June 1972

Impressive situations, with two fine contrasting pitches. It gains and traverses the lip of the smaller second roof system. Start at the pale open groove beneath the right end of the long roof.

1 **20m 5a** Climb the central and deepest of three faint groove-lines on good holds to pull out right to a good spike on the rib. Continue steeply up this with hard moves to gain a good ledge level with the lip of the roof. Belay here.
2 **25m 4c** Traverse left above the lip of the roof by a line of good hand holds, past a prominent thin diagonal crack-line then up to the base of the steep bottomless corner. Up this to a good spike at its top. Step round the edge and down to belay on a good ledge.
3 **35m** Move left 3m and easily up slabs to finish.

29 Guenevere ★★   60m HVS 5a

FA Rab Anderson & Mark Garthwaite 3 September 2000

Fine airy climbing. Climb steeply up the arête/rib immediately right of *Excalibur* to where that route swings round from the left. Move up slightly right then back left to climb a short, smooth leaning wall (good gear in the horizontal breaks). Bold climbing directly above (passing just to the left of a large detached flake/block) on good holds gains vague cracks in the wall/tower feature directly above. Continue up the cracks, moving up left just below the top. Easy ground gains the top of the hill.

The Pincer & The Contender, Jules Lines & Gary Latter climbing. Photo Rob Kerr

Achnaha
Buttress

Sron nan
Gabhar

Creag Meall
an Fhir-eoin

Ardnamurchan Ring Complex

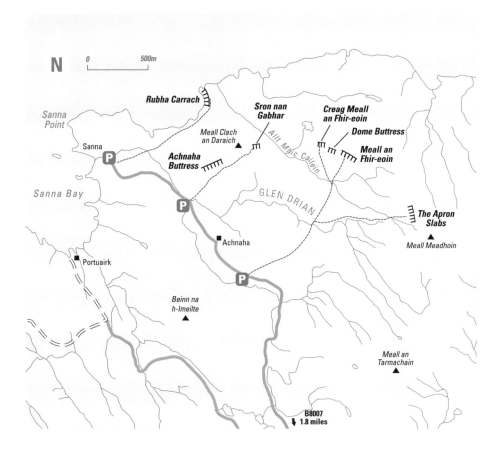

Meall an
Fhir-eoin

Apron
Slabs

ARDNAMURCHAN
(PROMONTORY OF THE SEA OTTER / SEA-VILLAINY)

This wonderful peninsula presents the most westerly point on mainland Scotland, offering a variety of climbing in a truly idyllic setting well away from the crowds. The outcrops on the north side of the road just before the road end at Sanna Bay offer a number of short routes on immaculate glaciated gabbro. The views towards the Inner Hebridean islands of Canna, Rum, Eigg and Skye would alone make the journey there worthwhile. The immaculate quality of the climbing makes it a wonderfully peaceful place to climb, well away from mainstream climbing venues. Worth combining with a trip over to climb on Garbh Bheinn.

All the inland crags are within what is called the Great Euchrite, more commonly termed the Ardnamurchan Ring Complex, a very distinctive tertiary volcanic intrusion, easily identified from the road. Though there are innumerable smaller crags throughout the area, only the biggest and best crags are fully described.

Access: The quickest approach is via the Corran ferry over Loch Linnhe then west along the A861 for 23.2 miles/37.1km to turn west onto the B8007 at Salen. Follow this for 19.8 miles/31.7km, turning right 0.75 miles/1.2km beyond Kilchoan towards Sanna Bay. The parking spot for the first two crags is reached about 1.9 miles/3km after the turn-off, about 200m north of the bridge over the Allt Uimha na Muice. For the majority of the remaining crags, continue for a further 1.6 miles/2.5km to park on the left side of the road, about 0.3 miles/ 0.5km beyond where the Allt Sanna (burn) runs beneath the road. 47 miles/75km from Corran – 1¼ hours.

From Fort William, take the A830 road towards Mallaig, turning south onto the A861 at Lochailort for 22.2 miles/35.5km to Salen then as above. 70 miles/112km – 1¾ hours.

ARDNAMURCHAN

CRAGS OF THE RING COMPLEX

The crags are grouped within three distinct areas, on the three main rocky knolls of Meall Meadhoin, Meall an Fhir-eoin and Meall Clach an Daraich forming the eastern and northern perimeter of the ring. They are described anti-clockwise, as encountered on the approach.

Mike Pescod bouldering on the side of Apron Slabs.

Bouldering: There is some good short bouldering above sandy landings on the beach about 10 minutes south of the car park at the road end, just beyond the last large flat building. In addition there is some good bouldering and lots of good short pitches on the slopes of Meall Canna, gained by ascending the first gully south of the car park. There is also some very good bouldering around the base and sidewalls of many of the crags, and many short unexplored walls dotted around, particularly on the upper slopes of Meall an Fhir-eoin.

HISTORY

The first routes recorded within the vicinity of the ring complex were a number of additions from Colin Stead and John Newsome in the early seventies, including a range of long routes on the western and southern slopes of Meall nan Con. The same pair also added the first route on the Apron Slabs with *Ne'er Day Corner*, Stead returning to add the fine *Gall*. Stead also added the first route on Creag Meall an Fhir-eoin, in addition to a number of shorter routes on Meall Sanna.

In the late eighties and early nineties Graeme Ettle, Grant Farquhar and Kev Howett developed the shorter right side of the impressive overhanging Rubha Carrach on the coast, Howett contributing the best route with *Beachcomber*. A strong team chanced upon this crag in 1997, with Rick Campbell producing the first route up the more impressive central section, *Nostromo*, climbed on-sight. On that visit the team spotted a couple of climbers at the base of the best looking crag, Creag Meall an Fhir-eoin. Gary Latter returned with friends a couple of weeks later. Charlie Prowse led *Thor* and the excellent *Yir*, and Latter added *Night Falls*. Prowse soon returned with friends, adding *Oswald*, together with the first route on the adjacent Dome Buttress, *Claude*. Margaret Riley and John Stevenson soon opened up a number of shorter buttresses, with the first routes on Achnaha Buttress,

along with further lower grade routes on Dome Buttress and Creag Meall an Fhir-eoin, including the excellent *Greta Gabbro* and *An Toiseach*. The prolific team of Dave Cuthbertson, Joanna George and Rab and Chris Anderson arrived in August, adding ten fine routes to Creag Meall an Fhir-eoin, including *Volcane*, *Minky* and *Up Pompei*, together with *Star Wars*, sharing some common ground with *Night Falls*. Rab and Chris soon added a couple of extremes on the Apron Slabs, including *Gift of the Gabbro*. Campbell and Paul Thorburn returned to Rubha Carrach in May 1998 to add *Heart of Darkness*. Swapping leads, Thorburn succeeded on *The Shipping News,* after a bold on-sight attempt the previous year. Cuthbertson, George and the Andersons visited Achnaha Buttress a couple of weeks later, adding another ten routes, the excellent *Wheesht* and the fierce *Shark Crack* falling to Joanna and Dave respectively. The following day Rab and Chris added the longest and hardest routes on the crags with *Western Front* and *Subduction Zone* respectively. The same weekend, Steve Kennedy and Cynthia Grindley developed Hooded Wall with a trio of fine routes, including *Etna*. The pair returned in the autumn to add a range of further fine routes nearby, including *Ring of Fire*, *Xenolith* and the bold *The Great Eucrite*. Julian Lines later visited this crag, on-sight soloing the fine arête of *Barbarella*.

1hr

NM 496 687 **Alt** 290m

MEALL MEADHOIN
(MIDDLE LUMP)

THE APRON SLABS

Meall Meadhoin is the highest (388m) and most easterly point visible from the road in the ring complex, containing a 90m high slabby crag down and left of the summit.

Approach: Follow a good path which heads north about 200m north of the bridge over the Allt Uimha na Muice (NM 469 677; 2.9km beyond turn-off) for about 1.7 km until just beyond a ruined croft at Glendrian. Leave the path and head north-east across rough ground in the direction of the slabs.

Descent: Down either side, best on the left.

Nesting restrictions: The crag is very close to a very important nest site and should not be climbed between March and the end of July.

1 Dance on a Volcano ★   70m E1 5b
FA Rab & Chris Anderson 17 August 1997

The blunt edge formed between the frontal face and the side wall on the left.

1 **45m 5b** Climb directly up the edge just left of *Ne'er Day Corner* and continue up easier ground to a belay.

2 **25m 4a** Scramble up slabs to the top.

2 Ne'er Day Corner ★★   75m VS 4c
FA p.1 Colin Stead & John Newsome 1 January 1971; p2 August 1972

The obvious corner and slanting crack leading up and around the left side of the roof.

1 **45m 4c** Move up the corner and follow the crack which slants up left towards the edge of the buttress. At the level of the roof step right and climb a wide crack then the slabby rib to a small stance.

2 **30m 4c** Continue up slabby ribs rightwards to finish on the summit block.

3 Gift of the Gabbro ★★   75m E2 5b
FA Rab & Chris Anderson 17 August 1997

The centre of the slab midway between the two corners.

1 **45m 5b** Climb the initial wall by a flange then the slab to a small ledge. Move up right to a thin crack in a shallow scoop and place the last wire for some distance. Pull out left at the top of the scoop then go up left to the base of a blind flange. Move right to a thin crack and follow this to a flat-topped spike (sling). Step left and up to the overlap and pull through this by the obvious flange. Continue for some way up and left to belay on the slabby rib as for *Dance on a Volcano*.

2 **30m 4c** Step back right into the groove and climb up right to follow a parallel line to *Dance on a Volcano* up short walls and slabs. Climb the final short wall centrally by an obvious 'ear'.

4 Toulouse Booze Cruise Blues ★   70m E1 5b
FA M.Harris & D.Balance 30 May 1998

The thin bottomless crack and slanting crack through the bulge. Start at the base of the right-facing corner.

1 **45m** Move left round left arête into a thin crack and ascend for 10m. Move right and follow a right-facing flake and the crack over the bulge leading to a large ledge. Traverse right 5m to belay beside a large block.

2 **25m** Continue directly up slabs.

The slabs on the right side of the crag are generally climbable anywhere at about Severe, on immaculate rock, though not easily protected away from cracks.

5 Leac Glas ★★★★   80m HS 4a
FA John Newsome & Colin Stead August 1972

Fantastic steady climbing with spaced protection. Start just right of the diagonal grassy fault.

1 **40m 4a** Follow the blunt grey rib past a superb bucket hold to a ledge below a crack.

2 **40m 4a** Finish up the crack and flakes above.

6 Solas ** 80m Severe 4a
FA Colin Stead 1970s; Variation Colin Stead 1980s

Follow a line up the slabs starting a few metres right of
Leac Glas keeping right of a curving crack, heading for
the prominent straight crack on the skyline. A variation
climbs the two curving cracks on the left.

7 Gall *** 80m Severe 4a
FA Colin Stead 1970s

Excellent climbing, quite bold after the initial crack. Start
at the foot of black seepage marks (small flake).

1 **25m 4a** Follow the right-slanting crack for 8m
(crux, well protected). Trend right and go up
to a narrow ledge then direct to a belay.
2 **38m 4a** Continue up good rock on the right
side of the fault to belay on a large terrace.
3 **17m** Finish up the same line on
easier ground to the top.

8 Leac Louise ** 70m Severe 4a
FA Gary Latter & Mike Pescod (both solo) 30 August 1999

The prominent triptych of discontinuous cracks on the
right side of the crag. Start 5m right of *Gall*.

1 **45m 4a** Follow the crack, stepping left onto
clean rock beneath some vegetation. Continue
up the second crack to a good ledge.
2 **25m 4a** The fine crack above, finishing either
by easier slabs or escape out right.

CREAG MEALL AN FHIR-EOIN
(CRAGGY LUMP OF THE EAGLE)

A good slabby crag of clean glaciated gabbro, clearly
visible on the hillside due north-east of the farm at
Achnaha, 1.2 miles/2km before the road end at Sanna.
The best and most varied of all the crags.

Approach: Follow a good path which heads north
about 200m north of the bridge for about 1.7 km until
just beyond a ruined croft at Glendrian. Head north-
east across rough ground in the direction of the crags.
Descent: Down either side of the crag.

NM 482 699 **Alt:** 140m   1hr

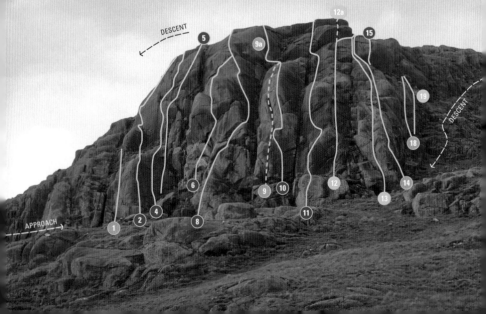

1 Crater Comforts *   60m VS 4c
FA Rab & Chris Anderson 3 August 1997

The crack-line running up the left side of the crag, immediately right of a thin grassy gully, to finish up the obvious prominent crack in the upper right side wall. Start at the lowest rocks beneath the crack next to a pointed flake just left of the edge which turns into a slab.

1 **25m 4c** Follow the crack and its continuation up a whaleback to where it thins to form a hollow flange. Step down and around the flange then step up right to belay just left of the thin crack in the left side of the smooth central wall.

2 **35m 4c** Step down into the grassy gully and after a few moves pull back onto the rock and climb the side wall to reach the obvious left-slanting diagonal crack and finish up this.

2 Volcane **   45m E1 5b
FA Joanna George & Dave Cuthbertson 3 August 1997

The prominent crack below the smooth central wall. Start just right of the toe of the buttress beneath a crack on the slabby left wall of the grassy sloping recess.

1 **15m 4c** Climb the crack to a ledge beneath the left side of a smooth wall, and continue to the shoulder to the left.

2 **30m 5b** Follow a short steep ramp to a break above, make a delicate step up and move right to a crack leading to a ledge. Continue up the crack and shallow corner to a large ledge below the top.

3 Trauma Crack *   45m E3 5a
FA Dave Cuthbertson & Joanna George 3 August 1997

The prominent curving crack on the right side of the smooth central wall. Good climbing but slightly contrived. Start as for 2 and belay down on the left of the crack.

1 **20m 5c** Climb the tapering groove and crack to a point very close to 4 (protection). Avoid possible escape on to that route and follow the crack which now bends back to the left (crux) to the ledge.

2 **25m 5a** Climb the continuation cracks and corners with a tricky move above a ledge to the large ledge below the top.

4 Magma Force **   50m E2 5c
FA Rab & Chris Anderson 3 August 1997

Start up the sloping grassy recess just right of 3 at the base of a heathery crack. Step up then move out left to climb the centre of the slab. Climb the short left-facing corner and continue up the left side of the rib to below a wide crack. An awkward move up a groove gains the crack directly. Climb the crack to a ledge, step right and climb via short steps and slabs to a short corner leading onto the flat ledge at the top of the crag.

5 Vulcanised *   50m E2 5c
FA Rab & Chris Anderson 3 August 1997

A parallel line just right of 4. Scramble to the top of the grassy recess then go up left to climb the crack and short right-facing corner. Continue up the slabby rib to a heathery ledge and climb a thin crack to beneath a steepening with a thin crack. Climb the steepening, continue above then step right to finish up the right edge of the crag.

6 Star Wars **   55m E2 5c
FA Rab Anderson & Dave Cuthbertson 4 August 1997

Takes the crack up the right side of the steep buttress. Start at the base of the crag well below the crack.

1 **30m 5c** Scramble up grass and rock to climb a short crack leading to the leaning cracked wall. Climb this past a niche into a diagonal break running up right then step up left and climb a steep crack to a ledge and belay just above.

2 **25m 5b** Cross the heathery garden above then climb the centre of the wall to gain and follow a slanting flake-line-come-crack up right. Finish up a slabby rib.

7 Night Falls **   45m E2 5c
FA Gary Latter & Charlie Prowse 8 July 1997

The prominent right-slanting diagonal crack. Start beneath the centre of the buttress.

1 **25m 5c** Move up and step left past a small juniper bush to a short crack leading up into a niche. Pull out right and over the roof on a superb jug. Continue more easily up the flake crack then by a fine thin crack up the slab to belay on large ledge.

2 **20m 5a** Climb the blunt rib which soon eases.

8 Return of the Jedi ★★   45m E1 5b
FA Rab & Chris Anderson 3 August 1997

Climbs the right side of the steep buttress. From the right side scramble up a heathery slab to a steep stepped groove/crack. Climb this then go up right along a horizontal break to the edge of the buttress. Step right around the edge and make some bold moves to gain the diagonal break of 7. Climb the crack just right of the edge and continue to the top.

9 Yir ★★★   55m VS 4c
FA Charlie Prowse, Rob Kerr & Gary Latter 8 July 1997

Just right of the central grass-filled fault is a prominent crack leading up into a slabby groove.

1 **45m** Follow these to a grass ledge at the top of the groove. Move right to the crest and continue up this past a further break to belay on large ledge just below the top.

2 **10m** Climb the crack above the belay.

9a Variation 15m 4b Move left across the grassy groove. Pull over bulge via a wide crack, move left and follow a thin curving crack.

10 Minky ★★   60m E1 5b
FA Dave Cuthbertson & Joanna George 3 August 1997

A direct line up the short slabby rib right of 9.

1 **45m 5b** Pull over a small overlap and follow a break slanting up to the left to a junction of cracks with 9. Go up a metre, step right and take a direct line up the whaleback by some thin poorly protected climbing to belay where the angle eases. E2 5b if climbed direct up slab (serious).

2 **15m 4b** Either climb the gully above, or move left and follow the surprisingly straightforward crack to the top.

11 Up Pompei ★★   60m E2 5b
FA Rab & Chris Anderson 4 August 1997

A direct line up the front of the second slabby rib. Low in the grade. Start at the lowest rocks.

1 **55m 5b** Gain and climb a crack up the crest of the initial short buttress. Follow a short crack in the left side of the rib and continue up into the centre. Step up left and follow the left side of the rib to easier ground. Continue to the headwall (possible belay), swing left and climb the short crack to a spacious ledge.

2 **5m** Climb the short wall above via the obvious step.

12 An Deireadh ★★   55m Difficult
FA unknown 29 June 1997, or before?

'The End'. The top of the right side of the buttress is split by a prominent short steep crack. Start directly beneath this, from a ledge at the base of the crack.

1 **46m** Follow the crack to belay on a small sloping ledge beneath the final steep crack.

2 **9m** Climb up to the crack and escape out right on good holds.

12a Direct Finish   16m Severe 4b
FA Rob Kerr, Charlie Prowse & Gary Latter 8 July 1997

The crack above the belay.

13 An Toiseach ★   50m Very Difficult
FA Margaret Riley & John Stevenson 22 July 1997

'The Beginning'. The crack up the third slabby rib, just left of the arête and right of the heathery groove-line between the ribs. Large gear.

1 **30m** Go up the corner to the crack and follow this to a very large ledge.

2 **20m** Continue up the slab behind and left of the belay to the large crack which comes up from the heathery groove-line between the ribs then climb directly up the slabs.

14 Oswald ★   55m HS 4b
FA Charlie Prowse, A.Simpson & T.Harper 17 July 1997

Start just right of the blunt rib at the right end of the crag. Follow the left of twin cracks for 5m then move out left to follow another crack and easier ground to finish.

15 **Tremor Crack** *   **10m E3 6a**

FA Dave Cuthbertson & Joanna George 4 August 1997

Attack the steep and strenuous overhanging crack in the headwall to an awkward exit. Gained easily by scrambling in from the right, or via 13 or 14.

16 **Bloody Crack** *   **10m E4 6a**

FA Mike Pescod & Nick Carter July 2002

The short 'elephant's arse' crack right of 14. Strenuous. Around the edge, right of the third slabby rib and up the slope is a short slabby wall with two right-slanting cracks.

17 **Oisean Bheag** **   **20m Severe 4a**

FA John Stevenson & Margaret Riley 22 July 1997

Pleasant climbing up the 'little corner' left of the cracks.

18 **An Rathad Ard**   **15m HS 4b**

FA John Stevenson & Margaret Riley 22 July 1997

The leftmost crack, starting below a triangular niche, leading to a belay below an overhanging wall.

19 **An Rathad Losal** *   **15m Severe 4a**

FA Margaret Riley & John Stevenson 24 July 1997

The lower, rightmost of the two cracks. Follow this to below the heather ledge then step left to finish as for 18.

DOME BUTTRESS 🌊 🚶

1hr

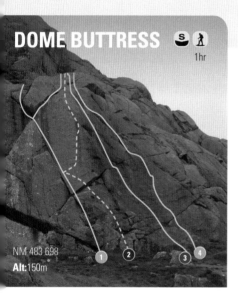

NM 483 698
Alt:150m

2 **Subduction Zone** *   **25m E3/4 5c**

FA Rab & Chris Anderson 17 May 1998

Bold climbing up the wall right of 1. Climb broken ground up the left edge of the slab, pull over a small roof and move up left to place a runner in the crack of 1. Step back right and climb the wall to reach a thin crack on the right edge. Move onto a foothold on the edge then make a couple of thin moves to reach the top.

3 **Lava Lout** *   **25m E1 5b**

FA M.Harris & D.Ballance 29 May 1998

A line close to the left edge of the slab. Start at the same point as 4, but climb the slab directly above to a small left-facing corner near the edge. Climb the corner to a small roof then step right into another left-facing corner which is climbed to the top.

The smaller buttress with a slabby right face 100m right of the main crag.

1 **Claude** **   **25m VS 5a**

FA T.Harper & Charlie Prowse 17 July 1997

Start at a large detached flake. Climb rightwards up the flake for 3m to gain the fine crack and up this to an overlap. Traverse left below the overlap to a steep groove, pulling through on a mega-jug to finish. Finishing out right along the break at the overlap is the same grade.

4 **Greta Gabbro** **   **25m VS 4c**

FA John Stevenson & Margaret Riley 24 July 1997

Well protected, the difficulties increasing with height. Start at the toe of the slab and head up right to a flake then go up a left-facing corner to the top.

The main fault up the centre of the slab is 5 *Canna Do It* Diff, the narrow crack just right 6 *Rum Do* S 4b.

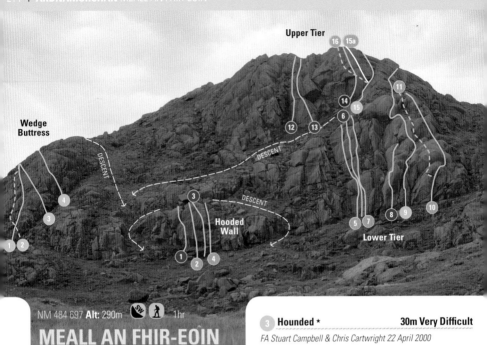

 NM 484 697 **Alt:** 290m   1hr

MEALL AN FHIR-EOIN
(LUMP OF THE EAGLE)
The area of slabs, walls and ribs lying on the main
summit knoll of Meall an Fhir-eoin.

WEDGE BUTTRESS

Between **Dome Buttress** and **Hooded Wall**, at a
slightly higher level. South Facing.

1 Fairy Ring *   50m Very Difficult
FA Steve Kennedy, David Hood & Cynthia Grindley 28 June 1998

The central crack system. Start at the lowest point and
follow the crack to a prominent protruding flake at 10m,
step right and follow a parallel crack to the top.

2 Fox *   45m Very Difficult
FA Stuart Campbell & Chris Cartwright 22 April 2000

Start 2m right of 1. Follow a left-slanting crack system
to ledge then a curving crack and groove slightly left
then cut back right to an obvious water-worn pink patch.
Finish up the crack above, trending left then right.

3 Hounded *   30m Very Difficult
FA Stuart Campbell & Chris Cartwright 22 April 2000

Start in a prominent black recess. Climb a wide
overhanging crack to a spike then the continuation crack,
crossing 2. Finish straight up slabs when the crack runs
out, to belay as for 1.

4 Foxed *   20m Severe 4a
FA Stuart Campbell & Chris Cartwright 22 April 2000

Start 5m up right of 3 at an inverted teardrop flake. Up
the left edge of the flake then a crack until it peters out,
continuing up flakes to belay as for 1.

HOODED WALL

A small slabby buttress 50m right of and slightly higher
than **Dome Buttress**, overlooked by a beak of rock.
Descent: Scramble down right before the slabby ribs.

1 Vesuvius *   20m E1 5b
FA Steve Kennedy & Cynthia Grindley 16 May 1998

The slim corner close to the left edge. Start by a pointed
undercut (often damp). Steep moves over the initial bulge
lead up rightwards to the corner/crack. Continue up the
slab left of the upper corner to finish just left of the beak.

EDGE BUTTRESS

HOODED WALL

2 Krakatoa ** 20m HVS 5b

FA Steve Kennedy & Cynthia Grindley 16 May 1998

The next crack line to the right. Surmount a bulge directly below the crack then climb the crack directly.

3 Etna ** 20m E1 5b

FA Steve Kennedy & Cynthia Grindley 16 May 1998

The crack right of 2. Initial moves up a steep slab lead directly to a steep wall at mid-height which forms the crux. Hard for the short.

4 Stromboli * 20m HVS 5b

FA Steve Kennedy & Cynthia Grindley 16 May 1998

The rightmost crack-line. Climb the lower slab directly to a short steep wall at mid-height. Surmount the wall and finish up a corner.

LOWER TIER

Some 50m right of **Hooded Wall** are two prominent whalebacks. The first three routes described climb the slabs just left of the left whaleback, by a grassy terrace.
Descents: From the summit easy slabs on the right lead to the rake between the tiers. Either go left down this, or right round the crest to descend more directly.

5 Vulcan * 65m VS 4c

FA Steve Kennedy, David Hood & Cynthia Grindley 28 June 1998

Start at a black streak on the left of the slab.

1 **30m 4b** Gain and climb a prominent crack running up the left side of the slab to the grassy terrace.

2 **35m 4c** Climb the slab and flake above for a short distance then move left to reach the obvious crack-line running up the left side of the upper slabs. Climb the crack then slabs up rightwards to a break in the upper wall. Pull through the break by a groove.

6 Dead Ringer * 65m E1 5b

FA Steve Kennedy, David Hood & Cynthia Grindley 28 June 1998

A more direct line up the slab. Start at a short undercut wall below a crack 2m right of 5.

1 **30m 5b** Steep moves lead into the crack which is followed to a slab. Climb the slab near the right edge to the terrace (joining 5).

2 **35m 5a** Climb the slab directly above the belay, but instead of moving left (on 5), continue to a break. Climb directly up the slab near the right edge (poorly protected) to a break in the upper wall. Finish up 5.

7 Western Front *   55m HVS 5b
FA Rab & Chris Anderson 17 May 1998

The slab to the left of the first whaleback has two
crack-lines in it. This route takes the right crack.

1 **45m 5a** After a bouldery start climb the crack
   then follow a slabby rib to heather ledges. Step
   right to climb a short buttress then go left round
   a rib and climb a groove up its left side (or the rib
   itself) to belay beneath a leaning barrier wall.

2 **10m 5b** The short, thin Y-shaped crack provides
   a fine sporting move to gain the slab leading
   to the upper terrace. The **Upper Tier** lies just
   above, providing a logical continuation.

8 Mirka **   30m E2 5c
FA Dave Cuthbertson & Joanna George 17 May 1998

The left whaleback. Ascend the slab to a steepening
left-slanting crack leading to triangular block. Navigate
around the block onto its top and an easing in the angle.
Step right and climb a crack in the whaleback to a ledge.
Either escape out right, or continue by easy grooves in
the crest.

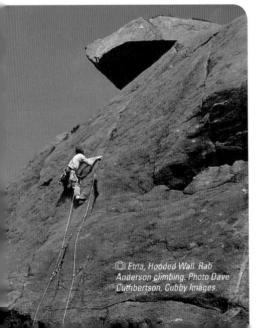

*Etna, Hooded Wall. Rab
Anderson climbing. Photo Dave
Cuthbertson, Cubby Images.*

9 Beth's Route *   120m Very Difficult
FA Davy Virdee, L.Curtis & E.Vokurka 9 May 1998

A series of short pitches, starting up the broad chimney
between the whalebacks.

1 **25m** Ascend the chimney then cracks and
   the slabby right wall of the gully.

2 **20m** Follow a crack up the rib up on
   the left to gain broad terrace.

3 **20m** Climb the V-cleft splitting the slab
   on the left then direct to the terrace.

4 **25m** Traverse across a right-slanting slab to an
   undercut layback. Use this to ascend the edge
   of the slab to a corner leading to easy ground.

5 **30m** Scramble up slabs.

10 Ringmaster **   40m VS 5a
FA Steve Kennedy & Cynthia Grindley 16 May 1998

The prominent corner immediately right of the right
whaleback. A bouldery undercut crack leads to the corner,
which is followed throughout. Very well protected.

11 Ring of Fire **   40m HVS 5a
FA Steve Kennedy & Cynthia Grindley 5 September 1998

A spectacular route up the rightmost whaleback. Climb
the corner of 10 for 7m then hand traverse the break out
left onto the crest of the whaleback. Climb the crest to
finish up a crack in the centre of the short finishing wall.

UPPER TIER
Above lies a grassy bay overlooked by a steep wall and a
prominent roof. This bay is gained easily by scrambling in
from either end, or via any of the previous routes.

12 The Great Euchrite *   40m E3 5c
FA Steve Kennedy & Cynthia Grindley 13 September 1998

Bold sustained climbing up the steep slabby wall just
right of the prominent vegetated corner on the left. Start
at a black streak near the centre. Climb to a small knob
and leftwards-slanting crack (protection) at 4m. Make
bold moves up and right to reach the right end of a ledge
above. Finish more easily up steep left-slanting cracks.

13 **Xenolith** *   40m E1 5b

FA Steve Kennedy & Cynthia Grindley 16 May 1998

Start by the large detached flake at the right edge of the
steep initial wall of 12. An easier slabby wall lies just
to the right, leading up to the left end of the prominent
roof. Climb the slab right of the flake to the ledge below
the steep upper wall. Climb the left-slanting cracks in the
wall to finish.

14 **Barbarella** **   20m E4 5c

FA Julian Lines (on-sight solo) 4 June 2001

The beautiful square-cut gritstone style arête. Start from
the left to gain the arête, which is climbed to a break. Pull
through the capping roof and continue easily.

📷 *An Deireadh, Creag Meall an Fhir-eoin.*
Charlie Prowse climbing.

15 **Pyroclast** **   45m Severe 4b

FA Steve Kennedy & Cynthia Grindley 16 May 1998

The far right end is defined by an easy angled corner with
an overhung left wall. Climb an easy slab then step up
left across a steepening into the corner proper, which is
followed directly to the top.

15a **Variation Finish** **   VS 5a

FA Stuart Campbell & Chris Cartwright 22 April 2000

From the ledge in the corner above the steepening, step
left to the base of a fine snaking crack up the immaculate
slab. Ascend the crack, finish directly up the slab.

16 **Fear of Flying** **   40m VS 4b

FA Steve Kennedy, Bob Hamilton & Pete Harrop May 2002

A good route in a wildly exposed position for the grade,
following parallel cracks running horizontally left above
the overhanging wall just left of 15. Climb the initial
corner of 15 before pulling out left into the cracks.
Traverse these horizontally left to the edge, continue left
a short distance then finish directly.

MEALL CLACH AN DARAICH
(HULL-SHAPED ROCKY LUMP)

The rocky ridge forming the closest section of the ring complex on the north side of the road.

Access: Park on left side of the road at NM 457 687, 0.5 miles/0.8km beyond the farm at Achnaha.

ACHNAHA BUTTRESS   15min
NM 462 696 **Alt:** 50m

A steep wall on the first rocky dome from the road.

Approach: Head in the direction of the crag across boggy ground and the burn after 200m to the crags.

1 Plocaig Rock ★   25m HS 4b

FA John Stevenson & Margaret Riley 21 July 1997

Start just left of the arête, on the west (sea-facing) end of the crag. Climb an obvious crack over a bulge (crux), continuing to a right-slanting crack. Keep left of the arête to finish up the slabby wall.

2 Wheesht! ★★   20m E2 5b

FA Joanna George & Dave Cuthbertson 16 May 1998

Scramble up onto the grassy terrace. Climb the first obvious crack up the left end of the crag with strenuous climbing to the niche.

The crack just right of 2 is 3 *Acrophobia* ★ E2 5c.

4 Pooper Scooper ★   10m Difficult

FA Chris Cartwright & Simon Richardson 10 October 1998

The obvious barrel-shaped scoop cutting through centre of the **Upper Tier**.

5 Soul Mining ★   10m E4 5c

FA Dave Cuthbertson & Joanna George 16 May 1998

Poorly protected climbing up the orange wall just right of 4 then black streaks above the terrace. Take a more or less direct line up the fingery wall midway between the black streak and the crack of 6.

6 Coal Mining ★   10m VS 5a

FA Joanna George & Dave Cuthbertson 16 May 1998

The obvious crack following the right line to the top.

7 Nicht Thochts ★   10m VS 4c

FA Joanna George & Dave Cuthbertson 16 May 1998

The rightward slanting seam right of 6. Join the horizontal crack for about a metre then break up left to finish up the wall above. A *Direct Start* up the wall just right is 5a.

8 Uisge * — 20m E2 5c
FA Dave Cuthbertson & Joanna George 16 May 1998

Right of the grassy gully splitting the crag is an orange scoop. Climb the wall starting at a pale streak to gain the scoop. Leave it following the rightmost crack, moving leftwards to the top.

A prominent scooped recess at the right side of the lower tier contains three cracks, taken by 9 *Achaye*, 10 *Achrobat* (both E1 5a) and 11 *Achtung* *, E2 6a (HVS 4c started further right).

12 Plocaig Walk — 15m Difficult
FA Margaret Riley & John Stevenson 21 July 1997

There is a dark slab below a roof near the right end of the main face. Climb the slab then easier ground to a terrace with a small wall. Go up this past a leaning block to the top.

13 Bondi Beach * — 15m E1 5b
FA Chris Cartwright & Simon Richardson 10 October 1998

The blunt scooped arête left of 14. Start up a small left-facing corner left of arête. Climb past a white streak, moving right and up to a blunt spike. Finish up the wall above.

14 Shark Attack * — 15m E3 6b
FA Dave Cuthbertson 16 May 1998

A painful, powerful boulder problem up the short steep crack on the steep east-facing side wall of the crag. Climb the leftmost crack in the wall, finishing up the easier wall above.

SRON NAN GABHAR (NOSE OF THE SHE-GOAT) 30min

NM 470 698 **Alt:** 50m

A prominent whaleback ridge on the right (eastmost) dome of the hill due north of Achnaha.
Approach: Head north-east skirting the right edge of the rocky ridge.
Descent: Down either end of the crags.

The broad slabby buttress on the right has a fine slab at its foot split by three thin crack-lines, the leftmost of which has a prominent triangular block set into it.

3 Ozone Layer * — 45m HVS 5a
FA Steve Kennedy, Cynthia Grindley & Mark Shaw 11 July 1998

The leftmost flake crack. An awkward undercut start leads into the crack which is followed to a ledge. Continue up the crack then directly on easier ground to finish.

The hairline crack just right is 4 *Acting Soft* E2 5c.

1 Mjollnir * — 50m HS 4a
FA Brian Davison & A.Richardson 29 May 1999

The left groove on the whaleback.

5 High Plains Drifter ** — 50m VS 5a
FA Rab & Chris Anderson 16 May 1998

The central crack then a short groove, continuing up excellent compact rock to the top.

2 Thor ** — 50m Severe 4b
FA Charlie Prowse, Rob Kerr & Gary Latter 8 July 1997

The prominent left-facing groove and crack up the centre. Scramble in from the left to belay beneath a short steep groove. Climb the groove and pull steeply out left onto the left-facing groove above. Up this and continue in the same line to finish more easily up the slabby ridge above.

6 Solar Wind * — 45m HVS 5a
FA Mark Shaw, Cynthia Grindley & Steve Kennedy 11 July 1998

The rightmost crack. Follow the crack to a ledge then continue by a vague groove leading to easier ground.

NM 461 707 35min

RUBHA CARRACH
(UNEVEN-SURFACED HEADLAND)

A long band of sea cliff extending leftwards to an impressive overhanging promontory. The rock is a strange pocketed basalt, very reminiscent of limestone in places. A big extensive cliff with much scope for future exploration. It is definitely 'terrain adventure'. Most of the crag is not affected by the tide while the sea is calm, except the northern (left) end.

Approach: From the car park at the end of the road at Sanna, head north towards a ruined cottage then follow the coast round to the cliff.

Descent: Down the scree-filled gully near the right (southern) end of the cliff.

The crag generally becomes more impressive from right to left, culminating in a steeply overhanging wall on the point before degenerating into poorer scruffier ground just beyond a prominent grooved arête. Near the right end is an amazing diagonal fault/gully. There is a superb cave at the base of this, extending back for just short of 100m to a small chamber with some fine stalactite formations; take a head-torch.

The freestanding pinnacle separated from the main cliff by the descent gully contains numerous shorter lines from HVS to E4 5c. Routes from right to left.

① Beachcomber ★★   35m E5 6b
FA Kev Howett 5 September 1993

The prominent steep thin flake-crack 15m right of the cave entrance. Climb easily up to the base of the crack. Gain the crack by spanning in from a large pocket on the right, and follow it with a difficult move to stand in the base of the groove. Continue up the groove to finish up an awkward crack in the headwall. Scramble up messy ground to a block belay a long way back. 60m rope required, or leave a spare rope.

② The Shipping News ★★★   50m E5/6 6b
FA Paul Thorburn, Gary Latter & Rick Campbell 3 May 1998

A long sustained route making full use of the brilliant pocketed band midway between the two roofs. Start 50m left of the deep huge cave towards the right end of the crag.

1 **25m 6b** A vague crack cuts through the two-tiered roof system. Climb up to underneath the second roof system then traverse left on a vague horizontal break heading for some large pockets after about 15m. Make hard moves up past a good sidepull to pull onto the less steep smoother rock above. Belay on large cams at a small grass ledge.

2 **25m 6a** Traverse left for 3m then climb the wall heading leftwards to pull out right over a protruding block to finish. Belay to Fs or hexes well back.

3 Nostromo **   35m E5 6a

FA Rick Campbell & Neil Craig 29 June 1997

50m further left is a prominent left-trending snaking black dyke. This route follows a direct line cutting through the centre of the dyke, aiming for a shallow left-facing groove above the dyke.

4 Heart of Darkness **   35m E4 6a

FA Rick Campbell & Paul Thorburn 2 May 1998

At the prow on the far left end are two prominent thin grooves. This route climbs the rightmost one. Start beneath a prominent pod-shaped chimney. Climb up to the base of the chimney then move out right and up to a small square ledge beneath where the grooves bifurcate (obvious from the ground). Make hard moves right across the wall to gain the deep groove on the right. Continue up this and the obvious line above. Well protected.

© *The Shipping News, Paul Thorburn on first ascent.*

📷 *The Gutter, Pine Wall Crag, Polldubh.*

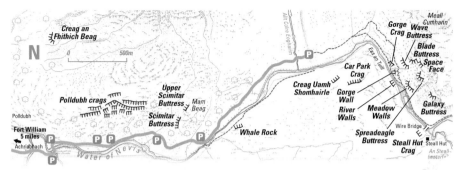

GLEN NEVIS

This splendid glen, celebrated as one of the most beautiful in Scotland, runs from the north end of Fort William south-east for 4 miles/6km, before turning east for a further 6 miles/10km. In a compact 4km central section over 70 crags flank the lower slopes of the mighty Ben Nevis massif and Sgurr a' Mhaim on either side of the glen.

The sheer variety and range of routes on offer, the sheltered quick drying southerly aspect of most of the crags, the quality schist and the short approaches (5 – 30 minutes) would alone make it an attractive venue. Combine these factors with the magnificent surroundings; stunning mountains, a spectacular waterfall, a unique gorge, and it all adds up to the best outcrop climbing venue in Scotland.

Many trees line the lower slopes and indeed sprout from many of the crags, including native oak, birch, ash, rowan and Scots pine, creating a relaxed friendly atmosphere and an often convenient means of retreat. Unfortunately, this sheltered nature of the lower crags can also act as a haven for midges in the summer, though in general the higher crags at Polldubh and above the Gorge tend to be more open in nature, and are often blessed with a favourable breeze. On some of the harder routes, the compact nature of the rock necessitates a good selection of RPs and micro-wires, and on some the use of tied down skyhooks. In contrast, many of the popular routes are well protected, making it an ideal introductory venue.

Access: Turn off the A82 (signposted Glen Nevis) at the roundabout at Nevis Bridge at the north end of Fort William. Follow the road for 4.9 miles/7.8km to cross the River Nevis by a bridge over the lower falls at Achriabhach, from where the Polldubh crags are clearly visible. The road now continues as single track with passing places. For Polldubh, park at a long lay-by on the right 0.5 miles/0.8km beyond the bridge, or by the roadside near the lay-by. For Whale Rock, continue for a further 0.4 miles/0.7km just round the bend to park on the left, just before a footbridge down on the right. For the remaining crags in the Car Park Area, The Nevis Gorge and Steall Meadows, continue for a further 0.8 miles/1.3km to a large car park at the road end, which can become very busy (full) with touroids in the summer.

GLEN NEVIS

"In its farthermost reach, Glen Nevis is a desolate moor. In its central section of 5 miles (from the great bend under Sgurr a Bhuic to Polldubh), it is one of the most beautiful glens in Scotland. The lower stretch of 4 miles to Bridge of Nevis gives a pastoral scene of green fields flanked on one side by forest and on the other by the huge bare slopes of Ben Nevis."

– W H Murray, Highland Landscape (The Aberdeen University Press/ National Trust for Scotland, 1962)

FORT WILLIAM

In the last decade 'the fort' has expanded to serve and exploit the constant stream of mainly foreign tourists that seem to invade throughout the summer months. In many ways it can be likened to a highland version of Chamonix, with a high street mall littered with loads of tartan knick-knack and woolly jumper shops in place of the somewhat more appealing street-side cafes.

Amenities: Many cafes, restaurants and pubs in and around the pedestrian precinct on the High Street. Morrisons supermarket (8–9 M-Sat; 9–5 Sun) at An Aird, midway between the rail and bus stations should provide all provisions. Late opening Spar stores in Claggan (first right off A82 Inverness road after Glen Nevis roundabout) and in Ballachulish. There is a cinema behind the **TIC** in Cameron Square in the centre of town. There is a limited bouldering wall within the Leisure Centre (Open 9–9 M–F; 10–6 summer weekends; 4.30 outwith summer; ☎ 01397 704359) which is on Belford road, a few hundred metres beyond the hospital heading out of town. Also swimming pool, sauna, squash, fitness suite & solarium. **Outdoor shops:** Nevisport, High Street (☎ 01397 704921; www.nevisport.com); Ellis Brigham Mountain Sports, Belford Road (opposite hospital) (☎ 01397 706220; www.ellis-brigham.com). These shops also provide regularly updated weather forecasts.

Accommodation: Masses of hotel, guest house and bed & breakfast accommodation, with the mile long southern approach road dubbed locally 'the golden mile', such is the profusion of B&B and guest house accommodation available. Bookings and information from **TIC** in Cameron Square (☎ 01397 703781; www.visithighlands.co.uk). **Glen Nevis Youth Hostel** (☎ 01397 702336; www.syha.org.uk) at the start of the tourist path up the Ben, 1.8 miles/3km along the Glen Nevis road.

Bunkhouses: Inchree Bunkhouse, Onich (☎ 01855 821287; www.inchreecentre.co.uk); Corran Bunkhouse, Corran ferry (☎ 01855 821235; www.corranbunkhouse.co.uk); Ben Nevis Bunkhouse, Achintee Farm, Glen Nevis (☎ 01397 702240; www.glennevis.com); Ben Nevis Inn (☎ 01397 701227; www.ben-nevis-inn.co.uk); Fort William Backpackers, Alma Road (☎ 01397 700711; www.scotlandstophostels.com); (☎ 01397 705623); Calluna, Fort William (☎ 01397 700451; www.fortwilliamholiday.co.uk); Bank Street Lodge (☎ 01397 700070; www.bankstreetlodge.co.uk); The Smiddy, Station Road, Corpach (☎ 01397 772467; wwww.highland-mountain-guides.co.uk); Farr Cottage Hostel, Corpach (☎ 01397 772315; www.farrcottage.co.uk); Chase the Wild Goose Hostel, Banavie (☎ 01369 840672; www.great-glen-hostel.com); Glenfinnan Sleeping Car (☎ 01397 722334); Grey Corrie Lodge, Roy Bridge (☎ 01397 712236; www.hotel-roybridge.co.uk); Aite Cruinnichidh, by Roy Bridge (☎ 01397 712315; www.highland-hostel.co.uk); Station Lodge, Tulloch, 5½ miles/9km east of Roy Bridge (☎ 01397 732333; www.stationlodge.co.uk).

Club Huts: Alex Macintyre Memorial Hut, Onich; Manse Barn, Onich; CIC Hut, Ben Nevis; Steall Hut, Glen Nevis; Riasg, Roy Bridge.

Campsites: There is a large official and very busy campsite (☎ 01397 702191; www. glen-nevis.co.uk) 1.5 miles/2.4km down the Glen Nevis road at NN 125 722 overlooking the tourist path up Ben Nevis. Wild camping discreetly further up the Glen, with popular riverside sites below Polldubh, or discreetly further up the glen. Wild camping is not permitted in the lower glen. There is also a small campsite on the right side of the road, 200m east of the roundabout on the Glen Nevis Road. Linnhe Caravan Park, Corpach (☎ 01397 772376; www.linnhe-lochside-holidays.co.uk); Lochy Holiday Park, Camagheal, Fort William (01397 703446; www.lochy-holiday-park.co.uk); Gairlochy Holiday Park, Spean Bridge (☎ 01397 712711; www.theghp.co.uk); Bunroy Park Caravan Site, Roy Bridge (☎ 01397 712332; www.bunroycamping.co.uk).

HISTORY

Climbing in the glen dates back to the mid-forties. During the war, Brian Kellet, (a pacifist working in the Forestry at Torlundy), would hire a bike and climb on the Polldubh crags in the evenings, though no routes are known to have been recorded from this period. After the war a small band of Fort William based climbers began exploring the myriad of crags at Polldubh. In 1947, Jimmy Ness and local surgeon Dr Donald Duff climbed *Pinnacle Ridge*, on the closest crag to the road. On his return from conscription in 1950, Ness added further routes with Alan Burgon, including the short *Severe Crack*, the first VS rated route on the crags, along with the fine long *Pine Wall*.

RAF mountain rescue teams, in particular groups from Kinloss, started using the crags in the late fifties. Ian Clough and Terry Sullivan were the most prolific, between them accounting for many of the best middle grade routes. Clough opened up Styx Buttress first with *Damnation*, then *Resurrection*, and with Sullivan the pair pioneered *Storm* and the long *Crag Lough Grooves*, both with 3 points of aid, along with many other excellent routes, including *Flying Dutchman* and *Phantom Slab*. Clough also led teams up *Spike Wall*, *Heatwave*, and with Eddie Buckley, *Vampire* and *Secretaries' Direct*. In the early sixties, gritstone expert Allan Austin, on honeymoon with his wife Jenny, made free ascents of *Storm* and *Crag Lough Grooves*. Ike Jones added the sparsely protected *The Old Wall* and Ken Johnson made a free ascent of *Clapham Junction* as well as adding a *Direct Finish*. In 1968 a German, Klaus Schwartz, had taken up an instructor post at Loch Eil Centre. Accompanied by fellow instructors, students and domestic staff, he

pioneered over a hundred routes, spanning just over a decade of industrious activity.

The talented John Cunningham made a fleeting visit, slotting in the thin and balancy *Twitch*. Alec Fulton climbed the unprotected top pitch of *Secretaries' Superdirect*, Schwartz later contributing the bottom pitch. Schwartz and Brian Chambers added what then became the longest route on the crags with *Autobahnausfahrt* Schwartz also established many aid routes, including *Black Friday*, *The Web* and *Withering Crack*. Similarly, the impressive overhanging Creag nam Fhithich Beag was developed in 1975 by Noel Williams and Andrew Wielochowski with numerous aid routes, including *Monster* and *Groanangasp*, along with *Steerpike* with some aid. Around the same time, at the other end of the Glen, Dud Knowles aided the wide diagonal crack up the even steeper Steall Hut Crag. In contrast, armed with a MacInnes ice axe, Schwartz set to work and cleaned and named *The Gutter* to produce the best route of its grade on the crags. Also around this time, Ed Grindley moved to the area, pushing standards on the crags with free ascents of *Fang*, *The Web* and *Withering Crack*. Two young Edinburgh climbers, Dave Cuthbertson and Murray Hamilton, made their first impression on the crags in 1977 when they bouldered out the short technical *Chalky Wall* early in the spring. Higher up, Aberdonian Brian Sprunt added *Diode* later that summer.

The pace of activity accelerated throughout the early eighties. Free ascents of *Autobahnausfahrt* and *Kaos* fell to Kenny Spence; *Wee One*, *Black Friday* and a new route *Tomag* to Hamilton. Dave Cuthbertson arrived on the scene adding a clutch of contrasting extremes, including

Soap Suds, and *Vincent,* before pushing standards with the futuristic forty-five degree overhanging *Sky Pilot* (E5 6b). His partner on many of these, Derek Jamieson, led, on-sight after Cuthbertson had cleaned, the bold *Risqué Grapefruit.* Grindley added good routes to Black's Buttress with *Land Ahoy* and *Shergar.*

The first modern foray out with Polldubh occurred when Hamilton, in the company of Lakes' activists Pete Whillance, Alan Murray and Dave Armstrong, attacked the steep 60m high Car Park Crag with wire brushes, coming away with four fine two-pitch E2s and the mega-classic *Quality Street,* a direct free version of an earlier aid line. 1982 saw the opening up of three important new crags in and above the gorge. Grindley discovered Wave Buttress, adding *First Wave, Ground Zero* and the stunning right rib of *Edgehog.*

Cuthbertson again pushed standards, first with his free version of *Groanangasp* on Creag an Fhithich Beag, renamed *Exocet* (E6 6a, 6b), along with his ascent of *Cosmopolitan* on the newly discovered Gorge Crag. Cuthbertson and Gary Latter added many other good routes here, including the classic *Travellin' Man* and *In the Groove,* Latter leading *All Our Yesterdays.* Grindley contributed the overlooked *Plague of Blazes,* and Noel Williams led a large Lochaber High School group up *Pupil Power.* Higher up the hill, Cuthbertson and Latter opened up a further big crag, Spreadeagle Buttress, with ascents of *Spreadeagle* and *Slip Away.*

The following year, Grindley continued to fill in the lines on Wave Buttress, with *Crackattack* and *Think Vertical.* Cuthbertson breached the centre of Galaxy Buttress with *Short Man's Walkabout,* added *The Singing Ringing Tree* to Spreadeagle Buttress and the sustained and fingery *The Handren Effect* to Creag an Fhithich Beag. New finds in the Car Park Area were the small though significant buttresses of Creag Uamh Shomhairle and Whale Rock, along with the first free route on Steall Hut Crag further up the

glen. Opposite, overlooking Steall Meadows, Grindley added the impressive 3m roof crack *Going for Gold.* 1984 and 1985 saw a dramatic increase in activity, with a dozen new crags opened up and over 70 extremes produced. Wave Buttress gave Kenny Spence *Walter Wall,* Hamilton *On the Beach* and Cuthbertson *Freddie Across the Mersey* along with the technical *Jodicus Grotticus,* which utilised two hammered RPs and a peg runner. In the gorge, Geordie Alan Moist opened up the spectacularly situated River Walls with *Gawping Grockles.* On Whale Rock, Cuthbertson contributed the excellent *Just a Little Tease,* employing side runners and two belayers to protect the crux. He also soloed a trilogy of bold unprotected routes on the slab of Upper Scimitar, culminating in the very committing *Jahu.*

The dreich summer of 1985 resulted in an unprecedented spate of activity, with almost fifty new extremes produced. Kev Howett and friends were resident in the glen at Achintee Farm, adding numerous hard routes during a cold dry February, including *Run for Home* to Whale Rock and *Easy Pickings* on The Gorge Wall, a route previously cleaned by another suitor.

Later that spring the pace of activity picked up, Cuthbertson, Howett and Latter accounting for more than forty extremes in a frenetic burst of activity. Cuthbertson breached the centre of the hanging slab of the River Walls with *Aquarian Rebels,* after Howett had unsuccessfully tried to snatch the route. That same day Cuthbertson boldly climbed on-sight the first route on the sculptured Meadow Walls with *The Mutant,* later completing a trilogy of good routes here with *Reptile* and *Tickled Pink.*

On a busy day in the gorge several new routes were climbed, including *Chimera* from Howett. Later, Cuthbertson slotted in two further hard pitches on Wave Buttress with *Washington* and the similarly bold *The*

> ... *The Snowgoose (Flight of),* at E6 6a an altogether different beast. This was the first of a number of hard additions to make use of tied down skyhooks for protection.

Edwardo Shuffle, in an attempt to straighten out his own *Jodicus Grotticus*. Down at Polldubh, both Latter and Cuthbertson led the previously pegged bouldery *Cubsville*. Up on Blade Buttress, Howett's attempt to gain the centre of the slab initially produced *Ugly Duckling*, which overnight mutated *"with some assistance from above"* (a rope was lowered at one point) into *The Snowgoose (Flight of)* at E6 6a, an altogether different beast. This was the first of a number of hard additions to make use of tied down skyhooks for protection. Across the way on Steall Hut Crag, Howett breached the impressive continuously overhanging front face with *Lame Beaver*, utilising a couple of rest points in the final easier crack. Cuthbertson made a free ascent two years later.

1986 saw Wave Buttress come under scrutiny, Latter plugging most of the obvious gaps, including *Straight Thinking* and *The Dark Crystal*. Up on Blade Buttress, the stupendous overhanging groove became the subject of a race, the resultant *Cruisability* eventually falling to Latter. Just up from here, Howett completed the first line on the Space Face with the wandering *Dancing on the Edge of Existence*, later straightened out with the superb *The True Edge* from Latter. Cuthbertson again pushed standards, this time on Whale Rock with his ascent of *Femme Fatale* (E7 6c). Many significant repeats of the harder routes also occurred around this period. Cuthbertson produced another difficult test piece the following year, when he snatched the very technical arête of *Liminality*, after another interested party had placed the pegs. The bold Mark McGowan was also active, his best effort the linking of two of Cuthbertson's routes to produce the serious and technical *Jodicus Direct*. Again new tactics (for Glen Nevis) came into use, when he pre-clipped the ropes into his high point on the second day, rather than re-climb the serious lower section. On Black's Buttress, Howett and Latter produced *Centrepiece*, protected by a skyhook and a *"little silver dagger"*. This peg later fell out, Mark Garthwaite climbing the route without in 1994 at E6.

The following year saw the big line of *Restless Natives* on Car Park Crag fall to a combined effort from Latter and Howett. A couple of days later, Howett forced his way up

Chiaroscuro on Spreadeagle Buttress, reportedly breaking some ribs in repeated falls from the finishing moves. There was a noticeable slowing down in the pace of activity over the next few years, as the number of remaining lines became fewer and harder. A fleeting visit from an on-form Johnny Dawes saw an impressive flashed ascent of *Jodicus Direct* (E6 6c). Later, on Steall Hut Crag, Mark McGowan added the difficult *Trick of the Tail*.

In the early 90s activity centred on the obvious hard potential of the severely overhanging Steall Hut Crag. Firstly in 1992, Murray Hamilton made a trip from his new home in France and free climbed the old aided crack-line. Hamilton decided to pre-place the protection prior to climbing this stunning crack-line in redpoint style to produce *Leopold*. The following year the neighbouring crack was redpointed by Latter, this time with the gear placed on the lead, to produce *Arcadia*. Whilst this route was being worked on, other parties were bolting sport projects that crossed both lines. The line of bolts coinciding with *Arcadia* were removed as there was also, unbelievably, extensive chipping and drilling of holds. The immensely powerful and talented Malcolm Smith made short work of the line of bolts at the right side of the crag to give *Steall Appeal*, which at F8b became the hardest sport climb in Scotland.

Bringing things fully up to date, Dave MacLeod has gone on to complete many of the more obvious harder remaining challenges, including the obvious gap on Creag an Fhithich Beag with *Juggernaut*, pushing standards further with a number of headpointed ascents; *Hold Fast* on Whale Rock, at E9 7a seriously raising the standard. Finally, in 2007 MacLeod moved to Fort William in order to work on the long standing sport project on Steall Hut Crag, bolted by Cuthbertson in 1993. As expected, the resultant *Ring of Steall*, at F8c+ became Scotland's hardest sport route. Prior to this MacLeod also added the superb *Stolen*, at a slightly more amenable F8b.

NN 145 694 **Alt:**130m (w) 30min

CREAG AN FHITHICH BEAG
(LITTLE CRAG OF THE RAVEN)

This is the first crag to come into view when driving up the glen and one of the most impressive, characterized by an overhanging front face broken by several overhangs on its right side.

Approach: The quickest approach is by crossing the river at a ford (NN 139 691) at a point about a kilometre downstream from the lower falls at Achriabhach, where the river runs close to the road, just beyond a large flat area of ground on the left (north) side of the road. (4 miles/6.4km from the roundabout). From the other side of the river (north), gain a path on the left and follow this to a stream (Allt na Dubh-ghlaic) just beyond a gate. Cross the stream and cut directly up through the trees by an ill-defined ridge to gain the left end of the crag. If the river is too high, or for those with hydrophobia, approach can also be made by starting along the track at Achriabhach Bridge (NN 145 685).

Descent: Down either side of the crag, easier on the left.

1 Hollow Wall ★★   9m VS 4c

FA A.Wallace 1975

On the short steep lower tier, directly underneath the left section of the crag. The crack near the left end, stepping left near the top.

2 Virtual Reality ★   25m E5 6b

FA Rab Anderson, Duncan McCallum & Johnny May (red pointed) 23 May 1992

The thin crack and hanging groove in the left wall of the crag. Reasonably well protected, though difficult to place.

The following two routes share a common start, a quartz intrusion on the left arête.

3 Liminality ★★★   25m E6 6c

FA Dave Cuthbertson (red pointed) 22 May 1987

A subliminal excursion up the edge of all things – or just a neat little arête? The prominent left-bounding edge of the crag. Up on quartz holds then left to a ledge on the left side of the arête. The thin crack on the right side is followed (2 stacked PRs, good RP #5 placement just above first PR) with hard moves to reach a PR at the top of the crack. Pull left to a further PR and up arête to top. **Note:** A 4' sling was pre-placed on the otherwise difficult to clip 3rd PR for the FA.

4 Caterpillar ★   27m E3 5c

FA Dave Cuthbertson & Ed Grindley 10 May 1984

The diagonal quartz vein then easier up a ramp to finish up a short steep wall.

5 The Dream of the Butterfly ★★   30m E6 6b

FA Gary Latter (red pointed) 14 September 1993

The horizontal fault emanating from the initial crack of 6 provides very safe strenuous climbing. Follow the fault past some PRs with a difficult section stepping down to better holds leading to the quartz recess on 4. Finish up that route.

6 The Handren Effect ★★★★   25m E6 6b

FA Dave Cuthbertson April 1983

One of the best pieces of wall climbing in the glen. Bold and sustained at a high standard. Start at an obvious inverted L-shaped crack. Up this past a pair of PRs with difficulty to reach a good flake hold (RPs behind this; situ nut above). Up a shallow runnel with hard moves to reach a superb bucket hold at the top of the wall. Stroll easily up the short corner above.

7 Juggernaut ★★★   30m E7 6b

FA Dave MacLeod 18 August 2002

Outstanding climbing up the wall in the centre of the crag, featuring fairly well protected but sustained strenuous climbing. Start up the left-facing scoop and step left to the PRs. Launch directly up the wall to reach a jug (good wire behind). Move up and left to the deceptive

break (RP) and dyno to a good hold directly above (crux). Move left and mantel onto the sloping ledge giving access to easy finishing rib on the left.

8 The Monster ★★   30m E5 6a

FA Andrew Wielochowski & Pete Webster (A3) 1975;
FFA Dave Cuthbertson & Alan Moist 16 June 1985

A strenuous well protected pitch. Start beneath a shallow left-facing scoop, as for 9. Climb directly, initially on good holds then continue up the wall above to an overhang. Go left to undercuts (F on left) and good footholds, and along an awkward jam crack with a hard move onto a ledge. Easier climbing up and rightwards to finish.

9 Steerpike ★★   45m E2 5c

FA Noel Williams & Andrew Wielochowski (1 PA & 1 tension traverse) 1975; FFA Dave Cuthbertson & Gary Latter 1982

Start just right of the inverted L-shaped crack, beneath a shallow left-facing scoop.

  1 **20m 5c** Up this on good holds past some old pegs to arrange a runner underneath the roof. Cross the gangway on the right (crux) to easy ground, and belay at the foot of the quartz groove.

  2 **15m 5b** Up the quartz groove directly above and pull rightwards onto a ledge and belay at an oak tree.

  3 **10m** Climb the tree and move right into a chimney, or abseil off.

10 Spring Fever ★★   25m E3 5c

FA Dave Cuthbertson, Kev Howett & Callum Henderson 30 May 1985

A fine route when combined with 9. Start from the hanging belay at the top of pitch one of that route. Climb thin crack and quartz overhang, as for that route, to a slab right of a hanging corner. Step down and swing wildly left for a jug then the obvious line leftwards.

⑪ Exocet ★★★   **40m E6 6b**

FA Andrew Wielochowski & Noel Williams (A3) 1975; FFA Dave Cuthbertson 18 May 1982; pitch 1 freed the following month

A direct uncompromising line through the overhanging prow up the steepest section of the crag. Start at the foot of a prominent diagonal crack-line up and left of an overgrown left-facing corner crack.

  1 **15m 6a** Swing right into the crack and up this to a hanging belay at the foot of a quartz groove (common to 9).

  2 **25m 6b** Undercut the roof leftwards for about 3m (very awkward) to a large flat hold above. Attain a standing position on this with difficulty and follow a line of holds trending leftwards to a resting ledge. Continue more easily above.

Note: The first pitch, although slow to dry, provides a very fine pitch in its own right at E3 6a – an excellent combination with *Spring Fever*. The section above the roof can also be gained from *The Monster*, providing a long exposed pitch at no change in the overall grade.

The Handren Effect.
Mark Garthwaite climbing.

POLLDUBH

The name Polldubh (literally the black pool) correctly refers to a pool in the River Nevis, just upstream from the lay-by at NN 153 685 below **Pinnacle Ridge**. Common usage has resulted in the frontage of crags on the hillside, extending for over a kilometre from the bridge at Achriabhach, being referred to as Polldubh.

The crags are many and varied, numbering around 40 in all, ranging from mere overgrown boulders a few metres high to fine 90m plus crags with two and sometimes three pitch routes. The obvious advantage of linking numerous routes within separate tiers is quite apparent, giving up to 300m of ascent.

CAVALRY CRACK BUTTRESS

NN 151 686 **Alt:** 140m   5min

The largest of the lower buttresses. The left face is split by prominent diagonal cracks, easily recognized by a large Scots pine sprouting high up with two further prominent Scots pines halfway up the left side of the front face.

Approach: Follow an initially boggy path from the Pinnacle Burn leftwards up to the base.

Descent: A steep path down the left side, skirting round the left side of a small broken buttress near the base.

1 The Old Wall ★★★   40m VS 4b

FA Ike Jones & party 1963

Steady open wall climbing on good holds. Protection is noticeably lacking. Start up a wide left-slanting heathery crack high up the left side of the base. Climb the initially vegetated crack for 6m to just past a tree. Move right and up before heading across the wall through *Storm* to finish on the right edge of the wall level with the pine on *Storm*.

2 Storm ★★★★   80m HVS 5a

FA Ian Clough & Terry Sullivan (3 PA) 3 May 1959;
FFA Allan & Jenny Austin 1962; True Finish: John Taylor
& Klaus Schwartz 1976

A well protected classic with fine situations, giving the best route of its grade on the crags. Omitting the final crux pitch by escaping out right from the tree belay to finish up *Fang* gives a great three star VS. Start a few metres up left from the very toe of the buttress, beneath a left-slanting ramp.

1 **21m 4b** Follow the ramp to belay on a ledge at the base of a long diagonal crack.

2 **27m 4c** The wide crack to a wonderfully positioned belay on the large pine.

3 **22m 5a** Ascend the shallow groove on the right to cross the bulge (crux) then much easier and trending slightly right up the wall above. *The True Finish*, E1 5b moves out left from above the crux and follows the shallow corner capped by a block overhang.

4 **10m** Scramble up easy slabs to finish.

3 Heatwave/Vampire Combo ★★   90m HS 4b

FA Ian Clough, J.Pickering, R.Henson, P.Brocklehurst & R.Porteous 22 May 1959

A good link. Start just left of the toe of the buttress, as for *Storm*.

  1 **20m 4b** Follow the ramp to belay on a ledge at the base of the long diagonal crack of *Storm*.

  2 **5m** Traverse the horizontal break right to belay at the base of a left-facing groove.

  3 **25m 4b** Climb the groove then continue up left-slant- ing cracks close to the right edge of the wall. The original route ascends the left wall of the gully at 4a.

  4 **40m 4a** Finish up slabs above, trending left to a short groove and direct above.

4 Drizzle ★   45m HS 4b

FA Ian Sykes & Jim Bell 1963; Pitch 2 Terry Sullivan 29 May 1959

Start above and behind a holly directly beneath the rightmost pine.

  1 **25m 4b** Follow the left edge of the *Vampire* slab to the big pines.

  2 **20m 4a** Continue up the right wall of the gully via an awkward step and a vertical dièdre near the top. Walk off right, or finish as for *Heatwave*.

5 Vampire ★   100m HS 4b

FA Ian Clough & Eddie Buckley 21 April 1959

Varied and enjoyable. Start 8m right of the buttress edge, beneath the rightmost pine.

  1 **30m 4b** Climb a short slab and traverse 3m right to a small birch. Move right along a ledge, follow left-trending flake crack and traverse left to the pine and belay.

  2 **30m 4b** Walk left 5m. Climb a groove then continue up left-slanting cracks close to the right edge of the wall.

  3 **40m 4a** Finish as for *Heatwave*.

6 Fang ★★   45m E2 5b

FA Bill Skidmore, Peter MacKenzie & Jim Crawford (aid) July 1963; FFA Ed Grindley & Ian Nicolson 19 April 1976

Bold open wall climbing. Start beneath an open left-facing groove down and right of the open slab of *Vampire*.

  1 **25m 5b** Go up a steep initial groove past an overlap then move steeply out right on good holds. Move up then pull leftwards along a diagonal crack to belay on a ledge.

  2 **20m 5a** The groove above, turning the roof on the right.

Storm, Neil Foss climbing.

PINNACLE RIDGE

NN 153 686 **Alt:** 100m   5min

The lowest of all the buttresses at Polldubh, immediately above the lay-by just beyond a small stream. Consequently the most popular and polished, but not indicative of what is on offer.

Approach: From the lay-by parking spot (NN 152 685), head up the well worn path just right of Pinnacle Burn, bearing right through the trees to the base.

1 Soap Suds ★   15m E4 6a

FA Dave Cuthbertson & Ian Sutherland 1981

Start at the left side of the wall beneath a curving overlap. Undercut rightwards and pull over the overlap at a good hold on the lip. Step right to gain better holds. Bold.

2 The Sugar Puff Kid ★   12m E4 6a

FA Dave Cuthbertson / Gary Latter (both led) 15 May 1985

Ascends the wall midway between 1 and 3.

3 Chalky Wall ★   12m E4 6a

FA Dave Cuthbertson & Murray Hamilton April 1977

The hard Polldubh test piece. Start 2m left of the prominent vertical crack of 4. Up past a flake with a hard move to gain holds in the start of a diagonal crack. Pull directly and somewhat blindly onto the rounded slab above.

4 Clapham Junction ★★   10m VS 5a

FA unknown 1950s (aid); FFA Ken Johnson 1964

The obvious crack, hand traversing right at the top. Technical and well protected. The 4a *Direct Finish* pushes the grade up to HVS 5a.

5 Severe Crack ★   9m VS 4b

FA Jimmy Ness & Alan Burgon 25 May 1950

The crack with a perched block near the top proves harder than its name would suggest.

6 Hodad ★   10m HVS 5b

FA Ike Jones & John Grieve 1967

The left-slanting diagonal crack on the second tier. Make a long reach right to finish.

7 Pinnacle Ridge ★★   45m Severe 4a

FA Jimmy Ness & Dr Donald Duff 1947

One of the most popular routes at Polldubh, with a polished first pitch. Start at the toe of the buttress.

1 20m 4a Climb near the left edge of the slab, first left onto the edge (good diagonal finger crack for protection) then back right and up to a small birch. Continue up the easy angled scoop/jam crack to a terrace. Step right and belay at good crack immediately below another birch.

2 25m Climb up then along the top of the large flake on the right (past a third birch) then up rightwards to follow a good crack up rough slabs to the top. The fine open scoop above the large flake can also be climbed at the same standard.

Variations: *Staircase* 15m S 4a (*FA Jimmy Ness & Alan Burgon 28 Sept 1950*) Start 6m right of the normal start and follow, wait for it, *"staircase like holds"* to the first tree. *Tip Toe* 25m HS 4a (*FA Jimmy Ness, M.Hutchison & R.Corson 23 Sept 1950*) Start immediately right of *Staircase*. Go up the slab to a small foothold, and (you guessed it!) tip toe left to good hand holds at 10m and traverse left. Either climb a niche or the crack to its right leading to the terrace. Poorly protected on the lower slab.

PANDORA'S BUTTRESS

Lies immediately above and to the left of **Repton Buttress**. The buttress has a slightly overhanging front face with twin diagonal leftward slanting cracks. Two rock tongues extend down on either side of the cracks into the trees.

Approach: From the lay-by parking spot (NN 152 685), head up the well-worn path just right of Pinnacle Burn then cross the burn and head up through the trees to the base.

 **Phantom Slab** ★★★   **25m VS 5a**

FA Terry Sullivan & Ian Clough 3 May 1959

Excellent sustained slab climbing, well worth the trouble of searching it out. Start by climbing the first two pitches of 2. Descend a few metres to belay beneath the right side of the slab. This point can also be gained by fairly straightforward down climbing or a short abseil from just left of the main pitch on 4. Traverse diagonally leftwards and follow a line up the left edge of the slab, finishing by moving slightly rightwards at the top.

 Pandora ★★   **65m Severe 4a**

FA Ian Clough & Eddy Buckley 20 April 1959

Good varied climbing.

1 **25m 4a** Climb the left of two rock tongues below the diagonal cracks to a large ledge.
2 **20m 4a** Continue up the rib to a tree on the right wall of a large corner.
3 **20m 4a** Up the corner to a large ledge then slabs on the left.

 Tomag ★★   **30m E4 5c**

FA Murray Hamilton & John Fantini 1981

Strenuous and sustained climbing taking the finely situated parallel cracks across the overhanging wall. Gain these from a short groove, and follow them round the arête on fist jams (large cam useful) then cut back right to the top.

4 **Flying Dutchman** ★★★   **60m Severe 4a**

FA Terry Sullivan & Ian Clough 3 May 1959

Deservedly popular with an exposed and sustained second pitch. Start on the lowest rocks, to the right of *Pandora*.

1 **27m** Climb the crest, or heathery grooves just to the right to a terrace.
2 **24m 4a** Go up slabs left of a dièdre to traverse diagonally left on good footholds to a short corner in the left side of the roof. Pull over the roof, up a crack and round a rib to belay on a capacious ledge.
3 **9m** Follow the ridge directly or scramble up easy ledges leading left.

4a **Direct Finish** ★   **6m VS 4c**

FA unknown 1960s

From the belay ledge, follow the thin rightward slanting crack.

NN 152 687 **Alt:** 160m   S   5min

REPTON BUTTRESS   5min

NN 153 687 **Alt:** 140m

Slightly below and immediately to the right
of **Pandora's Buttress**.

Approach: From the lay-by parking spot (NN 152 685)
head up the well-worn path just right of Pinnacle Burn
then cross the burn to the base.

❶ Three Pines *   30m Severe 4a

FA Terry Sullivan, Eddie Buckley & A. Flegg 17 March 1959

A popular route. Climb the rib immediately right of the
central gully to the pines. Follow the groove behind the
central tree moving right under the roof with interest to a
platform. Continue by a crack.

❶ₐ Three Pines Variations *   30m Very Difficult

FA unknown 1960s

Start 6m right of the original route and traverse up left
to the rib which is followed to the pines. Escape out left
then back right.

❷ Right Wall *   30m Very Difficult

FA unknown 1950s

Start on the right of the crag. Climb up to the right end of
the overhang, step left onto it and up to a tree. Traverse
3m to another tree and through yet another tree into a
cleft. Up behind this.

LITTLE BUTTRESS   10min

NN 153 688 **Alt:** 180m

A slabby crag with a large Scots pine at the left end of
a mid-height ledge. It lies just up and right of **Repton
Buttress**, about 100m left of **Pine Wall Crag**.

Approach: As for **Pine Wall Crag**, traversing left 100m.

Descent: Down the right side of the crag.

❶ Spike Wall **   55m Very Difficult

*FA Ian Clough, R. Henson, P. Brocklehurst & R. Porteous
28 June 1959*

A popular and delightful climb. Good value for the grade.
Start near some boulders.

   1 **30m** Climb the slab leftwards to the spike
   at 7m. Go over the spike and traverse left
   almost to the edge. Climb a recess and the
   ridge above to the big ledge with the pine.

   2 **25m** Climb the slab above on small quartz holds
   to finish on the rounded crest of the ridge.

❶ₐ Spike Direct *   30m Severe 4a

FA Ken Johnson 1960

Climb a groove just right of the rib for 5m then move right
towards the spike. Continue straight above the spike,
gaining the ridge by a crack on the right to reach a block.

THE ALP

Hidden from the road above and well right of **Pinnacle Ridge** and just beyond the origin of the Pinnacle Burn lies a large sheltered flat area of grass with two particularly fine contrasting crags, together with a strangely popular instantly-drying micro-crag.

Approach: From the lay-by parking spot (NN 152 685) head up the well-worn path keeping just right of the Pinnacle Burn, passing a boggy section just before the end of the burn. Continue past the 12m high smooth steep slab of **SW Buttress** to gain the Alp. **Pine Wall Crag** is just up through the trees on the left, **Styx Buttress** immediately in front.

SW BUTTRESS 🅂 🧗 10min

NN 154 688 **Alt:** 170m

A micro-crag, but very quick drying. It lies just above the origins of the burn.

Descent: By path down the right (east) side.

 Tear ★★　　　　　　　　　　**12m HS 4b**

FA Ken Johnson 1963/4

The vertical crack just left of centre with a technical but very well protected crux past the bulge.

 Scratch ★　　　　　　　　　　**12m VS 4c**

FA Ken Johnson 1963/4

Climb slightly rightwards up the slab, from just right of 1.

 SW2 ★　　　　　　　　　　**12m HVS 5b**

FA unknown early 60s

Start up the short corner just right of 2 to the diagonal break. Step right to a foothold and ascend thin cracks.

④ **SW Diagonal** ★　　　　　　　　　　**15m HVS 5b**

FA Ken Johnson 1963/4

Diagonal left-slanting crack with one hard move low down.

⑤ **Tee**　　　　　　　　　　**12m VS 5b**

FA Mike Hall (solo) 1971

Follow a direct line just right of the diagonal to finish up crack. Again, one hard move.

Tear, Penny Dunbabin climbing.

PINE WALL CRAG 10min

NN 154 688 **Alt:** 180m

A prominent 60m high ridge facing the glen, clearly distinguished by a large Scots pine at two-thirds height. **Descent:** Traverse leftwards on a path crossing a small burn then descend a short shallow V-gully leading left of the watercourse facing out, i.e. east, to large boulder field leading back to the base.

① Eigerwand ★   45m HS 4a

FA Ken Johnson 1960s

Start up left from the base beneath a large tree on a terrace at 8m. Climb up to the tree then a small gully on the left for 3m. Move right and follow a direct line, finishing up the centre of the superb headwall.

② Pine Wall ★★★   65m HS 4a

FA Jimmy Ness & Alan Burgon 1 June 1950

Excellent exposed climbing on perfect rock, making it one of the best climbs of its standard on the crags. Much variation is possible, although the described line gives the best climbing of the grade. Start at the toe of the crag, just left of *The Gutter*.

1 **35m 4a** Move up to a dièdre and climb this to a plat-form at 12m. Move left and cross a bulge then climb the immaculate slabs to the right of the rounded ridge to belay on large ledge where the angle eases.

2 **15m** Follow either the ridge or grooves left of it to belay beneath the steeper headwall.

3 **15m 4a** Pass an overlap on either side to reach a small recess just left of the crest, and continue more easily up this to finish.

③ The Gutter ★★★   65m Difficult

FA unknown 1940s?; after cleaning Klaus Schwartz 1976

A classic with fine situations – far and away the best route of its grade on the crags. Start at the lowest point of the crag.

1 **30m** Climb crack (awkward bouldery start) to a ledge at 12m. Continue in the same line by a deeper crack to belay just above a birch sapling.

2 **15m** Continue up a shallow groove just left of the crest of the ridge to belay on the big pine.

3 **20m** Move up left past the left end of a ledge to a good flake handhold on the wall then go out right to finish easily up the fine deep crack in the crest of the ridge.

The Gutter, Tom Lee climbing. Photo Dave Cuthbertson, Cubby Images.

STYX BUTTRESS 10min

NN 155 688 **Alt:** 180m

Immediately right of **Pine Wall Crag**, with a typically steep side wall and slabby front face.

Descent: Make a short step down into the open gully bounding the left side of the crag then easily down this.

1 Black Friday ★★   25m E4 6a
FA Klaus Schwartz & Blyth Wright (aid) 13 May 1969; FFA Murray Hamilton & John Fantini 1981

A well protected struggle up the prominent overhanging cleft splitting the centre of the left face. Climb up rightwards past a sloping ledge to the base of the cleft fault. Ascend this strenuously to easier climbing up the final wider cleft where the angle eases. Slow to dry.

2 Resurrection ★★★   30m VS 4c
FA Ian Clough & A.Lakin 5 April 1959

A Polldubh classic – sustained and well protected, taking the tapering ramp in the centre of the crag. Climb the slabby ramp with the crux at the narrow middle section, finishing by a slightly easier wide fault leading to a fine pine tree belay. Scramble to finish.

3 Damnation ★★★   30m VS 4c
FA Ian Clough & John Alexander 28 June 1958

Excellent varied climbing, improbable looking for the grade. Protection is good where it matters. Start 10m up right from 2. Go leftwards up a ramp, until it is possible to step up right to a rounded vertical rib leading to an overhang. Cross this slightly leftwards on good holds and continue directly up the fine cracked slab to finish.

4 Iche ★   30m VS 5a
FA Terry Sullivan & Ian Clough 11 April 1959

Start just left of the diagonal heather groove. Climb leftwards up the slab and cross the overhang 2m from its right end. Move left to a thin crack and follow this to finish up the slab above.

5 Right Wall ★★   50m Very Difficult
FA unknown 1960s

A long pitch on good clean rock. Near the right edge of the crag is a clean slab. Start near the left edge of this. Climb diagonally left to the edge of the slab and follow this, passing some pine saplings and keeping right of a recess to finish by a fine crack past another sapling.

ROAD BUTTRESS   5min

NN 154 686 **Alt:** 100m

200m right of **Pinnacle Ridge**.

Approach from 150m east of the lay-bys below **Pinnacle Ridge**.

1 No Entry ★ 20m VS 5a

FA Klaus Schwartz & Rebecca Morrow 3 June 1976;
Direct Start Ed Grindley 22 April 1978

Start just left of the groove of 2. Climb up to a curving crack and follow it to a heathery scoop.

2 The Web ★★ 20m E2 5c

FA Klaus Schwartz & Blyth Wright (A2) 29 May 1969;
FFA Ed Grindley & Willie Todd 5 June 1976

SECRETARIES' BUTTRESS   20min

NN 151 688 **Alt:** 250m

High up the hill, above and left of **Cavalry Crack Buttress** and about 100m left of **High Crag, Lower Tiers**. Easily recognised from the road by a three tier steep left wall split by two oblique faults, with a slabby frontal face.

Approach: As for **Cavalry Crack Buttress** then follow the path up the left side of the small subsidiary crag to the flat top of the main buttress. Continue slightly left and up past the left side of a further smaller buttress.

Descent: Down either side of the buttress.

1 Secretaries' Direct ★★★ 80m Severe 4a

FA Ian Clough & Eddie Buckley 21 April 1959

Excellent climbing, giving one of the best lines of its grade in the glen. Start below the shallow left-facing corner in the front face.

1 **15m 4a** Climb corner to the first ledge system. Move right 4m to belay below crack.

2 **18m 4a** Follow the central crack on superb quartz holds to the second fault system.

3 **47m** Easier up the slab to a horizontal ridge leading rightwards over several short steps.

The open groove with an obvious overhang halfway up. Layback round the first overhang on good holds and cross the top crux bulge directly. The layback crack of 3 can be gained by starting up 2 at E1 5b.

3 Wee One ★   25m E3 6a

FA Jim Mount & Brian Chambers (A2) 1973;
FFA Murray Hamilton & Kenny Spence 1980

Start just right of 2. Hard bouldery moves lead into a shallow left-facing groove (PR). Up this and finish by a layback crack.

4 Cubsville ★★   20m E5 6b

FA A. Gray & Jim Mount (A3) 1973;
FFA Gary Latter / Dave Cuthbertson (both led) 3 May 1985

Start in the centre of the crag. Climb the undercut groove to gain a crack above an overlap with difficulty and continue up this.

5 Withering Crack ★★   20m E3 5c

FA Klaus Schwartz & Jim Mount 11 October (aid) 1972;
FFA Ed & Cynthia Grindley 1978

The jam crack splitting two overhangs on the right side of the crag. After a bouldery start difficulties soon ease just above the first overhang.

6 Atree ★   20m VS 5a

FA Ed Grindley 31 August 1978

The groove to the right of 5 contains a tree. Reach this by a tricky wall and finish by a slab.

2 Secretaries' Super Direct ★★★   50m HVS 5a

FA Alec Fulton & Klaus Schwartz 28 July 1969;
p1 Klaus Schwartz & Jim Mount 19 May 1973

A fine exposed line heading for the left edge of the slabby face. Start below the corner of *Secretaries' Direct*.

1 **20m 5a** Move left across the steep slab to cross the overlap near the left edge and up this to the first ledge system.

2 **30m 5a** Follow the thin and exposed left edge of the slab to the second ledge (possible belay) Cross the gap and finish up easier slabs.

3 Twitch ★   15m E1 5b

FA John Cunningham & party 29 October 1969

The thin slab midway between the second pitches of *Super Direct* and the *Direct*. Unprotected, the difficulties easing as height is gained.

4 Vincent ★★★   60m E3 5c

FA Dave Cuthbertson & Ian Sykes 1981

Fine open climbing taking a diagonal line across all three tiers. Start at the toe of the crag.

1 **18m 5b** Up the wall to join the diagonal

crack and along this to a ledge.

2 **12m 5c** Move left round the overhang and up the wall (unprotected) to better holds just below the top. Up a slab to a ledge and belay.

3 **30m 5c** Descend about a metre, pull round onto the wall and follow a crack until a left traverse can be made to a ledge. Up cracks to the top.

5 Secretaries' Crack ★   20m Difficult

FA Jimmy Ness & Alan Burgon 11 May 1950

The fault splitting the second and third tiers of the crag gives one of the few deep chimney lines hereabouts. Follow this to a ledge on the front wall.

6 Ring of Fire Right-Hand ★★★   30m E3 6a

FA Murray Hamilton 1984

Fine open wall climbing with a gymnastic start. Start at the top left end of the buttress. Swing athletically right to a large flat hold above the lip of the initial roof and go up to a ledge. Break out right and follow an obvious line up the wall leading to the top crack on 4 and finish up this.

NAMELESS CRAG 25min

NN 152 689 **Alt:** 310m

Lies at the same level, and immediately to the left of the skull of **High Crag, Upper Tier.**

Approach: As for **Secretaries' Buttress**, cutting up the right side of that crag.

Descent: Down either side.

1 Savage Cabbage * 30m E4 5c

FA Dave Cuthbertson & Kev Howett 16 May 1985

The shallow hanging groove in the centre of the left wall. Climb the short groove to a ledge. Up then horizontally right to a poor PR at the base of the groove. Follow this with a hard move to reach a second PR (also poor) on the rib out right, then pull onto the slab on the left and finish more easily.

2 Risqué Grapefruit ** 30m E4 5c

FA Derek Jamieson & Dave Cuthbertson 1981

Thin bold climbing up the slightly slabbier right side of the face with a run out crux. Start under a short open groove in the centre of the face. Pull rightwards across the wall and round the arête onto a slab. Direct over a tiny overlap and up with some stretchy moves (crux) to reach a shallow scoop. Go up the shallow groove and leftward trending ramp to finish.

3 Faceless * 30m E2 5b

FA Gary Latter, Robert Lee & Dave Cuthbertson 3 June 1986

The deep-cut groove at the right end of the face.

4 Bitter Days * 25m E3 6a

FA Kev Howett 1 November 1987

The bulging arête, slab and roof forming the apex of the crag where the two faces abut. Start directly below the arête, reached by a narrow ledge system from the right. Climb the left side and swing round the arête and up the slab to good holds and protection under the roof. Pull through this to superb finishing holds. Spectacular.

The following routes are all on the shorter, slabbier right wall, facing up the glen. It is split into three walls by a pair of vertical, lichenous fault lines.

5 Quadrode * 20m E2 5b

FA Kev Howett /Gary Latter (both led) 1 November 1987

Bold steady climbing up the centre of the wall near the left end of the face. Start at a triangular. Easily on good holds to a runner placement in the second break (RP #3). Step left and follow obvious leftward trending holds with interest to finish at a good incut. PB in situ on top.

The central tower of rock formed by the two vertical fault lines is 6 *Cathode Smiles* * E2 5c.

7 **Triode** ★★   **20m E5 6a**

FA Dave Cuthbertson & Andy de Klerk 19 May 1987

Thin bold climbing up the blankest section of the face. Start beneath a shallow left-facing groove. Up this for about 6m then move right to a crack leading to horizontal break. Nut placement in slot above. Move left along the horizontal then up to a quartz hold. Continue on small holds to a series of undercuts heading out left to finish.

8 **Diode** ★★   **20m E2 5c**

FA Brian Sprunt & C.Hill 29 July 1977

A thin crack splits the right end of the face. Climb this direct passing a narrow roof at mid-height.

HIGH CRAG 25–30min

NN 153 688 **Alt:** 300m

LOWER TIERS

The biggest crag at Polldubh, composed of three tiers of slabs. The lower tier is scrappy, mostly obscured by trees; the second tier 70m high and much better. The routes are a little bit dirtier than the more popular shorter routes lower down, but not unduly so.

Descent: Down the left side, skirting left (west) round a short undercut slab near the base.

1 **Cervix** ★   **30m VS 4c**

FA Klaus Schwartz & Brian Chambers 11 October 1969

Start high up on the left wall above the gully and overlooking the subsidiary hanging slab down left. Go up the initial wall by a left-slanting crack with a strenuous crux at 10m. Finish up the fine steep slanting chimney.

2 **Crag Lough Grooves** ★★   **135m HVS 5b**

FA Terry Sullivan & Ian Clough (3 PA) 23 March 1959;
FFA Allan & Jenny Austin 1962

Varied climbing, with a hard crux section through the steeper final tier. Start left of a cave overhang, at the bottom left of the middle tier.

1 **30m 5a** Scramble to overhangs at 10m. Traverse 3m right across three small ribs into a red groove and follow this to a ledge and tree belay.

2 **40m 4c** Follow the crack up the edge of the slabs finishing by easier slabs on the right to a thread belay on the second terrace.

3 **15m 5b** Walk to the right a few metres. Cross the initial bulge and follow a prominent rightward trending gangway to a small stance around the rib.

4 **20m 4c** Follow steep groove above to slabs and a ledge.

5 **30m** Finish up easy slabs.

3 Kinloss Grooves ★   **65m VS 4c**

FA Ian Clough & Terry Sullivan 11 April 1959

Start at a tree below the first break in the overhang right of *Crag Lough Grooves*, left of a red wall.

1 **33m 4c** Climb to a small niche below the overhang at 9m, exit right and up to another niche. Continue up the slabs to a ledge.

2 **32m 4a** The slabs above, climbed anywhere, to the second terrace.

4 Autobahnausfahrt ★   **160m VS 4c**

FA Klaus Schwartz & Brian Chambers (1 PA) 2 September 1969

The longest route in the glen with pleasant and varied situations.

1 **35m 4a** Climb slabs near the right side of the base of the lower crag to the first terrace.

2 **15m** Climb the block and bulge above to a tree ledge.

3 **45m 4b** Surmount the overhang 5m above and head for a small groove and up this to the second terrace.

4 **35m 4c** Walk right and climb the steep slabs at the right end of the overhanging base, passing a heather groove at 8m on its left.

5 **30m** Continue straight up over a bulge to easy slabs, climbable anywhere.

UPPER TIER

Easily recognisable from the road, the steep left side of the crag bears a remarkable resemblance to a skull. The severely overhanging walls in the centre of the front face, either side of *Sky Pilot* give good, though limited hard **bouldering** above a wide grassy terrace. Worth knowing about for a rainy day – if you can bear the walk in.

Approach: As for **Secretaries' Buttress**, cutting up the right side of that crag to gain the left end of the terrace.

Descent: Down the left side.

5 Sky Pilot ★★★   **30m E5 6b**

FA Dave Cuthbertson 1981

The centre of the overhanging 45 degree wall is breached by a hanging crack, forming a block near the lip. Climb up and out on improving holds to the lip and step left to gain easy slabs. Bouldery.

6 Slatehead Slab ★★   **30m E2 5b**

FA Dave Cuthbertson & Gary Latter 27 October 1985

Right of the right eye (as you're looking at it) of the skull is a fine slab above a tree with a short wall at its foot. Gain the base by scrambling in from top right. From the tree traverse left then up the wall to pull left onto the slab at good side pulls. Follow the obvious line right across the slab to a good pocket at a break. Continue past another break to the top.

Vincent, Secretaries' Buttress. Jonny Baird climbing. Photo Dave Cuthbertson, Cubby Images.

BLACK'S BUTTRESS

NN 155 688 **Alt:** 300m

25min

Situated at the same level and well to the right of **High Crag, Upper Tier** about 60m above **Pine Wall**. The buttress is composed of a vegetatious lower tier marked by a clean left edge. Immediately above, separated by a wide flat grassy terrace (obscuring much of the crag from below) is a smooth 30m slab of immaculate rock. **Descent:** Traverse right and down steep grass to right.

 Zelos ★   **60m Very Difficult**

FA P1 Alec Fulton & Brian Chambers May 1969;
P2 Klaus Schwartz 15 February 1970

The first pitch is also a useful approach to the main crag.
- **1** **30m** Follow the clean left edge of the lower tier.
- **2** **30m** Continue 2m left of a small tree,
  again keeping close to the edge.

2 **Shergar ★★**   **30m HVS 4c**

FA Ed Grindley, Cynthia Grindley, Pete Long & Gordon Higginson
13 September 1981

Start left of the smooth slab on the left. Climb thin rightward cracks to gain a shallow left-facing corner.

 Land Ahoy ★★★   **30m E3 5b**

FA Ed Grindley & Davy Gunn October 1981

Brilliant climbing, sustained and unprotectable as far as the crack. Start midway between 2 and 4 beneath the left side of the smooth slab. Climb the wall direct to the crack in the upper half of the wall then more easily up this.

4 **Centrepiece ★★**   **30m E6 6b**

FA Kev Howett / Gary Latter (both led) & Dave Griffiths 11
October 1987; FA sans PR Mark Garthwaite 1994

Superb fingery climbing directly up the centre of the slab. Start at some quartz in the centre of the wall. Up to a prominent L-shaped hold at 5m (tied down skyhook on this). Hard climbing past this leads to a thin horizontal break. Pull direct past this to better holds (R #7 on side) and a reasonable stopping place. Poor RP placements in the incipient crack system above protect a further tricky move to reach a large flat hold. Easy climbing remains.

5 **Kaos ★**   **30m E2 5c**

FA Klaus Schwartz & P.Logan (3 PA) 7 July 1968; FFA Kenny
Spence 1980

Delicate and fingery with a poorly protected crux. Follow the obvious thin vertical crack then up and left with difficulty to gain a further crack and small ledge at 11m. Continue in the same line to the top.

6 **Crybaby ★**   **20m VS 4c**

FA Klaus Schwartz & Moira Horsburgh 29 June 1970; FFA Klaus
Schwartz & Loch Eil party 1972

Start midway between 5 and the rib on the right. Follow the crack rightwards past a small triangular niche to a ledge. Finish up a crack on the left.

NN 156 686 **Alt:** 130m (w) 10min

NN 157 687 **Alt:** 180m 15min

SCIMITAR BUTTRESS

The furthest right (eastmost) of the Polldubh crags, approximately 300m right of **Road Buttress** and slightly higher, on the rocky spur of Mam Beag (small breast).

Approach: From the small bridge 200m up the road from the lay-bys head slightly right up the hillside to the base.

Descent: Either scramble easily up or down the ridge to easy ground then down either side.

1 Wanderlust *   **25m Very Difficult**

FA Ian Clough 22 April 1959

Climb the wide right-slanting fault at the right end of the crag then follow an obvious left-trending line across the top of the wall. Finish up a short rough slab.

2 Razor **   **20m VS 4c**

FA Brian Sprunt & Andy Slater 1978

Start at the right end of the crag. From the base of 1 climb straight up to join 3. Follow this for a few moves then traverse left along a shelf to finish up the flake crack in a fine position.

3 Diagonal Crack *   **20m VS 4c**

FA R.Wilkinson & Doc Pipes (7 PA) 8 April 1958;
FFA Alec Fulton & Brian Chambers 1968

Steep climbing up the prominent right-slanting crack. Well protected on good holds.

4 Nutcracker Chimney **   **18m HS 4b**

FA R.Wilkinson & Doc Pipes 8 April 1958

Good well-protected climbing up the shallow flared chimney at the upper left side of the crag.

UPPER SCIMITAR BUTTRESS

A short steep isolated gritstone-like slab 150 metres up the ridge from the lower crag. All three routes are unprotected.

Approach: Continue up past the lower crag for a further few minutes.

1 Sweet Little Mystery *   **10m E4 6a**

FA Dave Cuthbertson (solo) June 1984

From the bottom left end of the crag, ascend diagonally rightwards to a steepening. Make an awkward step up to good break and finish directly.

2 Jahu **   **10m E6 6a**

FA Dave Cuthbertson (solo) July 1984

Climb the right trending scoop in the centre of the slab in its entirety. Very thin and committing, with a definite crux at mid-height.

The right side of the slab is taken by 3 *Where the Mood Takes Me* * E5 6a.

Car Park
Crag

Whale
Rock

Creag Uamh
Shomhairle

CAR PARK AREA

Between Polldubh and the road end car park are a number of crags, all on the lower slopes of Sgurr a' Mhaim, on the south (right) side of the road. **Whale Rock** is the first to come into view, across the river from where the road passes under a pair of distinctive Scots pines. Further on opposite the car park lies, not surprisingly, **Car Park Crag** itself, at 60m high, the largest steep and continuous crag in the glen. Below and right of this, level with the car park, is **Creag Uamh Shomhairle**.

WHALE ROCK   10min

A slabby front face, steepening and increasing in height towards the right end, where it forms a series of discontinuous scoops.

Approach: Cross the river at the bridge then the stream (Allt an t-Snaig) low down, near where it joins the river and follow a diagonal line direct to the crag from here.
Descent: Down either side of the crag, by steep ground.

NN 163 684 **Alt:** 200m

1 The Fascination Trap * 25m E1 5c

FA Dave Armstrong & Dougie Borthwick 4 July 1984

A diagonal left to right line across the slab, with a bouldery start. Just right of the heather gully is a thin crack in the slab. Up this to ledges then follow the obvious slightly rising traverse line with a further hard move across the slab to reach good holds leading into the top of 2. Continue in the same line to the top right of the crag.

2 Earthstrip ** 20m E2 5c

FA Dave Armstrong & Andrea Wright 7 September 1983

The central, widening crack line in the slab, easing towards the top.

3 Run for Home * 20m E4 6a/b

FA Kev Howett 28 February 1985

Thin sustained climbing on small edges up the diagonal hairline cracks starting 3m right of 2 joining that route at half-height. Many small RPs required.

4 Hold Fast *** 25m E9 7a

FA Dave MacLeod (headpointed) December 2002

A death defying line up the pristine wall. Start at the right edge of the small ledge (poor skyhook possible). Climb directly up the faint rib through a desperate technical and sustained crux to gain a tiny finger flake (no protection). Continue with further difficulty to a hard finishing move to gain a line of good edges leading leftwards into 3 and finish up this. (F8a/8a+) and hardest of 3 E9s in Scotland.

5 Femme Fatale *** 25m E8 6c

FA Dave Cuthbertson (headpointed) 27 July 1986

Very serious and technical climbing up the bulging scoops on the steepest section of the crag. Directly over the first bulge with difficulty (runners in opposition used to protect this – PR on ledge on left, and small RPs low down in crack on right) to a no hands rest and skyhook placement in first scoop. Move right and blindly place HB #2 & HB #1 in the thin crack to the right. Up rightwards into the second scoop to two poor PRs (now rusted & useless), and follow the diagonal crack out left to top. The route awaits an on-sight ascent.

Just a little Tease, Andy Nelson climbing.

6 Just a Little Tease ★★★ **25m E5 6b**

FA Dave Cuthbertson June 1984

Excellent, well protected climbing up the scoop and twin ragged cracks at the point where the crag bends around the hillside. Place a high runner on the right and a second opposing runner on the boulder at the foot of the previous route. Make difficult moves across the scoop to gain a good hold and protection. Attain a standing position

on this (rest possible) before following the cracks which lead strenuously to the top.

7 *Midgiematosis* ★, E2 5c follows a groove and cracks just right; 8 *Strategic Midge Limitation Talks* ★, E3 5c a thin crack climbing through a Caledonian pine sapling with interest.

CREAG UAMH SHOMHAIRLE
(SAMUEL'S CAVE CRAG)

10–20min
NN 170 689 **Alt:** 150m

The small buttress low down on the hillside, directly opposite the road end car park. The cave in question is the spacious open gully affair defining the left edge.
Approach: Direct from the car park, crossing the river at a weir or by boulder hopping if the water level is suitably low. Otherwise, especially after heavy snowmelt in the spring and particularly for those with hydrophobia, cross the river by the footbridge about a kilometre further downstream, as for Whale Rock, etc.

The wall left of *Choc Ice*, starting up the first few moves of that route is taken by 1 *Lord of the Midges* ★, E4 5c .

2 Choc Ice ★ **20m E1 5c**

FA Gary Latter & Ian Campbell 22 July 1983

The centre of the crag is split by a shallow groove line. Pull over the initial overhang (crux) and up the groove, exiting left.

3 Pagan Love Song ★ **18m HVS 5b**

FA Dave Armstrong & Andrea Wright 16 July 1984

Start at a shorter, undercut groove 3m right of the more prominent groove of *Choc Ice*. Up the groove to a holly below a small overhang then the crack through this.

4 Take Two ★ **18m HVS 5a**

FA Gary Latter & Ian Campbell 22 July1983

The short steep crack in the right wall of the crag.

NN 172 684 **Alt:** 350m

CAR PARK CRAG 🏔️ 👤 30min

The large buttress overlooking the car park, on the slopes of Sgurr a' Mhaim. It presents the highest vertical face of any of the crags in the glen, though others give longer, slabby routes, separated by grassy terraces.

Approach: From the car park, cross the river at a weir or boulder hop if the water level is suitably low. Otherwise, especially after heavy snowmelt in the spring (or for those with hydrophobia) cross the river by the footbridge about a kilometre further downstream, as for **Whale Rock,** then head steeply up the hillside directly to the crag. A pleasanter approach is to cross the River Nevis at the head of the gorge (either by boulder hopping or wading just upstream). Head up a good drovers track which zig-zags up the left of the crags then contour right (west) round the hillside for 200m to where the track levels out at a large flat terrace.

---

1 Restless Natives ★★   **90m E5 6a**

FA Gary Latter, Kev Howett & Andy Nelson 7 May 1988

Fine climbing up the deceptive looking grooves in the clean buttress at the left end of the crag. Start below a small niche about 5m up the wall.

  1 24m 6a Climb direct up into the niche (tied down skyhook and RP under overlap). Make hard moves up and right to better holds at the base of the slender bottomless groove. Up this and the continuation to pull onto a crack on the slab on better holds. Nut belay on small ledge.

  2 27m 6a Continue up the crack in the slab to reach an obvious line of holds leading out right into the centre of the prow. Follow this to a ledge (poor nuts above). Pull up the bulging tower above to the lip. Through the bulge slightly rightwards onto the bald slab, and up this (crux) to tree and nut belays on a grass ledge.

  3 39m 5a Finish up a rightward trending rib. Block belay well back.

2 Gobstopper Groove ★★   **60m E2 5c**

FA Dave Armstrong, Al Murray, Murray Hamilton & Pete Whillance 1981

Steep, well situated climbing. Start at the right side of a large tilted roof.

  1 35m 5b Climb the crack and groove to a large depression. Exit on the right and up a quartz band to a terrace.

  2 25m 5c Move onto the rib on the left and climb it by a shallow groove and thin crack.

3 The Mint * 60m E2 5c

FA Dave Armstrong, Al Murray, Murray Hamilton & Pete Whillance 1981

Steep well protected crack climbing.

1 **35m 5c** Climb a rightward trending crack 5m right of *Gobstopper Groove* to some small trees in the heather at 8m. Step left and follow the steep leftward slanting crack to the terrace.

2 **25m 5c** Finish up the top pitch of *Gobstopper Groove*.

4 Quality Street *** 70m E3 6a

FA Klaus Schwartz & Brian Chambers (HVS/A2) 20 June 1970; FFA Pete Whillance & Murray Hamilton 1981

Superb, sustained well protected climbing up the tram-line cracks on the left side of the smooth wall in the centre of the crag. Start on a raised ledge behind a large rowan, directly beneath the cracks.

1 **40m 6a** Climb the easier initial crack which leads to a ledge on the left, beneath the twin cracks. Follow these (crux) to pull out left on good holds. Traverse right to better holds in the shallow, left-facing groove. Continue up this to easier ground and a small ledge. Nut belay.

2 **30m 5a** Continue up the shallow right-facing corner then slightly left and directly up the easier slab. Tree belays further back.

Quality Street, Paul Thorburn climbing.

STEALL AREA

"... where crenellated crags tower"

– W.H.Murray, The West Highlands of Scotland, 1968
This section contains all the crags in and around the
Steall meadows, including the gorge. All are approached
from the car park at the end of the road (NN 168 692).

Both **Gorge Crag**, nestling in the trees and **Wave
Buttress**, directly above with a prominent quartz patch
in the centre, can be clearly seen from the car park as
can a number of crags on the hillside above.

EAS AN TUILL
THE NEVIS GORGE

This gorge has been described as one of the finest examples of its kind in Britain. *"The Nevis gorge, taken alone,
has no counterpart in this country and is internationally
famous. Its Himalayan character arises from a peculiar
combination of crag and woodland and water, which is
not repeated elsewhere in Great Britain."* – W.H.Murray,
Highland Landscape, 1962.

From the car park at the road end, a path follows the
true right bank of the river. The gorge itself extends for
about 1.5km, the river level falling some 130m in that
distance with the rocky side walls covered in native
pine, birch, oak and rowan. Above the gorge the scene
changes to one of Arcadian grandeur – the transition to
flat meadowland is truly stunning.

GORGE CRAG   15min
NN 175 691 **Alt:** 230m

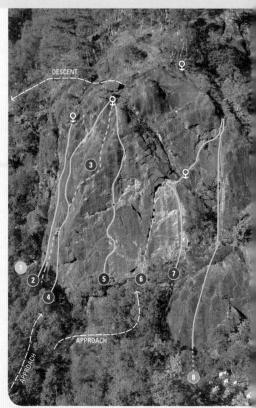

The first crag encountered in the gorge, easily seen from the car park. A slabby left wall sweeps round into a steep and imposing front face, with a couple of corner systems bounding the right side.

Approach: Along the path, the crag squats in the trees about 30m above the path, above a wooden boardwalk.

Descent: Either by abseil from trees at the top of *Plague of Blazes* or *Travellin' Man* (slings & maillons usually in situ) or contour left (north) from top of crag and down easy angled ground just before the stream.

1 Pupil Power *   30m Severe 4a
FA Noel Williams & Lochaber High School pupils June 1982

The prominent leftward trending stairway at the left side of the slab.

2 Plague of Blazes ***   30m E2 5b
FA Ed Grindley, Fiona Gunn, Noel Williams & Willie Lawrie 27 May 1982

An excellent pitch meandering up the centre of the slab. Start 5m up and left from the toe of the crag, at the leftmost of two thin crack systems running up the slab. Follow the zig-zag crack for 12m to a flake. Move left up into a recess; step right and up a slab to the final wall. Up this on good holds to finish at a Scots pine.

3 In the Groove **   39m E3 5c
FA Dave Cuthbertson & Gary Latter May 1982; p1 Gary Latter & Ian Campbell 24 July 1983

The diagonal steepening groove, trending right onto the front face, finishing in an exposed position.

1 **12m 5b** The shorter, right crack in the slab to the ledge.

2 **27m 5c** The groove above, and the subsidiary right groove past an obvious block (crux). Easier rightwards up ramp.

4 Travellin' Man ***   36m E2 5c
FA Dave Cuthbertson & Gary Latter 22 May 1982

Finely positioned climbing up the groove system splitting the rib between the left and front faces.

1 **12m 5b** Climb the cracked groove just right of the toe of the buttress to a ledge and belay.

2 **24m 5c** The groove above, stepping left (crux) to a crack in the slab. Up this and the easy ramp above.

Scramble up right over some boulders (or avoid by a detour round right) to gain the base of the following:

5 Cosmopolitan ***   30m E5 6b
FA Dave Cuthbertson & Gary Latter 20–21 May 1982

A fierce, well-protected technical test piece taking the wonderfully positioned hanging finger-crack in the headwall of the front face. Start below and left of a hanging left-facing groove in the centre of the overhanging wall.

1 **15m 6a** A bouldery start (crux) leads to a handrail (F #2 at right end) leading out right to the groove. Follow this, exiting out rightwards to a spacious ledge and belay.

2 **15m 6b** Gain the thin diagonal crack from the right with a hard initial move and up this to good holds just below the top. Brilliant.

6 Conscription ★ 45m E1 5b

FA Dave Cuthbertson & Gary Latter 19 May 1982

The obvious wide crack up the right side of the wall.

1 **20m 5b** Climb the crack then move right under a bulge to step right onto a ledge.

2 **25m** Finish up an easy flake to a tree belay further back.

7 All Our Yesterdays ★★ 45m E1 5b

FA Gary Latter & Dave Cuthbertson 19 May 1982

Good well protected climbing, often dry even in the rain.

1 **20m 5b** The corner crack, stepping out right onto a ledge.

2 **25m** Finish up the easy flake as for *Conscription*.

8 Mini Cooper ★ 40m HVS 5b

FA Willie Jeffrey, Noel Williams & Pete Hunter 11 June 1983

Start at the foot of a groove near the left side of the buttress below and right of the main crag.

1 **15m 5a** Gain the groove by some steep moves and up this to a terrace.

2 **25m 5b** Climb the steepening corner to the top of the flake on the previous two routes.

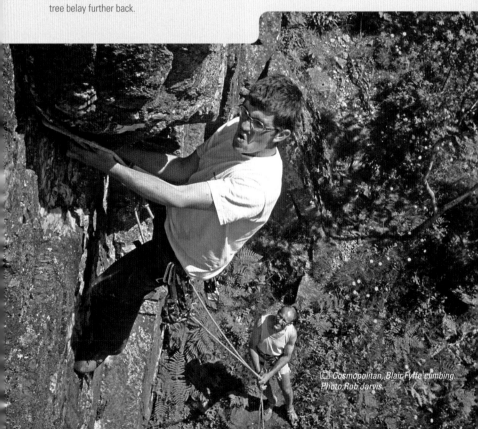

Cosmopolitan, Blair Fyffe climbing. Photo Rob Jarvis.

THE GORGE WALL   15min

NN 175 690 **Alt:** 210m

The steep buttress immediately above the path, about 100m beyond **Gorge Crag**.

Descent: Either by abseil from trees, or down the left side of the crag.

1 **Chimera** ★★★　　　　　　　　　　**30m E4 6a**

FA Kev Howett 11 May 1985

The spectacular overhung left arête. Climb the unprotected arête to gain better holds and protection in the upper groove. Follow this strenuously and make a difficult exit leftwards in a fine position.

2 **Easy Pickings** ★★★　　　　　　　　**30m E4 6a**

FA Kev Howett, Alan Moist & Calum Henderson 27 February 1985

Sustained varied climbing starting up the deceptive looking crack-line in the rib a few metres right of the arête. Up the crack with hard moves to reach a resting place. Up and left to swing into a ramp. From the top of this a hard mantel leads to a thin slab to finish.

THE RIVER WALLS   15min

NN 175 689 **Alt:** 200m

Extending left for about 100m from directly opposite **The Gorge Wall**. Steep slabs and walls rise abruptly from the river. The start of the routes may be inaccessible when the river is high. The most obvious feature is a prominent steep rectangular hanging slab split by thin vertical cracks with a shorter, wider left-trending crack on the left. Both routes start from the boulder choke at the bottom left of the hanging slab rising from the water.

Descent: Either by abseil from trees on top or down the extreme left or right side of the walls.

1 **Aquarian Rebels** ★★★　　　　　　　**24m E4 6a**

FA Dave Cuthbertson & Gary Latter 23 April 1985

Excellent climbing up the thin cracks in the centre of the slab, directly above a beckoning pool. Not easy to protect – small cams useful. Cross the scoop to gain the leftward crack of *Liquidator*. Arrange protection a short way up this then traverse right to follow thin cracks to a finish up the final steep crack.

2 **Liquidator/Gawping Grockles** ★ 48m E2 5c

FA Alan Moist & Dave Carr August 1984; p1 FA Paul Laughlan & Martin MacRae 4 May 1985

1 **12m 5b** Traverse rightwards across a scoop to the foot of the left trending hand crack. Follow this to belay on a grass gangway above.

2 **24m 5c** Up the crack to a ledge. Make a rising traverse right (difficult to protect) to a crack leading to a tree belay.

3 **12m 5b** Continue up a spidery crack-line in the headwall.

THE MEADOW WALL

NN 176 687 **Alt:** 250m ⓦ 🌤️ 🚶 20–25min

Situated on the left upon entering the flat meadows from the narrow confines of the gorge are a number of crags, the most continuous a long wall sculpted by glacial action. This curves round to the right past a pothole feature to eventually form a long terrace of unbroken rock higher up, with a prominent 3m wide roof in its centre just left of a steep gully. Left of and at a higher level than the sculpted wall are two shorter walls split by a further narrow grassy terrace.
Approach: The first two routes are approached directly up the hill from just beyond the head of the gorge.
Descent: Leftward along the terrace and into the wide open gully then down by the foot of **Wave Buttress**.

1 **Mutant** ★★ 40m E4 5c

FA Dave Cuthbertson & Gary Latter (on-sight) 23 April 1985

Start in the centre of the wall. Climb obvious steep scoops to a ledge (unprotected). Move left to the start of a diagonal crack. Gain elevated scoops above the crack and follow these to a small ledge. Go right round a prow and up a thin crack and ramp to finish on an easy slab. PB well back.

2 **Reptile** ★★ 40m E2 5c

FA Dave Cuthbertson & Kev Howett 21 May 1985

Follows a left-slanting diagonal line, taking in the obvious cracks. Start right of the centre of the wall at a scoop containing a thin crack. Up this to a ledge and trend left under a crack-line. Climb up a quartz wall to flakes at the junction with final twin cracks. Follow these with some interest to the top.

 The Mutant, Dave Cuthbertson on first ascent.

THE MEADOW FACE

The large expanse of rock, sweeping round to the right from the sculptured wall, directly overlooking the greater part of the meadows. More broken and easy angled lower walls lead to a broken terrace and a long band of walls above split centrally by a deep loose gully and dominated by a prominent roof system near the centre.

❹ Impulse ★★★   15m E8 6c

FA Dave MacLeod (headpointed) August 2001

A bold route up the front face of the leaning headwall high up on the left. Climb a narrow ramp to a cluster of poor Friends then launch boldly up the wall to a dynamic crux. Finish directly more easily.

❺ Going for Gold ★★★   45m E4 6a

FA Ed Grindley 26 August 1983,
p1 Davy Gunn & Ed Grindley 20 August 1983

A fine exercise in hand-jamming, tackling the prominent crack through the centre of the roof.

1 **25m 4c** Well left of the roof system is a shallow right-facing corner above the heathery terrace. Start below a shallow groove in the lower slab, below the upper corner. Climb a slab and gain the main slab by a break in the steep wall below the slab. Climb the faint groove followed by a rightward sloping crack to the terrace. Walk right along the terrace to a corner below the roof.

2 **20m 6a** Climb the roof past some evil flared jams to a good horizontal flake near the lip, and continue up the wide flake crack to the top. Very well protected – take some large cams for the upper crack.

GREY WALL

Up and left of the previous routes at a slightly lower level than **Wave Buttress** is a compact grey wall characterised by a right facing groove in the centre.

Approach: The best approach to the following route is to use a convenient terrace leading in from the left and abseil in (two PBs in situ at top). It is also possible to scramble up to the base.

Descent: Traverse left along terrace at top.

❸ Tickled Pink ★★   15m E3 5c

FA Dave Cuthbertson & Gary Latter 2 May 1985

Start beneath the groove. Climb the wall right of the groove to an escape ledge on the left then take the thin crack to finish. Better protected than first impressions would suggest, entirely from small RPs.

NN 176 690 **Alt:** 350m

WAVE BUTTRESS 🌞 🚶 25min

Clearly visible from the car park on the slopes of Meall Cumhann above and slightly right of **Gorge Crag**. A relatively exposed position ensures a fast drying time and often a midge free haven when the gorge is unbearable.

The crag is generally slabbier (75 – 85 degrees for the most) than most of the crags hereabouts, and split into two buttresses by a heather-filled gully. The left buttress has two obvious crack-lines: the left one *On the Beach* fading out at a horizontal crack at mid-height, and the continuous left to right diagonal crack of *Crackattack*.

Approach: Follow the main path through the gorge into the Steall meadows then a steep zig-zagging path up the hillside left of the wide, open gully, left of the **Meadow Walls**. Alternatively, the old drovers track, avoiding the precipitous section of the gorge, affords a slightly more direct approach. This branches off left from the tourist path just over 100m beyond where the path has been blasted across a stream and rises initially before contouring around the hillside above the gorge to link up with the zig-zag path from the meadows below Wave Buttress.

Descent: Either by abseil, or by an indistinct path along the top and down the right side.

---

① First Wave *   30m E1 5c

FA Ed Grindley & Noel Williams 20 April 1982

The left edge of the crag has a narrow right to left ramp with a series of ledges and short walls above. Start at some quartz blotches. Boulder diagonally rightwards to the foot of the ramp. Up this and follow a direct line to finish up a steep wall on good flakes.

② Freddie Across the Mersey *   30m E5 6a

FA Dave Cuthbertson, Dave Armstrong & Simon Reid June 1984

Climb a direct line 2m left of the vertical crack of 3. A bold initial section with difficult moves to reach the horizontal. Continue up and pull rightwards into the base of the big scooped groove and follow this to top.

3 On the Beach ★★★   30m E5 6a

FA Murray Hamilton & Rab Anderson April 1984

Bold open wall climbing with spaced protection in the upper half. From the pedestal follow the crack-line moving slightly rightwards to the horizontal break. Step left and follow the shallow runnel above to better holds at some quartz. Continue more easily above.

4 Jodicus Direct ★★★   30m E6 6c

FA Jodicus Grotticus – Dave Cuthbertson & Kev Howett May 1984; FA The Edwardo Shuffle – Dave Cuthbertson 20 June 1985; FA Direct Mark McGowan 20 July 1987

A direct uncompromising line up the wall in the centre of the buttress. A serious lower section to the break followed by a very technical sequence above protected by a PR. Start midway between the two cracks. Trend slightly leftwards to a tiny scoop then slightly right to the centre of the small overlap (HB #4 on side, pulling to left, in shallow horizontal above). Step left then make thin and committing moves to the horizontal break and protection (RPs #2 & #3). Climb the scoop above (RP #2 on left) to the PR. Desperate moves past this (long sling in situ) lead up and right into a scoop. Finish up the easier groove.

5 Ground Zero ★★   30m E2 5b

FA Ed & Cynthia Grindley, Noel Williams & Fiona Gunn 9 May 1982

Varied open wall climbing, with a bold lower section. Start just left of the diagonal crack. Climb directly up the wall past some thin flared cracks (RP #4 behind a good hold at the steepest section), moving slightly right on good holds to the base of a diagonal crack/ramp. Ascend the crack in the groove past an awkward bulge and finishing up the quartz staircase above.

6 Crackattack ★★   30m E3 5c

FA Ed Grindley & Barry Owen 14 August 1983

The diagonal crack. Well protected. Crux at the top.

7 The Dark Crystal ★★   30m E5 6b

FA Gary Latter 13 June 1986

The hanging flake and intermittent crack in the slab below 6. Start 2m right of that route, beneath a prominent

quartz blotch. Bouldery moves up the hairline crack lead to a good quartz hold and protection in the quartz crack. Pull right onto a flake and up to a good flat hold. Attain a standing position on this and follow the intermittent cracks in the slab above to a welcome respite on 6. The scoop to the left of the headwall provides a natural continuation. Gain the scoop from the right and up to rounded break (small Fs). Attain a standing position on this and pull over on the easy ramp leading left toward 5.

8 Bewsey Crack ★   30m HVS 5a

FA Ed Grindley & Noel Williams 23 May 1983

The shallow fading groove runs into a diagonal crack. Follow this into a sentry box near the top. Exit this on good holds.

9 The Gift ★   30m E4 6a

FA Kev Howett, Gary Latter & Dave Cuthbertson 12 May 1985

The line of the diagonal crack just right of the gully. Easily at first to a ledge then with difficulty to a break. Continue up the twin grooves formed by a huge block then the central groove on the right to finish by a tricky mantelshelf.

10 Straight Thinking ★★   30m E5 6a

FA Gary Latter 12 July 1986

A direct line following a vague crack-line running up the steepest part of the buttress, bisecting the crack of 9 low down. Start just right of the gully. Follow a vertical crack and continuation with a hard move to gain a good flat hold. Attain a standing position on this (good break for gear) from where bold climbing up the wall above (crux) leads to another break. Teeter up and right to finish at the same point as 11. Committing climbing on the crux.

11 Think Vertical ★   30m E3 6a

FA Ed Grindley & Barry Owen 9 August 1983

A fine natural line though it also happens to be a natural watercourse and therefore slow to dry. Start at the lowest point of the buttress, 6m right of the gully. Climb cracks leftwards into a right facing groove. Up this to a ledge and the steepening groove above (crux) to the top.

12 Walter Wall ★★   30m E4 6a

FA Kenny Spence & Spider McKenzie 28 April 1984

Serious though steady wall climbing up the shallow depression in the centre of the wall. Start at the toe of the buttress just left of 11. Up this a short way then easily right across a scoop to good holds above. Boldly climb the wall above with no protection to a good horizontal break and protection. Hard moves past this lead to a shelf. Exit rightwards.

13 Washington ★★   36m E5 6a

FA Dave Cuthbertson & Gary Latter 22 April 1985

Essentially a direct start and finish to *Walter Wall*, offering more sustained climbing with well spaced protection. Start just left of the prominent sharp arête of 14. Up a shallow left-leaning groove to some quartz holds at 6m (runner in a thin crack above). Move left to a shallow groove then make difficult moves across the wall into the scoop of *Walter Wall*. Continue up that route, taking in its crux. Avoid the rightwards traverse and climb a shallow groove to a bulge (runner in a thin crack). Turn this and up the slab above climbing rightwards to finish.

14 Edgehog ★★★   30m E3 6a

FA Ed Grindley & Noel Williams 26 April 1982

No prizes for guessing which route this refers to. Gain the arête from the right, and follow it to a large ledge at its top. Finish easily up the slab. Better protected than first impressions would suggest.

15 Teenoso ★   30m VS 4c

FA Ed Grindley 1 June 1983

The corner crack. A bit grassy, but worth doing anyway.

Edgehog, Iain MacDonald climbing.

SPREADEAGLE BUTTRESS

Situated a few hundred metres above and right of **Wave Buttress**. The crag is characterised by a prominent arching stepped roof/corner system on the left, sweeping over a steep square lower wall, which tilts back to form a steep slab in its upper section. There is a short corner on the right, running out at a wide ledge halfway up.

(w) 🚶 30min

NN 178 689 **Alt:** 450m

Approach: As for **Wave Buttress** then by a vague path diagonally right, crossing the open gully just right of that crag.

Descent: By an easy gully and down the rocky shelf on the right side of the crag.

 Slip Away ★★   30m E3 6a,

FA Dave Cuthbertson & Gary Latter June 1982

1 **18m 6a** The clean cut corner crack with the difficulties past an obvious smooth section on the right wall. Easier up the wide crack to a spacious belay ledge.

2 **12m 5b** Step left off the ledge and trend leftwards to finish up the final section as for 2.

 Chiaroscuro ★★   30m E7 6b

FA Kev Howett & Andy Nelson 10 May 1988

A varied pitch with much contrast; a hard and strenuous lower section leading to a bold upper half. It follows a fairly direct line up the blunt rib bisecting the groove of 3. Start beneath the scoop just left of the prominent corner-crack of 1. Up the scoop then climb leftwards past a series of vertical slots to an obvious projecting block on the arête. Climb into the hanging groove of 3 to break out left onto an obvious hanging block. Continue up the

wall above, keeping just left of the arête. This leads with increasing difficulty past a poor horizontal RP #2 slot (Tri Cam #1? also) to hard moves pulling over onto a sloping ledge. More easily leftwards up a slab.

 Spreadeagle ★★   30m E4 6a

FA Dave Cuthbertson & Gary Latter June 1982

The shallow hanging groove in the centre of the wall. Start left of the groove beneath an obvious scoop/depression. Up into this, and make a hard move rightwards at a horizontal hairline crack to better holds at the base of the groove and finish up this. The upper groove is often wet, though usually avoidable.

④ **The Singing Ringing Tree ★★**   30m E5 6a

FA Dave Cuthbertson 9 July 1983

In the centre of the wall left of the hanging groove of 3 is a short crack, running out at a bulge. Start beneath this. Up the crack to a good nut slot near the top and pull right (sling on large spike hold, RPs in thin crack down and right to hold it in place) on improving holds to an obvious flake crack. Much easier up the wall above, trending leftwards. The difficulties are short lived and concentrated on the initial steep start.

NN 178 690 **Alt:** 500m

BLADE BUTTRESS 35min

Above the right side of **Wave Buttress**, opposite
and slightly higher than **Spreadeagle Buttress**. The
buttress gets its name from the prominent hanging
blade-like arête forming clean cut grooves on either side.
Round to the right is a narrow, clean slab, sometimes
referred to as a pillar.

Approach: As for **Wave Buttress**, continuing up the
hillside, initially by an indistinct path, which veers off
rightwards to **Spreadeagle Buttress**.

Descent: Down a steep muddy gully on the left, or
alternatively head right into the wide open gully.
The first two routes start in the open bay beneath the
blade. Start by scrambling up into this.

1 Cruisability ★★★　　　　　**20m E5 6b**

FA Gary Latter 12 July 1986

The stupendous overhanging groove up the left side of
the blade. Gain and climb the flake crack leading to the
roof. Pull through this with difficulty, using a good incut
hold over the lip on the left. Continue up the groove,
pulling out right to finish. Strenuous and well protected.

2 Sabre ★　　　　　**20m E3 5c**

*FA Ken Johnstone & Gary Latter July 1984; Reclimbed after
disappearance of large flake – Gary Latter 19 June 1986*

The shorter, overhung groove up the right side of the
blade. Start at a short crack directly below the blade as
for the previous route. Up this into the groove and up
this (crux) to exit onto a jug ridden slab. Easily up this to
finish. Well protected.

3 Ugly Duckling ★　　　　　**30m E2 5b**

FA Kev Howett & Alan Moist 20 May 1985

Good climbing with a bold start. This route follows the
arête and crack up the left side of the narrow slab round
to the right from the previous routes. Start at a flake
belay at the base of the wall directly below the thin

crack. Up to roof, traverse left to the arête, and up this
(crux) to gain a good ledge. From the right side of the
ledge climb directly up the crack to the top. Friend belay
next to a large flake well back.

4 Flight of the Snowgoose ★★　　　　　**30m E6 6a**

FA Kev Howett, Gary Latter & Dave Cuthbertson 21 May 1985

Thin bold slab climbing in its upper reaches. Flight would
not be advisable. It climbs the centre of the narrow slab
after sharing a common start with the fledgling 3. From
near the top of the crack traverse right across the wall
then up to small ledge (tied down skyhook runners).
Ascend the wall with increasing difficulty to better holds
just below the top. Belay well back.

THE SPACE FACE 35min

NN 178 690 **Alt:** 550m

An imposing crag on the right side of the open gully
above **Blade/Spreadeagle** characterised by a distinctive
frontal face seamed with a series of criss-crossing cracks.

Approach: As for **Wave Buttress** continuing up the
hillside initially by an indistinct path then direct up the
right side of the open gully.

Descent: Scramble back a short way then traverse
leftwards and down the easy gully.

1 The True Edge ★★★★ 35m E5 6b

*FA Kev Howett & Alan Moist 10 July 1986; Direct (as described)
Gary Latter & Andy Nelson 17 June 1988*

Spectacular climbing up the hanging arête in a stunning
position. Very well protected after an initial bold start.
Follow the obvious crack-lines up the centre of the wall
avoiding the big easy flakes on the lower arête. Using
good underclings gain a good flake and finger-locks in the
base of the bottomless crack in the upper arête. Swing
round and layback up the overhanging left wall of the
arête to gain a good foothold in the crack. Swing back
round passing a further tricky section which enables
a good horizontal break to be reached. Saunter to top.
The main difficulties can be avoided by climbing the
finger-crack on the right at E4 5c.

The True Edge, Gary Latter climbing.
Photo Rick Campbell.

GALAXY BUTTRESS   25min

Beyond the **Meadow Walls**, and higher up the slope facing towards Steall Hut and the waterfall is a distinctive clean cut hanging slab above a long roof. Broken areas of rock lie on either side of this buttress.

Approach: Directly up the slope, leaving the path midway between the right end of the Meadow Walls and the wire bridge across the river.

Descent: Down the shallow gully/rake midway between the buttress and a narrow slab at the left side of the crag.

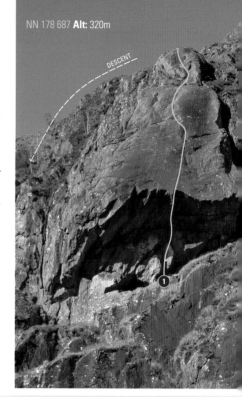

NN 178 687 **Alt:** 320m

DESCENT

1 Short Man's Walkabout ★★★   **45m E5 6b**

FA Dave Cuthbertson & Gary Latter 7 July 1983

Stunning, well protected climbing up a thin crack in the centre of the hanging slab. Start by scrambling to beneath a short right-facing corner and thin crack splitting the centre of the roof.

  1 **33m 6b** Up to a PR at the back of the roof (F #1.5 halfway out) and cross this with difficulty to a good fingerlock over the lip. Up the crack (no hands rest possible out right) to a ledge and belay.

  2 **12m 5a** Gain the scoop above, from the right.

STEALL HUT CRAG   30min

NN 176 683 **Alt:** 320m

This impressive crag lies not surprisingly on the hillside behind Steall Hut to the right of the waterfall. Though mostly permanently dry, it is also a strong contender for the midgiest crag in Scotland – be warned! *Stolen*, *Leopold* and *Steall Appeal* are *"virtually permanently dry"* in Summer and can be climbed in heavy rain, but the finishes of the others take a while to dry out.

Approach: Cross the wire bridge at Steall and head diagonally up the hillside behind the hut.

1 Lame Beaver ★★★   **25m E7 6b**

FA Kev Howett (2 PA) 31 May 1985; FFA Dave Cuthbertson 25 May 1987

A sustained pitch with sparse protection, breaching the left side of the extremely overhanging front face. Start

at the left end of the wall, about 2m from the left edge. Climb up past a shield of rock, heading for an obvious hold in the apex of the niche above (good small cam & R #3 behind this). Undercling the roof system rightwards with difficulty to gain good underclings in the niche on the right. Pull up and left using a good hidden pocket to jugs (crux). Superb climbing gains and climbs the easier flake crack in the headwall.

2 Stolen ★★★★   **25m F8b**

FA Dave MacLeod 30 July 2007

Brilliant and permanently dry climbing up the overhanging walls and bulges left of 4. Difficult climbing leads leftwards to the big tooth (no-hands rest). Follow the undercut groove above with more cruxes to a rest and yet another tricky section to gain the finishing headwall. Best F8b in Scotland?

3 Trick of the Tail ★★★   30m E6 6b

FA Mark McGowan 1 June 1989

A stunning pitch up the right to left diagonal crack/
groove dominating the centre of the crag. Climb easily up
a short slab leftwards to an old ring peg under the roof.
Up and left into crack, and up this to make a hard lunge
leftwards (crux) for a good undercling. Using this reach
a superb block hold in the base of the triangular niche,
and climb into this (no hands rest possible). Swing wildly
out right to better holds and climb the twin cracks above
with further difficulty to a recess and easy ground. Well
protected – many cams useful.

4 Arcadia ★★★★   25m E7 6b (F8a)

FA Gary Latter (red pointed) 20 September 1993

Two prominent diagonal cracks offer superb sustained
climbing. Both share a common start. The leftward
slanting crack, finishing up the final twin cracks as for 3.

5 Leopold ★★★★   25m E7 6c (F8a+)

*FA 1970s; FFA Murray Hamilton (protection placed on abseil
& pink pointed) 21 July 1992*

The wider right-slanting crack with a deviation out right
on good undercuts at the obvious shield of rock. Follow

good holds to pull out right into the crack. Follow this
on sloping holds past two cruxes until possible to pull
rightwards along a series of undercuts. Pass a final crux
above a resting jug to easier ground. Continue more
easily above. Bolts, then in situ wires, pegs and a cam.

6 Ring of Steall ★★★   25m F8c+

FA Dave MacLeod 1 August 2007

Brilliant technical climbing, the completion of a
longstanding project, bolted in the early nineties. Follow
5 to just beyond its crux, then move left to a big undercut.
A heinous boulder problem leads to the base of the
leftward slanting crack which leads with slightly easier
climbing to the top.

7 Steall Appeal ★★   15m F8b

FA Malcolm Smith 19 September 1993

"I believe this is Scotland's hardest sport route"
– Smith, 1993.

The line of 6 bolts at the right end of the crag. A hard
boulder problem start followed by a powerful undercut
move leads to some slightly easier climbing. Finish by
lowering from the final bolt.

Tower Ridge. Photo Dave Cuthbertson, Cubby Images.

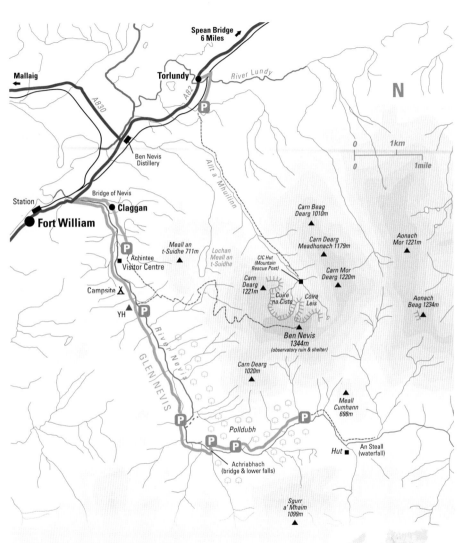

BEN NEVIS (THE BEN)

'Mountain with its head in the clouds' is perhaps the most likely possible translation of the name Beinn Nibheis. With the summit wreathed in clouds on average 200 days per year this interpretation certainly rings true. Avoid the summit if you can, as it is a bit of an eyesore, littered with memorials, plaques and discarded litter left behind by the hordes of tourists that trudge up the pony track.

Tower Ridge

North-East Buttress

Orion Face

Observatory Ridge

Minus Face

Douglas Boulder

"Nevis, the most massive, malevolent, most elevated lump of rock on these islands, is itself an island, humping hideous flanks from endless bogs, hard to equal for hidden depths of character." – Jimmy Marshall

In the Groove, Scottish Mountaineering Club Journal, 1971

Access: Turn east off the A82 at Torlundy, 1.2 miles/2km north of the A830 Mallaig turn-off and cross the railway bridge. Turn right and follow track for 0.5 mile/0.8km to a large car park.

Approach: (A) From the car park, follow the steep path diagonally up through the woods to the upper (guides) car park by the dam. Continue less steeply up the left (north) bank of the Allt a'Mhuilinn (stream of the mill) leading to the CIC hut in around 2 hours. **(B)** On foot from Fort William, either follow the pony (tourist) track starting from either Achintee or opposite the Youth Hostel in Glen Nevis, cutting off left (north) at the halfway lochan and following a path contouring round the hillside to the CIC Hut in 2¼ hours. **(C)** Alternatively, cut through the distillery opposite the A830 Mallaig turn-off, cross the railway and follow a path up the right (south) bank of the Allt a'Mhuilinn for 500m, cross a small bridge and head steeply up a path to join up with the usual approach at the dam.

The separate cliffs are described from **right to left**, as encountered on the approach.

"I've never seen a bigger hill,
I don't suppose I ever will,
But Everest is bigger still,
The very thought would
make you ill."

– Doug Benn

No. 5
Gully

No. 4
Gully

No. 3
Gully

Carn
Dearg
Buttress

Castle
Ridge

3 Gully
Buttress

Central
Trident
Buttress

South
Trident
Buttress

Organ Pipes

HISTORY

The first recorded rock climbs on the great towering masses of the North East face of the Ben occurred in September 1892 when the Manchester based Hopkinson family – brothers Charles, Edward and John and John's son Bertram descended *Tower Ridge*, three of them having ascended as far as the Great Tower the previous day. A few days later they all ascended *North-East Buttress*, adding in the space of a few days two classic ridges, which are today the two most popular routes on the mountain. These discoveries went unrecorded until a footnote appeared in the Alpine Journal in 1895. The first actual ascent of *Tower Ridge* occurred the previous year, when Norman Collie, Godfrey Solley and Joseph Collier made an ascent in full winter conditions, unaware of the Hopkinson's endeavours. The West Highland Railway opened up in the autumn of that year, greatly easing access. *The Direct Route* on the Douglas Boulder was ascended by William Brown, Lionel Hinxman, Harold Raeburn and William Douglas the following year.

Raeburn was prolific at the turn of the century, making a solo ascent of *Observatory Ridge* in 1901 to complete

the trilogy of classic ridges, returning the following year to lead the fine *Raeburn's Arête*. The Great War wiped out a whole generation, though significantly, the CIC Hut was erected in the 1920s as a memorial to Charles Inglis Clark, who was killed in the war. The left side of Carn Dearg Buttress was breached with the chimneys of *Route 1* from Graham McPhee and Albert Hargreaves in 1931. Hargreaves soon returned to cross the *Rubicon Wall* on Observatory Buttress, a bold and committing lead for the day. Later, the irrepressible Dr Jim Bell made numerous forays with various partners on The Orion Face, culminating in possibly the longest vertical route in mainland Britain with the aptly-named *The Long Climb* in 1940, setting a new standard on the mountain at Very Severe in the process.

Far and away the most active climber throughout the Second World War was Brian Kellett, a conscientious objector assigned to work on the forestry at Torlundy. Climbing mainly solo and after work, he repeated the majority of the established rock routes and added many important new routes and variations. On Carn Dearg Buttress, he pioneered the committing rising traverse of *Route II* in 1943, whilst the following year up on the Minus Face he contributed the fine *Left Hand Route* and *Right Hand Route* (both VS), the latter solo and on-sight. He also soloed the fine *1944 Route* on the South Trident Buttress. Ironically, Kellett and his climbing partner Nancy Forsyth were killed later that year, from a fall whilst roped together on the North Wall of Carn Dearg. After the war, Arnold Carsten and Tommy McGuinness pushed standards to HVS with *The Crack*, equalling Kellett's remarkable solo ascent of the eponymous *Kellett's Route* on Gardyloo Buttress two years previously.

In the fifties activity shifted to the obvious potential of the great sweeping slabs on Carn Dearg Buttress. In April 1954 two of the strongest English climbers of the day, Rock and Ice members Don Whillans and Joe Brown, snatched the plum line of chimneys near the right side of the buttress. The route was named *Sassenach*, after an understandably miffed Scotsman (George Ritchie) shouted up *"English Bastards!"* This much-eyed line had been attempted by the likes of Kellett in 1944 and the strong Aberdeen team of Patey, Taylor and Brooker the previous year, both teams attempting to traverse in from either side. At E1 with some aid, the technical difficulty was beyond the reaches of either party at the time. Talented southern teams continued to dominate over the next few years, with Cambridge climbers Bob Downes, Mike O'Hara and Mike Prestige adding *Minus One Direct* in 1956. When combined with the *Serendipity* and *Arête Variations*, added subsequently by Ken Crocket and Ian Fulton and Stevie Abbott and Noel Williams respectively, the route gives a superb E1. A few months later, Whillans returned with Downes, adding the plum line of *Centurion* up the centre of Carn Dearg Buttress and *The Shield* up the right edge. National pride was restored in 1959 when Edinburgh climbers Robin Smith and Dougal Haston put aside *"a mutual antipathy"* and teamed up to complete the fine hanging corner of *The Bat*. That same summer, Creagh Dhu climbers John McLean and Bill Smith added the similarly difficult (E2) *Subtraction* on the Minus Face. In a different vein, Ian Clough and Hamish MacInnes pegged their way up a

line of cracks up the overhanging right wall of Carn Dearg Buttress. *Titan's Wall* elicited the comment *"pegs shouldn't replace skill or supplement a basic lack of shame!"* in the SMC Journal.

Carn Dearg Buttress remained the main focus of attention, with Jimmy Marshall and James Stenhouse adding the superb sweeping traverse line of *The Bullroar*, and *The Shield Direct* (Marshall and George Ritchie) in the early sixties. McLean and Smith returned with Willie Gordon in 1962 to add the sustained *Torro*. A couple of years later, Brian Robertson and Jimmy Graham completed the complex line of *King Kong*, taking impressive ground between *Centurion* and *The Bat*, though employing much aid. Ian Nicolson and Norrie Muir freed the aid on the second ascent in 1970. The same pair added the inaugural *Heidbanger* on Central Trident Buttress, with Stevie Docherty and Bobby Gorman adding the neighbouring *Steam*. Docherty returned with Davy Gardner the following year to complete the excellent *Metamorphosis*. Muir and Nicolson also made impressive solo ascents of *Centurion*, unaware of each other's ascents until a later meeting.

Titan's Wall had attracted many attempts at a free ascent, with southern raiders Mick Fowler and Phil Thomas snatching the free ascent in June 1977 from under the noses of the locals. Dave Cuthbertson and Murray Hamilton made a further free ascent four days later, at the time unaware of Fowler's ascent. Round the corner, the glaringly obvious 'big banana groove' had been the subject of numerous attempts down the years. Cuthbertson, Willie Todd and Dougie Mullin added *Caligula* in 1978, climbing the initial groove before traversing out right, climbed on-sight. Murray Hamilton pushed standards to E4 in 1983 with his ascent of *The Banana Groove* in its entirety, after Kenny Spence had cleaned the line the previous weekend. The following weekend Pete Whillance added what remained the hardest route on the mountain for almost two decades with his ascent of the bold *Agrippa* up the exposed left arête of *Titan's Wall*. The following summer, Spider McKenzie made the second ascent, in addition to making audacious solo ascents of *Torro*, *Centurion* and *The Bat* in a morning. Rock climbing activity slowed down, with the only other addition of note in the eighties Willie Todd's *Boadicea* to the right of *Titan's Wall*. Finally, in 2001 Rick Campbell and Gary Latter completed the hardest route on the mountain with their ascent of the sustained continuous cracks of *The Wicked*, climbed ground up. They later returned in 2004 to complete the adjacent *Trajan's Column*.

---

1 Castle Ridge ★★   **270m Moderate**   2hr

FA Norman Collie, William Naismith, Gilbert Thomson & M.W. Travers 12 April 1895

The northmost and easiest of the great Nevis ridges. Although not matching the quality of the 'big three' classic ridges (*Tower, Observatory and North-East Buttress*), being both lower down and further north and west, it comes into condition much more readily than the others, particularly in the spring when the Orion Face is still in winter condition. Start at a tongue of rock above 'the lunching stone', an obvious large boulder on the path from Meall an t-Suidhe. Wander up slabs to get established on the main ridge or gain the ridge by an obvious traverse above **The Organ Pipes** from the **CIC Hut**. Once established on the ridge itself, like all the other Nevis ridges the correct route is well marked by crampon scratches. Follow the easy angled ridge then a clean cut left-slanting corner leading to easy bouldery ground. A steep blunt tower is the crux starting by an awkward corner before moving up right to climb wide crack in the steep nose. A short chimney above marks the last of the difficulties. Continue along the crest then a large tilted slab to gain the final boulder slopes of Carn Dearg. **Descents:** Either **(A)** traverse a short way south west to avoid the North Wall and descend the tortuous boulder field down to the south end of Lochan Meall an t-Suidhe, or **(B)** from the summit of Carn Dearg contour south to gain the zig-zags on the touroid path, or **(C)** descend by *Ledge Route* on Carn Dearg Buttress.

Castle Ridge, Jo George climbing. Photo Dave Cuthbertson, Cubby Images.

THE ORGAN PIPES 2hr

NN 165 723 **Alt:** 700m
The long low crag situated below **Carn Dearg Buttress**, 10 minutes up right from the CIC hut.

1 The Trial ★★   45m E3 5c
FA Wills Young, Andy Tibbs & Andrew Fraser 19 June 1988

An excellent pitch. Right of the main watercourse and at the right side of the crag is a dry area of buttress. At the right side of the steepest part is a corner which starts from a grass ledge. The route climbs the cracked arête on the smooth wall left of the corner. Start directly below the arête. Climb the clean wall to the arête, then the arête.

CARN DEARG BUTTRESS (RED CAIRN)

The showpiece cliff, the front face contains a series of slabs and overlaps, steepening on the right side of the buttress. Round the edge the north-west face presents a clean 100m high vertical to slightly overhanging wall with a fair concentration of high standard modern routes all finishing at a convenient central abseil point. The front face receives the sun until early afternoon; therefore an early approach is worthwhile.

Approach: Head directly up from the CIC Hut towards Coire na Ciste then follow a path cutting diagonally right across the screes to the base of the buttress. 15–20 minutes from hut.

Descents: Traverse leftwards down *Ledge Route* and down the lower reaches of **Number 5 Gully**, which often holds considerable quantities of snow well into the summer. This can be bypassed by an obvious fault on the left (west) side (about Moderate) or by continuing across a good path on the continuation of the upper shelf and down the lower reaches of Coire na Ciste.

Alternatively, in situ abseil anchors are in place on the belays of *Titan's Wall*, which provides fast descents for routes from *The Bat* rightwards. 60m ropes reach ground on stretch!

1 Ledge Route ★★   450m Easy
FA J.Napier, R.Napier & E.Green 9 June 1895

An exhilarating route, the easiest 'climb' on the mountain, it is in reality no more than a simple scramble. Start up **Number Five Gully**, the large gully defining the left side of the buttress. This usually holds much snow until well into the summer. If so, climb a fault line up the buttress to the right. Traverse out right on the first prominent shelf (often damp – crux) and continue round this until beneath a shallow slightly left-slanting scree-filled gully. This leads to another wide shelf. Follow this rightwards until it eventually leads to the easy angled crest of the buttress. Finish up this airily to the plateau.

NN 164 722 **Alt:** 800m
2¼hr

📷 Rick Campbell on the 'hoodie groove', pitch four of The Bat.

2 **Route 1 Direct ★★**   **180m Very Difficult**

FA Albert Hargreaves, Graham MacPhee & H.Hughes 17 June 1931; Direct Start Robin Plackett & W.Campbell 31 August 1941

The conspicuous chimney cleaving the left edge of the buttress. It provides a traditional struggle, saving its crux for the final pitch. Start to the left of the lowest rocks bounding the lower left flank of the buttress.

1 **30m** Climb just left of the right
    edge to belay by blocks.

2 **45m** Climb directly then a groove on the left to its top.
    Move right round the edge and up diagonal break
    then the wall above to belay on a second ledge.

3 **35m** Scramble to the top of the subsidiary buttress
    and walk right to the base of the chimney.

4 **25m** Grovel up the chimney (not as
    ferocious as it looks) then by a grassy groove
    to a recess. Go up the right wall to a belay.

5 **25m** Regain the chimney and climb
    it to belay on ledge above.

6 **20m** Continue up to gain the final chimney. This
    leads with interest to large block-strewn terrace.
    The path of *Ledge Route* lies just above.

3 **Route II Direct ★★★**   **235m Severe 4a**

FA Brian Kellett & W Arnot Russell 9 June 1943; Direct Start Brian Robertson & George Chisholm 19 May 1962

A superb high level rising traverse across the buttress. Committing for the grade – there is much steep ground both above and below! Start at a cairn on a large wet mossy lump (spring) right of *Route 1*.

1 **30m** Climb up the centre of a smooth slab to a small
    ledge, traverse right 1m to a smooth wall and up
    a small slanting corner. Traverse left to a stance.
    Continue up a small black crack to a flake belay.

2 **15m** Climb straight up for 15m to a
    large block below a groove.

3 **10m** Climb the groove and move out
    right to a shattered ledge.

4 25m Continue up broken ground to belay at the base of the chimney of *Route 1*.

5 15m Follow the chimney to a large chokestone at 10m then traverse out right on the slab to a small belay stance.

6 25m Continue out right to a large flake beneath the great overhangs.

7 10m Traverse the flake for 6m then up the rib to an inconspicuous thread belay low down.

8 40m Continue traversing the prominent fault to a platform on the edge of the buttress.

9 30m Scramble up the edge.

10 35m Follow the groove above mainly on the right wall to gain the crest of the buttress.

④ The Bullroar ★★★★   **280m HVS 5a**

FA Jimmy Marshall & James Stenhouse 30 May 1961

A long route following a committing rising traverse line across the centre of the buttress. Excellent positions with considerable exposure – not for timid seconds! Start 30m right of the *Direct Start* to *Route II* at a bottomless groove 6m right of a large vegetated right-facing corner with some large boulders at its foot. The wet streak on the main slab dries early in the day but returns by mid to late afternoon. The first pitch is often wet and a little dirty; thereafter the climbing is on immaculate rock.

1 35m 5a Pull over an awkward bulge into a bottomless groove and climb this

Unknown climbers starting the traverse (pitch 3) on The Bullroar. Photo Dave Cuthbertson, Cubby Images.

steeply (often wet) to belay at a thread 5m below the overlap at the top of the central slabs.

2 15m 4b Move right then go up a crack to just beneath the overlap. Traverse right across the slab on obvious weakness to belay just above.

3 28m 5a Step down and traverse right across the slab, dropping down to a (PR). Continue traversing the obvious line leading to a finely positioned belay in groove on the edge halfway up pitch 3 of *Centurion*.

4 30m 4c Climb the crack above then traverse right to a belay under the overlaps.

5 30m 4b Traverse right under the overlaps on excellent small flake holds to easier ground. Climb this to a large terrace above the chimneys of *The Bat* and *Sassenach*.

6 12m Traverse left from the left end of the terrace to an area of shattered rocks beneath an undercut groove.

7 20m 4c Climb the left-slanting groove to large ledge beneath undercut roof.

8 45m Negotiate the awkward slot to good holds and continue up the groove and continuation to grass ledge

9 50m 4c Continue in the same line to large ledge with loose blocks.

10 15m Finish more easily up the slabby wall above the broken edge on the left.

⑤ Torro ★★★★   **225m E2 5c**

FA John McLean, Bill Smith & Willie Gordon (1 PA) 25 July 1962; FFA Ian Nicolson & Ian Fulton June 1970

Excellent sustained climbing following a good natural line up the slabs left of *Centurion*. Start just left of the rib forming the left edge of the *Centurion* corner.

1 30m 5b Climb the steep initial groove to a flake then the groove above to a larger flake. Climb the right side of the flake and step back left and continue up groove to belay at a flake.

2 30m 5b Up a fault above then left and up a slim groove to PR on slab. Traverse left on a lip round the arête and up leftwards to belay on a ledge.

3 25m 5a Move up and right to a flake, step right and up rightwards up a slab to belay at an old relic.

4 20m 5c Follow a faint crack for 6m then step up left onto a higher slab. Climb up the edge of the slab to the roof, step left and cross this (crux) leftwards. Climb the groove above to a belay.

5 **35m 5a** Follow the fault for 5m then traverse right across the slab to a crack. Follow this to an overhang which is climbed trending leftwards, then by a groove to a grassy stance.

6 **20m 4b** Continue up the fault to a grass ledge beneath the long band of overhangs.

7 **30m 5a** Move up to the overhang then out left onto a steep slab, heading out left to another overhang. Step off a detached flake and delicately traverse left onto a large slab. Continue easily up rightwards for 12m to belay beneath the final overhangs.

8 **35m 5b** Traverse left into a steep little corner and follow this to a large grass terrace at the top.

---

6 **Centurion ★★★★**   **200m HVS 5a**

FA Don Whillans & Bob Downes 30 August 1956

A magnificent route based around the great central corner – the classic line on the cliff. So named because the overlapping slabs on the right reputedly resemble the armour plates of a Roman centurion!

1 **15m 5a** Climb the left wall of the corner by an awkward crack to fine stance on top of the rib.

2 **35m 5a** Traverse into the corner and climb it to a belay on a slab in an overhung bay. A brilliant pitch – the holds and protection just keep coming!

3 **25m 4b** Traverse left onto the edge. Climb easy grooves until level with the lip of the big overhang then step back right onto the lip and move up to a stance.

4 **20m 4c** Move back into the corner. Traverse left up across the wall on flakes then up the arête to a block belay.

5 **50m 4a** Climb slabby grooves in the same line past a block then continue up easier ground to join the *Route II* traverse. Trend diagonally left to belay on small muddy ledge.

6 **30m 5a** An intimidating exposed pitch. Move up to the overhang then out left onto a steep slab, heading out left to another overhang. Step off a detached flake and traverse left onto the slab on good hidden holds. Saunter rightwards up the fine

rough slab above to belay beneath some blocks.

7 **25m 4c** Traverse right for 6m and climb a spiky arête to a bulge. Surmount this, step left into an easy groove and climb this to the terrace at the top.

---

7 **King Kong ★★★★**   **275m E2 5c**

FA Brian Robertson, Fred Harper & Jimmy Graham 1+2 Sept 1964:
FFA gained from The Bat: Norrie Muir & Ian Nicolson June 1970

A fantastic long sustained route following an improbable and intricate line through the overlapping slabs right of *Centurion*. The original contrived start is seldom climbed (slow to dry) and the route is described by the more usual approach via *The Bat*.

1 **15m 5a** As for *Centurion*.

2 **15m 5b** Climb 6m up the corner then traverse right across the pink slab to belay at a perched block.

3 **35m 5c** Step left from the belay. Make a hard move up to gain a steep slab. Move up leftwards to gain an obvious line of weakness through the overlapping slabs and continue directly to reach an impasse at a large overlap. Undercling down and right to gain a thin crack springing from the lip of the overlap. Follow this diagonally rightwards across the slab above to belay at the right bounding rib.

4 **35m 5b** Climb directly up to gain a vertical crack in the red wall above. Climb this then trend up and right across the wall (bold) and up to belay at the top of *The Bat* corner.

5 **40m 5b** Move up from the belay then traverse left for 5m to the crack system left of *The Bat*. Climb this over a series of overlaps to move left to belay on a small grass ledge.

6 **25m** Climb easily by a grassy bay to a vertical wall then traverse left and up to a block belay beneath an overhanging wall capped by a small roof.

7 **40m 5a** Follow the crack through the roof and the continuation corner on the left to belay beneath a corner. *Route II* crosses here.

8 **40m 4c** Climb the corner, swing across to a spike then move left and continue up to a spike belay.

9 **30m** Continue slightly right then up to a grassy groove, moving left then up to finish.

Rick Campbell
nearing the top of pitch 4
of King Kong.

8 Trajan's Column ★★★   305m E6 6b

FA Rick Campbell & Gary Latter 7 September 2004
(pitch 2: 20 September 2003)

Fantastic varied climbing up the front face of the pillar right of the main pitch of *King Kong*.

1 **35m 5a** As for *King Kong* to the
large perched block belay.

2 **25m 6a** Move left, up then back right to a
position above the belay. Continue right and
up to a perch at the base of the main slab and
ascend straight up until it is possible to pull round
an arête on the right onto a sloping ledge in a
recess. (Spike belay on *King Kong* 5m higher.)

3 **30m 6b** A fantastic wildly-positioned pitch with
devious wandering climbing and spaced protection.
Step down right then make hard fingery moves to
gain good holds in the huge 'boot flake' and more
easily up this to a small overlap. Make committing
moves out right and up rightwards to a good incut
jug then straight up past a small useful flake to a
rest on the right arête below a smooth uninviting
groove. Traverse hard left into a parallel groove,
which is followed to a long thin overlap. Commit
right (scary) into the right groove (gear at last!)
and make a hard stretch up right to a good hold on
the arête. Continue back left to below the left side
of the final overlap and pull through this, keeping
close to the left rib leading to easier ground and
the belay common to *King Kong* & *The Bat*.

4 **40m 6a** Traverse out left along the obvious
fault line (*The Bullroar*) 10m beyond the crack
of *King Kong* to the crack splitting the slab. Pull
over the overlap and climb the slab to a slim
smooth hanging groove in the steep wall. Lean
out rightwards (crux) to gain two good incut jugs
then directly up the fairly sustained groove above,
belaying just above the final capping roof.

5 **15m** Climb easily up slightly left to belay at
the base of a small right-facing corner near
the right end of the big roof system.

6 **30m 5c** Climb the corner then move out
left into a slim groove and up this then the

fine rib to belay on a good ledge above.

7 **50m 4c** Move out right and up over vegetated ledges
to a loose wet corner. Climb this to pull out right onto
clean solid rock at a wide blocky crack. Move up left
and scramble up leftwards to a block belay on ledge.

8+9 **80m** Move out right and climb layback/jam cracks
up a slabby corner. Progressively easier scrambling
leads up leftwards to the top of the buttress.

9 The Wicked ★★★   107m E6 6b

FA Gary Latter & Rick Campbell 29 July 2000;
6 July 2001 & 22 September 2001

Follows a very well protected series of cracks up the left
wall of *The Bat*. Pitches 2-4 all overhang by 30 degrees.
Start immediately beneath prominent twin finger cracks
about 40m right of *Centurion*.

1 **20m 5b** Climb the lower slab direct, stepping
left up a tiny groove to pull onto the first
diagonal shelf on good holds. Belay at the
base of the rightmost of a pair of cracks.

2 **12m 6b** Make a long reach off undercuts to
a good spike hold then pull up into the crack
and layback this past good flat holds on the
right to a sloping hold at the top. Finish with
difficulty to belay on the shelf above.

3 **20m 6b** Step up left into the crack and follow
it with difficulty to good holds at the top. Pull
over on good flakes then climb a crack in
the arête, gained delicately from the right.
Belay on the next sloping shelf 5m higher.

4 **25m 6b** Climb the flake crack in the corner on the
left (*The Bat* descends here) then move right along
a wide crack (Camalot #4 useful). Climb the crack
on good holds with some hard fist jamming near
the top (F #4) to a good flake at the top of the steep
section. Continue more easily up the right-slanting
groove to pull round the arête then easily up the
shelf to belay near the base of *The Bat* corner.

5 **30m 6b** Climb the corner for 5m then move left and
arrange protection in the crack above. Step back
down and hand traverse left along the ledge to
step down into a short left-facing groove. Move up

left to a good jug and arrange protection (F #0.5) in the crack above. Return to the centre of the ledge. Climb straight up on small edges then traverse left along a horizontal crack past a good undercut (crux) to gain better holds. Continue directly on improving holds and protection to pull out slightly leftwards at the top to belay as for *The Bat*. Either abseil down *The Bat* in two rope lengths or continue up the groove above as for that route, traversing right along the terrace to abseil down *Titan's Wall*.

10 **The Bat** ★★★   **275m E2 5b**

FA Robin Smith & Dougal Haston (some aid) September 1959;
Independent finish Dougal Haston & Jimmy Marshall Sept 1959

A fantastic ultra-classic, restoring national pride. Immortalised in print and film, it still retains its once fearsome reputation.

1 **15m 5a** Climb *Centurion* pitch 1.

2 **35m 5b** Follow the *Centurion* corner for 6m then traverse right across a pink slab to a perched block. Continue moving right along a shelf to a block belay.

3 **25m 5a** Descend to the right for 3m to enter a bottomless groove and climb a short wall to a triangular slab. Follow the V-groove above then trend right along slabs to a belay beneath the left edge of the deep chimney of *Sassenach*.

4 **15m 5b** *The Hoodie Groove*. Climb a steep shallow groove on the left of the chimney then enter the main corner.

5 **30m 5b** Climb the corner to the overhang then launch into the wide corner crack above. Continue boldly to a ledge and belay, consciously trying not to emulate Haston: *"...as a black and bat-like shape came hurtling over the roof with legs splayed like webbed wings and hands hooked like a vampire..."* – Robin Smith

6 **35m 4b** Climb the groove to the left end of a large terrace. Either traverse right and abseil down *Titan's Wall*, or:

7-9 **120m 4b** Finish up the line of grooves above, belaying as required.

11 **Sassenach** ★★ **260m E2 5c with 2 PA (E3 6a free)**

FA Joe Brown & Don Whillans (some aid) 18 April 1954;
FFA Rab Anderson & Murray Hamilton 21 August 1983;
Patey Traverse: Tom Patey, Bill Brooker & W.Smith 1953

An old-fashioned neglected classic following the great chimney-corner line running the length of the right side of the buttress. A wild roof. So named, as an understandably miffed Scottish team shouted up *"English Bastards!"* as Brown & Whillans were completing the route. Below and right of the corner there is a large slab of rock leaning against the face. Start just to the left of this.

1 **25m 4c** Climb the sloping mossy ledges for 4m until possible to step right onto a nose. Climb this on good holds then traverse easily left and up wide corner crack to a stance and belay at the top.

2 **20m 5c** Continue up the corner with interest to the overhang. Traverse left (often wet – two slings for aid or free at 6a) then up the grooves above, moving leftwards to a stance and belay. *"Most sensational pitch I've done."* – Don Whillans

3 **10m** Up easily to the bottom of the corner.

4 **15m 5b** Climb the chimney past a tight constriction (crux) and belay where the angle eases. *"Good old-fashioned climbing"* – beware of several large loose spikes.

5 **35m 5b** Continue up the chimney to a large grassy terrace.

6 **20m** Move right across the terrace and scramble up easy rock to the foot of a V-groove capped by an overhang.

7 **35m 4b** Climb the groove for 10m then move out left onto a ledge. Continue up the crack above to enter another groove with a wide crack.

8 **15m 4c** Climb the groove and step right at its top.

9+10 85m 4b Climb the grooves above.

Note: The often wet crux pitch can be avoided by climbing pitch 1 of *Titan's Wall*, E2 5b then a 12m VS 4c pitch, the *Patey Traverse*, which traverses left round the arête and across slabs to a ledge at the base of *The Banana Groove*. Step down and left to a grass ledge at the base of the main chimney.

CARN DEARG BUTTRESS

2¼hr

Aussie Dave Smith on Centurion.

The Banana Groove ★★★   107m E4 6a

FA Murray Hamilton & Rab Anderson 21 August 1983

Right of *Sassenach* are two prominent hanging grooves. This climbs the leftmost groove in its entirety.

1 **35m 5b** Climb pitch 1 of *Titan's Wall* to belay near the left arête.

2 **12m 4c** Traverse left round the arête and cross slabs to belay at the foot of the groove.

3 **45m 6a** An exhilarating pitch. Climb the corner above and move left to the spike on the arête. Move up and right into the groove-crack and continue straight up the crack-line and ensuing shallow corner to pull out left onto a small sloping ledge.

4 **15m 5c** Continue up the groove to reach easier ground. Gain the spike abseil point on the right at the top of *Titan's Wall*.

Agrippa ★★★   80m E5 6b

FA Pete Whillance & Rab Anderson 29 August 1983

The stunningly positioned arête forming the left edge of *Titan's Wall*.

1 **30m 5c** Climb the slabby rib for 15m to a small overhang. Pull over to a sloping ledge and up the groove above to a shelf below another overhang. Straight up to the ledge and belay on *Titan's Wall*. A bit artificial.

2 **25m 6b** Move up left and climb a thin crack in the arête. Pull right to better holds and up to a large block. From a standing position on the block move round onto the left wall of the arête and up with difficulty to a good ledge and belay.

3 **25m 5c** Climb a slight groove on the right for a metre then up left across a wall to gain a flake in the arête. Climb this and continue on good holds, moving right to the spike belay on *Titan's Wall*. Abseil descent.

14 Titan's Wall ★★★★ 80m E3 6a

FA Ian Clough & Hamish MacInnes (A2) 19 April 1959;
FFA Mick Fowler & Phil Thomas June 1977

Steep, varied climbing (a modern classic), precursor to a clutch of short high standard routes in the vicinity. Start 5m right of the left edge of the wall.

1 **35m 5b** Follow cracks to an overhang near the edge. Cross this and continue up the crack-line slightly rightwards to a long narrow ledge. Move left along this to in situ belay above the huge roof.

2 **45m 6a** Traverse right along the ledge to the crack splitting the centre of the wall. Launch up this with continuous interest, soon easing near the top. Continue to a spike belay at the top of the wall. An excellent well protected pitch. Abseil descent.

15 Boadicea ★★ 100m E4 6a

FA Willie Todd & Alistair Cain June 1989

The main pitch climbs the well protected thin crack up the impending wall right of *Titan's Wall*.

1 **35m 5b** Climb pitch 1 of *Titan's Wall* to belay near the left end of the long narrow ledge.

2 **20m 5a** Traverse to the right end of the ledge. From the foot of the crack on *Titan's Wall* follow a curving crack to a stance on *The Shield Direct*.

3 **40m 6a** Return left to the crack, which now becomes vertical. Climb it, thin at first to reach an easier section by some flakes. Continue with

difficulty up the smooth section above to a belay.

4 **5m 5a** A short descent to the left leads to the abseil point at the top of *Titan's Wall*.

16 The Shield Direct ★ 212m HVS 5a

FA Don Whillans & Bob Downes 1 September 1956; Direct Start
Jimmy & Ronnie Marshall & George Ritchie (3 PA) June 1962

The steep smooth north-west wall is bounded high on its right by a 100m flake. Start 6m right of *Titan's Wall*, just left of the corner. Slow to dry.

1 **24m** Climb the wall for 7m, traverse right into the wide corner crack and climb to belay.

2 **15m 5a** Follow the crack until under the great roof. Move onto the left wall then climb a thin crack (crux, 3 points aid – often wet) to surmount the left edge of the roof. Continue up a short chimney to belay.

3 **18m** Continue up the chimney to a block belay.

4 **18m** Climb the steep groove above and traverse right to join the original route above the first chimney pitch.

5 **12m** Climb the narrow chimney until it is possible to step left to a small cave. Thread belays.

6 **40m** Step back into the chimney, climb a difficult bulge then up the corner to another chimney.

7 **35m** Up the chimney then a long grassy groove to the top of the flake. This is the 'lofty corner' of *Evening Wall*.

8 **50m** Finish up the rightmost of two grooves.

COIRE NA CISTE

This deep recessed coire containing twin tiny green lochans lies between **Carn Dearg Buttress** and the prominent projecting *Tower Ridge*. Between **Number 5 Gully** (bounding the left side of Carn Dearg Buttress) and **Number 4 Gully** lie the fine **Trident Buttresses**.
Approach: From the CIC Hut head directly south-west up the slabby buttress into the corrie then bear right and up the lower scree slopes of **Number 4 Gully** to the base of the cliffs. 45 minutes from the hut.

CENTRAL TRIDENT BUTTRESS

A steep rounded wall of excellent rock in its lower reaches, though care should be taken on blocky ground higher up.

Descent: Traverse left and down scree and easy slabs bounding the left side of the buttress or make a 45m abseil from block (sling & maillon in situ) near the top of *Steam*.

1 Steam ** 90m HVS 5a,

FA Stevie Docherty & Bobby Gorman Summer 1970

Start at an obvious right-facing corner groove near the left side of the face.

1 **25m 4c** Climb the corner to overhang which is passed on the left to a stance and PB.
2 **30m 5a** Climb the wall for 6m then move left to a corner. Climb this to a leftward-sloping ramp and belay in a greasy corner.
3 **35m 4c** Traverse diagonally up and right until a mantelshelf left onto a sloping ledge can be made (PR). Continue left and climb a steep wall to finish.

2 Heidbanger ** 80m E1 5b

FA Norrie Muir & Ian Nicolson 9 June 1970

Start 6m left of the base of the obvious crack system splitting the face.

1 **35m 5a** Climb a bulge moving right to the top of a steep groove at 6m and climb a short corner onto a band of slabs. Traverse rightwards to an arête and belay in a cave.
2 **30m 5b** Climb the hanging crack above then continue direct up the wall on fine incut holds to pull onto a ledge above. Continue up onto the next ledge and move out left to belay in a short corner.

3 **15m 4b** Climb the rib above on good holds then easily leftwards to a block belay/abseil on the left.

2a Cranium ** 20m E1 5b

FA Norrie Muir & Arthur Paul 19 June 1977

The prominent deep crack in the arête leading directly into the cave provides a good direct start to *Heidbanger*. Some large cams (up to 4") useful.

3 Metamorphosis ** 100m E2 5b

FA Stevie Docherty & Davy Gardner August 1971

The best line on the cliff on superb looking rock. Start just left of a prominent overhanging crack at the right end of the face.

1 **35m 5b** Climb rightwards to join the crack below the bulge. Surmount this and continue to below a corner. Go right and up to another corner (PR) which is followed to a ledge and PB.
2 **25m 5b** Continue past a recess to a ledge. Go right along the ledge and up to PB beneath an obvious flake (poor stance).
3 **25m 4c** Climb the flake and wall above then trend right to easier ground.
4 **15m 5a** Finish by a corner and wall above.

NN 162 720 **Alt:** 940m (E) 2¾hr

DESCENT

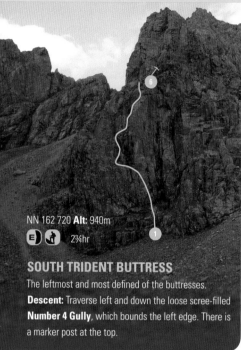

NN 162 720 **Alt:** 940m

(E) (🚶) 2¾hr

SOUTH TRIDENT BUTTRESS

The leftmost and most defined of the buttresses.
Descent: Traverse left and down the loose scree-filled **Number 4 Gully**, which bounds the left edge. There is a marker post at the top.

① 1944 Route ★★★   125m Severe 4a

FA Brian Kellett (solo) 30 July 1944

A superb route and a logical approach to the fine routes on the upper tier.

1. **30m** Start by scrambling up to the base of the steep wall about 30m right of the lowest rocks.
2. **25m** Go up left of the steep chimney then trend left to a belay ledge.
3. **25m 4a** From a large leaning block climb to the base of the second leaning groove from the left. Traverse right to belay beneath the rightmost (fourth) groove.
4. **33m** Climb into the groove then by a crack in the right wall to gain a system of ledges which are followed to a short steep corner.
5. **12m 4a** Finish by the corner.

> The following routes are all situated on the Upper Tier of the buttress, gained either via *1944 Route*, or scrambling in easily from the left.

② Sidewinder ★★   75m HVS 5a

FA Jimmy & Ronnie Marshall & Andy Wightman June 1964

Look for a triple-tiered corner rising steeply leftwards across the face 15m right of an obvious flake-chimney. Scramble from the ledge to the foot of the corner.

1–3 **4b 5a 4c** Climb the corners by cracks in three pitches (15m, 10m and 20m) to gain an easy slab.

4. **30m** Continue directly above by the continuation of the crack and a large flake to gain the crest of the buttress below the final tier.

③ Strident Edge ★★   75m VS 4c

FA Norrie Muir & D.Regan July 1972

Originally dubbed 'Pink Dream Maker', but renamed by the second ascentionists, thinking they were making the first ascent. The prominent sharp arête on the middle tier gives a pleasant and straightforward climb despite its fearsome appearance. Start 6m left of *Sidewinder*.

1. **15m** Climb rightwards to belay in the corner.
2. **36m 4c** Move airily out right and climb the steep cracked groove splitting the left side of the arête to belay on the crest.
3. **24m 4b** Finish up the left edge of the arête.

4 Devastation *   80m E1 5b

FA Colin Moody & Andy Nelson 12 July 1995

Fine varied climbing up the steep cracked groove round right of *Strident Edge*. Named after the numerous trundles on the first ascent! Start beneath the second corner right of that route.

1 **40m 5b** Climb the corner until it ends at the flake; move left to a niche above the overhang. Climb the steep crack above.

2 **40m 4a** On up.

5 The Slab Climb *   80m Severe 4a

FA Brian Kellet (solo) 30 July 1944

The crack up the left side of the slab. Start directly beneath the base.

1 **20m** – Ascend diagonally leftwards then traverse right and climb a short wall to the base of twin cracks.

2 **40m 4a** Climb the slab near the right crack towards an overlap, traverse left into the left crack and fol-low it to a ledge. Continue up to negotiate a steep chimney-slot with difficulty then easier grooves above. The crux chimney can be avoided by a flake crack above an overhang on the left, finishing up the final straightforward groove, as for *Devastation*.

3 **20m** – Continue more easily leftwards to finish.

6 Pinnacle Arête **   150m Very Difficult

FA Harold Raeburn, Dr William & Jane Inglis Clark 29 June 1902

Fine climbing up the right edge of the buttress, overlooking the steep north wall and a good finish to *1944 Route*. Start from the right end of the ledge running beneath the middle tier. Move over sloping ledges for 3m then up an awkward corner on the right. 10m of difficult rock leads to easier ground. Trend left to the crest and climb to the base of a steep wall which is climbed direct on good holds. One further short steep section leads up to the narrow shattered crest and the final tier of the buttress which gives scrambling to the summit plateau.

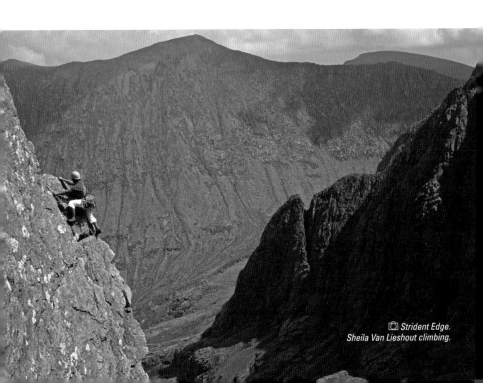

Strident Edge.
Sheila Van Lieshout climbing.

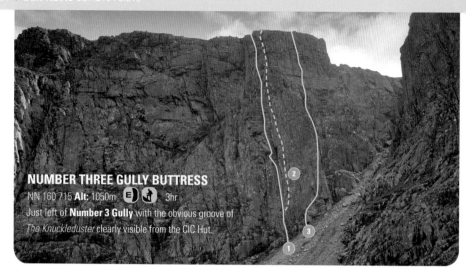

NUMBER THREE GULLY BUTTRESS
NN 160 715 **Alt:** 1050m ⓔ 🧗 3hr
Just left of **Number 3 Gully** with the obvious groove of
The Knuckleduster clearly visible from the CIC Hut.

Approach: From the CIC Hut head up into Coire na Ciste
as for the Trident Buttresses then head up scree to the
base of the cliff. 1 hour from hut.
Descent: Down the right bounding scree-filled
No. 3 Gully, or the more straightforward **No. 4 Gully**
(NN 158 717) 300m further right (north-west) along the
rim, which contains a metal indicator post at its top. Both
retain much snow well into the summer. Alternatively the
top of *Ledge Route* (large cairn) lies 400m further north
than **No. 4 Gully** and will always be clear of snow when
the cliffs are in summer condition.

① The Knuckleduster ★★　　　　**120m HVS 5a**
FA Jimmy & Ronnie Marshall 4 September 1966

Great climbing up the groove on the steep right side of
the buttress, though slow to dry. Start by scrambling up
to belay at the base of the groove.

1 40m 4c Follow the groove to belay
　beneath an overhang.
2 15m 5a Turn the overhang by a slab on
　the right to belay on the outer edge.
3 35m 5a Regain the groove by traversing
　left along horizontal ledge. Continue by
　a crack on the right wall to a ledge.
4 30m 4c Climb the wall on the right to gain the
　large platform of *Number Three Gully Buttress*.

② Last Stand ★★　　　　**90m HVS 5a**
FA Doug Hawthorn & Arthur Paul 2 July 1984

Steep and exposed climbing up the arête right of 1 *The
Knuckleduster*. Start below the prominent groove of 1.

1 30m Follow a diagonal line of weakness
　up and right to the foot of the arête.
2 40m 5a Climb by thin cracks on the right
　side of the arête to a ledge and belay.
3 20m 5a Continue directly by cracks, cross a
　bulge then finish more easily up further cracks.

③ Sioux Wall ★★　　　　**90m HVS 5a**
FA Ian Nicolson & George Grassam 4 September 1972

An excellent route on good rock, following an obvious groove
line just left of the centre of the steep face up right of 1.

1 25m Follow a diagonal weakness up and right. Climb
　past a large rock fin and up to a square-cut niche.
2 30m 5a Step left onto the steep wall. Climb
　this to a crack then move left onto a small ramp
　which moves back right to the base of the obvious
　corner/groove. Bridge up this to below a roof.
3 20m 5a Climb the steep crack above (hard to
　start) to a small overhang. Pull directly over
　this on large holds to a ledge and belay.
4 15m Climb the continuation crack to a large
　platform. Scramble to the top of the buttress.

Observatory
Ridge

Tower
Ridge

Minus
Face

12

11

8

Orion
Face

Douglas
Boulder

2

First
Platform

4

13

3

10

7   9

1

6

2

TOWER RIDGE 🚶 2½hr

DOUGLAS BOULDER 🔲 🚶 2¼hr

NN 167 719 **Alt:** 800m

A good direct approach to the base of *Tower Ridge*. Being one of the lowest lying buttresses on the mountain it is relatively quick drying and is often clear of the cloud when many of the other cliffs are shrouded in mist.

Approach: Follow a path heading south from the CIC Hut for 15 minutes to the base.

Descent: Abseil (slings in situ on blocks) or down climb down the back into the Douglas Gap and continue up *Tower Ridge*.

1 Direct Route ★★ 215m Very Difficult

FA William Brown, Lionel Hinxman, Harold Raeburn & William Douglas 3 April 1896

A good approach to *Tower Ridge*, following the groove splitting the centre of the front face. Start at the base of the lowest rocks. Climb easily up the large open groove until it steepens into an open chimney. Follow this for about 60m to a good ledge. Traverse right along this then ascend steep broken rocks to the top.

2 Tower Ridge ★★★ 600m Difficult

First Descent Jack, Edward, Bertram & Charles Hopkinson 3 Sept 1892; FA (in winter conditions) Norman Collie, Godfrey Solly & Joseph Collier 30 March 1894

A well trodden classic, the most popular of the classic ridges. Once the base is gained the way is obvious – just follow the crampon scratches! Approach by skirting left round the base of the Douglas Boulder and cutting up easy broken ground on the right to an easy-angled loose fault leading up to the Douglas Gap. Ascend a polished 15m open chimney to gain the crest. Follow this easily to a short steep wall and outflank this by a ledge leading up rightwards. A further easy-angled section leads easily to another short step, the Little Tower. Climb this by a choice of lines on good rough rock then another long almost level section leads to the Great Tower. This is again outflanked, this time by the Eastern Traverse – a metre wide ledge running out left round the corner. This leads to a deep chimney capped by a huge chokestone. Climb the chimney (15m) then continue out left then steeply on good holds to the top of The Great Tower. Follow the fine narrow crest which leads to the highlight – Tower Gap. Drop down awkwardly for 3m to the base of the gap (or jump the gap if you're mad enough!) then more easily up the other side. Continue easily, turning the final steepening by a ledge and groove on the right leading abruptly to the summit plateau.

OBSERVATORY RIDGE 2½hr

NN 168 716 **Alt:** 920m

The long narrow buttress projecting north from the summit sandwiched between two of the most famous winter routes around – *Zero Gully* and *Point Five*.

Approach: From the hut follow a good path up beneath the base of the Douglas Boulder, continuing slightly leftwards up scree to the base. 30 minutes from hut.

③ Observatory Ridge ★★★ 450m Very Difficult

FA Harold Raeburn (solo) 22 June 1901

Completes the trilogy of classic ridges with excellent clean continuous rock, particularly in the lower section. The hardest of the ridges, especially the lower third. Mostly of Difficult standard, especially the upper section (after about 180m), where the standard and angle eases considerably. The best route is well-scratched and obvious. Start at the lowest rocks. Scramble easily rightwards then traverse right to the right end of a grass terrace (65m). Continue just left of the crest by slabs and walls to steeper ground which is outflanked easily on the right. Follow cracks and grooves to gain the easier angled crest of the ridge which leads to the plateau.

NORTH-EAST BUTTRESS

NN 170 718 **Alt:** 850m   2½hr

This is the huge buttress projecting north-east from the summit plateau. Its north-west flank contains **Minus Face** and **Orion Face** – a great sweep of slabby buttresses rising up out of the usually snow-filled depths of the huge **Observatory Gully**. Separated by **Minus One Gully** and **Minus Two Gully**, the Minus Faces are numbered from right to left starting from the pronounced **Zero Gully** which separates the Orion Face from the broad *Observatory Ridge*. Routes below the First Platform are fairly quick drying with little run-off.

Approach: From the hut follow a good path up the right side of the burn up towards Coire Leis, which leads underneath the base of North-East Buttress. For the Minus and Orion Faces bear off right and up to the base of the chosen cliff. 20-30 minutes from hut.

Descent: For routes finishing on or near the First Platform, descend the easier lower section of **North-East Buttress**. For routes ending on the plateau, the quickest descent is to follow the path south-east down steep blocky ground (marker posts) to the abseil posts at the bealach at the top of Coire Leis and descend easy scree slopes (path) back down into Coire Leis.

④ North-East Buttress ★★★ 300m Very Difficult

FA Jack, Edward, Bertram & Charles Hopkinson
6 September 1892

Another great classic ridge. Start up left from the base of the ridge and traverse left beneath the lower rocks to gain a wide ledge which leads up right to the crest of the ridge. This leads to the First Platform, which can also be gained more interestingly by either *Raeburn's Arête* or *Bayonet Route*. Follow the crest of the ridge to a steepening and turn this by a shallow left-slanting gully. Trend rightwards up short chimneys and walls to gain a broad sloping shelf on the crest – the Second Platform. Continue up the narrow well defined ridge until a smooth overhanging wall bars progress. Outflank it either by a corner with large steps on the right, or more direct by following a right-slanting ledge to cross a bulge on good holds. The infamous Mantrap lurks a short way above. Attack this direct then continue by the '40 foot corner' which can be climbed direct or avoided on the left. Follow a small gully above which leads to easier rocks and the summit plateau.

⑤ Raeburn's Arête ★★★   230m Severe 4a

FA Harold Raeburn, Dr William & Jane Inglis Clark 30 June 1902

Fantastic climbing up the clean arête formed by the north and east faces of the buttress. Start directly beneath the arête, at the lowest rocks.

1 20m 4a Move up to a black overhang, bypass this on the right and continue to belay on a grass ledge.

2 35m 4a Climb the arête to belay on a ledge.

3 40m 4a Traverse 6m right then climb up to regain the arête as soon as possible.

4–6 135m Continue, keeping as close to the arête as possible to the First Platform.

⑥ Bayonet Route ★★   160m Very Difficult

FA Graham MacPhee & A.Murray 30 September 1935

Start from a large grass platform roughly midway between *Raeburn's Arête* and the right bounding chimney of the buttress.

1 45m Ascend a rib of rough rock veering slightly left to a grass niche at 20m. Traverse left across a rib and continue up a grassy groove to a belay.

2 20m Go out left onto the rib and follow it to beneath the left edge of the main overhang.

3 25m Gain the rib on the left and follow it until a right traverse leads into a grassy bay. Continue up the rib on the right of the bay.

5 30m The rib above.

6 40m Climb a corner to pull out left just above a prominent square-cut overhang. Continue by easier ground to gain the crest of the buttress. An ascent including the following two variations gives an excellent combination:

⑥ᵃ Direct Start ★★   35m Severe 4a

FA Jimmy Marshall & James Stenhouse August 1959

From the left end of the grass platform, follow the prominent corner, join the original route beneath the overhang.

⑥ᵇ Main Overhang Variation ★★   35m HS 4b

FA Brian Kellet (solo) May 1943

Bold and committing. From the grassy groove, climb a slab to a point beneath a V-notch in the main overhang. Gain this by cracks, exiting on the right. Trend left above the overhang to regain the original route.

THE MINUS FACE   NN 168 716 Alt: 950m 2½hr

The north-west flank of North-East Buttress contains The Minus and Orion Faces – a great sweep of slabby buttresses rising up out of the usually snow-filled depths of the huge almost corrie-like **Observatory Gully**. Separated by **Minus One Gully** and **Minus Two Gully**, the Minus Faces are numbered from right to left, starting from the deep pronounced **Zero Gully** which separates the Orion Face from the broad *Observatory Ridge*. All the routes finish at various levels on *North-East Buttress*, which can either be ascended or descended to finish.

MINUS TWO BUTTRESS

⑦ Left Edge Variation ★★★   80m VS 4c

FA N. & Bob Richardson & Alistair Walker 11 June 1988

An excellent start to *Left-Hand Route* providing better and more sustained climbing than the original lower pitches. Starts as for the Clough variation, but climbs the edge overlooking **Minus Three Gully** instead of the big groove.

1 31m 4b From the foot of the V-groove move out onto the left rib to climb up and left to a belay at flakes in a niche on the edge of the buttress.

2 37m 4c Descend right a metre or so then move up and right to climb a bulging groove then a further groove on the very edge of the buttress to a fine stance in a little bowl below an imposing wall.

3 12m 4c Pass this wall on the left then go up and right to belay above the crux of the original route. Continue as for the parent route.

8 Left-Hand Route ★★   **270m VS 4c**

FA Brian Kellett, Robin & Carol Plackett 20 June 1944

Good climbing up cracks splitting the front of the prominent raised crest of the buttress.

1+2 60m 4a Ascend the cracks splitting the front of the prominent raised crest of the buttress to gain a ledge at the base of a slab to the left of some stepped roofs.

3 10m 4b Descend a slab from the left end of the ledge and traverse left to a second slab which is climbed on small holds. The slabs above the ledge can also be climbed direct at 4c.

4 40m 4b Climb the slab keeping close to the left edge, then a groove to step right to belay.

5–8 160m Continue easier up more broken ground, better on the left, to gain the crest of *North-East Buttress*.

9 Right-Hand Route ★★   **275m VS 4b**

FA Brian Kellett (solo) 20 July 1944

Intriguingly, Kellett lost his trousers on the approach! It follows a line of cracks to the right of a large prominent corner just right of the centre of the buttress.

1 10m Follow cracks to belay in the corner.

2 40m 4b Continue delicately by either the cracks or the slab to a small stance.

3 40m 4b Move up for about a metre then traverse right for 4m. Cross a bulge and traverse left to a groove which leads to a belay.

4 20m Continue to easier ground.

5–8 165m Continue fairly steeply, climbable almost anywhere, to gain the crest of the ridge.

10 Subtraction ★   **275m E2 5b**

FA John McLean & Bill Smith August 1959

Start 12m right of *Right-Hand Route*.

1 35m 4c Climb the groove to belay below the left-trending overhanging continuation.

2 25m 5a Cross the overhang via the rib on the right and climb up to a belay.

3 40m Follow the arête to belay beneath a corner. Continue up the corner to belay in Minus Two Gully.

4 40m Continue by the corner to gain Minus Two Gully.

5 30m Cross the gully and continue up rightwards across Minus One Buttress to gain and follow the second obvious groove leading to a grass ledge on the right wall.

6 45m 5b Climb the overhanging groove and continue directly to a belay.

7+8 60m Finish more easily to gain the crest of *North-East Buttress*.

11 Long Division ★★   **190m E1 5b**

FA Colin Moody & Billy Hood 20 August 1995

A good direct line up the buttress right of *Subtraction*.

1 35m Climb the rib right of *Subtraction* to belay below the bulge.

2 35m 5b Climb the bulge just right of centre then follow the obvious steep crack to a belay below the overhanging nose. The last part of the crack is grassy and can be avoided by a step left.

3 30m 4b Go left round the nose then move right above it. Climb the rib past the right end of the roof to belay above.

4 40m 4b Climb the cracks left of Minus Two Gully.

5 50m Finish directly.

MINUS ONE BUTTRESS

12 Minus One Direct ★★★★   **315m E1 5b**

FA Bob Downes, Mike O'Hara & Mike Prestige (1 PA) 11 June 1956;
Serendipity Variation: Ken Crocket & Ian Fulton 27 August 1972;
Arête Variation: Stevie Abbott & Noel Williams (1 PA) 28 Aug 1983;
FFA Willie Jeffrey & Noel Williams 6 July 1984

A fantastic route *"of almost alpine proportions"* on superb rock throughout. When combined with the *Serendipity* and *Arête Variations* it provides one of the finest routes of its grade in the country. Start at the lowest point in the centre of the buttress.

1 25m Scramble easily to belay under a left-facing corner.

2 25m 4b Climb the corner then exit right onto a glacis and belay.

3 45m 4c Ascend a shallow groove in the wall

above to a block at 6m. Pass this by a crack on its right (it is also possible to climb on its left) then climb by short walls, moving left to a niche. Step right and climb to the top of a vast plinth.

4 30m 5b The crux pitch of the original route; a sustained and committing lead on perfect rock. Traverse right onto a nose above the overhang and climb it until it is possible to follow a ramp rightwards to finish at a block belay on a platform overlooking the final chimney of Minus One Gully.

5 25m 5b Traverse up and left until a hard move leads to a recess (crux). Climb this and continue to belay in a small grassy niche.

6 20m 4c Step left into a further recess and climb its slabby left wall. Climb the steeper rocks above until it is possible to break out onto right-trending slabs. Belay at a stack of detached blocks.

7 20m 5b On the left is a prominent slab capped by a long narrow overhang. Gain a foothold in the centre of the slab (crux), move up to the overhang (or climb straight above the belay to gain the traverse line – straightforward and more logical!) then traverse left on underclings to the arête. Cross the overlap with difficulty to a small exposed stance.

8 40m 4c Climb a crack in the crest above then continue more easily to a groove. Bridge strenuously up this to reach the great terrace.

9 40m 4b Climb to the top of a 12m pinnacle then continue easily to a leaning pedestal.

10 45m Finish up the finely-situated knife-edge arête to join *North-East Buttress* above the Second Platform and finish up that route.

THE ORION FACE

NN 169 717 **Alt**: 950m 2½hr

A vast mainly broken V-shaped slabby face extending from **Minus One Gully** rightwards to **Zero Gully**.

13 The Long Climb ★★★   **425m VS 4c**

FA Jim Bell & John Wilson 14 June 1940

Aptly named, this offers the longest vertical face climb in mainland Britain, of almost alpine stature. (Though *The Chasm* on Buachaille Etive Mor is longer, much more sustained and an altogether bigger day). An extensive snow patch usually lies in the basin until late in the season. It is usually better to skirt round the rocks on the left side of this to gain the base. Start to the left of the base of Zero Gully, by scrambling up to a large platform.

1 50m Go up an easy-angled ochre rib left of Zero Gully to a small platform.

2 45m 4c Follow a rib leading up from the left end of the platform to the base of the distinctive Great Slab Rib. Step round the rib on the left and move up to its base, or climb either directly up the rib or the groove on its right (both 4c).

3 40m 4a Traverse right onto the crest of the Great Slab Rib and follow fine parallel cracks to belay in a recess.

4 45m Head out and up right then climb easily to The Basin.

5 40m Continue easily across The Basin heading up to the base of the distinctive Second Slab Rib, which bounds the top right side of The Basin.

6 45m 4c Climb the slabby left edge of the rib then a short awkward wall either on the left or right to a belay.

7–10 160m The original route trends up slightly left (harder ground lies further left), aiming for the base of another 60m high Great Slab. Avoid this on the right by a line leading to a niche then a short difficult pitch gains the top of the slab. Continue easily to gain the crest of *North-East Buttress* and finish this. Much variation is possible in this upper section.

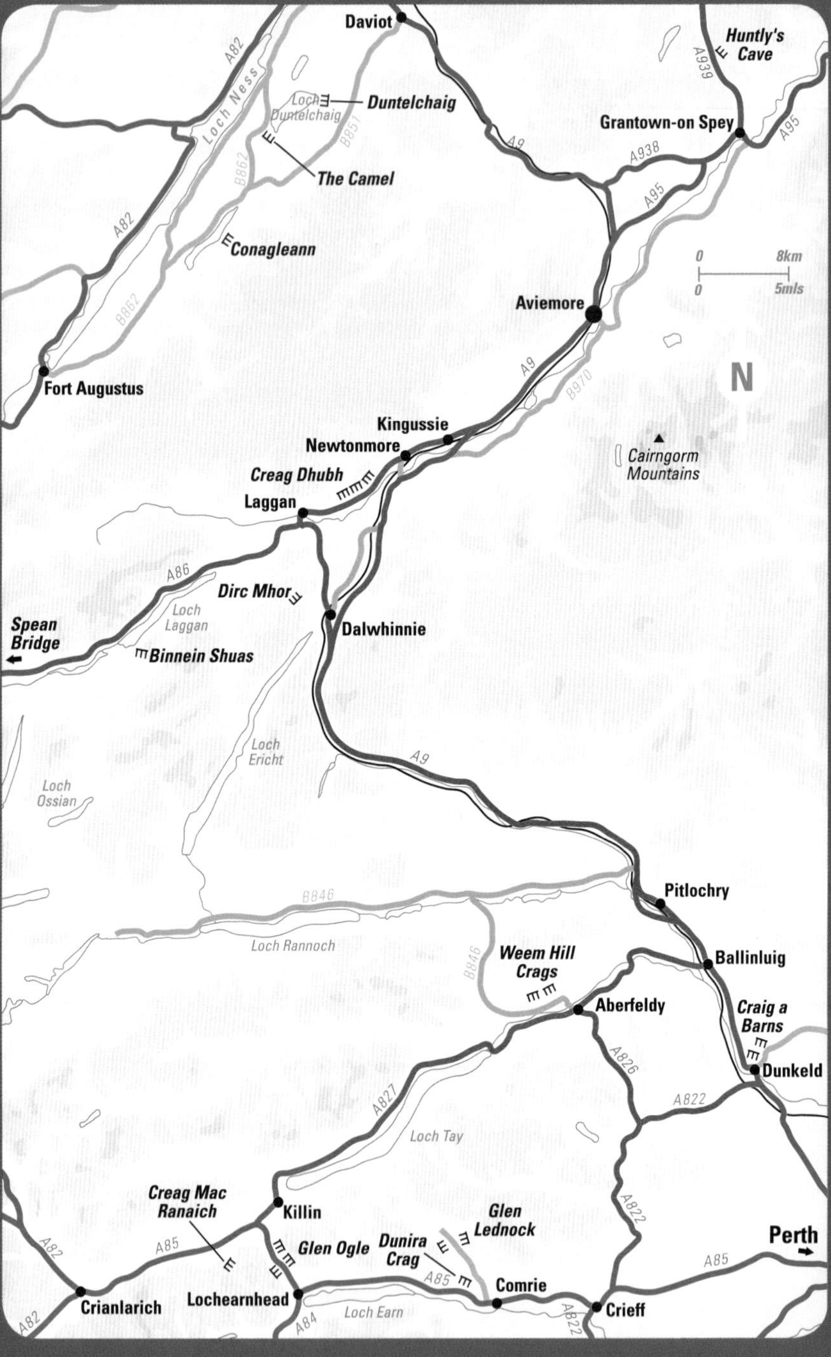

Daviot

Huntly's Cave

A82

Loch Ness

Loch Duntelchaig

Duntelchaig

A939

Grantown-on Spey

A95

The Camel

B862

B851

A9

A938

B862

Conagleann

A95

0   8km

0   5mls

A82

Aviemore

A9

B970

N

Fort Augustus

B862

Kingussie

Creag Dhubh

Newtonmore

Laggan

Cairngorm Mountains

A86

Dirc Mhor

Loch Laggan

Binnein Shuas

Dalwhinnie

Spean Bridge

Loch Ericht

Loch Ossian

A9

B846

Pitlochry

Loch Rannoch

B846

Weem Hill Crags

Ballinluig

Craig a Barns

Aberfeldy

Dunkeld

A826

A822

A827

Loch Tay

Creag Mac Ranaich

Killin

Glen Lednock

A822

Perth

A82

A85

Glen Ogle

Dunira Crag

A85

Crianlarich

Lochearnhead

A84

Loch Earn

Comrie

A822

Crieff

A85

CENTRAL HIGHLANDS

This is by far the largest area covered in the guide. The dominant rock type within the southern and central Highlands is schist. Within this area lie two of the most significant Highland outcrops – Creag Dhubh and Craig-a-Barns. Both played a leading role in the rising standards throughout the decades of the 70s and 80s. Binnein Shuas and the more recently developed great slash of Dirc Mhor offer the only climbing of note on micro-granite. Also within this area lies Glen Ogle (a definite contender for the least aesthetic glen in the whole of the Highlands), where the trend towards ever shorter and harder pitches has led to a cornucopia of miniature sport climbs. In a similar vein, though in an altogether pleasanter environment, the short steep buttresses on the thickly wooded slopes of Weem Hill provide the best mid-grade sport climbs thus far in the country. Other isolated sport venues amidst fine locations include the unusual conglomerate crag The Camel at the south end of Loch Duntelchaig just south of Inverness.

Accommodation: See also Northern Cairngorms (Strath Spey) introduction. **TICs:** Aberfeldy (☎ 01887 820276); Dunkeld (01350 727688); Pitlochry (☎ 01796 472215).
Youth Hostel: Pitlochry (☎ 01796 472308; www.syha.org.uk).
Bunkhouses: Trossachs Backpackers Hostel, Callander (☎ 01877 331200: www.scottish-hostel.co.uk); Comrie Bunkhouse, between Crieff & Comrie (☎ 01764 670140; www.comriecroft.co.uk); Culdees Bunkhouse, Fearnan, Loch Tay (☎ 01887 830519; www.culdeesbunkhouse.co.uk); Wester Caputh Independent Hostel (☎ 01738 710617 or 710449; www.westercaputh.co.uk) just off A984, 4 miles east of Dunkeld; Old Bunkhouse Lodge (☎ 01796 470022) & Pitlochry Backpackers (☎ 01796 570044; www.scotlands-top-hostels.com), both Atholl Road, Pitlochry; Dunolly House (☎ 01887 820298; www.dunollyadventures.co.uk) & Glassie Farm Bunkhouse (☎ 01887 820265; www.thebunkhouse.co.uk) both Aberfeldy; Adventurer's Escape, Weem (☎ 01887 820498; www.adventurers-escape.co.uk).
Campsites: Inver Mill Farm Camping & Caravan Site, Dunkeld (☎ 01350 777477); Aberfeldy Caravan Park (☎ 01887 820662); Beech Hedge Caravan Park, Meikleour (☎ 01250 883249; www.beechhedge.co.uk); Glengoulandie Country Park (☎ 01887 830495; www.glengoulandie.co.uk); Faskally (☎ 01796 472007; www.faskally.co.uk); Tummel Valley Holiday Park (☎ 01882 634221; www.parkdeanholidays.co.uk); Milton of Fonab Caravan Site (☎ 01796 472882; www.fonab.co.uk) all by Pitlochry; Blair Castle Caravan & Campsite (☎ 01796 481263; www.blairathollcaravanpark.co.uk); River Tilt Park (☎ 01796 481467), both Blair Atholl; Invernahavon Caravan Site, Laggan (☎ 01540 673534; www.laggan.com).
Club Huts: the Raeburn Hut on A889 between Dalwhinnie and Laggan.

"The one way to know mountains, and by knowing enter into possession, is to walk through them and climb on them. That double act is needed. In normal weather, one of the first intimate things that Scottish mountain country reveals to each explorer is the 'stone-glint' of its skeleton – the white light reflected off wet rock. Everywhere the bare bones break surface, exposed in slabs, protruding in ribs, outcropping in crags, or lifting up as whole mountains."
– W H Murray,
Scotland's Mountains
(Scottish Mountaineering Trust, 1987)

HISTORY

The first recorded climbs in the area came from one of the most active climbers at the turn of the century. In November 1903 Harold Raeburn and Charles Walker climbed two heavily vegetated gullies near the centre of Creag Dhubh, Scotland's biggest roadside outcrop. *"C.Walker who led then took us up the face above by steep and rotten grass ledges, which, but for the ice axe, we could not have ventured on."* The remaining clean obviously hard looking walls remained untouched for over half a century. The first recorded actual rock climbs in the area came in 1937 on Duntelchaig Crags by Richard Frere and friends Kenneth Robertson and Jimmy Walker. They climbed *Mica Slab, Mica Arête* and *Mica Chasm*. The following year Frere published the first outcrops guide in Scotland with *'A Guide to the crags in the neighbourhood of Inverness'.*

Sometime in the fifties B. Halpin, T. Abbey and S. Tondeur added one of the few easy lines on Creag Dhubh with *Rib Direct* and in 1959 Terry Sullivan and Neville Collingham added the first route to The Great Wall with *Brute* up the left side.

Around the same period (1957-60) the crags on the hillside of Craig a Barns overlooking the historic town of Dunkeld received their first recorded routes, though there are earlier records of others previously climbing on Polney Crag, including Jim Bell. Bell once famously stated *"any fool can climb good clean rock. It takes craft and cunning to get up vegetatious schist and granite."* and may have found the rocks a bit too clean for his liking! School-friends Robin Campbell and Paul Brian used Brian's home in Dunkeld as a base at weekends to produce many of the early routes on the crags. Amongst their additions were *Kestrel Crack, Beech Wall, Ogg's Hindquarters* and *Ivy Crack*, their first VS. Campbell led the classic *Wriggle* in 1959. The following year Edinburgh University MC members visited. Robin Smith, probably the best all round climber ever to come out of Scotland, left his mark when he soloed *The Groove*. Neil MacNiven completed the fine trilogy of VS routes with his ascent of *The Rut* and Campbell found the excellent *The End*. On Upper Cave Crag, Ferranti Club member Pete

Smith added the fine *Coffin Corner*. The two best lines on the more vegetated Lower Cave Crag gave Campbell *The Hood* whilst a young 19-year-old Dougal Haston contributed the bluntly named *Fuck Face*.

On a wet claggy day in May 1964 Tom Patey, one of the most prolific climbers of the era, visited the micro-granite cliffs of Binnein Shuas with R. Ford and Mary Stewart. With a tension traverse they climbed the upper section of *The Fortress*, gained from the garden, along with a couple of minor routes on the short lower tier beneath the main cliffs. In October that year Dougal Haston added the first worthwhile route on nearby Creag Dhubh with the classic *Inbred* up the right side of The Great Wall. The following year Haston and the Edinburgh Squirrels had a field day at Creag Dhubh, deliberately going out of their way to rile the SMC with a series of provocatively named routes. Haston, with James 'Big Elly' Moriarty and Arthur Ewing nabbed the plum line *King Bee*, the best route of its grade on the crags. Haston and Moriarty also added *Erse* and *Cuckold* with some aid. Up on Sprawl Wall, Fred Harper and Alasdair 'Bugs' McKeith put up *Jump So High* with some aid and the very fine *Gang Bang*. Also here, Hamish Small and Jimmy Graham established the best easy route on the crags with *Tree Hee*. Nearby, M. Harcus and G. Anderson added the similarly worthwhile *Raven's Squawk*. Other good routes that year were *Phellatio* from Ewing and Ian MacEacheran and the often damp *Cunnulinctus* from McKeith and R. Burnet.

The following year (1966) Bugs McKeith and party paid a visit to the 'great slash' of the Dirc Mhor adding the first route, *Holy Smoke* up the right edge of the impressive Sentinel Rock. Like nearby Creag Dhubh (from where it is clearly visible) the crag had first been visited by Harold Raeburn at the turn of the century, recording its potential in the SMC Journal at the time *"It is a perfectly dry ravine, from 250'–400' deep, with savage cliffs on either side, but much finer on the E than the W."*

Over the next two years Dundonians Doug Lang and Graham Hunter exploited the almost untouched potential of Binnein Shuas with no less than fourteen multi-pitch routes added in two summers, pride of place going to the celebrated *Ardverikie Wall*, a definite contender for the best Hard Severe in the country. Patey later acknowledged that it was possibly *"the finest route I've ever walked past"*. Unlike almost all the other crags in the area, most of the cliff is not composed of the more usual schist but mainly of micro-granite, though the routes on the far right of the East Sector are on schist. Amongst the other fine contributions on the cliffs from Lang and Hunter were a number of good lines on the West Sector including *Blaeberry Grooves*, *Kubla Khan* and the steep and exposed cracks of *The Keep*. Apparently the two were so concerned that other climbers might also come across the wealth of virgin rock that Lang managed to persuade the estate keeper to let him park his conspicuous white Volvo out of sight behind his cottage.

In 1967 at Polney Crag on Craig a Barns, Kenny Spence and John Porteous pushed standards with *The Way Through* through a couple of roofs. Harder and of more significance was Spence and Porteous's ascent in September of the bold and intimidating line of *The Hill* near the centre of Creag Dhubh's Great Wall. The gneiss crags at Duntelchaig saw a number of routes added throughout the sixties mainly by RAF Mountain Rescue Team members including aided ascents of some impressive lines on the overhanging Dracula Buttress. In the autumn of 1969 Bob Brown made the first free ascent of *Dracula*, at a solid E3 5c as hard as anything on any other Scottish outcrop at the time.

In the early seventies George Shields, resident in nearby Aviemore, added a number of good hard routes to Creag Dhubh with *Niagara* and *Mythical Wall*. Also around this time, Shields made the second ascent of Spence's testpiece *The Hill* at the same time as Ian Nicolson soloed the adjacent *Inbred*. Shields also made free ascents of both of *The Minge* and *Jump So High*, also adding a better *Direct Finish* to the latter with a point of aid. Robin Barley visited, adding the bold *Outspan* up the left side of the Great Wall.

The early to mid-seventies were very much a low point in Scottish climbing, following on from the great advances made in the two previous decades. Tom Patey and Ian Clough, two of the most prolific pioneers, died in 1970 and Haston was pursuing bigger things

abroad. Balnacoul Castle Crag in Glen Lednock was discovered by Robin Campbell in 1971. Naval personnel from Rosyth comprising Ian Conway, Dick Baker and T. Connelly took over development from 1973–4 with over 10 routes, culminating in *The Great Crack* with a point of aid from Conway. This soon received its free ascent the following year from two recent residents to the area, Ed Grindley and Ian Duckworth, Grindley soon returning to add the adjacent *The Chancers*. Huntly's Cave was developed variously by instructors from Joint Services at Grantown-on-Spey from the early seventies onwards, with Glenmore Lodge instructors, particularly John Cunningham and Bill March, later adding further routes. Later, Pete Boardman added *Pete's Wall*, Pete Livesey *Lime Street* and Martin Lawrence the athletic *Bo-Po Crack*.

In 1976 a new generation of young Edinburgh-based climbers, comprising Dave Cuthbertson, Murray Hamilton, Alan Taylor, Derek Jamieson, Rab Anderson and Mal Duff began exploring the crags of Craig a Barns. Cuthberston's first contribution on the new route front was the appropriately named *The Beginning* on Polney Crag, which he climbed after previously top-roping. On the altogether more impressive Upper Cave Crag, Jamieson added the first new route with *Tumbleweed*, so named because he fell from the top of the crag clutching a clump of heather prior to success. Hamilton freed *Squirm Direct, Squirm, Hang Out* and *Corpse*, culminating in an almost free ascent of the central crack and roof of *Rat Race,* resorting to one lonely peg on the final exposed roof. This was probably the most important free ascent in Scotland at the time. The route received its completely free ascent two years later from visiting American Mike Graham. Cuthbertson freed the bold open groove of *Rat-catcher.* Some of this group also showed an interest in Creag Dhubh, where Cuthbertson added the bold and rarely repeated *Run Free*, the steady though virtually unprotected *Ticket to Ride* and the popular *Strapadicktaemi*.

Things got off to an early start the following year when Cuthbertson and Hamilton produced the short brutal *Marjorie Razor Blade* at Cave Crag in February. On Lower Cave Crag, Hamilton freed the short hanging finger crack of *The Civer* to give the hardest route on the Dunkeld crags. Much of the main activity throughout the summer concentrated on the mountains, predominantly in Glen Coe, with major free ascents also on Ben Nevis and Creag an Dubh Loch. In the autumn, up on the Barrier Wall of Creag Dhubh, Hamilton freed *Muph Dive* while on the same day Cuthbertson added the excellent quartzy crack *Ruff Licks* in the centre of the wall.

In Glen Lednock Hamilton completed the fine trilogy of extremes on Balnacoul Castle Crag early in 1978 with *No Place for a Wendy*. At Cave Crag Cuthbertson freed (on-sight) the last remaining aid point on the roof of Coffin Crack to produce the short though athletic *High Performance*. In the centre of the crag Derek Jamieson pieced together the surprisingly delicate *Warfarin*. Cuthbertson rounded off that year's activities with *Case Dismissed* on Creag Dhubh's Barrier Wall. Completed on the second day's attempt and after abseil inspection it marked the start of a new era.

With few exceptions the majority of the harder additions from 1979 onwards adopted the practise of prior cleaning and inspection on abseil. That year a group of Stirling based climbers, Ian Duckworth, Neil Morrison, Rod Stewart and Bob Duncan added a dozen routes to the short granite crag of Creag na h-Iolaire, on the other side of Glen Lednock from Balnacoul Castle Crag. Amongst the best were *Black September* from Morrison, while the following year Duckworth and Morrison bouldered out *Disco Dancer* and *Disco Duck* respectively. Across the glen, Cuthbertson added the short arête *Gabrielle*. At Creag Dhubh he produced the boldest route on the crag yet with *The Fuhrer* up the left side of the Great Wall. The following weekend he went on to add what retrospectively became accepted as the first E5 in Scotland with the hanging arête of *Morbidezza*. Later on in the autumn the free ascent of the adjacent central groove of *Mousetrap* raised the technical standard to 6b for the first time on the crag. Pete Hunter, another Edinburgh climber, first top-roped then led with a peg runner the bold *Gotterdemmerung*. Cuthbertson soon removed the peg on the second ascent. The final notable addition that year was the adjacent very fine *Voie de*

L'Amie, again from Cuthbertson.

The early eighties saw the final phase of Cuthbertson's prolific development on both Creag Dhubh and Craig a Barns. At Cave Crag *Lady Charlotte* gave sustained wall climbing, the first of a clutch of E5s he climbed that spring. The same wall was soon crossed by the excellent *Pied Piper*. At Creag Dhubh the wandering *Instant Lemon* on Sprawl Wall from Jamieson soon received its *Direct* the following day. On the Great Wall a direct line through *The Hill* became *Over the Hill*. The following year, with a new guide in the offing, Cuthbertson produced almost 20 routes including a clutch of short hard routes on the Barrier Wall including *Galaxy* and *Ayatollah*. Waterfall Wall also saw a number of spectacular additions culminating in the finely situated *Acapulco*. One of the few remaining gaps on Cave Crag gave the hardest route yet – *In Loving Memory*. Although cleaned and inspected the peg was strangely placed on the lead. The following year (1982) Cuthbertson freed the last aid route on the crag, slipping wires over the old bolt heads to protect the bolt ladder of *Fall Out*.

In 1980 Allen Fyffe, Keith Geddes and Ado Liddell visited Dirc Mhor, adding *Working Class Hero* to the impressive Sentinel Rock. With Martin Burrows Smith, Fyffe returned the following year to produce *Positive Earth*. With so much potential remaining at the time it is hard to understand the cliff's subsequent neglect by this active group. Nearby, on Binnein Shuas, the first modern routes started to appear throughout the eighties. The plum crack-line of *Delayed Attack* fell to Geoff Goddard, beating a couple of other interested parties. The capping roofs on The Fortress gave a couple of bold on-sight routes to Mark Charlton with *Storming the Bastille* and *Ardanfreaky*. A few years later Kev Howett added the hard *The Wallachian Prince*, utilising the start of *Delayed Attack* to breach the wall to its left.

Clive Rowland and friends developed the fine isolated crags at Conagleann, adding a range of mainly easier routes on good rock including the fine VSs *The Raven* and *Toads Arête* along with the superb *Black Slab* on rock as good as anything on Cairngorm granite. On an evening visit to Creag na h-Iolaire in Glen Lednock in 1981, Kenny

Spence and John 'Spider' McKenzie produced the best routes on the crag with *Diamond Cutter* and *No Cruise*. Moving on almost a decade the next new addition came in 1992 when Kev Howett squeezed in *Sidewinder*. Across the glen the same year Rick Campbell added *Central Groove* at a surprising grade of E2 5c together with the fine flying arête of *Pole-axed*. More recently Gordon Lennox and Craig Adam have developed a couple of short steep buttresses higher up the hillside. On Hanging Buttress they climbed the finger crack of *Pump up the Jam* with a nut for aid, soon freed by Lawrence Hughes, renaming it *Hormone Warrior*. Lennox also climbed *Pump up the Groove* on-sight with numerous rest points, later cleaned up by Alastair Robertson at E5. Further up the Glen, Hughes and Howett developed Hideaway Buttress where Hughes put up *International Colouring in Contest* and Howett *Hide and Sneak*.

Finally here, Howett climbed the thin hanging crack on Ballindalloch Crag to give *Solutions to a Small Problem*. At Duntelchaig Duncan McCallum freed *Cyclops* in 1983. Much later (1991) Chris Forrest went on to add the hardest pitch on the crag with his *Wolfman*. Through the mid to late eighties, many of the remaining obvious harder gaps on Creag Dhubh were climbed with Gary Latter adding *Heather Wall* and the girdle of the Barrier Wall *Nobodies Fault But Mine*. Cuthbertson forced a more serious variation on his own *The Fuhrer*, dubbed *Colder than a Hooker's Heart*. Around this time Graeme Livingston made impressive on-sight solo ascents of many of the harder routes, including *The Fuhrer* and *Over the Hill*, going on to add a couple of pitches of his own with the technical *Apathizer* and the airy *Bratach Uaine*. A visiting Steve Monks stepped in to plug the glaringly obvious gap up the centre of The Great Wall with *The Final Solution*, beating Grant Farquhar to the line by a matter of days. Farquhar soon went on to produce the two most serious pitches on the crag with *Harder than Your Husband* and the short though nasty *Snotrag*, the first E6 on the crags. Lines either side of Heather Wall gave Paul Thorburn *This One* and Chris Forrest *Cross-Leaved Heath*.

The direction of Scottish climbing took a major turn in 1986 with the arrival of the first tentative placing of bolts.

Duncan McCallum climbed the strange diagonal crack up the centre of Cave Crag, which became *Rattle Yer Dags*, employing a bolt and peg for protection. Starting and finishing in the middle of nowhere this was rapidly superseded by Cuthbertson's ascent of the centre of the wall *Marlene (Original)* with the addition of another couple of bolts. Hamilton soon re-aligned the route, following a more obvious line of holds further left, which has now become the standard route everyone refers to as *Marlene*. Over the years more bolts have been added to make these routes complete sport routes. Hamilton then bolted and re-climbed *Fall Out Direct* adding a new start and finish. The following spring Graeme Livingston added an additional bolt, stringing both of Hamilton's pitches together to produce *The Silk Purse* (out of a pig's ear!). Also around this time bolts were added to other short pieces of rock on the crag. These were all subsequently removed and the central shield of rock is now considered by the majority as the only acceptable area for sport climbs on the crag. Down on the roadside Myopics Buttress in 1990, Ian Cropley and Duncan McCallum added their respective routes *The Vibes* and *Granola Head* based around an old aid route. More recently Neil Shepherd climbed the athletic roof of *The Chopping Block*. On Cave Crag Grant Farquhar stepped in and placed a couple of pegs to protect *Post Mortem*, beating another interested party who was intent on bolting the line. In 1992 the final remaining independent sport line on the crag gave McCallum, Rab Anderson and Johnny May *Hamish Teddy's Excellent Adventure*.

The early nineties saw the development of a number of contrasting crags in Glen Ogle, firstly with the biggest crag, Creag nan Cuileann. Here Kev Howett, Graham Little and Tom Prentice produced a handful of good steep extremes including *The Harder they Come* from Prentice and *Poison Ivy* and *Mind Bogle* from Howett. The following year Rick Campbell and Rab Anderson both led the powerful then bold thin roof crack *The Bigger they Fall*. The crags on the other (dark) side of the glen saw their first routes added that year with Campbell producing *Sugar and Spice*, the only traditional 'gear' route on this side of the glen. First to look at The Diamond with a sport climbing outlook was Paul Thorburn, who bolted two obviously hard-looking lines up the finest central section. Soon Rab Anderson, Neil Shepherd and George Ridge produced many sport routes. Anderson produced the fine *Children of the Revolution* and *Chain Lightning*, while Shepherd went on to add the longest sport route on the crags with *Scaramanga*. Thorburn eventually succeeded on his line *Off the Beaten Track*, whilst Duncan McCallum completed the adjoining *Spiral Tribe*. A young Iain Pitcairn later added *Digital Quartz* to complete a testing trilogy. Anderson, Shepherd and Ridge went on to develop many other shorter crags on both sides of the Glen. On the east (sunnyside) they accounted for over thirty routes mainly in the F6a – 7a range, on generally easier angled and better rock than the dark side.

In 1994 Rick Campbell knocked off the left arête of the steep retaining right wall of The Fortress with the pointedly named *Turning a Blind Eye*, though only after pre-placing a RP #0 on the bold top section. The following year Campbell returned and climbed the wide right-most of a trio of steep cracks above The Garden to give the thrutchy *Bog Myrtle Trip*. Later that month Neil Craig and Gary Latter completed the steep central crack to give *Wild Mountain Thyme*.

Around the same period Paul Thorburn discovered one of the most impressive pieces of schist in the country – Creag Mac Ranaich, high in the hills above Glen Ogle. With Campbell the pair added a fine collection of hard extremes culminating in the three-pitch crack-line *Toiler on the Sea*. The main as yet unclimbed feature is a stunning 30m wall overhanging by about 30 degrees. Further north, Kev Howett, Graham Little and a number of others developed the strangely neglected Dirc Mhor. In particular their trilogy of E5s *Fanfare for the Common Man*, *The Scent of a Woman* and *The Man with the Child in his Eyes* (on the barrel shaped Sentinel Rock) stand out as one of the best pieces of rock within the central highlands.

A significant find in 1997 was Weem Hill Crags with George Ridge, Neil Shepherd, Colin Miln and others producing around 50 routes, the majority of them bolted. Of more than 40 sport climbs, the largest buttress, Weem Rock in the centre gives the best selection of routes. Ridge added the excellent *The Screaming Weem*, Shepherd contributed the neighbouring *High Pitched Scream*, and Miln the short technical *The End of Silence*. On the slabbier front face Janet Horrocks and Isla Watson added the very fine long technical slabs of *The Long Good Friday* and *Confession of Faith*. Rab Anderson later added many further routes including a number of good easier lines. Aerial Buttress later received its hardest and best route with the superb *Saving up for a Rainy Day* from Gary Latter. Not all the activity was in the upper grades however and Mel Nicoll's *Looking for a Rainbow* and Bill Wright's *Back to Basics* are worthy finds.

Creag Dhubh received its hardest route late in 1997 with Dave Cuthbertson's bold and technical eliminate *Yes! Yes!* up the centre of Sprawl Wall. The obvious crack just to the right later gave Latter *The Meejies*. On Binnein Shuas, Paul Thorburn completed the hardest traditional route in the area with the bold and technical *Greatness and Perfection* breaching the impressive central roof of The Fortress. Another fine sport crag, The Camel, was bolted in the late nineties by Neil Shepherd and George Ridge. Shepherd completed the crag classic *Stone of Destiny* in 1999 to give one of the best routes of its grade in the country, later adding further good big pitches including *The Final Straw* and the superb *Paralysis by Analysis*. In 2007, Dave Redpath completed the testpiece *Ubuntu*. In Glen Ogle, Mark Garthwaite nipped in to climb the striking arête of *Arms Limitation* on the Concave Wall. Dave MacLeod completed a trilogy of hard longstanding projects here, first with *Cease Fire* on The Diamond. On Bond Buttress he added *Solitaire*, Dave Redpath completing the adjacent *Boldfinger*. In 2004 MacLeod completed the hardest pitch on the crags with his *Snipe Shadow* on Concave Wall. Just west of Comrie, Scott Muir developed the small tranquil sport crag of Dunira with 10 short routes including some worthwhile easier routes including the fine *Tullybannocher Tearoom*.

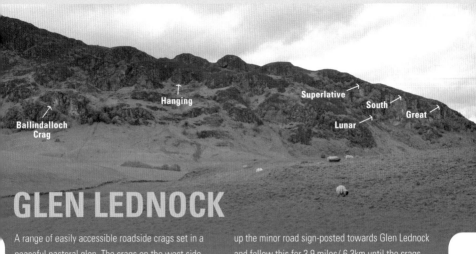

GLEN LEDNOCK

A range of easily accessible roadside crags set in a peaceful pastoral glen. The crags on the west side of the glen are schist whilst those opposite, though shorter, are composed of fine quality granite and dry much quicker. A number of short overhanging schist buttresses have been developed more recently, some of which stay dry during showers.

Access: The town of Comrie lies on the main A85 Perth – Lochearnhead road, 7 miles/11km west of Crieff. From a prominent right-angled bend at the west end of the town next to Deil's Cauldron restaurant, turn up the minor road sign-posted towards Glen Lednock and follow this for 3.9 miles/ 6.3km until the crags come into view. For **Ballindalloch Crag** and **Hanging Buttress** park at a passing place on the left, 100m before the turn-off leading down left to Ballindalloch Farm (3.4 miles/5.4km from Comrie). For **Creag na h-Iolaire**, park 0.6 miles/1km further on just before a cattle grid. For the remaining (northerly) buttresses on Balnacoul Castle continue for just over 1 mile/1.6km to a road leading down left to a bridge across the river. Park on the right just beyond the bridge.

BALNACOUL CASTLE CRAGS

Balnacoul Castle is the rocky hillside on the west side of the glen with a crescent-shaped band of crags extending across the hillside.

BALLINDALLOCH CRAG   15min

NN 736 265 **Alt:** 300m

The lowest and most southerly outcrop on the hillside above and right of Ballindalloch farm.

Approach: Park 100m before the turn-off leading down left to Ballindalloch Farm. Follow the track through the farm to a bridge over the River Lednock then head diagonally rightwards up the hillside to the crag.

1 **Mighty Mouse** ** 15m E6 6b

FA Gordon Lennox (headpointed) 4 June 1988

Climb the left arête of the crag.

2 **Solutions to a Small Problem** ** 18m E5 6b

FA Kev Howett & Lawrence Hughes 20 July 1997

Superb climbing up the thin hanging crack on the left side of the crag. Move up under the initial guarding roof. Cross the roof using a prominent jug and follow a slight groove to an overlap. Pull right into the base of the crack and follow it with difficulty to the top. Block belay above.

3 Hong Kong Phuey **   25m E6 6b

FA Gordon Lennox (headpointed) 22 May 2004

A direct line up the clean wall right of 2. Place a side runner at the first bulge on the route on the right. Start at a jug in the centre of the wall and climb up to the sloping ledge in the middle of the wall – bold and committing. Continue with interest to a good jug and better protection. Move up to the overlap and pull straight over on jugs.

NN 735 267
Alt: 360m

HANGING BUTTRESS   E   20min

A small overhanging buttress protruding from the centre of a large grassy bay in the centre of the band of crags on the hillside.

Descent: Down the gully bounding the crag's left side.

> The wall 3m left of 2 is 1 *Huckleberry Thin* * E4 5c. Sustained and quite bold.

2 Pump up the Groove **   20m E5 6a

FA Gordon Lennox & Craig Adam (several rest points)
4 June 1996: FFA Alastair Robertson 10 May 1998

The pocketed wall in the centre of the crag. Start just left of the boulder. Follow pockets to a small quartz niche. Exit direct from the apex of this then step up right to a shattered crack-line which leads strenuously to easy ground. Finish up an easy left-slanting groove.

> The short diagonal crack on the right is 3 *Hormone Warrior* * E4 6a.

📷 *Hormone Warrior, Rick Campbell climbing.*

RIGHT (NORTHERN) BUTTRESSES

The remaining crags on the hillside are described from right to left as encountered on the approach.

THE GREAT BUTTRESS

NN 735 270 **Alt:** 300m **E** **15min

The biggest of all the crags in the glen with a good selection of extremes.

Approach: Cross the fence and head south across the field to cross a small stream just beyond, then head slightly rightward up the hill and over the blunt ridge to traverse left to the base.

Line of flakes and obvious groove, starting as for 2 is
1 *Piggies Paradise* ★ E2 5b.

2 No Place for a Wendy ★★★ 45m E2 5b

FA Murray Hamilton 8 April 1978

Good climbing up the grooves in the right arête of the buttress. Scramble up right to belay on a slab beneath the prominent groove. Climb the initial dirty groove and step left into the main groove which is followed to the top.

3 Wendy's Day Out ★ E4 6a

FA Guy Muhlemann & Simon Richardson (1 PA) 20 July 1985; FFA Paul Thorburn & Rick Campbell July 1992

Sustained strenuous climbing up the hanging groove between 2 and 4. Start below a short crack just left of 2.

1 **20m 5a** Climb the crack for 3m then make a difficult move left to reach a sloping ledge. Traverse a metre further left then up the corner crack to the PB of 4.

2 **25m 6a** Up the impending wall behind the stance and over a small overhang to make a difficult exit into the smooth slab above. Up the overhanging groove on the left to reach 2 below its final crux and up this more easily to finish.

4 The Great Crack ★ 45m E2 5c

FA Ian Conway & party (1 PA) 15 May 1974;
FFA Ed Grindley & Ian Duckworth 1975

Good climbing up the prominent wide crack.

1 **20m 5b** Ascend the corner and crack through the overhang, continuing until moves up and right lead to a PB.

2 **25m 5c** Climb the wide crack above.

5 The Chancers ★   45m E2 5c

FA Ed Grindley & E.Brookes June 1975

The overhanging corners and grooves just left of 4.

1 **30m 5c** Climb corner until level with a gangway on the left. Swing up right to the foot of a steep, thin corner crack and up this to a large ledge and PB.

2 **15m 5c** Climb the open corner above to the top of the prow and finish directly by a steep crack.

6 Pole-axed ★★   15m E4 6a

FA Rick Campbell & Ian Taylor July 1993

Just up and left of Great Buttress is a prominent small buttress with a short isolated hanging arête. The base is easiest to approach by abseiling down the line of the route. Start up a short groove on the left then move right and up the arête strenuously.

NN 735 270 **Alt:** 300m   **E**

The following two routes are approached by scrambling up leftward to a bay with trees.

1 Central Groove ★★   30m E2 5c

FA Rick Campbell July 1992

Start directly below the prominent pink central groove. Up a small corner to a ledge, step left and up grooves to a larger ledge below the main groove. Up this past 2 PRs.

SOUTH BUTTRESS

Larger but more broken buttress 50m left of **Great Buttress**.

Descent: Walk right (north) to the top of **Great Buttress** and down its right (north) side or abseil from birch trees down the line of *Central Groove*.

2 Gabrielle ★   30m E4 6a

FA Dave Cuthbertson 11 June 1979

The short blunt right arête of 1. Follow 1 to the second ledge. Regain the groove on the right and climb up to a thin diagonal crack. Continue up the left side of the arête, stepping right at the top.

Carcase Wall *   75m VS 4b

FA Robin Campbell, J.Monan & Peter Murray-Rust June 1974

The longest route on the crags with a fine exposed final pitch. Start at the left edge of the buttress in an open groove 10m below a large rowan.

1 **25m 4a** Climb the crack to the first of two small trees. Step left and up the wider crack to a ledge next to the large rowan. Head up rightward and negotiate the large sloping rush ledge to reach a tree belay.

2 **30m 4b** Move up to a mossy streak in the centre of the wall and make steep moves up to a good flake crack. Up this to ledges then traverse right to P and nut belay beneath some overhangs.

3 **20m 4b** Step down and traverse right on a grassy ledge round the corner. Climb up on good holds then follow the slabby ramp rightward on undercuts to finish up a short corner crack. Tree belay.

LUNAR BUTTRESS

NN 735 269 **Alt:** 340m

A large bay left of **South Buttress** extends steeply up the hillside, leading to the base.

Descent: Walk left (south) and down below the base of **Superlative Buttress**.

1 The Grafter *   20m VS 4c

FA Dick Baker & Ian Conway 31 March 1974

Steep well protected climbing up the wall and corner crack at the bottom left end of the crag. Up broken rock to a ledge at the base of the corner. Up the thin corner crack then traverse left then back right to the foot of another corner. Finish up this exiting up a crack past an old tree stump.

Thin crack 1m right of chimney is 2 *Sunburst* * E1 5b.

3 Moonbeam **   35m VS 4c

FA Ian & T.Conway 10 October 1973

Good steep well protected climbing. Start beneath an overhang under the steep frontal face of the buttress. Up a short steep wall to a ledge. Move right and up the overhanging wall to a ledge below a groove. Up the groove to a small overhang, turn this awkwardly on the left and finish direct.

4 Moonshadow *   40m E1 5b

FA Ian Conway & Dick Baker (3 PA) 31 March 1974

The wall right of 3 gives a sustained strenuous pitch. Start as for 3 to the ledge. Move right and up the overhanging wall then traverse right 5m to the base of a groove on the wall overlooking a steep chimney. Ascend the groove to an overhang. Move left round this and traverse left round the large roof.

SUPERLATIVE BUTTRESS

NN 735 269 **Alt:** 340m

50m left of **South Buttress** is a sheep track up a shallow open gully, with a small rock step near the base.

Descent: Down the right (north) side.

1 Humdinger **   25m HVS 5a

FA Ian Conway & Dick Baker 3 April 1974

Exposed and spectacular. Start beneath an overhanging arête at the left end of the crag. Up a short wall split by a crack then up the groove to a ledge. Traverse left across the overhanging wall to the arête (PR), follow this to the top.

2 Little Brahma *   25m VS 4c

FA Ian Conway & Dick Baker 7 April 1974

Start left of the tree-filled corner. Traverse a grassy ledge left to a short groove. Step left on to a slab then up a wall first left then right to gain the base of the rightward-trending crack. Follow the crack to finish up a niche.

3 Barnstormer *   20m VS 4c

FA Ian Conway & Dick Baker 6 April 1974

Start at a slab below a large roof on the right side of the buttress. Climb the slab beneath the roof, traverse left and up to a sloping ledge below a short corner. Climb the corner, moving left to finish up a slab.

THE LOW WALL
NN 747,272
Alt: 280m

5min

CREAG NA H-IOLAIRE
(EAGLE CRAG)

A good collection of granite crags with a sunnier aspect than the schist crags across the glen.

Access: Park by the side of the road just before a cattle grid 0.4 miles/0.6km beyond the house 'Funtulich'.
Approach: Head directly across the easy angled slopes to the crag.

THE LOW WALL

The short wall low down on the left side of the crags.
Descent: Either walk left 50m from the top of the crag, abseil from trees or scramble down a grassy slanting rake/chimney fault (Diff) leading to the base of 4.

 Deuxieme   **10m MVS 4b**

FA Ian Duckworth (solo) 1979

The corner on the upper left side of the buttress. Start up a rib then step right and climb the corner past some saplings.

2 Premiere ★   **15m VS 5a**

FA Neil Morrison, Rod Stewart & B.Hogg 6 May 1979

The corner at the left end of the buttress. Climb this until it is possible to traverse right to a finely situated finger crack on the front of the buttress. Finish up this.

3 Junior's Jinx ★   **15m E1 5b**

FA Ian Duckworth & Neil Morrison 25 May 1979

Gain the final finger crack of 2 by climbing direct up the left edge of the buttress.

4 Strategies for Survival ★   **15m E1 5b**

FA Ian Duckworth, Bob Duncan & Neil Morrison 23 Sept 1979

The right edge of the leftmost buttress. Start up the grassy descent rake to pull out left onto the arête. Finish up this or the finger crack further left.

> *Oddball*, Very Difficult, takes a series of corners and ledges leading to the top end of the rake.

5 Get a Grip ★   **12m E1 5c**

FA Neil Morrison 19 September 1979

The slim groove in the rib left of 6. Climb the lower wall and groove, with the crux reaching a good layback flange near the top.

6 The Strangler ★   **12m E1 5c**

FA Ian Duckworth & Neil Morrison 25 May 1979

The recessed corner. Bridge up the corner, pull through a tricky bulge to finish up the easy upper groove.

Sultans of Swing ★   12m HVS 5a

FA Rod Stewart, B.Hogg & Neil Morrison 6 May 1979

The prominent right-slanting diagonal crack leads to a slight niche. Finish slightly rightward up the wall above.

8 Cranium Wall Direct   10m E2 5c

FA Gordon Lennox & Craig Adam July 1994

The centre of the wall, climbing through the L-shaped niche past a PR and finishing slightly rightward.

9 Cranium Wall ★   10m HVS 5a

FA Ian Duckworth & Chris Calow 1980

Start at the right end of the steep orange wall. Direct up to an overhang on the right, move right to a good jug and finish direct just left of the tree.

CENTRAL WALL

Some 50m up rightwards from the right edge of **The Low Wall**. All the routes belay well back from the top.
Descent: Abseil from trees down either end of the crag or traverse steep grass leftward for 100m then cut down to follow a vague path skirting back down to the base.

10 Black September ★★   20m E3 6a

FA Neil Morrison 29 May 1979

Excellent sustained well protected climbing. Start at the highest point of the wall. Climb to a good hold at 4m

then span left to a good incut. Move left again then direct to a ledge. Climb the wall just left of the initial thin crack to a reasonable flake. Step right and finish up the fingertip crack.

11 Jessicated ★   20m E1 5c

FA Ian Duckworth & Neil Morrison 10 June 1980

Start beneath twin diagonal cracks just left of the shallow corner of 12. Climb the cracks to the ledge then pull through the bulge near its right end. Climb the wall to finish up a shallow corner.

12 Tigger ★   25m HVS 5a

FA Neil Morrison & B.Hogg 6 May 1979

A wandering natural line. Start below the corner in the centre of the wall. Up this to the ledge at half-height. Traverse down left on the ledge to gain a slab on the left side. Follow this delicately up and left to finish up a slim corner.

13 Disco Dancer ★   20m E2 6a

FA Ian Duckworth May 1980

A bouldery start leads to fine climbing up the left edge of the wall. Start 2m right of the shallow corner. Hard initial moves lead (sometimes) to better holds and a horizontal break. Move right along this then break leftward through the overlap and climb the left side of the upper wall on good diagonal slots. Move diagonally left through a break in the overhangs to finish up 11.

The Disco Duck *   20m E2 6a

FA Neil Morrison 2 October 1980

A good slightly easier companion to 13. Start directly beneath a small vertical slot 4m up. Boulder past the slot then make a hard move left to a junction with 13. Pull through the overlap then shimmy up the diagonal crack and up on good holds to gain the grass ledge. Finish easily up a slim corner crack.

HIGH WALL

A further 60m diagonally up the hillside from the **Central Wall** is an acutely overhanging wall lying above an easy-angled ramp.

Descent: A 25m abseil from trees (belays also) at the top of the crag.

 Diamond Cutter ****   30m E3 6a

FA Kenny Spence & Spider Mackenzie June 1981

Brilliant well protected climbing up the flake crack and hanging corner at the left side of the wall. The best pitch in the glen. Start a short way up from the base of the wall. Up diagonally left to the diagonal crack of 16 and

up this to a ledge. Move up to the flake crack splitting the bulge on the left and up this to an easing below the corner. Finish spectacularly up this (crux) mainly by its right arête in a superb position.

16 No Cruise **   30m E4 5c

FA Spider Mackenzie & Kenny Spence June 1981

The wide diagonal crack gives a sustained and strenuous pitch. Take some large Fs or hexes. Start as for 15 to gain the crack and follow this to a bulging V-groove just short of the top. Pull out rightward round the bulge then up and right.

17 Sidewinder *   25m E4 6a

FA Kev Howett & Dave Douglas 18 June 1992

A strenuous pitch up the centre of the crag. Start 7m further up the large ramp from the other routes. Move left onto the top of a large protruding block. Step left into the crack of 16 and up this to beneath a prominent fin. Climb direct using holds on either side of this then continue up the right slanting groove to a rest near the top. Swing out left on a sharp protruding hold to finish up a short jam crack.

Harry McCaffery starting up the wandering Tigger, Central Wall.

THE HIDEAWAY CRAG

🆂 🧗 20min

NN 723 287 **Alt:** 370m

A small schist crag on the hillside a few hundred metres left of and level with the dam at the head of the glen. The main feature is a very overhanging lower right wall.

Access: Continue up the road for just over a mile past **Creag na h-Iolaire**, through a gate past farmhouses taking left branch of road (marked 'Private, locked gate') to park just beyond the bridge over the River Lednock.

Approach: Follow the track past the locked gate then steeply up the hillside on the right.

Descent: Down steep grass at either side.

---

1 Goldie ★ 20m E2 5c

FA Lawrence Hughes & Kev Howett 28 April 1996

Lies on the small buttress to the left. Start just left of a large aspen, below the scrappier buttress further left. Up a bulging wall into a hanging groove which leads rightward into the vegetated fault forming the left side of the slim buttress. Cross this and traverse out right across the lip to pull onto the slab above. Finish more easily.

2 International Colouring in Contest ★ 20m E4 6a

FA Lawrence Hughes & Kev Howett 18 July 1996

Start below a hanging flake at the left side of the main buttress. Climb up to the flake and wildly gain good holds above it. Swing onto the wall above and climb the cracked slab to the bulging headwall. Exit left.

3 Hide and Sneak ★★ 20m E5 6a

FA Kev Howett 18 July 1996

Good climbing up the left-slanting weakness through the centre of the wall. Follow the fault diagonally left to gain a large protruding hold at the lip. Pull into a groove above on the left and up this to the left side of the upper roof. Pull up and right into a hanging niche above the roof. Move left onto a large flake and leave this to finish round rightward of a huge block at the top.

4 Suffer in Silence ★★ 20m E5 6a

FA Rick Campbell & Neil Craig August 2000

Start in the recess right of 3 beneath a large roof. From a standing position on the shelf to the left make committing moves up under the roof. Move left under the roof with surprising ease to a crux move right into a groove above. Continue up to finish directly through the large roof above.

5 Stiff Upper Lip ★ 20m E4 6a

FA Rick Campbell & Alastair Robertson (ground up) August 2000

Climbs through the curious 'lip' right of the roof of 4. Start in the recess under roof and move right up a ramp until it is possible to pull up and span left onto the undercut 'lip'. Move up with difficulty to ledge above and continue straight up to easy ground.

 *Strath Earn Shangri-La, Karen Latter climbing.*

DUNIRA CRAG

NN 742 248 **Alt:** 350m 🆂 🧗 40min

A small secluded schist crag in a tranquil open location high on the hill of Creag Liath just west of Comrie with a grand outlook over Strath Earn.

Access: Follow the A85 west of Comrie for 2.4 miles/3.8km to turn off right (north) up a tarmaced single track road signposted 'Dunira – Private'. This is the next road east of another, signposted 'Private Road Access to Whitehouse only'. From the west continue past St Fillans for 2.1 miles/3.4 km to gain this road, which is 0.3 miles/0.5km beyond another dirt track with a gatehouse on the left (not recommended). Follow the road for 0.3 miles/0.5km then turn right at crossroads and follow the road for 0.5 miles/0.8km to park at an obvious widening on the left beyond the entrance to 'Greystones' and just before a 'No Vehicle Access' sign.

Approach: Continue east along the track taking the left fork past the farm and follow this until it curves back round a large field. Just before the track starts to level out cross a ladder by a large gate on the right to follow a vague path steeply up the right bank of the stream to the end of the tree line. Cross the stream and negotiate the boulder field leftwards up to the base of the crag.

---

1 **Strath Earn Shangri-La** ★   **14m F4+**

FA Scott Muir 2004

The right edge.

2 **Tullybannocher Tearoom** ★★   **14m F5**

FA Scott Muir 2004

The left-slanting groove, breaching the roofs near the top on huge holds.

③ Dun Moanin' 13m F6b

FA Scott Muir 2004

The short wide crack then the centre of the pillar on the right. Pull rightward through the final roof on good holds to the LO of 1.

④ Dunira or Die ★ 13m F7a

FA Scott Muir 2005

The right edge of the wall on good holds then easily to the roof. Pull up and left then back right with difficulty.

⑤ The Fort Dundurn Gurner ★ 13m F6c+

FA Scott Muir 2004

Head for the mid-height undercut flake then through the roof with interest.

⑥ Glen Bolt'achan Big Guns ★★ 13m F6c

FA Scott Muir 2004

Fingery climbing direct up the wall.

⑦ George's Bush ★ 13m F6a

FA Scott Muir 2004

The fine flake-crack leading up left into the wide fault climbed on some great holds.

⑧ Twenty Shilling Woodworm ★ 13m F6a

FA Scott Muir 2004

The fault of 7 gained from the start of the next two routes.

⑨ Whitewash 10m F6b

FA Scott Muir 2004

Eliminate gaining the break of 10.

⑩ The Whitehouse 10m F6a+

FA Scott Muir 2004

Make a tricky move to gain the top of the flake. Traverse left along a handrail then gain and follow the right-slanting break.

GLEN OGLE (HIGH GLEN)

Glen Ogle is the open 5 mile/8km long glen running south-east to north-west from the A84/A85 junction at Lochearnhead to the A85/A827 junction at Lix Toll, some 2 miles/3km south-west of Killin, close to the west end of Loch Tay. It is a strong contender for the least aesthetic glen in the entire Highlands, with a steady procession of trucks and caravans trundling up the road. A number of small schist crags situated on both sides of the glen provide a wide range of short bolted routes of all grades from F5+ upwards, together with a handful of traditionally-protected routes on Creag nan Cuilean. The rock on the east tends to be easier angled, and better and more importantly, receives the sun.

Nesting restrictions: From March – July peregrine falcons and buzzards nest on some of the crags. If present, move to another crag well away from the nesting site.

Access: Travelling from the south via Lochearnhead the majority of the crags are approached from a small rough parking spot on the west side of the A85 road opposite the viaduct 2.2miles/3.5km beyond the village. The remaining crags, **Creag nan Cuileann** and **Mirror Wall,** are approached from a smaller lay-by on the east side of the road 0.4 miles/0.6km further.

← Mirror Wall

← Bourneville

→ The Asteroid

← Creag nan Cuileann

MEALL BUIDHE (YELLOW HILL)

The hill near the top of the east side of the glen.

P

NN 578 265 **Alt:** 350m **E** 🏃 20min

THE ASTEROID

The black slab above the lower parking spot is **The Asteroid** (not visible from the road). Five pleasant 10m routes, F5+ and F6a on good rock, though slow to dry. Not well equipped, with single bolt anchors at the top.

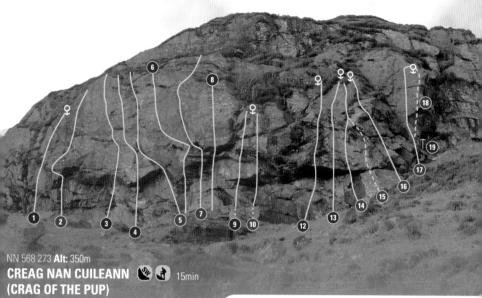

NN 568 273 **Alt:** 350m

CREAG NAN CUILEANN 15min
(CRAG OF THE PUP)

The largest crag high up on the east side of the glen.
Fortunately (or unfortunately, depending on your
viewpoint) the traditionalists got here first.

Approach: From the lay-by at the top of the glen on
the east side of the road head diagonally right up the
hillside to the crag.

Descent: All the trad routes finish on a large grassy
ledge just short of the top. Traverse right along this and
down the right side of the crag.

1 Idiot Wind ★★ 10m F7b

FA Rab Anderson 11 October 1998

The steep little wall at the left end of the crag just right
of a short, roofed chimney. 5B to LO.

2 Merlyns Flight ★ 30m E3 6a

FA Kev Howett 24 August 1992

Climbs the prominent break through the roof at the left
side. Start just right of a short hanging corner formed by
a block under the roof. Exit out left on a horizontal crack
and just before its end climb the crack above onto the
slab. Finish directly up the wall.

3 The Bigger They Fall ★★ 25m E5 6c

FA Rick Campbell & Rab Anderson (both led) 13 June 1992

A powerful well protected start leading to a bold
headwall. Start 5m left of 5. Climb to the bulge and
struggle up the thin crack (awkward to place R #2 at the
start) to its top. Move up left to a small roof (F #0 or #0.5),
pull over and continue to a quartz niche (F #1.5 in pocket
below) then wobble up the pocketed headwall to the top.

4 The Harder They Come ★ 30m E4 5c

FA Tom Prentice & Kev Howett 3 August 1991

Climb a short crack immediately left of the central fault
to join the fault at a holly. Pass the tree then traverse a
ledge left into the centre of the wall and climb a very thin
crack with difficulty to a deep horizontal slot on the left.
Continue direct, exiting out left.

5 Pruner's Groove ★ 30m E2 5c

FA Graham Little, Tom Prentice & Kev Howett 1991

The central fault. Climb up leftward to the right end of
the roof. Cross this on good holds, foot traverse a good
break left to the groove and finish up this.

6 Mind Bogle *   30m E5 6a

FA Kev Howett 3 August 1991

The roof and quartzy scoop right of the central line of 5. Quite serious. Start under the stepped roof right of 5. Up the initial wall to beneath the roofs. Pull out left through the arête of the lower roof to gain the base of a prominent white break that leads left. Up to join 7 at the crack. Step hard left into the break and follow it with difficulty to pull onto the wall just right of 5. Continue direct about 3m right of 5 through the bulges near the top. Friends essential.

7 Poison Ivy **   30m E3 5c

FA Kev Howett & Tom Prentice 11 May 1991

The prominent crack-line splitting the wall on the right. Start below the roofs below the crack just right of 6. Up into the roofs and out left to the base of the crack. Climb it to a small shelf near the top, exiting out right onto grass ledge.

> The following nine sport routes are all located at the right side of the main wall. The first three routes all start from a boulder at the base, directly beneath the centre of the aspens at 10m. Roof and wall is 8 *Fight or Flight* F7a+; roof and bulge immediately right of the blocky groove 9 *Slaphead* F7a.

10 Fat Chance *   10m F6c

FA George Ridge 24 September 1998

The short thin crack in the bulge just right of the blocky groove.

11 Fight the Flab *   10m F6c+

FA Rab Anderson 24 September 1998

The roof left of 12 then the short blunt slabby nose. Approach from the right as for 12. **Take great care** with the block under the line – do not stand on the left/lower block.

12 Let it All Hang Out *   10m F6c+

FA Rab Anderson 30 August 1998

Thug through the roof close to its widest point then the slab above to a LO in the trees.

13 Happy Campus *   10m F6c+

FA Rab Anderson April 1999

Line through roof immediately right of 12.

14 Hang On! **   10m F6c

FA Janet Horrocks 19 September 1998

The small roof just right of 13, finishing up the featured wall and slab above.

15 Step on It   10m F6a

FA George Ridge September 1998

Start right of 14. Climb the wall, moving up left into 14 to finish.

16 Life in the Fat Lane *   12m F6b+

FA Rab & Chris Anderson 29 August 1998

Short steep crack at right side of wall. LO on the heather ledge, beyond the rowan.

> Round the edge and up the slope a little is a short blunt arête.

17 Chasing the Bandwagon *   10m F6a+

FA Colin Miln 3 July 1998

Line up wall left of the arête.

18 Reaching the Limit *   10m F6c

FA Rab Anderson 4 July 1998

Climb on and just left of the arête, sharing the first two bolts and LO of 17.

19 Clutching at Straws *   10m F7a

FA Rab Anderson 20 June 1998

Aptly named. The steep leaning side-wall and arête climbed on its right side.

Set back to the right is a pale clean slab, with a diagonal line of aspens cutting up left from the centre.

① Dazed and Confused   **15m F6a**

FA Janet Horrocks 29 August 1998

The leftmost route on the recessed section, using a tree to gain the mid-height ledge.

② Having a Little Flutter ★★   **12m F6c+**

FA George Ridge 29 August 1998

The wall to the left of the thin crack in the headwall.

③ Ceuse Jimmy ★★   **12m F6c**

FA George Ridge 30 August 1998

The line up to, then following a prominent thin crack in the headwall.

④ Kinmont Times ★   **10m F6a+**

FA George Ridge 30 August 1998

Right to left-slanting crack on a recessed section, finishing on the left edge as for 1. Direct to the LO is 6b+.

⑤ Lichen Virgin ★   **12m F6a+**

FA Janet Horrocks 30 August 1998

The hollow flake, wall and groove bounding the right side of the recessed section.

⑥ Loose Living ★   **12m F6a**

FA George Ridge 1998

The prominent shallow groove and direct continuation.

⑦ Ghost Trail ★★   **12m F6b+**

FA Rab & Chris Anderson 14 June 1998

The pale streak on the right edge of the wall, sharing the same LO as 6.

About 80m right of **Creag nan Cuileann** at the same level as the upper (rightmost) wall lies **Bourneville**, a long 7m high vertical pocketed wall. Twelve routes, mostly F6b except (from left) 1 F6a; 2 F6a+; 6 F6a+ and 7 F6b+.

MIRROR WALL
NN 569 276 **Alt:** 480m ⓢ 🚶 30min

A compact sunny off-vertical wall, which has the unique distinction of harbouring the highest (in Alt) sport routes in the country. A fine peaceful venue with the pleasantest outlook of any of the crags.

Approach: As for **Creag nan Cuileann** then head steeply leftward (rough going on heather) up the hillside to the crag, which is the lowest of a number of small buttresses just left (west) of the stream.

❶ Munrobagger ★   **12m F6b+**

FA George Ridge 23 May 1998

The shallow hanging groove on the left, starting and finishing up the curving crack.

❷ Blind Faith ★   **12m F7b+**

FA David Redpath 1997

The line of red hangers up the wall right of the scoop. Shallow finger pockets allow a shallow scoop to be gained then easier above. Blind climbing.

❸ Take a Hike ★★   **12m F7a**

FA Janet Horrocks 29 May 1998

The left line of staples taking the blank looking wall to a thin crack near the top.

❹ Cony the Calvinist ★   **12m F6c**

FA David Redpath 1997

Climb the broad shield right of 3 on good pockets that are hard to find.

❺ Fat Eagle Flies Low ★★   **12m F6a+**

FA Janet Horrocks 29 May 1998

The right line of staples.

❻ Retribution ★   **12m F6c+**

FA David Redpath 1997

The next line right of 5. More pocket pulling, some of which are slightly painful.

❼ Bad Religion ★   **12m F6c+**

FA David Redpath 1997

A bit contrived, leading into 6 at half-height.

8 *Carry on up the Corbetts* F6a+ is the rightmost line.

THE WEST (DARK) SIDE VIADUCT CRAGS

A good introduction to small, dirty, usually wet and midgy crags ...
sorry, I mean Scottish sport climbing. It can only get better!

Bond Buttress

Concave Wall

The Diamond

SGORRACH NUADH
(NEW PRONGED/PEAKED/CLIFFY)

This is the hill on the west side of the glen with the old dismantled railway and viaduct running parallel to the road, beneath all the crags.

BOND BUTTRESS   30min

NN 567 264 **Alt:** 370m

The biggest crag on the hill, worth the extra hike up there. It sits in a fine elevated position out of the trees (i.e. could be midge free!).

Approach: Head up the open hillside slightly leftward from the viaduct. In summer avoid the bracken by heading west along the top of the viaduct for 200m until just beyond the stream then cut up the hill, bearing rightwards higher up.

 Solitaire ★★★   20m F8a+

FA Dave MacLeod September 2003

The blunt arête. Climb a diagonal flake crack then launch directly up the arête with very sustained fingery climbing to eventually gain a good break. Easier climbing leads to the groove of 2 and the top.

 Scaramanga ★★   20m 7a+

FA Neil Shepherd 10 July 1993

The fine left-trending groove on the right side of the crag. Often wet.

 Boldfinger ★   20m F7a

FA Dave Redpath September 2003

Climb 2 to the ledge beneath the roof. Break out right through the bulges on good holds then using a hold in the groove above, move up rightward past one lonely bolt to a break with a final long reach to the finishing holds. Dirty and not well bolted

10min

NN 568 265 **Alt:** 310m

THE DIAMOND

The left side of the buttress has the best concentration of hard routes on any of the crags.

Approach: Follow a prominent narrow track diagonally down to a small wooden bridge across the stream then steeply up to the viaduct. Cross the fence and follow a path diagonally up rightwards to the crag.

The minuscule route left of the main wall is 1 *Midge Patrol* F6b+. Routes 2 and 3 are projects.

4 Easy Over *   15m F7a

FA Rab Anderson 1993

The black streak above the boulder to a tiny groove onto the shelf. Pull over the roof on large holds, move leftward and finish up slab to LO.

5 Digital Quartz **   15m F8b

FA Iain Pitcairn 1993

Start beneath a prominent quartz boss. The lower wall is the technical crux, the headwall F7b+.

6 Cease Fire **   15m F8a+

FA Dave MacLeod September 2001

From the cave sustained crimping leads to a rest at a quartz hold. Excellent moves on finger pockets (crux) lead to a jug rail and the top.

7 The Link **   15m 7c+

The easiest line up the main face. Follow 6 to the horizontal traverse line then move left and finish up 5.

8 Spiral Tribe **   15m F8a

FA Duncan McCallum 1993

Follow the line of BRs direct from the first BR on 10.

9 Off the Beaten Track ***   15m F8a

FA Paul Thorburn 1993

The right line on the main wall.

10 Children of the Revolution **   20m F7b

FA Rab Anderson 12 July 1992

Start at the right side of the wall. Follow the fault leftward to the large ledge beneath the roof. Pull over the roof on good holds and follow a direct line up the headwall to LO.

11 Chain Lightning *   5m F7b+

FA Rab Anderson 1993

The short hanging groove in the blunt right arête of the main wall, past a shelf at 2/3rds height.

12 One in the Eye for Stickmen *   15m F7a

FA Neil Shepherd 13 June 1993

The cracked grooves 3m right of 11. Start just left of the prominent white streak near the base of the crag.

13 Old Wives' Tail *   15m F6b

FA Neil Shepherd 12 June 1993

Climb *Metal Guru* to the second BR then follow the left-slanting ramp.

14 Metal Guru ★★   15m F6c+

FA Rab Anderson 20 July 1992

The thin crack up the vertical wall right of the main face.

15 is a project

16 Sugar and Spice *   15m E3 6a

FA Rick Campbell & Rab Anderson 4 June 1992

The original line on the crag, before the boltnasties arrived! Start directly beneath the wide slanting crack/ pod type thingy.

17 Gross Indecency   12m F7c

FA Rab Anderson 3 July 1993

The prominent short V-groove at 4m then the wall 2m right of the crack of 16.

18 The Trossachs Trundler   12m F7c

FA Malcolm Smith 1993

The thin V-slot 2.5m right of 17.

19 After the Flood *   12m F6c

FA George Ridge 24 May 1993

The line of resin bolts right of 18.

20 is a project. PR and BRs midway between.

21 Arc of a Diver ★★   12m F6c

FA Rab Anderson 5 June 1993

Left-facing groove through the left end of the lower roof.

22 Climb and Punishment   12m F7b+

FA Rab Anderson 1994

Bouldery start then powerful above ledge.

23 Wristy Business *   8m F6c+

FA Rab Anderson 1993

The groove to a ledge then the steep wall above.

24 Raspberry Beret *   8m F6b+

FA Chris Anderson 4 July 1993

The featured wall starting from the ledge.

25 *Ship Ahoy* F6c is a scruffy wall at the right extremity.

CONCAVE WALL

A very steep crag high up on the right. From The Diamond traverse right past a number of smaller crags for a few hundred metres then directly up the hill from the right edge of the last crag. 10 minutes further.

1 Northern Exposure *   12m F6c+

FA Dave Redpath 3 August 1998

Start up 2 then cop out onto the vertical wall.

2 Arms Limitation ★★★   18m F7b+

FA Mark Garthwaite July 1999

The prominent overhanging arête climbed on its left side.

3 Snipe Shadow ★★   10m F8b

FA Dave MacLeod April 2004

The similarly overhanging wall to the left. A sustained sequence on finger pockets leads to a desperate crux sequence and nice finishing dyno for the top jug. Top end 8b.

4 Embrace My Weakness *   8m F7c+

FA Dave Redpath 8 August 1998

The left micro-route – originally bolted for a warm-up! Up on ledges to get established, move up to the flake then take your pick of the micro finger edges to finish.

CREAG MACRANAICH

 1¼ – 2hr

(MACRAINACH'S CRAG) NN 548 250 **Alt:** 750m

A readily accessible series of crags with a remote mountain feel. The climbing is situated on a number of small buttresses from 20 to 50m high scattered on the east and south side of the hill. The best and largest crags lie under the summit plateau on the east side and so far have produced a number of routes of widely ranging character. Lying west of Glen Ogle access from here or Lochearnhead is simple and relatively short making the location useful for day trips from the central belt. The most impressive buttress, Main Crag, displays not only the awesomely steep prow but also has a very steep, though disjointed sidewall, the home of a classic three pitch E6 crack – there's not many of them in Scotland! The rock is compact mica schist displaying a degree of horizontal banding and is often encrusted with garnets. It is also covered in a hard lichen, necessitating ruthless wire brushing to produce quality climbs.

Access: From the A85 at the head of Glen Ogle (NN 563 276) park on the west side of the road just beyond the forestry plantation (travelling from the south).

Approach: (A) Probably best even though the going is tougher is to approach from the north. From the parking spot at the head of Glen Ogle (NN 563 276) cross the disused railway by a bridge and head up the left side of the plantation. Follow a shallow valley south until you can contour round right (west) to the base of the final steep approach slopes. A number of sheep tracks criss-cross this. A useful variation, and also the best return route if climbing near the summit, is to branch west from the valley to gain the col (NN 551 261) between the two hills. Head south along the plateau to gain the descent south of the Main Crag. Same approach time, though useful in high summer to avoid the long heather. **(B)** Easier going but longer and rather boring is the approach from the south. 300m after crossing the inflow to Loch Earn (south of the village) follow a small road and park just before a farm at NN 582 277. Head through the farm, then along a fence between two fields to gain a track starting from a bridge. Follow this onto the moor and continue until due south of the crag. Head over the bog then diagonally up to the crag.

MAIN CRAG

The most impressive crag, the steep prow can be seen in profile from the A84 south of Lochearnhead, high on the south end of the east face of the hill. Right of the vegetated but impressive central corner lies the awesomely-steep prow, overhanging at 1 in 3 and harbouring the stunning line of *Head On*. The left wall of this sports two hard slab routes and the wall left again is split by a low wide ledge and a discontinuous ledge high up but, more importantly, is cleaved by the striking crack line of *Toiler on the Sea*.

Descent: Down a wide grassy gully some 100m south of the crag.

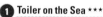

1 **Toiler on the Sea** ★★★ 50m E6 6b

FA Paul Thorburn & Rick Campbell 20 May & 28 June 1995

The striking crack-line in the wall left of the central vegetated corner. The second and third pitches overhang at an angle of 1 in 2. Start 5 metres left of the corner.

1 **12m 6b** Gain the diagonal crack and follow it past some small niches to a difficult finish.

2 **18m 6b** Climb the prominent overhanging crack with a difficult section at 5m to a rest in niche. Gain the belay ledge above with difficulty.

3 **20m 6a/b** Climb the groove above to a spike and rest. The crack and strenuous groove (F #4) lead to good holds. Finish directly through bulges past some hollow rock to a peg and nut belay 15m further back.

② Complicity ★★   35m E5 6a

FA Paul Thorburn 3 August 1996

The centre of the slab, left of 3. Start at the toe of the slab. Climb a small right-facing corner and gain the flake above (PR). Move up and gain the thin crack above and follow it to a sloping ledge. Climb flakes on the left then move back into the centre of the wall. Move up to finish by a short diagonal crack.

③ Sidewinder ★★★   50m E6 6a

FA Rick Campbell August 1994

Serious climbing up the slabbier right wall of the corner. Start round on the right side of the arête, at the left end of the very steep prow at some blocks.

1   **35m 6a** Climb boldly up to a PR in a corner. Move round arête and up left to a flake shield. Climb straight up (crux) past a scarred flake to gain protection in a smaller flake above. Continue boldly past broken flakes with a traverse out left to gain a good large nut placement 6m from the top. Return right and finish up the cleaned strip.

2   **15m 4c** Continue up easier ground to a belay.

PYRAMID CRAG

This lies 300m north of the main crag at the same level and is characterised by a large right-angled corner system in the centre.

Descent: Down and right to a scree filled gully to the right of the crag.

④ Charge! ★   20m E4 6b

FA Paul Thorburn & Rick Campbell 28 June 1995

The book-shaped corner. Technical. Gain the flake line from the right and follow it to its top. Climb the corner with difficulty to pockets. Better holds lead left round the bulge to easy ground left of the arête. Spike belay 20m further back.

Left-Hand Crack, Polney Crag Deziree Wilson exiting the corner onto the final easy wall.

Paul Donnithorne starting up
The Way Through, Polney Crag.
Photo Alan Leary.

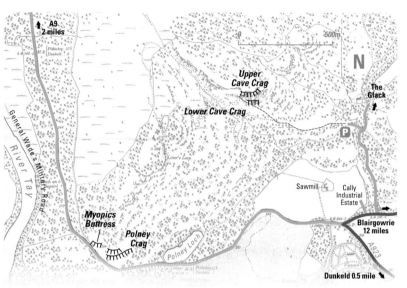

CRAIG A BARNS

This is the thickly wooded hillside overlooking Dunkeld (fort of the Caledonians), the gateway to the Highlands'. There are two main contrasting crags, the steep and imposing overhanging walls of Upper Cave Crag, catering mainly for the extreme climber and the slabbier walls of Polney Crag, offering a fine selection of routes in the lower and middle grades. The rock is schist and dries relatively quickly after rain.

Accommodation: Caravan and campsite at Inver (NO 016 421) on the south side of the A9, 0.6miles/1km west of the main turn-off. Numerous hotels and B&Bs in and around Dunkeld. Wester Caputh Independent Hostel (☎ 01738 710617 or 710449) lies just off A984, 4 miles east of Dunkeld. Wild camping, discreetly, is possible in woods up and left of Lower Cave Crag.

Amenities: TIC in the main square in Dunkeld (Mar-Oct, 01350 727688); bank with ATM in square also. Range of shops in main street, including a couple of supermarkets and numerous cafes. Late opening Spar supermarket in Birnam (1.3 miles/2km from Dunkeld). There is also a good wee cafe in the log cabin Post Office and General Store in Birnam, 0.8 mile/1.3 km from the A9 turn-off if travelling from the south. Peculiarly, it closes for lunch! and on Sundays. Also here, there is a good café/gallery in the Birnam Institute or Katie's Tearoom few hundred metres further north, adjoining the petrol station. Bar meals available in many hotels – try the Taybank Hotel (often live folk music) or the Royal Dunkeld Hotel in the main street opposite the chip shop and baker's. Public toilets at the car park at the north end of town.

"The pass into the Highlands is awfully magnificent; high, craggy and often naked mountains present themselves to view, approach very near each other and in many parts are fringed with wood, overhanging and darkening the Tay, that falls with a great rapidity. After some advance in this hollow, a most beautiful knoll, covered with pines, appears in full view and soon after the town of Dunkeld, seated under and environed with crags, partly naked, partly wooded, with summits of great height."

– Thomas Pennant,
A Tour in Scotland, 1774

POLNEY CRAG 🅂 🇸🇪 🧗 5min

NO 012 432 **Alt:** 180m

The large sprawling dome-shaped crag immediately above the old A9 road. The crag provides the best and most readily accessible low-mid grade routes in the area with a good selection, particularly in the Very Difficult to E1 range. This is the most popular crag in the Highlands, particularly at the weekend and on summer evenings.

Access: Follow the A923 through Dunkeld and continue straight on for 0.9 miles/1.4km past the turn toward Blairgowrie. Park on the right hand (east) verge by a litter bin, just beyond Polney Loch (below the main bulk of crag) or park a few hundred metres further north directly below **Ivy Buttress**. From the north follow the A923 (signed Blairgowrie) for 2.8 miles/4.5km to the same spots.

Approach: Straight up the path behind the parking spot to the crag. For routes on **Ivy Buttress** continue round the road for a few hundred metres then cut up directly by steep path.

Descent: For routes on the left side of the crag (*Kestrel Crack* leftward) traverse left and round by a path leading down a steep muddy gully back to the base. For the

DESCENT

30

32

28

27

31

22

23

24 25

**Hairy
Gully**

26

29

Right Section

routes on the **Upper Buttress** scramble or abseil down a shallow gully about 30m right of the top of *Ogg's Hindquarters* (pine and birch tree at top) to gain the start of the path above the finish of *Kestrel Crack*. There is an easy (though dirty and slightly loose) gully down the centre of the main section of the crag – **Hairy Gully** (Moderate). If intending to do a number of routes here it may be quicker to set up a fixed abseil down this. A broken path of sorts heads right along the top of the crag then down the right end of the crag – **take particular care in the wet**. In situ slings and maillons have been left on the pine trees at the top of 21 *The Creep* & **Hairy Gully** – please use these if intending to abseil.

IVY BUTTRESS

A shorter more broken buttress close to the road, bounding the left edge of the crag.

1 **Hot Tips ★**   **15m E4 6b**

FA unknown 1969; FFA Dave Cuthbertson & Rab Anderson 11 June 1980

The prominent hanging groove in the arête. A hard bouldery start to get established in the groove, which after a few hard pulls, soon relents. Finish much more easily past a huge cracked block.

2 **Ivy Crack ★**   **30m VS 4b**

FA Paul Brian 1958

The prominent slabby corner.

  1 **15m 4b** Tricky initial moves lead to steady climbing up the corner crack to a tree belay.

  2 **15m** – Climb easily up a series of blocks directly above the belay.

3 **Poison Ivy ★**   **15m VS 5a**

FA Robin Campbell 1961

A good well protected problem up the short right-facing corner down and left of the main slabby corner of 4.

4 **Consolation Corner ★**   **30m Very Difficult**

FA Paul Brian & Robin Campbell 1957

A good first pitch. Start round on the right side of a large block pinnacle just right of a huge beech tree.

  1 **15m** Climb a short wide crack on the right side of the block to the top of the pinnacle (or 4a gain the same point from the start of 3). Step left and up the corner to a tree belay on a ledge on the left.

  2 **15m** Direct by two ribs and occasional rock above. Tree belay on the left at the top.

UPPER BUTTRESS

A series of disjointed crags directly above **Ivy Buttress**.
Approach: Via any of the routes on **Ivy Buttress** or the left end of the **Left Section** or by scrambling up the narrow muddy gully at the left end of **Ivy Buttress**.

5 **Left-Hand Crack ★★**   **12m E2 5c**

FA Neil MacNiven 1961 (2 PA); FFA John Mackenzie 1974

The steep corner towards the left end of the buttress immediately above the path. Abseil or lower from a small beech at the top of the difficulties (sling & maillon in situ).

The following two routes are situated just above the path above a maze of jumbled boulders.

Mottled Rib *   45m Severe 4a
FA Dave Cuthbertson & G.Saxon May 1980

Start beneath a groove with a tree at the top, 10m left of 7. Climb the steep initial groove, step left and up the main groove past the tree. Continue up to the second juniper bush and some good protection in the recess just above. Traverse right 3m into the centre of the slab and up this on good pockets.

Ogg's Hindquarters **   30m Very Difficult
FA Robin Campbell 1959

Fine varied climbing. The route starts from 'Duncan Ogg's Hole', reputedly the hide-out of a local infamous cattle rustler. Start from the top of the boulder. Bridge up the overhanging groove (yes, the grade is right!) then step right onto the hanging slab and continue past a juniper bush. Traverse leftward into the centre of the slab. Follow the obvious line, pulling out slightly left then back right at the top. Tree belays further back.

MAIN CRAG
LEFT SECTION

Anon *   35m Difficult
FA unknown

The easiest worthwhile line on the crags. May be a smidgin harder than Difficult for the initial crack, but very well protected. Start at the left side of the recessed slabby bay, beneath twin cracks.

1 **15m** Follow the cracks to a ledge then traverse left to beneath the well defined square-cut corner.

2 **20m** Climb the corner (easier than it looks) to finish slightly rightward up slabby rock.

Kestrel Crack *   35m Severe 4a
FA Robin Campbell 1957

The slab and wide hanging flake in the centre of the recessed bay. Follow a vague crack-line leading up to beneath the centre of the flake (or cleaner and better – the start of *Anon*) then the flake above (large hexes useful) which leads to a large ledge (possible belay). Continue easily up the slabby corner above.

Twisted Rib **   45m Very Difficult
FA Robin Campbell 1957; Direct Finish Paul Brian 1959

Good open climbing up the right defining rib of the slabby recess.

1 **15m** Follow the initial rib (poorly protected, but on good holds) to a ledge. Go left and up a short easy corner to a tree then move back right to a huge flake belay on large ledge.

2 30m Traverse a long way rightward on disjointed ledge then ascend a slab diagonally rightward to a grassy bay. Finish up the groove right of the grass.

11 Beech Wall ★★   35m HS 4b
FA Robin Campbell 1959

Start, not surprisingly, behind the beech tree. Climb the short steep initial groove then move right and up the second groove. Continue more easily directly to steep headwall (possible belay on grass ledge). Finish up fine shallow left-facing flake groove.

12 Piker's Progress Direct ★   35m HVS 5a
FA Ian Rowe 1969

Start below a break in the left side of a line of overhangs, 10m right of the beech tree. Climb the initial wall past a large flake then move leftward up the steep wall (crux) to a break in the overhang formed by a huge block. Pull strenuously right into a short slabby groove then traverse right to the prow to finish up the final rib of 14.

13 The Way Through ★★   30m E2 5b
FA Kenny Spence & Russel Sharp July 1967

Good steep climbing up the centre of the double roofed wall. Start in the centre of the wall. Climb to the lip, pulling diagonally right to a slab beneath the second roof. Break through this on good holds at its widest point (good slot for gear on lip) then continue to cracked blocks beneath the prow. Pull over the overhang above at a thin crack then finish easily.

The following four pitches all share a common start, at the prominent break at the left side of the large overhang near the base.

14 Piker's Progress ★   35m VS 5a
FA Robin Campbell 1960

Move up to beneath the roof then traverse a good break leftward to a groove cutting through the left side of the roof. Make awkward moves up right past a PR (crux) onto a slab on the lip. Move up the cracked groove above then traverse left to cracked blocks under the prow at the

base of 15 (possible belay). Traverse left round the prow and finish up the rib.

15 The Groove ★★   30m VS 5a
FA Robin Smith (solo) 1960

Follow 14 as far as the cracked blocks. Continue direct up the fine right-slanting groove above.

16 The Rut ★★★   30m VS 5a
FA Neil MacNiven 1960

Excellent sustained well protected climbing up the short hanging groove above the common start – the best line on the crag. Finish by stepping left into the final section of 15.

17 Wriggle ★★   35m VS 5a
FA Robin Campbell 1959

Follow the common start through the break in the roof then make an exposed traverse on good pockets above the lip of the roof rightward to a blunt rib. Finish up this.

18 Twilight ★   30m E1 5b
FA Dave Cuthbertson & Rob Kerr 2 November 1980

A fine direct line cutting through the traverse of 17. Start below the holly bush at the right side of the long low roof. Up a groove just left of the holly to a roof. Pull out left through the roof to the slab of 17 then direct up the blunt rib climbing through a bulge at the top.

19 Holly Tree Groove ★★   30m Very Difficult
FA Robin Campbell 1960

The diagonal right-slanting ramp line. Start just right of the holly bush. Climb a short awkward wall on the right to step up left into a short groove. Move up and follow the ramp to a ledge at its end, finishing up the open chimney above.

20 Recess Route ★   30m Very Difficult
FA John Proom 1960

The wall right of 19. Start on a small ledge with a block, below a faint rib. Climb the wall first on the left then right to reach a large grassy recess. Finish up the final open chimney of 19.

21 The Creep   **30m Severe 4a**

FA Robin Campbell 1960

Poorly protected climbing, taking a parallel line right of
20. Start just right of 20. Move up into the short corner
then climb rightward up the slab to a small sloping ledge
beneath the right edge of the first overlap. Move left
through the overlap on big holds then up and right to the
right side of a grassy recess. Finish up the easy-angled
shallow groove above.

22 Dynamo *   **30m VS 5a**

FA Rab Anderson & Dave Cuthbertson 10 June 1980

Fine varied climbing. Start at the left side of a long

grass ledge at the base of the wall, gained by walking
left from the base of 23. Follow a shallow right-facing
groove in the prominent black seepage streak to a
foot-ledge on the right below the overlaps. Pull through
the overlap at a slight weakness (crux), step left then
direct up the wall to finish up a steep crack just right of
the final chimney of 20.

23 Cuticle Crack ** **   **30m Severe 4a

FA Paul Brian 1960

Popular and polished, climbing the prominent deep crack
3m left of **Hairy Gully**. Follow the crack moving right
along the top of a large protruding block. Finish directly.

RIGHT SECTION

24 Bollard Buttress   **30m Difficult**

FA Robin Campbell 1959

Poorly protected climbing up the wall just right of **Hairy
Gully**, starting 5m left of 25.

25 Bollard Buttress Direct   **30m Severe 4a**

FA Paul Brian 1960

Protection is only just adequate. Start at a thin crack with
'Bollard Buttress' painted on the rock. Follow the crack
then a shallow groove. Finish up a rib leading slightly
rightward.

26 Springboard *   **45m VS 4b**

FA Robin Campbell 1960

A good though wandering route. A short way right of
Hairy Gully is a jumbled mass of boulders piled up
against the crag. Start just left of these, at the lowest
point of the wall. Climb first leftward then back right and
up to a deep horizontal break under the overlap. Hand
traverse this right and up into the short brown groove. Up
the corner (unprotected) moving out left under the roof at
the top to a slab. Climb left up an overhung recess to a
slab and finish rightward up this.

27 Springboard Direct *   **40m E3 6a**

FA Dave Bathgate (3 PA) 1960; FFA Derek Jamieson 1978

A technical and perplexing problem, previously severely
undergraded (E1 5b!). Follow 26 to the overlap. Make
hard moves to become established in the slim groove
above. Fiddly protection.

28 The Chute *   **30m VS 5a**

FA Robin Campbell 1961

Start at the base of the brown groove of 26. Step up
then move right immediately to follow a slim groove to a
quartz bulge. Cross the bulge with difficulty to a tiny ash
tree then move up rightward, traversing right round the
top of a large flake to finish up easy slabs.

29 The End *   **35m VS 5a**

FA Robin Campbell 1960

Excellent varied climbing. Start at the base of the narrow
clean slab on the lower tier, immediately right of the
jumbled boulders.

> **1 15m 4c** Up the left side of the slab under a shallow
> left-facing corner. Climb the corner to a bulging
> nose, up this and the delicate slab above to ledge.

2 20m 5a Break through the central weakness in the bulging wall above (crux) then direct up the slab to step right to below the break in the largest part of the overlap. Pull through this and finish easily up the fine slabs. Tree belay.

30 Barefoot /The Beginning ★★   35m E2 5c

FA Pitch 2 Dave Cuthbertson, Derek Jamieson & Murray Hamilton 1976 (previously top-roped); Pitch 1 Dave Cuthbertson & Pete Hunter 31 August 1980

A logical combination with a serious second pitch. Start in the centre of the narrow slab, just right of 29.

1 15m 5c Easily up the slab to a very thin crack. Move left then back right to better holds on the blunt arête near the top.

2 20m 5b Climb the short right facing tapering groove then left and across a steep wall onto the slab. Up this directly to the roof, crossing this at a prominent break. Continue more easily.

31 Terminal Buttress ★   45m VS 4c

FA Robin Campbell 1959

Start at the corner near the right side of the lower slab.

1 15m Up the corner to ledge.

2 30m 4c Climb through the bulge just left of the weakness of 29 (crux) to gain the recess above. Step right and up a crack in the overlaps to finish up slabs.

32 Spirochaete ★   30m VS 4b

FA J.Cameron & C.Norris 8 December 1969

The last worthwhile route on the crag before it degenerates into the hillside. Start at the right side of the crag, behind a large birch tree. Climb a short right-facing layback groove then traverse out right to a small beech tree (runner). Move back left and finish quite boldly up the slab.

MYOPICS BUTTRESS 1min

NO 009 433 **Alt:** 140m

A short steep buttress very close to the road with a trio of short action-packed sport routes.

Access: Drive round the bend heading away from the main crag (north) and park on the right, just before the start of a private track.

Approach: Zig up left then back right to the crag.

1 The Chopping Block ★★   15m F7b

FA Neil Shepherd 15 September 1996

The left line (right of project). Follow good holds up to the roof. Cross this using a good flange to gain a good spike hold (crux) on the lip. A good quartz pocket above soon leads to more reasonable climbing up the headwall, to share the same LO as the following route.

CAVE CRAGS

Two steep crags in a fine secluded setting high on the hill, much quieter than the nearby Polney Crag and with a finer outlook.

Access: Leave the A9 and follow the A923 through the historic town of Dunkeld, complete with its own Cathedral. After 0.3 mile (0.5km) beyond the town, turn right towards Blairgowrie then take the second un-metalled track on the left (by a post-box, signposted The Glack). Follow this for 0.35 miles/0.6km to turn left and into the large 'Cally Car Park'.

Approach: From the car park follow the obvious well worn forest track traversing the hillside westwards, until a narrower path forks off on the right (just before the forest track starts to descend). Follow this to just beyond large fallen yew tree then cut up the hillside just before the stream. **Lower Cave Crag** lies 30m right of the 'cave', a man made structure supposedly erected for one of the Duke of Atholl's 'paramours'! For **Upper Cave**

The Vibes ★★   **15m F7c**

FA Ian Cropley 1990

The central line with a hard crux moving out left to underneath the roof. Climb the lower wall with a long reach right to good holds, to hard moves up left to the main roof. Pull through the roof on good holds. Easier up short final wall to LO.

Granola Head ★   **15m F7c**

FA Duncan McCallum 1990

The right line. Cross the initial roof with difficulty then up to a good ledge beneath the final overhanging arête. Climb this with difficulty to an abrupt finish.

Crag cross the stream (next to the cave) and follow the steep path directly up the hillside, re-crossing the stream just beyond a large mossy boulder, to follow the path steeply up to the left end of the crag. 15 minutes.

LOWER CAVE CRAG   10min

NO 018 437 **Alt:** 220m

A dank and often overgrown crag in the trees overlooking the path, though with a few good exposed routes well worth seeking out.

Descent: Scramble up through the boulders and trees to the base of the upper crag then left and down the approach path for that crag.

> The obvious hanging finger crack and roof at the left end is *The Civer* ★ E3 6a; an early testpiece.

 The Hood ★★   **30m VS 4c**

FA Robin Campbell & partner 1959

Good exposed climbing, staying dry in the rain. Start near the right end of the crag just left of where the face changes direction.

1 **18m 4b** Climb the wall to the centre of a long roof then traverse right along a juggy break beneath the roof and pull round the arête onto a ramp, which leads back left. From the top of the ramp step right to gain ledges and easy ground leading up to a large roof. Bypass this on the right to gain a large block belay on the right edge beneath an overhanging corner.

2 **12m 4c** Step up onto the slab and traverse left onto the arête. Step up to the base of the prominent overhanging crack and swing out left to finish up a slabby rib.

The Hood Direct ★   **35m HVS 5a**

FA Brian Robertson & partner 1963

Start just round the arête from the normal route at a short leaning corner cutting through the overhanging walls at the base.

1 **20m 4c** Clamber out of a tree and go up the short

corner past the lower roofs to below a bigger roof. Traverse awkwardly left to gain the base of the ramp of the normal route. Follow this to the left then step right onto easy ground at a large roof. Bypass this on the right to a ledge.

2 15m 5a Follow 1 onto the slab and climb leftward to beneath the overhanging crack. Finish strenuously up this crack on painful jams.

3 Fuck Face ★   **35m HVS 5a**

FA Dougal Haston 1959

A good direct line up the smooth corner right of 2.

1 10m 4c Gain the corner from the left and climb it by thin bridging to pull onto a large slabby area.

2 25m 5a Pull onto the steep wall on the right (PR) and climb through the bulge with difficulty. Finish up the easier upper wall, trending right to finish.

4 Cherry Tree Ridge Direct ★   **27m Severe 4a**

FA Robin Campbell 1959; Direct Ron Hockey & John Proom

The blunt rib just beyond the vegetated gully at the right end of the crag. Climb the rib over grassy ledges to the base of the steep corner on the left side. Climb this, stepping right at the top to finish up the edge.

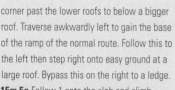
The Hood, Lower Cave Crag, Mike Brownlow climbing. Photo Dave Cuthbertson, Cubby Images.

UPPER CAVE CRAG  15min

NO 018 438 **Alt:** 270m

Regarded by many as one of the best 'roadside' crags in Scotland. Once dry, much of the crag is often climbable even in heavy rain, with the sport routes on the central wall usually climbable well into the autumn.

Descent: There is a well worn path down the left side of the crag, scrambling past a birch tree at the upper left end of the crag. Another possible descent is down the centre of the slabby vegetated face left of *Flook* on the right side of the crag at about Diff. standard. At the bottom head left (facing out) across a mossy slab to the base of the corner of *Flook*. Avoid in wet conditions. A 25m abseil from the pines at the top of *The Gnome* or 35m abseil from tree at the top of *Mousetrap* (slings & maillons in situ) are other options. It is also possible to traverse a long way right through lots of vegetation and down the right side of the crag – take a machete!

❶ The Ramp ★ 40m HS 4b

FA Paul Brian 1957

Bounding the left side of the steep section of the crag is a large ramp, split by a large ledge at mid-height.

1 15m – Climb the ramp by a crack on its right side to a spacious belay on the ledge. A fine easy pitch on its own – about Difficult. (Abseil descent from tree).

2 25m 4b Continue up the corner crack in the back of the ramp, which widens and steepens before a ledge/pinnacle thingy. Make steep moves up the wall above (often dirty – crux) to a heathery finish.

> The following three routes all start from the large platform half way up *The Ramp*.

❷ Voie de L'Amie ★★★ 30m E3 5c

FA Dave Cuthbertson, Rab Anderson & Mal Duff September 1979

A fine contrasting pitch, quite bold in the lower half. Start just left of the scoop of 3. Direct up a shallow groove to a bulge. Hand traverse diagonally right on improving holds to the ledge on 3. Finish with interest up the superb thin pocketed crack above.

❸ Hang Out ★ 40m E3 5c

FA M.Forbes & G.Miller (5 pts aid) 1972; FFA Murray Hamilton, Dave Cuthbertson & Derek Jamieson 1976

The shallow rightward trending scoop above the right side of the ledge. Quite bold.

1 20m 5c Up the wall then head rightward and up the scoop to a ledge.

2 20m 5a Follow the diagonal crack rightward to finish up the final left-facing groove of 6.

❹ The Pied Piper ★★★ 43m E3 5c

FA Dave Cuthbertson & Mal Duff 24 April 1980

A brilliant left to right girdle of the crag, crossing some impressive ground. Start on the commodious ledge half way up *The Ramp*.

1 23m 5c Follow the horizontal crack (2 PRs) into 6, step down then continue rightward to the larch (possible belay). Move up rightward to good holds then out right. Reverse down a short way to a good flake then follow the obvious line across the big open groove of 9 to belay on the lip of the lower roof of 11.

2 20m 5c Finish up the top pitch of 10.

❺ Lady Charlotte ★★★ 45m E5 6a

FA Dave Cuthbertson & Mal Duff April 1980; Pitch 2 Dave Cuthbertson & Ken Johnstone April 1980

The classic hard route, taking the intricate pocketed wall the full length of the left side of the crag. Start about 6m up *The Ramp*. Finishing up 2 in one 35m pitch gives a fantastic outing.

1 25m 6a Up a tiny right-facing groove to a good foot ledge. Step left then climb direct to good holds in the horizontal crack of the girdle (F #2 in pocket just below). Make a hard move up to the hollow hanging flake above, up this then out leftward on good holds to the final section of 3. Easier up this to belay on a ledge. A harder *Direct*, 6b is possible by stepping out right from a pocket above the hanging flake to a hidden PR in tiny groove then directly up the wall to the ledge.

2 20m 5c Reverse the traverse of 2, pull over bulge

and up wall to small niche. Finish up thin crack. A bold pitch with minimal protection. Alternatively, finish up the brilliantly-situated final crack of 2.

6 Rat-catcher ★★ 45m E3 5b

FA Alan Pettit & Ken Martin (A3) 1969;
FFA Dave Cuthbertson & Murray Hamilton 1976

Bold steady climbing with little protection and some suspect rock. It follows the shallow open groove up the wall left of the larch. Direct up the wall and leaning corner, turning the bulge on the right to PR at 12m. Move slightly right then back left to a further PR in the horizontal break. Continue in the same line to the top.

7 In Loving Memory ★★ 35m E6 6b

FA Ken Martin (A3) 4 October 1969;
FFA Dave Cuthbertson & Martin Lawrence 1981

The short but action-packed overhanging wall above the larch, starting up that. Monkey up the tree to its uppermost branches. Step onto the wall and up past a PR (rock in small pocket just above) to poor holds in a small recess (RP #3 in short pale crack up on left). Continue to a good jug. Head up leftward to finish up a short tiny right-facing corner.

Crossing the spectacular top roof on Rat Race, Climbers Gary Latter & Mick the Fish. Photo Ian Campbell.

8 Morbidezza ★★ 35m E5 6a

FA Dave Cuthbertson 24 June 1979

The blunt hanging arête in the centre of the crag, just left of the open groove of 9. An optional (bit contrived & crux – 6b) boulder problem start up the overhanging right rib of 9 leads to a scoop. Move left into the groove of 9, up this for a few metres then left to the arête (possible rest in tree out left). Up this by a crack to a large flat hold at its top then finish up the left side of the large cracked block.

> The central groove just right of the larch tree is the often wet 9 *Mousetrap* ★ E4 6b.

10 Warfarin ★★★ 45m E2 5c

FA Derek Jamieson, Grahame Nicoll & Mal Duff 5 September 1978

A surprisingly balancy route meandering up the centre of the crag. Start below a hanging right-facing groove, 3 metres left of the central crack of 11.

1 **25m 5c** Boulder up the steep wall to the groove, up this (PR near top) then move up leftward into the groove of 9. Up this for a few metres to traverse right on the lip of the roof to a hanging stance on 11. N & PB.

2 **20m 5c** Up to the roof and some old PRs then follow good line of holds diagonally right under the roof to a tricky finish.

11 Rat Race ★★★★ 40m E4 6a

FA Neil MacNiven (to top roofs)/Brian Robertson & John McLean (on bolts) 1963; FFA Pitch 1 Murray Hamilton with 1 PA on new direct top pitch 1976; FFA complete Mike Graham 1978

The showpiece of the crag with a sustained first pitch. Start beneath the pea-pod in the centre of the crag.

1 **20m 6a** Climb the pod (awkward) or the wall on the left to a good F #1.5 placement and PR just above. Continue up the crack with a hard section to gain the niche (good no-hands rest). Jug hauling above leads to a hanging stance on the lip of the roof.

2 **20m 5b** Direct to the roof then out rightward for 6m to a good flange in the roof (old PRs). Cross the roof leftward to finish up a short wall. Belay far back on pines.

THE SPORT WALL

12 Marlene ★★★★   **20m F7b+**

FA Murray Hamilton September 1986;
First red pointed Steve Lewis 13 September 1986

The most popular sport route in Scotland and justifiably so. Very sustained with a bouldery start and no desperately hard moves. Follow the left-hand line of bolts, moving right past the 4th BR with a long reach to the base of the diagonal crack. Up this and pull blindly up left at its top to LO.

13 Marlene with Ultima Necat finish ★★★   **20m F7c**

FA Dave Cuthbertson (original – 3 bolts in total) 3 August 1986;
Ultima Necat – Mark McGowan 8 July 1987

The original start, giving much harder more sustained climbing. From the second bolt, pull out right and up to a good finger-lock (BR). Straight up with difficulty to the 4th bolt, step left and direct past a further BR to the same LO.

14 The Silk Purse ★★★★   **25m F7c+**

FA as Fall Out M.Forbes & G.Millar 8 December 1969 as bolt ladder; FFA (escaping out right) Dave Cuthbertson & Gary Latter 1982; as Fall Out Direct (in 2 pitches, with new bolts) Murray Hamilton & Rab Anderson 21 September 1986; as described Graeme Livingston April 1987

The classic hard sport route – a long stamina pitch. Follow the right-most line of bolts with a hard move left to join 12 just before the start of the crack. Up the crack to its end then make hard moves up and right to some barn-door-layback moves up the scoop to reach good quartz pockets. The final few metres relent, leading to a LO under the projecting roof.

15 Hamish Teddy's Excellent Adventure ★★★
                               25m F7b+

FA Duncan McCallum, Johnny May & Rab Anderson (all redpointed!) 1992

Finely situated climbing up the upper right arête of the bolted wall on good holds. The easiest link is to combine this with the lower section of 12, giving a 7b+ overall. Numerous other combinations are possible, such as The Silk Teddy … use your initiative!

16 Squirm Direct ★★   **20m E3 5c**

FA Dave Bathgate (5PA) 1960;
FFA Murray Hamilton & Alan Taylor 1976

The right edge of the central bolted wall has a prominent groove leading to a bulge. Gain the groove by swinging left on good holds from the lower right-trending groove. Up this to a crucial PR at the bulge, pull through this and pull out left to a recess (old PRs). Move out rightward up easier ground to gain the belay ledge on the ordinary route.

17 Squirm ★   **35m E1 5c**

FA Neil MacNiven (1 PA) 1960;
FFA Murray Hamilton & Alan Taylor 1976

Good climbing on the main pitch with a short well protected crux and fine airy finish. Start 10m right of 16.

1 15m 4b Up easy broken ground
to a large belay ledge.

2 20m 5c Climb the green wrinkled slab with
difficulty past a PR (crux) to easier ground.
Head out left and finish spectacularly up the
right side of the arête on huge flakes.

 Corpse ★★   **30m E2 5c**

FA Neil MacNiven (3 PA) 1960;
FFA Murray Hamilton & Alan Taylor 1976

Good climbing with a short well protected crux. Start just
left of the big open corner. Easily up to the base of the
shallow right-facing groove. Up this (difficult to protect)
to a glacis on the right (PRs). Move out to the right end
of this and finish up the short strenuous crack sprouting
from its right end.

 Post Mortem ★   **30m E4 6b**

FA Grant Farquhar 7 October 1990

A good well protected 'stiff' direct finish to 18. From the
left end of the glacis, climb past 2 PRs to pull blindly
rightward onto a ledge. Belay further back.

[📷] The classic hard Upper Cave Crag sport
route, The Silk Purse. Grant Farquhar displaying
his stylish tartan trews on an ascent in the late
eighties. Photo Rick Campbell.

19 Coffin Corner ★★   **25m HVS 5a**

FA Pete Smith & Ferranti Club members 1960

The large left-facing corner near the right side of the crag.
Easy ground leads to the base of the corner. Follow this
past some threads to pull out right at its top. Block belay
just above. Easier ground remains.

20 High Performance ★★   **20m E3 6a**

FA George & R Farquhar 1960;
FFA Dave Cuthbertson (on-sight) 10 October 1978

Gymnastic climbing through the roof just right of the
big corner. Scramble up rightward to the roof. Climb
the crack in the roof (overhead protection) to a good jug
on the lip and PR just above. Step right and up shallow
groove past a possible no-hands rest (a cheval!) to finish.

21 Death's-head ★★   **30m E1 5b**

FA Dave Cuthbertson, Alan Taylor & Murray Hamilton Oct 1976

Start just right of the prominent cracked roof of 20,
gained by easy scrambling from either side. Follow the
cracked groove, turning the bulge on the right. Step
back left and up the short left-slanting groove to finish
on good holds. Protection is reasonable, though fiddly
to place.

 The Crutch ★★   **35m Severe 4a**

FA Andy Wightman 1959

Fine well protected climbing and the best route of the
grade on the crags.

1 15m 4a Start a few metres right of the 'cave',
down and right of the prominent S-shaped crack.
Up past a small beech tree then diagonally left
to the base of the shallow corner (possible belay).
Up this to belay on slabby ledges on the right.

2 20m 4a Move left and make a tricky step left to
gain good holds on the slab. Traverse left into the
short right-facing groove (left of the final groove of
24) and up this on good holds. Continue easily up
vegetated ramp/gully to tree belay. A good direct
single pitch can be climbed by pulling straight up
onto the final slab past a good undercut flake.

📷 Coffin Corner,
Sam Forrest nearing
the top.

23 Marjorie Razorblade ★★★   25m E2½ 5c
FA Dave Cuthbertson & Murray Hamilton March 1977

The characteristic offset S-shaped crack in the steep wall right of *The Crutch*. A thug's delight.

1   **15m 5c** Climb steeply on good holds directly up to the base of the crack (possible belay). A combination of jamming and laybacking may lead to a belay on slabby ledges above.

2   **10m 5a** Step left across *The Crutch* to a short steep left facing groove. Up this to easier ground. Round to the right is a wide vegetated slab. Overlooking this is a shorter steep back wall, with a holly bush low down in the centre.

24 Flook ★   30m Very Difficult
FA Pete Smith 1960

The dièdre bounding the right edge of the slab. Near the top, traverse left onto large blocks and finish up the short corner above the large roof.

25 Tumbleweed ★   25m E2 5b
FA Derek Jamieson & Dave Cuthbertson June 1976

Scramble up the gangway for 10m to below the holly bush. Up to a ledge beneath the holly then follow a gangway/ramp up leftward to the base of the corner. Step right and climb a shallow groove and wall rightward to the top. Sparsely protected. So named as the first ascentionist plummeted from the finishing moves clutching a handful of heather!

26 Summer Days ★   30m E3 5c
FA Dave Cuthbertson & Rab Anderson November 1978

Start on the right side of the wall, near the arête. Follow the left rising crack leading to the holly bush. Pass this with interest to finish directly up the strenuous shallow groove in the wall above.

27 The Gnome ★   25m E1 5c
FA Brian Robertson 1960; FFA Mick Couston 1974

The right arête of the wall. Start at the foot of the arête. Climb by cracks on good holds up the left side to move right to a ledge beneath short open groove. Up this with interest past a PR to top.

28 Tombstone ★★   20m E2 5b
FA Dave Cuthbertson & Mal Duff 10 October 1978

Steep and sustained with good protection. The prominent groove right of 27 gives steep jamming and bridging. Scramble up to large ledge at the base of the crack. Follow the crack to overhang, cross this and continue on good holds in the same line to finish.

High Pitched Scream, Weem Rock. Sadie Renwick reaching the sanctuary of the final juggy top out. Photo Dave Cuthbertson, Cubby Images.

WEEM HILL CRAGS

A fine varied selection of quick drying, mainly sports crags set in the thickly wooded hillside above the village of Weem, overlooking the River Tay and Aberfeldy in the heart of rural Perthshire. The crags have a very sunny aspect, particularly in the spring and late autumn when there are no leaves on the trees.

A peaceful place to climb. The rock is generally an excellent schist, often encrusted with many garnets in its upper reaches, giving good friction. The majority of the routes are all very well bolted, some over-bolted with some of the bolts less than a metre apart, making it possible to effectively top-rope some of the routes.

The name Weem is a phonetic corruption of the Gaelic uaimh, meaning cave, though there are no proper caves as such on the hillside. There is a fine forest walk past St David's Well, a small spring at the base of a short steep crag. In the 7th century a Christian missionary, St Cuthbert, lived here as a hermit. In the 15th century a local laird, Sir David Menzies, *"gave up the grand life for religion"*. There are many local legends about Weem Rock (St David's Well) and its caves. One says that a demon guarded a huge treasure in a cave and fought off his foes by changing form. It was said that while St Cuthbert occupied this cave the Devil occupied another lower cave.

Access: Leave the A9 at Ballinluig and follow the A927 west for 10 miles/16km to Aberfeldy. Turn north at cross-roads at the west end of the town (signposted Kinloch Rannoch) and follow the B846 across Wades Bridge over the River Tay to reach the village of Weem after 1 mile/1.6km. For **Weem Rock**, **Hanging Rock** and **Aerial Buttress**, park alongside the wall on the main road next to the church. For the **Secret Garden Crag** and **Easter Island Buttress**, continue through the village for a further 0.3 mile/0.5km to park in the large car park on the right, near Castle Menzies.

Amenities: Aberfeldy has all the usual requirements – a supermarket, some tea-rooms, several pubs and a couple of wee book shops. The Black Watch, The Fountain and The Breadalbane Inn are all good, the latter two also providing bar meals. For lunches and snacks the Mill Restaurant does good food at reasonable prices. Closer to the crags there is a good tea-room in the Castle (open 10.30 – 4.30 1 April – mid October; 2.00 – 4.30 Sunday). House of Menzies (open 10.00 – 5.00; Sunday 11.00 – 4.00) on the main road half a mile west of the castle is also very good, with great cakes. For supplies of chalk, climbing gear, etc. there is a small outdoor shop, Munros in Bank Street, just east of the cross-roads (☎ 01887 820008). The Weem Hotel immediately underneath the crags is rather handy for an après climb pint & good restaurant.

Accommodation: Adventurer's Escape bunkhouse next to the Weem Hotel www. adventurers-escape.co.uk (☎ 01887 820498). Masses of hotels, guest houses and B&B establishments in the area. Info/brochure from **TIC** in the Square, Aberfeldy (☎ 01887 820276). There is also a Caravan and Campsite (☎ 01887 820662) at the east end of the town. Wild camping is a bit more of a problem as much of the surrounding area is heavily farmed.

It is advisable to locate and stay on the approach paths described or take a machete as the undergrowth is very dense. Deer ticks are a bit of problem but only seem to be encountered if you stray from the paths.

WEEM ROCK 🌑 🅂 🔰 10min

NN 845 502 **Alt:** 200m

An excellent crag with two contrasting faces. The left side of the crags sports a couple of wildly steep lines, overhanging at about 30 degrees. Further right the front face has an excellent slab with some good long pitches, together with a number of shorter routes further right.
Approach: Walk up the steep road at the side of the church for just over 100m to a wide grassy track on the right, just beyond Tigh na Sgoill (old schoolhouse). Walk along this for 50m then cut up left at the second telegraph pole (prominent Scots Pine ahead) to gain the main Weem Forest Walk. Follow this right for 200m, cutting back left at a hairpin. After about 100m, midway between some small wooden seats and some steps on the path, cut steeply up right on a small path through the undergrowth to scramble steeply over fallen trees and rocks to reach the left end of the crag.

SIDE WALL

The acutely overhanging left wall.

❶ The End of Silence ★★   15m F7a+

FA Colin Miln 29 March 1997

Technical fingery climbing up the narrow lower wall, soon relenting in its upper half.

❷ The Last Temptation ★★   25m E2 5c

FA George Ridge & Janet Horrocks 10 April 1997

The hanging right-facing groove up the right side of the overhanging wall. Climb a short steep crack into the groove. At the top, pull over the small roof on good holds. Step right and follow a crack behind a sapling to a tree belay or move up right to the LO of 4.

❸ The Screaming Weem ★★★   20m F7a+

FA George Ridge 13 April 1997

Excellent sustained climbing up the central line of resin bolts left of the blunt arête, to share a common LO with 4. Difficult moves around the 3rd bolt and a long reach for a good hold on the lip of the roof. The blunt arête, gained by moving out right from the 5th B is 3a *Last Gasp* ★ F7a+.

❹ High Pitched Scream ★★★   15m F7a

FA Neil Shepherd 13 April 1997

Excellent steep climbing. Scramble up shrubbery at the left end of the grotty slab then shuffle right along a narrow ledge to BB at the base of the route (or climb dirty lower slab direct past a bolt!). A strenuous fingery start on small holds soon leads to a line of good incut holds, sharing the final few moves and LO of 3.

There are two further similarly graded routes just to the left, though the penalty of messing up a clip and landing in the shrubbery (including hollies!) in the gully accounts for their neglect.

FRONT FACE

❺ The Real McKay ★   20m F6a

FA Persons Unknown June 1997

Finely situated climbing up the right side of the arête with difficult moves past the 2nd bolt. Continue much easier up the groove, finishing up a pleasant cracked groove.

❻ Back to Basics ★★   25m VS 4c

FA Bill Wright, Mel & Grahame Nicoll 26 August 1997

The line of cracked grooves a few metres right of the left arête. At the overhang move right and climb another groove to finish.

7 The Long Good Friday ★★   20m F6c+
FA Isla Watson 25 May 1997

The line up the left side of the slab with the crux passing a prominent triangular slot just above half way.

8 Confession of Faith ★★   20m F6c
FA Janet Horrocks 12 April 1997

The central line with the difficulties just above mid-height.

9 Mannpower ★   20m F6a+
FA Dave Pert 12 April 1997

The prominent thin intermittent crack at the right side of the slab. Start up the wall just left of the corner then follow the intermittent crack, passing the small roof with difficulty.

10 On the Tick List ★   20m E2 5b
FA Neil Shepherd 31 March 1997

Start on the ledge up to the right. Follow the slightly diagonal fault trending leftward to the LO of 9.

11 Boom Head   15m F6a+
FA Neil Shepherd 24 August 1997

Line 2m right of 10 (3m left of the left-facing groove) direct through the first bulge, skirting the right side of the isolated upper roof.

12 Blinded by the Night   18m HVS 5a
FA George Ridge 4 October 1998

Central corner to LO.

13 Staring at the Sun   18m F5+
FA George Ridge 10 October 1998

The arête just to the right of the corner.

14 The Soup Dragon   15m F5+
FA Janet Horrocks 20 September 1997

The line up the left side of the shorter face on the right.

15 Scooby Snacks ★   15m F6a+
FA George Ridge 21 August 1997

Start beneath the centre of the shorter, more broken slab near the right side of the face. Follow the left-hand line of bolts to a 3 B LO common with 16.

16 One Step Beyond ★   15m F6a
FA Isla Watson 24 August 1997

Start beneath a ledge at 3m. Climb up past the ledge then direct up the slab with steep moves to gain the LO.

17 Down to the Last Heartbreak   15m F6a
FA George Ridge 30 June 1998

The line up the wall right of 16.

18 The Trial of Brother No. 1 ★   15m F6a
FA Colin Miln 7 September 1997

The centre of the scooped wall to a LO just beneath a prominent curving overlap at the top.

19 Lap Dancing ★   15m F6b+
FA Rab Anderson 13 September 1998

The wall between 18 and 20, surmounting the roof at the top.

20 The Llama Parlour   10m F6c
FA Janet Horrocks 28 September 1997

The steep technical wall 4m left of 22.

21 The Protection Racket ★   10m F6a+
FA George Ridge 21 August 1997

Strenuous climbing up the prominent left-facing groove at the right end of the face with the crux where the angle eases.

> The left edge of the groove is 22 *Lighten-up* F6a; wall at the far right end 24 *Bark Bacherache* F6b

23 Crowing at the Enemy ★   10m F6b+
FA Rab Anderson 10 October 1998

The shallow groove on the far right.

HANGING ROCK

NN 847 502 **Alt:** 200m 10min

A short steep wall with some good very fingery sport climbs and a traditional crack. An excellent very sheltered sun trap in the spring. It is located on the right side of the hill, deep in the undergrowth and consequently hard to locate in the summer.

1 **The Glass Ceiling ***   **15m F6c**

FA George Ridge 31 May 1997

Climb the wide overhanging crack on the right side of the wall then hand traverse the top of the crag to the LO common with 5. Good, though a bit contrived.

2 **Alien Artefact ***   **12m F7b**

FA Neil Shepherd 31 May 1997

Start at the next line of bolts left of 1. One thin move past the second bolt then good edges to a huge LO staple.

3 **The Chemical Generation ***   **12m F7b**

FA Colin Miln 24 March 1997

Start down behind the boulder. Up to the good juggy break then past some thin cracks and a good quartz

Approach: (A) Follow the approach as for Weem Rock to the bend in the path then continue in the same direction (north-east) on a vaguer path heading diagonally rightwards up the hillside for 100m (past some short bouldering walls) then cut directly up the hillside for 100m to the crag, which lies immediately behind a very dense stand of conifers. **(B)** Contour right from Weem Rock then head up behind the dense stand of pine trees.

pocket to good holds above the bulge. A few further moves to gain the LO.

4 **Crushed by the Wheels of Industry ***   **10m F7a+**

FA George Ridge 29 April 1997

The line 2m right of the crack. Sustained and fingery.

5 **Drop Dead Gorgeous ***   **10m E3 6a**

FA Neil Shepherd 28 May 1997

Well protected climbing up the crack on good holds.

6 **Remanufacture ***   **10m F7c+**

FA John Gaskins May 2003

The leftmost line with an inordinately hard crux.

AERIAL CRAG 20min

NN 847 505 **Alt:** 300m

A short buttress situated almost directly above Hanging Rock. A good open crag with a fine outlook from the top. The two pitches up the left wall are very steep and stay dry in the rain.

Approach: Continue steeply up from the left side of Hanging Rock for about 10 minutes, cutting out right about 50m above some dead elms just above a band of small outcrops running up the hillside).

Descent: By abseil from a variety of trees on top or head left and down grassy slopes left of the leftmost outcrops.

1 **Communication Breakdown ***   **12m E3 6a**

FA Kev Howett & Grahame Nicoll 4 August 1997

The thin discontinuous crack at the left end of the steep left wall, finishing up an awkward V-groove at the top.

2 **Saving Up for a Rainy Day *****   **18m E5 6a**

FA Gary Latter & Rick Campbell 31 August 1997

Excellent sustained well protected climbing taking the obvious challenge up the centre of the wall. Climb the steep finger crack to a break at its top. Move out left along the break and up to good holds then climb the flange to a good nut placement in quartz near the top of the flange. Climb the wall above slightly rightward on thin slots to gain good flat holds at a small ledge. Stand on this and finish more easily.

The crack up the left side of the arête is 3 *The Porn Channel* E1 5c; 4 *The Choice of a New Generation* E2 5c takes the right side of the arête to finish up 3.

5 Kissing the Witch * 10m F6b
FA Janet Horrocks July 1997

The left-most line of bolts up the wall.

6 Static in the Air * 15m E3 5c/F6c
FA George Ridge May 1997 (with bolts); FA sans bolts Kev Howett & Lawrence Hughes 16 August 1997

The thin hanging crack-line on the left side of the front face. Gain the crack from the left by stepping off the boulder and follow it quite boldly near the top to finish past a block and sapling. Tree belay above the ledge.

SECRET GARDEN CRAG

A good steep slabby face with a prominent roof running across the right side of the crag at mid-height.
Approach: Follow the forest walk (signed St David's Well) past two zig-zags. Turn left and follow a good path at the back edge of the walled garden then drop down a short way (culvert across path) to pick up a path cutting up through the rhododendrons to the crag's base.

1 100 Ways to be a Good Girl * 8m F6b+
FA Janet Horrocks 5 April 1997

The grey streak at the left end, cutting through three small roofs.

2 Batweeman * 10m F6b
FA Isla Watson 22 March 1997

The cracked left-facing corner and technical wall above. The best of the easier routes to warm up on.

3 Forbidden Fruit * 12m F6b+
FA Isla Watson 12 April 1997

Start just right of the arête, 3m right of the groove. Climb on sloping holds to a ledge then with interest above.

7 Cracking Good Reception * 15m HVS 5a
FA unknown 1997

Follow the deep crack immediately right of 6.

8 Strong Signal * 15m HVS 5a
FA Grahame Nicoll & Kev Howett 2 August 1997

The shallow groove in the centre of the front face just right of 7.

9 Moving the Aerial * 15m E1 5b
FA Kev Howett, Grahame Nicoll & Alastair Todd 4 August 1997

Start just right of 8. Climb up and move right round a blunt rib into a shallow groove. Up this then move out left and up past the left side of a small overlap to finish.

The following crags are all best approached from the castle car park:

NN 837 498 **Alt:** 200m 10min

4 Faithless * 15m F6c+
FA George Ridge 30 March 1997

The left side of the highest section, breaching the left side of the mid-height roof.

5 The Missing Link ** 20m F6c+/7a
FA Isla Watson 17 June 2000

Excellent sustained climbing. Climb the bottom section of 4 through the roof then traverse diagonally left via a golden BR to finish up the top crux headwall of 3.

6 The Watchtower * 15m F6c
FA Colin Miln 2 March 1997

The central line through the roof.

7 Caledonia Dreaming * 15m F6c
FA Neil Shepherd 9 March 1997

Start just left of the arête. Follow the crack just left of the right arête with spectacular moves on good holds through the body-length roof.

8 Don't Knock the Block 15m F6a+

FA Janet Horrocks 21 February 1998

Right arête of front face. Up to the first BR on 9, step left to the arête. Follow the arête to a ledge, step left above the roof and finish directly.

9 Brass Monkeys 6m F6a+

FA George Ridge 8 March 1997

A minuscule route (more of a boulder problem!) up the wall at the right side of the crag.

EASTER ISLAND
BUTTRESS 🔵🔵 10min

NN 838 497 **Alt:** 170m

A good little crag about 50m down and right of the main crag. There are rather a lot of bolts on the tiny triangular-shaped lower wall (about twenty-five!)

Approach: As for the **Secret Garden Crag** until about 50m below the crag to gain a vague path branching off horizontally right.

1 Looking for a Rainbow ★ 25m Very Difficult

FA Mel & Grahame Nicoll 26 July 1997

Follow the slabby ramp, finishing up the prominent V-corner on the left to an oak tree belay. Abseil descent.

2 Left on the Shelf ★ 20m F6c+

FA Rab Anderson 22 June 1997

Follow the left line of bolts to the top of the initial wall, step left past a couple of good pockets (BR on slab above) and pull over the roof on good holds to finish up the easier arête in a fine position.

3 President Shhean Connery 8m F6c+

FA Colin Miln 20 April 1997

Rather closely spaced bolts just a tad close to 2. The 4th bolt is about 3m up!

4 The Republic of Scotland ★★ 8m F7a+

FA Colin Miln 20 April 1997

The line of bolts up the centre of the wall. Excellent climbing on good edges.

The right arête is 5 *Right in the Face* ★F6b.

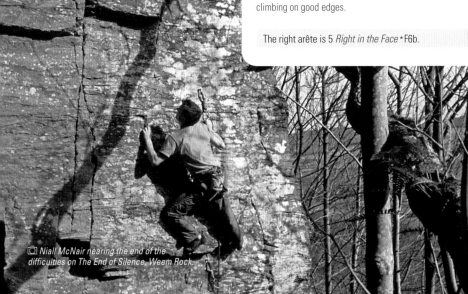

📷 *Niall McNair nearing the end of the difficulties on The End of Silence, Weem Rock.*

DIRC MHOR

(THE GREAT SLASH) 1½ hr

NN 591 861 **Alt:** 560m

This impressive defile lies about 5 kilometres (3 miles) west of Dalwhinnie. It is a narrow kilometre-long slot lined with cliffs, particularly on the east side, where, at their northern end, they culminate in **Sentinel Rock**, an impressive 80 metre barrel-shaped buttress. The rock is micro-granite, similar to but of even better quality than the nearby Binnein Shuas. Both **Sentinel Rock** and **Ship Rock** dry quickly, though many of the other crags seep for several days.

Access: Follow the A889 for 1 mile/1.6km north of the distillery at Dalwhinnie to park on the east side of the road opposite a track signposted 'Old Drovers Road to Feagour'.

Approach: Follow the track which leads to a new house after 1km. Continue through the courtyard of the house then on an ATV track which follows the Allt an t-Sluic westwards. Follow this *"yellow brick road"* criss-crossing the burn then the burn heading up into the Dirc Mhor. Avoid the rough going boulder-choke in the base of the Dirc by cutting up left to contour into the base of **Sentinel Rock** on a good path.

SENTINEL ROCK

The showpiece, a stunning barrel-shaped 80m tall buttress standing guard over the lower reaches of the Dirc.

Descent: From the boulder-strewn terrace above the crag continue up more broken ground over the top of the small hill then head left (north) and return round to the base of the crag. Alternatively, a 45m abseil from an in situ sling and crab on block on the top right side of the crag leads diagonally rightward to the third grass ledge.

1 Working Class Hero ★★★   85m E2 5c

FA Allen Fyffe, Keith Geddes & Ado Liddell 1 August 1980

The ramp and corner up the left wall. Start at the base of the large slanting slab.

1 **15m 4b** Climb the big slab to belay at its top.

2 **30m 4c** Gain and climb the small right-facing corner in the overhanging wall above which leads to the clean cut ramp/corner line. Follow this spectacularly to a niche and exit out right onto a large ledge cutting across the front of the buttress. A stunning pitch.

3 **40m 5c** Step up to the large ledge which leads diagonally right across the face to a corner. Up this to the top of a pinnacle. Traverse diagonally right using a thin crack and from its end traverse back hard left. Easier rock leads to the top.

2 The Man with the Child in his Eyes ★★★
85m E5 6b

FA Kev Howett & Graham Little 24 June 1995

The left arête of the front face. Start as for *Working Class Hero*.

1 **15m 4b** Climb the big slab to a belay.
2 **30m 6b** Climb a small groove in the wall just right of the corner of *Working Class Hero* for 4m until it is possible to span out right around the arête to gain a big flat-topped flake. Move up to join *Fanfare for the Common Man* at the left end of its belay ledge. Up the arête past a quartz fin where hard moves gain a prominent hold in the arête. Continue up the thin crack on the left side of the arête with sustained difficulty until an exit left near the top gains a belay at the left end of the large ledge.
3 **15m 6a** Follow slabby rock up and left to gain the thin crack near the arête. Up this to belay.
4 **25m 4c** Trend leftward to the base of the left trending ramp. Follow the crack directly above to broken ground. Scramble rightward to reach the boulder strewn terrace.

3 Fanfare for the Common Man ★★★ 90m E5 6b

FA Kev Howett & Graham Little 16 July 1994

Brilliant climbing up the left side of the front face. Start as for *Working Class Hero* at the lowest point of the crag.

1 **25m 5a** Climb the easy angled slab for 10m (as for *Working Class Hero*) to a point where a prominent flake crack breaks the right wall. Ascend this then traverse right along a fault to step up onto the right of two sloping ledges. Move left to take an awkward belay at the junction of the two ledges. Climbing direct from the fault to the ledges via a short steep diagonal crack is 6a.
2 **25m 6b** Step up onto the higher ledge then move left to the base of a slight groove. Up this to a thin horizontal crack. Pull up bulging rock with increasing difficulty to a hairline horizontal crack then make committing moves left and up to gain better holds. A sequence of good holds lead to the large ledge. A superb pitch.
3 **20m 5c** Climb easy rock just right of the belay to gain a right-trending ramp shared with *Working Class Hero*. Follow this to the start of a less distinct left-trending ramp. Ascend this to a deep incut hold below bulging rock. Go directly over the bulge to a thin flake then move left to gain a flange. Move left and up to ledge.
4 **20m 4a** Climb a left-trending stepped groove then scramble back right and up to gain the block strewn terrace.

4 The Scent of a Woman ★★★ 95m E5 6b

FA Kev Howett & Graham Little 30 July 1994

The central line up the front face completing a great trilogy.

1 **25m 6b** Climb the flake as for *Positive Earth* then continue up the overhanging corner cutting through the roof to a rest above the lip. Move right then up the pod on the right side of a big block to a pedestal.
2 **30m 6b** Step right and up into a short, shallow right-facing groove. Pull out left to gain a thin crack which leads up to join the left-trending diagonal crack of *Positive Earth*. Follow the continuation of the diagonal line up left on good holds then traverse di-

agonally left to under a prominent isolated roof in the centre of the face. Climb directly up the two-stepped overhanging wall above, with hard moves over the final lip then move up right to gain a rock ramp which leads to a belay at the right end of the large ledge.

3   20m 6b Move left up a short slabby wall to a right-trending ramp. From this follow a less distinct left-trending ramp (common with *Fanfare for the Common Man*). Move right and up to a diagonal crack in the bulging wall then move up and right to gain a sharp edge. Make difficult contorted moves up to reach an undercling (F #0). Undercling rightward to gain a poor crack in a bulge. Strenuous moves on scarcely adequate holds lead up to a belay ledge.

4   20m 4a Climb a short slabby corner then broken ground leading to the terrace.

⑤ Positive Earth ★★   85m E1 5c
FA Martin Burrows-Smith & Allen Fyffe 23 August 1980

A line up the right side of the face heading for the big corner. Start at the toe of the buttress.

1   20m 4c Climb the corner until it steepens then escape up the right wall onto a large slab. Follow a line diagonally up the wall above to belay at large prominent blocks.

2   20m 5c Move slightly left into a niche. Climb the thin diagonal crack which leads leftward with a hard bouldery move to reach a good small triangular ledge. Up the wall above on good holds leading into the base of the corner.

3   15m 4a Climb the corner and exit left under the roof to belay on the large ledge on the front of the buttress.

4   30m 4c Finish up the fine vertical crack above.

⑥ Holy Smoke ★★   80m VS 4c
FA Bugs McKeith & party 23 August 1966

An excellent superbly positioned top pitch. Start at the lowest of three grassy slabs, above and right of the lowest rocks. The first (4c) pitch of *Positive Earth* would provide a fine start.

1   20m 4c Climb a short wall then rightward to

the large blocks of the first belay of *Positive Earth*. Continue up the wall above by a crack on the right to the third grassy slab.

2   25m 4c Climb the corner then move left onto the wall of the buttress. Continue up to belay on small ledges on a slab below the big corner.

3   35m 4c Climb the left arête of the corner to the roof then go left to the large ledge. From the top of the pinnacle above, hand traverse up and rightward in a wild position until a narrow ledge leads right. Directly up then left to a slab. Follow the crest to the top.

> The deep groove and cracks on the left side of the projecting rib on the right is 7 *Slowhand* ★ HVS 5a, –.

> **Descent:** Continue up steep broken ground above the crag then head right (south), eventually reaching the top of the descent gully about halfway along the crags.

⑧ Scorched Earth ★★   50m E1 5b
FA Janet Horrocks & Kev Howett 25 June 1995

Ascends the clean-cut slab sandwiched midway between two corners. Start below the corner between two small rowans.

1   20m 4c From the start of the big corner scramble horizontally rightward along the grass ledges then the slabby wall leading up and right to an easy slab. Traverse right and up to a chokestone belay beneath the open chimney on the right side of the slab.

2   30m 5b Climb a crack-line up the centre of the slabby wall then large knobbles to the easier central slab. Follow this slightly left to near its left arête just below the top of the crag. Step right into a short ramp and make a hard exit. Belay at small rock outcrop 15m further back.

SHIP ROCK

Two hundred metres further south up the Dirc is a short steep projecting buttress above an area of easy angled slabs and grass.

PORT WALL

Belay on Fs and Ns on large block 10m back from the top.
Approach: All routes are approached from the left. Scramble up easy ground then climb a short corner and arête (Severe 4a) which leads to the left end of the wall.
Descent: Scramble up heather then walk right (south) to the top of the descent gully.

⑨ Spurlash ★★ 15m E4 6b
FA Kev Howett 28 August 1994

The deep central crack. Start off the left end of the ledge. Move left under a small roof to gain a flake. Pull over the roof rightward to gain the crack, which leads with difficulty to a shelf and large flake. Pull up the wall above and finish up the fine deep crack in the pale coloured rib.

⑩ A Deep Green Peace ★★ 15m E4 6a
FA Kev Howett & Tom Prentice 11 August 1994

The thin crack immediately right of the deep crack of 10. From the left end of the ledge follow a very thin crack diagonally right into a short corner. Up this then make strenuous moves out right to gain and climb the thin crack to the shelf. Stand on the shelf and step left to the big flake of 9 and finish up this.

⑪ Murderous Pursuit ★★ 15m E3 6a
FA Kev Howett & Janet Horrocks 13 August 1994

The shallow scoop in the right side of the wall just left of the arête. Climb up to a vertical quartz-studded 'bore-hole'. Gain the thin flake crack above and follow it to a jug at its top. Pull up and right to a small flake then step right to pull onto the shelf. Finish up the cracks above.

⑫ Breaking the Wind ★★ 15m E4 6b
FA Kev Howett & Lawrence Hughes 13 August 1995

The arête. Start up 11 to just past the 'bore-hole'. Reach out right round the arête to gain a crack. Follow this into the short hanging groove, exiting onto the easier wall above.

⑬ Close to the Wind ★★ 30m E5 6b
FA Gary Latter (on-sight) 9 July 1996

Excellent well protected climbing. On the overhanging right (starboard) wall of the crag is a very prominent crack directly above the right side of the blocky ledge. Climb the crack on good holds to a good undercut flake at half-height. Continue with difficulty up the thin finger crack above, which leads to an easy-angled slab. Finish more easily up the rib (just right of 12) to belay a long way back.

DESCENT GULLY BUTTRESS

One hundred metres beyond **Ship Rock** is a further projecting buttress of clean white rock which forms the left side of the only descent gully on the entire east side.

The fine white arête is 14 *Carry on up the Kyber* ★E1 5b.

⑮ Nature's Raw ★★ 45m E1 5b
FA Kev Howett & Grahame Nicoll 28 September 1997

Excellent climbing up the grey wall right of 14. Scramble up to underneath the short corner immediately right of that route. Climb the corner passing a perched flake with care to gain a sharp flake forming the top of the corner. Step immediately right into the centre of the face and climb up, then right to gain a slight recess near the top right side. Finish onto the easy slabby rock at a junction with 14, then up the final blank looking corner, which is well protected and covered in good holds.

16 *Bournville* ★E1 5b climbs clean brown wall high up the gully.

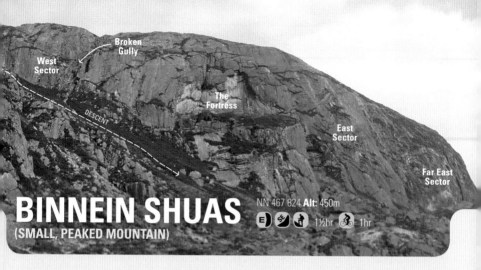

BINNEIN SHUAS

NN 467 824 **Alt:** 450m

1½hr   1hr

(SMALL, PEAKED MOUNTAIN)

A fine cliff offering a good range of routes with an idyllic outlook. The cliff has a beautiful remote feeling despite its accessibility. Being further east it can often be dry and sunny here when nearby Glen Coe & Ben Nevis are enshrouded in cloud (but has a more westerly climate than Creag Dhubh and the Cairngorms). The rock on the left side of the crag is composed of micro-granite and feldspar, while the right (Far East Sector) is composed of horizontally bedded mica schist, similar in character to nearby Creag Dhubh.

Access: Along the A86 Spean Bridge – Newtonmore road. Park at a large lay-by on the south side of the road at NN 432 830 just east of a concrete bridge over the River Spean, about a mile/1.6km west of the west end of Loch Laggan. This is 14.2 miles/22.7km west of the A889 Laggan turn-off (4.3 miles/6.9km west of the Creag Meaghaidh car park) and 14 miles/22.4km east of Spean Bridge.

Approach: Cross the bridge and follow a good land-rover track through a couple of gates (bikes will have to be carried over stile at first gate), which curves round leftwards behind the hill to the shore of Loch na h-Earba in under an hour. From just before the bridge a rougher boggy path heads diagonally across the hillside on the north side of the loch to reach the cliff in a further 25 minutes.

Descent: Follow a vague path heading left above the top of the cliffs then down the scree in the diagonal gully bounding the left side of the **West Sector**.

WEST SECTOR

From the left the first crag of any height is a fine 25m rectangular wall seamed with lots of vertical cracks.

1 **Blaeberry Grooves** ★★   **75m VS 4c**

FA Graham Hunter & Dougie Lang 17 September 1967

An excellent well protected main pitch up the deep crack system in the centre of the rectangular wall.

1 **30m 4c** Climb the crack which lies back in its upper section. Belay on the heather terrace beneath a crack system in the centre of the hanging slab.

2 **45m 4a** Climb the steep wall on good but well spaced holds to a good spike at the top. Pull onto the slab and continue easily by the central crack. Belay just beneath the top.

WEST SECTOR

② Gorgon *   **90m HVS 5a**

FA John Mackenzie & N.Fraser 1969

5m right of *Blaeberry Grooves* is a deep slot which peters out at half height.

  1 **30m 5a** Climb the offwidth slot with interest, continue direct in the same line to the heather terrace.

  2 **40m 5a** Up slabs to the foot of a dièdre and up this with difficulty to a leftward traverse.

  3 **20m** Finish up the easier slabs above.

To the right of the wide **Broken Gully** the crags gain height.

③ Cube Wall *   **120m HS 4b**

FA Graham Hunter & Dougie Lang 17 September 1967

A good main pitch up the rock to the left of the prominent vertical dyke. Start 2m left of the dyke beneath a shallow right-facing groove with a crack in the back.

  1 **35m 4b** Layback up the groove then move out onto a ledge on the left. Move diagonally left to a vertical crack system and up this trending rightward to enter the grassy left-facing corner higher up. Up this to belay on a grass ledge at its top.

  2 **20m 4b** Up the wall above to a heather terrace.

Either walk left along a path into **Broken Gully** and make a 40m abseil from tree or flake or:-

  3 **40m** Climb a short layback crack above a large boulder then follow an easy groove rightward, cutting through *Kubla Khan* to a poor belay at a quartz knob.

  4 **25m** Finish directly up an easy slab.

④ Kubla Khan **   **107m HS 4b**

FA Graham Hunter & Dougie Lang 25 June 1967

Fine climbing up the pale wall just right of the prominent vertical dyke at the left side of the cliff. Start just right of the dyke.

  1 **15m 4a** Climb the cracked lower wall directly underneath the prominent white streak to a good ledge.

  2 **45m 4b** Follow the cracks up the slab just left of the pale streak, transferring right to a further set of cracks up the pale streak to a thread belay below a huge boulder (possible abseil descent, 50m ropes gain easy ground on left). A brilliant pitch.

  3 **12m** Walk up heather on the right to the wide grassy terrace.

  4 **35m** Up a boulder on the left and finish up pleasant easier slabs. Tied off clump of grass or sprig of heather for belay!

5 The Rubaiyat ★★   70m E1 5b

FA Gary Latter & Judy Hartley 30 August 1996

A direct line up the right edge. Start down and right of
Kubla Khan beneath twin parallel cracks.

1 **20m 4c** Climb direct, passing a tiny rowan sapling
near the top to pull onto a heather terrace.

2 **50m 5b** Climb an easy niche which leads to a flared-
crack in the slab. Follow this past a thin section
low down (poorly protected crux) and continue in
the same line to a prominent right-slanting break.
Shuffle right along this and continue in the same line
to finish up a wider crack. Move out left to belay as
for Kubla Khan. Either continue up this or abseil off.

THE FORTRESS

The centre of the buttress above a large grassy terrace
has a huge capping roof. Approach by scrambling up a
grassy ramp and short corner containing a rowan to gain
the left end of the terrace.

7 Greatness and Perfection ★★★   40m E7 6c

FA Paul Thorburn & Rick Campbell June 1998

Start in the centre of The Fortress 3m right of the
prominent dirty chimney (Storming the Bastille ★E3 5c)
cutting through the huge roof. Pull over the bulge into a
scoop on the left then a gain very shallow left-hand runnel
and follow it to good nut placements at 12m (very serious).
Continue with difficulty to the roof (large Fs) and undercut
this rightward. Climb the thin diagonal finger crack with
a fiendishly hard move to reach better jams above the lip.
The easier upper crack leads to a nut belay in a bay.

8 Ardanfreaky ★★   105m E3 6a

FA Mark Charlton, John Griffiths & Alan Moist 27 May 1984

A somewhat vegetated line through the right side of
the roofs. Pitch 2 is worth the effort. Start below grassy
cracks at the right side of the huge roof.

1 **21m 5c** Climb the line of grass (yes, there is a
crack in there somewhere) to move right into the
corner and up this to a ledge. Your mate's pitch!

6 The Keep ★★   95m HVS 5a

FA Dougie Lang, Graham Hunter & M.Main (3 PA) 16 July 1967

A good route with a finely situated main pitch up the left
edge of the steep central section of The Fortress. Start
from the right end of a grassy ramp leading up to The
Garden (rowans at left end).

1 **10m 4b** Up the short steep hand/fist
crack to a block belay on a ledge.

2 **35m 5a** Climb the edge on good holds to the
prominent twin cracks splitting the steeper wall
above. Up these with interest and continue
more easily in the same fault line. An easy slab
leads to a belay on a small grass ledge.

3 **50m 4a** Move out leftward and up the
centre of the easy unprotected slab.

2 **18m 6a** Pull over the roof above on good holds into a
corner. Traverse left under the large roof to a curious
drooping flake. Step up to the roof and continue
traversing in a fine exposed position into a short hanging corner. Struggle up this to move left on to a ledge.

3 **39m 5b** Follow the diagonal crack rightward then
slabs above in the same line to a tree belay.

4 **27m 4b** The corner crack to the top.

9 Wild Mountain Thyme ★★   45m E5 6b

FA Neil Craig/Gary Latter (both led) & Rick Campbell
31 July 1995

Right of the central roofs is a steep wall with three
prominent cracks. This follows the right-slanting diagonal
one. Amble up an easy slab to a crack and along this to an
undercut. Move up to better holds then make a hard move
back right which soon leads to easy ground. Finish up the
easier vertical crack over the bulge as for the next route.

10 Bog Myrtle Trip ★★   40m E4 6b

FA Rick Campbell 6 July 1995

The deep crack on the right side of the wall. Follow the
crack with difficulty to some good finger slots then up the
excellent hand crack to a bulge. Cross this on good holds
then trend slightly right to belay at the back of the terrace.

11 Fortress Direct ★★   140m HVS 5a

FA Tom Patey, R.Ford & Mary Stewart (1 tension traverse) 16 May 1964; Lower part Rab Carrington & Jimmy Marshall July 1970

Described starting up the *Variation Start*, which gives the best line. Start on the steep right wall, about 20m up right form the toe of the buttress beneath a short left-facing groove with a roof low down.

1 **45m 5a** Up this and undercut left round into an easier groove. Up this and, at its top, traverse left and follow twin cracks to a large grassy terrace. Belay at the right side of the wall.

2 **30m 5a** Traverse out right to a triangular overhanging niche with a crack rising from its roof. Climb the fine crack, step right at the top and up to a large ledge.

3+4 65m The edge above.

EAST FACE

12 Turning a Blind Eye ★   50m E6 6b

FA Rick Campbell & Paul Thorburn 11 June 1994

The left arête of the steep right face of *Fortress Direct*. Start up the rib just right of the last route. Climb the

lower 30m (about HVS) to a small overhang beneath the steep upper section. Climb first up left to an in situ RP #1 then up and back right to a flake on the right wall. Finish straight up.

13 The Wallachian Prince ★   45m E5 6b

FA Kev Howett & Andy Nelson 1988

It bites. Good climbing up the wall left of *Delayed Attack*, gained from that route's lower crack. Up the crack to a large flake. Break out diagonally left to an arête then up to a small roof. Up right of the roof then step left along the lip to a small ledge. Struggle with the thin crack in the bulge above then blindly past a small flake to finish up a short hanging groove.

14 Delayed Attack ★★★   45m E3 6a

FA Geoff Goddard 30 July 1983

The superb right-curving crack up the right side of the face. Follow the crack with a hard section over the overhang and up a small groove. This leads to a short wide hand and fist crack in a fine position to the top. Very well protected.

THE EAST SECTOR

This is the area of rock right of **Hidden Gully**, an aptly-
named left-slanting feature splitting the much steeper
the Fortress from the generally slabbier **East Sector**.
The gully only becomes apparent from below.

15 Flypaper *   120m HVS 4c
A Graham Hunter & Dougie Lang 24 June 1967

Start about 60m up **Hidden Gully** where it begins to narrow.

1 **40m 4c** Up the red wall then over an
   overhang to beneath a small birch tree in the
   corner. Traverse right to a thread belay.
2 **30m 4c** Move back horizontally left for 8m then
   up directly for 9m, trending leftward to a terrace.
3 **50m 4c** Ascend the prominent red streak
   on good holds to a flake on the right. Climb
   the wall above the flake on small holds to
   reach and finish up a layback crack.

16 Hurricane *   155m HVS 4c
A Colin Ogilvie & Miss C.Stock 11 September 1976

Start beneath prominent rock scar about 6m below the
first step in **Hidden Gully**.

1 **40m 4c** Up a shallow corner past the rock
   scar. Continue by a faint groove to a rowan
   then up left to a belay at another tree.
2 **25m 4c** Gain a rib on the right and
   climb easily up this to a belay.
3 **50m 4c** Move down right onto a fine slab.
   Climb this centrally to an overhang. Cross the
   overhang and continue up the slab above, trending
   right to a small flake belay on a terrace.
4 **40m** Finish easily up the slab.

17 Hairline Grooves *   135m Severe 4a
A Graham Hunter & Dougie Lang 17 September 1967

A diagonal line across the slab. Start beneath a prominent
water worn fault a short way up **Hidden Gully**, down
and right of the prominent pink rock scar of *Hurricane*.

1 **30m 4a** Climb up to a spike at 6m then the

crack above to an area of dark grey schist.
Move up to belay on light-coloured rock.
2 **40m 4a** Move out rightward and up a
   vertical crack leading into a short groove.
   Traverse right and up 3 metres to the flake
   belay common with *Ardverikie Wall*.
3 **45m 4a** Follow the thin crack above and its
   wider continuation to a *"perfect thread belay"*.
4 **20m** Easily to a terrace.

Ardverikie Wall. Martin Grant nearing the top of the crucial third pitch.

18 Ardverikie Wall ★★★★   **185m HS 4b**

FA Graham Hunter & Dougie Lang 24 June 1967

'This route can be considered a classic. Its appearance belies its grading and, with the exception of the first [originally 12m] pitch and some lichen on the rib, is on perfect rock throughout and with magnificent situations. The pioneers can think of no other route of the same grading of comparable quality." – Doug Lang

Scottish Mountaineering Club Journal, 1968

A classic route on immaculate rock, possibly the best route of its grade in the country. Expect other parties at weekends. It follows a direct line up the face right of Hidden Gully. Start 8m left of a boulder which forms an arch. Harder and more direct variations may be made.

1 45m 4a Climb the rib on good holds leading to a point overlooking a short corner on the right. Move back left and continue steeply up the rib then by an immaculate slab slightly rightward and back left to ledge and flake belays. A brilliant pitch.

2 30m 4a Move right and up the beautiful flake groove to its top. Step up right to a ledge then straight up to a flake and nut belay at base of obvious thin right-slanting crack.

3 30m 4b Climb the crack then more easily up an ill-defined rib leading to easy-angled left-slanting grooves which lead easily to a large flake belay in a scooped area.

4 30m 4a Climb up to an obvious traverse line leading leftward to good holds at flake-cracks sloping left to right. Follow these, pulling easily over a small bulge then scramble to a thread belay at the back of the grass terrace.

5 50m Easy slab to a block belay on the left. Alternatively, walk left along the terrace and finish up the fine top pitch of *Flypaper* (HVS 4c).

FAR EAST SECTOR

Just beyond *Ardverikie Wall* the rock changes from the micro-granite to horizontally bedded mica schist, with some large areas of quartz. Though much of the cliff is broken and vegetated, there are a few worthwhile lines.

19 Soft Shoe Shuffle ★   **143m HVS 5a**

FA Graham Hunter & Dougie Lang 24 May 1968

Good climbing up the steep clean slab about 70m right of *Ardverikie Wall*. Start on a flat rock ledge below an overhang.

1 13m 4c Surmount a awkward overhang to reach a flake. Traverse right to an obvious crack and climb this to a flake belay on a ledge.

2 12m 4c Traverse left under an overhang for 8m, break through the overhang and go up to belay on a ledge. (The crack directly above the belay can be followed, finishing out right to the belay at the end of pitch 3 – HVS 5a).

3 18m 4b Climb the corner on the right then go diagonally right following a line of flakes to a flake belay at the left side of the slab.

4 40m 5a Continue up the obvious steep quartz band on the left and climb directly, breaking through several bulges on good holds to belay at the back of a terrace. Abseil descent (nut & maillon in situ).

5+6 60m of easy climbing leads to the terrace.

20 Eastern Chimney ★   **90m Severe 4a**

FA J.McDowell & D.Todd 24 May 1969

Well protected climbing on good rock up the prominent wide chimney 100m right of *Ardverikie Wall*.

1 45m 4a Gain the chimney by climbing the initial rib on the right. Continue to belay on grass ledge.

2 45m 4a Continue up the chimney then break left and up a prominent corner and easier rock above. Scramble to the terrace.

NN 671 958 **Alt:** 370m 🚶🚶🚶 10–20min

CREAG DHUBH

With over 150 routes of up to 100m this is far and away the largest roadside crag in Scotland. The rock is horizontally bedded mica-schist and something of an acquired taste. For those looking for well-protected routes, this is not the first place that immediately springs to mind and it has, perhaps unjustifiably, earned itself the moniker 'Creag Death' among the unconverted. The style of climbing – steep walls usually with flat or sloping holds and often well-spaced protection often dictates a bold approach.

Many of the routes dry quickly, with any seepage lines obvious from the approach. It is often a good retreat when it's wet further west around Nevis & Glen Coe and it's often possible to climb here most of the year. Although there are numerous easier routes, the best climbing and by far the highest concentration of routes is from HVS upwards, though there is still enough of interest in the lower grades. A good selection of cams will be found particularly useful, particularly in the smaller sizes. Double ropes will also be found useful, as most of the routes involve abseil descents. It's worth carrying some spare bits of tat and maillons/krabs to backup existing abseil points; also it might be worth assessing the current state of the trees before launching into the abyss!

A good overview of the crags can be gained from the field opposite the parking spot.

Access: Creag Dhubh overlooks the infant River Spey and the A86 Spean Bridge–Kingussie road, some 3.3 miles/5.3km south-west of Newtonmore (4.2 miles/6.7km east of Laggan). Park in a lay-by on the north side of the road, opposite the westmost of two small ox-bow lochans.

Accommodation: There are a couple of good camping spots beneath the crags, one on flat ground beyond the stream 300m west of the parking spot, the other up right of the parking spot, in line with **Sprawl Wall**.

Approach: Go through the gate at the car park and follow the path which soon rises steeply, scrambling over a boulder field near the top to gain a horizontal path just beneath the crags. **The Great Wall** is just up to the left, with the **Lower Central Wall** closer on the right. **Sprawl Wall** lies well up and right of here, above a large boulder field. The continuation of the crags just left of **The Great Wall** soon becomes **Waterfall Wall**. Higher up and left lies the initially-hidden **Little Rock**, with **Bedtime Buttress** the furthest left, with a prominent large projecting roof high on its right side, well seen in profile.

Crags are described as logically encountered on the approach, first from **The Great Wall** rightward, then leftward.

THE GREAT WALL

NN 671 958 **Alt:** 360m   10min

The showpiece of the crags, in its centre a superb 45m gently overhanging wall containing many of the best routes on wonderful folded contorted schist.

Descent: Usually by abseil from trees (slings in situ) at the top of all the worthwhile climbing. From the top of *King Bee*, abseil more or less straight down the arboreal *Nutcracker Chimneys* (45m; 25m). For routes left of *Brute*, abseil from an aspen (slings in situ) at the right end of a grass ledge 55m to the ground or split at multitude of bolts on the second stance of *Brute*. Routes from *Outspan* to *Inbred* all converge at another convenient tree (40m).

---

1 King Bee ★★★   115m VS 5a

FA Dougal Haston, James Moriarty & Arthur Ewing April 1965

Excellent climbing with a short well protected crux. The classic of its grade on the crag. Start at a prominent rib at the left end of The Great Wall.

 1 **25m 4c** Up the slabby right side of the rib to a small tree then left and up a shallow corner to a tree. Traverse right under a roof and climb to belay at a small tree just above.

 2 **35m 5a** Traverse diagonally left (past a possible belay) to a tiny groove in the rib. Make a difficult move over the bulge (good protection) and continue to a nut and PB on a quartz slab beneath a roof. (50m abseil possible from here).

 3 **25m 4c** Move out right to break through the roof just left of a large perched block. Up vegetation rightward to a tree belay on the right. Either abseil off, or:

 4 **30m 4c** Pull up the wall above the rightmost tree and trend diagonally left on clean rock to gain the upper grass slopes.

1a Kingbee Direct ★★   **20m HVS 5a**

FA Kenny Spence & R.Gough September 1967

An excellent exposed direct on the first pitch. From the first small tree, climb up the left side of the arête then step right (F #3 in break) and pull spectacularly through the roof on good holds to a belay just above.

2 Erse ★★   **75m E3 5b**

FA Pitches 1 & 2 Dougal Haston & James Moriarty May 1965 (aid on P.1); FA Pitches 3-5 Dougal Haston & Joy Heron May 1965; FFA unknown

A serious first pitch and fairly aptly named, as that's what you would land on from a great height! Start just left of *The Brute*.

1 35m 4b Climb a small shattered groove crossing some overlaps then boldly up the wall above to a V-notch in the roof. Cross this on good holds and go up to belay on a long ledge.

2 40m 4c Ascend the wall and crack to a ledge beneath a roof. Turn this by a bulge on the left and continue up a groove.

3 Jump for Joy ★★   **57m E2 5b**

FA Dave Cuthbertson, Bob Duncan & Alan Taylor August 1981

Good climbing up the wall between 2 and 4.

1 30m 5b Climb *The Brute* corner to the ledge. Move left and climb a wall to an old PR under the right end of roof. Step right and pull over an overhang. Move back left and up a groove to BB.

2 27m 5b Climb a wall and quartz groove to a roof, pull over this and continue to tree belays.

4 The Brute ★★   **110m VS 5a**

FA Terry Sullivan & Nev Collingham October 1959

Good climbing on the lower pitches. Start at an open groove just left of a large birch near the left end.

1 15m 4c Ascend the groove then step right and up to a ledge.

2 30m 5a Move diagonally right under the roof to cross it by a crack at its smallest point (PR). Continue to move left to belay at a plethora of bolts. Make a 30m abseil to the ground, or:

3 25m 4b Climb the big corner on the right to a tree belay.

4 40m 4b Finish up the slabby wall on the left.

5 Outspan ★★★   **45m E2 5b**

FA Robin Barley & Brian Griffiths 13 April 1971

Excellent bold climbing, steady at 5a after the initial boulder problem start, following a wandering line up the left side of the impressive main section of the wall. Start at the thin crack near the centre of the wall (8m right of the birch). Climb direct to an obvious handrail and follow this left for 4m. Ascend directly up the steep black wall on good holds (bold) to a horizontal break. Move right along this to a bulge (PR), pull over this and go up right to a large flake, continuing diagonally rightward to join 11 on long ledge. Follow this easily leftward to tree belay.

6 The Fuhrer ★★★   **45m E4 5c**

FA Dave Cuthbertson & Ian Duckworth 17 June 1979

An excellent serious pitch up the left side of the wall. Start at a thin crack near the left side of the wall directly beneath a prominent plaque of rock at 6m. Up the wall to a good rounded spike then the quartz scoop diagonally left to gain the plaque. Stand on the top of this then traverse right and up to the PR on 5. Pull over the bulge and go up right to a large flake. Climb the quartz wall diagonally leftward to a broken ledge, finishing up the steep shallow groove which leads to tree belay.

7 Colder than a Hookers Heart ★★   **45m E5 5c**

FA Dave Cuthbertson, Gary Latter & Calum Henderson 23 October 1985

Very good but serious climbing, taking an eliminate line based on 6. Climb to the spike on 6. Move slightly right to a small overhang (poor F & RP #1 on right), pull over this and directly up the wall above to the PR on 5/6. Trend left and up the overhanging wall to a jug at the base of the quartz wall. Up this going slightly left to a crack in the arête above the girdling break. Climb the crack past a dubious block and trend right to the tree belay on 11.

8 Harder than your Husband ★★   40m E5 6a

FA Grant Farquhar & Ian Marriott 21 May 1988

The most serious pitch on the wall, taking a fine central line. Start as for 9. Gain the ledge and continue up the bulging wall to a good finger jug about 3m below the traverse into the niche. Break out left and climb the quartz bulges up into the slanting niche (protection). Continue to the girdle ledge then move left to finish up 6.

9 The Final Solution ★★   40m E5 6a

FA Steve Monks & Willie Todd May 1987

A serious pitch just right of the centre of the wall. Start at the foot of the boulder to the left of 10. Climb the initial wall via a series of bouldery moves to stand on a ledge. Step left and climb directly up the bulging wall to gain a small niche at 15m – F #2. Climb directly out of the niche and up the wall passing through the second niche of 10 traverse to the tree belay at the top.

10 The Hill ★★★   60m E2 5b

FA Kenny Spence & John Porteous September 1967

A tremendous route, serious on the first pitch and very exposed on the second. Start on a large flat block beneath the rust coloured streak 5m left of 11.

  1 20m 5b Climb direct past a useless PR (good nut) to a flake runner and traverse right 5m to the triangular niche of 11.

  2 30m 5a Traverse left to a smaller niche, then continue by a slightly descending traverse to another niche. Climb straight up on big holds to below small overlaps, then make a descending traverse left to a slight niche. Continue directly on steep easier ground to finish up the final section of 11. Either abseil off or:

  3 20m 4c Climb the bulge and mossy slab starting from the right end of the ledge. Belay well back.

10a The Hill Variation ★★★★   45m E2 5b

An excellent more direct single pitch variation is possible by climbing direct from the PR to the first small niche on the second pitch. Continue as for the normal route to the long ledge on 11 and follow this up left to the tree belay.

10b Over the Hill ★★★   40m E3 5c

FA Dave Cuthbertson & Rob Kerr 24 October 1980

An excellent direct pitch through 10 giving sustained varied climbing. Follow 10a to the first small niche then move diagonally right to a small spike. Step back left and climb straight up the wall with difficulty to join 11. Follow this up left to the tree belay.

11 Inbred ★★★   55m HVS 5a

FA Dougal Haston & T. Gooding October 1964

The original route to venture up the Great Wall and one of Haston's best rock routes. A fine natural line and a good introduction to the crag. Start near the right end of the ledge, directly beneath a large spike.

  1 25m 5a Straight up the crack system to a PR, then trend leftward to pull into the triangular niche from the left. Step down and move right, then direct pulling through a bulge (just left of a large quartz patch) to the left end of the belay ledge. BB and large block on right. A more direct line perhaps nudges the grade up to E1 5a.

  2 30m 4b From the left end of the ledge follow a leftward trending line to a tree belay.

12 Strapadicktaemi ★★   50m E1 5a

FA Dave Cuthbertson & Rab Anderson 10 September 1976

Sustained climbing on good holds – a little bolder than *Inbred*.

  1 25m 5a Start up 11 for 5m then follow a thin crack cutting diagonally right until above the tree then direct, trending slightly left through bulge to the belay on 11

  2 25m 5a Traverse right 3m then climb the left-slanting crack to a bulge. Step left and continue up another crack which leads to the top.

LOWER CENTRAL WALL

The shorter wall starting 50m right of **The Great Wall**.
Descent: Abseil from trees at the top of all the routes.

NN 672 958 **Alt:** 350m [S] [🏃] 10min

---

13 **Rib Direct** *   **95m Severe 4c**

FA B.Halpin, T.Abbey & S.Tondeur, date unknown

The left-defining rib of the crag with a fine upper pitch.

1 10m 4a Climb diagonally left to belay on the large tree.

2 20m Continue up the groove to belay just above
a dead tree, at the base of a steepening.

3 20m 4c Negotiate the bulge above and continue
up the slabby corner to a tree belay.

4 45m 4a Traverse right and move up leftward to
a tree then finish up the rib in a fine position.

---

14 **Ticket to Ride** ★★★   **30m E3 5b**

FA Dave Cuthbertson & Alan Taylor 9 September 1976

Serious sustained climbing up the prominent black streak
just right of the obvious quartz patch. Low in the grade.
Start below the quartz streak. Climb up and right across the
quartz to a spike. Ascend direct to a small niche, moving left
through a horizontal quartz band to finish up the steep wall.

---

15 **Cunnulinctus** *   **65m VS 4c**

FA R.Burnet & Bugs McKeith November 1965

The vegetated chimney with a couple of holly bushes at
10m. Often damp in the lower half, but not unpleasantly so!

1 30m 4c Climb the wall on the right, moving

leftward into the chimney at the holly.
Follow this to a ledge and tree belay.

2 35m 4b Continue up the chimney, moving out right to a tree belay.

---

16 **Phellatio** ★★   **35m HVS 5a**

FA Arthur Ewing & Ian MacEacheran May 1965;
Direct Finish (as described) Ken Crocket & Colin Stead 4 June 1972

A popular companion to *Cunnulinctus*! Good steady
climbing starting up the shallow left-slanting groove 9m
right of the chimney of 15. Ascend the groove to a ledge
at 15m (possible belay). Continue directly up the wall
above, passing through a niche to finish slightly leftward
up the headwall. Tree belay.

---

17 **Mirador** *   **30m Severe 4a**

FA Ian MacEacheran, Jock Knight & R.Burnet October 1965

Start at the base of a short groove on the left bounding
rib of the deep gully. Climb the groove then move right
and follow the rib to the top.

📷 *Tony Stone running
it out on Ticket to Ride.
Photo Claire Penman.*

SPRAWL WALL

NN 674 960 **Alt:** 410m S 🖐 🏃 20min

The prominent overhanging black-streaked wall at the top right end of the crags above the large boulder-field bounding the right edge of the crags. The main (right-most) streaked section of the crag is the slowest of the crags to dry, taking a couple of days after heavy rain (check from parking spot).

Approach: From the parking spot follow a small path diagonally right to a flat knoll, from where the wall can be viewed. Continue diagonally right, negotiating the boulder field.

Descent: Either walk off right (east) and down the right edge of the cliff or abseil from large birch at the top of the centre of the main cliff.

 Tree Hee ★★   **70m Severe 4a**

FA Hamish Small & Jimmy Graham April 1965

Good climbing up the left edge of the slabby right wall of the buttress. Start round right from a short overhanging wall at the toe of the buttress.

1 30m 4a Traverse easily diagonally up left to a shallow left-facing groove near the edge. Up this to a good ledge on the arête, directly beneath a holly tree.

2 40m 4a Cross the overlap just right of the holly then trend slightly left up the slab. Bypass the final overlap on the left.

2 Jump So High Combination ★★★   **40m E2 5c**

*FA Fred Harper, Bugs McKeith & Arthur Ewing (5 PA) May 1965;
FFA with Direct Finish George Shields & party early 1970s;
FFA Murray Hamilton & Kenny Spence 1978*

One of the best pitches on the crag – sustained and varied. Start beneath a shallow left-facing groove beneath the ledge on the overhanging left section of the crag. Climb the groove then boldly up to move right to a ledge (old PR). Step left and finish up the finely situated crack in the headwall, negotiating the turf at the top with interest.

The following four routes all start from a large ledge at the base of the left side of the clean overhanging wall, gained by scrambling up rightwards then over some blocks to gain its left end.

3 Instant Lemon ★★   **45m E3 5c**

FA Derek Jamieson & Dave Cuthbertson 29 September 1980

Excellent serious climbing meandering up the left side of the wall. Start at the left end of the ledge.

1 20m 5b Climb the easy broken quartz flake then step onto the wall and follow the prominent handrail out right, then direct up the wall at its end to large ledge.

2 **25m 5c** Traverse left on superb holds for 5m, move up then follow a line of holds in a pale streak leftward to enter a groove which is followed rightward to finish up the right side of a corrugated overhang.

4 Instant Lemon Direct **   40m E5 6a
FA Dave Cuthbertson, Pete Hunter, Derek Jamieson & Cameron Lees 30 September 1980

A bold bouldery start since the disappearance of the PR.

1 **20m 6a** Climb directly up the first white streak 3m to the right of the flake, passing a small rectangular flake to join the end of the hand traverse. Move out right to belay.

2 **20m 5b** Traverse left and climb a stepped ramp then finish diagonally rightward up a wall and slab.

5 Yes, Yes *   30m E7 6b
FA Dave Cuthbertson & Joanna George September 1997

An eliminate, giving serious technical climbing direct up the wall right of 4. Start from a thread belay at the right end of the ledge.

1 **14m 6b** Climb the pale wall to a small overlap and step right into the niche on the right. Continue on good holds steeply for about 3m (protection in a succession of thin cracks to the left, the third being in the black wall above the prominent handrail which runs diagonally right across the wall). Stand on the handrail and reach left for a small hold and so to a poor PR in a little left-facing corner. From the top of the corner, rock over and make a long reach left for a good finishing jug. Continue up and right to belay at the thin crack of 2. Note: The PR fell out in Spring 2007 and will need replacing.

2 **16m 6a** Climb a thin crack 2m left of 2 until it peters out. Go left and boldly up to a large recess and protection. Continue to finish up the right side of the corrugated overhang, as for 3.

6 The Meejies **   14m E5 6a
FA Gary Latter & Lawrence Hughes 10 August 2000

A direct line up the centre of the wall. Climb easily up the crack into the niche then up to the obvious handrail. Gain a standing position on this then continue with good protection to finish on good holds. Finish up any of the routes above.

The Meejies. Dave MacLeod climbing.
Photo Dave Cuthbertson, Cubby Images.

WATERFALL WALL 15min

NN 667 956 **Alt:** 360m

The steep impressively-situated walls flanking the waterfall (Cadha an Feidh).

Descent: By abseil from trees. There is a small tree and fairly new single bolt directly above *Acapulco* (slings & krab in situ – 45m to ground). For routes from *Oui Oui* leftward, abseil from any of a number of trees at the top.

> The obvious groove up the left side of an overhung recess is 1 *Tip Off* ★ VS 4c; the prominent wide flake crack beneath the right side of the steep wall 3 *Epar* ★ VS 4b, 4a.

2 Hayripi ★★   45m HS 4b

FA Dougal Haston & Mike Galbraith June 1965

The shallow right-facing corner on the right side of the buttress.

1 20m 4b Ascend a ramp and corner leftward to a belay ledge.

2 10m 4a Traverse right to a small overhang then climb a ramp and groove to a belay ledge.

3 15m 4a Finish up the groove at the right end of the roof (*Epar*).

4 Face Value ★★   35m E3 5c

FA Dave Cuthbertson & Rab Anderson June 1981

A good pitch with spectacular moves through the initial roof. Belay on the ledge at the top of the first pitch of 3. Climb easily up to the roof about 2m left of its right end. Pull left through the roof and move out leftward above the lip to a good foot ledge and protection. Continue on excellent rock up the wall above, left of a prominent quartz vein. Tree belay up on left.

5 Independence ★★   40m E3 5c

FA Dave Cuthbertson, Rob Kerr & Calum Fraser 5 April 1981

An excellent pitch. Start beneath a shallow groove at the right side of the steep wall. Climb easily up right trending grooves to pull round a rib onto a small ledge beneath a roof. Climb up to an old PR over the roof, cross this and continue quite boldly on reasonable holds to a small ledge and protection. Continue up the wall, stepping out right to finish.

6 Acapulco ★★★   **42m E4 5c**

FA Dave Cuthbertson & Rab Anderson June 1981

Excellent climbing forging a line up the centre of the wall with a serious first pitch. Start at the base of the wall.

1 **12m 5b** Follow the left-trending quartz seam to a good ledge. Unprotected. This pitch can be avoided on either side.

2 **?0m 5c** Climb the short corner on the right then direct up the wall. Trend slightly leftward to a prominent flange over the roof then move right to a prominent block on the roof. Pull over to a good ledge. Trend leftward up the wall to a large ledge then direct from the right side to finish. The block can also be gained directly at 6a – not quite as spectacular.

7 Bratach Uaine ★★★   **35m E4 6a**

FA Graeme Livingston & Andy Cunningham August 1987

Well positioned climbing up the blunt left arête of the wall. Follow 8 to the roof, traverse right along the prominent break to a good jug on the arête and pull through the roof just to the right (crux). Continue steadily up the right side of the arête.

7a Snotrag ★   **35m E6 6b**

FA Grant Farquhar & Clare Carolan May 1989

A short, though hard and committing start takes the arête all the way, to join the ordinary route at the crux roof. Much more sustained. Boldly climb up the arête to gain a large 'fin' and protection. Continue with some *a cheval* moves to join 7 at the jug.

8 Wet Dreams ★★★   **35m E2 5c**

FA Dave Cuthbertson & Rab Anderson June 1981

A brilliant well protected jug haul. Steep and sustained. It takes the big left-facing corner right of the waterfall, bounding the left side of the very steep Waterfall Wall. Start by scrambling up slabby ground (often wet) to a ledge at the base of the corner. Climb up to the first roof and pull through this (crux). Continue up the corner and through a second easier roof then left and up past 2 PRs and a clump of trees to traverse right to belay at a large birch.

9 Niagara ★★   **65m E1 5b**

FA George Shields & Chris Norris April 1971

A very exposed line through the slabs and roofs right of the waterfall. If the first pitch is avoided the route is HVS. Start at two parallel flakes 10m up the waterfall slab.

1 **25m 5b** Traverse across the flakes and pull up to a ledge beside some quartz. Move left to another flake, up it then return right to the top of the quartz. Climb a short green groove then trend left to ledges with trees.

2 **10m 4c** Pull out left onto a recessed slab at the right end of a smooth overhanging wall. Climb the slab to trees, traverse right through these and up to a ledge.

3 **30m 4c** Spectacularly hand traverse left to avoid a roof and climb the arête above.

10 Oui Oui ★★★   **80m Difficult**

FA R.Burnet & Bugs McKeith October 1965

A fine route for water-nymphs, climbing under the waterfall with an excellent main pitch. Start to the right of the waterfall.

1 **20m** Climb grot and vegetation to belay in a flake crack beneath a steep corner on the right wall.

2 **35m** Continue up the slabby corner, (cleanest further left) passing behind the fall, to P and nut belay on good ledge.

3 **25m** Continue diagonally up left past some perched blocks to a tree belay on a grass terrace. Abseil descent.

11 Brass ★   **30m Severe 4a**

FA Allen Fyffe & Bill March April 1972

Good climbing following a wandering line up impressive ground, though slow to dry. A gully slants leftward from the slabby lower section of the waterfall to a level grassy section. Start left of here, level with a grass ledge in the centre of the wall. Traverse right to the ledge then trend leftward to the left end of the roof. Continue leftward passing its left end, finishing up a large groove.

Oui Oui.

LITTLE ROCK 15min

NN 668 957 **Alt:** 410m

Well to the left of Waterfall Wall, higher up the slope is an overhanging yellow wall with a stepped ramp-line running below it. The steepest crag here.

Descent: Traverse left and down the easy open gully, or abseil from the birch on the left of the top of the crag.

❶ Cross Leaved Heath ★★   15m E4 6a
FA Chris Forrest 1992

Good sustained climbing up the left side of the wall. Start up the initial crack as for 2. Ascend the crack then step left and move up into the tiny right-facing corner. Move up past this with difficulty, finishing directly.

❷ Heather Wall ★★   15m E4 6a
FA Gary Latter 16 June 1985

Good sustained climbing, with bigger holds than 1. Start beneath the leftmost crack 3m right of the corner. Climb the crack then direct to a large incut block at the base of the tiny left-facing corner. Continue straight up, trending slightly right to finish up another crack.

❸ This One ★   15m E4 6b
FA Paul Thorburn & Gary Latter 1991

Another good sustained workout, though close to 2 in the central section. Start 2m right of 2 beneath a couple of prominent quartz slots. Climb past these and place a small cam in the short vertical slot above. Make hard moves to gain a large incut plaque directly above then climb straight up until a step right at a good thin horizontal break leads to some sloping holds to finish past a cracked block.

❹ Un Petit Mort ★   12m E1 5b
FA Rusty Baillie & Martin Burrows-Smith 1976

Steep and strenuous climbing on huge holds up the widening crack at the right side of the wall.

BEDTIME BUTTRESS

The Barrier Wall

Lower
Right Wall

6

Lower
Left Wall

5   4

3
2
1

LOWER RIGHT WALL   15min

NN 668 956 **Alt:** 350m

A prominent quartz-streaked slab down and right of the prominent huge beak-roof.

Approach: (A) From the parking spot, walk west along the road a few hundred metres to a gate 100m beyond the bridge over the burn. Follow a good track up the left side of the burn until opposite the crags. Cross a fence and burn to scramble steeply up to the base. **(B)** Continue traversing left from the base of **Waterfall Wall**.

Descent: Abseil from trees on the terrace.

1 Porn ★★   45m E1 5a

FA John Porteous & Mike Watson 11 April 1970

Good open climbing up the left-trending line. Start beside a fallen tree.

  1 **35m 5a** Climb a short steep wall and thin
      crack to gain a corner on the right. Follow
      the corner and a left-trending line until a
      right traverse leads to a small cave belay.

  2 **10m 4c** Climb the thin crack on the right to a big tree.

2 Most Girls Do ★   40m E1 5a

FA Simon Richardson & Roger Webb & June 1985

A good direct line up the centre of the wall with good but well spaced protection. Start just right of 3 but climb straight up to the more prominent right crack. Climb this then move slightly right through a bulge and up to join 1. Go straight up to finish up the top pitch of 1 to the tree.

3 Cuckold ★   45m E2 5b

FA Dougal Haston & James Moriarty May 1965;
FFA Pete Boardman & partner 1974

Fine climbing with two good contrasting pitches. Start below a thin diagonal crack.

  1 **35m 5a** Gain and climb the crack. Traverse
      delicately left where the crack fades into
      a corner. Up this to a small stance.

  2 **10m 5b** Direct up the quartz to the overhang. Turn
      it on the left then up to a ledge and tree belay.

LOWER LEFT WALL   15min

NN 667 956 **Alt:** 350m

A more broken lower wall with a roof forming an alcove at the base.

Descent: Traverse left and down open gully at left end of crag (**The Barrier Wall** approach), or abseil from trees.

4 Downtown Lunch * **80m HVS 5b**

FA Fred Harper, Arthur Ewing & Bugs McKeith May 1965

A good first pitch. Start 5m right of the next two routes, at the right end of the initial roof.

1 **25m 5b** Step up right to a ledge with a small roof on its left then move back left to gain the main slab above (crux). Follow the obvious line, trending slightly leftward to belay at blocks.

2 **25m** Scruffy ground leads to the right end of the terrace beneath the Barrier Wall.

3 **30m 5a** Go up the gully round the right end of the Barrier Wall to a ledge on the left then a groove. Step left onto the front face to an easier finish.

5 Quickie * **30m HVS 5a**

FA Dave Cuthbertson & Rab Anderson 19 September 1977

Another useful approach. Start at the left end of the initial roof. Ascend a short wall to the roof, turn this on the left then move right about 3m and follow a line diagonally leftward to finish by a short crack.

6 Negligee * **40m VS 5a**

FA Ian MacEacheran & R.Burnet May 1965

Good climbing with an awkward start. Climb 5 to the roof and continue up a groove and corner.

Andy Nelson leaving the triangular niche on the classic test-piece The Hill, The Great Wall. Photo Dave Cuthbertson, Cubby Images.

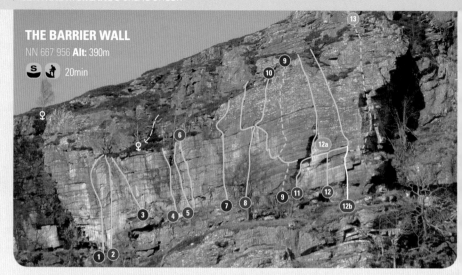

THE BARRIER WALL

NN 667 956 **Alt:** 390m

20min

This is the Upper Tier of **Bedtime Buttress**, the furthest crag from the road, high up on the extreme left of the crags. The angle varies from just off the vertical to slightly overhanging, providing a fine range of short extreme pitches. Very quick drying.

Approach: (A) From the parking spot walk west along the road a few hundred metres to a gate 100m beyond the bridge over the burn. Follow a good track up the left side of the burn and a narrower continuation then cut up the hillside to the short broken crags high on the left. Traverse right 200m along the terrace to the base of the wall.

(B) continue traversing left from the base of **Waterfall Wall** and scramble up a broken gully just left of the

Lower Left Wall leading to the left end of the main crag. **(C)** From the top of **Little Rock** head west for a few hundred metres, cross a hollow and head to a point 50m left (west) of a prominent small Scots pine at the top of the crag. Carefully scramble down a shallow recess to some small trees (see descent details below).

Descent: The quickest descent is by a short 10m abseil from the trees at the top of the left side of the wall, overlooking the 'crevasse', reached with care by some precarious but straightforward scrambling. Otherwise, traverse the length of the crags (c 200m) left (west) and descend down birch (just beyond a lone pine), cutting back along the terrace to the base of the wall.

1 The Art of Relaxation ★★   **15m E4 6a**

FA Dave Cuthbertson & Roy Williamson May 1981

Start just left of the prominent overhanging crack of 2. Up the wall to a good break on the left, move slightly right and continue up a crack to a ledge and tree belay.

2 Case Dismissed ★★★   **15m E3 6a**

FA Dave Cuthbertson & Rab Anderson 12 October 1978

Superb strenuous and well-protected climbing, taking the steep hanging finger crack up the longest section of wall

just left of the 'crevasse'. Direct up the wall to gain the crack and up this. At its top step up and right onto a foot ledge. Up the quartz crack on the left to a block overhang, finishing out left to a ledge and tree belay.

3 Cadillac ★   **12m E4 6a**

FA Dave Cuthbertson & Rab Anderson June 1981

Start on the top of the 'crevasse' to the right of 2. Step onto the wall and traverse left to join 2 at the top of the crack.

Three routes follow lines up the short wall further right. 4 *C'est la Vie* E3 6a takes a thin crack to the niche, exiting leftward; 5 *Hands Off* E2 5c follows diagonal cracks to the right side of the same niche, finishing direct and 6 *Legover* E2 5c ascends the wall direct above the start of 5, finishing slightly right.

7 Galaxy ** 15m E4 6a

FA Dave Cuthbertson & Martin Lawrence 26 April 1981

Sustained climbing up the wall left of 8. Climb directly up the wall by vague hairline cracks to gain the top break. Move left then back right, finishing by a short finger crack.

8 Ruff Licks *** 15m E3 5c

FA Dave Cuthbertson & Rab Anderson 19 September 1977

A fine introduction to the harder routes on the wall. Low in the grade. Start at a thin crack below the quartz crack containing a tiny sapling at 2/3rds height. Up the thin crack to gain the wider quartzy crack and up this to the sapling. Move left and finish up the thin crack.

9 Apathizer ** 20m E5 6b

FA Graeme Livingston & Willie Todd September 1986

Strenuous fingery climbing, though well protected, taking a direct line through the diagonal line of 10. Start 2m left of the right-facing corner of 11. Climb the wall to a ledge and thence a quartz pocket (protection). Go left until some good holds enable a traverse rightward to reach some flakes. Go up and slightly leftward to make some hard moves into the horizontal break. Leave the break with difficulty to finish up the slab above.

10 Ayatollah *** 20m E4 6a

FA Dave Cuthbertson, Rob Kerr & Calum Fraser 6 April 1981

Excellent sustained climbing with improving protection. Start as for 11. Up the corner to a roof, move left then up to a good slot. Traverse left about a metre then up to break. Move left then up to another break and small circular quartz recess. Continue up and left on small quartz holds to gain good break at junction with 8. Move right and up to finish on a slab.

11 Muph Dive ** 25m E2 5c

FA Dave Bathgate & Dick Holt (3PA) May 1965; FFA Murray Hamilton & Adge Last 19 September 1977

The stepped right-facing corner near the right end of the wall. Climb the corner, finishing up a fine easier slab at the top.

12 Muffin the Mule * 20m E1 5c

FA Dave Cuthbertson & Dougie Mullin 14 October 1977

Well protected climbing up the wall right of the corner. Start up a thin crack (awkward) which leads to a good horizontal break. Traverse this rightward to a ledge then directly up the slabby wall above.

12a Left Start * 20m HVS 5a

Good climbing and the easiest line on the wall. Start up 11 for 3m then hand traverse right along the break to make awkward moves down to better holds in a recess. Continue round right to join the normal route on the upper slab and finish up this.

12b Direct Start * 20m E2 6a

Gain the ledge by the shallow overhanging groove.

13 Downtown after Lunch ** 30m HVS 5a

A good pitch. Climb 12a to the ledge at the end of the traverse. Climb a groove above the right end of the ledge then step left and finish more easily.

📷 *Gary Latter at the start of the crack of Case Dismissed. Photo Jonny Baird.*

HUNTLY'S CAVE

NH 025 327 **Alt:** 180m 5min

An excellent steep little crag situated in a pleasant open wooded gorge with a stream running through it. The rock is schist, generally vertical or overhanging, with the bedding plane dipping down at an angle forming lots of excellent incut holds and blocky roofs. All the routes are well protected.

Although it faces north it is often sheltered from the wind by a stand of mature larches just to the north. Unfortunately this sheltered location makes it very midgy for most of the summer months – much better as a spring or autumn venue. The cave that the crag takes its name from lies beneath a boulder about 50m downstream from the far left end of the crag. First ascent details for the earlier routes are not available as the crag was only written up in the early eighties, hence the somewhat uninspiring route names.

Access: From the south follow the A939 for 2.9 miles/4.7km beyond Grantown-on-Spey to park at either side of the road a few hundred metres north-west of a trio of farmhouses at Glaschoil. There is a tiny quarry-like feature (space for two cars) on the left (south-west) side of the road. If approaching from the north these parking spots are just beyond where the old disused railway cutting runs alongside the north-east (left) side of the road for about 500m.

Approach: Cross a stile and follow path down through the trees for just over 100m to cross the old railway line and another stile. Continue down the path for about 150m to arrive at some level slabs of rock at the top of the crag.

Descent: By a good muddy path zig-zagging down the left (facing out) side of the crag.

Routes described from right to left.

1 Hanging Groove   10m E1 5c

Start 2m left of the prominent cave-like block chimney at the right end of the crag. Ascend the wall to cross the roof at a small jammed block. Finish up a short crack and the hanging groove.

2 Huntly's Jam *   10m E2 5b
FA Nick Sharpe 1987

Follows the right arête of 3. Cross the initial roof (crux) then follow the easier arête, finishing up its left edge.

3 Pete's Wall **   15m E2 5c
FA Pete Boardman 1970s

A good well protected pitch. Start just right of 4. Climb the initial wall to break through the long low roof at its smallest point to gain a good incut break (crux – reachy). Continue directly up the wall past further good breaks near the top.

4 Right Hand Groove *   10m Very Difficult

Well-defined groove, finishing past a horizontal birch tree.

5 Slot Direct *   10m Severe 4a

The leftmost of the three grooves.

6 Left Rib   12m Very Difficult

Start from a smaller subsidiary groove at the base of 5. Move left to a recess then past a pedestal. Step left ound the edge and finish by cracks leading to the slot.

7 Dead Tree Wall *   15m VS 4c

A bit of a misnomer as the tree is long gone. Start below the prominent roof a few metres down and left of 6. Climb the crack through the right end of the roof, hand traverse left a move then cross the roof and climb the wall just right of a groove. Continue more easily to a spectacular finish through the split roof left of the more prominent 5.

8 Central Crack *   20m HS 4b

Start as for 7. Traverse left beneath the roof to the arête, move up then back right. Trend leftward to gain and follow the deep crack to finish out leftward beneath the final roof. A Direct Finish over the roof to the right is possible at VS 4c.

9 Lime Street **   20m E4 5c
FA Pete Livesey late 70s

Very sustained and strenuous climbing up the innocuous looking right wall of 10, unfortunately slightly escapable near the top. Start off the blocks at the base of 10. Move up rightward to the small roof and pull through this to a huge hold. Continue up the flake, step left and up the cracked groove and the good hand crack which curves towards the top roof of 10. At the top of the crack move up rightward to layback up a line of small flakes just left of the arête. Finish more easily up the final wall.

10 Double Overhang ***   20m HVS 5a

Excellent climbing up the central left-facing corner system.

11 Bo-po Crack *   20m E3 6b
FFA Martin Lawrence 3 October 1980

A well protected technical problem through the thin roof crack left of 10. Start 2m left of 10. Up the scooped wall to the crack then through the roof and up the wall to good ledges. Finish up the final crack of 13 to the rowan tree.

12 Diagonal **   30m VS 4c

Start up 10 to the roof.

1 20m 4c Traverse left underneath the roof and step out left (crux) and up into the left-facing groove. Follow this then continue out left and up to belay in a recess beneath the final roof.

2 10m 4b Move up above the belay then out right round the roof and easily to finish.

13 Diagonal Direct *   25m E1 5c

Start a few metres right of 15. Ascend the green scooped wall and up the first corner of the normal route. Pull out right (possible belay under roof). Finish direct over the roof (crux) and the easier short wall above.

14 Slabby Groove ** HVS 5a

A bit of a misnomer, though the groove is easier angled than many of the other routes. Start up 13 but move left onto the arête. Step left and up the left side of the arête then make a hard move into the deep cracked groove. Continue directly up past small ledges to finish up the wide crack of 15.

15 Cave Route *** 25m Severe 4a

An excellent route amidst impressive surroundings, which can be split into 3 pitches. Start beneath the large bay towards the left end of the crag.

1 **18m 4a** Climb the easy initial corner to a large ledge. Traverse left 3m above the ledge then up blocks on the arête and move back right to thread belay on a large block in the 'cave'.

2 **12m 4a** Step up right and finish up the exposed wide bottomless crack – not as fierce as it looks!

Alternative Finish: Stick insects can squeeze through the narrow chimney running back from the 'cave' or the similarly thin slot at the base of the bottomless crack.

15a Cave Route Direct *** 10m MVS 4b

A better way of climbing the middle section is to continue up the right side of the flake/corner above the first ledge. Very well protected.

16 Huntly's Wall ** 25m E3 6a

FA unknown 1970s

The luminous yellow wall bounding the left-edge of the crag, with a spectacular finish through the capping roof. At the far left end of the crag is a short easy left-trending ramp. Start up the ramp for a few metres then move onto the wall on the right and up to the roof. Pull through this and up by the line of a thin finger-crack (crux) to gain a good ledge. Move easily up to a good horizontal break beneath the final roof. Pull out right onto the lip then use a good incut hold to reach up rightward to good holds. Finish past some keyed-in blocks.

Deziree Wilson breaching the first roof on the crag classic Double Overhang.

DUNTELCHAIG (ROCKY FORT) NH 643 317 **Alt:** 250m

A collection of steep gneiss crags overlooking the north-east end of Loch Duntelchaig, which lies to the east of the north end of Loch Ness. Good evening crags in a pleasant setting.

Access: Turn off the A9 just south of Daviot (7 miles/11km south of Inverness) along the B851 Fort Augustus road. Follow the road for 4.5 miles/7km to turn off right 0.2 miles/0.4km south of Inverarnie. Follow the single track C-class road turning left at the T-junction just beyond the River Nairn. Continue, passing through Dunlichity and along the shore of a small loch to a small unmetalled road on the left leading to a parking area on the left at Loch Duntelchaig.

DRACULA BUTTRESS   10min

The first large buttress on the approach, with prominent roofs on the left.

Approach: Pass a locked gate and continue down the forestry track on the east side of the loch for 450 metres then scramble up the left side of a mass of jumbled boulders to the left end of the crag.

Descent: Down the grassy ramp on the right.

 Cyclops ★★ 30m E4 6a

FA unknown; FFA Duncan McCallum 6 August 1983

Just right of the lowest point of the buttress is an overhanging right-facing corner with an ivy-covered right wall. Climb the corner to the lip of the roof and continue up the corner to a ledge. Climb more easily up the next corner to a belay. Either escape left or finish up easy slabs above.

2 Wolfman ★★ 30m E6 6b

FA Chris Forrest & Roy Henderson August 1991

The hanging groove in the arête. Now much harder following the removal of 4 PRs used on the first ascent. Start at the large block at the foot of 3. Head out left to the arête and pull over a bulge to the base of the groove. Up this with difficulty using a hidden hold on the left to pull out right to a good rest. Traverse right to join 3 in the middle of its roof pitch and finish up this.

3 Dracula ★★★ 30m E3 5c

FA unknown (A1); FFA Bob Brown & Fred Williams Autumn 1969

Superb athletic climbing through the spectacular roof crack. One of the hardest pitches in Scotland for its day.

> **1 15m 4c** Climb the prominent corner past an awkward bulge to a fine belay perch below the roof.
>
> **2 15m 5c** Follow the roof crack out left past some thin jams near its end to an easy finish up the front face. Very well protected and worth knowing about for a rainy day.

4 Vampire ★★ 30m E3 6a

FA Ado Liddell & Martin Burrows-Smith 1976

The next roofed corner above and right of *Dracula*. Start 15m right of *Dracula*.

> **1 20m 5a** Follow a left-slanting line of flakes (poorly protected) to the base of the corner then up this to a sloping stance under the roof.
>
> **2 10m 6a** Make some precarious moves to gain excellent holds on the lip. Finish up the overhanging groove above.

THE MAIN CRAG (w) (climber) 15min

A fairly rambling and generally uninspiring crag, sloping up from left to right above the jumble of boulders immediately right of **Dracula Buttress**.

Dracula Buttress

Approach: Directly through the boulders from the track.
Descent: Follow a path rightward then cut down just beyond the Chasm block, a large prominent block delineating the right extremity of the crag.

1 Misty Crack ★   30m E1 5b

FA Allen Fyffe & Ado Liddell 1982

The roofed corners and crack bounding the right side of the main slab. Start at the lowest point of the crag. Climb the first corner to exit right, then the second corner, exiting left on to mossy slabs. Traverse right just above the lip of the roof then up (possible belay) to finish up the fine crack in the steep headwall. Tree belay. Abseil descent.

2 Monolith Crack ★   35m HVS 4b

FA Ian MG & Richard Frere (in descent) 24 June 1937

The huge corner in the upper crag directly above a large aspen. Start at a crack 8m left of the monolith.

1 **15m** Climb the short wide crack above a rowan tree then by vegetated slabs trending up left to belay on the aspen.

2 **20m** Climb the offwidth crack in the corner with sustained interest (poorly protected) then an easy lichenous slab to a belay.

3 Monolith Recess ★   35m E1 5b

FA Ado Liddell & party 1978

A huge flake sits against the face at the lowest point of the crag.

1 **20m 5a** Climb the left side of the block then the fine layback crack above. Continue up more broken ground to belay at the base of the prominent crack in the headwall.

2 **15m 5b** Attack the fine crack, finishing strenuously on good jams.

④ Drum ★   **60m Very Difficult**

FA Ian MG & Richard Frere 24 June 1937

Good varied climbing up the right side of the crag. Start a short way up the vegetated ramp that runs up under the right side of the crag, directly beneath a prominent tree on the face at 12m.

1 **12m** Climb a short right-facing corner over a chokestone then up to the tree.

2 **13m** Continue up the offwidth corner-crack above then out left along a large flake crack and up past a tiny pine to belay at the left end of large ledge.

3 **15m** Climb the crack above the right end of the ledge, soon easing.

4 **20m** Continue up the fault in the same line, crossing a chokestone steeply on huge holds.

The following three pitches start from a cluster of trees on the heather terrace at the top right of the crag.

⑤ Drumhead ★   **18m MVS 4b**

FA Ian Sykes, Pothecary, John Hinde, Grant & Bell 1962

Walk left then up a heather groove to belay at large block. Climb the fine flake crack through two overlaps then easily up slabs to a block belay.

⑥ Mica Arête ★   **20m MS 4a**

FA Richard Frere 1937

From near the left end of the terrace climb an easy groove then up the right-facing groove above. Ascend the V-groove on the left, then a short crack leading onto the arête. A further shallow groove leads to a final slab.

⑦ Mica Chimney   **20m Very Difficult**

FA Richard Frere 1937

Follow 6 to the V-groove and continue up that to finish by a deep slot.

⑧ Top Corner ★   **20m HS 4b**

FA R.Bell & R.Todd 1964

Gain the terrace then scramble up and right to a tree belay at the base of the prominent corner. Climb this direct, exiting left.

THE SEVENTY FOOT WALL   15min

The steep clean wall below the right end of the **Main Crag**. The central section is unfortunately frequented by abseilers from a local outdoor centre, witnessed by the two muddy streaks down this part of the crag.

Approach: Continue along the forestry track beyond **Dracula Buttress** for a further 200m to where the wall becomes visible and follow a small well-worn boggy path crossing a stream to the base.

Descent: By a well-worn path down the right side.

① Slings ★★   **15m E1 5b**

FA Duncan McCallum or Allen Fyffe & Sammy Crymble April 1980

Sustained climbing with a perplexing finish. Right of a blocky crack right of the pillar is a thin crack. Climb the crack into a right-facing groove, up this to the roof and pull out right to finish.

② Razor Flake ★   **15m HVS 5a**

FA Duncan McCallum & John Mackenzie July 1978

The central wall has a huge sharp-edged flake above its base. Gain the right edge of the flake and hand traverse it leftward. Follow a crack to a ledge at half-height, finishing up the thin cracks above, moving left near the top to a muddy finish. The *Direct Start* is 5b.

③ Seventy Foot Wall ★   **15m HVS 5b**

FA unknown, circa 1970

The next crack-line to the right. A serious start up the wide flake crack leads to a prominent break in the overhanging headwall.

NH 602 288 **Alt:** 250m

10min

CREAG NAN CLA

THE CAMEL

A fine, fairly recently developed steep sport crag of unusual conglomerate. It lies near the top of an open gully, which doesn't get much sun and can be quite breez (keeping the midges at bay!). Take up to **15 quickdraws** for some of the routes.

Environmental restrictions: Due to nesting birds of prey, there is a complete ban on the crag from February – July. Additionally, due to the presence of rare lichen (the site is a SSSI), it has been agreed with SNH that no climbing takes place left of the first route described. Failure to adhere to these restrictions could jeopardise access to this fine venue.

Access: From the south: Turn off the A9 just south of Daviot (7 miles/11km south of Inverness) along the B851 Fort Augustus road. Follow the road for 7.8 miles/12.4km to turn off right (north, signposted Loch Ruthven) just less than a mile beyond the prominent crag of Brin Rock up on the hillside. Follow the single track C-class road for 4 miles/6.4km to park on the roadside directly beneath the crag. **From Inverness:** Follow the A862 through Dores heading towards Errogie for 11 miles/17km to the south-western tip of Loch Duntelchaig then turn left (south) up the single track C-class road for 0.7 mile/1.1km to park directly beneath the crag.

Approach: Head straight up the hill to the crag.

1 Inverarnie Schwarzenegger ★★★ 25m F7a

FA Neil Shepherd 11 August 2000

The leftmost line of resin ring bolts, easing after the crux at 20m.

2 Stone of Destiny ★★★★ 30m F6c+

FA Neil Shepherd 12 October 1999

One of the best routes of its grade in the country and almost always dry. Follow a sustained line up the centre of the wall with the main difficulties centring around the biggest 'pebble' on the cliff.

3 Paralysis by Analysis ★★★★ 25m F7a+

FA Neil Shepherd 7 August 2004

Superb sustained climbing up the continuously overhanging wall just right of 2.

4 There's Sand In My Pants ★★ 26m F6c+

FA Ali Robb 7 August 2004

Head for the huge hanging fissure at 10m which leads with interest, finishing more easily past a ledge to share the LO o

5 The Final Straw ★★★ 30m F7a

FA Neil Shepherd 5 August 2000

Stunning climbing up the huge hanging ramp. Make hard moves up the wall to gain the easier ramp. Continue up fina groove and capping overhang to gain the LO.

📷 *Deziree Wilson getting to grips with the Stone of Destiny.*

6 Giza Break ★★   28m F7b+

FA Neil Shepherd 24 September 2005

Line through ramp of 5 to share same LO.

7 Ubuntu ★★★   25m F8a

FA Dave Redpath 20 October 2007

Breaches the centre of the sweeping bulge. Start easily
up the slab, then tiring moves on undercuts lead right to
a powerful crux off small edges to a handrail. Continue
following the cool line of cobbles above.

8 Two Humps Are Better Than One ★★   23m F6b

FA Neil Shepherd 30 August 1998

The prominent ramp near the top of the gully, with crux
just below LO. Unfortunately, dirtier than other routes
here and bolting a little unfriendly.

CONAGLEANN

A fine collection of buttresses with a pleasant outlook. The central buttress containing the described routes is composed of granite while peculiarly the neighbouring crags on either side are quartzite.

Access: Turn off the A9 just south of Daviot (7 miles /11km south of Inverness) along the B851 Fort Augustus road. Follow the road to the village of Errogie. Continue for a further 1.3 miles/2km then turn left and cross the causeway splitting Loch Mhor turning left then right (following signs for Easter Aberchalder). Continue up the track on the right to park at a cottage or park by the farm and walk an extra 10 minutes.

Approach: Continue up the land rover track for a further 25–35 minutes (depending on where parked) and go through a gate in the deer fence beneath the base of the central buttress, **Raven's Roost**.

RAVEN'S ROOST

An immaculate clean lower front face capped with a very lichenous easier upper slab.

Descent: From the terrace at the top of the main slab make 50m abseil from a small tree on the left or scramble right down a grassy tongue past some small trees and down easy ground at the left edge of the **Eastern Slabs**.

 The Raven ★★   **50m VS 4c**

FA Clive Rowland & B.Ledingham 1981

Immaculate climbing in the lower section, degenerating in the easier lichenous upper half. Climb the stunning right-slanting diagonal hanging flake (very well protected), moving up and slightly right at the top to gain the upper slabs. Trend right then back leftward past a crack near the top.

NH 579 206 **Alt:** 400m   ½hr

2 Croak * 25m E1 5b

FA Martin Hind & G.Lowe 1998

The blunt rib up the centre of the front face. Start beneath a short steep crack 3m left of 3. Climb the flake crack and trend slightly left and follow the rib steeply to gain a good right-slanting flake crack which leads to a belay in a small recess on the arête. Either traverse right to the in situ nut at the top of 4 or finish up the upper slab of 3.

3 Toad's Arête ** 50m VS 4b

FA Clive Rowland & B.Ledingham 1981

Good climbing up the line of huge flakes just right of the right arête of the front face. Climb steeply over a tricky initial bulge and continue on huge holds in a fine position, trending right. Above, move left onto the slab and climb a direct line up the centre to belay just short of the top on rope stretch.

4 The Falcon * 25m E2 5b

FA Gary Latter & Sean Roberts 2 August 2000

The impressive right-facing flake up the centre of the orange scooped wall at the right side of the crag. On the first ascent the prominent upper section of the flake was gained via the wall on the right (loose rock near the base of the flake). This was removed on abseil and a direct ascent would be more logical. Gain a ledge on the right wall of the flake and go up until an obvious traverse line leading left into the top of the flake. Traverse left using a good spike to a small ledge and continue leftward to a cleaned ledge. Climb straight up on good flakes then more easily up the edge of the slab. Trend right on ledges to an in situ nut in a large flake. Abseil off.

EASTERN SLABS

The slabs flanking the upper right side of **Raven's Roost**.
Descent: Either make a 50m abseil from a small tree on the left or scramble down either end of the crag.

5 Black Slab *** 50m Very Difficult

FA Clive Rowland, Richard McHardy & Paul Nunn 1981

Excellent climbing on immaculate rock up the black streak up the left side of the slab. Slow to dry. Not well protected.

1 **15m** Climb either the slabby corner or its right rib.
2 **35m** Continue directly up the immaculate slab moving out left to belay at a small tree.

6 Ash Slab ** 50m HS 4b

FA Clive Rowland, Richard McHardy & Paul Nunn 1981

Excellent climbing up the top slab. Start 10m right of 5.

1 **30m 4b** Ascend a slabby depression then the steep wall to the right of the overhanging section. Move left along a big turfy ledge and go up a blocky groove and the rib just left of a tree to gain a ledge.
2 **20m 4b** Finish up the rib above.

7 The Streak * 40m VS 4b

FA Clive Rowland & B.Ledingham 1985

Up right of 6 beyond a shallow gully is a rib barred by a large roof at the base. Scramble leftward up vegetation then follow the water streak in a vague scoop.

Approaching the top of the immaculate Black Slab.

Colleen Maclellan pulling through the crux bulge on Final Selection Direct, Stag Rocks, Cairn Gorm.

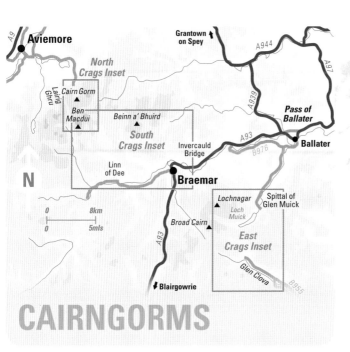

CAIRNGORMS

The mighty rampart of the high sub-arctic granite plateau of the Cairngorms forms the largest nature reserve in Europe, covering a vast area of around 770 square kilometres. Bounded on the west by the A9 Perth – Inverness road, the high Cairngorms are divided roughly from north to south into three plateaux by the long Lairig Ghru and Lairigh an Laoigh passes. These high, windswept and barren plateaux include four summits over 1220m, forming the largest tract of high land in Britain. Within this area are to be found some of the finest, and most remote, alpine-like corries in the country. In contrast, ski developments high on the northern slopes of Cairn Gorm afford convenient short approaches to a range of cliffs and corries. East of the A93 Glenshee road (the highest trunk road in Britain, rising to 670m) and the River Dee lies a broad rolling tableland dominated by the famed Lochnagar, in the heart of the Balmoral estate. Further east lies the mighty Creag an Dubh-loch, for the rock climber the finest mountain cliff in Britain with a frontage of over a kilometre of rock rising to almost 300m.

HISTORY

The first to explore the cliffs were the quartz diggers and botanists as far back as the tail end of the 18th century. The first actual recorded rock climbs of any worth date from the early years of the 20th century with Harold Raeburn and party ascending *Pygmy Ridge* in 1904. Numerous disintegrating gullies in Lochnagar and elsewhere were climbed, perpetuating the belief that the rock in the Cairngorms was poor. The Great War wiped out a whole generation of climbers. On the remote Beinn a' Bhuird in July 1933 Sandy Wedderburn, Pat Baird and E.Leslie ascended *Mitre Ridge* on the same day as the neighbouring eponymous *Cumming-Crofton Route*. Various Dundee climbers including Symmers and Ewen made attempts on Lochnagar's *Eagle Ridge* but it was the irrepressible Dr Jim Bell and Nancy Forsyth who completed this regal route in 1941. In many ways this particular route had a similar effect as *South Ridge Direct* on Arran in turning around the groundswell of opinion on the quality of rock climbing to be found in the whole of the Cairngorms. Where many of the previous additions were, with a few notable exceptions, on poor rock, the quality of the rock away from the gullies and on the cleaner ridges and open faces was soon realised. Other quality routes appeared throughout the decade, including *Savage Slit* in Coire an Lochain from Richard Frere in 1945. In Coire Sputan Dearg, R.Still and Miss E.J. Lawrence's ascent of *Crystal Ridge* in 1948 soon became a classic. The following year eight further routes appeared in the coire including *Hanging Dyke* from Allan Parker and J.Young and *Snake Ridge* from Bill Brooker and party.

Development picked up throughout the fifties, Ian Brooker and Miss M. Newbigging adding the first route on Hell's Lum Crag with *Deep-Cut Chimney*. Tom Patey and Bill Brooker picked the plum *Squareface* in the remote Garbh Choire. The first route to venture onto steep rock on Creag an Dubh-loch was *Vertigo Wall*, a very bold venture by Patey, climbed in the rain in tricounis. A similar psychological breakthrough occurred the following year (1955) when Jerry Smith climbed *Pinnacle Face* on Lochnagar in rope-soled shoes. On the same day Patey and John Hay added the first route on the Crimson Slabs of Creagan a'Choire Etchachan; *The Dagger*, with some aid. Other classics soon sprung up in the coire including *Talisman* from Bill Brooker and Ken Grassic and *Djibangi* from Hay.

In the Loch Avon basin Ronnie Sellars and Mac Smith climbed the classic *Afterthought Arête* and the surprisingly straightforward *Final Selection* on Stag Rocks. Over the next couple of years Sellars and G. Annand moved

onto the open slabs of Hell's Lum Crag with *Devil's Delight* and the fine *Hellfire Corner*. On Shelter Stone Crag across the way the same pair forced *The Citadel*. Though grassy and nowadays justly neglected it was the first route to break through the main bastion. Marking an end to the decade Jimmy Marshall sprung *The Mousetrap* up the edge of the slabs at the base of Creag an Dubh-loch's Central Gully Wall.

In July 1960 the chairlift opened on Cairn Gorm with the access road to the car park at 650m on the slopes of Coire Cas markedly altering the ease of access to both the Northern Corries and the Loch Avon basin. Activity slowed down in the early sixties, though Ronnie Kerr's ascent of *The Sheath* on Creagan a'Choire Etchachan in boots gave possibly the first HVS in the massif. With his superb eye for a line, Robin Smith with Graham Tiso added the best line on Hell's Lum with *The Clean Sweep*. Smith returned the following year (1962) in the company of Creagh Dhu strongman Davy Agnew to thread *The Needle* up the full length of the Main Bastion on Shelter Stone Crag. This route was a significant breakthrough in that it was the first extreme in the Cairngorms. Sadly it was Smith's last great climb, as he was tragically killed in the Pamirs later that summer.

Creag an Dubh-loch saw an intense period of activity as standards rose throughout the latter part of the sixties. Jim Stenhouse and Brian Lawrie established the first route on The Central Slabs with *Dinosaur* in 1964. The following year Edinburgh Squirrels Dave Bathgate, Arthur Ewing and Jim Brumfitt made an epic ascent of *The Giant* with much aid, including a forced bivouac beneath the big corner. Mike Forbes and Mike Rennie grabbed a couple of plums on The Crimson Slabs with the very fine *Scabbard* and the hard *Stiletto*. Around this period routes were recorded on Eagles Rocks, though Freddy Malcolm and others climbed here in the fifties. In 1967 Yorkshire brothers Robin and Tony Barley breached the Broad Terrace Wall with *Culloden* and Brian Robertson and Allen Fyffe added another line on the Central Slabs with *The Blue Max*.

The slabbier front face of Central Gully Wall saw *King Rat* from Fyffe and John Bower and *Cougar* with aid from

Mike Rennie and Paul Williams the following year. Major routes appeared on the Shelter Stone Crag that year (1968) with *Steeple* from Kenny Spence, John Porteous and Mike Watson and *The Pin* from Rab Carrington and Jimmy Gardiner, the first route to breach the *"manifestly impossible"* Central Slabs. The wealth of good unclimbed rock on Creag an Dubh-loch soon came in for scrutiny. Three classics of *Black Mamba, Falseface* (some aid) and *Goliath* fell in one day to teams comprising Fyffe and John Grieve, Graeme Hunter and Dougie Lang, and Brian Findlay and Mike Rennie respectively. Fyffe and Grieve stayed on for the rest of the week, adding a further four routes, their best contribution being *Pink Elephant*. Lang and Hunter returned the following year, adding *Sword of Damocles* with aid, and Ian Nicolson and Dave Knowles added their *Dubh Loch Monster*.

Around this period Stac an Fharaidh was developed mainly by John Cunningham and George Shields, then Bill March, with *Whispers, Pippet Slab* and *Linden* being the best additions. Carrington and Nicolson's ascent of *Haystack* in 1971 remained the hardest route in the area until the late seventies. Dougie Dinwoodie and Bob Smith were the most active, both on Creag an Dubh-loch and Lochnagar, whittling away at reducing the aid and finding good new lines on Lochnagar, culminating in *Black Spout Wall* on-sight with some aid in 1976. Standards were raised in 1977 when Dave Cuthbertson and Murray Hamilton made free ascents of *Cougar* and *The Giant*, the latter route unfortunately suffering a huge rock fall fairly recently. The compelling line of *Cupid's Bow* on the Shelter Stone's Central Slabs was climbed by Dinwoodie with some aid but on-sight and without chalk. The first of a new generation of routes to be cleaned and inspected on abseil appeared in 1979 when Hamilton and Spence climbed the technical *Sans Fer*. Not all the activity was in the extreme grade however, and one particularly noteworthy find was Dinwoodie and party's *Magic Crack*, far and away the best rock route in Coire an t-Sneachda. Cuthbertson completed *The Missing Link*, a bold sweeping line across the Central Slabs, previously attempted by others.

1982 saw the start of a new phase of activity in the Cairngorms. On the Shelter Stone Crag Hamilton and Rab Anderson added *The Spire* and made a free ascent of *Cupid's Bow*, whose second removed some of the pegs. Pete Whillance added *The Harp* and the bold *The Run of the Arrow*, a line previously attempted on-sight by Dinwoodie whose high point was for many years marked by the welcome sanctuary of two hammered nuts just beneath the crux. The main activity that summer was a number of impressive routes on Creag an Dubh-loch, with Hamilton and Whillance to the fore. The bold *Slartibartfast* started things off closely followed by *The Naked Ape, The Ascent of Man, Voyage of the Beagle* and a host of others. The following year Hamilton, with Spence and Anderson, added *Flodden*, the first route to breach the smooth steep left side of the Broad Terrace Wall. Aberdonians Dougie Dinwoodie and a young Graeme Livingston soon made their own contributions with their *Perilous Journey*. The following year, after Dinwoodie had put much effort into cleaning, and made several attempts on the line, Hamilton stepped in and nabbed the hardest route yet with the pointedly named *Cannibal*. Dinwoodie soon completed a number of routes on the False Gully Wall including the tellingly named *The Snake*. The Aberdonians, with Dinwoodie and Livingston to the fore, completed many further hard routes with *The Improbability Drive* from Livingston and *Fer de Lance* and a host of others from Dinwoodie.

On the Shelter Stone Crag early nineties activity was dominated by Rick Campbell who established a trio of hard slab routes, all E7 and of very different character.

… Hamilton stepped in and nabbed the hardest route yet with the pointedly named *Cannibal*. Dinwoodie soon completed a number of routes on the False Gully Wall including the tellingly named *The Snake*.

Preceding these cutting edge routes, Campbell made the much sought after long awaited free ascent of *Thor* in 1989, then the bold *Aphrodite* the following year, the crux climbed on-sight. *The Realm of the Senses* and *L'Elisir d'Amore* soon followed. Also here, Rab Anderson contributed the fine *Stone Bastion*, the crucial final corner pitch gained by abseil and redpointed. Two of the most active climbers on the Dubh-loch in the nineties, Wilson Moir and Rick Campbell, went on to add their own desperates on the Central Gully Wall, both climbed on-sight (though Dinwoodie had cleaned both in the late 80s). Moir's *The Shetlander*, and Campbell and Paul Thorburn's *Hybrid Vigour* raised the standard. The first two pitches of the latter route had previously been climbed by Dinwoodie back in 1987 via an indirect start.

Around this period nearby Lochnagar was brought thoroughly into the nineties by Moir with a series of good hard pitches including *The Existentialist*. The following year Moir and Neil Morrison climbed the evocatively-named *Steep Frowning Glories* up the full length of the cliff, another line that had been previously cleaned by Dinwoodie. At the Dubh-loch, slab aficionado Julian Lines went on to top-rope and then lead the thin pitch of *Buddha*, the first E7 on the crag and now the most popular of the hard routes with no less than five ascents to date, including an on-sight. The final phase of development on the cliff has seen two further hard additions, with Thorburn adding another excellent high standard route with the stunning arête of *The Origin of Species* on the Central Gully Wall. Gary Latter forced *An Spearag* up the centre of the False Gully Wall.

On the smooth glacial polished slabs around the base of Hell's Lum Crag, Lines added another E7 when he soloed the short thin smearing pitch of *Firestone*. Lines later completed a further trio of hard thin slab pitches in the vicinity including *Devilicious* and *Devil's Advocate*. Although the two big crags of Creag an Dubh-loch and The Shelter Stone Crag still continue to attract the majority of climbers in the extreme grades, others have journeyed further afield in the search for new unclimbed rock. In the remote Coire Sputan Dearg, Moir contributed another two fine hard routes with *Flying Saucers* and

Bolero. Significantly, Lines also repeated all three of the Shelter Stone E7s, Thorburn beating him to the second ascent of *The Realm of the Senses* and Lines stringing together the logical combination of *The Realm of the Senses/L'Elisir d'Amore*. In his own inimitable style, in June 2003 Lines went on to produce what many consider one of the most impressive displays of bold committing climbing in the country with his audacious ascent of *Icon of Lust* heading straight up the slabs from the start of *The Realm of the Senses*.

Final development on the cliffs includes the fine oft-tried line of *The Seventh Circle* from Iain Small in Hell's Lum, and a number of fine extremes on the West Wall of Mitre Ridge on Beinn a' Bhuird from Pete Benson and Guy Robertson, including *Spear of Destiny* and the superb *Freebird*.

CAIRNGORM OUTLIERS

The Red Craigs in Glen Clova have been climbed on since at least the late thirties, W. Ward and John Ferguson adding the fine *Flake Route* and Ferguson and Graham Ritchie *Parapet Route* around this period. In the 50s D. Brown climbed the fine *Alder*, George Malloch the classic *Proud Corner* and *Special Brew*, and Ian Sutherland and Donald Watt *High Level Traverse*. Many of the earlier partially aided routes were freed in the mid-seventies with Ged and Ian Reilly freeing *Special Brew* and *Guinness*; Steve Scott and Reilly freeing *Zig-Zag Direct*, and Murray Hamilton *The Red Wall* and *Witches Tooth*. Further up the Glen the excellent isolated granite crag of Juanjorge received its first routes with Hamilton climbing the superb *Roslin Riviera* and Kenny Spence *Ladies of the Canyon*.

A large number of quality harder routes appeared throughout the eighties. Neil Shepherd contributed *Wandered* and *The Wildebeest*, Dougie Dinwoodie *Empire of the Sun*, Colin MacLean *The Sorcerer*, and Hamilton freed *Roman Candle*. Dundonians Grant Farquhar and Graeme Ettle were the most prolific throughout the late eighties. Ettle headpointed the very bold *DRI* and *Cinderella* with a rest point (freed on second ascent by Gary Latter), and Farquhar added

The Whoremistress, *The Supernatural Anaesthetist* and the hardest addition with *A Vanishing Breed*. Farquhar returned in 1995 to add the stunning and difficult *Times Arrow* up the centre of Juanjorge.

The Pass of Ballater was developed mainly by Aberdonians from the sixties onwards. Throughout the seventies a steady trickle of quality routes appeared, with John Mothersele adding the fine *Black Custard*, Brian Lawrie *Medium Cool*, Dave Wright getting *Blutered* and Guy Muhleman freeing *Little Cenotaph*. Standards leapt considerably with Yorkshire raider Jerry Peel's ascent of his eponymous *Peel's Wall*, at E4 6a possibly the hardest pitch in Scotland at the time, alongside Cuthbertson's similarly-graded *Chalky Wall* at Polldubh.

Bob Smith freed the excellent *Anger and Lust* in 1980 soon followed by Murray Hamilton's free ascent of *Bluter Groove* in 1982. Alastair Ross added a number of routes including *Silent Spring* and the late Bob Smith left his mark with his headpointed ascent of what was later dubbed *Smith's Arête*. Throughout this period Dougie Dinwoodie produced a wealth of excellent extremes including *Rattlesnake*, *Cold Rage*, *Lech Gates*, *Demon Drink* and *Drambo*. Graeme Livingston also added a number of hard lines including *Captain Copout* and *Distemper*, with Willie Todd releasing his *Hot Temper*. Bringing things to a fitting close, Tim Rankin headpointed the technical and bold *Wife Beater*, at E7 6c far and away the hardest pitch on the crags.

📷 Scott Birse on the wonderfully situated Afterthought Arête, Stag Rocks, Cairn Gorm.

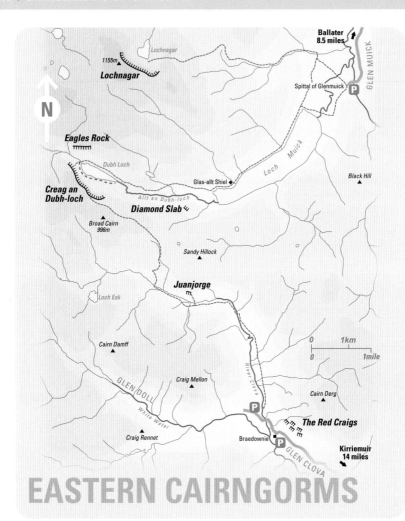

EASTERN CAIRNGORMS

Accommodation: Ballater is the nearest town with numerous hotel and B&B establishments though there is a dearth of bunkhouses and Youth Hostels, except The Schoolhouse (☎ 01339 756333; www.theschool-house.com). **TIC** in Station Square (☎ 01339 755306). **Amenities:** Fish & Chip shop in Golf Road, the next road west of the square. Bar meals in many hotels. Lots of tourist cafes/tearooms in Bridge (main) Street – the Silver Teapot does good breakfasts, as does Station Cafe. Bank with ATM here also. Public toilets in the main square behind the church. For pubs try the Barrel Lounge of The Glenaden Hotel in Church Square. For young ravers there is often a disco in the back on a Saturday evening. Outdoor shop: Lochnagar Leisure (☎ 01339 756008) in Station Square. Mountain bike hire: Wheels and Reels (☎ 01339 755864).

Campsite: Ballater Caravan Park (☎ 01339 755727) at south end of town (signposted) at (NO 371 954). There are spots for wild camping in upper Glen Muick.

GLEN CLOVA

THE RED CRAIGS

Glen Clova lies in the southern edge of the Cairngorms and The Red Craigs provide many easily accessible, fast drying routes all within 10–15 minutes walk from the road. A south-west aspect makes it possible to climb on the crags for most of the year, though it should be remembered that they lie at an altitude of over 300m (1000ft). The climbing and setting is somewhat reminiscent of the Lake District (without the lakes and the crowds). The rock is diorite, a coarse grained form of granite varying from rough and rounded to smooth and angular.

Access: Follow the A90 north from Dundee turning off to Kirriemuir. Bypass the town and continue north on the B955 following the signs for 'the glens'. From Aberdeen the shortest route is to leave the A90 at Finavon and follow the B957 to Tannadice then by minor roads to Memus and Dykehead. On reaching The Clova Hotel pass over the narrow bridge and continue up the glen for 2.9 miles/4.7km. Park on the verge on the left just beyond a long thin stand of larches and pines beneath the crags or a few hundred metres further on in the quarry on the right.

Accommodation: The Clova Hotel (☎ 01575 550222) has a bunkhouse and serves good pub food and even better ale. For the impecunious, there is a capacious (sleeps 12 comfortably) but draughty howff under the boulders below the **South-East Crag**. There are also two club huts near the crags – Whithaugh (NO 300 742) belonging to the Forfar & District Hillwalking Club – bookings via Clova Hotel and the Carn Dearg MC Hut just beyond Breadownie Farm at NO 286 758.

The Red Craigs, on the right (north) side of the road near the head of the glen, consist of six crags in all – the slabby **South-East Crag**, with the steep **Central Crag** just up to its left, the **Upper** and **Lower North-West Crag** and the two-tiered **The Doonie**.

Approach: Head directly up the hillside to the crags.

Upper Doonie

Lower Doonie

P

Upper North-West

Lower North-West

Central

South East

SOUTH-EAST CRAG

The eastmost (furthest right) crag on the hillside, with the best easier routes

Descent: Scramble off to the left and down the open gully running underneath the base of **Central Crag**.

1 Three J's Chimney ★　　　**12m Very Difficult**

FA J.Scroggie, J.Scott & John Ferguson July 1938

Just right of the left edge of the crag is a short chimney. A tricky start leads to better holds and protection. (The nearest city, Dundee, used to be famous for the 'three J's' – jute, jam & journalism.)

2 The Wildebeest ★★　　　**20m E4 6a**

FA Neil Shepherd 1986

Good sustained climbing tackling the roofed niche in the upper right side of the wall. Start beneath a prominent orange coloured wall. Step off a boulder and climb directly up the wall to a ledge below the niche. Climb the niche, pulling through the roof on good holds to finish more easily.

3 Parapet Route Direct Start ★　　　**12m HS 4b**

FA unknown

Start above and right of the lowest point of the wall right of the vegetated gully. Follow a corner-crack fault line leading to the terrace.

The following routes all start from a long grassy terrace, gained either from the right or by starting up the previous route.

4a Parapet Route Direct ★★　　　**45m MVS 4b**

FA Ged & Ian Reilly 1970s

Start 4m further right than the normal start at another short shallow left-facing corner near the right end of the terrace. Climb cracks above, stepping left to a ledge beneath a prominent steep crack (possible belay). Climb up into the hanging corner finishing up the final section of the ordinary route.

4 Parapet Route ★★　　　**45m Severe 4a**

FA John Ferguson & Graham Ritchie 1 September 1940

Start just right of 5 beneath a short left-facing corner. Climb the corner and the short steep chimney just right then move diagonally left to a groove. Ascend the groove, stepping right delicately to a crack leading to a large flake. Finish steadily up the right rib of the wall above.

NO 297 756 **Alt:** 330m

15min

5 Central Crack ★★★   40m HS 4b

FA unknown

An excellent well protected pitch on superb rock up the
shallow left-facing corner.

6 Flake Route ★★   40m VS 4b

FA W.Ward & John Ferguson 27 August 1939

Start beneath a short chimney at the left end of the
terrace. Climb the chimney and step left and up over
some blocks to a projecting block on the arête. Pull over
this and up to a large flake. Move up diagonally right to a
rounded boss then direct to finish on better holds.

📷 *Ianes Auchterlonie storming up Central Crack
in his Californian pants, man!*

CENTRAL CRAG   15min

NO 295 757 **Alt:** 400m

The overhanging wall with a distinctive orange patch
above the descent rake for **South East Crag**.

Descent: Scramble up the hillside to an old fence
then follow a vague path rightwards and down the
scree filled gully.

1 Empire of the Sun ★★   30m E4 6a

FA Dougie Dinwoodie & Jeff Hall 1986

Good well-protected climbing starting up the orange
patch. Climb slabs then directly up a crack in the loose
orange rock to a slabby ledge. Gain the flake on the left
then move up and left to another flake. Move up right
along a crack until it is possible to pull up to small flat
ledge (crux). Climb direct to belay on a large ledge. Finish
up the short (5a) wall above.

NO 293756 **Alt:** 330m

10min

LOWER NORTH-WEST CRAG

The prominent crag directly above the approach path.
Descent: Down a path at the right side of the crag.

① Cauldron Crack ★★   20m HVS 5a
FA unknown

The overhanging recess up the right side of the pillar
gives a good steep pitch on huge holds. Climb the lower
corner to huge flake holds at the roof. Move out left then
step back right (PR) past a holly to gain a ledge. Finish up
the short wall.

② Witches Tooth ★   20m E1 5b
FFA Murray Hamilton & Dave Brown 1976

Well protected climbing up the left side of the pillar.
Climb the crack leading into a niche. Step left into a
corner crack and follow this and the short wall above.

③ Monster's Crack ★   20m HS 4b
FA Andy Mitchell 1954

The prominent left-facing corner crack. Climb the lower
corner past assorted shrubbery, finishing up the short
steep corner crack on the right at the top.

④ Cinderella ★★   30m E5 6a
FA Graeme Ettle 1987 (headpointed with 1 PA);
FFA Gary Latter & Kev Howett 6 July 1988

A good reasonably protected pitch up the leaning wall
round to the right of 5. Start at the large pointed flake on
the ledge left of 3. Climb the thin crack (PR) and the ramp
leading left to a large flat hold (small Fs in break on left).
Stand on the hold and up steeply to another PR (or R #4
placement). Swing into the corner on the left then step
back right to finish easily.

⑤ Proud Corner ★★★   30m VS 4c
FA George Malloch 1950s

One of the best pitches on the crags, following an
exposed well protected line up the blunt right arête of
the *Beanstalk* dièdre. Start beneath a pair of cracks on
the arête. Follow either of the cracks or the arête to a
good ledge at 10m. Climb large flakes up the arête to a
PR on a small triangular slab. Continue directly on good
pockets to reach a small ledge, move right then directly
by a tiny corner to finish.

⑥ The Beanstalk ★   30m Severe 4a
FA Tom Patey 1954

The great recessed dièdre in the centre of the face. Easily
up broken rock to a short chimney then the crack on the

right to a ledge. Continue slightly rightward to a tree, finishing up the steep crack behind. The corner on the left provides a slightly harder finish at VS 4c.

 Wander ★   **30m HVS 5b**

FA W.Divers & Ken Sturrock 1957

Start beneath a prominent vertical crack 6m left of the corner of 6. Go up the crack to a ledge then move left and climb the shallow corner to a tree. Make an exposed step out right and finish up a crack past ledges.

 Wandered ★★   **30m HVS 5a**

FA Neil Shepherd 1982

Very good well-positioned climbing up the open wall left of the corner. Start up the crack as for 7 to the ledge.

Follow the steep flake crack on the right to gain a large ledge. Move up into the recess on the left, step round the arête and finish up the exposed final wall on good holds.

9 Twenty Minute Route ★   **45m Moderate**

FA J.Nisbet & John Ferguson March 1939

The broken rib bounding the left side of the main face. Start below a corner crack at the lowest rocks.

1 **10m** The corner to belay on the large terrace.

2 **10m** Left slanting crack to tree belay.

3 **15m** Climb direct behind the tree to gain a bulging slab or move out left onto the rib and gain the same position.

4 **10m** Cross the bulging slab and move out left to easy ground.

UPPER NORTH-WEST CRAG

A fine varied crag high on the slope just up and left of the top of **Lower North-West Crag**.

Descent: Follow a path up and left to a small cairn at the top of the descent gully bounding the left side of the crag.

1 **20m 5c** Climb up to a good hold, step right onto the grey slab and pull over the bulge to a spike. Continue past large sloping ledge above then easily to a flake belay.

2 **20m 5a** Move up left then back right beneath a small roof to the crack and finish up this.

Routes from right to left.

1 The Red Wall ★★   **35m E1 5b**

FA B.Forbes (Aid) 1950s; FFA Murray Hamilton & Dave Brown 1976

Fine climbing up the central crack in the smooth red wall. Start beneath a steep flake crack in the initial grey wall.

1 **20m 5b** Climb the steep flake crack right of a large detached flake to gain a huge sloping ledge. The easy open quartz chimney above leads to a belay.

2 **15m 5b** Step out right and climb the fine crack on immaculate rock to the top.

2 Kremlin Control Direct ★   **40m E2 5c**

FA Alistair Ross & Ged Reilly 1985; Direct – Simon Stewart & Catherine Smith 1986

The leftmost crack-line in the smooth red wall at the lowest point of the crag. Start below some blocky overhangs at the left side of the steep grey wall.

3 Alder ★★   **30m VS 4b**

FA D.Brown 1951

Excellent airy climbing crossing some unlikely looking ground for the grade. Start in the right side of the overhung recess behind the large aspen (not an alder!).

1 **10m 4b** Follow wide cracks to a nut and PB on a large ledge.

2 **20m 4b** Move out right then back left and finish directly.

4 Puddin' Fingers ★   **25m E2 5c**

FA Alec 'Tam' Thomson & Ian Shepherd (3PA) 1982; FFA Grant Farquhar, Graeme Ettle & Simon Stewart 1985

The steep flake crack on the right side of the overhanging wall. Start behind the rightmost aspen. Climb the steep initial flake crack continuing in the same line.

⑤ Sorcerer's Apprentice *   25m E2 5c

FA Colin MacLean & Ged Reilly 1985

Sustained climbing up the steep crack in the right side of the overhung recess. Start up and left of the rightmost aspen below a steep flake. Climb the flake then move out right and up the crack passing a tiny rowan near the top.

⑥ The Supernatural Anaesthetist *   25m E4 6a

FA Grant Farquhar & Simon Stewart September 1987

Sustained technical climbing up the hanging orange groove on the left side of the overhung recess. Start up 7 to the huge hanging flake. Make hard moves right into the groove and ascend this with interest. Near the top step out right then back left to finish at a projecting flake.

⑦ The Sorcerer **   25m E3 5c

FA Colin MacLean & Ged Reilly (in two pitches) 1985;
FA in one pitch Murray Hamilton 1985

Good well protected climbing. Start at the second aspen a short way up 9. Step right and up a short groove and slab to a large block. Undercut this leftward to good flakes in the corner and up to beneath the huge hanging flake. Undercut this spectacularly leftward then finish up an easier flake groove. Belay just beneath the top or further back.

⑧ A Vanishing Breed **   35m E6 6b

FA Grant Farquhar & Arthur Collins 1990

Steep powerful climbing up the wall high in the centre of the crag. Start at the base of the cleft of 9. Gain the wall via a crack, which is followed until it peters out. Move up and step right to a large sloping shelf and protection (2 RURPs in situ; R #1 down and right; Tri-cam #1 up and left in crozzly pocket). Climb the wall above bearing right to join 7 at the end of its flake.

⑨ High Level Traverse & Direct Finish **   40m HS 4b

FA Ian Sutherland & Donald Watt early 50s
Direct Finish D.Thomas, J.Fleming & 'Goggs' Leslie April 1950

A fine unusual route with two contrasting pitches. Start at the back of the overhung bay down and right of the huge overhung cleft-fault.

1 **20m 4b** Move up left to the base of the cleft and enter it with difficulty. Squirm more easily up it to spike and nut belay on ledge at its top.

2 **20m 4b** Traverse left across the exposed slab and round the corner to the base of a short narrow chimney. Move up this with interest then continue up the wide flake-crack to finish more easily.

NO 293757 **Alt:** 400m
15min

⑩ Zig-zag Direct ★★　　　　　　　**45m HVS 5b**

FA Doug Lang 1960s; FFA Steve Scott & Ian Reilly 1974

A good sustained meander. Start at cracks in the slab, down and right of the prominent cracked roof of 11.

1　**20m** Zig up and right across the slab to a large block (PR). Pull over the block and climb the crack on the right to belay on a pedestal above a deep cleft.

2　**25m** Climb the corner above then zag out left at a prominent hand rail beneath the capping roofs.

⑩ₐ Zig-zag Double Direct ★★　　　　**40m E2 5c**

FA Mick Tighe (pitch 1) 1972; FFA Simon Stewart & Grant Farquhar 1985

An excellent well protected pitch. Start beneath the large open corner of 10. Follow the steep crack-line through the roof then out rightward as for 10. Continue easily

up the corner to negotiate the capping roof (crux) which soon leads to good holds and the top.

⑪ Roman Candle ★★　　　　　　　**18m E3 6a**

FA Davie Crabbe, J.Howe & Doug Lang (A3) 1964; FFA Murray Hamilton, Rab Anderson & Duncan McCallum 24 September 1983

A short steep athletic problem tackling the roof crack at the left end of the crag. Up easy slabs to the right-facing corner in the roof. Climb the corner and hand traverse out to the lip (PR). Pull over strenuously to gain the slab above.

⑫ Just Another Sparkler ★★　　　　**15m E3 6a**

FA Murray Hamilton & Neil Shepherd 1985

The flakeline in the steep wall just left of 11. Strenuously gain and climb the flake with difficult finishing moves pulling onto the easy slab above.

📷 *Malcolm Davies pulling through the crux moves of Just Another Sparkler.*

THE DOONIE

The dome-shaped mass of rock on the left side of the hillside, above the quarry. The upper and lower tiers are split by a large left-slanting diagonal terrace.

LOWER DOONIE 10min

NO 290758 **Alt:** 300m

The generally broken lower crag though with a fine clean wall near the left end.

Descent: Down the diagonal terrace then steep grass at the right side of the crag.

1 Ant Slab ★★   25m Difficult

FA Unknown

A good pitch up the clean pink slab on the right side of the crag. Follow a diagonal crack up right then another back left into the centre of the slab. Direct up this to a block belay.

2 Special Brew ★★   50m HVS 5a

FA George Malloch 1950s (sling aid); FFA Ged & Ian Reilly 1974/75

A good exposed route up the centre of the main face. Start below a pink right-sloping ramp, just right of 3.

 1 **15m 4a** Follow the vegetated ramp then
    move up and right to belay at a peg.
 2 **20m 5a** Move up and left to a PR at a small ledge.

Climb the steep juggy cracks above to a short corner (PR). Traverse right to belay on the large ledge.

 3 **15m 4c** From the right end of the ledge climb over the large detached block and continue in a fine position to the top.

2a The Furstenberg Finish ★★   30m HVS 5a

FA Grant Farquhar & Simon Stewart 1988

A good left finish. From the short corner on the second pitch step right then up the wall to a shelf beneath a prominent V-niche. Traverse left with a tricky move to gain better holds in the groove on the left. Finish more easily up this.

2b Special Brew Direct ★★   25m E3 5c

FA Nick Sharpe & Graeme Ettle 1985

A good well protected line cutting through the original route. Climb directly up the grooves above the belay to gain the large belay ledge on the right. Climb the wall directly above the left side of the ledge to finish.

③ Guinness ★★   50m E1 5b

FA Fred Old, George Malloch, Frank Anderson & Alex Ferguson (2PA) 1958; FFA Ged & Ian Reilly 1974/5

The crag classic on superb rock. Start 5m up and right of the toe of the crag directly beneath an overhanging beak roof.

UPPER DOONIE   15min

NO 291759 **Alt:** 300m

The sprawling walls directly above the steep grassy descent rake for the **Lower Doonie**.

Descent: Abseil from trees at the top of the crag or walk off left and down the diagonal grassy terrace.

Routes from right to left.

④ Dancin' in the Ruins ★★   35m E3 5c

FA Simon Stewart & Chris Cracknell 1986

A good varied first pitch up the right side of the wall right of 5. Start below a tongue of rock projecting from the roof.

  1 **20m 5c** Climb the slab, move left and continue to a small niche (often wet) at the left side of the diagonal roof. Swing rightward through the roof on huge holds and continue steeply to belay at a small aspen.

  2 **15m 5b** Move up and left then step right and finish up a right-facing groove just right of a steep crack containing loose blocks. Belay on a metal fence post.

⑤ The Whoremistress ★★   35m E4 6a

FA Grant Farquhar & Graeme Ettle 1988

An excellent long sustained pitch up the centre of the alcove. Start in the alcove below a square-cut recess with a small tree down and right of prominent evergreen bush. Up the recess and the V-groove above to a large diagonal shelf. Move up into the groove above with difficulty (poor PR). Climb direct up to the left side of the overhang and cross this using a prominent small flake on the wall above (crux). Step left into wide vertical crack and finish more easily to a ledge and tree belay on the right.

  1 **20m 5b** Gain and climb the grey concave slab leading directly to a good belay ledge.

  2 **25m 5b** The black leaning corner above past a large ledge (possible belay). Finish up the wide crack on the right past a PR.

③a Variation Finish ★★   30m E1 5b

FA Martin Hendry 1960s

Move up and right below the 'beak' overhang to finish up right slanting cracks.

⑥ DRI ★★   45m E6 6a

FA Graeme Ettle & Grant Farquhar (headpointed) May 1987

A very serious pitch up the blunt arête in the centre of the crag. The last runners are below half-height and the route remains unrepeated. Start beneath twin cracks in the right side of the arête. Climb the crack to a good ledge on the front face. Climb the arête on its left side passing a prominent side-pull to reach good holds near the top. Pull onto the slab above. Continue more easily up the wall above to finish up the final layback crack of 7.

⑦ Vindaloo Direct ★★   45m E1 5b

FA J.Cadger & J.Thomson (A2; 3 bolts) 1972;
FFA Simon Stewart & Grant Farquhar 1986

A fine varied pitch with an exciting finale. Start beneath a crack 5m up and left of the blunt central arête of 6. Climb the initial steep crack, move left round the overlap and up the slab to a recess above. Traverse right round a block on huge holds then finish by a short fierce layback crack.

⑧ Larch Tree Wall ★   35m Very Difficult

FA unknown

Start at the top left end of the diagonal terrace. Climb the pocketed wall just right of the prominent lower crack then directly up the compact cracked wall above. Finish more easily up the upper rocks. The larch fell over in 1999.

JUANJORGE

NO 265 795 **Alt:** 500m   1¼hr 45min

A fine isolated wall of immaculate granite in the upper reaches of Glen Esk, which forms the upper right branch at the head of Glen Clova.

Access: Continue up Glen Clova past the Red Craigs for a further 0.6 mile/1km to car park (charges) and information hut.

Approach: From the car park at the head of the Glen go back across the bridge and follow the track (on the east side of the River Esk) north through the forest. Just over 100m beyond the farm at Moulzie follow the track down left and cross the River Esk. Continue round the track for a further 1.5km then re-cross the river and head diagonally leftwards up the hillside to the crag.

Descent: Abseil from trees at the top.

1 Granite Heids ★   25m E1 5b

FA Dougie Dinwoodie & A. Gunn April 1987

Start below the leftmost of two grooves, left of 2. Climb the groove until it is possible to move out left onto the edge (crux). Finish out right to a tree belay.

2 Rhiannon ★★   25m E3 6a

FA Dougie Dinwoodie & Greg Strange 1986

The obvious corner line to the left of the smooth face. Climb straight up the slabby face below the corner. Pull over a bulge and go up a short groove to flakes right of the base of the corner. Climb the sustained corner to the top. Tree belay.

3 Time's Arrow ★★★★   30m E6 6b

FA Grant Farquhar & Clare Carolan 4 July 1995

The compelling central line through the triangular niche. Move up then step right to the base of a thin diagonal crack. Up this passing a Lost Arrow. Make difficult moves (crux) through the niche to gain the crack sprouting from its apex. Continue up the sustained crack to join 4 at its final moves.

4 Roslin Riviera ★★★   35m E4 6a

FA Murray Hamilton & Greg Strange 21 June 1983

Excellent well protected climbing. Climb the groove in the toe of the crag to its top then follow the left-slanting diagonal crack with a hard move to a resting place. Continue up the crack until a step left is possible to another crack, which leads after a couple of moves to a horizontal break. Finish above a small tree.

5 Ladies of the Canyon ★★   30m E5 6b

FA Kenny Spence & Murray Hamilton July 1983

Climb a short crack and step left into the scoop in the wall 5 metres right of 4. From the top of the niche make a hard move right to holds which lead left to a crack. Follow this through the roof to easier ground.

LOCHNAGAR (LOCHAN OF THE NOISY SOUND)

"Yet still are you dearer than Albion's plain.
England! Thy beauties are tame and domestic,
To one who has roved o'er the mountains afar;
Oh! for the crags that are wild and majestic,
The steep frowning glories of dark Loch na Garr."
- George Gordon, Lord Byron, 1806

The north-east corrie of Lochnagar presents an almost 1.5km long crescent of cliffs encircling the loch after which the mountain is named. Although there are substantial areas of grass and vegetation on the cliff including large areas of loose rock, especially in the gullies, there are also many excellent routes throughout a wide spectrum of grades, all on immaculate Cairngorm granite.

The correct name for the mountain should be Beinn Chiochan, or hill of paps, whilst the individual tops are Cac Carn Beag and Mor (little shit cairn & big shit cairn) — little wonder that the name was altered shortly after Queen Victoria purchased the estate!

Access: From Ballater head east out of the town over the River Muick. Turn right and follow the B976 south for 0.6 miles/1km then turn left at the bridge of Muick up the minor C-class single track road up Glen Muick for 9 miles/14km to the car park at the road end at the Spittal of Glenmuick.

Approach: From the car park follow the track for a few hundred metres to the visitor centre. Turn right (signposted) and head north-west across flat ground crossing the River Muick by a bridge to a path cutting through the woods. Continue by a good land-rover track up first the left then the right side of the Allt-na-giubhsaich (stream of the pinewood) for just over 2.5 km to just short of the summit of the bealach. Follow a narrower but well constructed path west up the hillside for 1.5km passing the Fox Cairn Well to gain the col between the large flat mass of Cuidhe Crom on the left and Meikle Pap. Follow a small path cutting down into the corrie, which drops down until about 50m short of the lochan before rising up to a large monument from where all the routes can normally be viewed. 2hrs.

Descent: The fastest descent is by either branch of *The Black Spout*. The Left Branch lies 300m north-west from the top of *Eagle Ridge*, with a prominent large cairn about 50m from its top. This is relatively straightforward with an 'entertaining' through route beneath a chokestone near the base, just before reaching the main branch. If these are filled with snow continue north-east along the rim of the corrie, descending by easy slopes beyond **West Buttress**.

2hr

EAGLE RIDGE NO 247 856 **Alt:** 970m

1 **Eagle Ridge** ★★★★   **250m HS 4b**

FA Jim Bell & Nancy Forsyth (1 PA) 24 July 1941;
FFA S & Mrs Thomson June 1944

*"…for difficulty, narrowness and steepness altogether
superior to any of the well-known Nevis ridges."* – Bell
A majestic route, more popular than all the other rock
routes in the corrie put together. It dries quickly and the
rock is clean, making it possible (at VS) in the rain. Start
beneath a prominent slabby V-groove just inside the
open scree-fan of Douglas-Gibson Gully. Climb the groove
then continue more easily up shallow gully, trending right
to negotiate a chimney containing some chokestones

(30m).Trend back leftwards, ascending a 10m inset
corner on the right then steeper rock to regain the crest.
Move up right to a recess then continue steeply, moving
left to a *"splendid sentry box"*. Continue up the smooth
arête, finishing by a small corner to a ledge on the crest.
Ascend the 'whaleback' crest for 20m then a short slab
corner leading to a knife-edge on the crest. The crux
looms above – a vertical 4m wall split by a jam crack
where a few moves (well-protected) lead to a good ledge.
Continue along the almost level crest to a square-cut
projecting overhang. Swing up onto the 'coping slab'
above and mantelshelf from some cracked blocks into
a V-recess finishing rightwards up easy-angled slabs to
blocks just below the top.

TOUGH-BROWN FACE 2hr

NO 246 857 **Alt:** 950m

The lower wall of overlapping slabs presents one of the
finest faces in the Cairngorms. There is more vegetation
than, say, Creag an Dubh-loch, though mainly on the
ledges and routes give fine sustained technical climbing.
Descent: All the routes end on the **Great Terrace,**
crossed by the Tough-Brown Traverse, then traverse
right until overlooking the initial groove of Backdoor
Route, which starts just below the prominent bend in
Raeburn's Gully. Descend on vegetation easily right for
15m to a sling on a block and PB. A 45m abseil from here
gains the scree fan in Raeburn's Gully.

The area of rock near the left side of the cliff has suffered two massive rock falls in recent years, the first in June 1995, then again early in 2000, destroying or drastically altering many fine routes here and leaving a mass of unconsolidated blocks at the base. **Great care should be taken in this area.**

❷ Tough-Brown Integral **   160m E2 5b

FA Rob Archbold & Greg Strange August 1983

A sustained direct combination searching out the cleanest available rock. Start just right of the rockfall scar.

1 **35m 5a** Ascend a shallow corner crossing a bulge at 10m. Move right and go up to a tiny ledge then follow the prominent horizontal traverse line right, climbing up to beneath a prominent 10m corner.

2 **10m 5a** Follow the corner, continuing up to a good ledge.

3 **30m 5b** Traverse rightward along a narrow rising foot ledge to a corner crack-line (*Post Mortem*). Follow this past a roof to belay at a perched block.

4 **25m 5b** Go up the corner above the block, stepping right beneath a roof into a second corner. Go up this to step back left to an awkward rest beneath a bulge. Go up the crack above to reach some jammed flakes then head out left to gain a large ramp. Belay in a grassy niche.

5+6 **60m 5a** – Finish up the final two pitches of *Post Mortem*.

❸ Post Mortem **   150m E2 5b

FA Mike Forbes & Mike Rennie (A3) August 1970;
FFA Andy Nisbet & Steve Kennedy 2 August 1981

Very fine sustained climbing up the shallow cracks in the centre of the face, though slow to dry. Start 5m right of a large pointed block.

1 **35m 5a** Mantelshelf onto a shelf continuing up more shelves and making a detour out right into an often wet crack. Move back left to a shelf leading to The Terrace.

2 **30m 5b** From the left end of terrace go up a short left-slanting ramp then step left into a groove and follow it for 5m (crux) until it is possible to traverse left to a good rest. Ascend a short slab under a roof then traverse back right to regain the crack. Follow the corner crack past a roof to belay at a perched block.

3 **25m 5b** Continue up a corner above, stepping right under a roof to a further corner. Climb this stepping left to an awkward rest beneath a bulge. Continue up a crack to jammed flakes leading out left to a large ramp. Belay in a grassy niche.

4 **40m 5a** Continue up the ramp to a break, descend right to a lower ramp and mover awkwardly round a corner. Climb up to the continuation of the main ramp and follow cracks to its tip then make a big step up round a block.

5 **20m** Follow line of flakes left to gain the Tough-Brown Traverse.

❹ Mort **   110m E1 5b

FA Mike Forbes & Mike Rennie (10 PA) 11 June 1967;
FFA Dougie Dinwoodie & Bob Smith August 1976

The right-slanting crack starting near the centre of the face. Start at the large pointed block as for *Post Mortem*.

1 **35m 5a** As for *Post Mortem*.

2 **35m 5b** Climb steeply to the right side of a downward pointing 'tooth' in the roof. Cross the roof by the rightmost of twin cracks to a poorly protected mantelshelf (crux). Ascend the right side of the rib on the left, pulling up left onto the top. Ascend the left crack above to a grassy ramp and belay 5m up this.

3 **40m 5a** Either traverse left under a small roof or traverse higher (5b but cleaner) into a continuation groove and up this to a grass trough. Belay by a large perched block.

BLACK SPOUT PINNACLE 2h

NO 248 856 **Alt:** 1000m

The large triangular buttress on the right side of the corrie demarcated on either side by **Raeburn's Gully** and *The Black Spout*. On the left side is the fine 100m apron of the lower slabs leading to more vegetated ground above. Further right, higher up the lower reaches of *The Black Spout*, the slabs gradually steepen, merging with the steep *Black Spout Wall*. From the top of the pinnacle follow an obvious line bearing left down an easy slab to gain the col (25m). 30m of easy rocks (exposed) above lead to the plateau.

5 Pinnacle Face *   95m VS 4b

FA Jerry Smith & J.Dennis 4 September 1955

A major breakthrough in Cairngorm climbing, first ascended in rope soled shoes. Start about 10m above the lowest rocks at the corner of *The Black Spout*.

1 **35m 4a** Follow either of two grooves, both awkward to start. The rightmost V-groove leads to a delicate traverse left at 10m to a short chimney in the left groove. Continue up the chimney then by left-trending cracks.

2 **25m 4b** Go up to a corner and pull onto the slab on the right. Trend left up a slabby fault to belay on a large grass ledge.

3 **25m 4b** Continue left crossing the large prominent fault to twin cracks. Follow either of these continuing up the rightmost crack where the other fades then traverse rightward on flakes to belay in a niche.

4 **10m 4b** Go up the steep corner above to a ledge. Traverse easily right on grass ledges leading to a descent to The Springboard.

6 Pinnacle Grooves **   70m VS 5a

FA Rob Archbold & Greg Strange 29 June 1975

Fine well protected climbing up the grooves in the centre of the *Pinnacle Face*. Start beneath the rightmost groove of *Pinnacle Face*.

1 **30m 5a** Climb the groove to grass ledges on the right at 15m. Move right then go left and up to a large downward pointing flake. Layback up its left side to step into a smooth groove on the left and climb this to a grass stance and belay.

2 **15m 5a** Continue up a groove left of the prominent overhang to a grass ledge on the right.

3 **25m** Step left then go up about 9m. Here grass ledges lead horizontally right for 15m to the start of *The Link*.

The following 5 routes all lead to a series of large vegetated ledges dubbed **The Springboard**, from where a 45m abseil can be made from a large block in the centre – slings in situ.

7 The Nihilist **   45m E1 5l

FA Brian Lawrie & Dave Innes August 1976; Direct Start Guy Muhlemann & Greg Strange 28 August 1983

Superb sustained climbing following the prominent twin grooves leading to the right end of The Springboard. Start immediately left of the smooth wall near the base of 8.

1 **25m 5b** Climb up to obvious holds and make a difficult move left before swinging up to a large ledge (the *Direct Start* gains this by the prominent V-groove). Move up to a higher ledge then gain a steep narrow slab with a bulging wall above. Traverse right to an *"apparently desirable mantelshelf ledge"*. Continue traversing right to gain the main groove descending a little to a belay.

2 **20m 5a** Make a long reach to gain steep cracks above a prominent hooded overhang. Continue more easily up right to make a hard exit by a wide crack onto The Springboard. Combining the first pitch of this route with the second pitch of *The Extremist* gives a very good and sustained E2 5b and the fastest drying line on the pinnacle.

8 **The Extremist** ★★   **40m E5 6b**

FA Wilson Moir, Paul Allen & Julian Lines 16 June 1996

Excellent sustained climbing. Slightly harder technically than *The Existentionalist* but better protected. Start just right of the V-groove of *Nihilist Direct Start*.

1 **18m 6b** Climb an awkward corner/ramp to its top. Make hard moves up and right into the obvious niche. Continue up the crack above to belay above the overhanging wall.

2 **22m 5b** Continue in the same line up twin cracks slanting left to join and finish up the corner.

Wilson Moir on the first ascent of The Extremist. Photo Paul Allen.

9 **The Existentialist** ★★★   **42m E6 6b**

FA Wilson Moir & Paul Allen 8 July 1995

One of the best pitches in the Cairngorms, climbing the impressive smooth wall at the base of *The Black Spout*. Start at a small corner 10m right of *Nihilist Direct Start*. Climb boldly up into the little corner. Climb it and the crack above to a ledge. Continue up a superb flake crack until it is possible to exit by the left crack. Finish up *The Nihilist* to reach The Springboard.

10 **The Link** ★   **100m VS 5a**

FA Ken Grassick & Bill Brooker 16 June 1956

The time honoured upper continuation to *Pinnacle Face*. Start in the rightmost of three faults at the top of The Springboard.

1 **15m** Make a short awkward traverse into a vegetated V-groove which is followed to belay on the rib on the right.

2 **25m 4c** Move up the rib a short way then step back into the groove and follow it to a prominent triangular overhang. Climb up and right round a huge block to a small recess beneath an overhang. Cross this and climb a good crack slightly right to belay behind a further huge block.

3 **30m 4c** Follow the prominent right-slanting crack moving out left near its top to a steep groove and go up this to a large overhang. Pass this on the right using a 'sometimes rotating' block.

4 **30m 5a** Break through the overhang above by good cracks.

11 **Black Spout Wall** ★★★   **170m E3 5c**

FA Dougie Dinwoodie & Bob Smith (2 PA) 8 & 10 August 1976; FFA Brian Lawrie & Neil Morrison September 1983

Very good climbing particularly on the lower pitches, following the prominent crack-line in the pillar left of the great overhung recess in the centre of the wall. Start on a large grass ledge right of the crack.

1 **40m 5c** A very fine pitch. Shuffle left along a small ledge and climb the deep mossy crack to a pinnacle at 15m. Cross the bulge above then ascend the smooth dwindling groove to flakes and a large PR on the right. Descend to the lip of the overhang and swing left into the scoop at the base of a ramp. Go up the ramp crossing an overhang at its top to gain better holds 3m above. Move down diagonally right to a ledge and PBs directly above the initial cracks.

2 **30m 5c** Climb directly up the wall above, crossing a bulge to gain a groove and climb this by a thin finger-crack then the easier upper groove, which leads to an exit out left to ledges near *The Link*.

3 **40m 4b** Traverse right 7m, then follow slabby shelves up and right to gain the arête above the great overhangs. Go up this to a little ridge.

4 **25m 5c** The left-slanting 'inhospitable crack' lies to the left. Climb the long right fork of the forking system leading to the apex of the wall.

5 **35m** Finish up the crest to the top of The Pinnacle.

12 **Steep Frowning Glories** ★★★　　　**155m E5/6 6b**
FA Wilson Moir & Neil Morrison 21 July 1996

An excellent modern companion to *Black Spout Wall* with a stunning well protected crux pitch breaching the great overhangs. Start 5m right of *Black Spout Wall*.

1 **14m 5c** Climb a crack up a pillar (just left of a shallow corner) to ledge.

2 **18m 5c** Continue up the crack to a

roof. Go left and pull out onto a ledge leading left to *Black Spout Wall* PB.

3 **18m 6b** Go back right along the ledge and climb cracks diagonally rightward gaining the pedestal under the roof crack from the right. Climb the roof crack (full set Fs #0-4 desirable) to belay just above.

4 **45m 5c** Climb the continuation crack and corner and continue up to join *Black Spout Wall* at the right-slanting shelves. Go along these and the arête to belay beneath the gable wall.

5+6 60m Continue up *Black Spout Wall*.

13 **Drainpipe Crack** ★　　　**35m E2 5c**
FA Dougie Dinwoodie & Colin MacLean 4 August 1982

Excellent sustained jamming, though, as the name suggests, seldom dry. Start beneath the right line up the steep wall right of *Black Spout Wall*. Follow the steep crack into a recess beneath the final overhang. Cross the overhang with difficulty to finish up the right crack.

14 **The Black Spout** ★　　　**250m Easy**
FA J.Gibson & W.Douglas (winter conditions) 12 March 1993

Separating the main face from West Buttress is a huge scree-filled gully. Hidden from the corrie floor the Left Branch has one entertaining pitch, a traditional through route beneath a huge chokestone just above the fork. In descent either branch proves straightforward.

WEST BUTTRESS   2hr
NO 246 859 **Alt:** 980m

15 **Black Spout Buttress** ★　　　**250m Difficult**
FA T.Goodeve, Willie Ling & Harold Raeburn 17 April 1908

The best easy route on the cliff though the lower buttress is very vegetated and probably better avoided by traversing in from the fork on *The Black Spout*. Start about 10m right of *The Black Spout* at the top of a grass cone. Climb the chimney fault then scramble for approx.

60m to a level arête at the end of the lower buttress. Continue along the arête then a ridge of piled blocks to a 'deceptively difficult' short chimney. Easy climbing above then leads to a short wall, which is started centrally and finished on the right by an awkward corner. Now go up a fine 10m on good holds then a ledge on the left to regain the crest, which leads easily to the top.

Broad
Terrace Wall

Central
Slabs

Central
Gully Wall

Central
Gully

False
Gully
Wall

North-West
Gully Buttress

2½hr   1¾hr

NO 233 826 **Alt:** 700m

CREAG AN DUBH-LOCH
(CLIFF OF THE BLACK/DARK LOCH)

Undoubtedly the finest mountain cliff in Britain with a kilometre long, 300m expanse of impeccable granite. Superb routes of all grades from VS to E7, with the finest selection of extremes to be found anywhere.

Access: From Ballater head east out of town crossing the bridge over the River Dee then turn right and follow the B976 south for 0.7 miles/1.1km. Turn left at the Bridge of Muick up the minor C-class single track road up Glen Muick for 8 miles/13km to the car park (pay & display) at the road end at the Spittal of Glenmuick.

Approach: Follow the land rover track past the toilets and visitor centre for 800m to a narrower track on the right crossing the outflow of Loch Muick then by the land rover track along the north side of the loch as far as the Glas-allt-Shiel (royal shooting lodge) – 4.5km/1 hour. Continue through the woods by a narrower track which leads after a further 3km and 250m of ascent to the Dubh-Loch. Mountain bikes can be taken to the head of Loch Muick, saving around 40 minutes.

Accommodation: There is a small draughty howff sleeping two in the boulder field directly below **The Central Slabs** and superb campsites by the golden sandy beaches around the west end of the Dubh-Loch. There is also a bothy at the rear of the Glas-allt-Shiel. Wild camping in upper Glen Muick.

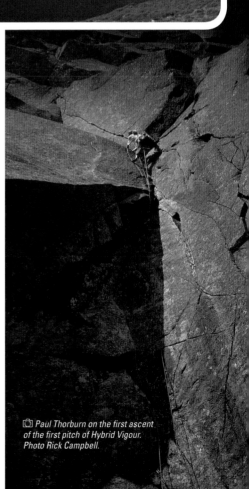

📷 *Paul Thorburn on the first ascent of the first pitch of Hybrid Vigour. Photo Rick Campbell.*

BROAD TERRACE WALL

The steep dark crag high on the left side of the cliff, steepest in its centre where the smoothest section leans out over The Grass Balcony. The huge corner fault of *The Sword of Damocles* demarcates the left edge of the steepest section, clearly visible even from the head of Loch Muick. Further left the face curves round to a slabbier section before petering out into vegetated ground above **South-East Gully**. This is the last section of the cliff to dry due to a large patch of snow at its top, which usually results in seepage until at least the end of June.

Approach: Gain the grassy Broad Terrace under the frontal face by zig-zagging up the left side of the broken and copiously vegetated lower crags, starting near the base of **South-East Gully**.

Descent: Traverse left (east) just past the loose gully bounding the left side of the crag and scramble down the vegetated rock ridge. Near the base veer left and down a slabby rock ramp (Diff) in the side wall of the gully. In wet conditions or if unsure of the line, continue traversing further east past the end of the cliffs and down the easy-angled grass slopes.

1 **The Eye of Allah** ★★ **100m E3 5c**

FA Wilson Moir & Chris Forrest 7 September 1991

1 **30m 4b** Start up *The Last Oasis* and follow the fault easily to belay below a steepening.

2 **30m 5b** Climb the corner above then step left onto a rib and follow a thin crack left to a ramp. Follow the ramp easily to belay at its left end.

3 **25m 5c** Climb a finger crack to a shelf then use a good flange to traverse right and pull into a corner. Exit right to a belay ledge below a slanting corner.

4 **15m 5b** Climb exposed hanging slabs on the left and finish up blocks above.

2 **Alice Springs** ★★★ **95m E2 5c**

FA Murray Hamilton & Pete Whillance 29 July 1983

Excellent climbing on immaculate rock up the crack-line in the centre of the wall.

1 **20m** Start up the fault of *The Last Oasis* and follow it easily to below a steepening.

2 **40m 5c** Climb the corner above, as for *The Last Oasis* then step left onto the rib and follow a thin crack left to ledges. Climb

the prominent finger crack to a ledge.

3 35m 5b Move up to the base of a corner, step right on to a rib and reach a crack on the right. Follow this and the continuation groove above to finish.

③ The Bedouin ★★ 95m E4 6a

FA Wilson Moir & Colin Stewart 27 July 1989

The obvious line between *Alice Springs* and *The Last Oasis*.

1 35m 4b Climb *The Last Oasis* to the top of the second steep step.

2 45m 6a Step left on to edge and go up to enter the left-facing corner. Climb this to a small overlap. Climb the bulge (crux) and move up to an undercling. Use the short corner on the left to gain the next break and follow the twin grooves to ledge. Zig-zag up the walls above finishing through a steep slot to ledges. A fine sustained pitch on immaculate rock

3 15m Easy rocks lead to the top.

The less prominent leftmost of the two faults is the aptly named 4 *The Last Oasis*, VS 4b,4b,4c – a natural drainage line, giving good climbing when dry.

⑤ The Sword of Damocles ★★★ 95m E2 5b

FA Graham Hunter & Doug Lang (12 PA) 20 June 1970;
FFA Dougie Dinwoodie & Bob Smith July 1977

The huge corner system, the most prominent line on the wall. Start at an easy chimney next to a steep wall.

1 15m 4c Climb the chimney then traverse left across the wall to a ledge at the base of the big corner.

2 35m 5a Follow the corner past a ledge on the left. Continue up the corner above to a large flake below the hanging chimney.

3 15m 5b Climb the chimney (very sustained) to large ledge at its top.

4 30m 5a Move right and follow a short corner to a white slab. Climb the chimney on the right or left, or climb further right if damp. Finish easily up giant steps and broken ground. A useful variation if the top chimney is wet. From below the hanging chimney, cross the first bulge until

below the first old bolt. Traverse the left wall to the edge, move up the arête and traverse left then up the short pale groove of *Mirage* leading to the large ledge at the top of the chimney.

⑥ Flodden ★★★★ 120m E6 6b

FA Murray Hamilton, Kenny Spence & Rab Anderson 22–23 July 1983

A stunning right to left diagonal line, crossing some impressive ground with two hard contrasting pitches. Low in the grade. The last hard pitch takes a lot of seepage and is slow to dry. Up vegetation to the base of the wall then scramble up a flake on the left and traverse right along a good ledge to belay atop a large flake.

1 30m 6b Up an easy crack in the back of a left-facing groove to underneath the roof. Layback and jam this with difficulty (Fs #2-3) and follow this until it narrows just above a jug on the right wall. Difficult moves traversing left lead to a good flake. Up this and a groove to belay in a short right-facing groove below a big roof.

2 15m 6a Gain a good crack in the groove above the roof with difficulty. Up this and foot traverse right along a ledge to a thin left-trending diagonal crack. Up this and boldly up a scoop to a ledge. Belay at P at left end of ledge.

3 10m 5a Step down left onto a lower ledge, left and up a flake to belay at top of a pedestal.

4 25m 6b Move left off the ledge and up to under the rectangular roof (poor rest – extend runners under roof, otherwise excessive rope drag near end of pitch). Move left to a good rest under the next roof. Move over a flake to good nuts then step left to a good rest on a slab. Climb the slim groove above to a good nut slot, step down and move left across the slab to a good finger edge. Up the steep corner above on improving holds to belay in the base of the corner.

5 40m 5a Climb the left rib of the groove above then more easily up occasional rock and much vegetation to the plateau.

7 Culloden ★   125m E2 5c

*FA Tony & Robin Barley (4 PA) July 1967; FFA Jeff Lamb
& Pete Whillance 1975*

The first route to breach the Broad Terrace Wall. Though
quite lichenous the situations are impressive. The route
follows the first line right of the two big roofs at the right
side of the smooth wall heading for a prominent large
V-groove at mid-height. The highest section of the Broad
Terrace has some piled blocks. Start down left of these

and climb up left to belay on a large obvious platform.

1 **45m 5a** Climb direct up grooves, cracks and a flaky
wall to move right onto the top of a huge flake.

2 **35m 5c** Up the overhanging crack and the large
hanging groove to ledges. Continue up the
shallow grooves to belay beneath a bulge.

3 **45m 5c** Move left and follow a shallow corner
then back right above the bulge. Continue by a
groove and short walls finishing up easy ground.

THE CENTRAL SLABS

Overlapping slabs sweep the centre of the cliff for 300
metres at this point. The slabs are set at too high an
angle for friction climbing; therefore the routes follow
natural lines. Although the routes are slightly contrived
with many of the lines interchangeable, the generally
delicate nature of the climbing, with the overlaps providing variety, gives many enjoyable routes. The routes are
broken into two distinct halves by a slanting mid-height
terrace reducing the overall seriousness as escape is
possible rightward onto **Central Gully Buttress**.
Descent: From the plateau, walk right (north-west)
and go down **Central Gully**. If filled with snow early in
the summer, go down the easy crest of **Central Gully
Buttress**, cutting down left into the lower reaches
of **Central Gully**. Near the base, a small ledge leads
horizontally left (10m above a greasy ramp) to short wall
of blocks just above the gully floor.

1 Dinosaur/Pink Elephant ★★   320m HVS 5a

*FA Jim Stenhouse & Brian Lawrie (1 PA) 25 July 1964;
FFA Dougie Dinwoodie & Ian McIvar 1974;
FA (Pink Elephant) John Grieve & Allen Fyffe 14 June 1969*

A good combination giving the best line on the left side
of the slabs. The last (crux) pitch up the big groove is
unfortunately slow to dry. Start at the lowest rocks.

1 **25m** Follow broken cracks to a grass rake, or
scramble leftward up the rake to the same point.

2 **40m 4b** Follow the main crack system above to

a stance 5m below the long lower overlap.

3 40m 5a Surmount the overlap above and go up the slab over an awkward bulge. Go up slightly higher and follow a toe traverse left (careful not to go too high). Step up left then go slightly down into the prominent shallow corner. Climb this using the left rib to the top of a large flake.

4+5 80m 4c Go up a grassy niche and climb the bulging corner above. Break right over the big left-slanting overlap to reach slabs then follow the obvious line up into *Dinosaur* Gully and follow its right branch to The Terrace.

6 20m 4b Follow the prominent corner on the right side of the Sea of Slabs to under bulges.

7 45m 4b Continue up grooves above, break through the overhang by a short bulging slot and continue up slabs.

8 25m 5a Follow a tapering slab leading up left to the right end of large grass ledge below the upper overhangs. Traverse right to a slabby knife edge then drop into the big upper groove.

9 45m 5a Follow the groove, overcoming a steep step by the left wall then regain the groove. Finish up the groove or by rocks on its left side.

❷ The Blue Max ✶✶   335m E1 5b
FA Brian Robertson, Allen Fyffe & W.Wilkins (2 PA/A1)
16 – 17 September 1967; FFA John Fraser & party 1975

Excellent sustained climbing, though the crux section is contrived. The route breaks through the main overlap at a conspicuous rockfall scar. Scramble up the grass rake to a large block.

1 40m 5a Follow the crack-line directly above the block over a difficult bulge. Continue up cracks then move right to belay at the base of a left-facing corner.

2 35m 5a Follow the corner to small ledges and go up to make a thin traverse right over a smooth slab to belay under the main overlap.

3 25m 4c Break through the overlap by a right traverse across the wall immediately above the rockfall scar then go up by cracks to belay.

4 40m 5b This is the line of *Cyclops*. Move

diagonally left and traverse along the top of a huge diamond-shaped block beneath the overlap. Step right through the bulge by a crack which twists back into the groove. Continue up the groove to belay on the rib. A fine well protected pitch

5 40m Continue up the rib then go straight up the succeeding crack and corner to a roof. Turn the roof on the right by cracks leading to a small ledge. Continue up walls for 10m to belay on a long grassy ledge.

6 30m 4c Move up grooves to a some large blocks then up two diagonal cracks leading onto the arête on the right. Step round the arête and continue more easily leftward up the slabs to the right edge of the upper slabs.

7 40m 4c Turn the crescent-shaped groove of *Cyclops* by a smaller groove on the right (or a wide V-groove round the right edge) to a junction below short twin grooves. Climb the left-hand groove and continue slightly leftward up easier slabs above by cracks to a grass stance immediately beneath a small rounded bulge.

8 40m 4c Gain the slab and traverse left to the short left-facing Quartz Corner. Climb the corner to exit right to the rib before it becomes vegetated. Continue up the fine rib to gain and climb grassy grooves.

9 35m Finish up the grooves, moving onto the right wall near the top to gain broken ground.

❸ Cyclops ✶✶✶   290m HVS 5a
FA Greg Strange & Mike Freeman 19 May 1973

The classic route on the Central Slabs following a direct line of cracks up the lower slabs and utilising the wall of *The Blue Max* to breach the main overlap. Start at the foot of the grass rake of *Dinosaur* at the top of a tongue of slab encircled by a ring of grass.

1 30m 5a Follow the left of twin parallel cracks right of a brown corner to pull onto a hanging flake from the right side. Go up the edge to a good ledge under a small overlap (crux).

2 35m 4c Climb the bulge above then climb the prominent crack to a scoop with a constricted groove above. Follow the groove over a long grass plug and continue to belay at top.

3 35m 4c Climb direct through the overlap by traversing right across the wall immediately above the rock fall scar (as for *The Blue Max*) then continue up the superb finger and hand crack to the second overlap.

4 50m 4c Follow the continuation fault, then directly up cracks in the steeper pink water washed rock. Continue up leftwards over grassy ledges to a large grass ledge and thread belay.

5 10m Scramble up left to belay at the base of an obvious crescent-shaped groove near the right edge of the upper slabs.

6 25m 5a Climb the difficult short flared groove (crux) continuing more easily up the crescent groove above (junction with *The Blue Max*) to its top, then climb a short cleft on the left to a ledge.

7 20m 4c Continue up cleaned cracks up and left to grass ledge.

8 40m 4c Gain the slab above and traverse left to the short left-facing Quartz Corner. Climb the corner to exit right to the rib before it becomes vegetated. Continue up the fine rib to gain and climb grassy grooves.

9 45m 4b Finish up the grooves, moving onto the right wall near the top to gain broken ground.

4 Black Mamba ★★★　　　　　　　**335m VS 4c**
FA Allen Fyffe & John Grieve 7 June 1969

The classic on the slabs, giving excellent sustained climbing. Right of the grass ring of *Cyclops* is a grass ledge 20m up the slabs. Start from grass at a low point in the slabs.

1 20m 4c Climb a delicate shallow crack-line leading to the left end of the grass ledge.

2 45m 4b Climb the grassy crack system directly above then the shallow V-groove just right of the long corner to finish up the upper part of the corner. Belay on a ledge on the left at the top of the corner, directly beneath a prominent rock scar in the main overlap.

3 45m 4b Breach the overlap using the cracked groove on the right, then follow easier cracks above to ledges.

4 45m 4b Step round large flake and follow cracked slabs to a shallow gully containing a large pointed block. Continue leftwards up easy slabs to turfy groun

5 20m Climb leftwards over turfy ledges, then directly over short walls to smaller grassy ledges (The Terrace) beneath the crux pitch of *Cyclops*.

6 40m 4b Climb up and diagonally left beneath small bulges (left of the *Cyclops* groove) to gain a pink rib and slab close to *Pink Elephant*.

7 25m 4b Traverse back right to gain the cleaned cracks, (common to both *Cyclops* and *The Blue Max*) and follow them left to a grass ledge.

8 40m 4c Gain the slab above and traverse left to the short left-facing Quartz Corner. Climb the corner to ex right to the rib before it becomes vegetated. Continue up the fine rib to gain and climb grassy grooves.

9 45m 4b Finish up the grooves, moving onto the right wall near the top to gain broken ground.

5 Buddha ★★　　　　　　　　**40m E7 6c**
FA Julian Lines & Eddie McTavish (headpointed) 31 August 1995

About 75m up and right of *Black Mamba* is a small isolate blank-looking slab/wall topped by a right curving overlap. Start in centre of slab. Climb scoops then move right to arrange protection in cracks. Gain and climb twin converging cracks until they disappear then make desperate moves to better holds. Abseil off. Superb climbing and a soft touch - graded for an on-sight ascent. Possibly E6 6b for the tall.

Rick Campbell on the thin Buddha, if there is such a thing?

CENTRAL GULLY WALL

The massive convex face forming the right side of Central Gully, sweeping round to the longer slabbier frontal face where the lines tend to follow longer easier crack lines. The wall is steepest where it overlooks the gully, split by three huge corner systems (taken by *The Giant, Goliath* and *Vertigo Wall* respectively). Lower down near the mouth of the gully the wall forms a maze of walls and overlapping slabs. The majority of routes finish in an area of vegetated blocks beneath the plateau. After prolonged wet spells many weeps emanate from this area for several days. If a route has wet streaks on it try something else. Many of the harder routes first climbed in the early eighties utilised pegs either for runners or belays – most of these are currently (2008) in a very poor state, increasing the seriousness considerably.

Descent: Traverse left (south-east) & down **Central Gully**.

Routes from right to left, as approached up the gully.

1 Cougar ★★★   **125m E3 5c**

FA Mike Rennie & Paul Williams (16 PA) 15-16 June 1968;
FFA Dave Cuthbertson & Murray Hamilton June 1977

A brilliant route threading its way through the right side of the hanging slabs, saving its crux for the top pitch. Start at the base of Central Gully, at the top of a mound with embedded rocks.

1 **20m 5a** Traverse right into the initial corner and follow it (often wet) into a notch. Continue up and left to reach a good ledge beneath an overhang.

2 **40m 5c** Climb cracks heading up left over a bulge. Continue up the corner above to a capacious belay on the *Cougar* slab.

3 **35m 5b** Traverse left along a crack and step down into a recess beneath a short overhanging corner crack. Climb this strenuously on good holds then leftward on good flakes to belay beneath a short overhanging wall.

4 **30m 5c** Climb the wall to gain a slab beneath the final bulging band. Move right and mantelshelf onto a block then climb the crack above to an overlap. Make a short leftward traverse under the overlap, continuing left to reach a good rounded spike. Step up and traverse left beneath a bulge then up left to gain a good ledge beneath a roof. Scramble to the plateau.

2 Voyage of the Beagle ★★★★   **160m E4 6a**

FA Murray Hamilton & Rab Anderson 12 August 1983

An excellent sustained route, though generally on less steep ground than its companions. At the top end of the grade. Start beneath a hanging left-facing groove, 6m left of *Cougar*.

1 40m 6a Climb a flake crack on the right up into the groove. Follow the groove initially with difficulty then more easily to a small square-cut ledge. Move left across the wall then regain the corner. Step down left to gain a thin slanting crack leading back into the fault which leads to a belay at the start of the slab.

2 15m Easily across slab to belay at some ancient Ps.

3 40m 6a Climb up left and place runners on the upper slab. Return and step down to gain the lower slab. Cross the slab with some thin moves to gain the arête. Step left round the arête and straight up to enter a groove (*The Ascent of Man*) and up this to its top. Move left to gain a groove leading to the belay at the end of second pitch of *The Naked Ape*.

4+5 65m Finish up *The Naked Ape* (25m, 6a; 40m, 5c).

3 Cannibal ★★★★   **140m E6 6b**

FA Murray Hamilton & Rab Anderson 9 June 1984

Excellent sustained climbing, taking a direct line of increasingly hard pitches through the *Cougar* slab. Start up the arête right of the overhung alcove.

1 30m 5c Climb the crack just left of the arête until moves can be made round the arête into another crack. Climb this until it fades then step left to gain a crack on the crest. Climb this steeply to a stance on the slab above.

2 10m 6a Move up left and gain holds which lead to a PR below the roof. Pull out right until a crack above the roof leads to a stance and PB on the higher slab.

3 30m 6b Move up to a left-slanting corner and climb this to a roof. Traverse left and pull into the recess (PR) then pull over its right wall onto the *Cougar* slab. Belay at the right end of the slab as for *Cougar*.

4 40m 6b Above and slightly right is a stepped corner. Climb the first step then swing right to the arête

and move up until the corner can be regained. Continue up the corner and pull out right below a steep nose. Climb the wall right of the nose to gain a short crack then pull onto a block on top of the nose. Follow a slab left below a roof to a stance.

5 30m 5a Climb the crack above. Scramble to the top.

4 Perilous Journey ★★★   **135m E6 6b**

FA Dougie Dinwoodie & Graeme Livingston 18 August 1983

Another fine sustained route up the steep frontal face. Start as for *Cannibal*. Unfortunately the original start was obliterated by the huge rockfall from *The Giant*. None of the pegs are of any use.

1 30m 6a Climb the initial crack of *Cannibal* then take the curving crack leftward into the groove of *Hybrid Vigour*, stepping left to a thread belay.

2 20m 6b Go up the slabby wall above to a slabby shelf. Move up left along a creaking flake to arrange protection in a jug. Return to the shelf and make a hard mantelshelf move (crux) onto a smaller shelf above. Go left and step up delicately to reach good flake holds leading to a poor PB on the slab.

3 30m 6b Step down left and traverse the lip of the slab to an *"evil sloping perch"* at the end. Swing left round the overhanging nose and make hard moves across left and up past a PR. Climb up and step right to follow a vague groove system then twin cracks with difficulty to a PB. Good nut up left on the arête.

4 25m 5b Move up left round the arête into the groove of *The Ascent of Man*. Go up this a short way then continue to make an awkward move across a slab on the right to reach the hanging crack. Climb the crack and continue to the top of the great blocks of *Cougar*.

5 30m 5b Climb a shallow recessed corner, as for *Cougar*, then go left up a shelf. Climb a bulging nose past a spike then slightly right then left to join the left traverse of *Cougar* just below the rounded spike. Traverse left along a bulge then climb direct to easy ground.

5 **Hybrid Vigour** ★★★   80m E6 6c

FA Rick Campbell & Paul Thorburn July 1994; Pitches 3 & 4 Rick Campbell & Paul Thorburn (alts.) & Neil Craig 1 July 1995; Pitch 1 gained from R & pitch 2 – Dougie Dinwoodie & G.Thomson 5 July 1987

An impressive on-sight effort taking the big overhanging alcove near the base of the gully.

1 **35m 6b** Climb the groove past a PR to a rest where it starts to impend. Avoiding the wet flakes on the right wall climb the groove via a hard undercut move to better (but wet) holds in the groove above. Continue up the easing groove and the vertical section above (PR) to belay on a slab.

2 **10m 6c** Move left and delicately gain a slab under the big overhang. Gain holds on the lip to the right and make wild moves over the bulge. Step left and go up a delicate groove to belay as for *Voyage of the Beagle*.

3 **10m 6b** Move up left onto the slab beneath the overhanging wall. Follow the weakness left to a higher slab and belay as for *Perilous Journey*. A desperate, poorly protected pitch. A pleasanter, though less independent option is to follow *Voyage of the Beagle* out left to the cracks of *Perilous Journey* and up these to gain the same belay.

4 **25m 6a** Move back right past stacked blocks then hand traverse right past a PR into a niche in the overhanging wall. Pull round the corner onto a shelf at the base of an overhanging crack. Finish up the crack in a spectacular position.

6 **The Ascent of Man** ★★★   130m E5 6b

FA Murray Hamilton & Rab Anderson 24 July 1982

Climbs the prominent groove and crack-line between *Cougar* and *The Giant* with an inordinately hard 3m crux section. Start directly beneath the prominent steep groove.

1 **30m 6b** Climb a crack for 3m and traverse right along a ledge to gain the lower groove. Follow this up and traverse left across a slab to regain the crack. Climb this to the break in the roof (ancient PR) and pull into the groove above, which is followed with much interest to a hanging PB.

2 **30m 6a** Step up and move across right to gain a subsidiary groove. Climb this and move across left to gain a crack which leads to a leaning wall. Step up left to climb the short crack above and hand traverse right into a groove. Up this to belay at its top.

3 **35m 5b** Climb the short corner above then up left along a slab and down into a recess occupied by a large detached block.

4 **35m 5a** Step back up right and climb cracks to enter a groove system which is followed to grassy terrace. Scramble off right.

7 **The Origin of Species** ★★★★   70m E6 6b

FA Paul Thorburn & Gary Latter 22 September 1997

A long sustained and serious main pitch following the stunning blunt arête cutting through *The Naked Ape*. Take all the micro wires you can muster. Start 2m down from the start of *The Naked Ape*.

1 **15m 5b** Climb the shallow groove parallel to the larger groove of *The Naked Ape* to a flake and nut belay on small ledge.

2 **40m 6b** Continue up the groove above, past a PR at a prominent rock scar to a wide crack with a chokestone (F #4). Move up the flakes above then traverse right along horizontal break to the base of the arête (skyhooks on good flake on right). Move up the arête with committing moves to stand on the sloping shelf on the left. Follow the thin crack above with difficulty to a good hold at its top. Continue up leftward to the horizontal break of *The Naked Ape* and follow this boldly right then up to the PR on the arête. Climb the steep thin groove above, exiting onto the slab with interest. Belay in the niche beneath the right end of the roof.

3 **15m 6a** As for *The Naked Ape*. Move across the slab to a good foot hold. Pull over the roof slightly rightward then up with a hard move past PR to a good ledge above. Finish up the steep jam crack to spike and nut belay. 50m abseil reaches the ground on the stretch.

Unknown climbers on the second pitch of Goliath.

The lowest and most impressive of the three great corner systems is 9 *The Giant*, E3 5c, 6a, 5a,?
A massive rock fall has removed the final corner pitch, leaving a crack line on the right wall which looks possible at a similar grade, or finish up *Goliath*.

10 Goliath Eliminate ★★   160m E2 5b

FA Norrie Muir & Steve Docherty (4 PA) 22 May 1971;
FFA Brian Davison & Andy Nisbet August 1983;
Shelf Variation Jim McArtney & Brian Lawrie 1967

Good sustained climbing, though a bit of a misnomer – it shares about 3m of climbing with *Goliath*. Start 10m left of the huge poised block.

1 **20m 5b** Traverse right on a grass ledge. Hand traverse right and mantelshelf onto the block. Chimney up the back to the top of the block, move right along the shelf and up to belay on a ledge.

2 **10m 5a** Pull over the bulge above then step right and up to belay at the end of the first pitch of the normal route.

3 **30m 5a** Climb the steep corner and move up to a shelf. Move right up the slabby shelf to a ledge at the top.

4 **30m 5a** Continue up rightward to belay beneath the rock scar of *The Giant*.

5+6 **70m** Traverse left and finish as for *Goliath* (40m, 30m).

11 Goliath ★★   150m HVS 5a

FA Brian Findlay & Mike Rennie (4 PA); 7 June 1969;
FFA Ian Nicolson & party 1970

The large slabby right-slanting corner in the upper cliff gained by a traverse in from the left. Start 30m up and left from a huge perched block.

1 **40m 4b** Move up diagonally right on small ledges then traverse right across slabs to P and nut belay below and right of two small left-facing corners in the steep wall.

2 **40m 5a** Climb either of the steep corners and move up to a shelf (crux). Continue up the fault line to belay on the right.

3 **40m 4b** Go across the slab on the left then climb to a ledge leading left to a huge slab. Climb the slab for 10m and continue to belay on a

8 The Naked Ape ★★★   126m E5 6b

FA Pete Whillance, Pete Botterill, Murray Hamilton & Rab Anderson 1 August 1982

A bold and impressive route based around the big arête right of *The Giant*. High in the grade. Start below a groove leading directly up to the main corner system of *The Giant*.

1 **33m 5b** Climb the groove and where it forks keep right up a flake crack to reach a ledge and belay at the top of the initial ramp of *The Giant*.

2 **27m 6b** Climb the smooth groove above the belay mainly via its left rib to reach a PR on the right at 10m. Move up right onto the steep slab, traverse right to the arête and step up to a PR. Continue traversing right along an obvious foot ledge and step up to a good ledge and belay.

3 **24m 6a** Follow the leftward slanting slabby corner to a niche below a roof and place a runner in the lip. Climb delicately down leftward to a good foot hold near the arête. Step up left and climb a break in the overhang to gain a sloping ledge. Up a short steep wall (PR) to a ledge and belay in a niche.

4 **42m 5c** Climb the overhanging crack above to a large ledge. Step up right and climb cracks to enter a groove system. Follow this to a grassy terrace at its top. Scramble up right (as for *Cougar*), to the plateau.

long ledge midway up the great corner.

4 30m Move up to a ledge above then traverse right and up to finish up wide easy cracks close to the right edge of the slab. Scramble to the plateau.

12 The Israelite ★★   125m E4 6a

FA Pete Whillance & J.Moore 5 June 1982

The smooth orange-coloured water-worn groove just left of *Goliath*. An excellent main pitch, though unfortunately slow to dry. Adequately protected with lots of small wires. Start as for *Goliath*.

1 25m 4b Traverse easily right across slabs (as for *Goliath*) to a small stance and PB below the line of the groove.

2 45m 6a Climb the slab above then slightly leftward until a traverse right can be made to a crack leading up to an overlap. Climb the overlap on the right to enter the main groove and follow it direct to where the angle eases. Traverse right to the belay of *Goliath*.

3 20m 5a Up the obvious thin crack in the centre of the slab to a large ledge and belay below the huge corner.

4 35m 5b Climb the corner direct to the top. Scramble to the plateau.

13 Bombadillo ★★   135m E4 6a

FA Pete Whillance, Murray Hamilton & Rab Anderson 31 May 1982

Follows grooves in the nose of the buttress, right of *Vertigo Wall*. The pegs on the crux pitch are in a bad state. Start as for *Goliath*.

1 15m Traverse easily right across slabs to a grass ledge and belay below the huge corner of *Vertigo Wall* (part of the first pitch of *Goliath*).

2 45m 5c Step down and right then up to gain the slab above. Climb the slab and shallow groove to exit left by a rock scar to ledges. Move right and climb a slab rightward then up a hidden flake crack to gain a niche. Move left and pull up into a prominent V-groove. Climb this and continue to a large ledge. Belay 6m right along the ledge.

3 42m 6a Climb the broken wall rightward to a ledge below an overhanging groove. Hand traverse left across a steep wall and pull

up onto the slab above (poor PR). Traverse delicately back right to the groove (PR) and climb it to where the angle eases. Follow an obvious leftward slanting ramp line to the arête, move left to a crack then up to a ledge and belay.

4 33m 5b Up a vague crack above the belay for 5m then traverse right to an obvious thin crack. Follow this until a good ledge leads right onto the arête. Up the arête to the top. A superb pitch. Scramble to the plateau.

> The huge recessed scoop/open corner is the character building 14 *Vertigo Wall* VS 4c.

15 The Wicker Man ★★   150m E3 6a

FA Pete Whillance & Rab Anderson 4 September 1982

The conspicuous crack-line in the centre of the wall left of *Vertigo Wall*.

1 30m 5a Climb up for 6m to a grassy bay below a leftward trending groove. Follow the left wall and rib of the groove to a ledge and belay at a large perched block.

2 35m 6a Step right and climb twin cracks in a giant groove to a ledge below a small square-cut overhang. Climb the thin right crack into a triangular niche. Step left and climb the crack near the edge to a ledge. Continue more easily up the obvious corner crack to a belay on the right.

3 25m 5a Continue up the corner and slabby groove above exiting right at the top. Up grass ledges for 6m to belay at a large embedded flake. 50m abseil from here gains the base.

4 30m *"The sphagnum moss pitch."* Move left around the corner and follow easy ledges leftward and then back diagonally right to reach a belay below the bulging headwall.

5 30m 5b Move up right onto a glacis and climb the overhang at its narrowest point to reach a rightward slanting groove. Climb the crack on its right to the plateau.

📷 *Gary Latter on the perplexing crux of The Shetlander. Photo Dave Cuthbertson, Cubby Images.*

The following routes lie on the front face, described from left to right.

🔟 The Shetlander ★★   **60m E6 6c**

FA Wilson Moir, Neil Morrison & Niall Ritchie 9 August 1995

The crack-line left of *The Wicker Man* with a very hard well protected crux.

1 **15m 5b** Climb the flaky crack-line to gain a tufty break. Follow this leftward to belay at the base of a right-slanting corner.

2 **30m 6c** Go up the right-slanting corner then climb a crack leading into another corner, which leads to a resting place beneath the steep section. Continue up the crack-line to reach a semi-rest at flakes. Climb the desperate bulging groove above to a P and nut belay in a niche.

3 **15m 6a** Go up from the belay until it is possible to step right. Move up right then back left to finish up a crack.

🔟 The Mousetrap ★★★   **195m VS 4c**

FA Jimmy & Ronnie Marshall & Robert Anderson November 1959

A good direct line up the crack system near the left side of the front face. Well protected and reasonably quick drying. Start up left from the lowest point of the toe of the wall beneath a deep easy groove.

1 **25m 4a** Climb the groove then traverse left and climb the wide cracks to belay beneath a steepening below and left of the main crack.

2 **45m 4c** Follow the wide crack (crux), or more easily by the rib on the right and up to the recess above. Continue up the recess to a block belay near the top. A fine long sustained pitch.

3 **25m 4c** Up the steep flake corner on the left, step left past a flake and up a small groove and cracks above to a belay beneath an overlap.

4 **50m 4c** Continue up the crack-line to a small spike belay near the left end of a heathery ledge.

5 **50m 4b** Continue in the same line then scramble diagonally left for 25m to a block belay. Scramble to the plateau 40m above.

18 Dubh Loch Monster ★   200m E1 5c

FA Ian Nicolson & Dave Knowles (1 PA) 18 June 1970;
FFA Jeff Lamb & Pete Whillance 1975

The thin crack right of *The Mousetrap*. Very sustained at 5a with one move of 5c.

1 **30m 4b** Follow the cracked slabs to beneath a chimney break.

2 **40m 5c** Climb the chimney (crux) then continue by an awkward wall and the crack-line to beneath an overhanging notch.

3 **10m 5a** Move left and up the arête then move back right to a large ledge.

4 **25m 5a** Follow cracks to above a double bulge. Climb the first bulge, move right 2m and cross the second bulge with difficulty. Continue up slabs to beneath a short wall.

5 **45m 5a** Move left to a break and up this to gain the slab above. Move left 2m and pull over a short wall into a corner. Follow the corner for 5m then the rib on the right over two bulges, turning the second on the left and move right to a ledge.

6 **50m** Climb slabs diagonally rightward to a crack at the right end of the overlap. Climb the crack then a steepening corner. Finish up the crack above to easier ground.

19 King Rat ★★★   220m VS 4c with 2 PA (E1 5c free)

FA Allen Fyffe & John Bower (5 PA) 9 June 1968;
FFA Phil Thomas & Mick Fowler June 1977

The prominent crack system right of *The Mousetrap* only spoilt by inordinately hard moves through the prominent roof. Start directly below the prominent large roof at 50m, close to the left wall of the large recess at the lowest point of the wall.

1 **40m 4b** Climb steep rocks at the back of the recess for 15m then traverse the left wall on

flakes to a ledge on the open face. Climb direct up the crack-line to a large grass ledge.

2 **20m 5c** Move right from the ledge and up cracked slabs to a shallow cave under the roof. Move awkwardly up left into a corner and up this to a ledge.

3 **50m 4b** Follow the cracked ribs above until beneath a short vertical wall. Move left up slabs to below a short leaning corner.

4 **10m 4b** Follow the corner to ledges.

5 **30m 4c** Climb a short wall to gain a slab beneath a roof. Cross the bulge 3m left of the roof then traverse right along a narrow slab above the roof and up to ledges.

6+7 **70m 4b** Move into the upper crack system and follow it to grass ledges. Scramble away left

📷 *Rick Campbell on the immaculate crux wall of The Improbability Drive.*

A good area of rock high on the right side of the cliff with plenty of good varied extremes. The wall holds the sun the longest (until around mid-day). The smooth-looking barrier wall above the slanting shelf and grassy terrace invariably provides the crux pitches of almost all the routes. This can be gained by an unpleasant VDiff. scramble (rope advised!) up the vegetated gully at the left end of the lower rocks. A much better (safer!) alternative is the first pitch of either *Sans Fer* or *Falseface*, both leading to the far right end of the terrace.

Descent: Either walk left (south-east) and down **Central Gully** or head out right (north-west) and down easy slopes beyond the last outcrops.

Routes from right to left as encountered on approach.

1 Falseface ★★ 110m E2 5c

FA Graham Hunter & Doug Lang (13 PA) 7 June 1969; FFA Bob Smith & Dougie Dinwoodie July 1977

The right side of the lower wall beneath the terrace has a prominent right-facing corner. Start below and left of this.

1 20m Climb up and slightly rightward to gain a grass shelf leading into the corner.

2 20m 5c Layback strenuously up the corner to a belay at the right end of the terrace.

3 35m 5b Up the short wall above to move right into a hidden chokestone chimney and up this to a ledge on the left beneath an overlap. Gain the sloping ledge above, cross the overlap then traverse right to better holds. Move up and back left then up a series of grooves to a large ledge.

4 35m 5a Move back left and into a steep corner which is followed to near the top. Go along the right wall and up a detached flake to ledges and easy ground.

2 Sans Fer/ Iron in the Soul ★★★ 120m E4 6b

FA Sans Fer Murray Hamilton & Kenny Spence June 1979; FA Dougie Dinwoodie & Brian Lawrie 22 August 1984

The first route to breach the smooth barrier wall above the grassy terrace and the start of a new era. This combination links the best pitches by the most direct line. Start in the centre of the lower face 10m left of the prominent corner of *Falseface*.

1 40m 5c Climb up to a niche and slab heading for a prominent finger crack. Climb this painfully to belay on a sloping ledge at the right end of the grassy terrace. Walk left 15m to the base of the crack.

2 20m 6b Climb the crack with a difficult rounded exit to a superb incut jug at the back of the ledge. Belay just above.

3 30m 6a Climb the bulge above and go up cracks and a corner crack slightly left under the next bulge. Layback right and go over the bulge to follow a flake crack curving up and left in a slab. Go on up a short corner to belay on the ramp of *Sans Fer*.

4 30m 5a Move left up the ramp and climb a short cleaned crack then step right and follow further cracks and blocks leading to easy ground.

3 An Spearag ★★★   **30m E6 6b**

FA Gary Latter 23 September 1997

Varied climbing with a short well protected technical crux. Midway between *Sans Fer* and *Slartibartfast* is a thin crack leading to a prominent orange streak high on the wall. Start below this. Climb the crack with a tricky move to clip a PR in the horizontal break. Make hard moves to become established in the break level with the PR. Step right and continue past some underclings to a prominent undercut flange. Pull onto the sloping shelf above (at the end of the traverse on 2) and follow the groove of 2 then break out left for 4m to the base of the prominent right-slanting ramp-groove. Belay on the small shelf (P) down on the left 3m right of the belay on 4.

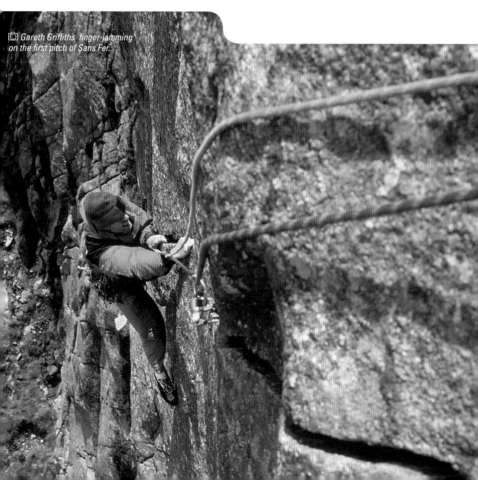

📷 *Gareth Griffiths finger-jamming on the first pitch of Sans Fer.*

4 **Slartibartfast** ★★★   **75m E5 6b**

FA Murray Hamilton, Pete Whillance & Rab Anderson 30 May 1982

Takes the most prominent crack and groove line in the
centre of the wall. Start below a crack in the middle of
the wall.

  1 **21m 6b** A ledge on the wall just right of the crack
     gives access to a small groove. Climb the groove un-
     til it peters out (RP #3 out in slot on right). Move up
     and left (bold) to follow the crack and shallow corner,
     moving right at the top to belay on sloping ledges.

  2 **21m 6a** Climb the obvious corner containing three
     small overhangs and belay on a slab above.

  3 **33m 5c** Continue in the same line
     via steep cracks to the top.

5 **The Improbability Drive** ★★★   **70m E6 6c**

FA Graeme Livingston & Dougie Dinwoodie 15 August 1984

Bold sustained climbing on the initial wall, leading to
a difficult well protected final move. Start 10m left of
Slartibartfast, just right of an obvious crack.

  1 **20m 6c** Climb right up little foot shelves using diago-
     nal cracks then up the wall to gain a horizontal break.
     Go straight up the wall to a semi resting place at
     the next break. Climb the twin cracks directly above
     using mainly the left one, with a hard move to gain
     a good jug at the top of the wall. PB on slab above.

  2 **20m 6a** Climb directly up the bulge just
     left of the belay then slightly right to
     climb the third roof of the second pitch of
     Slartibartfast and belay on slab above.

  3 **30m 5c** Climb the prominent groove on the right
     rib then veer slightly right and make an awkward
     move up a notch into the *Sans Fer* niche. Stride
     across black gunge, then straight up through
     a roof to easy ground and a block belay.

6 **Fer de Lance** ★★★   **65m E6 6b**

FA Dougie Dinwoodie & Jeff Hall 10 August 1987

The wall crack at the left end of the wall gives the
longest and steepest pitch on the smooth barrier wall.
Initially bold, then sustained and well protected.

  1 **30m 6b** Climb the sustained crack past a PR
     low down and up past two shake-outs to gain
     an awkward shelf. Climb the bulging wall
     above moving right and up a corner past a
     spike to exit left onto a ledge. PR 6m higher.

  2 **35m 5c** Climb up past PR and go up diagonally
     right into the corner of *Slartibartfast*. Climb this
     past the bulge above then step left along a
     shelf. Climb the bulging crack above, step left
     and pull up onto a big flake. Move up left to
     easier ground, finishing up a grassy groove.

NORTH-WEST GULLY BUTTRESS

The furthest right extremity of the cliff has a prominent
short isolated area of pink slabs amongst the generally
more broken rocks right of the gully itself.

1 **Jezebel** ★   **50m E3 6b**

FA Graeme Livingston & Alastair Ross 11 August 1984

A direct line up the centre of the slab with a hard friction
crux. Start just right of the lowest point of the buttress
beneath a steep slab with twin parallel cracks.

  1 **10m 5c** Climb the overhanging wall then up to
     belay at the base of the large corner on the right.

  2 **15m 6b** Climb the twin cracks with hard friction
     moves into the scoop on the left. Climb this and the
     big corner above to belay beneath a wide crack.

  3 **25m 5b** Up the crack and corner above then
     left to easy ground. Belay on the right.

② **Baal** ★★   **50m E4 6a**

FA Wilson Moir & Julian Lines 15 July 1996

Basically this is *Jezebel* Direct. Better than the original.

1 **10m 5c** As for *Jezebel*.

2 **20m 6a** Climb *Jezebel* cracks direct, with
a final move up and right from the left
crack to reach a good break. Traverse left
to belay at the base of big corner.

3 **20m 6a** Climb a steep thin crack up the arête

above and continuation flake, curving right
on the bare slab-arête which leads to the
belay. Easy climbing leads to the top.

③ **Late Night Final** ★   **60m HS 4b**

FA Allen Fyffe & John Grieve 9 June 1969

1 **40m** Climb the big corner to its top.

2 **20m** Continue up cracks to an overhanging
corner in a steep wall. Climb this to a
grassy niche then move right and up.

EAGLES ROCK   NO 235 834 **Alt:** 850m 🟢 🧗 1½hr

This is the large slabby mass of cliff overlooking the
north-west end of Creag an Dubh-loch. Away from the
waterfalls at the upper left end the slabs are very quick
drying and unlike Creag an Dubh-loch receive the sun in

the afternoon. Protection is often sparse.

Approach: As for Creag an Dubh-loch, following the
path round the north side of the Dubh-loch then heading
directly up the hill side on the right to the base.

A LIKELY STORY SLAB

The overlapping greenish slab right of the
lower section of Diagonal Gully.

Descent: Either traverse left and go down the
left-bounding Diagonal Gully or make a 50m
abseil diagonally rightward (southwards) from
a thread (sling and maillon in situ) just above
obvious large block at the top of the slab.

1 Fraud Squad ★★   **70m E2 5b**

FA Alistair Ross, Ged Reilly & C.Harper 16 June 1984

Start just left of *A Likely Story* by a white trickle mark.

1 **30m 5b** Climb to an overlap and traverse left and up to a scoop with horizontal quartz bands. Move out left from the top of the scoop onto a bald slab. Pad up and right to a belay on the right side of a V-notch.

2 **30m 5b** Climb the crack through the double overlap and follow the blind pocketed crack above or the slab just to its right to the base of a thin curving flake. Move left to belay.

3 **10m 4c** Go through the overlap and finish up mossy cracks. The final pitch of *A Likely Story* provides a better finish.

1a Fraud Squad Direct Start ★   **30m E4 5c**

FA Julian Lines & Charlie Ord (on-sight) 12 July 2000

Pull straight over from the first overlap and ascend direct up the centre of the rippled scoop. Continue direct to the belay. Bold.

2 A Likely Story ★★★   **75m HVS 5a**

FA Graham Hunter & Doug Lang (2 PA) 25 August 1968; FFA Allen Fyffe & John Grieve October 1970

An unsung Cairngorm gem. Start in the centre of the overlapping greenish slabs.

1 **25m 5a** Move up slightly left to an overlap, traverse right 2m and cross this then follow an obvious corner which leads to a ledge.

2 **20m 5a** Use a flake to gain the corner above and follow this then make a delicate traverse right under the overlap into a notch. Pull through the overlap and continue to a belay of sorts in a triangular depression.

3 **30m 4c** Traverse leftward along the slab beneath a steep wall, finishing up a prominent crack in the slab with a steep finish on good holds.

3 Ripping Yarn ★   **80m E1 5b**

FA Julian Lines & Eddie McTavish 31 August 1995

1 **30m 5a** Start 5m right of *A Likely Story*. Pad up a blank slab, move right into a V-notch. Above step left to the base of a smooth slab. Climb the slab via a line of small features until the angle eases. Step left to belay as for *A Likely Story*.

2 **50m 5b** Climb *A Likely Story* for 5m then pull out left through a V-notch. Climb a slab above to a steep wall, pull through via an ear onto the slab above then climb the slab veering left to finish as for *A Likely Story*.

📷 *Karen Latter starting up Fraud Squad.*

THE PASS OF BALLATER

Upper Tier

Western Section

Middle Tier

Gully
Wall

Central Section
Front Face

NO 367 971 **Alt:** 300m 🇸 🇼 👤 10min

P

CREAG AN T-SEABHAIG
(HAWK CRAG)

A compact selection of sunny crags situated on the pine and larch covered hillside of The Pass. Excellent granite yields a range of routes from VS upwards. Being a bit of a sun-trap, it is often possible to climb here in the winter months. A popular weekend venue for Aberdonians, it is about an hour's drive from the granite city.

Access: The Pass lies behind the hill of Craigendarroch, on the north side of the town of Ballater itself. Travelling from the east, turn off right from the A93, 1.4 miles/2.2 km before Ballater and follow the B972 for 1.1 miles/1.7km to a parking space on the north side of the road. From the west turn left off the main A93 road into the pass just beyond (east of) a large lay-by on the south side of the road. Follow the B972 for 0.7 miles/1.1 km to a parking area directly beneath the Central Section of the crag.

Approach: Head directly up a worn path immediately above the parking spot to the **Central Section**. For the **Western Section** walk west along the track past the gate for 300m to just beyond a large fallen block then up an eroded path leading to the left end; or cut up the right side of the crag for the Upper Tier.

CENTRAL SECTION – FRONT FACE

Directly above the parking area.

Descent: Either by 25m abseil from trees (sling and maillon in situ on Scots pine at top of *Blutered*), or down either side of the crag after gaining a well worn path at the top.

 **Giant Flake Route** ★★   **30m MVS 4b**
FA Greg Strange & Raymond Simpson 1967

A rightward diagonal line across the front face. Start 10m right of the left edge of the front face, beneath a small larch at 10m. Climb a short difficult boulder problem wall (crux) to a good ledge at the base of the short left-facing corner. Up this onto the top of the flake. Traverse right along a large ledge and continue up another short corner on good holds continuing rightward on large flakes to finish at the large Scots pine.

② Convoy ★   25m VS 4c

FA Jim McArtney, Derek Pyper & Alan Corbett early 60s;
FFA unknown

A direct line cutting through 1. Start 4m right of 1. Climb
the groove to the large ledge on 1. Up the short corner
then direct to an alcove and over the roof on good holds.

③ Drambo ★   15m E6 6b

FA Dougie Dinwoodie & Alastair Ross 1985

A serious route breaching the centre of the wall, gained
from the left arête. Climb the arête to the resting ledge
on the left (runners at small ledge on the arête just
above). Traverse along the break right into the centre of
the wall (two RP #5s here – last worthwhile protection).
Climb up to a handrail then step up, moving out left to
good finishing holds.

④ Bluter Groove ★★   20m E3 6b

FA Jim McArtney, Derek Pyper & Alan Corbett 1965;
FFA Murray Hamilton, Pete Whillance & Rab Anderson 1982

A short well protected technical problem. Start beneath
the prominent central groove. Climb the groove, initially
using the right arête then bridge into the groove to reach
a good jug on a block at 6m. Continue more easily above.

⑤ Wife Beater ★★   20m E7 6c

FA Tim Rankin (headpointed) May 2005

Superb technical climbing. Just right of 4 is a thin crack
up the wall. Climb the desperate bouldery crack and
move up to a junction with 6; follow this and then 7 up to
a good undercut and the last protection. Make very thin
committing moves up and left to a sloping break just right
of the arête, continue straight up the right side of the arête
to pull over on 'thank god' holds. Finish up the easy upper
wall on the left. A good micro wire can be placed from
the left to protect the initial hard moves. Linking the initial
hard crack and the top of 7 would give an excellent E6 6c.

⑥ Blutered ★★★   20m E1 5a

FA Dave Wright, Alison Higham & Guy Muhleman 1976

Excellent sustained climbing. Start 5m right of the
prominent groove of 4. Up easily to a large flake then
leftward and along flared horizontal break to good holds
on the arête. Step into the groove and up this by a superb
hand crack. Direct up easier ground to the pine tree.

Demon Drink **   **15m E5 6b**

FA Dougie Dinwoodie 1985

Good well protected climbing. Follow 6 to the left edge of the wall. Move up right and across to protection. Step left and go straight up to the next protection. Make a long reach for a knob directly above (crux) then finish on superb holds.

 Doctor Dipso **   **15m E4 6a**

FA Dougie Dinwoodie 1985

Good climbing up the right side of the wall. Climb 7 to the large flake. Move up to 2 PRs then make hard moves up and left to protection in a hollow sounding flake. Climb straight up to another runner placement then head up rightward to good holds on the arête. Finish more easily up this.

9 **Larup Head** *   **20m E3 5c**

FA Graeme Livingston & Colin Jamieson 1985

A good pitch up the highest section of the wall. Start 8m right of 8 at some undercut flakes directly beneath a trio of horizontal breaks. Climb up the wall past these to a good ledge, move left and continue up the wall, finishing up the prominent crack on the right.

10 **Alcoholics Anonymous** *   **15m E1 5b**

FA Alastair Ross & Ian Davidson 1985

Start just right of 9. Climb directly through a shallow niche to gain a ledge. Finish more easier up the sparsely protected small corner above.

11 **Strawberry Ripple** *   **8m VS 5a**

FA Brian Lawrie, Ged Reilly & G.Stephen 1980

A slight route, with good technical climbing at upper limit of the grade. Climb the short discontinuous crack in the small slab on the right edge of the crack to a rounded finish.

Paul Thorburn on the technical Bluter Groove.

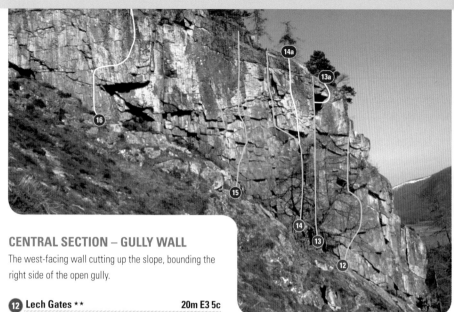

CENTRAL SECTION – GULLY WALL

The west-facing wall cutting up the slope, bounding the right side of the open gully.

12 Lech Gates ★★   20m E3 5c

FA Dougie Dinwoodie & Graeme Livingston 1983

Start 6m down and right of 13, down and right of a smooth corner. Climb blocky flakes rightward to a shallow corner. Move up the crack on the right then traverse out left to under the roof. Pull round left and finish up steeply up the crack.

13 Anger and Lust ★★★   20m E2 5c

FA 1971; FFA Bob Smith & A.Williams 1980

The prominent roof-capped corner behind the larch. If you get lost on this one, give up! Follow the corner to finish spectacularly by undercutting left into the deep crack through the left side of the roof (crux) leading to good finishing holds.

13a Right Finish ★★★   6m E4 6b

FFA Dougie Dinwoodie & Watty Taylor 1985

A short well protected finish. Traverse right along the lip of the roof to a good jug. Step left and finish up the short corner.

14 Cold Rage ★★   20m E3 6a

FFA Dougie Dinwoodie & Colin MacLean 1983

Start just left of 13. Climb the initial thin crack (crux) to

a niche and up the crack to the overlap. Traverse left to climb the crack and groove above.

14a Hot Temper ★★   15m E5 6b

FA Willie Todd & Graeme Livingston September 1986

A strenuous well protected direct finish to 14. Follow 14 to the recess below the roof. Pull directly over the roof and climb the wall above which soon eases.

15 Distemper ★★   15m E5 6b

FA Graeme Livingston & Willie Todd September 1986

The steeply overhanging small pink corner left of 14. Climb hollow flakes up to a small roof then move round right into the main corner, which is climbed past an undercut out on the left wall. Pull awkwardly onto the small ledge above and finish more easily.

16 Captain Cop Out ★★   15m E4 6a

FA Graeme Livingston & Colin Jamieson 1984

Start up the slope on the upper wall, left of a large overhang. Climb up a crack to a protruding split block. Make a right rising traverse across the wall to finish at an obvious break.

WESTERN SECTION – MIDDLE TIER

Descent: Either by abseil from trees at the top, or down a worn path down the left end.

1 Razor's Crack *   8m VS 4c

FA Greg Strange & Dave Stuart 1971

The S-shaped crack at the left end.

2 Jumbled Blocks Crack *   10m Very Difficult

FA 1960s

Also a useful descent. The prominent corner and crack near the left end, just right of the S-shaped crack. Polished.

3 Stinker *   10m E1 5b

FA Dougie Dinwoodie & Brian Lawrie 1981

Further right is a prominent mid-height roof. This climbs the well protected crack.

4 Lime Chimney   10m Very Difficult

FA Dave Stuart & Greg Strange 1971

The prominent short chimney, the finish is usually dirty.

5 Lucky Strike *   15m VS 5a

FA Mike Freeman, Greg Strange, Dave Stuart & Raymond Simpson 1971

The stepped left-facing corners. Start immediately left of a rock scar. A bouldery start leads to better holds.

Continue up the steep black-streaked corner to large ledge and tree. Finish up the upper corner behind the tree.

6 Flake Traverse *   25m HVS 5a

FA unknown

Start 3m right of 5. Follow an obvious traverse across the wall to join the final pitch of 7. Continue traversing right into the final quartzy cracks of 8 and finish up these.

7 Pretzel Logic *   20m E3 5c

FA unknown; FFA Mike McDonald & Brian Sprunt 1980; upper corner Tony Barley & Jerry Peel 1977

Start at a short corner 4m right of 5, just right of the arête. Climb the corner until a rising traverse out right can be made to gain the crack system. Follow this to the base of the final imposing corner and finish up this in a fine position.

7a Direct Start *   8m E3 6a

FA Graeme Livingston, Colin McLean & Alastair Ross 1983

The short left-facing groove gives a problematic start to a good hold at its top. Direct up the painful quartz-filled finger crack to finish up the final corner.

8 Rattlesnake ★★   20m E3 6b

FA Dougie Dinwoodie & Brian Lawrie 1981

A fine line taking the prominent quartzy cracks up the right edge of the wall. Start a few metres right of 7a. Up the initial corner with difficulty, either direct or from the right. Finish up the striking cracks.

> 8a Avoiding the initial troublesome groove by starting up 9 gives a very fine E2 5c. ★★

9 Supercreeps ★   20m E1 5b

FA Alastair Ross & P.Garden 1982

Start 2.5m right of 8 in a small vegetated corner. Up the corner then out right to the left end of the long slab beneath the overlap. Pull directly over the overlap and up to a shallow niche. Continue directly to a small overlap then up rightward to finish at the same point as 11.

UPPER TIER

Descent: Either by abseil from trees on the top, or down obvious worn paths at either end.

1 Janus ★   10m E4 6b

FA Alastair Ross & Marion Sutherland 1990

A good well protected technical pitch. Start just left of 2. Climb short crack then move left into another crack which is followed to the top.

2 Left-Hand Crack   10m VS 4c

FA Stan Falconer & party 1975

The crack on the right side of the short smooth wall, near the left end of the crag.

3 Original Route ★   10m VS 5a

FA Davy Duncan & party late 1960s

Further right is a corner. Gain this awkwardly then go up right to a ledge. Finish by deep cracks in the wall above.

10 Medium Cool ★★★   20m VS 4c

FA Brian Lawrie & Dougie Dinwoodie 1971

Spectacular exposed climbing up the right side of the large hanging slab. Start beneath the right end of the slab next a fresh rock fall scar. Climb a short left-facing corner onto ledge then traverse down left on the hanging slab to gain small pine. Continue left along good break under the overl to a ledge then back right through the overlap and up to a large pine. Climb the slab boldly behind the tree to a fine belay on the large larch.

11 Silent Spring ★★   25m E2 5a

FA Alastair Ross & P.Garden 1982

Fine bold slab climbing in an exposed situation with a run-o upper section. Follow 10 to the second pine (possible belay) then boldly run it out up the left trending runnel to the top.

12 Scary Monsters ★   30m VS 4c

FA N.Smith, N.McNeil & Alastair Ross 1980

Good climbing, though the upper corner often becomes choked with larch needles.

> **1 10m 4c** Follow 10 to belay on the tree.
> **2 20m 4c** Foot traverse left along the prominent break then move up and left into the corner. Finish up this.

4 Fingerwrecker ★   10m HVS 5c

FA Brian Lawrie & Greg Strange 1979

The obvious thin crack just left of 6. Follow the painful initial crack (not using the boulders) to gain a scoop.

5 Wrecker's Traverse ★★   18m E3 5c

FA Alastair Ross, Neil Morrison & Ged Reilly 1984

Follow 4 to the scoop. Move up right then traverse the obvious break right across 6 to attain a standing position on 7. Finish boldly up this.

6 Peel's Wall ★★★★   12m E4 6a

FA Jerry Peel & Tony Barley 1977; Right Finish: Neil Morrison 1999

The classic test-piece of the crag, and one of the hardest pitches in Scotland in its day. Start in the centre of the wall. Gain a good undercut flake then direct with long reaches to the horizontal break. Continue direct with an awkward move to gain a narrow ledge finishing out rightward. The *Right Finish* E4 6b moves right from the horizontal break finishing up the wall and slab just right of a blind vertical crack.

7 Smith's Arête ★★★　　　　　　**10m E5 6a**

FA Bob Smith (headpointed – 1 runner pre-placed) 1983

The prominent square-cut arête left of the central corner. Poorly protected. Climb the lower edge to the horizontal break and better protection at two-thirds height. Continue more easily directly up the final slab.

8 Little Cenotaph ★★　　　　　　**10m HVS 5b**

FA aided; FFA Guy Muhleman, Greg Strange & Rob Archbold 1975

Well protected climbing up the central square-cut corner. Wide bridging leads to a ledge on the right. Finish by the shallow corner (crux) on the left.

9 Dod's Dead Cat ★　　　　　　**15m E2 5c**

FA Ewen Todd & Robin Patterson 1986

Follow 8 to the horizontal break. Traverse out left along this to join 7 and finish up this.

10 Pink Wall ★　　　　　　**8m VS 5a**

FA Greg Strange & C.Anderson 1972

The centre of the wall right of 8 with a boulder problem start. Finish up an easy corner above the ledge.

11 Black Custard ★★★　　　　　　**15m E1 5b**

FA John Mothersele & Mike Freeman 1971

A fine well protected struggle up the steep left-slanting quartzy crack near the right end of the crag. Follow the crack up to a black roof and pull over this to good holds, finishing easily.

Luke Arnott starting up Little Cenotaph.

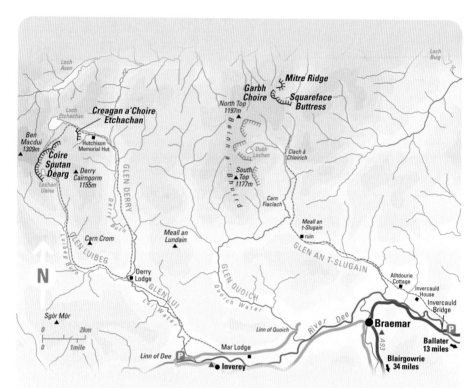

SOUTHERN CAIRNGORMS

DEESIDE

Accommodation: The peculiarly self-proclaimed 'award winning Highland village' of Braemar is the main centre, with numerous hotel and B&B options. **TIC** (☏ 01339 741600). **Bunkhouses:** Gulabin Lodge, Glenshee (01250 847614; www.cairngorm-mountainsports.com); Rucksacks Braemar (☏ 01339 741517); Braemar Lodge Bunkhouse (☏ 01339 741627). **Youth Hostels:** Braemar (☏ 01339 741659); Inverey, 5 miles west of Braemar (☏ 01339 741017); Tomintoul (☏ 01807 580364). **Campsites:** Invercauld Caravan Club Site, Braemar (☏ 01339 741373; www.caravanclub.co.uk); a couple of miles south of the town along the west bank of the Clunie Water, (the river running into the south end of Braemar) is a popular place to wild camp. Club hut at Muir of Inverey.

Amenities: There is a small supermarket in the village; Outdoor shop is Braemar Mountain Sports (☏ 01339 741242; www.cairngormmountainsports.com) which also does mountain bike hire.

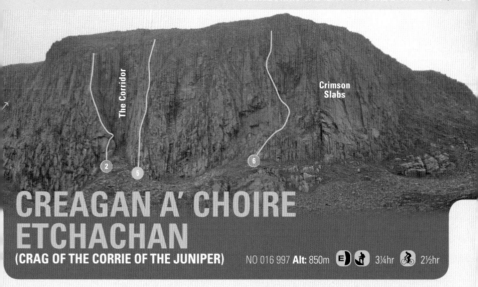

CREAGAN A' CHOIRE ETCHACHAN

(CRAG OF THE CORRIE OF THE JUNIPER) NO 016 997 **Alt:** 850m **E** 🚶 3¼hr 🚴 2½hr

A big slabby crag in an idyllic setting on the east side of Derry Cairngorm, part of the Ben Macdui massif. A visit here could also be combined with Coire Sputan Dearg, which lies less than an hour away (40 minutes from the top of the cliff)

Access: From the centre of Braemar follow the C-class road west along the south side of the River Dee for 6 miles/9.6km to Linn of Dee. Continue for a further 200m along the north side of the road back towards Braemar to a car park (pay & display) in the forest on the left.

Approach: (A) From the car park at the Linn of Dee follow the signposted path to meet up with the track from the locked Derry Gates to reach Derry Lodge in a little over 4km. Turn right at the public phone 200m beyond the lodge, cross a footbridge and head north up Glen Derry

re-crossing the Derry Burn (footbridges) after 2.4km and the Glas Allt Mor after a further 3km. Continue, then cross the Coire Etchachan Burn to gain the Hutchison hut after a further 1km. The cliff lies 750m further west up the slope. Cycles can be taken to at least the second footbridge or a couple of kms further.

(B) From the North (Coire Chas car park on Cairn Gorm). By any of the routes to the Shelter Stone near the head of Loch Avon. Continue steeply south-east up the path on the slopes of Carn Etchachan to just beyond Little Loch Etchachan. Follow the path left (east) for 200m then contour due south to gain the base of the cliff.

Accommodation: The compact Hutchison Memorial Hut (NO 023 998) beneath the cliff in Coire Etchachan makes an ideal base, sleeping six people at a squeeze.

THE BASTION **E**

NO 016 997 **Alt:** 900m

The large buttress at the left end of the crag, between the loose and vegetated **Forked Gully** and the prominent slabby recess of **The Corridor**.

Descent: Traverse left (south) 200m beyond **Forked Gully** and down steep grass and scree slopes.

1 Quartzvein Edge ★★   120m Moderate

FA Kenny Winram, G.Greig & Mac Smith 15 June 1952

A popular route following the left edge of The Bastion overlooking Forked Gully. Start at the base of Forked Gully above a detached block. Climb a 3m wall with inset quartz then follow the edge to a gravel patch at 35m. Layback up a left-slanting groove and continue to the lower of two shelves. Follow the shelf which develops into an open chimney ending in jumbled blocks poised over the gully. Either finish up a scree funnel or by the right side of a false tower.

2a Talisman Direct Start ★ 40m E1 5b

FA Andy Nisbet, Steve Kennedy & N.Mollison 13 July 1981

The prominent corner system just left of the arête below the start of the normal route. Start at the lowest point of the buttress. Ascend the corner to an overlap (PR) then follow the continuation corner on the left. A traverse back right on good holds across a steep wall leads to the arête, which is followed to the belay on *The Talisman*. Either finish up this or abseil off.

2b Talismaniac ★★ 40m E4 6a

FA Julian Lines & Sue Harper 4 August 1996

Essentially an extended start to *Talismanic* giving a superb bold pitch. Start right of *Talisman Direct Start*. Climb the centre of the scooped wall to a bulge. Pull through this to gain an obvious quartz blotch. Move delicately right then up the arête to better holds to join the normal route.

2c Talismanic ★ 30m E3 5c

FA Wilson Moir & Niall Ritchie 10 June 1990

The left arête. Start at the base and pull onto the edge using big holds and go up to a perch. Continue boldly for 4m then follow cracks to the belay.

2 The Talisman ★★★ 105m HS 4c

FA Bill Brooker & Ken Grassick 24 June 1956

Excellent varied climbing taking the crest of the wall overlooking The Corridor. Start behind a huge boulder at the base of The Corridor.

1 **35m 4b** Ascend the wide flake-crack rightward to a ledge on the right then follow the easier slab slightly leftward. An obvious traverse left leads to a fine belay on the edge.

2 **22m 4c** Traverse left to the base of a thin groove and follow this to an awkward overhanging alcove at its top. Negotiate this with interest (very well protected) to gain a fine belay stance.

3 **48m 4a** Finish up the crest, starting initially on the right wall.

📷 *Jo George starting the traverse on the first pitch of The Talisman. Photo Dave Cuthbertson, Cubby Images.*

Talking Drums **   115m E2 5b

FA Colin MacLean & Andy Nisbet 4 July 1986

Sustained well protected climbing with a sensational finish up the headwall. Start at the lowest point of the buttress.

1 40m 5b Climb *Talisman Direct Start.*

2 25m 4c Follow the obvious thin diagonal crack leading right past a triangular block and through the girdling bulge. Move slightly back left and up to a poor belay under the headwall.

3 25m 5a Gain the base of a shallow groove via two small scoops and follow the groove to a good foothold at its top. Move right and up on hidden holds to a hand traverse and mantelshelf leading right to a PB.

4 25m 5b Make a delicate move up to gain a small ledge and PR then swing down right and across the wall to reach the base of a corner crack. Follow this to finish.

JUNIPER BUTTRESS

The buttress right of the large recess of **The Corridor**.

4 **The Hex** *   80m HS 4b

FA Greg Strange, Mike Forbes & Brian Lawrie 10 July 1971

A short but steep route on excellent clean rough rock. Start at a shallow pink bay.

1 40m 4b Climb a vague rock fault to a system of grass cracks and belay at top of cracks beneath a bulge.

2 40m 4b Step left and follow the continuation fault to a point where the cracks become grass choked. Step right to the crest and into *Pikestaff* and finish up the last 6m of that route.

5 **Pikestaff** *   120m Very Difficult

FA Tom Patey, Bill Brooker & John Hay 7 August 1954

Follows the left rib. Go up The Corridor flank of the rib to a point just beyond a ferny trough which climbs to a large grass platform on the buttress. Start beside a curious little pocket in the rock. Climb over short walls and then up alongside the trough to within 5m of its top. Slant up the Corridor wall for 18m by cracks until a break on the right leads to a crest. Follow the rib directly ahead. First comes a smooth nose, then easier rocks to a pointed belay. Take off from a flake on the left (crux) and finish the pitch by moving right. A final 35m pitch leads to easy ground. Scramble to the plateau.

THE MEADOW FACE

 Carmine Groove **   140m VS 4b

FA Greg Strange, D.Stuart & Dougie Dinwoodie 17 July 1971

The obvious red groove left of the overhangs on the upper section of the cliff. Slow to dry, though it provides two superb pitches on steep clean rock. Start directly below a recent rock scar in the lower overhangs.

1+2 60m Scramble up right to the upper meadow.

3 20m 4b Start up the groove above the left edge of the meadow, moving right to a flake, then back left to re-enter groove. Follow this to belay below an overhang.

4 25m 4b Step left onto a steep red slab and climb directly up the corner to a roof. Exit right to a small ledge and follow a thin crack in the slab to ledges.

5 35m – Move right and follow a narrow grey rib soon leading to easier ground.

THE CRIMSON SLABS

The very fine sweep of slabs bounding the right end of the cliff.

⑦ Scalpel Direct ★★   **120m E1 5b**

FA Dougie Dinwoodie & Greg Strange 11 July 1977;
Direct Finish Andy Nisbet & Alastair Ross 20 October 1985

The very shallow tilted corner towards the left edge of
the slabs. Fairly bold in its upper reaches. Start 4m right
of the left-bounding Red Chimney.

  1 **40m 4c** Ascend the arête overlooking
corners on the left to a ledge. Step into the
edge of the overlap then direct over a small
bulge. Step right to a small stance.

  2 **45m 5b** Go up the shallow corner until it finishes at
an overlap. Step right and place good runners in *King
Crimson* then return to make a rising left traverse
(crux) to the arête of a curving corner. Continue up
cracks just right of the arête leading to easier ground.

  3 Either continue up broken rock (35m), or move right
to *Djibangi* and descend via the terrace or by abseil.

⑧ In the Pink/King Crimson ★★   **125m E3 5c**

FA King Crimson: Alastair Ross & Greg Strange 25 August 1984;
In the Pink: Andy Nisbet & Alastair Ross 27 October 1985

An excellent combination with the main pitch on
immaculate pink rock midway between the corners of
Scalpel and *Djibangi*. Start in the alcove as for *Djibangi*.

  1 **35m 4c** Climb a flake crack midway between
Djibangi and *Sgian Dubh* then move left round
a bulge and up to join *Djibangi*. Climb its
small corner to a small ledge at its top.

  2 **45m 5c** Go out left to a prominent jug, then climb the
slab to a shallow flake with unexpected but crucial
runners. Climb straight up the pink rock to gain a tiny
foot ledge and arrange runners under a shallow curving overlap. Move up left to grey rock and continue to
beneath an obvious notch in the main overlap. Move
right then cross the overlap just right of a small corner forming the notch. Continue directly, pulling left
into a small groove (F #0) and follow this to broken
ground beneath an area of clean cracked slabs.

  3 **45m 5a** Climb directly up the slabs by cracks
passing through a break in the overlap and
right of a large block. Scramble to finish.

⑨ Djibangi ★★   **135m VS 4c**

FA John Hay, R.Wiseman & A.Cowie (2 PA) 22 July 1956;
FFA early sixties

The leftmost and less prominent of the two corner lines
on the slabs. The first pitch of *Sgian Dubh* provides a
better start, more consistent in standard with the main
pitch. Start at the base of a prominent pink right-facing
corner in a grassy alcove beneath the line.

  1 **20m** Climb diagonally left to a large
platform on the edge of the slabs.

2 25m Trend back right and ascend a small corner in the centre of the slabs then easier to the base of the main corner.

3 30m 4c The fine corner, stepping right to a P and NB on the rib at the top. Either make two abseils (40m; 30m, or one 60m) from PBs or continue up the inferior upper slabs.

4+5 60m Move back left into the corner and climb it then move out left and follow the obvious groove leading to a huge block. Climb round this and continue up a rib to easy ground.

🔟 Sgian Dubh ★★   105m HVS 5a

FA Andy Nisbet & Miss M.Bridges May 1978

The right arête of the main *Djibangi* corner. Start at the left side grassy alcove as for *Djibangi*.

1 30m 4c Follow a series of shallow left-facing corners leading up to the base of the main *Djibangi* corner.

2 35m 5a Ascend the arête overlooking the corner making a short deviation out right in the mid section. Abseil as for *Djibangi*, or:

3 40m Grassy grooves lead out rightward to the terrace.

11 Stiletto ★★   110m E1 5c

FA Mike Forbes & Mike Rennie (3 PA) 17 August 1966;
FFA Dougie Dinwoodie & Adair McIvor 1976

Sustained well protected climbing tackling the impressive vertical crack slicing into the slabs, midway between *Djibangi* and *The Dagger*.

1 25m 4b Go up the lower continuation of the crack to belay beneath the crack

2 40m 5c Cruise up the crack.

3 45m Traverse right into *The Dagger* and follow it easily to the terrace.

12 The Dagger ★★   130m HVS 5a

FA Tom Patey & John Hay (4 PA) 4 September 1955

The great sweeping corner dominating the right side of the slabs. The original line on the slabs with a classic main pitch. Start in the grassy alcove as for *Djibangi*.

1 25m 4b Traverse right and up a little for 5m then move back left into a short corner. Continue slightly left again to gain easy ground leading rightward to the base of the main corner.

2 35m 5a Go up the corner to a hanging belay on a huge spike beneath an overhang.

3+4 70m Move left below a bulge to avoid the overhang then move into the grassy groove above and scramble to a large platform beneath the final slab (terrace descends right from here). Climb the slab by a crack slanting right then direct to finish.

13 Scabbard ★★★   106m VS 4c

FA Mike Rennie & Mike Forbes September 1966

The wonderfully situated arête overlooking *The Dagger* corner – very quick drying. Start by a right-facing clean–cut corner directly below the line.

1 28m 4c Ascend the corner then continue directly by cracks to belay at the base of the arête

2 28m 4c Go up the prominent finger crack and continuation cracks to a small overlap. Continue up the edge to the spike belay at the top of the corner.

3 50m 4b Move right and down a short way, and pull out right to an edge. Follow cracks and blocks to gain the terrace at its highest point.

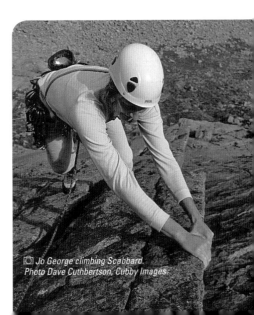

📷 *Jo George climbing Scabbard.*
Photo Dave Cuthbertson, Cubby Images.

The central of three corners at the right end of the cliff is the sustained poorly protected 14 *Scythe* E2 5b.

 Sabre ★   **45m VS 4b**

FA Steve Kennedy & Charlie McLeod 28 July 1982

The rightmost corner. Start up an awkward pale-coloured slab. Surmount an overlap and finish up a cracked slab leading to the terrace.

 Delicatessen ★   **40m VS 4c**

FA Andy Nisbet, Rick Allan, Brian Davison, Steve Kennedy & Guy Muhlemann June 1983

The best continuation to routes ending on the terrace. Above the top of the terrace is an area of mainly vegetated slabs descending rightward. This route climbs the clean cracked arête bounding the right edge. Follow the arête directly, staying close to the crest.

Karen Latter nearing the top of the classic Cyclops (see page 403), The Central Slabs, Creag an Dubh-loch.

BEN MACDUI
(HILL OF MACDUFF)

Crystal
Ridge

Grey Man's
Crag

Glissade
Gully

Central   Spider
Buttress   Buttress

Snake
Ridge

Main
Spout

Terminal
Buttress

COIRE SPUTAN DEARG
(CORRIE OF THE RED SPOUTS)

NO 003 991 **Alt:** 1090m   3½hr   2½hr

This coire lies high on the east side of Ben Macdui, at 1309m Britain's second highest mountain. The slabby rock is rough, clean and very quick to dry. With short routes and easy descents it is often possible to climb several routes in a day. A pleasant open friendly atmosphere makes this is one of the best lower grade venues in the whole of the Cairngorms.

Access: From the centre of Braemar follow the C-class road west along the south side of the River Dee for 6 miles/9.6km to Linn of Dee. Continue for a further 200m along the north side of the road back towards Braemar to a car park (pay & display) in the forest on the left.

Approach: (A) From the car park at the **Linn of Dee** follow the signposted path to meet up with the track from the locked Derry Gates to reach Derry Lodge in a little over 4km. Cross the footbridge over the Derry Burn and follow it downstream to pick up the track heading west up Glen Luibeg. After 2.5km break off right up a path up the right (east) bank of Luibeg Burn for 2km to a fork. Continue up the right fork then in the same direction for a further 3km to the cliff. (3 hours). Cycles can be taken as far as the Luibeg Burn (3 km from cliff).

(B) From the Hutchison Hut head up the side of the stream in the grassy bay to the left of the cliff and over the col between the summit and Derry Cairngorm (1 hour).

(C) From the north (Coire Cas car park on Cairn Gorm) the fastest approach is to follow the path up the ridge on the west side of Coire an Lochain as far as Lochan Buidhe, then contour round the north-eastern slopes of Ben Macdui, heading south-east across the upper reaches of Garbh Uisge Mor. Descend down the scree-filled **Glissade Gully** (NO 002 990) beneath the south end of a tiny lochan to arrive in the centre of the corrie (2½ hours).

Accommodation: The closest base is the Hutchison Memorial Hut (NO 024 997) in a wonderful situation beneath Creagan a' Choire Etchachan. Further away, though still a useful base is Bob Scott's Bothy (NO 043 932) just south of Derry Lodge. Good camping spots are numerous, including just beyond Derry Lodge; Robbers Copse (NO 015 938) – the stand of Caledonian pines just beyond the ford over the Luibeg Burn; the flat grassy area just beyond the confluence of the Allt Carn a' Mhaim 1.5km further up the burn; or under the cliff itself. There are also some draughty howffs in the corrie, best suited for dry sunny weather.

Descent: The scree-filled **Glissade Gully** in the centre of the corrie between **Grey Man's Crag** and *Snake Ridge* provides the easiest descent.

GREY MAN'S CRAG

① Crystal Ridge ★★   110m Difficult

FA R.Still & Miss E.Lawrence 1 September 1948

The great slabby ridge abutting the left side of the steep upper left side of the main buttress.

  1 15m Scramble up to a large platform beneath the main slab.

  2 50m Continue, keeping close to the crest of the slab.

  3 45m Continue in the same line to reach more broken ground. Scrambling remains

② Zircon ★   120m E2 5c

FA Simon Richardson & John Ashbridge 7 June 1992

Good sustained climbing up the wall left of *Amethyst Pillar*. Start 10m below a chimney.

  1 10m 4c Step onto the slab on the right and move up to a large ledge.

  2 35m 5c Follow *Amethyst Pillar* for a few metres, then the crack system trending left. Pass below a long narrow rectangular roof. Climb the steep crack system 3m to its left and exit strenuously on big holds to reach a ledge.

  3 25m 5a Continue up the left-facing chimney groove directly above.

  4 20m 5c Gain a sloping triangular ledge from the right and follow a line of flakes diagonally left across the wall to a steep finish on the left arête.

  5 30m 4a Finish up easy cracks and grooves.

③ Amethyst Pillar ★★★   100m HVS 5a

FA Final crack: Jim McArtney & James Stenhouse 13 July 1964; Lower section: Rob Archbold & Dave Nichols 10 June 1979

Superb steep climbing up the left side of the buttress. Star at the base of the prominent left-slanting chimney fault.

  1 40m 4c Move out right onto the steep slabs, starting about 5m below a 'curious round niche'. Climb up by cracks, pulling left over a bulge to the obvious hanging corner. Step left beneath a small roof, step down left and traverse left across steep wall by a flake ledge to belay at its end.

  2 25m 4c Above is a shallow cracked groove with a bulge. Climb this and exit right onto the crest of the ramp.

  3 35m 5a Move up right and climb a prominent vertical crack above a pedestal using a jammed flake on the initial bulge. Finish up slabs.

④ Grey Slab ★★★   117m HS 4b

FA M.Higgins, John Innes & Brian Lawrie 14 September 1963

A brilliant route following the prominent left trending ramp in the centre of the buttress. Start by scrambling up broken ground to a good platform 10m beneath the corner

  1 12m 4a Climb the cracked groove to gain the right end of the ramp. P & NB.

  2 20m 4b Climb the ramp to a grass ledge.

  3 40m 4a Continue in the same line to an overhang,

turn this on the left and climb to a ledge. Climb the slab or the corner on the right until forced to move left at the top. P & NB on small ledge.

4 45m 4a Step down and move into the chimney on the left and finish easily up this. Alternatively, the short slab above the belay (4c) can be climbed to gain the chimney higher up.

5 Ferlas Mor ★★   **120m HS 4b**

FA John Mothersele, Greg Strange, Dave Stuart, Brian Lawrie & Dougie Dinwoodie 22 May 1971

Ferlas Mor is the big grey man, a spectre reputed to haunt the slopes of Ben Macdui, first witnessed by Norman Collie in 1891.
A fine companion to *Grey Slab*, taking a direct line up the centre of the crag.

1 12m As for *Grey Slab*, or climb the fine long layback crack on the right (20m VS 5a).

2 30m Swing up right and climb grooves and ribs on the edge overlooking *Grey Slab* to a basalt fault. Climb this to a ledge below the crux of *Hanging Dyke*.

3 36m Move left and continue up grooves to a

small stance level with the top of *Grey Slab*.

4 44m Go up and right and follow the crest via a short chimney and easy rib to top.

6 Hanging Dyke ★★   **105m Very Difficult**

FA Allan Parker & J.Young 29 March 1949

Start to the right of the lowest rocks at the foot of a broad slab. The dyke goes up the centre of the slab.

1 30m Follow the dyke to a small ledge then climb a grass-filled crack to a good stance beneath a crack-seamed slab.

2 30m Climb a wide slab inclining left by a series of parallel cracks to a sloping corner. The dyke steepens, forming a rib to the left of a groove. Climb the rib for 18m on small holds (crux), until the dyke falls back into a chimney. Spike and NB on ledge on right.

3 45m Follow the continuation of the dyke up left on the crest then by the left wall of a grassy groove. Scramble out right, then up a wide easy grassy gully to finish.

📷 *Dave McGimpsey on the final jamming pitch of Amethyst Pillar. Photo Andrew Fraser.*

📷 *Karen Latter moving up the ramp on the fine second pitch of the classic Grey Slab.*

SNAKE RIDGE

There are two ridges right of **Glissade Gully**, this is the rightmost one.

7 **Snake Ridge** ★★   **130m Severe 4a**

FA Bill Brooker, D.Sutherland & C.Hutcheon 25 June 1949

An excellent climb. One of the original classics of the corrie. *Snake Ridge* is the second of the long ridges to the right of **Glissade Gully**, so named from *"its fancied resemblance as seen from the top, to a snake, head down"*. For easier recognition its lower rocks fan out into three ridges *"giving a fair impression of inverted Prince of Wales feathers"*. The left side of the ridge is low and angles easily into a grassy gully running alongside.

1+2 60m Start on the left *"feather"* and follow the crest directly for two pitches to a platform and belay below a step on the ridge.

3 15m Climb this on the left to a stance and spike belay on the right.

4 25m 4a The crux pitch follows. Go up a short wall and use good holds to pull up into a groove. Continue rightward up the groove to the crest, or (easier) leave the groove and climb to a good hold on the left.

5 30m Further climbing leads to the broken upper buttress.

THE CENTRAL BUTTRESSES

Three buttresses close together, right of *Snake Ridge*.

8 **The Black Tower** ★★   **110m Severe 4a**

FA Tom Patey, 'Goggs' Leslie & Mike Taylor 21 April 1952

Fine climbing up the central buttress, unfortunately marred by a horribly wet and slimy approach pitch. Start to the left of the buttress.

Starting 15m above the lowest rocks follow a prominent groove on the left flank of the buttress. This leads in 25m to easier ground. Climb broken slabs on the left to a platform 9m above, and at the foot of a steep 6m groove, close to the true crest of the tower. The groove, *"entered from the right by a Severe movement"*, gives access to a platform and block. The steep slab round the corner on the left is climbed by a 6m crack to a short arête. Traverse delicately for 5m across the slab on the right until it is possible to regain the crest and the summit of the tower by a short crack. The tower is connected to the plateau by a shattered arête. Clean, rough rock throughout.

9 **Flake Buttress** ★   **110m Moderate**

FA J.Tewnion, E.Smith, Mac Smith, Kenny Winram 22 May 1949

Good varied climbing up the right buttress. More difficult variations have been made on the lower section. Start just right of the lowest rocks.

1 18m Follow a grassy depression rightward to a stance on the broken crest.

2+3 92m Continue in the same line until a flake crack leads back left to a short right-angled corner. Swing up left on good holds. Go up a chimney on the right and then by easy ledges to a stance and belay below an overhang on the crest. Behind a huge flake on the left climb a vertical crack on grand holds and continue up slabby blocks to a gap. Ignore the easy ground on the right and take the arête straight ahead to the plateau.

SPIDER BUTTRESS

The slabby buttress high up in the coire, between *Flake Buttress* and **The Main Spout**.

10 Bolero ★★   50m E5 6b

FA Wilson Moir & Tim Rankin 27 July 1997

1 **30m 6b** Start up the initial corner of the big low angled corner, then go right to climb the small left-facing corner, pulling out right at its top to the PR on *The Skater* (the PR is a joke but other gear can be arranged). Step up then reach left to climb the arête (crux) to a ledge. Continue up the easier arête above to a belay.

2 **20m 5c** Traverse 5m right and pull over the overhang via a flake layaway. Continue up the hanging slab to the top.

11 The Skater ★   45m E4 6a

FA Colin MacLean & Andy Nisbet 26 July 1984

Ascends the left edge of the buttress overlooking the large easy-angled corner. Start at the base of this.

1 **30m 6a** Ascend a shallow corner just right of the arête of the large corner exiting right. Move diagonally left across the slab to a jug on the arête and poor PR (good F). Climb the slab on the right to the prominent corner at the left end of the cigar-shaped overhang. Climb the corner to a belay.

2 **15m 4b** Continue up and slightly left over easy blocks, finishing by a short overhanging crack

12 The Fly ★★   45m VS 4c

FA Dougie Dinwoodie & Brian Lawrie 19 June 1971

A good well protected pitch up the steep cracked wall near the centre. Climb a crack leftward then move up right to gain a horizontal crack. Traverse this across the wall and climb easily up left to the prominent deep S-shaped crack. Climb the crack then either the slab or the deep flake crack on its right to finish.

13 Flying Saucers ★   55m E4 5c

FA Wilson Moir & Tim Rankin 27 July 1997

1 **35m 5c** Start up the initial crack of *The Fly* to gain the left arête of the wall. Climb the arête to its top and arrange bombproof runners. Continue up the unprotected scooped slab-rib which runs up rightward to a horizontal break. Step right and ascend a short crack leading to a belay.

2 **20m 4c** Go directly up from the belay to climb flakes up the slab above.

THE MAIN SPOUT – TERMINAL BUTTRESS

The largest piece of rock on the right side of the base of **The Main Spout**.

Descent: Down the grassy shelf slanting down leftward into **The Main Spout**.

14 The Chute ★   45m HVS 5a

FA John Ingram, Brian Findlay, Greg Strange & Dave Stuart 13 June 1970

The leftmost of a series of grooves and corners on the wall left of the descent route. Follow the corner to a *"curious jammed block"* and go behind the block. Step left and climb the left-slanting crack to a shallow groove left of a prominent overhanging prow. Follow the groove to a good platform. Scramble to finish.

15 Terminal Wall ★★   70m HS 4b

FA Brian Lawrie & Jim McArtney 8 September 1963

Fine exposed climbing following a series of cracks and grooves up the left edge of the wall at the right side of the corrie. Start just right of a short gully and prominent fault. Climb straight up over an overhang then left to a stance on the edge. Move right, climb cracks above then a fault to a sloping ledge leading right. From the end of this ledge go straight up and make an awkward move left round a corner on a hidden foot hold. Finish by cracks and split blocks.

BEINN A'BHUIRD (TABLE HILL)

A vast mountain, with its extensive summit plateau containing a series of fine corries cutting into its eastern slopes, together with the even remoter Garbh Choire at the head of An Slochd Mor (the great pit).

Access: Turn north off the A93 (signposted Keiloch), 2.8 miles/4.5km east of Braemar, 0.2 miles/0.3km east of Invercauld Bridge over the Dee. Park in the small car park up on the right (pay & display).

Approach: Mountain bikes recommended. Follow single track road (signposted Water of Quoich) north-west through the forest past Invercauld House. Take the right fork 500m beyond the farm at Alltdourie (signposted Slugain) through a plantation and onto a new track up Gleann an t-Slugain which reverts to a stalkers path at the ruined Slugain Lodge. Leave bikes here. Continue until the path splits 500m beyond. Take the right fork and follow it north, passing the huge boulder of Clach a' Chleirich, then the stream which leads north in a further 2km to the col of The Sneck (the notch), 15km.

On foot: If the Dee is running low, ford it just downstream from Braemar Castle and head north to pick up the track at the bottom of Gleann an t-Slugain. This reduces the approach on foot by around half an hour.

Accommodation: There is a small howff sleeping two or three people at NO 098 995 at the base of Dividing Buttress, under the second largest boulder immediately beneath the lowest slabs (200m west of Dubh Lochain). Otherwise, excellent wild camping in any of the corries or the upper reaches of Glen Quoich.

GARBH CHOIRE (w 🥾 🏃)
(ROUGH COIRE)   4hr   3hr

A fantastically remote corrie, with grand views north over the head of An Slochd Mor.

Descent: From the top of the path at The Sneck, head west up the rim for a few hundred metres to drop down to an obvious grassy hollow on the right. Contour west from here to pick up a path which descends diagonally across scree slopes into the base of the corrie. A prominent narrow scree fan a few hundred metres north of the top of *Mitre Ridge* provides a convenient descent from the other end of the corrie.

SQUAREFACE BUTTRESS

NJ 111 013 **Alt:** 950m

High up on the left side of the corrie, ending abruptly on the plateau, and roughly midway between The Sneck and *Mitre Ridge* is a fine steep buttress with a superb slabby west wall. Very quick drying.

Approach: Easiest from the plateau. Follow a path west round the rim for about 250m beyond the top of the buttress. Just beyond a shallow gully, follow a vague path diagonally down to the base. From the corrie floor, follow the diagonal scree and boulder-filled rake tortuously up to the base.

1   Squareface ****   90m Very Difficult

FA Tom Patey & Mike Taylor July 1953

The best route of its grade in the entire massif, well worth the long approach. Start at a large flat area beneath the centre of the slab.

1   **40m** Move slightly left and follow a crack/groove over small bulge at mid-height to large platform. Continue u the ridge to belay on a ledge on the left side of the arê

2   **25m** Traverse right for 9m past the first prominent crack then direct up the slab to another obvious traverse line leading back left to a fine belay ledge

on the arête. Thread and nut belay.

3 25m Follow the obvious line up rightwards to a good horizontal crack. Climb the obvious wide fissure, then rightwards to a fine wide left-facing layback flake (the fissure continues at Severe). Climb the flake to its top then move up rightwards pleasantly. A stunning pitch.

Angel's Edgeway ★★   65m VS 4b

FA pitch 2 W.Gault & A.Kane 1959; complete Brian Findlay & Greg Strange 17 June 1989

Good situations and exposure, cutting through *Squareface*. Start right of *Squareface*, left of a corner crack.

1 30m 4a Ascend slabs to where they steepen. Move right and climb the crack through a bulge which leads to the belay on *Squareface*.

2 15m 4b Step out right and follow a line just right of the arête to share another belay with *Squareface*. A fine exposed pitch

3 20m 4a Follow *Squareface* to the good horizontal crack. Traverse left and layback the prominent hollow flake, then easy ground to finish.

Unknown climbers on the finely positioned top pitch of Squareface.

MITRE RIDGE   NJ 107 014 **Alt:** 950m

Mitre Ridge ★★   220m HS 4b

FA Sandy Wedderburn, Pat Baird & E.Leslie 4 July 1933; Variation Start: Charles Ludwig & D.Dawson September 1933

One of the great classic Cairngorm ridges, despite some vegetation and loose rock. After the first pitch (avoidable), the climbing is Very Difficult. Start beneath large groove midway between the lowest rocks and the right edge of the ridge.

1a 35m 4a Climb slabs then the groove and a short bulging wall to belay.

1b 25m The first pitch can be avoided by following a line of weakness (Moderate) leftward from the ridge to belay at the top of the original first pitch.

2–6 Follow the general line of a rising shelf round to beneath a deep chimney on the west face. Follow the chimney and enter a shallow gully which leads in 12m to a shoulder on the ridge. Make a delicate traverse right then climb direct to the base of the steep wall beneath the first tower. Gain the large grass platform above either directly by 5m inset right-angled corner or, slightly easier, by moving leftward over a slab and climbing a splintered chimney. Climb the wall and continue to the col between the first and second towers (junction with *Cumming-Crofton Route*). Either turn the second tower on the left or direct by a steep crack to finish along a narrow arête and final tower.

THE WEST WALL

Steep and impressive, but well endowed with holds.

The Fundamentalist ★★   175m E2 5c

FA Simon Richardson & Iain Small 15 July 2005

An excellent route taking the right edge of the front face of *Mitre Ridge*. Pitch 3 is sensationally exposed. Start directly below the well defined pillar split by a crack that lies just left of the initial corner of *Cumming-Crofton Route*.

1 30m 5a Scramble up to the crack and climb it through

an overlap to a good platform on top of the pillar.

2 30m 5b The route continues up the slim hanging groove in the edge (between the corners). Move right, then back left into the hanging groove and climb it to exit on easier ground on the front face of *Mitre Ridge*. Continue easily up the edge where *Mitre Link Variation* joins from the right.

3 35m 5c Go up to the foot of the first tower and climb the right edge on hidden holds.

4 20m Scramble along the ridge to the notch below the Second Tower.

5 20m 5c Climb the wall on the front face of the tower past a prominent protruding flake. Strenuous and awkward to protect.

6 40m Scramble to the plateau.

③ Cumming-Crofton Route ★★   155m Severe 4b

FA Stephen Cumming & John W.Crofton 4 July 1933; Pitch 5: Jim Bell May 1935

A classic and the most impressive of all the pre-war routes in the Cairngorms. Start directly beneath the large open corner bounding the left end of a steep clean wall. Scramble up slightly left to a small platform.

1 25m 4b Climb the obvious open chimney passing a steep projecting flake with interest (crux) at mid-height. Belay in a cleft at the top.

2 15m 4a Move up to ledge above then climb diagonally rightward up a smooth slabby groove until it ends at a bulge. Move up then step left round the rib to belay at base of corner.

3 20m 4a Climb the flaky corner to a good ledge on the right.

4 45m 4a Climb the wide crack in the left wall then the general line of the corner. Cross a loose gully to large blocks then up to belay on the crest of the ridge.

5 25m 4a Step off the top of the large block and up to a ledge above. Traverse a wide flake right round the edge. Step down into corner and up this, stepping left up a flake on good holds to the top of the first tower. Continue along a level section to a large block belay.

6 30m Continue along the airy crest, via a good ledge down on the left side to drop down into a gap. Finish easily on the left of the final wall. Thread belay.

④ The Spear of Destiny ★★   50m E5 6a

FA Pete Benson & Guy Robertson 26 August 2007

The smooth slab and bulging wall left of *The Empty Quarter* heading for then through the obvious arrow-shaped niche. Superb sustained climbing on beautiful rock. Start below a big open groove 10m down from *The Empty Quarter*.

1 15m Climb the easy groove, or cracks on its left wall, to belay comfortably on a perched block thread belay.

2 35m 6a Step left onto the slab directly above the belay and move left to reasonable holds by a good diagonal crack (protection). Stand up on these, tip-toe a little further, then step left to where a series of moves leads directly to the obvious jug. Continue up to another diagonal crack, climb past this, then traverse rightward into the niche. Turn this on the left, step back right, then climb sustained cracks into the obvious fault and easy ground. Either continue up *The Chancel* or abseil off (in situ thread on left).

⑤ The Empty Quarter ★★   95m E3 5c

FA Dougie Dinwoodie & Greg Strange 6 August 1983

An excellent well protected pitch up the shallow vertical corner at the right side of the wall.

1 40m 5c Scramble up to a ledge then move right onto the wall and ascend to the corner. Climb a good crack leftward until it is possible to move up to a small foot ledge beneath an overlap. Step left, move under the bulge, then pull over and climb diagonal cracks in the wall to easier ground. Traverse left and follow an obvious line to gain the terrace.

2+3 55m 4c From the middle of the terrace, climb the wall above, then continue straight to easy ground below the Second Tower.

⑥ Bounty Hunter ★   60m E2 5b

FA Guy Robertson & Pete Benson 7 September 2007

The fine crack system right of *The Empty Quarter*.

1 35m 5b Climb the crack over an overhang, then

trend left past another. Continue directly up the
wall above to a ledge and belay below a tower.

2 25m 5b Start up a groove in the right arête, swing
left onto the front face at an obvious break, then
climb directly to easier ground which leads to a
platform. From here either abseil off or scramble
up left to the col behind the First Tower.

© Photo Pete Benson.

THE SLOCHD WALL (THE PIT)

7 Slochd Wall ★★★   **110m HVS 5a**

*FA Mike Rennie & Greg Strange (A3) 30 August 1969;
FFA Brian Lawrie & Andy Nisbet 3 July 1979*

Excellent clean climbing taking the large vertical corner
above the left end of the roof system. Start at the foot of
North-West Gully.

1 15m Climb the gully to the first depression.
Traverse onto the wall on the left via a
grass shelf to an obvious belay stance.

2 30m 5a Go up a crack rightward, then
slightly leftward up a steep slab on the left of
a corner to a large overhang. Swing right under
the overhang into a shallow corner which leads
with difficulty (crux) up into the main corner.

3 15m 4c Traverse left into another corner
to step right onto a large ledge.

4 20m 5a Go up the rib at the left end of the ledge
for a short way to swing left to regain the corner.
Climb this, bypassing the overhang on the left. Trend
diagonally left to an arête and belay just above.

5 30m Continue up the edge to finish by a crack.

8 Freebird ★★★   **100m E4 6a**

FA Guy Robertson & Pete Benson 7 September 2007

Brilliant climbing up the right arête of *Slochd Wall*
corner; start as for that route.

1 30m 6a Climb *Slochd Wall* to just past the
bolt, step right under the obvious slot and
make hard moves up right to a rest on the
arête. Continue directly through bulges and

up a slab (crux), to belay just left of overhangs.

2 30m 6a Pull right through the overhangs into a
hanging groove, step right again, then go back left
and climb cracks up the wall in a superb position.
Belay at the right end of the second big ledge.

3 40m 5a Climb cracks in the right side of the upper wall.

9 The Primate ★★   **110m E1 5b**

*FA John Anderson & Andy Nisbet 9 July 1979;
Pitch 1 Greg Strange & R.Ross 8 July 1984*

The wide crack splitting the right side of the roof system. A
fine companion to *Slochd Wall*. Start as for that route.

1 15m As for *Slochd Wall*.

2 25m 4c Follow the obvious right-slanting
crack to gain cracks which lead to a ledge below and right of the roof crack.

3 25m 5b Traverse left and follow the crack with a *"fasci-
nating sequence of moves"* through the roof. Continue
up the crack to a grass terrace beneath the final wall.

4 45m Climb short walls to a left-slanting groove
in the headwall, then the groove leading
almost to the left edge to finish up a crack.

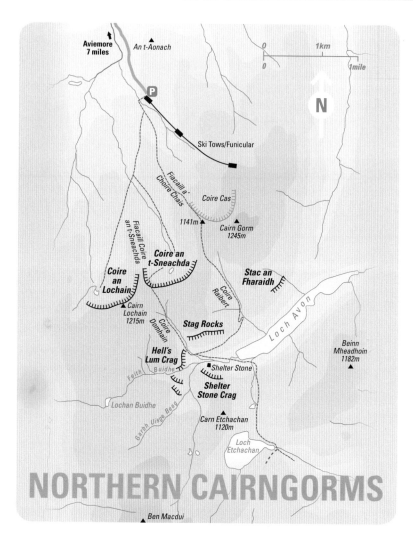

Amenities & Accommodation: Aviemore (the Las Vegas of the Highlands!) is the most convenient base though it has all the charm of a new town designed by wee men in suits sitting at a drawing board. There are a multitude of eating and drinking establishments here, though much better towns can be found in all directions (anywhere away from Aviemore!). There is a large Tesco supermarket in the centre of town. For good food try the Old Bridge Inn just off the B970 (Cairn Gorm road) at the south end of town. For pubs The Winking Owl seems popular with climbers. There is also a bar in Glenmore Lodge (☎ 01479 861256) where a variety of self catering chalets and B&B accommodation are also available. **TICs** Kingussie (☎ 01540 661297); Aviemore (☎ 01479 810363); Grantown-on-Spey (☎ 01479 872773).

10 miles south of Aviemore, The Tipsy Laird Restaurant and Bar (☎ 01540 661334) at the north end of the High Street in Kingussie does particularly good food. They also have a bunkhouse and provide a variety of B&B and self catering accommodation. Innumerable **Bunkhouses:** Pottery Bunkhouse, Laggan Bridge (☎ 01528 544231; www.potterybunkhouse.co.uk); Newtonmore Independent Hostel (☎ 01540 673360; www.highlandhostel.co.uk); Strathspey Mountain Hostel, Newtonmore (☎ 01540 673694; www.newtonmore.com/strathspey); Craigower Lodge, Newtonmore (☎ 01540 673319; www.activeoutdoorpursuits.com); Happy Days Hostel (☎ 01540 661175; www.happydayshostel.co.uk) & The Lairds Bothy (☎ 01540 661334; thetipsylaird. co.uk) both Kingussie; Glen Feshie Hostel (☎ 01540 651323) and Kirkbeag Hostel (☎ 01540 651298) both at Kincraig; Bothan Airigh, Insh Village (☎ 01540 661051); Aviemore Bunkhouse (☎ 01479 811181; www. aviemore-bunkhouse.com); Fraoch Bunkhouse, Boat of Garten (☎ 01479 831331; www.scotmountain.co.uk); Lazy Duck Hostel (☎ 01479 821642; www.lazyduck. co.uk); Nethy Bridge Hostel (☎ 01479 821370) both Nethy Bridge; Carrbridge Bunkhouse (☎ 01479 841250; www.carrbridge-bunkhouse.co.uk); Slochd Mhor Lodge, by Carrbridge (☎ 01479 841666; www.slochd.co.uk); Ardenbeg Bunkhouse (☎ 01479 872824; www.ardenbeg. co.uk) and The Stop-Over (☎ 01479 872529/873121) both in Grantown-on-Spey. **Youth Hostels** in Kingussie

(☎ 01540 661506); Aviemore (☎ 01479 810345); Loch Morlich (☎ 01479 861238). Climbing Club Huts are Milehouse, 1 mile from Kincraig; Mill Cottage in Feshiebridge; and the Raeburn Hut on A889 between Dalwhinnie and Laggan.

Campsites: Dalraddy Holiday Park, Aviemore (☎ 01479 810330; www.alvie-estate.co.uk); Edinkillie Campsite (☎ 01479 820238); High Range (☎ 01479 810636; www.highrange.co.uk) all Aviemore; Glenmore Camping & Caravan Site (☎ 01479 861271; www. forestholidays.co.uk); Coylumbridge (☎ 01479 812800); Grantown-on-Spey Caravan Park (☎ 01479 872474; www. caravanscotland.com); Boat of Garten Caravan & Camp Park (☎ 01479 831652).

Outdoor Shops: Cairngorm Mountain Sports www. mountainsports.com (☎ 01479 810903) also have a café upstairs and do the cheapest mountain bike hire in town; Nevisport www.nevisport.com (☎ 01479 810239); Mountain Spirit www.mountainspirit.co.uk (☎ 01479 811788); Ellis Brigham www.ellis-brigham. com (☎ 01479 810175) all in Aviemore. **Climbing Walls:** small leading and bouldering wall in Glenmore Lodge (☎ 01479 861256; www.glenmorelodge.org. uk); small leading and bouldering wall in Dalfaber Industrial Estate, Aviemore (☎ 01479 812466; www. extreme-dream.com); modern (2000) leading and bouldering wall in Inverness Leisure Centre (☎ 01463 667505; www.invernessleisure.com) with some routes climbed on leader placed protection.

📷 *Prore, Coire an Lochain. Scott Muir climbing.*
Photo Dave Cuthbertson, Cubby Images.

NORTHERN CORRIES OF CAIRN GORM STRATH SPEY

Clearly visible from the A9 are three great corries scooped into the northern slopes of Cairn Gorm. The east most is Coire Cas, of interest purely to the skier. Further west lie the two most accessible cliffs in the Cairngorms, Coire an t-Sneachda and Coire an Lochain.

Due to the large amounts of broken rock in the corries they are better known as superb and very popular winter venues. Nevertheless, they are of some interest to the rock climber with a few particular routes as good as anything of their grade in the area.

COIRE AN T-SNEACHDA
(CORRIE OF THE SNOW)

NH 995 031 **Alt:** 1000m

1hr

The central of the three great northern corries (korin'tray-achk) lies midway between the ridges of the Fiacaill a' Choire Chais and the Fiacaill Coire an t-Sneachda.

Approach: From the Coire Cas car park, cut down right past the bottom T-bar to follow a signposted path heading diagonally right (south-west) then head up the left (east) side of the Allt Coire an t-Sneachda (stream). Continue along the path up into the corrie.

Descent: By the Goat Track, a well-worn path right of the main mass of the crag. This follows a zig-zagging line, steeply at first, then heads diagonally right (east) under the cliffs.

ALADDIN'S BUTTRESS

The large buttress left of the centre of the corrie, bounded on its left side by the scree-filled zig-zag gully of *Aladdin's Couloir*.

1 **The Magic Crack ★★★★**　　　　**100m HVS 5a**

FA Greg Strange, Mungo Ross, J.Wyness & Dougie Dinwoodie 16 May 1981; Start as described: Allen Fyffe & Martin Bagness July 1984

A contender for the best HVS in the Gorms, with a superb final pitch up an immaculate finger crack. Unfortunately winter ascents since the late nineties have greatly scarred the route. Start at a deep left-facing corner by a

huge beak of rock.

1 **35m 4c** Follow the corner then the broad blunt rib above to large spike belay on platform.

2 **25m 4c** Follow the rib to gain the thin crack on the right, which leads up into corners.

3 **40m 5a** Move right and follow the immaculate finger crack. Higher up cross an overlap and finish up the cracked wall leading to easier ground. It is also possible to abseil (slings in situ) back down the line in 2 rope lengths.

2 Damnation ★   90m E1 5b

FA D.Sharp & B.Taplin (1 PA) 1969; FFA unknown

A good main pitch up the rightmost corner. Start up from
the lowest rocks.

1 **45m** Follow easy cracked slabs and corners to a
huge spike belay at the base of a pale corner.

2 **45m 5b** Climb the initial corner then the main
one to finish up the cracked wall on the left.

3 Pygmy Ridge ★★   90m Moderate

FA Harold Raeburn, W.Gordon, G.Almand, A.Roth 1 April 1904

High up in the centre of the corrie is a prominent ridge.
Either scramble up much broken ground to the base of
the route, or gain the base by scrambling or abseiling
down its right (west) side from the corrie rim. Follow the
well defined rib, crossing a horizontal rib.

FLUTED BUTTRESS

NH 992 029 **Alt:** 1080m

The broken buttress high on the right side of the corrie
overlooking the Goat Track.

4 Fingers Ridge Direct ★   110m VS 4c

FA Allen Fyffe & Martin Bagness 9 July 1984

This is the direct line up the slabby rib culminating in
some distinctive pinnacles just short of the plateau.
Pleasant climbing though escapable in places. Start in
the middle of the ridge.

1 **35m 4b** Climb directly up pink slabs, cross an
awkward bulge and belay in the open groove.

2 **20m 4b** Work up and right to a stance by Red Gully.

3 **30m 4c** Follow the diagonal crack
in the fine slab to ledges.

4 **25m** Go up the next diagonal crack
to join the normal route.

Scott Muir and Jo George on the
fantastic final pitch of The Magic Crack.
Photo Dave Cuthbertson, Cubby Images.

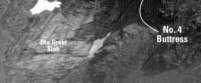

COIRE AN LOCHAIN
(CORRIE OF THE LOCHAN)

The westmost of the three great northern corries lies west of the Fiacaill Coire an t-Sneachda, beneath the summit of Cairn Lochan, the most westerly of the Cairn Gorm tops.

Approach: From the Coire Cas car park, cut down right past the bottom T-bar to follow a path heading diagonally right (south-west) to cross the Allt Coire an t-Sneachda (stream) after about 10 minutes. Continue along the path, branching off left after 75m, to follow a narrow path up into the coire, skirting round the right side of the boulder field to arrive at the lochan. Head steeply up the hillside to the base of the chosen cliff.

The buttresses are numbered left to right.

Descent: Down either end of the coire. For the western descent, from the top of *Savage Slit* continue west along the rim of the coire for 400m, then down gravelly ground, skirting back round on grass right (east) to the base of **No. 4 Buttress**.

NO.1 BUTTRESS

NH 985 027 **Alt:** 1030m 1½hr

The buttress on the left side of the corrie, with a steep right side rising out of **The Vent**, a short well defined gully funnelling into easy angled open ground above.

1 **Ventriloquist** ★★   80m HVS 4c

FA John Lyall & B.Kellet 2 August 1990

Good climbing up cracks near the left side of the front face. Start beneath a chimney crack 5m left of *Ventricle*.

1 **30m 4c** Climb the chimney crack then move right and follow a crack-line up into a recess. Pull out right to beneath a wide crack.

2 **20m 5a** Climb the crack with difficulty then trend up right by two short corners to a ledge.

3 **30m 4c** Move up left to a line of flakes and traverse right to a thin crack. Move up the crack, bypassing the steepest section by a short detour on the right. Above, cross the 'crevasse', finishing up a deep crack.

② Ventricle ★   95m E1 5b

FA John Cunningham & George Shields (1 PA) summer 1968; FFA unknown

The line of cracks and grooves on the left wall of **The Vent**. Start near where the face changes aspect.

1 **15m 5b** Climb the initial overhanging crack (crux), move right along a ledge and climb a wall near the right edge to belay in a small mossy recess.

2 **15m 5b** Climb directly above the belay heading for prominent groove, with an awkward move to gain the belay ledge.

3 **20m 4c** Follow the right most of the two shallow grooves to reach a steep groove. Climb this until a traverse can be made to

a block belay at the top of a groove.

4 **45m 4b** Follow the wide crack in the groove, finishing up the steep wall to ledges.

③ Daddy Longlegs ★★   70m HVS 5a

FA George Shields & Brian Hall (11 PA) 25 August 1968; FFA Brian Davison & Andy Nisbet 29 August 1983

The steep groove and cracks high on the right side of the buttress. Start 15m beneath the chokestone in **The Vent**.

1 **35m 5a** Climb the groove, step right into another groove and up this past an overhang to ledges.

2 **10m** Scramble up left.

3 **4c 25m** Follow two vertical cracks in the wall right of the wide corner crack of *Ventricle*.

NO. 4 BUTTRESS

NH 982 027 **Alt:** 1030m 1½hr

Bounding the right edge of the corrie, down and right of the two branches of **Y Gully** is a fine buttress with a number of excellent prominent corner lines. By making a 50m abseil down the chimney of *Savage Slit* a number of routes can be climbed in one visit, retrieving the abseil anchor on the final ascent.

Approach: Follow a path heading steeply up right, then back left under the base of the buttress.

① Procrastination ★   70m Severe 4a

FA John Cunningham & George Shields summer 1968

The narrowest central corner line on the front face.

1 **10m** Climb easily up to the start of the corner.

2 **40m 4a** Climb the corner, bypassing a small roof on the right.

3 **20m 4a** Move back left and follow the continuation of the groove to a large ledge. Go up the wall above, scramble to above *Savage Slit* and continue easily to the top.

② Fall-Out Corner ★★★   95m HS 4b

FA Tom Patey, R.Ford & Mary Stewart (1 PA) 17 May 1964

On the right side of the pillar is an equally fine right-facing corner – the line. Start beneath the corner.

1 **10m** Go up to belay beneath the roof blocking the corner.

2 **35m 4b** Cross the roof and climb the excellent sustained corner to its top. Belay in the corner just above a long ledge on the right.

3 **20m** Continue up the corner, finishing over some jumbled blocks to belay on large platform.

4 30m Drop down into the 'crevasse' and move
left, finishing up the final pitch of *Savage Slit*.

③ Prore ★★   **100m VS 4c**
FA G.Bradshaw & B.Taplin 5 July 1969

Excellently situated climbing up the prominent curving
right arête of 4, starting and finishing up that route.

1 15m Climb as for *Savage Slit*, then move
out right to belay beneath the arête.
2+3 60m 4c Climb the right side of the arête
to belay on large platform at the top.
4 25m Finish as for *Savage Slit*.

EWEN (NO. 3) BUTTRESS

The large sprawling buttress towards the right side of
the corrie, sandwiched between the prominent wide
right-slanting gully fault of **The Couloir** and the left
branch of **Y Gully**.
Descent: By 50m abseil (sling usually in situ) from last
crest before plateau.

① The Vicar ★★   **70m E1 5a**
FA George Shields & S.Wilkinson (5 PA) 25 July 1968;
FFA Brian Davison & Andy Nisbet 29 August 1983

A disgusting first pitch, though worth the effort to
gain the excellent top pitch. Start just right of a huge
overhanging groove-recess.

1 35m 5a Climb the slimy overhanging groove, then
move up left towards to the back of the recess to
beneath the second overhanging groove. Traverse
right and mantelshelf onto a ledge with large blocks.
Go up a steep crack to belay on the next ledge.
2 35m 5a Follow the shallow corner and its left wall for
20m then move out onto the arête and finish up this.

② Siberia ★★   **60m E3 5c**
FA Ian Taylor & Chris Forrest August 1996

The stunning arête. Start as for *The Demon*.

1 30m 5c Go up for 3m then step left into a
groove and follow it to the roof. Pull leftward
over the roof, follow cracks in the arête and

④ Savage Slit ★★★   **80m Very Difficult**
FA Richard Frere & Kenneth Robertson 17 July 1945

*"It appeared to be very deeply cut in places, and to
penetrate into the depths of the mountain."* – Frere.
A compelling line tackling the unmistakable wide
chimney slot in the huge left-facing corner up the centre
of the buttress. Start directly below the main corner.

1 10m Climb easily up to belay at the
base of the corner proper.
2 45m Climb the chimney above, mainly by its
right edge to a large ledge at its top. Can be
split at 20m, but an excellent long pitch.
3 25m Finish up the gully above, with a short
steep rock step at the top to gain easy ground.

⑤ Bulgy ★   **80m VS 4b, 4b**
FA George Shields & R.Doig (1 PA) 21 August 1968

The left arête of *Savage Slit* finishing up the wide crack
through the prominent twin roofs.

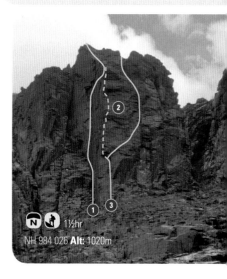

NH 984 026 **Alt:** 1020m   1½hr

pass the next roof round on the left.
2 30m 5c Follow twin cracks until a move left
gains the edge. Climb the roof using a flake on
its left side and continue more easily to the top.

3 The Demon *   60m E2 5b
FA Brian Davison & Andy Nisbet 29 August 1983

Intimidating climbing up the steep section up the centre of the buttress. It starts below the arête of *Siberia* and heads diagonally right to follow a crack-line which comes up from the base of the wall. Start just right of the toe of the arête.

1 **30m 5b** Climb up for 3m then step left into a shallow groove and follow it to a roof. Traverse right under the roof, then go up slightly right into a thin crack. Follow this to a small stance at the top of the crack.

2 **30m 5a** Move up and right on steep layback flakes to enter the main crack system. Follow this to easy ground.

📷 *Cairn Gorm plateau.*

THE LOCH AVON BASIN

Loch Avon (pronounced 'aan') lies in a deep 300m hollow between Cairn Gorm and Ben Macdui. The western end of the loch is overlooked by a variety of contrasting cliffs, dominated by the imposing **Shelter Stone Crag** at the head of the corrie. **Hell's Lum Crag** sits glistening opposite while further east not far below the Cairn Gorm plateau are **Stag Rocks** and **Stac an Fharaidh**.

Access: From the A9 take the turn-off just south of Aviemore and follow the B9152 north (parallel to the A9) for 1 mile/1.6km to turn off right along the B970 (on the southern fringes of the town) which passes through the Glen More Forest Park before climbing steeply up to the large extensive car park (NH 990 060) 630m/2000 feet up the northern slopes of Cairn Gorm (7 miles /11km).

Approach: From the Coire Cas car park at the chairlift follow the track up the left side of the first tow passing underneath the tow at the first station. Continue up the wide vehicle track for about 10 minutes past a couple of zig-zags to gain a recently constructed path (marked Fiacaill path) leading up onto the ridge, Fiacaill a' Choire Chais (tooth of steep corrie). One hour of ascent to cairn at top of ridge (·1141).

Accommodation: Clach Dhion (stone of the shelter), a renowned howff is situated low down in the corrie at the base of the boulder field beneath the **Shelter Stone Crag**, near the stream at NJ 002 016. There is a cairn on top. Less popular and not quite so claustrophobic howffs exist further up the boulder field. There are also many superb camping spots by the stream and around the head of the loch and on some beautiful golden sandy beaches along the shores of the loch.

Bouldering: There is some excellent bouldering around the base of the boulder field, including a finely situated long 6a arête above a pool just above the path.

HELL'S LUM CRAG
NH 995 017 **Alt:** 920m ⛷🧗 1¾hr

The extensive crags on the south-east flank of Cairn Lochan at the head of the Loch Avon basin, sandwiched between the streams of the Feith Bhuidhe and the Allt Coire Domhain. Many of the routes on **The Frontal Face** and **The Left Sector** take a lot of drainage, though many of the other lines dry quickly.

Approach: From top of Fiacaill a' Choire Chais (·1141) follow a path on the right which contours initially south then south-west across the hillside (not marked on 1:25,000 map) for a little less than 2km to gain a well worn path down the east side of the Allt Coire Domhain. The cliff comes into view on the right just beneath the steepest section of the path. Cross the burn level with the base of the cliff, just beneath a large boulder on the path. Forty-five minutes from top of ridge (·1141).

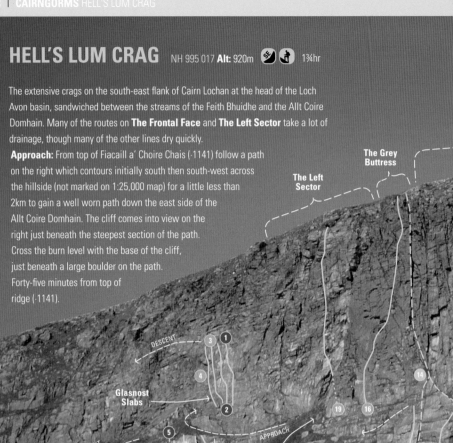
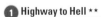

THE FRONTAL FACE

The main highest section of the crag, gradually steepening as height is gained.

1 **Highway to Hell ★★**   20m E2 5b

FA Julian Lines (on-sight solo) August 1995

The slabby right-angled arête at the far right end of the cliff. Climb it boldly on its right side.

2 **Sneer ★**   120m Very Difficult

FA Alasdair 'Bugs' McKeith (solo) 27 June 1963

A varied route on very clean rock up the overlapping slab at the right side of the cliff. Climb the obvious large open corner about 30m right of *The Escalator* to easier rock. Go up rightward by easy grooves finishing up the right of two obvious cracks through three overlaps on the often wet upper slabs.

The Frontal Face

3 Two Little Devils *   30m E1 5c

FA Julian Lines & Keith Crymble 21 September 1995

10m right of *The Escalator* is a steep slab with a
Y-shaped crack system. Climb this to easier ground
(superb gear). Climb the wide crack above to a glacis.

4 Dust Devils *   30m E4 6b

FA Julian Lines & Robin McAllister 30 August 1998

Desperate (very close to E5 6c!) padding up the slab left
of *Two Little Devils* protected by a side-runner at the top
of the Y-fork in its crack-line. Climb the blank slab to a
ledge then the bold rib above to easier ground. Take the
single crack through the headwall.

5 The Escalator ★★   150m Moderate

FA Graeme Nicol, Tom Patey & Miss E Davidson
30 September 1955

The prominent fault towards the right end of the cliffs. Clean sound rock but often a watercourse. Easy scrambling up a gully leads to a large platform below the steeper section where an easy shelf leads off to the right. Pleasant climbing up pink water-worn rock leads to a finish just left of the top of the watercourse.

6 The Devil's Alternative ★★★   180m E1 5a

FA Allen Fyffe & Bob Barton 1 August 1981

Interesting climbing on excellent rock following a direct line up the right side of the slabs. Start at a greenish buttress just left of the depression of *The Escalator.*

1 **45m** Climb the buttress by shallow cracks to a huge terrace.

2 **45m 5a** Twin cracks rise above the overlap. Gain these from a scoop on their right and climb them to the next overlap (*Auld Nick* crosses here). Work left across the overlap to the glacis.

3 **45m 5a** Above is a stepped wall. Zig-zag up this to gain a short left-leaning corner, above which moves up and right lead to the next glacis.

4 **45m 5a** Climb into a niche in the grey wall above, go leftward to a horizontal crack then make a hard move to easier ground. An easier rib now leads to the top.

7 Auld Nick ★★★   160m Severe 4a

FA G.Brown, Ian Houston & Ian Small 11 October 1963

Excellent sustained climbing up the right side of the slabs. Start at a prominent crack in the slab 20m down left from *The Escalator* depression.

1 **45m** Follow the crack to belay beneath the first overlap.

2 **45m** Continue up the right-facing corner, then the crack in the slab to the next bulge. Move right along horizontal crack then diagonally up right.

3 **20m** Ascend the left-facing corner over a series of steps to belay beneath a right-tapering roof.

4 **30m 4a** Pass the roof on the right then continue leftward, passing a block to a large ledge. Continue up the thin crack above the centre of the ledge to belay beneath large grey block.

5 **20m** Climb either side of the block then scramble to the top.

8 Prince of Darkness ★★   140m E2 5b

FA Bob Barton & Allen Fyffe 10 August 1984; Variation p2 (as described) Paul Thorburn & Julian Lines summer 1999

Good though slightly meandering climbing with a particularly fine top pitch. Start just right of the base of the diagonal fault.

1 **25m 4a** Climb the crack in a green slab to grooves. Belay below an obvious single crack splitting the slab.

2 **45m 5b** Move to the base of the crack. Make a bold move to start the crack and follow this (good gear), moving up to belay below the prominent red slab.

3 **30m 4b** Climb cracks in the big red slab to a good ledge.

4 **40m 5b** Climb corners to easier ground.

9 Devilicious ★   20m E5 6a

FA Julian Lines (on-sight solo) 5 September 1998

Immaculate padding up the concave slab just right of the start of *The Clean Sweep.* Start just right of a pink streak. Climb through the first overlap into the centre of the scoop then direct through the upper overlap and continue nervously to a good hold.

10 The Clean Sweep ★★★   190m VS 4c

FA Robin Smith & Graham Tiso September 1961

The crag classic. Start down and left of the prominent left-slanting diagonal fault leading into *Deep-Cut Chimney* beneath a left-facing corner at the right side of the slab.

1 **30m 4c** Follow the corner for a short way to gain a groove. Climb this to gain cracks on the crest of the green whale-back leading to a belay beneath the fault.

2 **50m 4a** Climb the slab above the fault moving left and up corners to P & NB on top of a huge block below the pink corner.

3 45m 4c Climb the superb corner then the continuation fault to a large ledge on the right underneath an overhang. A fine sustained pitch – very well protected.

4 30m 4b Continue up the rib above to belay where it opens out into a large open corner.

5 25m Traverse right round the rib and follow a slightly wandering line to a large grassy ledge near the top.

6 10m Climb the short steep wall on the right, scrambling to finish.

11 Hellfire Corner ★★   185m VS 4b
FA George Annand & Ronnie Sellars 14 September 1958

Good climbing up the large corner to the left of *The Clean Sweep*. Slow to dry. Start at a crack at the lowest point of the slab.

1+2 60m 4b Climb the crack and left-facing corner leading to the large diagonal fault.

3 45m 4a Ascend the short deep left-facing corner leading up into the main corner system which is followed to a belay beneath a large overhang.

4 20m 4b Continue in the same line up a depression and corner to an awkward move onto a platform beneath the main corner.

5 20m 4b Continue up the steepening corner, chimneying through the overlap in a fine position to move out right to a large ledge.

6 40m Finish more easily up the right-facing corner left of the big fault above.

12 The Bats, The Bats ★★   50m HVS 5a
FA Blair & Allen Fyffe 14 August 2003

A good pitch on immaculate rock following the crack lines in the clean pink slab left of *Hellfire Corner*. Climb the clean crack into the short shallow right-facing corner. From the top of the corner trend left to gain the prominent crack and climb it to where it disappears then move right to a square nose. From the right side of the nose follow another crack to the fault. Descend by traversing left.

13 Salamander ★★   155m HVS 5a
FA Dougie Dinwoodie & J.Tweddle 18 September 1971

A direct line parallel to *Hellfire Corner*. Start below an obvious right-facing corner.

1 40m 4b Climb directly and delicately up the corner and follow this to a ledge. Continue upwards passing a prominent overlap by a bulging slab on the left to reach a platform.

2 20m Follow easier rocks to a glacis.

3 20m 5a Climb twin cracks up steep slabs left of an obvious corner to a platform.

4 20m 4b Climb directly by a black bulge just right of a short corner and go up slabs trending rightward to an obvious shallow scoop.

5 30m 4b Continue up slabs to reach a shallow groove. Follow this to break through the upper overhangs by a striking chimney slit. Thread belay.

6 25m Continue direct through an open funnel to easy ground.

📷 *Alan and Sam Leary on the crux third pitch of The Clean Sweep. Photo Dave Cuthbertson, Cubby Images.*

14 Deep-Cut Chimney ★   **150m Very Difficult**

FA Ian Brooker & Miss M.Newbigging September 1950

A good climb up the impressive slit with a spectacular and unexpected finish. Though vegetated in its lower part the walls are close enough to back and foot and avoid the greenery. Start either directly below or by the easy terraced fault cleaving the smooth lower slabs. Once in the chimney proper there are a number of pitches to be overcome, mostly fern and grass-grown, hence climb them back and foot leaving the herbage untouched. About 50m from the top the rock scenery becomes quite remarkable; the chimney cuts far into the cliff and chokestones are jammed well out between the walls forming a tunnel. Back and foot outwards below the final overhang to reach a crazy pile of boulders wedged in the outer jaws. The finish comes with startling suddenness.

15 Devil's Advocate ★   **50m E4 6a**

FA Julian Lines & Tang Hui Li 23 June 1999

A slightly contrived line but with superb climbing and amazingly quick drying. Start at a thin vertical crack in a slim green buttress just left of the obvious Direct Start to *Deep-Cut Chimney*. Climb the crack to a small foot ledge at 4m. Step up and make a very thin move up and left to better holds. Place a runner in the crack above, step down and move right onto a slab. Make awkward moves up and slightly left to below twin hairline cracks. Climb between these (marginal RPs) to the top. F #3 for belay.

THE GREY BUTTRESS

A very quick drying buttress due to its detached nature lying between *Deep-Cut Chimney* and **Hell's Lum**. The front face is steeper lower down, lying back in the upper section where the lines become less defined.

16 Hell's Lump ★★   **100m VS 4c**

FA Jimmy Marshall & James Stenhouse September 1961

Start at a pink and green slab 45m right of Hell's Lum.

1 **40m 4c** Climb a line of quartz up the slab to gain a large flake at 15m. Continue by the groove and crack above for 12m. Move up rightward to turn the overhangs by a layback crack on the right and gain a grassy bay

2 **18m 4a** Continue up to the recess above.

3 **22m 4b** Follow the recess then by cracks and corners, trending slightly rightward.

4 **20m** Climb the rib to finish.

17 Chariots of Fire ★★   **45m E4 6a**

FA John Lyall, Andy Nisbet & Jonathan Preston 4 August 1991

A sensational route with flaky rock adding to the excitement. Although overhanging all the way the crux is short and well protected. Gain the start by a 40m abseil from the 'viewing block', a large flat rock from where one can lie and peer into The Lum.

1 **15m 5b** Climb out rightward into a shallow corner, actually a big flake. Follow this briefly then go rightward again into another corner. Go up this to belay below a roof.

2 **15m 6a** Make a high traverse left onto the overhanging wall then pull up to good holds (crux). Traverse left to a spike then go up to a line of flakes leading leftward to a small ledge.

3 **15m 5a** Continue up the flakes then straight up over the bulge to the viewing block.

18 The Seventh Circle ★★★   **50m E6 6b**

FA Iain Small & Gary Latter 10 August 2007

The stunning slim groove and hanging crack in the wall just below the main pitch in The Lum. Gain the base by a 60m abseil from 8m left of 17 abseil point (starting down front face).

1 **23m 6b** Climb the groove, moving out left then back into the groove, past a PR. Pull over small overlap, stepping left to a good rest. Return and make difficult moves up and right to get established in the crack, which leads with difficulty to good ledge.

2 27m 6b Traverse left into good flake crack and follow this past projecting block to rest on wall on right. Step left and pull over the roof with difficulty leading to better holds above. Continue more easily up crack to good ledge above. Scramble out rightwards to finish.

THE LEFT SECTOR

When dry the clean pink rock immediately left of **Hell's Lum** gives some excellent climbing.

 Styx ★★   **105m VS 4c**

FA Bill March & D.Mardon 27 July 1969

Good climbing, though slow to dry. Start 15m up the gully on the left wall.

1 35m 4b Climb a prominent left-slanting groove until the angle eases then the ochre slab on right to a belay.

2 35m 4c Climb to the corner (chokestone) and exit left onto slabs below a large overlap. Surmount this by bridging on left. Climb the slab above and bypass the next overlap on the right. Climb the obvious line, surmount the overlap on the left and go straight up to belay below an obvious overhanging crack. A superb pitch.

3 35m 4b Climb the crack and take a straight line up the obvious crack to an overhang. Surmount this on the right using jugs and go up to finish.

GLASNOST SLABS

The clean red slab, left of the three faults running up the cliff, and above **The Lower Slabs**.

Approach: Walk left from the base of **Hell's Lum**, then scramble up to a squat green ledge at the base, gained from the left.

Descent: Either by abseil or scramble left on rock ledges, then down.

1 Independence ★★   **40m E1 5b**

FA S.Elishashvili, John Lyall & Andy Nisbet 29 July 1991

Climbs into and out of the left-facing crescent-shaped niche. Bold in places. Start down and right from the ledge. Climb up to the big niche, over the bulge up and right, then return left into the crack (protection). Follow this to easy ground.

2 Perestroika ★   **35m E2 5c**

FA S.Elishashvili, John Lyall & Andy Nisbet 29 July 1991

From the ledge, climb direct to left-slanting crack in the fine pink slab. Continue straight up to finish up further left-slanting crack.

Iain Small on the first ascent of The Seventh Circle.

3 Glasnost * 　　　　　　　　35m VS 5a

FA S.Elishashvili, John Lyall & Andy Nisbet 29 July 1991

Fine well protected climbing. From the bottom left of the slab climb direct to join and follow a left-slanting crack-line splitting the fine pink slab. Above the steep step, either move right and follow another crack to easier ground, or continue leftward to finish as for 4.

4 Anarchy * 　　　　　　　　45m VS 4c

FA Allen Fyffe & Mark Diggins 7 August 1999

Pleasant climbing up the vague rib defining the left side of the slab. Climb shallow grooves up and left to an easing. Move right into a short left-facing corner then climb the wall above to a left-facing slanting groove with a crack on its left wall. Follow the groove and the continuation fault to easy ground.

THE LOWER SLABS

A small slabby lenticular-shaped buttress of very clean rock directly below and left of the chimney of Hell's Lum. 50m high at its centre tapering into the hillside at both ends.

Descent: Down either side of the slab.

1 Firestone ** 　　　　　　　　25m E7 6b

FA Julian Lines (headpointed) August 1995

Devoid of holds and protection. 30m left of the right end of the buttress is a featureless black slab with a pink streak up its centre. Climb the pink streak directly up the holdless slab. It steepens at 12m and a blind flake hold out left helps extraction. Easier to the top.

2 Cerberus * 　　　　　　　　50m E3 5c

FA Julian Lines (on-sight solo) August 1995

The crack-line on the left side of the smooth slab gives good climbing. Continue up and left to a belay at the back of the grass terrace.

3 Hell's Gate * 　　　　　　　　50m HVS 4c

FA Paul Allan & Neil Morrison 14 August 1996

Climb the cracks left of 2 to easier ground. Trend left to finish directly into a right-facing corner.

4 Firestarter * 　　　　　　　　40m E3 6a

FA Julian Lines & Robin McAllister 30 August 1998

Climb a thin crack in the slab to where a white streak comes down. Move left and right up the slab (or harder direct above a short corner) to a capping bulge. Pull through the bulge via tiny holds.

5 Mars * 　　　　　　　　45m E1 5b

FA Mark Diggens & Allen Fyffe 7 August 1999

Start as for 4 over the initial bulge, then move left up thin cracks. Finish up the green crack in the rib left of the corner of 6.

6 Pluto * 　　　　　　　　45m E1 5a

FA Julian Lines (on-sight solo) August 1995

Good climbing on fine clean rock. Start at a white streak near the lowest point. Climb up to a left-facing corner, then move right via a very thin crack to a hairline crack. Climb the crack, which eases after 5m, aiming for right-facing corner near the top. Climb the corner and pull out left to finish.

Steve Evans climbing Purge, Stag Rocks.

STAG ROCKS 🏃 1¾hr

This is the collective name for the long face of dark rough granite crags on the southern slopes of Cairn Gorm. Quick drying, the cliffs rise in two sections separated by the open scree-filled **Diagonal Gully**.

Y-shaped Gully

Diagonal Gully

Approach: From top of Fiacaill a' Choire Chais (·1141), head down the path close to the left (east) bank of the Allt Coire Raibert and traverse right (west) to the base of the crag. In clear weather the prominent Y-shaped gully (NH 000 022) can be descended to gain the base of *Afterthought Arête*. The long open Diagonal Gully (with scree chute almost reaching the loch – NH 001 022) gives the fastest approach to **The Right Section**, though care is required especially on the steep grassy upper section. Alternatively, for **The Left Section**, follow the **Hell's Lum** approach to pick up a vague path contouring left underneath the steep clean **Cascade Wall**. Cross a couple of wet shelves then regain the path which leads across the Y-shaped Gully to the base of *Afterthought Arête*. 35 – 40 minutes from ·1141.

Descent: As for the approach.

THE LEFT SECTION NH 001 021 **Alt:** 950m Ⓢ

① Afterthought Arête ★★★   180m Moderate

FA Ronnie Sellars & Mac Smith September 1956

The excellent exposed ridge defining the left edge of Stag Rocks, bounding the right side of the wide scree-filled Y-shaped gully. Avoid the initial steep start (Severe 4a) by moving in from the right further up the slope. *"After this the rocks develop into an excellent, steep knife-edge for 75m and maintain their interest to the top."* Climbed in three full rope lengths. Finish more easily over broken boulders.

② Serrated Rib ★   150m Moderate

FA Jock Nimlin (solo) July 1930

The rib on the right overlooking Diagonal Gully. Climbed in three rope lengths, the middle pitch mainly heather.

THE RIGHT SECTION

NJ 001 022 **Alt:** 950m

Final Selection ★★★   50m Difficult

FA Ronnie Sellars & Mac Smith November 1956

The last defined arête near the top of **Diagonal Gully** gives a very fine route. The right side of the arête is steep, the left a cracked slab angling into a large right-facing groove.

1 **40m** Start up the large groove then break out right onto the arête. Continue up the edge and cracks on the left of the edge to a platform on the right just below the level of a prominent overhang.

2 **10m** Finish easily up the corner on the right.

The arête can be followed more directly by stepping right from the base of the initial groove, finishing steeply on good holds over the small overlap above the belay ledge at Severe 4a.

Purge ★   55m Very Difficult

FA B & D.Taplin 7 August 1969

The groove down to the right of *Final Selection*.

1 **40m** Climb up into the groove and follow it to belay at the right end of the ledge at its top.

2 **15m** Move slightly right then trend left to finish up the edge of the final easy groove on *Final Selection*.

LONGBOW CRAG

NJ 002 022 **Alt:** 950m

Very quick to dry, this slabby crag forms the right extremity of **Stag Rocks**, taking its name from the large roof system midway up the left side of the crag. The upper section of the crag ends in broken ground well below the plateau.

Longbow Direct ★   145m VS 5a

FA Derek Pyper & Jim McArtney August 1962

Good varied climbing up the left side of the face left of the roof. Start at the pink water-worn fault beneath the left side of the face.

1 **30m** Go up the right side of the fault to beneath steep wall.

2 **25m** Traverse across wall for 2.5m then trend left across slab to a ledge at the foot of a prominent steep red wall.

3 **25m 5a** Climb straight up the wall and overhang on jugs then traverse left across a smooth slab and climb a thin crack to a belay.

4 **20m 4c** Hand traverse right then ascend a short corner and over an overhang to reach the Longbow roof. Traverse right under the roof for 6m then swing round the arête to belay.

5 **45m** Either climb the crack above or the crack up the slab on the left, both leading to easier ground. Make for the square-cut chimney and finish up this. Scramble to finish.

The Sand-Pyper Direct ★★   150m HVS 5a

FA C.Sands & Derek Pyper (1 PA) October 1962; FFA unknown; Direct Finish Mick Geddes & J.Higham 1 July 1972

Good climbing, increasing in difficulty as height is gained. Start 25m right of *Longbow Direct* near the centre of the face.

1 **25m 4a** Go over a slab to and climb a crack and rib for 10m, passing a ledge on the left then straight up slabs to a ledge below a long diagonal overlap.

2 **30m 4b** Go up the wall on its right edge between overlaps and traverse left for 3m. Climb a shallow right-facing groove then trend left over ledges to belay on a ledge beneath a large cracked overlap.

3 **25m 4c** Traverse right and up on slabs for 12m then cross the overlap near its right end. Head diagonally back left to a grass ledge.

4 **25m 4c** Follow the diagonal fault right over the block. Step left over the overlap then follow the groove left to a grassy ledge.

5 **45m 5a** Climb the short corner above to
the roof, step right into the next corner and
return left as soon as possible (crux). Continue
up the corner to a ledge then a pleasant
hand crack, finishing by easier ground.

③ The Tenements *   150m Very Difficult

FA 'Goggs' Leslie, Mac Smith & M.Petrie 14 August 1955

The cleaner rocky buttress on the right side of the large
grassy fault leading to a grassy amphitheatre. Start at
the left edge of the rocks.

1 **20m** Zig-zag up cracked slabs and blocks to a ledge.
2 **30m** Move left into a recess, exit right
awkwardly then head up leftward on

good bubbly rock to easier ground.
3 **35m** Follow the large open groove.
4 **30m** Turn the overlap on the right
then trend back diagonally left.
5 **35m** Continue *"gravitate naturally by slabs
and little pitches"* trending diagonally
left to finish at a prominent chimney.

📷 *Martin Fitzsimons on
The Sand-Pyper Direct.*

50min

STAC AN FHARAIDH 🏔 🚶
(PRECIPICE OF THE LADDER)

NJ 014 029 **Alt:** 950m

These glaciated slabs lie on the southern flank of Cairn Gorm overlooking Loch Avon. The slabs are divided into an **East** and **West Flank** by a broad gully and are broken by overlaps or steep walls which provide the cruxes of most of the routes. On the west flank the top overlaps extend into a steep wall providing climbing of a different character.

Approach: From the top of the Fiacaill a' Choire Chais head south-east skirting round the east side of .1082 and down the west (right) bank of the Feith Bhuidhe (yellow bog-stream) that drains south-east into the loch. The best line lies about 50m right (west) of the stream, involves some easy-angled scrambling and is almost always very wet and slippery. Continue down grass slopes to skirt round beneath the base of the crag. A slightly longer approach is to descend easier slopes 300m east (left) of the Feith Bhuidhe then contour back west below some broken rocks to the crag, re-crossing the stream just before the crag.

Descent: As for the approach described above.

WEST FLANK

1 Mack's Dilemma ★★   130m VS 4c
FA George Shields & S.Wilkinson 24 July 1969

A good route up the left edge. Start at the left edge of the slabs.

1 **30m** Climb cracked slabs to belay 6m beneath a right-facing corner.

2 **20m** Climb the corner and continue up the rib with a short excursion to the left to gain a block platform

3 **20m 4c** Continue over an awkward bulge then the rib above to a ledge.

4 **25m 4b** Go up the right side of the arête for a short way, move left onto the edge and continue up to a large ledge

5 **35m** Climb easier ground in the same line to finish.

2 Speakeasy ★   120m VS 4c
FA Allen Fyffe & Blyth Wright 17 June 1978

A pleasant climb taking a line parallel to and right of the left edge of the slabs. Start at the left end of the long block. Climb the slab over two small overlaps to a belay in the corner in the large overlap. Exit left from the corner on to the ledge and traverse on the shelf above this to a small corner. Climb the corner, move right then back left with an awkward mantelshelf then straight up to a grassy ledge. Follow the fault above into a short deep chimney. Climb this and the crack above. A short easy pitch then leads to the top.

EAST FLANK

3 Whispers ★★   130m VS 5a
FA John Cunningham & George Shields Summer 1969

On the extreme left of the right slab are two cracks – the right is the route. Very quick drying – one of the first routes to come into condition early in the spring.

1 **45m 4a** Climb the second crack system from the left. Go straight up cracks (heathery, sometimes wet) to belay at an easing in the angle.

2 **40m 4b** Continue up the same crack system, at one point quite near left edge and up to belay at the base of huge triangular flake.

3 **45m 5a** Move up to the top of the flake then traverse right past PR for 6m. Move up rightward through a bulge and make thin moves onto the slab above. Climb past a flake-crack onto the ledge above then traverse diagonally leftward and straight up to belay on a grass ledge.

4 Bellows **   140m HVS 5a

FA Rab Carrington & Jimmy Marshall 5 July 1970

Good climbing up a crack-line 12m right of and parallel
to *Whispers*. Start directly beneath the prominent
right-facing corner beneath the first overlap system.

  1 25m Climb easy vegetated crack to belay
at the base of a steep grassy corner.

  2 35m 5a Climb the corner then step right to a
good foot hold on the lip. Move right into the
crack system and follow this up the slab then an
easy enormous flat scoop to belay in the short
left-facing corner crack below the overlap.

  3 35m 4c Climb a series of sloping ledges up leftward to a
crack then move up and left over an overlap and follow
cracks to belay at the base of the huge triangular flake.

  4 45m 5a Continue up the wide crack to a PR
then traverse right. Move diagonally right
through the crux bulge of *Whispers*. Continue
up past a ledge then boldly up a thin rounded
crack finishing more easily trending left.

5 Pushover *   140m HVS 5a

FA John Cunningham & Glenmore Lodge party Summer 1969

A good line up the centre of the slab though slow to dry.
Start at the crack at the left side of the large boulder.

  1 45m 5a Follow the sustained crack taking the right
fork of the Y at 10m to beneath the bow-shaped
overlap. Sustained and poorly protected.

  2 12m 5a Pull onto the overlap and move left until the
upper slab can be gained. Move up this to a ledge.

  3 40m 4c Trend up and leftward to a steeper wall which
is climbed by a series of cracks to below mossy blocks.

  4 43m 4b Climb over the blocks and up slabs
to a chimney to finish up the wall above.

6 Pippet Slab ***   135m Severe 4b

FA John Cunningham & Bill March 14 June 1970;
Direct Andy Nisbet & party 1987

The right crack-line. Fine climbing though quite run-out at
times. First 5m is the crux. Start 3m right of the boulder.

  1 45m 4b Climb either of the twin grassy cracks
which converge at 15m crack then continue in the

same line to a ledge and chokestone belays.

  2 30m 4a Trend left up a easy crack to a grassy ledge
below a wall. Now step up right and traverse right
along a ledge to regain the line (can be climbed
direct up the crack at Severe). Continue up thin slab
bearing slightly left to small stance and nut belay.

  3 40m Climb directly up a shallow corner above
some overlaps to belay in a small wet recess.
This pitch is slow to dry but a faster drying Direct
Variation, HVS 4c ascends the smooth slab
forming a vague rib just left of the corner above the
overlaps. Perfect rock but very sparsely protected.

  4 20m Up a recess onto a slab, which leads to short
overhanging wall. Climb this to the top of the crag.

7 Linden **   70m Severe 4a

FA Bill March, L.Rae & S.Matthewson 4 June 1970

An excellent little route up the prominent sloping ramp
high on the right side of the slab. Start in the large
grassy bay on the right where a narrow grass strip runs
up leftward to a wide right-facing flake crack.

  1 25m 4a Climb a short crack 6m right of the corner,
move left then follow thin flakes up the blunt arête
(poorly protected). Step right past a large pocket
then up to belay in cracks at the base of the ramp.

  2 45m 4a Climb the ramp then the flake crack
and a short steep corner to a glacis. Move
out right up a slab to a P and nut belay at the
right edge of the slabs. Scrambling remains.

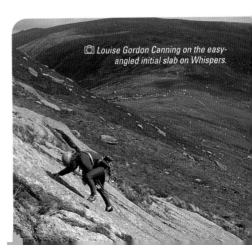

📷 *Louise Gordon Canning on the easy-
angled initial slab on Whispers.*

SHELTER STONE CRAG

NJ 002 013 **Alt:** 850m 2¼hr

With a series of excellent routes from E1 – E7 the Shelter Stone Crag is far and away the best cliff in the northern Cairngorms for the extreme climber. As the most accessible high standard cliff in the Cairngorms it is consequently relatively popular. The 'big three' routes on The Bastion often have several teams on them on most summer weekends, even in poor weather.

Approach: From the Choire Chais car park at the chairlift follow the track up the left side of the first tow passing underneath the tow at the first station. Continue up the track to gain a newly constructed path (marked Fiacaill path) leading up onto the ridge (Fiacaill a'Choire Chais – tooth of steep corrie) (1hr of ascent to top of ridge). Walk due south and down Coire Raibert (Robert's Corrie) by a path on the left bank of the burn. Cut across the stream bed a couple of hundred metres short of Loch Avon and follow a worn path west to the head of the loch. From here cross the stream and follow a path which weaves through the massive boulder field up to the base of the crag. If going in for a day trip and climbing on **The Bastion** (or intending to top out from **The Central Slabs**) it is worth walking round the rim of the corrie and gearing up at the top of the cliff, thus avoiding climbing a further 300m back out of the corrie floor.

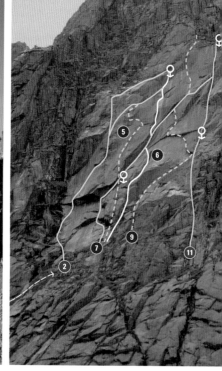

THE CENTRAL SLABS

In many ways the showpiece of the crag, this 100m sweep of steepening slabs lies sandwiched between two large areas of unpleasant grass and broken ground – dubbed the Low Ledge and High Ledge respectively.
Approach: A short awkward corner near the left end provides access to the Low Ledge – an extensive long right-slanting grass terrace at the base of the slabs proper.

Descent: Either continue by much vegetated scrambling above the slabs and traverse right on the plateau to descend as for the routes on **The Bastion**, or abseil. In situ anchors are in place at the top of *The Run of the Arrow* (P and nut) down to *Thor* dièdre then from 2 PRs to Low Ledge, or from 2 PRs and long sling 10m up and left from the top of *The Pin* then by thread on belay again to Low Ledge. Scramble back right (facing out) along this and down awkward short groove to base of cliff.

LOWER TIER

❶ Freya *   50m E3 5c
FA Julian Lines & Lawrence Hughes 4 July 2001

Climbs good clean hairline cracks in a slab to the right of the obvious grey right-facing corner. Start at the toe of the slab 8m right of the corner. Climb directly up the slab on reasonable holds for 15m to reach a scoopy groove on the left, just right of the corner. Make thin moves up and right then direct, passing a couple of overlaps to gain the ledges beneath the main routes.

MAIN FACE

❷ The Harp **   80m E3 6a
FA Pete Whillance & Ray Parker 27 July 1982

Excellent well-protected climbing on the third pitch. Start down and left of the lower left-facing corner of *Thor*.

1 **15m** Move leftward across slab to an old PB in a recess left of the main slabs.
2 **15m 6a** Move right and up to a weakness in the overlap. Through this (crux) and easily up a slab to belay 5m above.
3 **50m 5c** Up crack/groove and move out right to join the left-trending diagonal fault of *Snipers*, which provides a more logical finish. Alternatively, move out rightward to belay as for *The Run of the Arrow* (30m) finishing up the final pitch of that route (25m 5a).

❸ The Immortal Start *   35m E4 6a
FA Julian Lines & Rick Campbell 20 July 1996

A good alternate start to many of the routes on the slab. Start at the left end of the lower slabs at a right facing corner leading into an arching roof. Climb the

📷 *Paul Thorburn on the third pitch of The Harp.*

corner easily to the roof, pull over and follow a crack-line upwards to its termination (RP #1 at its top). Move right to gain better holds, step up above a small overlap and delicately traverse right to gain the huge loose flake/block on the initial corner of *Thor*.

4 Aphrodite ★★★   95m E7 6b

FA Rick Campbell & Alistair Moses July 1990

A long sustained and serious main pitch, following a superb uncompromising line up the left side of the slabs. Start at the base of the left-facing corner leading up to the base of the *Thor* dièdre.

1 35m 5a Climb the corner, moving out left round a prominent overhang. Continue up, teetering past a large loose flake near the top to belay beneath the main roof.

2 10m 6b Cross the overlap past 2 PRs with difficulty to a ledge above. Follow the thin crack leftward to a good nut placement. Return to belay at P and nut placement just above the lip of the roof. An additional 10m of rope required to arrange a satisfactory belay for the next pitch.

3 50m 6b Move up and right into a weakness leading into *The Run of the Arrow*. Follow that route to the crucial protection then move up and right and up again to a tiny foot ledge. Continue directly up to good foot holds in the scoop where *Cupid's Bow* traverses in from the right. Belay/abseil point at the base of the flake crack on *Cupid's Bow*.

5 The Run of the Arrow ★★★   105m E6 6b

FA Pete Whillance & Tony Furnis 24 July 1982

The main pitch follows the faint fading crack up the slab down and left of *Cupid's Bow*. It is very bold, with two sustained hard sections. The route has become a grade harder (much more serious) since the removal of the hammered nuts (which were poor anyway) just before the last protection.

1 40m 5a Climb easily up rightward to a grassy platform at 10m (possible belay) above a small niche. Move left around the rib and follow a crack up into the base of the *Thor* dièdre. Climb the dièdre for 6m to belay at 2 PRs.

2 40m 6b Move up the short corner above the belay and pull left onto the slab. Out left on good holds to thin twin parallel cracks (many small nuts). Up these with difficulty to an easy middle section leading to a large flat hold. Step right precariously to place protection (F #0 under overlap, Wallnut #9 on side or old style R #7 and good small nut in between; F #Z2 also). Make hard delicate moves left and up leading to better holds and continue leftward to belay.

3 25m 5a Follow the obvious rightward slanting line for 12m to a flake crack. Finish up this.

6 Cupid's Bow ★★★   95m E4 6b

FA Dougie Dinwoodie & Dick Renshaw 27 May 1978 (4PA); FFA Murray Hamilton & Rab Anderson 4 June 1982

Superb climbing with an excellent sustained main pitch up the bow-shaped corner above the *Thor* dièdre. Start at the base of the left-facing corner of *Thor*.

1 10m Climb easily up rightward to belay on a grassy platform above a small niche.

2 40m 5a Go straight up the cracks on the left then traverse right into a shallow corner. Go up this then move left onto the rib and traverse into *Thor* dièdre. Go up this for a short way to take a stance in slings beside a ledge of sorts.

3 45m 6b Move up the dièdre then swing out left onto a good ledge below the bow. Climb the corner with difficulty (crucial F #0) until it is possible to gain the left rib. Move up this past an awkward bulging section at the top of the corner. Continue up the continuation of the bow until it kinks to the right. Step left onto a difficult slabby grey wall and climb this to traverse right by small ledges to beneath a prominent flake-crack in the headwall. Finish by moving left up this.

7 Thor ★★★★   110m E5 6b

FA Mike Rennie & Greg Strange (A2) 7 September 1968; FFA Rick Campbell & Neil Craig 15 July 1989

One of the most striking natural features on any crag in Scotland, following an exquisite sweeping line across the slabs. Start down and left of the huge dièdre.

1 40m 5b Climb up into the left-facing corner. At the prominent stepped roof move left onto the slab on the left and up this. Near the top step right across large perched flake and undercut round right and up into the main dièdre. Belay at 2 PRs 6m up this.

2 24m 6b Continue up the dièdre to awkward RP placements above an obvious flake/side pull above the overlap. Gain a good side pull in the alcove (good golo and PR) and cross this to belay on the worryingly hollow flake at a clutch of Ps. It is worth leaving the last two PRs clipped as a backup for the next pitch.

3 46m 6b Continue across beneath the overlap past a PR to reach a crescent-shaped crack then a good horizontal and a further PR above the overlap. Traverse right with a long reach then follow a series of rising ledges rightward to reach *The Pin*. Finish direct up the crack.

8 The Missing Link ★★   **115m E4 5c**

FA Dave Cuthbertson & Derek Jamieson summer 1981

A fine bold diagonal pitch across the slab, with the technical crux leaving the *Thor* dièdre.

1 35m 5a As for *Aphrodite*.

2 15m 5b Up the dièdre to the hanging stance below ledge common to *Cupid's Bow*.

3 40m 5c Traverse right and follow the long narrow overlap (2 poor PRs) to gain a hollow sounding flake. Traverse this to its end and pull into *The Pin*. Climb up a short way to belay.

4 25m 5a Finish up *The Pin*.

9 The Realm of the Senses ★★★   **105m E7 6c**

FA Pitch 1 Andy Cunningham & Allen Fyffe summer 1990; Pitch 2 Rick Campbell & Gary Latter 29 August 1993; Pitch 3 Rick Campbell (previously top-roped) 23 July 1994; as described Julian Lines & Paul Thorburn 1 August 1999

Magnificent sustained climbing with two hard contrasting pitches. Start as for *Cupid's Bow* to belay under a steep wall.

1 30m 5c Move up the initial wall then follow thin tapering ramp up rightward to good

ledge at the base of the left-facing corner.

2 30m 6c Very sustained with three separate hard sections – by far the safest of the E7 pitches on the slabs. Follow the tapering left-facing corner with increasing difficulty to good runners at the overlap. Move left past 2 PRs with increasing difficulty to join *The Missing Link* at its first PR. Follow this past the downward pointing PR to gain a standing position on the hollow flakes. Place crucial runners above the overlap, move back down and traverse left above the overlap to gain a flake leading to the *Thor* belay.

3 45m 6b The L'Elisir d'Amore pitch. A serious pitch taking an initially left-trending diagonal line across the upper slab with a 25m fall potential from above the crux. Gain the old PR in a pocket 8m above the *Thor* overlap. Make hard moves up to a hold at the top of the pale streak (good crucial R #4 in the back of the hold). Move left up a flake to its termination. Make a thin and bold move left to good foothold in the pink streak. Move precariously up the streak to a line of poor pockets that lead in extremis to a rest in a short corner and some poor RPs and a Camelot #0.1. Climb out of the corner using the left wall then straight up on reasonable holds and follow the holds curving rightward until they run out. Make a thin move to gain a flake groove on the right and continue up it to the top. Scramble up and right to a 2 PB in short overhung corner.

10 Icon of Lust ★★★★   **115m E8 6c**

FA p.1 Julian Lines & Lawrence Hughes (on-sight) August 2001; p2&3 Julian Lines & Paul Thorburn 30 June 2003

A monumental voyage up the full height of the slabs taking a direct line through *The Realm of the Senses*. Start 20m down and left from the initial crack of *The Pin*.

1 35m 6a The serious pitch! Climb a cracked groove to a ledge at 10m. Pull onto a bleached slab and climb it veering right into a vague left-facing corner at its top (good gear). Go straight up the steep wall on small positive edges to pockets over the top, step left and pull onto the ramp and follow this rightward to the belay.

2 **25m 6c** A brilliant pitch, desperate and bold. Follow *The Realm of the Senses* groove to the overlap, step right and pull through the overlap with disbelief, sketch up the slab to a weird pocket (F #00), move diagonally leftward, very thin, to join *The Missing Link* amidst its crux. Gain good holds and gear then traverse down and left above the overlap to gain a flake leading to the *Thor* belay.

3 **55m 6b** Extremely bold, a cool head required. Climb *Thor* to the crescent crack, step up into pockets and make thin moves up and left to a jug in the red streak. A precarious stretch left enables a 00 cam to be placed blind, the only protection in 25m of climbing. Climb the red streak to a pocket, step right and up the right edge of the red streak

past a flat hold into a scoop (frightening). Climb a vertical wall past a PR (RP #2 1m above) to gain flakes in a scoop, move diagonally left along flakes and onto the slab above. Continue up the slab to a grassy ledge and possible belay. Continue up the wall above to the apex of the slabs, PB.

⑪ The Pin ★★★   **70m E2 5b**

FA Rab Carrington & Jimmy Gardner August 1968 (2 PA); FFA Ben Campbell-Kelly & Mike Kosterlitz, early 70s

Good sustained climbing up the prominent vertical crack-line near the right edge of the slabs. Start directly beneath the crack.

1 **35m 5b** Follow the crack (belay possible at 20m) through an awkward bulge high up then slightly right and direct to a good thread belay.

2 **35m 5b** Continue in the same line up the steep wall above the belay then the fine crack above.

Julian Lines starting the tenuous traverse on the crux pitch of The Realm of the Senses. Photo Dave Cuthbertson, Cubby Images.

THE MAIN BASTION

This steepening 250m tapering wedge dominates the
head of the Loch Avon basin.

Descent: From the plateau head out right (west)
beyond the broken scree-filled Pinnacle Gully then
down the mainly grassy buttress just before the stream.
Cut back right across the top of the boulder field to
regain the base.

 Haystack ★★★   **280m E3 5c**

FA Rab Carrington & Ian Nicolson (1 PA) summer 1971;
FFA unknown

Excellent climbing heading for the stunning steep wide
crack on the upper left side of the front face. Start at
the toe of the buttress beneath the leftmost of two
right-facing corner systems.

1   **30m 4c** Follow the right-facing corner
to the base of a short corner.

2   **40m 4b** Climb the short corner then exit left
onto slabs. Continue up and left to a good
grass ledge beneath a shallow corner.

3   **40m 4c** Climb the corner then move out right and
cross the overlap above by a prominent crack. Move
left and follow a right-slanting corner to terraces.

4   **40m** Follow short walls and grassy ledges
leftward to beneath the steep wall.

5   **40m 5c** Follow the steep line of weakness
(common to *Steeple*) but continue direct through
a slight break then move right up a ramp (above
the *Steeple* ramp) to belay in a slight recess.

6   **45m 5a** Make delicate moves left onto a ledge
and follow pleasant cracks left to a break in
the arête. Follow an initially steep crack to
gain a ledge beneath an overhanging wall.

7   **30m 5c** Climb the impressive wide overhanging
crack, more difficult above the prominent flake.

8   **30m 5a** Move right and follow a short vertical
crack in the wall above finishing more easily.

13 **Steeple** ★★★★   **250m E2 5c**

FA Pitches 1-6 Kenny Spence & Mike Watson (2 PA); Pitches 7–9
John Porteous, Kenny Spence & Mike Watson August 1968;
FFA Jeff Lamb & Pete Whillance May 1975

Excellent sustained climbing linking the lower and upper
corners by a good natural line. Start beneath a prominent
right-facing corner system (the rightmost of two) up right
from the toe of the buttress. This is left of the steep
grassy gully which splits the lower section of the face.
Scramble 6m up the gully and belay at the start of a
large corner.

1   **30m 5a** Climb the corner passing two small
overlaps to belay beyond the second.

2   **25m 5a** Continue up the corner
above, exiting left at the top.

3   **45m** Climb by short walls and grass ledges
to a terrace below the steep crux wall.

4   **35m 5c** Climb the steep line of weakness
and move right with difficulty then more
easily up the rightward-slanting ramp.

5   **45m 4c** Climb the obvious line of

layback cracks up and right to the foot of the wonderfully situated upper corner.

6 **40m 5b** Climb the corner past a niche to belay on ledges on the left.

7 **30m 5a** Finish by a thin crack on the right, which leads by ledges and cracks to the top of the crag.

14 The Spire ★★   265m E4 6a
FA Murray Hamilton & Rab Anderson 5 May 1982

Two good independent pitches above the grass terrace at one third height. The penultimate pitch is disappointing and *Haystack* or *Steeple* would give a better finish. Follow the first three pitches of *Steeple* (30m 5a; 25m 5a; 45m) to belay on the grass terrace beneath a groove midway between the crux pitches of *Steeple* and *The Needle*.

4 **45m 6a** Climb the steep shallow groove, pull right over the bulge at the top and continue up to the *Steeple/The Needle* belay ledge. Climb directly above to belay at a large pointed block. A superb pitch.

5 **40m 6a** Above is an obvious ramp. Gain the ramp with difficulty and follow it and cracks above to belay to the left of the large

blocks at the base of the *Steeple* corner.

6 **10m 5a** Continue up a short crack above the ledge to belay beneath the impressive main overhanging crack of *Haystack*.

7 **40m 5a** Climb up rightward across the wall via grooves to the arête overlooking the *Steeple* corner. Continue up the wall to grass ledges at the base of the final *Steeple* crack.

8 **30m 5a** Finish as for *Steeple*.

15 The Needle ★★★   260m E1 5b
FA Robin Smith & Davy Agnew 8 June 1962

The crag classic, with excellent varied climbing – the first extreme climbed in the Cairngorms. It follows an inspired line up the centre of the cliff, heading for the prominent chimney splitting the upper cliff. Start directly below the upper chimney, about 30m up right from the right-facing corner of *Steeple*.

1 **30m 4b** Climb straight up a slab with a step left onto a nose at 20m then direct to a ledge and block belay.

2 **45m 5b** Go up, first right then left then by a line of twin zig-zag cracks to a short steep wall at 40m. Pull up rightward onto the steep rib and up to belay below the grass terrace.

3 **25m** Cross the terrace, straight up the slab and flake crack on the left to the top of a huge block.

4 **30m 5b** Go up left for 6m then step right and up a flake crack to traverse left along a thin ledge leading to a bulging crack. Climb the crack to belay on ledges.

5 **20m** From the left end of the ledge move up then go diagonally rightward up a slabby ramp to ledges. Continue right to belay.

6 **35m 5a** Go diagonally up and right along the 'crack for thin fingers'. Above this break out right then up and left by blocks and ledges.

7 **20m** Go up grooves to the foot of the chimney-crack splitting the final rocks of the crag.

8 **35m 5a** Climb the chimney-crack (the Needle Crack) to a ledge and loose blocks.

9 **25m** Continue by the line of the chimney to thread a pile of chokestones and emerge on plateau.

16 Stone Bastion *   245m E4 6b

FA lower pitches Rab Anderson & Chris Anderson 17 May 1992; top pitches – Rab & Chris Anderson 23 July 1994 (reached on abseil, and redpointed); Pitch 3 Paul Thorburn & Gary Latter 31 July 1995

The highlight is the fine sustained and strenuous top pitch, tackling the big corner right of *The Needle*. The climbing below is generally wandering and disappointing and the top pitch would be better approached by abseil from the plateau or from *The Needle*. Start up and right of *The Needle*, at the right end of a long grass ledge.

1 **45m 5a** Climb up for 10m then along a diagonal fault to a short groove. Up this then right across a slab and up onto a higher slab. Straight up on big holds to belay.

2 **25m 5b** Move right to a large loose flake. Up a left-slanting ramp and continue up to a shallow right-facing groove. Up this to good holds then easily to a thread belay on the terrace as for *The Needle*.

3 **50m 6b** Climb pitch 3 & 4 of *The Needle* until halfway along the traverse. Pull straight over the roof into a shallow hanging groove and up this with difficulty. Belay on the right at the top.

4 **45m 5a** Move round right and up the 'crack for thin fingers' pitch of *The Needle*.

5 **25m 4b** Traverse right along a grass ledge and up an easy ramp to a ledge and loose blocks.

6 **15m 5a** Move up the corner past loose blocks to a ledge beneath a wall (PR above). Traverse left and step down to a lower ledge then across to belay at the base of a corner.

7 **40m 6a** Up the corner to a ledge then a crack in the right wall or corner. Above climb a superb slab on horizontal breaks to the top. Belay in a recess. A brilliant three star pitch. Scrambling remains.

📷 *Paul Thorburn on the first ascent of third pitch of Stone Bastion.*

Dave McGimpsey & Robin McAllister (aka The Doobie Brothers) completing the first ascent of Moon Safari. Photo Andrew Fraser.

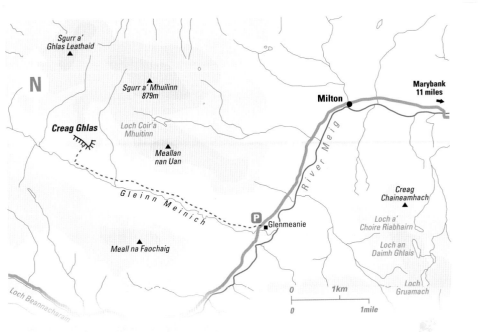

EASTER ROSS

Strathconon runs west from the coast around Conon Bridge and Maryburgh. Although there are numerous roadside crags dotted around, one large crag, Creag Ghlas, stands out.
Accommodation: Riverside Chalets Caravan Park, Contin (01997 421451); hotels and B&Bs in most local towns. **TIC**, Strathpeffer (01997 421415).
Amenities: Small supermarket and petrol station at Contin on A835.

HISTORY

Although climbed on since the late sixties, the first worthwhile routes didn't appear until the nineties. Based locally, Bob Brown and Lord John Mackenzie added a series of good lines, with *Glass Slipper*, the excellent *Hall of Mirrors* and *Salamander* standing out. Later, with Mackenzie in the lead, they added another classic with *Victory Crack*. Later developments in the autumn of 1998 produced a number of good single pitches around the base, including *Super Discount* from Dave McGimpsey, *Spider in a Dark Room* from Andrew Fraser and *Moon Safari* and *Tales of the Old Days* from Robin McAllister. Dave returned with Andy Nisbet, adding *Toad Hall*, but it was left to slab maestro Julian Lines to round things off with his very impressive on-sight ascent of the bold *The Unknown Soldier*.

SGURR A'MHUILINN (PEAK OF THE MILL)

CREAG GHLAS (GREY CLIFF)
WEST BUTTRESS

¾hr 1¼hr

NH 246 545 **Alt:** 400m

This compact slabby schist buttress rises to 150m at its left end. A good range of cams and large nuts are required for protection. An accessible location with a remote feeling and fine views.

Access: From the A835 Inverness – Kyle of Lochalsh road, turn south at Moy Bridge for 0.75 mile/1.2km to Marybank. Follow the minor C-class road west from the village, along Strathconon, passing Lochs Achonachie and Meig. Just beyond the tiny settlement of Milton at the head of the strath, the road bends round south-west. Park at NH 284 527 (1.3 miles/2km beyond Strathanmore) at the start of the forestry road (opposite 2 houses, named Glenmeanie) which heads west (right) up Gleann Meinich (14.3 miles/23 km from Marybank). It may be possible to drive (rough going – 4WD recommended) up the forestry road if the gate is open for 3.1 miles/5km to park on the right opposite a clearing, directly underneath the crag.

DESCENT

Approach: Cycle (recommended option) or walk up the forestry road for just over 3 miles/5km, then head steeply up the hillside on the right (north) for 30 minutes towards the crag.

Descent: For routes on the right: go right and into a wide heathery gully behind the right edge, and down this via a scramble down a rock rib. This can become quite tricky in the wet. **For routes on the left:** head up and leftwards to another shallower gully bounding the left end of the cliff. Leave this where it steepens and go down steep heather on the right (west) until possible to cross below the gully. Follow ledges back below the cliff.

1 Salamander ★★★   **140m VS 5a**

FA Bob Brown, John Mackenzie & Colin Powell
12 August & 24 September 1994

The best and most enjoyable route on the cliff, if not in the whole of Easter Ross. It takes a central line giving sustained climbing which is quick to dry. Start beneath the sweep of smooth slabs split by a prominent dog-leg crack.

1 **25m 4c** Climb the crack to a narrow ledge; a superb well protected pitch.

2 **25m 4c** Trend up right on hidden edges to a narrow heather ledge and shuffle left along this to some holds. Climb the slabby wall above, exiting left along a diagonal crack, to block belays on the left.

3 **20m 5a** Make an awkward move into a scoop and ascend over loose blocks to the middle of the overlap. Traverse left under the overlap and move round to a good ledge.

3a **20m HVS 5b** Harder but better. Step right from the belay and climb the thin crack, which is difficult (but very well protected) for the first 6m, soon easing with the lessening of angle. Easier to the overlap, step right and up the right edge to easier ground. Belay at some spikes.

4 **20m** Climb easily over more broken ground leftwards to a belay beside a large hollow flake.

5 **25m 4c** On the left is a hidden corner; climb up the edge, step left on to the slab and undercut into the corner. Layback this to belay on the rock glacis below the top wall.

6 **25m 4b** Left of the big block is a superb narrow chimney which narrows to a crack. Follow this pleasantly to the top.

2 Toad Hall ★★   **145m E2 5b**

FA Dave McGimpsey, Andy & Gill Nisbet 3 September 2000

Start at a cairned ledge beneath the central rib, which has a steep pale side-wall with a heather chimney at the base.

1 **45m 5b** Increasingly fine climbing. Step up right onto a higher ledge then climb next to the right bounding wall of the rib and up a short step to heather. Step left immediately onto the bounding

wall and climb this, initially close to heather but soon diverging into a crack about a metre from the arête. Follow this, sometimes using the crack to the right, to gain the arête. Follow the arête to the ledge.

2 **20m 4c** Climb the right edge of the main slab, then continue on the main slab trending left before returning back right to the top of the slab.

3 **20m** Scramble up left to a big flake at the base of the next slab.

4 **20m 5b** Go 5m farther left to gain and climb a right-slanting crack to a terrace (initial runner high on left recommended).

5 **40m 4b** Climb a line of flakes up the next wall. Go left to a big flake at the base of the final blocky wall. Stand on it and climb the wall above.

3 Hall of Mirrors ★★★   **80m E2 5b**

FA Bob Brown, Graham Cullen & John Mackenzie 30 October 1993

A magnificent sustained main pitch with a big feel to it. It follows the obvious crack system up the striated side-wall of the central rib.

1 **50m 5b** Sustained and well protected – take a double set of cams. Climb cracks and flakes to a small overlap. Pull over and follow the main crack to a hanging belay beside a small spike about 6m below the overhung ledge. Either abseil off (belay in situ), or:

2 **30m 4c** Traverse left round rib onto steep slab. Continue up the arête by delightful flake cracks to an awkward step right. Continue up and left to the right end of the heather terrace above. Scramble down then up to reach the descent gully.

4 Glass Slipper ★★   **65m VS 5a**

FA Bob Brown, John Mackenzie & Martin Hind 7 June 1992

A fine route taking an implausible line. Further up and right is a steep slab with a prominent curving overlap running up its right side. Start below the central crack of the slab.

1 **10m 4c** Climb the crack up the slab to a flake below the curved overlap.

2 **20m 5a** Gain the overlapped corner above, then

follow this tenuously to an easing. Traverse
left along the hand-rail to a narrow stance.

3 35m 4c Climb the steepening cracks above to
a stepped ledge. Climb the spike on the right,
then traverse left below the top slab to a wide
crack. Finish easily up this. Scrambling remains.

*Ged Reilly psyching up for the fine
layback/jam crack on Hall of Mirrors.
Photo Forrest Templeton.*

VICTORY SLAB

Left of *Salamander* at a higher level is a steep slabby wall split by a pair of cracks towards the right end. Gain the terrace at its base by a chimney corner, or the easier corner to the left.

Descents: Abseil from in situ anchor at top of *Victory Crack*, or scramble off left along the exposed ledge.

5 **Chameleon** ★★   60m E2 5c

FA John Mackenzie & Bob Brown 31 August 1998

Left of the heather corner that lies left of the *Salamander* slab is another steep slab with a shallow right-trending curved overlap. The route takes shallow cracks running rightwards straight through this feature. There is an optional first pitch (which was soloed) that avoids heather. Start below the overlapped slab to the right.

1 **15m 4b** Climb two short slabs and move to a short crack below the overlap.

2 **45m 5c** Climb boldly up to and through the overlap with more unprotected and delicate climbing to the base of the thin crack. Climb this (crux), which is well protected by wires to a wobbly flake and small ledge. Move up rightwards through an overlap and make a delicate step up right to the edge, which is followed more easily to the heather ledge. An excellent sustained pitch.

6 **Spoils of War** ★★   45m E1 5b

FA Bob Brown & John Mackenzie 4 November 1995

A well protected pitch up the very pronounced crack to the right of 8. Start to the right of the crack to avoid heather. Traverse left on flake hold to the main crack. Follow the crack past a wide section to a little tree and step left to the thin parallel section, which leads with difficulty to the top.

> The crack close on the left to *Spoils of War* is taken by 7 *Garibaldi*, E3 6a, 6a.

8 **Victory Crack** ★★★   25m E2 5c

FA John Mackenzie & Bob Brown 20 August 1995

An excellent pitch, well protected by wires and small cams. Climb the left steeper discontinuous crack. Very sustained with the crux at the top.

📷 *Brian McCreadie fighting fit on Victory Crack. Photo Ged Reilly.*

9 The Unknown Soldier ** 25m E7 6b

FA Julian Lines & Rich Biggar (on-sight) 18 July 2002

An eliminate offering extremely bold slab climbing on impeccable rock. Start 2m left of 8 and just right of 10. Climb directly up the bald slab to some quartz blocks at 12m (RP #5). Stand on the quartz and make a long reach for a fingerhold. Make a rock over onto this and stand up (crux). Reach a good hold on the left and clip the PR on 10. Stand on a good hold and move diagonally left, then up to a horizontal break. Step left to a vertical crack and finish up this, as for 10.

10 Tales of the Old Days ** 30m E5 6b

FA Robin McAllister, Dave McGimpsey & Moose Harrison September 1998

Start to the right of a slabby recess left of 9. Climb the thin slab to gain the right edge of a crescent shaped crack and follow this to a good pocket at half-height (first good gear). Continue up and right to an awkward mantelshelf move. A long stretch (6a) or dyno (6b) gains the top break (poor cams). Follow this leftwards to a short finishing crack. Very bold in its lower half.

11 Beware the Greeks * 20m E3 6a

FA Julian Lines, Robin McAllister & Dave McGimpsey September 1998

The slab and hanging crack 4m left of 10. Climb the bold slab to gain the crack (assortment of dubious gear). Climb the crack, mainly on its right side.

12 Super Discount * 16m E3 6a

FA Dave McGimpsey, Robin McAllister & Andrew Fraser 19 September 1998

The twin crack-line on the left. The left and lower crack is climbed to an awkward transfer to the upper right crack. Climb this with interest to crux moves (Camalot #0.1) near the top.

The rightmost of the twin cracks is taken by 13 *Prix Choc* E2 5c.

THE LOWER TIER

Left of and below the main crag, beneath *Victory Slab* is a subsidiary slabby wall, seamed by cracks and with a square recess near its right end.

14 Moon Safari ** 25m E2 5b

FA Robin McAllister, Dave McGimpsey & Andrew Fraser 20 September 1998

An excellent route up the largest buttress at the right end of the crag. The improbable lower section is climbed left of centre, with holds appearing when least expected. Move slightly rightwards to the upper section, which gives technical and intricate climbing and is climbed right of centre, moving across left at the top.

15 Gloaming Wall * 20m MVS 4b

FA Bob Brown & John Mackenzie 24 September 1994

Left of the recess at the right end of the slab is a heathery crack. Start to the right and pull through the overlap. Climb a thin crack to the top.

16 Glazed and Confused * 20m E1 5b

FA Andrew Fraser, Robin McAllister & Dave McGimpsey 20 September 1998

The wide central wall, climbed in the middle. Move easily up the lower part of the wall and over the central bulge to reach a hairline crack through the upper wall. Fine moves up this lead to a nubbin, a good ledge and the top.

17 Spider in a Dark Room ** 20m E1 5b

FA Andrew Fraser, Robin McAllister & Dave McGimpsey 20 September 1998

The thin central crack. *"Sheer fun".*

18 Centipede Crack * 20m HVS 5b

FA John Mackenzie & Bob Brown 24 September 1994

Start below a thin crack on the left side of the slab. Climb thinly up to the crack (crux) then more easily up the crack to finish delicately.

ACKNOWLEDGEMENTS

Special thanks go to my regular climbing partners and buddies over the many years it's taken to put this book together – Paul 'Stork' Thorburn and Rick Campbell and especially to my wife Karen for her unstinting support both on and off the rocks. For assistance with the computing side and technical boffinry special mention must also be made to Colin Martin and Alan Cairns.

The following climbers have all assisted by helping with photographs and/or commenting on the text at various stages of production, many making my job last a wee bit longer by going out and discovering many worthy new routes.

Craig Adams, Robert Adie, Malcolm Airey, Paul Allen, Emma Alsford, Rab & Chris Anderson, Innes & Gwen Auchterlonie, Dan Bailey, Jonny Baird, Finlay Bennet, Gary Benson, Rich Biggar, Bob Brown, Dave Brown/Hot Aches Images, Jim Buchanan, Hannah Burrows-Smith, Dr Leanne Callaghan, Billy Gordon Canning, Louise Gordon Canning, Trevor Carpenter, Andy Cave, Mark Chadwick, Nick Clement, Neil Craig, Pete Craig, Noel Craine, Martin Crocker, Adrian Crofton, Steve Crowe, Smiler Cuthbertson, Ben Darvill, Malcolm Davies, Paul Donnithorne, Al Downie, Robert Durran, Phil Ebert, Graeme Ettle, Dr Grant Farquhar, Lee Fleming, Iain Forrest, Andrew Fraser, Tess Fryer, Allen Fyffe, Blair Fyffe, John Garbutt, Dr Mark Garthwaite, Dave Griffiths, Gareth Griffiths, Davy Gunn, Alan Halewood, Matt Harding, Bill Hart, Sue Harper, Rik Higham, Dan Hill-McManus, Dave Hollinger, Lawrence Hughes, Glenda Huxter, Murdoch Jamieson, Rob Jarvis, Hugh Jenkins, Susan Jensen, Paul Johnstone, Ross Jones, Steve Kennedy, Rob Kerr, Helen Konkol, Chris Lane, Mike Lates, Graham Lawrie, Alastair Lee/Posing Productions, Gordon Lennox, Julian Lines, Andy Lole, Ian MacDonald, George MacEwan, Lord John Mackenzie, Colleen Maclellan, Dave MacLeod, Karin Magog, Gaz Marshall, Robin McAllister, Dr Darren McAuley, Harry McCaffery, Chris McDaid, Dave McGimpsey, Niall McNair, Paul McNally, Iain Miller, Colin Miln, Wilson Moir, Colin Moody, Martin Moran, Neil Morrison, Mike Mortimer, Chris Murray, Fergus Murray, Kev Neal, Andy Nelson, Grahame Nicoll, Andy Nisbet, Roger Palin, Mike Pescod, Tom Prentice, Charlie Prowse, Carl Pulley, Kath Pyke, Jon Rabey, Tim Rankin, Tom Redfern, Dave Redpath, Mike Reed, Ged Reilly, Simon Richardson, Ali Robb, Alastair Robertson, Guy Robertson, Peter Robins, Kevin Rutherford, John Sanders, Klaus Schwartz, Alan Shand, Neil Shepherd, Dave Simmonite, Iain Small, Craig Smith, Malcolm Smith, Neil Smith, Nick Smith, Andy Spink, Tony Stone, Emily Strong, Paul 'Tat' Tattersall, Ian Taylor, James Thacker, Louise Thomas, Pete Thomas, Mick & Kathy Tighe, Dave Turnbull, Mike 'Twid' Turner, Nic Turner, Sheila Van Lieshout, Crispin Waddy, Ron Walker, Alan Wallace, Raymond Wallace, Isla Watson, John Watson/Stone Country Press, Rueben Welch, Tim Whitaker, Sam Williams, Deziree Wilson, Trevor Woods, Andy Wren, Blyth Wright and Stuart Younie. Special thanks to Kev Howett for magnanimously collating many of the descriptions for the Barra Isles. Apologies in advance to anyone I've missed.

Also a special thanks to the many clients, unfortunately too numerous to mention, who, often unwittingly, assisted in checking out routes, both classic and obscure.

Particular thanks to Don Williams of Bute Cartographics for the excellent maps, to Jim Buchanan/Wild West Topos for his superbly crafted topos of all the Gairloch crags, also Steve Crowe for additional topos, and Mark McGinnes for additional design input and assistance with software.

All photographs are by the author or in his collection unless otherwise credited. Many thanks to all who contributed photographs, in particular Dave Cuthbertson/Cubby Images, credited separately.

Finally, particular thanks to authors or their estate for permission to reproduce quotations: Doug Benn, Andrew Fraser, Doug Lang, Jimmy Marshall, Anne Murray (estate of WH Murray) and Bill Skidmore.

Also thanks to the 'old fox of Glen Coe' Hamish MacInnes for the foreword, and not forgetting Peter Wood (the designer) and Franco Ferrero (the gaffer!) at Pesda Press for all their patience and hard work.

ROUTE INDEX